THREE AFRICAN TRIBES IN TRANSITION

THREE AFRICAN TRIBES IN TRANSITION

Volume I of Contemporary
Change in Traditional Societies

Edited by Julian H. Steward

EDWARD H. WINTER

T. O. BEIDELMAN

ROBERT A. MANNERS

STANLEY DIAMOND

UNIVERSITY OF ILLINOIS PRESS Urbana, Chicago, London

Photographic credits: *Perspectives on Modernization* (Figs. 1-18). Except where individually credited, all photographs by Julian H. Steward. *Tanganyika* (Figs. 19-42). Except where individually credited, all photographs by E. H. Winter. *The Kipsigis of Kenya* (Figs. 43-64). Except where individually credited, all photographs by R. A. Manners. *The Anaguta of Nigeria* (Figs. 65-95). Photographs by Olga Diamond.

Illini Books edition, 1972
originally published in a clothbound edition, 1967

Manufactured in the United States of America
Library of Congress Catalog Card No. 66-25557

ISBN 0-252-00282-2

Foreword

Interest in contemporary change or modernization of traditional societies has become so great and research so extensive since World War II that facts are accumulating faster than new theoretical constructs can be devised to give them meaning. In an effort to develop and test a systematic approach to the problems of modernization, a project of cross-cultural research was developed in 1956 at the University of Illinois under the auspices of Studies of Cultural Regularities, and a substantial grant enabled work to begin the following year.[1]

A fundamental assumption of the project was that the participation of several persons in a single, unified program would better clarify the underlying problems and yield more comparable data than the findings of independent studies of single cases of modernization. The project members were selected because they were interested in the general purpose of the research and because they had specialized knowledge of different world areas which would insure a truly cross-cultural selection of cases for field research.

PERSONNEL AND RESEARCH AREAS

The personnel consisted partly of members of the Department of

[1] We are indebted to the Ford Foundation for the principal grant that made this project possible, but the Foundation is not responsible for the nature of the field work or for the publications that have followed it. The University of Illinois provided the salaries of the project director, Julian H. Steward, and of Charles Erasmus and Louis Faron, who were then research associates connected with Studies of Cultural Regularities, and it gave us office space and other facilities. We are also pleased to acknowledge support from the National Science Foundation to F. K. Lehman for his research in Burma and Thailand in 1962 and to Robert Manners for extended work in Kenya.

Sociology and Anthropology (now the independent Department of Anthropology) of the University of Illinois and partly of persons at other institutions who had previously been associated with my research and who obtained leave to join the project. The substantive monographs of field research are grouped by general areas: West Africa, East Africa, Southeast Asia, Japan, Mexico, and Peru.

The project had been planned during several years with the help of Charles Erasmus, Louis Faron, Frederic K. Lehman, Robert Murphy, and Eric Wolf, who had been my research associates at the University of Illinois at various times after 1952, and with the advice of Edward Winter, who was a member of the teaching faculty at the University, Stanley Diamond, and Robert Manners, who had been one of my colleagues in the study of Puerto Rico in 1948-49. The present project also included Toshinao Yoneyama, who had begun field work under me while I was director of the Kyoto American Studies Seminar in Kyoto, Japan, in 1956. T. O. Beidelman, a graduate student of anthropology at the University of Illinois, became Winter's assistant on the project. Sol Miller, a student while I was at Columbia University, joined us to work in Peru. Richard Downs was invited to join us because he had made Indonesia his special field for many years. Shuichi Nagata, then a graduate student at Tokyo Metropolitan University, Japan, assisted Yoneyama during several months of field work at Kurikoma in northern Japan, and later conducted independent study for six weeks.[2]

RESEARCH PROCEDURES

The project was divided into three phases: first, a half-year of joint discussion and preliminary planning; second, eighteen months of field research; and third, a final period of discussion and preparation of manuscripts.

[2] All of these persons have since moved on to other positions. Manners is with the Department of Anthropology at Brandeis University, Faron with the Department of Anthropology at New York State University, Stony Brook, Long Island. Erasmus is in the Department of Anthropology at the University of California at Santa Barbara, and Winter in the Department of Sociology and Anthropology at the University of Virginia. Diamond is now a member of the Anthropology Departments at the New School for Social Research and Columbia University, Lehman is on the staff of the Department of Anthropology at the University of Illinois, Downs is at the University of New Hampshire, Miller at the New School for Social Research, Beidelman at Duke University, and Yoneyama teaches anthropology at Konan University, Japan. Nagata, after completing his doctorate in anthropology at the University of Illinois, is now in the Department of Anthropology at the University of Toronto, Canada.

During the first phase, most of the project members spent one semester at the University of Illinois preparing for the field work and discussing problems and procedures. Those who could not be in residence at Urbana managed to attend occasional conferences. The principal subject of discussion was the meaning of modernization, the kinds of information or relevant phenomena to be investigated in the field, and the value of a possible taxonomy of contemporary societies as compared with identification of processes of change in understanding cross-cultural differences and similarities.

We did not expect at this time to outline any definitive or universally applicable procedures, for it became clear that the methodology of studying modernization must take into account such a wide and variable range of phenomena that it must be adapted to each empirical case. Because our field studies included such dissimilar societies as African tribes, Malayan rice farmers, Japanese rural communities, Mexican collective farm workers, and Peruvian hacienda and plantation laborers, many of the methodological implications of the project have become clear only after the field research. The most fruitful result of our deliberations was an awareness that each field study must break the bonds of the traditional, narrow ethnographic approach and consider the factors of the larger context that have influenced and are manifest in each society.

The second phase consisted of field work of about eighteen months in each case. During this time, there was a constant exchange of reports and ideas between project members. Meanwhile, my wife and I visited Kenya, Tanganyika, Malaya, and Japan. We lacked time to visit the other areas, but I had previously traveled in Mexico and Peru.

During the third phase, which was devoted to preparation of manuscripts, we had frequent discussions among the project members who were at Urbana and held several conferences that were attended by those who had returned to their own institutions. In fairness to the authors, it must be stated that some manuscripts were completed five or six years ago but that publication has been delayed by the usual complications inherent in a project of this size. Delay, in turn, stimulated some of the authors to revise their manuscripts. Manuscript revisions, however, consisted of further clarification of matters already discussed rather than of attempts to bring field materials up to date.

Some profound changes have occurred everywhere during the last five years. Most of the nations have been affected by political changes that will inevitably have repercussions on the local societies. Kenya and Tanganyika (now Tanzania) have won their independence. This has led to withdrawal of many Europeans, especially land owners, and it has certainly altered the strongly segregationist policies of these former colonies. Everywhere, the problem of foreign investment creates national political problems, and leads to conflicting ideologies regarding national policy. There are communist positions and others labeled "communist" because they advocate redistribution of foreign-owned lands and other wealth. There are views which stress the need for foreign capital and technical skills. The independent governments are too new to have settled into a permanent pattern. Factionalism based upon tribal backgrounds, individual struggle for control, and issues concerning relationships to other nations continue to plague each government. In parts of Southeast Asia, war and the threat of war together with internal movements that are designated "liberation" or "communist" keep any government off balance. Malaysia has been threatened by external invasion, while Singapore, its largest city and center of commerce, has become independent.

Whether national political change expedites or retards the effects of technological, economic, and other factors, the new contexts will necessarily require many changes in the course of time. Whether socialist or capitalist ideologies are finally adopted and whether these will profoundly affect the influence of particular factors upon local societies remains to be seen.

Meanwhile, marked changes have been clearly evident during the last five years in Japan, Mexico, and Peru, whose governments have been most stable. In Japan, there has been a great increase of farm mechanization, which had barely begun at the time of our studies. There had emerged a small landless farm wage-labor population, and this may grow, especially as accelerated urban development draws larger numbers of people from rural communities. Possibly a revolution in the basic pattern of farming and farm life will occur if a rural, wage-labor proletariat replaces farm family workers. Changes in the Yaqui-Mayo area of Mexico may occur if the opportunities created by the great irrigation works and new towns exert such pressure as to revise the arrangements that bind these Indians to the farm collectives. In Peru, increasing industrialization, together with expanding networks of roads, is giving the hacienda and plantation societies greater opportunity and potential mobility. Five years can bring great changes in the lives of workers who shift to new job situations.

That our studies have not brought change up-to-date is unimportant, however, because change is never ending. The lasting value of the studies is that the trajectory of change in each case was viewed against the background of the society that was traditional prior to the penetration of modernizing factors. The processes and trends observed five years ago had been operating for many decades, and they had been effective in different degrees. They can be better assessed through new research a decade or so hence, when their effects will have become more evident. It is even possible that at some future time, perhaps not very distant, world affairs will have become so altered and national contexts of modernization will incorporate such fundamentally new factors that societies of today will become traditional with respect to new trends and processes.

I had originally planned to publish an explanation of the general purpose and method of the project in the first of these volumes and to postulate tentative explanatory formulations of the substantive results of the field work as a concluding section of the third volume. Discussion with project members subsequent to the research, careful analysis of the manuscripts, and consideration of the larger implications of our project, however, soon made it very evident that adequate treatment of modernization must involve the larger dimensions of any culture change and that explanatory formulations of change would have to include far more cases than those studied by our project. What had been intended as reasonably brief statements, therefore, will be made into a separate book that will enlarge and supersede my *Theory of Culture Change* (1955).

This forthcoming book is the product of a lifelong interest in problems of culture change and of studies of modernization that began twenty-five years ago when I established the Institute of Social Anthropology at the Smithsonian Institution, began research in Latin America and started a series of publications. This interest was continued and the methodology developed in the study of Puerto Rico (Steward *et al.*, 1956). It would be impossible now to give full credit to each associate who has stimulated and contributed to my thinking. In acknowledging the very basic contributions of my colleagues to the theoretical views that have resulted from the present project, I cannot guarantee that any of them wholly agree with what I have formulated.

The introduction to the present volume is limited to a statement of our general goal and the relevance of the studies to this goal. It will necessarily anticipate certain theoretical points explained more fully in the forthcoming book, but it does not explore their ramifications. This introduction is divided into four major headings: the broad purpose of the project; the meaning of modernization as contrasted with other kinds of culture change; some definitions that are offered to avoid the morass of semantic confusion but that have theoretical implications explored elsewhere; and a brief account of our field studies with special reference to larger categories of societies they represent and also to categories that are not included in our studies.

JULIAN H. STEWARD

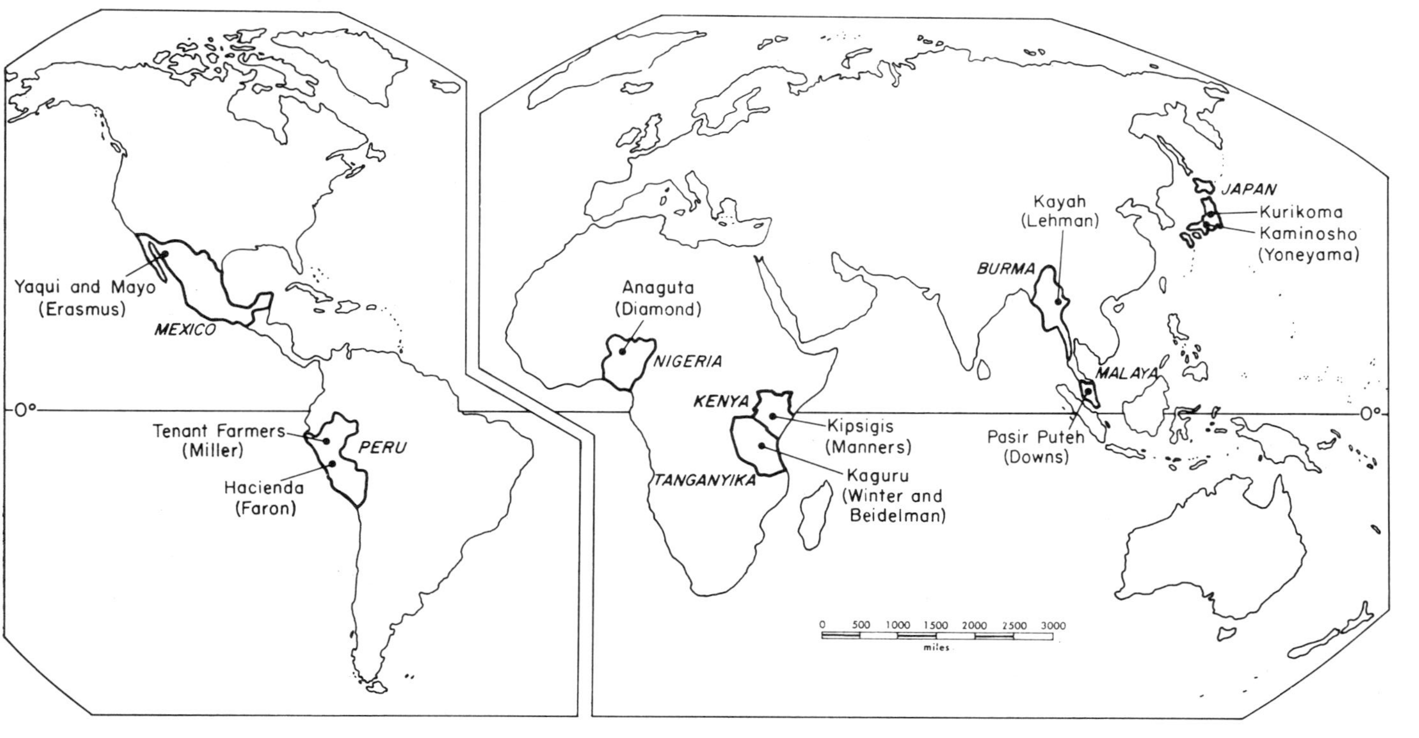

Location of research for the three volumes.

Contents of the Three Volumes

Contents

Perspectives on Modernization: Introduction to the Studies

JULIAN H. STEWARD

PURPOSE AND GOALS

The general purpose of our project was to investigate the effects of the modern, industrial world culture on various traditional, rural segments of national populations. This purpose, however, required more than a descriptive or ethnographic account of what the local societies are like today. The underlying interest was to determine the processes or evolutionary transformations that have affected traditional societies. The methodology that has been developed for cultural studies, however, is very inadequate in many respects for dealing with modernization.

It is a commonplace in science that any experiment may disclose phenomena that seem irrelevant and do not fit established categories. Whether in nuclear physics, biology, or cultural studies, new phenomena may remain in limbo until their properties are determined and theories can be devised to accommodate them. There is consequently a time for experimentation and observation and a time for contemplation, digestion of facts, and revision of theories. New experiments or observations may then test the theories and establish the categories of relevant phenomena.

During the last few decades, especially since World War II, anthropology has devoted attention to societies and to subsocieties or subcultural groups that have become modernized or transformed in some degree owing to influences from the rapidly changing industrial world. Meanwhile, other social sciences, including sociology, economics, psychology, geography, and political science, as well as certain of the humanities, have also become interested in contemporary changes among traditional societies of diverse cultural heritages. A common interdisciplinary interest in cross-cultural comparisons is emerging, but methodologically the more delimited problems, conceptualizations of data, and particular methods tend to be those traditional to each discipline. In some respects, therefore, an excess of undigested data exists.

But the obverse is also true. Each new theory gives relevance to facts that were previously ignored; earlier studies may be very deficient in certain data that are crucial to modern problems. This paradox of an abundance of undigested facts and paucity of relevant facts can only be resolved by attempting to rephrase the whole methodology of studying culture change. In this effort, special attention must be paid to the nature of causal factors, the meaning of processes, and the conceptualization and categorization of phenomena observed in any study.

I think it can be said fairly and without derogatory implications that anthropological analyses of change are still bound by traditional methods. Studies of modernized societies ideally should fit a methodology that applies to any segment—whether an ethnic minority or people who have been wholly "assimilated" to some subcultural group—of any nation in the world. But anthropology has moved into this broad field very recently and very cautiously. It has limited its investigations mainly to ethnic minorities, immigrants, and other enclaves within modern industrial nations or to aboriginal populations who remain on their native lands but have become linked with the larger society.

The methodology is still largely traditional in several respects. It studies the ethnology of the small group and records modern changes, but it does not trace them to the larger context. There continues to be emphasis upon lingering ethnicity of the society studied; that is, on the traditional pattern, value system, cultural personality, and other normative factors which are presumed to prevent change. Anthropology has also tended to treat change in terms of "acculturation," a concept that is inadequate despite many attempts to redefine it, and "diffusion" of culture traits, which may be very misleading applied to the modern world. If studies of contemporary ethnic enclaves within larger societies or of native communities are limited by the ethnographic method, they record as relevant only those phenomena that can be locally observed.

Specialized wage labor, dependency upon a market for basic commodities, subjection to laws of all kinds, influence by political ideologies, and the many other phenomena contingent upon the place of the society in a larger state system are viewed only on the local level. One anthropologist has said of national political change, "It should be observed at the village pump level." Yet none of these phenomena are completely described merely as parts of an ethnography because each is a local manifestation of something much larger. No society has a complete, self-sufficient, and independent structure. This limitation is tacitly acknowledged by the common reference to the subject matter as a "subsociety" or a "subculture."

The many intrusions of external influences and institutions into the local society cannot be understood solely in terms of their interactions within the local society. A descriptive ethnography cast in the traditional mold, therefore, tells us little about modernization. Virtually every facet of the subculture has such a close linkage with the institutions and features of the larger society that the subsociety could not exist in isolation from its context. Consequently it cannot be understood if described as an ethnographically independent unit. The many factors that penetrate the local society from the larger sociocultural system create a dependency relationship that initiates processes of internal transformations or evolutionary changes.

There are many methodological problems to be explored in connection with studies of modernization. The adequacy of such traditional concepts of process as "acculturation," "diffusion," and "assimilation" must be re-examined. The meaning of evolution in any empirical study of culture change must be clarified. Processes of change must be related to particular causal factors and to substantive effects. Instead of assuming universal evolutionary processes and transformations of whole cultures through universal stages, changes in technology, humanistic achievements, and especially social structures of systems must be assessed (Steward and Shimkin, 1962). That there is differential evolution of the components of a culture must always be viewed as a possibility, and various particular lines of evolution must be inferred from the empirical data of substantive cases. In addition, the very generalized concepts of ethnic minorities, subcultures, and subcultural groups or subsocieties must be broken down into useful categories and related to the different contexts of modernization. The extent to which rural and urban areas are modernized in similar and different ways must be examined, and the concept of urban placed in the context of modern national institutions and traditional cultural heritage.

Special importance will be ascribed to the heuristic value of distinguishing institutional factors of the state-level context, of identifying the agencies that mediate these factors to the local societies, and of determining the nature of processes of change. Distinctions will be drawn between individual agents who mediate national institutions to local societies and local associations which represent these institutions on a community level. Emphasis will also be placed upon features of the natural environment that not only facilitate or inhibit change but that require cultural ecological adaptations in each case.

These matters will be considered here, but they require full exposition of methodology that will give a longer time perspective and a wider substantive coverage. This is reserved for a future book.

THE MEANING OF MODERNIZATION

Modernization is used herein to designate sociocultural transformations that result from factors and processes that are distinctive of the contemporary industrial world. It means more than culture change, for change may be essentially cumulative when culture traits are merely incorporated into the existing pattern of a society. Modernization is evolutionary in that basic structures and patterns are qualitatively altered. This use of evolution, however, does not imply general world stages of transformations. To the contrary, it refers to specific alterations of particular societies that must be determined empirically in each case and that may or may not be cross-culturally similar.

In order to place this concept of modernization in perspective, it is necessary to discuss such other processes as culture trait transmission, institutional dependency of a social segment on a larger sociocultural system, and those state-level institutions that are distinctive of the modern world.

In any change, culture traits, practices, and ideas are transmitted from one society to another. In culture trait distribution studies, this has been designated "diffusion," and it has generally implied a cumulative process by which the inventory of a society is enlarged. So far as interest has centered on the normative aspects of society, the transmission or borrowing of traits has been viewed in terms of the screening effects of the existing pattern and value system. Many societies are extraordinarily conservative and resistant to change, and they tend to reject traits that would create imbalance.

All societies, however, have been transformed, whether over centuries, generations, or only a few decades. Although some borrowed traits may be mere embellishments or elaborations of existing systems, others entail new adaptations to the natural environment and the social environment. Whereas a folk legend may be added to the cultural inventory, domesticated crops may eventually create new social structures as they are utilized in certain environments, and patterns of warfare may deeply modify the nature of society owing to its reactions with other societies.

Trait transmission from state-level societies to simpler societies may operate as between tribal societies. In one respect, however, it may be so different that it is quite inadequately conceptualized as "diffusion" in the traditional sense. Whereas diffusion between tribal societies ordinarily implies that the borrowing society incorporates the trait as part of its largely self-sufficient system, borrowing by a simple society from a complex state often involves adoption of traits upon which it comes to depend but which it cannot reproduce itself. The simple society, therefore, becomes institutionally dependent upon the state, for example, through trade.

There is of course some interdependency of tribes upon one another for subsistence that may amount to a kind of symbiosis. The Negrito-Bantu exchange of game and vegetable produce in Africa is a case in point. Dependency upon trade, however, became more absolute when metallurgy controlled by state specialists reached the bronze age and even more so the iron age. In later periods, when iron and steel tools were mass produced, societies well beyond the political limits of states became dependencies of the manufacturers. Prior to important contacts with Europeans, certain American Indian tribes were socially transformed owing to new kinds of land use that followed the introduction of steel traps, axes, and other hardware through the fur trade and rubber trade. Other traits of European origin than hardware, however, had similar effects; for example, the horse among the Plains Indians which was supplied through a continuous flow from the Spanish Southwest.

State institutions may influence local societies that are outside their political control in other ways. Their market for slaves may initiate slaving activities, which extend from one tribe to another, some tribes becoming slavers and others victims. Militarism has frequently involved traditional societies in warfare, which spreads as a kind of chain reaction to other societies. Populations dislocated by a state or colony may move into areas where their presence induces profound changes.

In the early history of state development, native populations seem to have become dependencies of the state through politico-religious control and exaction of labor and farm produce rather than through transmission of traits distinctive of state-level institutions. They may have been required to help construct temples, palaces, and burial monuments, but they were observers more than participants in ruling class ceremonialism and activities. Their community culture remained traditional, even into feudal periods of only a few centuries ago. There may have been some dependency of rural populations on state specialists for iron tools, but most farm tools were traditional, wooden types until modern mass-produced steel tools became widely disseminated. Metallurgy among tribal and peasant populations has always been restricted in output and applied primarily to weapons.

The early lower-class populations were even denied the opportunity to modify many aspects of their traditional culture owing to various prohibitions and sumptuary laws. Change occurred mainly among those persons who were removed from their communities to serve special state purposes. A fixed, traditional peasant culture of feudal or Tokugawa Japan is described in Volume II.

Where state control has been strongly authoritarian, the institutional interdependency has been principally based upon extraction of wealth by the ruling class. The exploited received little in return. Exploitative systems, however, have taken many forms: exaction of tribute, expropriation of lands and other wealth, and binding of labor through slavery, land shortage, taxation, and other means. Each has had somewhat different effects on the traditional society.

The period of colonization affected native societies in several ways. The sovereignty of local states was made subordinate to that of the empire, but the institutional means of exploiting the native peoples varied. In densely populated native states like those of central Mexico and Peru, Spanish religion, laws, and methods of land use were directly imposed. In tribal areas, such as Africa, maximum use of land and labor required means of binding the labor, conversion of some areas into plantations with new crops, and encouragement of local tribesmen to produce new commodities. In the era of mercantilism, the colonies were linked with the larger world through commerce which involved mainly the interests of the hacienda or plantation owners, who exchanged local produce for the amenities of civilization which they obtained mostly from Europe.

As industrialization and technological change began to penetrate the colonies, however, traditional modes of production had to be altered. Technological innovations increasingly required new skills and new adaptations of society to the land. Government institutions began to create agencies to disseminate knowledge of basic education, farming methods, and health measures, and the state created local cooperatives in many areas. Plantations also developed as distinctive contexts of modernizing factors. Transportation facilities and communications networks drew local societies more closely into the orbit of effective national institutions.

In the contemporary world, free access to factors of change is denied traditional societies in a decreasing number of cases. Members of these societies are becoming involved with and dependent upon more and more state-level institutions, and they are adopting more culture traits from the national inventories. Strongly modernized segments of highly industrialized nations have become so dependent upon the facilities and institutions of the larger society for meeting their basic physical needs and for satisfying nearly every want that neither families, communities, nor subsocieties could survive by their own efforts. Some nations have reached the point where common household or family tasks of a generation ago, such as dressmaking, truck gardening, or home repairs, have become either nostalgic memories or do-it-yourself hobbies.

Modernization, therefore, is more than assimilation of a traditional society into a state or transmission of traits of the contemporary industrialized state to an ethnic group. It consists of those processes by which qualities unique to the modern world affect any component of urban or rural populations. The contemporary world culture (Steward, 1956a) has a vast repertory of scientific knowledge, technological applications of science in industry, transportation, communications, health, and other fields, international economic institutions, religions, political alliances, and humanistic achievements. All nations contribute in some degree to this culture, and, under certain preconditions, any may potentially draw from it. State-level institutions of nations of different cultural heritages and ideologies are affected in various ways by these larger, supranational potentials, but each nation has a combination of modernizing factors that provides a new context of change for its basic populations.

Distinctively modern features include: highly mechanized productive processes on the plantation and in the factory that require special skills and afford special opportunities; applications of science to farming and medicine with consequent population increase;

Fig. 1. In Kurikoma, Japan, national level institutions are represented by the school house and by voting for members of the Diet. Chairs, tables, and men's clothing are Western traits diffused from the cities.

development of transportation networks that range from roads for bicycles and trucks to ships and airplanes which may leapfrog over marginal areas; utilization of formerly latent resources, such as oil, minerals, uranium, and others; cultivation of new cash crops on lands that frequently had not been used, for example, coffee, tea, rubber, and sisal; capitalization of field production and processing that often exceeds the capacity of the richest families and leads to corporate enterprise. These trends have drawn increasing numbers of people from the farms into urban areas, which variously combine such functions as government, industry, commerce, transportation centers, religion, education, and recreation. Each city, therefore, contains a large number of potential modernizing factors that may transform any component of its population.

State-level institutions respond to these characteristics of modernizing trends. Government legislation covers many aspects of culture from regulation of industry, trade, union activities, and price controls to land tenure, marriage, property rights, education, and health practices. Government may provide such facilities as transportation networks, electricity, irrigation and flood control measures, schools, medical aid, farm loans, marketing assistance, and many others. It may encourage some activities, and it may prohibit others through restrictions on production, trade, and even social mobility.

Although it is beyond the scope of present considerations to compare modernization in a capitalist or so-called free enterprise system with that in a socialist system, it must be recognized that the processes previously discussed pertain mainly to the Western world, where our studies were made. A subsequent review of our data will disclose that one of the most common consequences of modernization has been that members of the society have acquired an incentive for private gain. A profit motive is not of course limited to the modern era, but it has been rapidly induced by modernizing factors.

In the traditional societies individuals either did not produce a surplus or were not permitted to retain enough of their surplus to reinvest it in the means of production or to spend it in ways that would change their customary behavior patterns. The tribal societies were essentially on a subsistence basis. The rural peoples of Malaya had been stripped of most surplus by their sultans and those of feudal Japan by their lords. Workers on traditional haciendas of Mexico and Peru were so bound by indebtedness and other means that they received little more than bare essentials for life.

Acquisition of the profit motive came when restrictions were removed and individual effort could be rewarded. Societies which had previously lacked private land tenure now formalized a system of family landholdings whereby the family could retain its profits. The Kipsigis dispersed over nearly all their territory and each family claimed land on which to produce truck garden vegetables. In many areas people became sharecroppers, renters, or wage laborers on plantations. Owing to improved productive methods and the abolition of all restrictions, the Japanese peasants now produce for their own profit; and even their cooperative farm labor is declining. Among the Kelantan Malays, many individuals are beginning to value what money can buy for their own use and are ascribing less importance to giving to others.

The transition from the traditional to the modernized has entailed conflict between the many earlier patterns of cooperation and sharing and the recent goals of maximizing individual profit. In societies which had lacked the opportunity for private enterprise prior to the penetration of industrial influences, the conflict is still evident in the factionalism between the older and younger generations. Differences in value orientation distinguish the Yaqui, who retain a traditional pattern of costly religious ceremonies that dissipate individual wealth, from the Mayo, who are abandoning this pattern and striving for individual gain by independent farming or wage labor.

Whatever the outcome of modernization within a socialist plan as compared with a capitalist system may be, modern technology imposes certain inescapable requirements. A modern factory must have special categories of workers and of managerial personnel. Genuine mechanization of farming requires use of heavy machinery on large tracts of land and costly processing equipment. Networks of transportation must be developed. People must be educated for many special skills required in the contemporary world. Systems of communications must keep the public informed.

The general trend of modernization in both socialist and capitalist nations seems clearly to be a reduction of the percentage of the population that operates as "free individual enterprise" and an increase of the number of salaried workers. Each year in the United States the number of independent farmers, shopkeepers, manufacturers, and even professional workers is decreasing while the number of salaried employees of large corporations and of the federal government is increasing. Similarly in Russia and China, socialism has meant allocation of incomes in ways that amount to salaries rather than equal division of the profits of any enterprise. In other words, convergent evolution is occurring in the modernization of both capitalist and socialist systems, and this is particularly evident in many aspects of the change in contemporary Russia. The basic incentive to produce more goods in both systems will probably be increased salaries.

Industrialization is also affecting the urban segments of modern nations more rapidly than rural populations because industries as well as other state functions are usually centered in cities. In Japan, the growth of the industrial complex has wrought profound transformations in the urban centers as compared with the basically traditional nature of the rural societies. These societies have maintained their traditional family structure by preserving the small family farm of about two acres through primogeniture. Until now it has used only hand tractors for small plots and avoided heavy machinery which could cultivate farm units of several hundreds of acres and would free the farm family to increase its income through other work.

Mechanization of Japanese farms to the extent that is now possible would throw more people on the labor market than it could absorb, and it would completely disrupt the rural societies. In a system of private enterprise, there are many cooperative credit unions, marketing associations, and processing arrangements, but producers' cooperatives or collective organizations are rare. Once farming becomes highly mechanized and capitalized, as on the coastal plantations of Peru, Puerto Rico, Hawaii, Malaya, Kenya, Tanganyika,

Figs. 2 and 3. In northern Japan (Kurikoma), the hand tractor is an improvement over the horse for cultivating plots of a fraction of an acre mainly because it need not be fed all year.

California, and many other places, the fate of the small individual farmer is to lose his land to larger corporation-owned productive units. This might not happen in Japan, but it may be significant that the largest rural productive unit in Japan in 1959 was a corporation farm of 2,600 acres, which is about two hundred times the size of the next largest farm.

Our only case of a true cooperative production unit is the Mexican *ejido*, especially among the Yaqui Indians. This collective farm has been allotted, financed, and controlled by the government. Owing to the very context of free enterprise in which it exists, the purchase of machinery, advancement of loans in lieu of wages, and other features have bound the workers to it through perpetual indebtedness. The *ejido* communities, moreover, are preserved in part by the traditional Yaqui pattern of distributing individual wealth through ceremonies rather than accumulating it as private wealth. But the Yaqui, and much more so the Mayo, are beginning to look to outside opportunities for free individual farms or even wage labor.

The present project deals with the *processes of modernization* of rural societies within the orbit of the Western, capitalist industrial world, but it describes no thoroughly *modernized societies.* Most of the societies studied in the field are only somewhat modernized. Few of their members employ the latest technology in farming or other productive activities, travel in automobiles, enjoy extensive schooling, have television sets in their homes, belong to national associations, participate politically in national affairs, or share in the innumerable features of a completely industrialized society. No society is, in fact, ever completely modernized, because modernizing factors are continually changing and processes are never ending. One can only say that some societies, such as the farm communities of Japan, are strongly modernized in their cultural goals and sophistication, that the tribal societies of Africa are partially modernized, and a few, such as the Kayah of Burma, are still wholly traditional.

Conceptualization of Phenomena of Modernization

The basic problems of methodology that will be discussed more fully in my separate volume must be anticipated here in order to indicate how conceptualization of the data relevant to modernization gives comparability to our studies, whether the comparisons disclose cross-cultural regularities of any kind or features distinctive of each case. There are five categories of data or concepts necessary to the problems: (1) traditional society or base-line culture; (2) state-level context of factors; (3) agencies by which these changes are mediated to local societies; (4) internal processes of change that are initiated by external factors; and (5) substantive manifestations of change in each society.

THE TRADITIONAL SOCIETY

Because the process of change operates through time, some knowledge of that which is being changed is necessary; that is, a starting point, traditional society, or base line is needed. In most cases, the specific factors of modernization began to take effect only a few generations ago and at most not over a century ago. These factors are barely incipient among the Kayah of Burma, and they have been effective in varying degrees elsewhere.

It is not necessary to trace change indefinitely from the past, although a fairly long, pre-modern period would give better perspective. In many cases, the virtual absence of historic records precludes any great time depth.

THE CONTEXTS OF CHANGE

In the contemporary world, societies are being increasingly affected by the context of supracommunity or supratribal institutions. Some of these institutions, such as corporations which control mines, plantations, commerce, and manufacturing, or religious organizations, may be international. Most are organized on a state basis. Some are governmental institutions, and others are privately managed. Most institutions are mediated through centers or sublevels found in regional and urban foci. The effectiveness of these institutions depends upon the local natural and social environments and in turn it modifies these environments.

Any context of modernizing institutions and factors is inseparable from the cultural heritage of the area. Long-standing state, urban, and community institutions may be perpetuated and yet acquire new functions within the modern world. Some may decline and disappear; and others may remain as mere symbols. Traditional culture traits may persist in new contexts or be replaced by new traits under a variety of preconditions. Neither the institutional contexts nor the culture trait inventories are fixed; both are constantly undergoing transformations.

The members of any segment of a state society are never affected by the totality of state institutions. They acquire special economic roles as farm producers, laborers, middlemen, managers, and salaried employees, and as such they are inseparably linked with the larger institutions, but shipping, manufacturing, and distribution involve other aspects of economic institutions that do not directly affect their behavior. They are subject to particular laws, but they are not part of the larger law-making apparatus. They may have unequal access to education and other facilities. They may be given special advantages, or they may be subjected to certain restrictions.

MEDIATING AGENCIES AND MECHANISMS

The modernizing effects of a complex national society upon its segments result partly from culture trait transmission and adaptive interactions between neighbors or adjoining groups and partly from the influence of national institutions. Within preconditions set by financial means and other circumstances, a local society will adopt new practices and material goods because it has been influenced by other societies, perhaps even those in urban aeras, and stimulated by mass media of communications. National institutions, however, are mediated to the local or traditional society by several different mechanisms and agencies. These agencies are logically distinguishable, and in some cases represent developmental stages.

Three categories are: first, individual agents who link the traditional society with a state institution; second, forced regimentation of the members of the society; and, third, organizations or associations which represent local levels of national institutions.

Individual agents may transmit certain traits to societies which live outside the effective political control of states, as in the case of traders who introduce steel traps and tools. Where the traditional society is territorially localized within a nation, as on Indian reservations of the United States and in many colonial areas, mediating agents may include administrators, missionaries, law enforcement officials, health personnel, teachers, merchants, farm experts, and others who live among but are not members of the local societies. Such agents deal directly with individuals of the local society in the absence of local organizations or associations which can perform appropriate functions.

The Kelantanese Malays exemplify a society which lacked traditional associations that could perform modernizing functions. Formerly ruled by the sultan's agents, their present associations are loose semi-secret groups controlled by strong men. These have inhibited the effectiveness of colonial and national agents in various fields.

Whether traditional associations can acquire new functions is an empirical question. It is unlikely that large clan or lineage groups could become corporate entities for production in a system of private profit and free enterprise, although such change may be possible in a socialist system. Many American Indian tribes responded to modernizing influences by accepting new organizations, such as stockmen's associations. The Kipsigis of western Kenya first made extensive use of individual government agents, and then began to develop their own agencies, such as tribally financed and administered schools, local markets, and cattle auctions. Among the Sonjo of Tanganyika, the former warrior age-grade became a wage-labor group until it passed into the next older age-grade of farmers. Among the Nyango-Irigwe of the plateau of Nigeria, the men's dancing groups became commercially oriented organizations that helped tribesmen make the transition to the city. In Yugoslavia, traditional patrilineages of dairy farmers were made into communes without substantial change. The kinds of native kin groups and associations that are amenable to assuming new functions, however, merit detailed comparative analysis.

The Anaguta retained traditional structure, but their adaptations to the suburban situation was as fragmentary groups, which did a little subsistence farming, some cash farming, and some menial work. They were not thoroughly integrated with national institutions, however, except as a kind of rural proletariat, and, instead of relating to their larger context through associations, they created special leaders to represent them in external affairs—a system much like the governors of certain Rio Grande Pueblos—who had no functions within the villages.

In Japan, modernization has reached the point where many local associations are linked with national institutions. In some cases, traditional societies have acquired new functions, and in others local chapters of national organizations have been created. Norbeck (1962) has estimated that Japanese rural communities usually have between fifteen and twenty-five associations. A community in Miyagi Prefecture has twenty-one, ten of which were introduced by the government. Older organizations include ceremonial groups, fire brigades, and various work associations, and new ones are 4-H Clubs, farm cooperatives, Parent-Teachers' Associations, and recreational clubs. The new organizations not only cooperate with agents from the outside but they send their own representatives to regional meetings. The development of national associations with local chapters has proliferated into all areas of behavior in the United States: Boy Scouts, 4-H Clubs, Future Farmers of America, the Rotary, Lions, and other business societies, fraternal orders, religious groups, scientific and professional organizations, labor unions, and many others. Every kind of national association transmits some influence to the local subsociety or social segment, even though affiliation with these may interlock.

To judge by reports from China, it is possible in a socialist country to create associations which become a precondition rather than a consequence of industrial development. Although there is different opinion about the amenability of the Chinese people to accepting the many nationally oriented and affiliated associations, the effects of these innovations have been impressive. I am less concerned at this point with assessing China, however, than with raising the basic problem of what characteristics predispose any segments of society to accept authoritarian, socialistic programs that may fundamentally reorganize their traditional structure. Cultural goals, aspirations, access to land, occupational and status mobility, and a history of inhibiting factors in their larger context may be important considerations in cases like China.

PROCESSES OF CHANGE

The basic factors of modernization that are mediated to the local societies through various agencies initiate internal processes of change. These processes may be designated evolutionary in that they lead to structural transformations or modifications.

There are many categories of processes. Those processes by which special cultural traits are transmitted involve such modern factors as mass media of advertising and communications and increased mobility that potentially spread knowledge of what others do and create new desires. Contemporary trait transmission also has the precondition of financial means of adopting new practices, since most innovations create a dependency on the larger society. The concept of diffusion as understood in its use for tribal societies is hardly applicable.

The more basic processes of change include a wide variety of transformations that are caused by institutional factors. This causal aspect of process has not been clearly conceptualized nor have the more substantive processes been distinguished by appropriate terms. "Secularization," "individualization," and many other terms are too general to have substantive meaning. For such a fundamental process as that through which a society becomes a specialized dependency of a larger state there is no term. Missionization is fairly specific in its implication of a special context of factors. The modern mechanized plantation is usually an even more definite context of factors than the mission. Strikingly similar processes are involved in the growth of slums throughout the world.

Fig. 4. Workers migrate from jobs near cities close to Lake Victoria to their remote native villages on the upper Albert Nile in Uganda, traveling five days by rail, barge, bus, and again barge.

Fig. 5. Homes of resident laborers on rubber plantation in Kelantan State, Malaya, who subsist by a wage economy.

In each of the studies included in these volumes, a number of general processes will be recognized. The societies are becoming specialized economically, the lands are becoming individualized (i.e., family owned) in many cases, and traditional social cohesion is being weakened as each family is drawn into a cash economy. The distinctive native social structure is becoming weakened and factionalized along lines of generations, conservatives and progressives, and other dichotomies. The people are becoming detribalized as they acquire structural ties with external institutions and as their outlook becomes more national. Many individuals and families are leaving their communities to become modernized in the particular context of a plantation or an urban center.

The causal role of processes must await further detailed comparisons, for it is quite clear that a single factor may generate several processes, as the rubber trade in the Amazon that led to tribal disintegration, development of family rights to wild rubber tracts, and eventually to dependency upon external markets even for food. It is also evident that processes resulting from several factors may have similar effects. A nucleated settlement, for example, may result from warfare, resettlement for administrative purposes, restriction of inhabitable sites, or the creation of a factory or plantation town.

An inherent part of the concept of process must be culmination or at least sufficient transformation of the society to disclose the nature of the process. The early native Meso-American and Andean cultures culminated in essentially theocratic states owing to the processes of intensive plant domestication, demographic growth, internal specialization, and centralization of states around religious centers. The process of militarism began slowly but later culminated in the great empires found by the Spaniards in the fifteenth century.

Among our studies, the modernizing processes had not begun among the Kayah, they are barely discernible among the Kaguru, but they have wrought tremendous change among the Kipsigis. It is difficult today to assess the effectiveness or culmination of any process, for new factors are introduced so rapidly that some persons consider that the era of industrialization is being supplanted by one of automation. In most of our studies, however, it is clear that certain processes are only incipient. The Malays of Kelantan have not quite broken through tradition to manifest important modernization. The hacienda workers of Peru have continued to be affected by earlier processes even while new ones become operative. The Yaqui of Mexico have been so strongly bound by government controls that the influence of many processes that are transforming their neighbors is inhibited.

If processes are to be related causally to institutions of the larger complex and to social transformations of the traditional groups, they will have precise meaning to the extent that they can be stated in substantive terms. This requires that they be inferred empirically from substantive studies. Many will be found to have operated cross-culturally, but it cannot be assumed a priori that any particular combination of factors, processes, and results will be universal.

SUBSTANTIVE IMPLICATIONS OF PROCESS

Any analysis of the effects of modernization must first take into account the cultural heritage of each society in order to determine the extent to which it has been modified or readapted and whether it has retarded or shaped the effects of processes in special ways. It is very possible that structures may be drastically transformed while outward embellishments of the culture retain traditional features of the heritage. There are, however, no a priori criteria by which to judge what is important in change and what is not.

After the nature of transformations is determined in individual cases, comparisons will disclose similar changes in other cases. It does not follow, however, that all features of traditional societies or states will be transformed in identical ways. At present, comparisons may disclose modifications of only parts of societies, such as productive processes, religion, or special aspects. Whole cultures may converge to similar types, but the present categories used to describe such societies—peasants, farmers, plantation workers, urbanized peoples—are far too general to have much heuristic value.

Further breakdown into more significant niches, however, cannot be accomplished by means of prior taxonomic criteria. Even if this were possible, a taxonomy, as the members of our project agreed, would be more useful for the light it throws on process than for its own sake.

It is clear that many factors of modernization have been operating in widely separated parts of the world. They are causing certain foreseeable convergences among dissimilar traditional groups and perhaps parallel developments among types that were cross-culturally similar. It need hardly be stressed, however, that any theory which postulates that modernization will cause certain cross-cultural regularities does not presuppose that all societies and cultures of the world will be reduced to a complete and monotonous homogeneity or identity. Quite the contrary. Just as mountains, mesas, and other features of the natural landscape retain interesting, varied, and ever-changing topography because tectonic forces offset the universal eroding processes which would reduce the earth's surface to a featureless peneplane, it can be expected that special combinations of processes of culture change together with differences in the cultural heritages and in local environmental and social adaptations will perpetuate a varied cultural topography.

There are certain obvious cross-cultural similarities or regularities: for example, the weakening of extended kinship systems, commercialization of various kinds, individualization of productive effort and land tenure, acquisition of new skills, a broader view of the world, and new goals. The Mexican, Andean, Asian, and African farmers, however, are by no means identical; nor are these or any other farm societies entirely unique. Persisting features of the cultural heritage are modified by new factors; old forms acquire new functions. Even if the traditional cultures were entirely swept away —a very remote and unlikely possibility—special environmental features and particular combinations of factors of change would continue for a long time to create local differences in rural communities. Cities as well as rural areas will perpetuate certain sociocultural differences and affect peoples within the orbit of their influence in distinctive ways despite many similarities of modernization. The cities of India, China, Europe, the United States, and Latin America not only reflect the contexts of their larger national settings and cultural heritages, but they differ because of their special functions and the nature of the social segments which comprise their populations.

A major task is to assess the significance of the heritage of cultural areas so that the cross-cultural operation of similar modernizing factors within different settings can be recognized.

SOME DEFINITIONS

In order to avoid misunderstandings which are so often purely semantic a few definitions are given at this point, although some are discussed fully elsewhere. These are intended solely to clarify my own usage. Other persons will ascribe different meanings to these terms.

Modernization. This term has been clarified previously and it is necessary only to add that my colleagues agreed most emphatically that modernization in no way implies that the transformations and new qualities of the contemporary world are superior, better, or indicative of progress or improvement according to value judgments. Neither does it imply deterioration or worsening of contemporary life, as some persons view modern trends. The term is neutral.

Culture change has so many meanings that it is used here only in a general sense. It may signify increased culture trait content and richness within an unchanging structure; or it may imply structural and ideological modifications and transformations that exhibit new qualities.

Cultural evolution generally implies structural modifications and transformations that result from internal processes, whether these processes are initiated by internal or external factors. Evolution may be viewed in world stages (White, 1959), each connected with factors that induce "revolutionary" processes—for example, the agricultural revolution—or it may be delimited to signify transformations in particular societies. Whether the evolutionary changes in any society are to be considered "revolutionary" is a matter of definition. Some traditional societies may be gradually modified without losing their identity, while others are so completely disrupted that their members are merged or assimilated into totally different sociocultural segments of a larger state society.

Acculturation is rejected here because its meanings are too varied and ambiguous (Acculturation . . . , 1954; Murphy, 1964). Change of any kind induced by the interaction of tribal-level sociocultural systems with one another might better be distinguished as "transculturation" than acculturation. Of the many kinds of transformations caused by the linkage of a traditional society with state-level institutions, "modernization" has meaning that is specific to contemporary changes. These involve much more than trait dissemination.

Assimilation is subject to certain misunderstandings. A traditional society cannot of course assimilate the totality of a state culture. It may adopt only a limited number of traits, and the adoption always has preconditions. The term is more meaningful with reference to how the native society is assimilated into the larger society as a special segment, but this process requires the corollary concept of culmination. A traditional or native society may retain some degree of ethnic distinctiveness, but, as a special type of rural society or as a subsociety of an urban center, it accommodates to the total institutional and structural framework (including other subsocieties) of a region, city, state, or nation. A traditional society, however, may so lose its "ethnicity" that it is assimilated into pre-existing segments of the state. Assimilation in this second sense may be incomplete and difficult to assess, for the members of any segment of a larger society are not necessarily homogeneous. They may become variously affiliated with different occupational groups, neighborhoods, religious organizations, and associations.

Native refers both to a culture and a society which have become established in a certain area. It is to be distinguished from "traditional" in that the latter refers specifically to the sociocultural systems prior to modernizing trends. "Native" is in no way derogatory; it does not suggest that the people are backward, primitive, underdeveloped, or inferior. It generally designates the society or people indigenous to a place, such as New York City, rural Malaya, or East Africa. A native society may be either traditional or modernized.

Traditional refers to the characteristics of the native society or state that existed before modernizing influences began to transform it. Because the processes of modernization have become discernible in most areas only in recent decades, traditional usually means what many living persons remember or were told of the former way of life. In some cases, the traditional culture still survives with great strength.

Traditional should not be confused with aboriginal or pre-colonial. Where colonialism was introduced only in the last century, some traditional societies were aboriginal tribal groups and others were segments of older state structures. In much of Latin America, however, colonialism reached many aboriginal societies four and a half centuries ago, and transformations occurred during several major periods prior to modernization. Latin America, therefore, has many types of traditional societies which represent a variety of structures and blends of Hispanic and Indian traits.

Culture heritage. In a very literal and narrow sense, a cultural heritage is that which has been transferred from one generation to another. It is convenient, however, to distinguish the basic, longstanding features that give the major culture areas and subareas their distinctive character from those which merely are traditional in the pre-modern sense. The heritages of Japan, Southeast Asia, East Africa, West Africa, and Europe are rooted in many centuries of development. Much of Latin America has the twofold heritage of Spain and the aboriginal Indian.

Culture type. I use cultural or social type to designate the structure, rather than culture element inventory, of a society. Structure includes not only kinship relations but those arrangements and interactions between the members of the society for carrying out subsistence, ceremonial, war, recreational, and other activities (see Lehman, 1964). The values, goals, and attitudes pertaining to these activities are inherent in the structure. This meaning of type must be sharply distinguished from that which conceives type as a culture element content and that has been the basis of the culture area type and of such contemporary types as Gillin's Indian, Mestizo, and Hispanic types in Latin America (Gillin, 1949), wherein the mestizo is a mechanical mixture of aboriginal and Spanish traits.

State very broadly subsumes many kinds of sociocultural systems which consist of differing subsocieties and which have supracommunity or supratribal institutions and organization. It includes nations, empires, colonies, princely states, sultanates, chiefdoms, feudal estates, and other sociopolitical categories which will be made clear in their contexts.

Tribes in aboriginal times were societies which, though not necessarily strongly integrated sociopolitical units, had sufficient cultural homogeneity to constitute the group with which the individual identified. But no single definition applies to all so-called tribes. In a negative sense, tribes lacked state-level institutions. Today, "tribe" or "tribal" is a useful, if often imprecise, term because, despite tremendous variations in the nature and cohesiveness of tribes, it may continue to be the primary and even maximal group of identification.

Community has various meanings according to the context, but it is often even more specific than "tribe" in designating the group of primary identification and social interaction. As subcultural differences begin to cluster around occupations, social and religious affiliations, statuses, and other features, subsocieties may cut across towns and lose their purely local integration. These groups are communities by extension of the definition.

A small localized community, as contrasted with a town, usually exemplifies a number of regionally similar communities which belong to the same tribe or to some other subcultural rural category. Such communities, therefore, are the social units usually chosen for ethnographic analysis. The culturally homogeneous community is characteristically fairly small, ranging from a few dozen people to a maximum of a few hundred.

Larger communities, which are more commonly called towns, usually have internal diversity and consist of a number of subcommunities or subcultural groups which are distinctive in certain ways. Some localized communities that develop around plantations, mines, or other special enterprises include a hierarchy of authority and different kinds of workers. These communities, like other heterogeneous settlements, might better be designated towns, as in the case of "company towns." (See also Arensberg and Kimball, 1965.)

Subcultural group, subsociety, and social segment have been used to designate those social groups within a large society that are distinguishable by ethnic background, occupation, religion, race, status, or other common characteristics and yet share certain features with other social segments. Subcultural groups or subsocieties within a certain nation all conform to national laws, they potentially acquire many culture elements of the national inventory, and they are influenced by national institutions. Whether they occupy urban centers or rural areas, there is also a patterned interaction between these groups.

These terms, however, can be very misleading because of their inherent imprecision. An ethnic minority may eventually lose most of its distinguishing characteristics, especially its community-level features, and merge with members of other ethnic groups which achieve a certain degree of subcultural homogeneity and distinctiveness. If any category of subcultural group is distinguished solely on the basis of shared culture traits, however, there is no way to measure it, for it depends upon the unanswerable question, "How different is different?"

The more meaningful diagnostics of a subcultural group are its structural features. These may result from tradition, from the effects of supracommunity institutions, and from interactions with other groups. The extent to which the effects of any particular structures, such as those pertaining to employment, religion, political affiliations, or associations, are manifest in a random way in a subsociety or have some inner consistency is a matter of empirical investigation. Subcultural groups crosscut and interlock with one another in many respects, but it is highly improbable that their interconnections are wholly fortuitous.

Levels of sociocultural integration is a concept that underlies the entire theoretical approach to modernization and is fundamental to the distinction of contexts of different kinds. This was provisionally formulated fifteen years ago (Steward, 1951, 1956a), and it will be amplified in the future. The present relevance of the concept may be explained briefly.

The basic level and, among all historically known human societies, the irreducible social unit (certain modern slum dwellers excepted) is the nuclear family, which is based upon complementarity of the sexes. The family is the core of the household, although the domicile may include additional relatives, and the family may be formally extended in different ways. Such primary groups as tribes, bands, and villages have suprafamilial levels of culture which pattern the interaction of families; for example, hunting, farming, or military endeavors, ceremonial groups, and associations of various kinds. Supracommunity institutions usually are those of a state—or, today, a province or region—which affect community and family behavior through creating an economic, religious, military, political, or other dependency relationship between the subcultural group or social segment and the state, but these institutions are less parts of local behavior than family and community patterns. Production for a market, for example, will influence a local society by making it dependent on external sources for manufactured goods, and this may bring profound internal changes, but the larger institutions involved in the market economy—transportation of goods, manufacturing, processing, capital investment, and many other features—are in no way part of the patterns of the family or local community. Many higher level institutions, such as those concerned with international commerce in raw materials and manufactured goods, are supranational. (See, for example, Wolfe, 1963.)

The factors and processes of modernization, therefore, must be identified according to their levels of sociocultural intergration; for state-level institutions require mediating agencies in order to affect families and communities. It cannot be assumed that the different levels are identical cross-culturally. There are many kinds of states, and a state may have several internal levels of integration.

THE SUBJECT MATTER OF THE RESEARCH

Criteria of Selection

There are two general categories of criteria on which the choice of societies for field research might be based. The first category pertains to the nature of the societies that are being modernized—whether they are independent tribes, segments of larger social systems, representative of different culture areas or subareas of the world, or structural types which crosscut basic culture areas. The second category includes characteristics of the modernizing context, such as economic, political, religious, and other state institutions, colonial or national ideologies and policies, plural societies, and caste or racial prejudices. Agencies that mediate various external influences to the local society, such as traders, missionaries, and government officials, are factors of this category.

Choices are usually made on the basis of criteria of the first category because of their intrinsic interest, such as ethnically distinctive tribes, traditional rural populations, and racial cr other minorities of urban societies. The effects of modernizing influences are too complex and variable to afford a clear basis for selection. The problem is not whether markets, sources of wage labor, means of acquiring skills, participation in political activities, religious and recreational institutions, and many other factors are present as potential influences in a national, urban, or regional context. It is to determine which factors are active or effective influences in each case. This is an empirical problem which must take into account inhibiting factors of the context, such as territorial inaccessibility, restrictive laws, limitations of local environmental potentials, and inherent conservatism of the society, as well as the factors of demonstrable effectiveness.

Both sets of criteria, however, are necessary to give comparability to the studies. If native societies are chosen from dissimilar areas in various parts of the world, each case represents a distinctive cultural heritage. It is the cross-cultural occurrence of particular modernizing factors that affords a basis for assessing the similarities and differences of their effects.

By placing our choices in the perspective of these criteria, the comparability of our data is more apparent. Neither culture area, culture type, nor context, however, is entirely adequate for comparative purposes of modernization without finer categorization of each. Some of the smaller distinctions will be evident in our studies. At present some implications of these criteria for the choices made and those which might have been made must be briefly sketched.

The criteria of native culture area and culture type are mutually exclusive in some respects, for each area includes many subareas and types, and some types may crosscut widely separated areas. To accord primary importance to culture area is to follow traditional anthropological procedure, for most interest has, until recently, been area oriented. Choices made from areas, moreover, afford the advantage that any similarities in modernization cannot be ascribed to the continuity of the cultural heritage or to transmission of modern practices between neighboring societies.

The area criterion alone, however, is inadequate, for the basic cultural heritage may be manifest in such different structural types as independent tribes, states, or empires. In the absence of any generally accepted criteria that make finer distinctions between various categories—such as food collectors, hunters, farm communities, feudal societies, colonial empires, capitalist states, communist nations, and the many segments of each—our choices of traditional societies have been made within two very crude categories: native tribal societies and rural segments of states.

Our tribal societies represent varying degrees and kinds of modernization, ranging from the isolated and essentially aboriginal Kayah of Burma and the conservative Anaguta of Nigeria through the slightly modified Kaguru of Tanganyika, the strongly transformed Kipsigis of Kenya, and the government-controlled Yaqui and Mayo of Mexico. In part, these differences result from the length of time the tribes have been subjected to external influences. The Yaqui and Mayo have been under some Spanish influence for nearly four centuries, whereas the other tribes have been affected for little more than a half-century. In part, the dissimilarities reflect the interaction of particular modern contexts and local conditions.

Five of our societies had been parts of very different kinds of native states: the Moslem sultanates of Malaya, the Japanese Empire, and the Inca Empire of Peru. In the study of the modernization of the populations of most states, many kinds of segments might be chosen: independent farmers, laborers on rural estates (Japan excepted), various occupational, ethnic, and racial groups both in rural and urban areas, and special classes of rulers, priests, warriors, and others. Any segment or subsociety chosen would have to be understood in terms of its regional or urban context, its national context and basic heritage, and the larger area and even world context. For no nation today is a wholly self-sufficient entity. The general state context includes not only institutional factors, but such structural features as classes based upon wealth, heredity or race, castes, plural, closed societies, and other factors that permit or inhibit social mobility.

There is a danger in studies of modernization of making an a priori dichotomy between rural and urban contexts and assuming that the processes differ fundamentally in each category. Throughout history, tribal societies as well as the so-called peasant societies within feudal states have been rural, whereas urban centers have always been distinguished as the "containers of civilization." It is a quality of modernization, however, that certain rural populations may be even more subject to change than some segments of cities. Resident laborers on many mechanized plantations, for example, may live in a more modernizing context than certain migrant slum dwellers of cities. The basic farm population of Japan has been reached by more modernizing factors than many rural or urban segments of other nations.

The Societies Selected

The significance of the various criteria for selecting societies for field study is more apparent in retrospect than it was in the initial stages of planning the project. In the beginning, it was of primary importance that the project members be interested in undertaking studies that would have comparability with reference to modernization; that is, that they pay attention to change and to the national, regional, and local environment factors involved in change. It was equally important that they have some familiarity with the areas of proposed research and that these include at least some of the major cultural areas.

Practical considerations, however, partly determined some choices. Malaya was substituted for Indonesia owing to difficulties in working in the latter area. Japan was included partly because its distinctiveness and great industrial development lent challenging diversity to the project, and partly because, with the help of Toshinao Yoneyama, I had begun studies of rural communities in 1956 while director of the Kyoto American Studies Seminar.

Research in the other areas followed our original plan and afforded cases which represent several categories.

AFRICA

All three of our African societies—the Anaguta of Nigeria, Kaguru of Tanganyika, and Kipsigis of Kenya—remained independent tribes until less than a century ago, although the Kaguru and Anaguta had been somewhat affected by earlier slaving activities. After a period of competition among European nations for control of portions of Africa, Tanganyika, Kenya, and Nigeria eventually became British colonies but today they are independent nations. The potential influences upon these tribes was therefore similar to the extent that they reflected British policies, but more specific factors in the local contexts entailed special policies and brought different responses.

Similarities consisted mainly of features of British sovereignty. Kenya was first administered by the Imperial British East Africa Company in 1888, and incorporated along with Uganda in the East Africa Protectorate in 1895. Tanganyika, which had been penetrated by Arab slavers, was settled by Germans, especially missionaries, in 1884, and it became German East Africa in 1886. After World War I, Kenya became a British Crown Colony and Tanganyika became a League of Nations Mandate under England and later, in 1946, a United Nations Trusteeship under England.

Foreign settlement and exploitation of both territories was first expedited by railroads which ran from their coasts through their interiors. The railroad in Kenya to Lake Victoria was completed in 1901, and that in Tanganyika was extended to Lake Tanganyika in 1914. Expropriation of the rich farmlands for plantations began early in the present century but the construction of other facilities was accelerated after World War II. The general effects of modernization, which included loss of native lands, led first to local unrest, later to strong anticolonial feelings as in the Mau Mau uprising among the Kikuyu of Kenya, and finally, since our field research, to the independence of each colony.

Nigeria had been subject to Portuguese slavers three centuries ago, and later to other slavers. By 1885, it became a British colony and in 1914, the Protectorate of Nigeria. Unlike East Africa, however, Nigeria was not settled by colonial planters who expropriated land and found means of binding labor to their estates. Instead, it utilized a system of indirect rule to extract wealth. In the powerful Moslem tribes of the north, it found strong governments to meet this function. In much of East Africa, the British government had to appoint chiefs where they did not exist, but it took great pride in the model of indirect rule developed in Nigeria.

With the help of the local rulers, or Emirs, the British developed trade routes through the low coastal plains to the north. At first they extracted natively produced wealth in palm oil and later in cacao, peanuts (groundnuts), and tin. The existence of the large, powerful tribes, such as the Fulani and Hausa, as well as small, refugee groups, such as the Anaguta, were basic to the structure of Nigeria when it achieved independence as the Federation of Nigeria in 1960 and later as a member of the British Commonwealth in 1963.

East Africa. The general native culture of East Africa was somewhat distinctive in its combination of a little farming, cattle raising, and considerable warfare among tribes which often numbered many thousands. British policy in this area, moreover, led to extreme segregation and prohibitions on native participation in modern life that was surpassed only by South Africa. The ratio of Europeans to Africans has an interesting relationship to segregation. In South Africa, the ratio is 1:4, in Kenya where segregation was also strong, 1:150, in Tanganyika where Africans were permitted slightly more freedom, 1:440, and in Uganda, where equality far surpassed the other countries, 1:640.

The restrictions reflect European domination of the economy, especially where farmlands and other sources of wealth have been expropriated and native labor has been required. It was strongest in the areas of white settlement in Kenya and Tanganyika. Uganda was colonized late, it lost far less land to foreigners, and it has been less exposed to modernization.

Migrants from Asian (India) and Arab countries have filled the gap between the Europeans—who are the owners of plantations and mines, the ruling class and the major businessmen—and created an intermediate social sector of entrepreneurs, storekeepers, and skilled artisans. The ratio of Asians and Arabs to Africans is 1:25 in South Africa, 1:40 in Kenya, 1:85 in Tanganyika, and 1:85 in Uganda.

The Europeans, Indians, and Africans are strongly differentiated in every way. They are racially, culturally, and religiously distinct, and they are segregated by occupation and residence. Except for the higher echelons within the government, whose agents make occasional contacts with the Africans, the Indians have far more intimate relationships with the native population, especially in their role of entrepreneurs in marketing cash crops and maintaining stores in the small towns. It is only on the lowest level, in the African village, from which Indians are precluded, that the Africans themselves have become very small businessmen.

Europeans have to a great extent, although not always, expropriated lands for plantations in areas of marginal value to the native population. With the exception of sisal, which will grow in hot, arid country, it happens that tea and coffee, which are the principal plantation crops, are suited to comparatively high, cool, and rainy country. In East Africa, the hot, coastal lowlands were left to the Arabs. The great, semi-arid plains of the interior supported vast herds of wild game and considerable numbers of domesticated cattle and goats, but they did not attract European plantations or any important numbers of stock raisers. European plantations have been concentrated in the higher altitudes, near or in the zones of greater rainfall and dense native forests. In Tanganyika, they occurred in the southern highlands and around such great mountains as Kilimanjaro and Meru, while the arid lands of Kaguru country were little affected. There are forested mountains in Kaguru territory, but most are too steep to be suitable for plantations. In Kenya, there is a vast territory around and to the north and west of Nairobi that is known as the White Highlands because so much of it has been converted into European-owned plantations. Some of these plantations have encroached upon native lands to the extent of causing serious land shortage and dislocation of the people. The Kikuyu, among whom the Mau Mau arose, were one of the most seriously affected tribes. Farther west, across the Rift Valley, the Kipsigis have lost half their lands to Europeans, especially to large tea plantations, but these plantations are still being extended into forest lands of altitudes of seven thousand feet and more. Under new land uses and with markets for new crops, the Kipsigis still have sufficient land to have become specialized in truck gardening.

Tanganyika: The Kaguru. The Kagura have responded very slowly to the modernizing factors in East Africa, because these factors have been concentrated in the areas of white settlement. The 80,000 members of this tribe live in dispersed clusters of 20 to 40 houses and raise cattle and crops in their generally arid and unproductive territory. It was in this area that the famous "Operation Groundnut"—a colossally unsuccessful attempt to introduce peanuts as a cash crop—cost the British government several million dollars. Although crossed by the highway to the coast, the area has attracted few European plantations or towns. The principal cash crop of the Kaguru has been castor beans, which is marketed by Indian middlemen. Castor beans, however, have fluctuated on the world market and afford the Kaguru a very uncertain and meager cash income. This linkage to a world market has a different effect than production of truck garden vegetables for a local market, for the latter is assured and the crop can be varied. It has been said that the Kaguru might profitably raise tobacco, but the missionaries have so far discouraged this on moral grounds.

Owing to the small budget of Tanganyika, there are few agencies that mediate national factors to the local communities. Secondary roads are few, impassable, or nonexistent. The Kaguru have little access to more than primary government or mission schools which might give them the training necessary to find employment in the few towns. Wage labor on plantations provides one source of income in Tanganyika, but, like some of the highland Indian migrants to coastal plantations in Peru (described in Volume III), this may entail long trips for temporary employment, and its effect may be limited to material goods purchased elsewhere and adopted as conveniences or luxuries.

Kenya: The Kipsigis. Unlike the Kaguru, the Kipsigis occupied a territory which had sufficient elevation in most parts to give native farming an importance perhaps equal to that of herding and to at-

Fig. 6. Wheat farm of thousands of acres in the White Highlands of western Kenya, where Europeans have forced back the natives.

Fig. 7. A tea plantation of 28,000 acres in traditional Kipsigis territory affords a market for Kipsigis truck garden produce and employment for non-Kipsigis resident native labor.

Fig. 8. Land shortage has created cheap labor for the tea plantations in Kenya.

Fig. 9. The tea plantation provides housing, schools, medical care, and other facilities. Hexagonal, cement, aluminum-roofed houses were built (right), but the workers preferred their native-type wattle-and-daub, thatched roof houses (left).

tract European plantations. It is on the western fringe of the White Highlands, and about half of the Kipsigis land has been lost to Europeans, principally to tea plantations of many thousands of acres.

In order to provide transportation and communications, this area has been linked with Nairobi by a good highway, and even partly by a railroad spur, and local roads have been constructed where needed by Europeans. The European town of Kericho has developed in Kipsigis territory, while the smaller town of Sotik provides stores and servicing personnel which help link the Kipsigis with outside institutions. Most important, however, the Europeans need market vegetables because their plantations are strictly monocrop, and the rainfall and fertility of Kipsigis land is such that the natives can provide these foods.

The Kipsigis number about 200,000 persons. Despite the loss of lands to Europeans, their opportunity for cash cropping prevented their being forced to labor on the plantations. Instead, within a generation, they have changed from a pastoral people with small gardens to excellent farmers. Hence, they are regarded as the "show piece" of Kenya. Individual landholdings of about twenty acres, and the settlement of families on their own farms instead of in small groups as formerly have been made possible through pacification of the country as well as economic ties and land potential.

These new developments have not destroyed tribal identification, but they have become preconditions for further transformations. Where government or mission schools are not available, some of the tribe are building their own. They have been taking advantage of government services in farming and cattle breeding, although government regulations had strictly delimited their milk and tea production. Internal factions are developing, especially along the common lines of generations, and the youths are keenly aware of the local and even national potentials for a better life.

West Africa: the Anaguta. Many factors in the British colonial context had comparatively little effect on certain tribes of Nigeria owing to the presence of powerful kingdoms, or incipient states, which, as in other parts of West Africa (Diamond, 1951), dominated small, marginal tribes. The Anaguta, who lived between the coastal plains and the northern plateau, were but one of several small groups which had been victimized by the strongly organized Fulani and Hausa. The relationship of the Anaguta to their native neighbors as well as the British policy of indirect rule made the effects of colonialism unlike that of most of East Africa.

Fig. 10. The Anaguta live in loose clusters of traditional-type houses near Jos. Here, a woman tends a cassava plant in front of her hut. *Photo by Olga Diamond.*

During the early period of slaving, the powerful tribes drove the smaller ones, such as the Anaguta, into the refuge area between the coastal plains and the plateau. The Anaguta became involved with external institutions mainly after the British discovered the tin mines in the Jos area, where a town of some 50,000 Africans and 1,200 Europeans grew up within traditional Anaguta territory. Anaguta land was not expropriated for plantations, but their territory was compressed through urban expansion and prohibition of their rights to use forest reserves for farming or firewood. Although the tribe has retained its traditional social structure, it has become a rural proletariat in that it is forced to live by means of small subsistence plots, a little cash cropping, beer making, and miscellaneous menial chores—a haphazard accommodation. The Anaguta

Fig. 11. Although the town of Jos is within traditional Anaguta territory, the numerous and powerful Ibo, Hausa, and Fulani have become more important economically and socially in the city. Above, the home of a rich Ibo trader is next to a traditional dwelling in Sabon Gari (New Town). *Photo by Olga Diamond.*

population, according to some estimates, may have dropped from 5,700 in 1934 to 2,500 in 1959.

The people have little education and few have been missionized. Their history as a small, fugitive group has placed them at a disadvantage with the stronger tribes. Their present drift seems to suggest eventual loss of ethnic and social identity.

In the analyses of the formation of new nations in tribal areas, much attention has been accorded the processes of detribalization and the creation of a national outlook. It is expectable, however, that racial and ethnic distinctions will, as in the case of the Anaguta, also give way to class distinctions within the native population, and, although this process is already evident in urban centers, it will also occur in rural areas. A traditional inequality of tribes will be an important factor in class formation.

SOUTHEAST ASIA

As a general culture area, continental Southeast Asia is characterized by a considerable number of features drawn during many centuries from China, India, and the Moslem world. It is very diversified internally, however, for many small civilized states developed on the basis of a stable population of producers of irrigated rice in the low river valleys, while more primitive, isolated, and basically tribal societies of the hills, such as the Chin and Kayah of Burma and the Montagnards of Vietnam, carried on swidden farming in the mountain ranges that transect this area. The isolated mountain people of Malaya and the Philippines were food-gathering Negritos.

Two very general categories of rural populations were associated with tribal and state societies in Southeast Asia: the hill tribes, which are exemplified by the Kayah; and the rice producers of the small princely states, represented by the rural Malays. The hill tribes lacked institutional integration with the states; the rice farmers were the basic rural populations who came under the economic, political, and religious control of the state rulers.

European conquest of Southeast Asia first achieved control of spices and other luxury goods. Later, Europeans established plantations of new cash crops such as rubber, and extracted mineral and other resources, mostly from areas not already devoted to rice. In pre-colonial times, the hill tribes had not produced sufficient surpluses to make them true economic dependencies upon the local states, and their territories contain few resources of value to Western capitalism. As a result, they have remained economically, politically, and culturally marginal.

Within Southeast Asia, therefore, the two rough categories of native societies, variable though each is, are somewhat more precise structurally than such catch-all categories as "peasants" and "tribes." The local states combined a cultural heritage drawn from China and India within strongly centralized governments whose rulers were supported by a class of rice farmers and by trade, especially in Malaya. The hill statelets or subnuclear systems were weakly unified, they had no basic class of workers that was distinct from rulers, and they so related to the states as to create a patterned local adaptation to the orbit within which they functioned.

Burma: Kayah, a Hill Tribe or Statelet. The Kayah are a loosely unified people who numbered about 50,000 in 1941 and occupied some 3,600 square miles in the mountains of eastern Burma. They had formerly belonged to the Kayah "State," which, together with the adjoining Buddhist Shan and Burmese States and the other societies that comprise modern Burma, came under British control by 1884. They remained part of modern Burma when it became independent in 1948. Very little is known of the pre-colonial culture of the Kayah, and today the traditional Kayah structure seems to have been strengthened rather than modified by the few modern influences that have been mediated to it through Burma proper.

The Kayah population is only 14 persons per square mile as compared with 90 persons per square mile in Burma as a whole. The latter figure is not very different from that of the entire state of Kelantan in Malaya, including the mountainous regions, which had 78 persons per square mile in 1947. The fertile agricultural plains of Kelantan, however, had between 232 and 666 persons per square mile, depending upon local productivity. I have no comparable demographic figures for the plains of Burma, but the intensive, irrigated rice farming obviously created density far greater than in the hills.

The economic basis of the Kayah population is rice cultivation, but irrigation is little used and there is no important category of surplus that has financed or structured an economic dependency upon the adjoining states or the Burmese nation. Kayah society is grouped in permanent villages of thirty or more families, and the villages are loosely unified under charismatic, rather than purely hereditary, leaders whose power is sanctioned by local "pagan" religious beliefs and by access to slight wealth. The unity was "subnuclear" (Lehman, 1963) in that it was a diminished form of Burmese political structure, but it lacked the Buddhist religious apparatus which was an essential adjunct to true monarchical government. The lack of participation in the institutional life of the colony and the modern nation of Burma explains the perpetuation of the traditional nature of Kayah society.

In recent years, the only extractive wealth for an external market in Kayah territory has been a few minerals and teak wood, but these are too distant from the villages to have provided them wealth or employment. A single major road traverses the territory, and a few stores and other outposts of the state culture are scattered along it. A few schools and fewer missions have been established in Kayah territory. These mediating factors of external influence have affected a few individuals, but the basic structure of Kayah society remains marginal and traditional. Lack of the preconditions necessary to massive transmission of culture traits has also left the Kayah culturally marginal.

Malaya: Rural Society of Kelantan State. Malaya was formerly divided into many small, princely states which became Moslem sultanates during the fifteenth century. Kelantan had been dominated by various neighboring states, but finally came under the control of Siam or Thailand, which still holds the upper half of the

Malay Peninsula. Toward the end of the nineteenth century, the introduction of rubber and exploitation of tin gave Malaya great importance to the European world, and in 1909 Kelantan, along with other states, came under British control. After World War II, England made great efforts to modernize it in preparation for independence in 1957. The west coast had been more deeply influenced by factors of the external world during and subsequent to colonialism than Kelantan, which lacks tin and which has remained more traditional for several reasons.

The very great population of Kelantan has made it a state of rice imports. The average household rice land is 1.75 acres in Jeram kampong, but many holdings are much larger and many much smaller. There is also much sharecropping. A principal cash crop is rubber, and, although it is estimated that half the rubber of Malaya is produced by the native population—the Jeram household averages only 1.64 acres of rubber—their production and processing methods are so poor that the rubber loses half or a quarter of its value. Each household also has about two acres of fruit trees and vegetables, but these are so inadequately tended that their yield is minimal. It is only in recent years that the government programs are beginning to improve farm production, but shortage of land and neglected irrigation works limit their success.

Other factors deter the effectiveness of modernizing factors. The local communities (*kampongs*) are loosely nucleated villages of a few hundred people (Jeram had 700 inhabitants) who have had no strong ties to the state since the strong rule of the sultans was replaced by a bureaucracy. The villagers lack internal institutional structuring. Each is under an appointed state official who has limited power and little influence. Local authority is vested in men of personal prestige, wisdom, and physical courage, but there is a tendency to keep their identity secret. Because these men have no connection to the state they are not agents of modernization.

The absence of strong community institutions has caused communities to relate to one another through intermarriage, visiting (facilitated by the new system of roads), and splitting and wide dispersal of landholdings. The typical farmer, moreover, has difficulty accumulating capital in the form of land or cash, while traditional values inhibit the drive for monetary rewards. Finally, the state of Kelantan is 85 per cent rural, as defined by people living in communities of less than 1,000. Kota Bharu, its largest city, has only 38,000 persons. Whereas Malaya as a whole is 50 per cent Chinese, Kelantan is only 6 per cent, for the Chinese are attracted to cities and commerce. Consequently, there are few urban opportunities and these

Fig. 12. A traditional Kelantan Malay house surrounded by various fruit and nut trees.

Fig. 13. West coast Malay chief's house retains advantage of elevated floor and airy construction of the traditional house, but has concrete steps. Granary is in rear.

Figs. 14 and 15. Natives in Pasir Puteh, Kelantan, use rubber hand press and then work rubber on the ground, producing crude, inferior sheets.

Fig. 16. Native methods cannot compete with the clean rubber (drying, above) produced in the plantation processing plant.

have been largely preempted by Chinese, while the small total number of Chinese has provided few mediating agents who might create a culture ferment, as they have elsewhere.

Although modernization has been slow in Kelantan, the very lack of traditional community institutions may permit innovations and, if cities and industries grow, potentials exist for individuals now in the rural communities. A break-through to a desire for new opportunities is, in fact, beginning, especially among the younger generation. They are seeking education in addition to that provided by religious schools, they are taking advantage of facilities offered by the state, and they hope for new occupational roles and statuses. The Europeans, Chinese, and Malays are still clearly distinguishable racially, ethnically, and religiously, but they are not hierarchical, castelike social segments, as in Africa. Malays are the ruling class and the lower class, but the latter will change as it has access to and opportunity to use modernizing factors.

LATIN AMERICA

The Indian societies studied in Mexico and Peru differ from our other cases in that they had been influenced by European institutions for 400 years prior to the era of modernization. In the densely populated pre-Columbian states, the Spaniards found native societies amenable to labor on their haciendas and in their mines and towns. They not only utilized the general native segment of society that had performed public labor and served in households, but they increased the labor force by expropriating native lands, by introducing livestock, horses, grapes, and other plants and animals for their own special use, decreased subsistence lands, and by resettling whole communities in order to administer them more effectively. The hacienda of early Spanish colonialism in the highlands of Peru differed from that of more recent colonial plantations of other nations in that it directly expropriated the principal agricultural lands and the laborers attached to them, whereas twentieth-century plantations of Africa and Southeast Asia usually preempted lands of marginal value in the native economy and were forced to bind a labor force to them by taxes or other means.

In the early periods of Spanish colonialism the principal wealth was mineral, but in time export crops such as sugar, coffee, cotton, and others were grown in areas near the sea lanes. In the period of modernization, the haciendas on which these crops were grown became more mechanized and commercialized monocrop plantations. Wage laborers, sharecroppers, and specialists in the managerial hierarchy were drawn into these plantation contexts, where they lost identification with their native villages. Increasing industrialization, urbanization, and other factors of modernization provided larger and more varied contexts of change.

Where haciendas and mines did not directly affect the local populations—especially in areas such as northern Mexico, the tropical forests of South America, and some of the isolated highland communities of the Andes—missionaries, often aided by soldiers, created new population centers where they introduced European crops, imposed Catholicism over the aboriginal religion, and caused various transformations of the local tribes. Their influence remained after the missionaries withdrew, and few Indians of Latin America today can be considered wholly aboriginal.

The four centuries that followed the Spanish Conquest are divisible into major periods of change, depending upon each area. Mexico's independence from Spain in 1821 and Peru's in 1824 followed rebellion by the landlords more than the Indians and eliminated Spain's economic and political restrictions but did not introduce fundamentally new institutions that might affect the basic populations. Modernization began to penetrate these areas most rapidly where agricultural wealth could be produced for export and transportation was developed, and it has followed more slowly in remote, marginal areas.

The traditional cultures of our studies in Mexico and Peru, therefore, are not aboriginal. Even to view them as a mechanical mixture of Spanish and Indian traits has little meaning. The aboriginal sociocultural systems have undergone a succession of structural transformations, even down to the community and family levels, that represent responses to external institutions of different kinds. As a reference point for analysis of modernization, each traditional society is one that had already been modified by state institutions and by haciendas, missions, and other local contexts.

Mexico: Yaqui and Mayo. Some 6,000 to 10,000 Yaqui and 30,000 to 34,000 Mayo Indians lived in 1959 on the arid coast of southern Sonora, Mexico. The history of their societies has been described in great detail by Spicer (1961, 1962), starting with the first missionary contacts in 1553, then the period of mission villages from 1617 to 1767 when the Jesuits were expelled, a following period of comparative autonomy until 1887, and the modern era after 1887. Spicer's analysis of change deals with the nature of Spanish-Indian contacts, culture trait borrowing, and assimilation.

Erasmus' study stresses the institutional linkage of the Indians to the larger context, and it consequently considers the changes after the Mexican Revolution as the beginning of modernization, for the *ejido* or collective farm was introduced after this time.

The pre-Columbian Yaqui and Mayo had been rather simple farming tribes which are classed in the general aboriginal culture area of the Greater Southwest. During their century and a half of influence, the Jesuits introduced not only livestock and new crops but a system of annual ceremonies and societies responsible for these ceremonies. These social features survived after missionary withdrawal and continued through the period of comparative autonomy into periods and situations of hacienda domination. They are important today because the obligations to support these ceremonies place value on giving and obviate the opportunities for accumulation of individual wealth.

The traditional societies and cultures are those that existed prior to the Mexican Revolution of 1910, when the principal institutions to which the Indians had been linked were haciendas, where they were held through debts virtually in slavery. When the haciendas were broken up, the Indians were placed on *ejidos*, which were financed and regulated by the government. They were advanced loans, required to buy machinery and to grow certain crops, and paid in the form of loans rather than wages. The Indians consequently had little chance to leave the *ejidos*. Meanwhile, the construction of large irrigation systems in the area, especially during the last two decades, reduced natural flooding and productivity of Indian lands, and the people who sought a cash income turned increasingly to cutting wood, weaving mats, and producing other handicrafts. Mestizos and whites entered the area in great numbers at this time to create new irrigated farms and swell the population of towns and cities. The Indians, however, were too bound to their *ejidos* to take advantage of the new opportunities.

More isolated and traditional, the Yaqui adjusted to the *ejido* situation better than the Mayo, for they continued their traditional ceremonial pattern which prevented accumulation of individual wealth. So long as this continued, the minor influence of schools and other governmental or private institutions made no great difference. The Mayo, however, were losing their traditional structure and the means of maintaining it earlier than the Yaqui. Many Mayo had married outside the tribe, and all had fairly intimate contacts with the larger society. The Mayo *ejidos*, therefore, have weakened, individuals are seeking private wealth through unrestricted production for profit and through wage labor, and communities will probably change in response to new goals and activities.

Peru: Hacienda and Plantation. The aboriginal empire of the Inca of Peru had amalgamated a diversity of local states under a strongly centralized government. These included farmers and pastoralists who were dispersed in the highlands up to an altitude of fifteen thousand feet and farmers who were nucleated in communities of irrigation farmers on the arid coast. The Spanish Conquest of 1532 replaced the Inca imperial institutions with those of Spain, but the basic rural population today is largely of Indian descent and, in certain areas, features of Indian family and community-level culture have survived.

The fundamental changes in the context of Peru since the Spanish Conquest have been contingent on its economic, political, and religious dependency upon external powers—at first, upon Spain, and after 1824, upon the larger world of industry and commerce. Sketches of the general changes in post-Conquest Peru by Kubler (1946) and Faron (in Volume III) show adaptations of policies and transformations of local communities that responded to the kind of wealth extracted for an external market. Miller in Volume III has given a general picture of the plantation and hacienda in modern Peru.

The initial Spanish policy was theoretically indirect rule, or exaction of tribute, through the *encomienda,* a system that granted individuals the rights to take wealth from, but not interfere with, the native peoples of given territories. Mines, however, were taken by the Spaniards almost immediately, and haciendas, or individually owned farmlands, were quickly expropriated from the Indians. Owing to Spanish restrictions on overseas trade and emphasis upon mineral wealth, the early haciendas served the mines and towns rather than foreign markets. The traditional pattern of the hacienda, which still is somewhat manifest in certain areas, was a large landed estate that was controlled by a paternalistic *hacendado,* largely self-sufficient in producing its own food and meeting other needs; it drew its labor force from various sources—especially dispossessed Indians, a native class of more or less bound laborers (*yanacona*), and more recently, African slaves, Chinese and Japanese immigrants, and finally, highland Indians.

Native Indian communities (*comunidades indígenas*) began to be absorbed very early on the coast, and today they survive mainly in isolated portions of the highlands. Even in the highlands, however, they are being pressed by the expansion of private estates, especially those devoted to livestock. This has brought violent rebellion in some areas and generally caused an overflow population to migrate to the coast to find employment. Highland haciendas have been devoted mainly to food production, because the transportation to the seaports has been too expensive to permit export crops.

The highland hacienda has remained more traditional than that of the coast. Its labor force has included sharecroppers from Indian villages who helped expand the hacienda by clearing new lands, for which they received rights to cultivate certain portions. Former bound labor remained, and as long as the hacienda store (the familiar pattern of the "company store") persisted, the workers remained in debt. As population increased and new land became unavailable many landless families became wage earners.

The highland hacienda studied by Sol Miller was unusual in that the *hacendado* or *patrón* was a railroad, not a person, but attitudes toward management were similar to those on personally owned plantations. During the present century, and especially since World War II, increasing industrialization and particularly the expansion of a network of roads, educational facilities, and population pressures has given the workers new orientations. Already, there is a diversity of opportunities on the hacienda. The status groups within the community depend largely upon their rights to cultivate lands of varying fertility and their position in the managerial hierarchy of the hacienda.

The modern highland hacienda can no longer meet the needs of its people. Many individuals and families who need, or believe they need, additional money, drift to the lowlands, first as temporary, contract laborers, later as permanent settlers. Many other highland families who have no land and little employment opportunity also seek a livelihood on the coast. In the community of the coastal plantation, they eventually lose identity with their native villages and merge with families of diverse provenience into a laboring proletariat. Many other highland families, however, find no regular employment on the coast, and they are forming slums around Lima and the other cities.

The development of the traditional societies of the coastal areas differs from that of the highland principally because the coast converted to special export crops and became exposed to modernizing factors much earlier. Chancay Valley studied by Louis Faron exemplifies many processes characteristic of the coast generally.

Initially, the haciendas of this valley produced food for Lima. By the middle eighteenth century it began to grow sugar for export, and increased its production after Peru's independence from Spain in 1824 when sugar could be shipped to any market. Slaves had been imported, though freed in 1855, and some 80,000 Chinese immigrated to Peru in the nineteenth century to become bound laborers because local Indian communities supplied insufficient manpower.

The marked changes caused by modernizing factors began about 1900. Cotton became the principal crop, and so many sharecroppers were brought in that the cultivated land was increased threefold and the population fourfold. Japanese arrived to create highly efficient farmers and hacienda managers; the Chinese became largely absorbed into the Indian population. With World War II, the Japanese lost their hold on farm wealth. Meanwhile, mechanization began to create a trend toward larger farm units and fewer sharecroppers and independent farmers. Needed farm labor is being drawn today from surplus highland populations of communities like those described by Miller.

Some of the traditional concepts of the hacienda linger in that the *patrón* has much personal influence, but the trend toward complete depersonalization of the hacienda as a purely cost-accounting production unit with labor bound through indebtedness has been checked by a liberal government. Personal services given free to the *patrón* and use of the hacienda store to force indebtedness have been abolished. Better prices to the sharecropper have been guaranteed, and the law has required that 20 per cent of the land in the Chancay Valley be devoted to food cultivation. At the present time, therefore, Peru is caught between the increasing need to produce food for its expanding industries and cities and the trend toward mechanized plantation monocrop production for world markets.

These processes are affecting the people of Chancay Valley in various ways. Cash returns are increasing, but easy access to coastal towns, especially Lima, is providing avenues of escape for those who do not find a satisfactory niche in the local arrangements.

JAPAN

The uniqueness of Japan among the nations previously mentioned highlights the significance of the contexts of these other countries. Japan was never conquered by a mercantile or capitalist nation and consequently never had its lands expropriated by foreigners to create large plantations. With very few exceptions, Japan's farms are family owned and family worked, and they rarely exceed two acres, which is only a little larger than the Malay rice paddy of Kelantan. Efficient rice production, now supplemented by many vegetables, however, has supported an increasingly industrialized and urbanized nation.

Japan is also distinctive in the general homogeneity of its race, religion, language, and ideology, so that, with the exception of the Eta, a small outcast group, everyone has potential mobility. Changes, therefore, will come about as a result of industrialization, which is steadily reaching the rural people, rather than through upheavals or disjunctions that have followed conquest elsewhere.

The survival of the small farms in one of the world's most industrialized nations may seem to be something of a paradox. Railroads and a few bus lines have been the principal means of transportation, but automobiles and roads are now entering the national scene to an important degree. Rural electrification and education, however, are second to no other nation, and government services in the form of marketing arrangements, farm organizations, improved agricultural methods, health measures, and other kinds of rural assistance, together with the organization of local chapters of national associations, have already created a very sophisticated farm population.

Our two communities, Kaminosho, a hamlet (*buraku*) in the Nara Basin, and Kurikoma, a hamlet in the northern mountains, were traditional societies for the purposes of our research in the feudal period which ended about 1870. Under the lords of the Tokugawa period, they were primarily rice producers, but change in their culture was inhibited by sumptuary and other restrictive laws and by prohibitions on territorial, occupational, and status mobility. The two communities differed mainly as they adapted to local environments and were able to produce special crops for outside trade.

Today, the feudal restrictions have been removed, travel and considerable migrations to cities occurs, better production enables the people to purchase many new kinds of goods and to adopt new customs, and local associations are powerful agencies for introducing new methods of farming, processing, and marketing. In Kaminosho, which is suburban to Osaka, members of many families commute daily to work in the city. Kaminosho has been more modernized than Kurikoma owing to its greater wealth and access to the city. Both communities, however, have remained traditional and rural in their social structure.

The modern as well as the feudal peasant society was based on a family which maintained use and usually ownership of lands, which it cultivated mainly by its own labor, through a system of primogeniture. Although surplus was taken from the farmer as tribute, rents, or taxes at different periods, the basic owner-cultivator farm of about two acres was preserved. Farm families have always been integral parts of the hamlet (*buraku*). In feudal times, the hamlets functioned autonomously, except for obligations to the lords. Today, they are still the primary society, although linked with many national institutions. Perpetuation of the farm family and hamlet is, in fact, facilitated by industrialization which is draining off younger sons and daughters to urban centers and relieving stresses that might endanger the traditional structure.

Modernization of farming methods has begun, but it has not yet affected social arrangements pertaining to the small farm. Rural Japan is so highly electrified that nearly every farm has outlets in the fields for threshing machines. Many communities have privately or village-owned gasoline powered hand tractors, but these are no more than substitutes for horses in the north and oxen in the south which are suitable for cultivating tiny farm plots. Tractors need not be fed and therefore do not compete with food crops. Fertilizers, herbicides, and insecticides can be used on farms of any size. A small class of migratory farm laborers is beginning to appear in the southern area, probably in response to the new diversity of crops and the production of two and sometimes three crops a year.

Fig. 17. Traditional, thatched house (left) near Kurikoma, Japan, is still preferred, but two-storied wood and aluminum house (right) is more economical for it requires less space and land must be used to raise special thatching reeds. Electrical power lines are visible in all Japanese rural landscapes.

A radical and revolutionary transformation of farm cultivation and the nature of farm social structure could occur if heavy machinery were introduced. Although steeply terraced land must always be cultivated by hand or by small tractors, there are large areas where the dikes separating farms could be eliminated and heavy machinery could cultivate units of hundreds of acres. This is done in the United States with exceptional productivity. Probably it will be done some day in Japan. But as long as farm income suffices and urban centers cannot absorb the enormous labor supply such cultivation would release from the land, the present methods of farming, of land ownership, and of inheritance, and the present structure of the rural community will continue.

A few localities, however, have experienced incipient changes owing to special factors. In the mountains north of Kaminosho, the introduction of liquid fuel for household purposes has released community forest lands, which were sources of firewood and charcoal, and considerable acreage has been devoted to the dry farming of vegetables. Dairy farming, formerly confined mainly to Hokkaido, has been initiated in cleared forest lands of northern Honshu, where repatriates from Manchuria hold about six acres each and live in dispersed settlements rather than the traditional

Fig. 18. During rice planting, all family members are busy and "even the cats have hands." Cooperation between families continues in Kurikoma, but labor exchange tends everywhere to be replaced by wage labor.

type of hamlet. There is even one corporation-owned farm of 2,600 acres—by far the largest in all Japan—devoted to dairy cattle, poultry, hay and other produce and worked entirely by wage labor. But these are all exceptions.

Some Omissions of Subject Matter

We obviously had to omit many major categories of subject matter because any project is limited in scope. The omissions may have affected the general conceptual scheme for viewing modernization in some degree, and they would certainly have restricted hypotheses not based on additional cases.

One important area omitted is India, which is distinctive especially for its basic caste structure, its earlier princely states, its rich religious and philosophical heritage, and its enormous population. India alone could have afforded many kinds of samples. Field study of societies within mainland China and within the Russian sphere would have been impossible and use of the literature would have been an enormous task. Among the communist nations, no less than among capitalist colonies or spheres of influence, however, programs of directed change are of interest as much because of their unexpected results as because of their partial success. These considerations are for the future.

Many culture areas and structural types among American Indians were omitted from the field research because a fairly long familiarity with them and a vast literature gave them lower priority. Knowledge of these Indians, however, was an important factor in developing the research design of the project and it underlies many of the thoughts expressed in this introduction and to be expanded in my later volume. Indians of the United States have received more attention than any tribes in the world, and much of the early theory of acculturation and assimilation was based on this research. Some reassessment of the reservation context, which is highly distinctive, however, will be in order. In addition, my project, Studies of Cultural Regularities, has recently been extended to a study, not yet published, of the modernization of the very conservative Hopi by Shuichi Nagata. Nagata's data will be utilized according to the methodology explained here.

Field work in South America outside the Andes was omitted because my colleagues and I had previously paid it considerable attention (Steward, 1946-50; Steward and Faron, 1959; Faron, 1961, 1964; Murphy and Steward, 1955; Murphy, 1960). There is, moreover, a growing literature on the subject which has been taken into account.

Our field studies in Africa, Southeast Asia, Japan, Mexico, and Peru were principally of certain communities of rural agrarian societies and of some plantations. While many other kinds of rural societies and urban peoples were omitted, they are no less important in understanding the processes of modernization and will therefore be fitted into the broad conceptual scheme subsequently.

Bibliography

Acculturation: An Exploratory Formulation
1954 "Social Science Research Council Seminar on Acculturation, 1953," *American Anthropologist*, Vol. LVI, pp. 973-1002.

Arensberg, Conrad M., and Solon T. Kimball
1965 *Culture and Community*, New York, Chicago, Burlingame.

Barnett, Homer G.
1953 *Innovation*, New York.

Broom, Leonard, and John I. Kitsuse
1955 "The Validation of Acculturation," *American Anthropologist*, Vol. LVII, pp. 44-48.

Diamond, Stanley
1951 *Dahomey: A Proto-State in West Africa*, Ph.D. thesis, Columbia University. (In press.)

Erasmus, Charles J.
1961 *Man Takes Control: Cultural Development and American Aid*, Minneapolis.

Faron, Louis C.
1961 *Mapuche Social Structure*, Urbana, Ill.
1964 *Hawks of the Sun: Mapuche Morality and Its Ritual Attributes*, Pittsburgh.

Gillin, John
1945 *Moche, A Peruvian Coastal Community*, Institute of Social Anthropology, Washington, D.C.
1949 "Mestizo America," *Most of the World* (ed. Ralph Linton), pp. 156-211, New York.

Heath, Dwight B., and Richard N. Adams (eds.)
1965 *Contemporary Cultures and Societies of Latin America*, New York.

Katz, Elihu, Herbert Hamilton, and Martin Levin
1963 "Traditions of Research of the Diffusion of Innovation," *American Sociological Review*, Vol. XXVIII, pp. 237-52.

Kroeber, A. L.
1952 *The Nature of Culture*, Chicago.
Kubler, George
1946 "The Quechua in the Colonial World," *Handbook of South American Indians* (ed. J. H. Steward), Vol. II, pp. 331-411, Bureau of American Ethnology, Washington, D.C.
Lehman, F. K.
1963 *The Structure of Chin Society*, Urbana, Ill.
1964 "Typology and the Classification of Sociocultural Systems," *Process and Pattern in Culture* (ed. Robert A. Manners), pp. 376-98, Chicago.
Lewis, Oscar
1961 *The Children of Sanchez*, New York.
Murphy, Robert F.
1960 *Headhunter's Heritage*, Berkeley.
1964 "Social Change and Acculturation," *Transactions of the New York Academy of Science*, Ser. II, Vol. XXVI, pp. 845-54.
Murphy, Robert F., and Julian H. Steward
1955 "Tappers and Trappers: Parallel Process in Acculturation," *Economic Development and Cultural Change*, Vol. IV, pp. 335-55.
Norbeck, Edward
1962 "Common-Interest Associations in Rural Japan," *Japanese Culture: Its Development and Characteristics* (eds. Robert J. Smith and Richard K. Beardsley), pp. 71-83, Viking Fund Publications in Anthropology, New York.
Redfield, Robert, Ralph Linton, and Melville Herskovits
1936 "Memorandum for the Study of Acculturation," *American Anthropologist*, Vol. XXXVIII, pp. 149-55.
Rubin, Vera
1959 (ed.) *Plantation Systems in the New World*, Pan American Union, Washington, D. C.
1961 "The Anthropology of Development," *Biennial Review of Anthropology* (ed. Bernard J. Siegal), pp. 120-72, Stanford.
Spicer, Edward H.
1961 (ed.) *Perspectives in American Indian Culture Change*, Chicago.
1962 *Cycles of Conquest*, Tucson, Ariz.
Spiro, Melford E.
1955 "The Acculturation of American Ethnic Groups," *American Anthropologist*, Vol. LVII, pp. 1240-51.
Steward, Julian H.
1946–50 (ed.) *Handbook of South American Indians*, 6 vols., Bureau of American Ethnology, Washington, D.C.
1951 "Levels of Sociocultural Integration: An Operational Concept," *Southwestern Journal of Anthropology*, Vol. VII, pp. 374-90.
1955 *Theory of Culture Change*, Urbana, Ill.

1956a *Anthropological View of Contemporary Culture Change*, Kyoto American Studies Seminar, Kyoto, Japan.
1956b (*et al.*) *The People of Puerto Rico*, Urbana, Ill.
1959 "Perspectives on Plantations," *Plantation Systems in the New World* (ed. Vera Rubin), Pan American Union, Washington, D.C.

Steward, Julian H., and Louis Faron
1959 *Native Peoples of South America*, New York.

Steward, Julian H., and Demitri B. Shimkin
1962 "Some Mechanisms of Sociocultural Evolution," *Evolution and Man's Progress* (ed. Ralph W. Burhoe), pp. 67-87, New York.

Wagley, Charles, and Marvin Harris
1955 "A Typology of Latin American Subcultures," *American Anthropologist*, Vol. LVII, pp. 428-51.

White, Leslie
1959 *The Evolution of Culture*, New York.

Wolf, Eric
1955 "Types of Latin American Peasantry," *American Anthropologist*, Vol. LVII, pp. 542-71.
1959 *Sons of the Shaking Earth*, Chicago.

Wolfe, Alvin W.
1963 "The African Mineral Industry: Evolution of a Supranational Level of Integration," *Social Problems*, Vol. XI, pp. 153-64.

Vogt, Evon Z.
1960 "On the Concepts of Structure and Process in Cultural Anthropology," *American Anthropologist*, Vol. LXII, pp. 18-33.

Tanganyika: A Study of an African Society at National and Local Levels

EDWARD H. WINTER

T. O. BEIDELMAN

Preface

In this study we shall be concerned with presenting a picture of the principal social, political, and economic aspects of Tanganyika as a whole. Once this has been done, we shall focus our attention upon one relatively small area, Ukaguru, the country inhabited by the Kaguru, one of the many Bantu-speaking groups inhabiting the territory. In this first part, our personal observations are used primarily as a background against which to assess the veracity and appropriateness of the published sources upon which it is, for the most part, based. In an attempt to give a rounded account of the conditions in Tanganyika which will be meaningful to someone with no previous knowledge of East Africa and one which will serve as a framework into which the second part of the study can be fitted, we have been obliged, of necessity, to traverse ground which is familiar to the specialist. However, we hope that, by unearthing some relatively little known facts and putting them together in certain ways, we have made some contribution to the study of Tanganyika and of colonialism in general. In the second part, by contrast, primary importance is accorded to material collected in the field. Published information about the Kaguru is extremely scanty, and some of it is unreliable. The material presented here does not, in any sense, represent a "complete" report. It has been presented in a particular way for the purposes of this study, and may be seen as constituting an introduction to the study of the Kaguru.

The present tense is used throughout in reference to the years 1957-58, the period during which we carried out our investigations in Tanganyika. This study was written in 1959 and revised early in

1960. Many profound changes have taken place since then. For example, the whole system of chieftainship by which the Kaguru were administered for decades has been abolished, as have similar systems throughout Tanganyika following independence. Indeed, the name Tanganyika itself no longer exists on the map, having been replaced by Tanzania following the union with Zanzibar. However, we have retained the word Tanganyika in order to emphasize that we are concerned, not with presenting the most up-to-date picture of conditions in a part of East Africa, but rather with what we considered to be deep-seated conditions and trends as they existed near the end of the colonial era.

Part I. Tanganyika: The National Level

PHYSICAL SETTING

Tanganyika is a large territory of some 360,000 square miles. It is about four times the size of the United Kingdom. Behind the coast there is a wooded plain which extends inland in most places for more than a hundred miles. The country then rises to the East African plateau with altitudes ranging from 3,000 to over 4,000 feet. In various areas there are isolated mountain peaks such as Kilimanjaro and Meru, small mountain ranges and highland areas which stand above the plateau. There are no navigable rivers but three of the great African lakes are found on the borders of the country: Lake Victoria on the northwest, Lake Tanganyika, which runs along most of the western boundary, and Lake Nyasa whose northern tip extends into Tanganyika.

Vast areas receive very little rainfall. In about one-third of the territory there are very slight chances of receiving the yearly 20 inches of rain which many experts consider the lower limit for agriculture under East African conditions (East African Royal Commission, 1953-55, p. 255). Furthermore, two-thirds of the country is infested with tsetse fly, the vector for human sleeping sickness, and trypanosomiasis, which affects livestock. In terms of rainfall and general climatic conditions, the most favorable areas are the highlands. Unfortunately, many of these are already densely populated. Tanganyika presents man with a harsh environment which poses a multitude of problems for those who try to cope with it. The failure of the gigantic groundnut scheme in the postwar period is merely the most publicized failure in human adaptation to Tanganyikan conditions. In many areas, such as that occupied by the

Gogo, periodic famines still occur. In such places the problem, even today, is not so much the one which will be chiefly discussed in the pages which follow, that of raising cash incomes and standard of living, but instead, that of keeping the inhabitants alive.

HISTORY

There have been Arab settlements on the East African coast for over a thousand years. In 1498 Vasco da Gama rounded the Cape of Good Hope and soon afterwards these coastal towns came under Portuguese control. In the seventeenth century the power of Portugal declined and at the end of the century, in 1698, Fort Jesus at Mombasa fell to the Arabs and soon afterwards all of the East African towns were once more in Arab hands with the exception of those in the south, in what is now Portuguese East Africa.

It is extraordinary that neither the Arabs nor the Portuguese appear to have penetrated the interior until the nineteenth century when Arabs, based upon Zanzibar, began to extend operations inland in search of ivory and slaves. The arrival of the Portuguese was important, however, in that it led to the introduction of certain New World crops such as tobacco and potatoes and, most important of all, maize, which rapidly became the staple crop in a very large part of present-day Tanganyika.

Soon after the Arabs had established caravan routes to the Great Lakes, they were followed by European explorers. Burton and Speke traveled from the coast to Lake Tanganyika and in 1858 Speke reached a southern arm of Lake Victoria. In 1863 the first mission, a Roman Catholic station, was established on the coast. Thereafter missionaries, both Catholic and Protestant, penetrated the interior.

In 1884 the Gesellschaft fuer Deutsche Kolonization was organized. On behalf of this company, a party of Germans under the leadership of Dr. Carl Peters went to East Africa. After a very short time, Peters returned to Europe with a number of chiefs' signatures on treaties between themselves and the company. The German government lent the company its official support. Protests from the Sultan of Zanzibar concerning the treaties made by Peters were silenced by the appearance of German warships off Zanzibar. A French, English, and German Commission was sent out to East Africa and the final result was an agreement between the British and German governments in 1886, delimiting their spheres of influence. As a result of two agreements which he was forced to sign in 1888 and 1890, the Sultan of Zanzibar lost all his rights over territory on the Tanganyika mainland.

The German company retained politicial control for a very short time. Almost at once they were faced with a revolt led by an Arab named Bushiri and German troops had to be called in to suppress it. In 1891 the German government took over formal control of the territory. Vigorous efforts were made to develop the area economically and a widespread African uprising called the Maji Maji Rebellion was successfully suppressed in 1905-7. All German activities were brought to a halt by the outbreak of the First World War. General Lettow-Vorbeck fought a brilliant campaign against tremendous odds and managed to have a force still in operation when he received news of the armistice. The Africans were the chief sufferers and many thousands of them died as soldiers, conscripted porters, and innocent bystanders.

After the war, German East Africa was granted (with the exception of the densely settled northwestern part, the present-day Ruanda-Urundi, which came under Belgian control) to Great Britain as a mandated territory under the supervision of the League of Nations. After the Second World War, Tanganyika's status was that of a trusteeship territory under the supervision of the United Nations Trusteeship Council.

INHABITANTS

As a result of censuses carried out in 1948 and 1957, reliable figures on the population have become available for the first time. Unfortunately, only certain large totals are as yet available for the 1957 census and in certain places we shall have to use figures from other years. The first census showed the population to be much larger than had previously been thought. The second census refuted conclusively the view held by certain people in the thirties that the population was decreasing. The population is not only increasing, but it is doing so rapidly. In the nine-year period, the total population rose by a million and a third from 7,410,000 to 8,700,000 (Colonial Office, 1957, p. 3). This rate of increase poses serious problems for the future, particularly in view of the limited areas available for agricultural expansion and the failure of the modern economy to provide additional employment opportunities to keep pace with the growing population.

The inhabitants of Tanganyika are often discussed in terms of three categories: African, European, and Asian or Indian. In a sense, these are real social groups because they are meaningful in terms of social behavior between members of these categories. Thus, one does not expect to find Indians and especially Africans in a hotel in an area where there are large numbers of European settlers. However, a rigid color bar is no longer in effect and although Africans seldom enter such places, should they do so they would be served. The three groups have different standards of living, pursue different occupations, and above all, their physical differences are great enough to be readily visible. The only possible confusion occurs in the case of certain Indians and Europeans from the Mediterranean.

This broad classification ignores the tremendous heterogeneity of the population. Each of these categories, particularly the African, contains a multitude of very different groups. With the exception of the Europeans, no group has any great sense of unity. This is particularly marked in the case of the Africans, but it is also true to a very large extent of the Indians whose social lives revolve within their own particular ethnic or religious groups. There seems to be little feeling that they owe loyalty to one another at any level beyond this. What unity there is among the Indians is forced upon them by the fact that they are treated as a unit socially, economically, and politically by the Europeans and Africans.

To turn first to the Africans, there are some 120 tribes recognized for census purposes. Although anthropologists and others have defined the word "tribe" in a number of different ways, there is no harm in using it as long as its meaning in any particular context is clearly understood. The term "tribe" as it is used in East Africa has no political implications. Although, in recent decades, under European rule, many of the tribes have been organized into centralized political units, this was not the case under aboriginal conditions when a tribe of 20,000 or more people might have been organized into a multitude of small, independent political units. Even today many tribes are not unified. Tribe refers to an ethnic group, i.e., an aggregation of people who share a common way of life and who usually have a language of their own. The tribes vary tremendously in numbers. At one end of the scale are the Sukuma who numbered over 1,000,000 in 1957, followed by the Nyamwezi with 363,000. At the other end of the scale are the hunting and gathering Hadza of whom there are but a few hundred. Some nineteen tribes have populations in excess of 100,000 while an additional twenty-four have populations of over 50,000. The first six tribes in numerical order comprise just over a third of the total population.

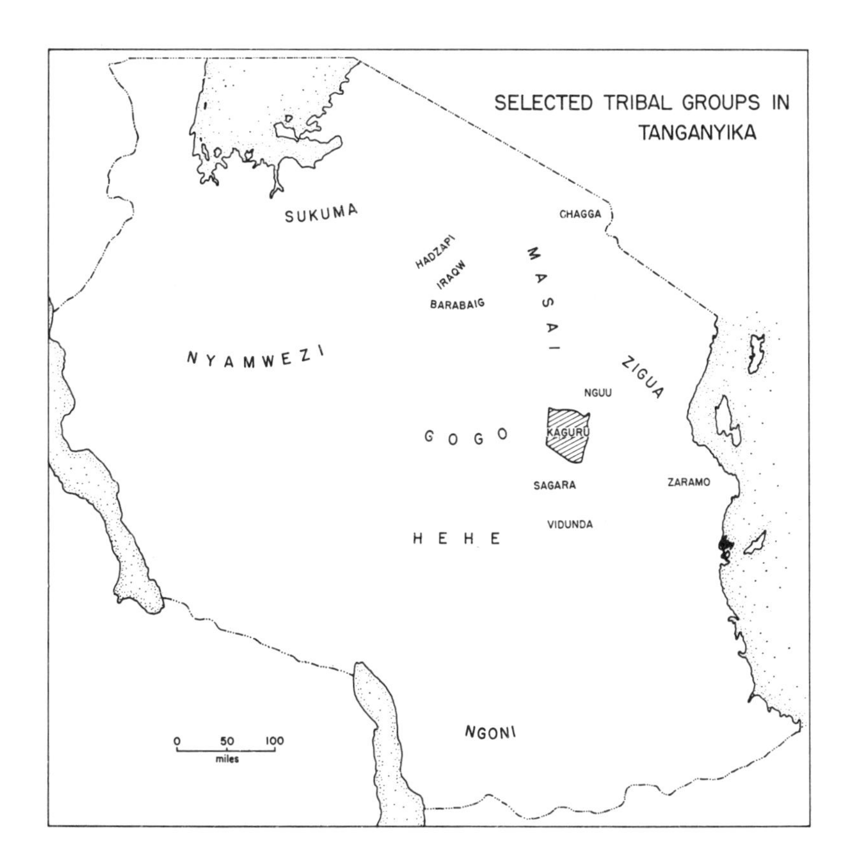

The language situation in Tanganyika is extremely complex since practically every tribe has its own language, which is unintelligible to members of other tribes. The majority of the languages, however, are Bantu and the differences between them are comparable to the differences between the Romance languages, such as Italian and Spanish. Other languages found in the north are Nilotic, Kushitic, Nilo-Hamitic, and Khoisan. In the last century, Swahili, the Bantu language of the coast, began to penetrate the interior with the Arab slavers, and it is now the lingua franca of Tanganyika as well as a much larger part of eastern Africa. At the present time, most adult men in the interior have at least a smattering of Swahili, but this is not true of the women who usually know only their own language. Swahili is the official language of the territory and is used by administrative and other government officials in their dealings with the African population, even though English is the official language in the Legislative Council. Swahali is the language used by settlers in dealing with their labor, and it is also employed by some missionaries. It is the language used by the so-called detribalized Africans who now live in towns and in other places outside the older tribal framework.

There is great variation among the various tribes in such things as matrilineal or patrilineal descent, marriage customs, family types, music, religion, etc. For example, a systematic comparison of the Masai of the Rift Valley and the Haya on the shores of Lake Victoria would show only a small number of similarities in their cultural inventories. Rather than commenting further upon this diversity, a few generalized remarks will be made about the basic types of economy pursued. Fishing is of importance only along the coast itself and on the shores of Lakes Victoria, Tanganyika, and Nyasa. The people who live in the coastal hinterland are almost entirely agricultural although a few sheep and goats are kept. On the interior plateau cattle people are encountered. Actually, only a few people such as the Masai and Barabaig, who form a minute proportion of the population, are entirely pastoral. Most people pursue a combined pastoral-agricultural economy with agriculture as the basis of subsistence. While rice has been grown on the coast for some time, maize is the principal grain wherever conditions are favorable. Elsewhere reliance is placed upon more drought-resistant sorghums and millets. The principal root crops are sweet potatoes and cassava; beans are also grown in considerable quantities. In a few areas of high rainfall, such as the slopes of Kilimanjaro and in Bukoba, plantains form the basis of the diet.

Of the non-indigenous groups, the Arabs were, until the present century, the most important. Today, although some Arabs have settled in the interior, they have not spread in any numbers from the towns and small trading centers on or near the old caravan routes. In 1952 there were 13,000 Arabs in the country, of whom 2,500 lived in Dar-es-Salaam and Tanga. Upon the arrival of the Germans they lost their ancient authority along the coast and their newly acquired power in the interior. Today, most of them make their living as small-scale merchants and traders. They now play a very peripheral role in the economic and political life of the country.

Numerically, the Indians are the most important of the non-indigenous groups.[1] It is widely believed among the Europeans in East Africa that the present Indian population derives from the

[1] A good survey of Indians in East Africa may be found in Hollingsworth, 1960.

coolies who were brought over to work on the Uganda railway. In fact practically all of these men, who were Punjabis, were repatriated at the expiration of their periods of contract (Morris, 1956, p. 195). The bulk of the East African Indian population is Gujerati-speaking. The areas from which they came, Gujerat, Cutch, and Kathiawar, have a long history of contact with the Arab towns of the East African coast. In the early nineteenth century there are said to have been three or four hundred Gujerati in Zanzibar, and when Sultan Said moved his capital from Arabia to Zanzibar in 1840, he found a thousand of them in residence (Moffett, 1958, p. 399). The Sultan gave them preferential treatment and used them in the collection of customs duties. In the nineteenth century, when Zanzibar was the political and economic capital of the east coast, the Indians had already acquired a position of dominance in trade. It was the Indian merchants who financed the Arab slave caravans (Moffett, 1958, p. 299). In Tanganyika itself, Indians were found in small numbers in the Arab coastal towns. When the Germans imposed European law and order upon the country, many Indians moved inland seeking trade wherever it could be found. They reached all corners of the territory.

The Indian population has increased very rapidly. At the end of the German period they numbered just over 9,000. Since the First World War, their number has increased both by immigration and by natural means. In the early days of British rule, Indians were recruited for various types of government work since they had skills which were unobtainable among the African population and since they were cheaper to employ than Europeans of the same calibre. In recent years the government has attempted to make it extremely difficult for new Indian settlers to enter Tanganyika but, even so, the rate of immigration has been about 3,000 a year (Moffett, 1958, p. 300). It has been estimated that the Indian population in East Africa has one of the highest rates of increase in the world. Martin thinks it likely that the natural rate of increase may be as high as 3 per cent per annum which means that the population will double every twenty-four years; he attributes this to the higher standard of living which Indians enjoy in East Africa as compared to India (Martin, 1953, pp. 247, 341). For instance, in East Africa they have access to medical services of a standard usually not available in their homeland.

The Gujerati-speaking population dominates the retail trade of Tanganyika and much of the wholesale trade as well. It is responsible for purchasing most of the African-produced crops and transporting them to the railways.

In addition to the Gujeratis, there are some 3,000 Sikhs from the Punjab. While some Sikhs work as traders in the more remote and wilder parts of the territory such as Masailand, they are principally skilled artisans. Another very distinct subgroup within the Indian population is formed by the Goans, who number about 3,000 (Moffett, 1958, p. 300). The Goans from Portuguese Goa also have a longstanding history of contact with the East African coast. They are Roman Catholics with Portuguese names and they refuse to be classified as Indians. They occupy a great many government clerical positions and due to their high reputation for honesty they are often given posts which involve the handling of money. They also run small shops, particularly those catering to the European trade. They are seldom found in up-country trading centers and appear unable to compete with the Gujeratis.

This breakdown of the Indian population into the dominant Gujerati-speaking group and smaller Punjabi and Goan groups only touches the surface of the complexities involved. Among the Hindus, who are slightly outnumbered by the Muslims, there are all the categories traditionally associated with caste in India. Among the Muslims the situation is somewhat simpler although it too has its complexities since they do not form a single corporate group but instead are divided into a number of sects. The most important of these are the Shia Ismailia Khojas, the followers of the Aga Khan (Moffett, 1958, p. 301), who numbered about 17,000 in 1952, and the Shia Itnasheri Khojas who numbered about 4,000 (Morris, 1956, p. 465).

The Ismailia Khojas deserve special comment. Although they form only slightly more than a quarter of the Indian population, they are the largest corporate Indian group. Furthermore, they are by far the best organized. In many towns in Tanganyika their communal building, the Jamat Khana, is the most impressive architectural feature. They have developed their own medical facilities and they have spent a great deal of money on schools for their children. In addition, they have communal funds which extend loans to members of their sect, thus permitting them to pursue an aggressive policy of commercial expansion.

The fact that the Ismailia Khojas are Muslims would seem to provide a source of contact with the African population or at least with that portion of it which has been converted to Islam. But the Khojas, and indeed the majority of the other Indian Muslims, are

Shias while the African Muslims are Sunnis in the tradition given to them by the Arabs. To date the Ismailia Khojas have made no serious attempt to convert the African population to their own religion.

The Indians play a very important role in the modern economy of the country. They were the pioneer traders who opened up the hinterland and who, by displaying imported goods in their shops, provided one incentive for the production of cash crops by the Africans. Today, in small settlements, all of them are engaged in trade. In the larger towns, they also work as clerks and artisans. A few of them are wealthy and have plantations and other interests, but these are exceptional.

Although a few Indians talk of returning to their homeland, the great majority of them have thrown in their lot with East Africa. Under the leadership of the Aga Khan, the Ismailia Khojas, in particular, are making an effort to fit themselves into the larger East African society by such means as the abandonment of traditional Indian dress for the women and the use of English instead of Gujerati as the language of the home.

About two and a half thousand Somalis (Moffett, 1958, p. 305) have infiltrated into Tanganyika by way of Kenya. They play an important role as buyers in the cattle trade, and in some areas they have successfully established themselves as small traders. In physical appearance and dress they are quite distinct from the bulk of the African population from whom they hold themselves aloof. Despite the color of their skins and the location of their homeland, they insist upon being considered as Asians together with the Arabs, a matter which came to public attention when they refused to be enumerated with the African population in the 1948 census.

Next to the Indians, the Europeans form the largest element of the non-indigenous population. Since political power rests in their hands, since they own most of the plantations and many of the largest business firms, and since they are responsible for the missionary effort, their importance in the modern life of the country is out of all proportion to their number. Although the European population remains extremely small in terms of the total population of the country, it has increased rapidly in recent years as the following figures show (1957 figure: Colonial Office, 1957, p. 96):

1931	8,228
1948	10,648
1957	20,534

As might be expected, the British are numerically predominant in the European community, despite the presence of people from most European countries, the United States, and the various Commonwealth nations. Of other groups, the most notable are the Afrikaners and, in particular, the Greeks. The Greeks, of whom there were 1,300 in 1952, came into Tanganyika during the German period and were employed primarily in the construction of the railway lines. Since then, they have concentrated upon agriculture, and now, for the most part, they consider themselves permanent settlers. In many places, Greek estates pioneered the production of export crops and at the present time they produce more sisal than the British (Guillibaud, n.d., p. 129). The Greeks tend to concentrate in certain areas and they have relatively little social contact with the British; for one thing, many of the older Greeks speak no English. The general situation is epitomized by the fact that in the town of Arusha in northern Tanganyika, there is not only a European club but a Greek club as well.

As far as occupations are concerned, most of the Europeans are employed by the government (2,600 in 1952), work in the mission field (1952: 2,000), are employed as businessmen or by commercial firms (a category for which no figures are available), or work on the land as owners or employees of large-scale farming enterprises (1952: 1,300) (Moffett, 1958, p. 303; Colonial Office, 1957, p. 57).

Most of the Europeans view Tanganyika as a place in which to spend their working life or a part of it, returning afterwards to the country of origin, usually Britain. Only a small proportion of them can be classified as settlers, people who have sunk their roots into the country and see it as a permanent home for themselves and their children. Although, in a sense, the settlers form the core of the European population, they carry much less political weight than they do in neighboring colonial territories. This can be attributed to their small numbers, the fact that they are scattered in different parts of the country instead of being concentrated in a solid block as they are in Kenya, and that, in a British territory, so many of them are of non-British, particularly Greek, origin.

SYSTEM OF GOVERNMENT

Tanganyika is of considerable interest in a worldwide typology of political systems because it represents an extreme example of the bureaucratic state. The civil servants are not only powerful servants of the state, as is the case in western Europe, but they *are* the state.

The entire country is virtually run by less than 300 selected and trained men of the administrative class. They formulate policy and implement it throughout the country. At certain levels they also exercise judicial powers.

At the apex of the system is the Governor. Although it need not be the case, he is almost invariably a colonial administrator who has come up through the ranks. It is general practice to select a man from another colony, so that while he has had many years of administrative experience, at the time of his arrival he usually has no detailed knowledge of local conditions. While he is ultimately answerable to the Colonial Office in the person of the Secretary, he has a great deal of leeway in pursuing his own policy. He is the representative of the Queen and as such he is the figure about whom all ceremonial life revolves. He is provided with an impressive setting in the form of an enormous official residence with extensive grounds and ceremonial paraphernalia, such as an elaborate uniform which is worn on formal public occasions. A recent Governor made it a practice to have a brass band accompany him on his tours of rural areas. To some extent, Provincial and District Commissioners are duplicates of the Governor on a more restricted scale.

The Secretariat, headed by the Chief Secretary, is located in the capital at Dar-es-Salaam. There too are found the headquarters of most of the departments, Medical, Agricultural, etc., which are grouped together into ministries.

The Governor is assisted and advised by an Executive Council with which he meets regularly. This is made up of representatives of the general public in addition to official members. The proceedings of this council are confidential. In addition, there is a Legislative Council whose deliberations are open to the public and reported in the local press. In this Council, which was set up in the mid-twenties, parliamentary procedure is followed. The government introduces legislation which is debated and then passed, ministers explaining their policies and answering questions directed to them by members of the Council. The government retains a majority so there is no chance that its legislative program will be upset. Until 1945 the membership of the Council consisted of European and Asian members only, so that African interests were represented primarily by the officials. Since 1945, African members have sat in the Council. All the members of the Council who were not civil servants, sitting ex-officio, were nominated by the government.

This does not mean that the Council consisted of a group of yes-men, for the European settlers are notoriously outspoken, particularly in criticism of the government. In the latter part of 1958 elections for certain of the representative seats were held for the first time. Due to the nature of its composition, the Legislative Council has served as a place where the government could obtain an expression of public opinion or at least certain sectors of it, where advice and criticism of the government could be freely aired, and where senior government officials responsible for the formulation of policy could be forced to defend their acts publicly.

For purposes of administration, the country is divided into eight provinces, each headed by a Provincial Commissioner. The provinces in turn are divided into more than fifty districts. It is at the district level that territorial policy is really implemented in terms of the local population. At the provincial headquarters, most of the major departments of the government are represented by officials who oversee the work of their departments throughout the province. Thus there are posts such as that of Provincial Medical Officer, Provincial Veterinary Officer, etc. This organization is duplicated at the district headquarters where there is a District Commissioner, who is in overall charge, assisted by from one to four or five junior administrative officers. Again, depending upon the nature of the district, its relative importance, etc., there will be a number of European specialist officers, who have a great deal of autonomy in the pursuit of their departmental programs vis-à-vis the local administrative officers. In a small district there may be only one or two, while in a large district there may be a dozen or more such people representing most of the major departments.

Judicial Organization

There is a system of African courts which operates within the framework of the system of native administration to be described below. At the head of the territorial court system is the High Court of Tanganyika in which sit the Chief Justice of the territory and five other judges. The rest of the territorial courts are district courts. Here the judge is an administrative officer or a resident magistrate. The latter are men with legal training who are stationed in the principal towns. They also tour the outlying districts to hear cases, thus relieving the administrative officers of a part of this time-consuming work. All cases involving Europeans or Asians are heard in the territorial courts where those involved may be represented by legal counsel. Cases involving Africans reach the district courts on appeal from the African local courts although some, such as those dealing with manslaughter, must be heard, even initially, in a district court with a European judge.

Government at the Local Level: Immigrant Communities and the Towns

At the local district level, the focus of administrative attention has always been upon the political institutions of the indigenous African population. The Europeans and Asians have only been formally integrated into the system at the level of the national government through the seating of non-official representatives of these groups on the Legislative Council. At the district level the immigrant population have been dealt with atomistically as individuals except where they have formed local associations of farmers or traders whose representatives may approach the District Commissioner on matters of common concern.

The growth of the towns has posed special problems in terms of political organization, for in a sense towns have come into being in a system which has had no place for them. This is because the political system was originally devised to deal with the affairs of the entire territory at the level of the central government, while the local district government concerned itself with African affairs. Though there were old Arab towns on the coast and a few in the interior which grew up in the nineteenth century along the caravan routes, they were very small entities. Relatively little systematic attention was given to the administration of these centers. The smaller trading centers were administered directly by the District Commissioner, while in the large towns advisory boards consisting of certain official members, such as the Medical Officer, and Europeans and Asians nominated by the District Commissioner were brought into being.

African administration was seen as the problem of African political development in the rural areas. Africans in the towns (and on the European-owned estates as well) were completely outside the scope of a system based upon the principle of indirect rule. In any case, as the Royal Commission has said, "For many years Africans were regarded as temporary inhabitants of the towns, in which they worked as unskilled labourers. When urban administrations found it necessary to provide them with accommodation it was on the assumption that they would work for short periods in the towns, unaccompanied by their families and would then return to their area of origin" (East African Royal Commission, 1953-55, pp. 200, 201).

The towns were seen as European and Asian communities in which the Africans were merely visitors. Now it has been realized that a permanent African town population has come into being, consisting both of a middle class composed of educated and more highly paid people, such as clerks, and a large proletarian group. The government is now trying to grapple with the problems presented by this segment of the population and furthermore, it is now regarded as desirable to foster a permanent urban population. Formerly, urban Africans were referred to by the negative term "detribalized," the assumption being that certain social elements had been taken away and that the African had entered a social vacuum. Now it is increasingly realized that such people are individually adapting to, and collectively building a new and specifically urban social structure.

African Administration

While important changes have taken place in recent years, the local system of African administration retains the form imposed upon it in the mid-twenties when Sir Donald Cameron was Governor of Tanganyika. It was he who introduced into Tanganyika the principle of indirect rule, developed by the British in India and introduced into Africa by Lugard. The reasoning behind the adoption of this principle in Tanganyika, its adaptation to local conditions, and its implication on both the local and national levels can be understood most readily by quoting the words of Cameron himself. In a speech delivered in 1926 he said:

> What I have asked myself on many occasions, is the one matter that is of paramount importance in a country like Tanganyika. It is, I believe, to make secure the future of the native; not in his capacity as a producer, but in his capacity as a member of the State.
>
> Except where he has been detribalized, with the pathetic results that can already be seen in East Africa—as well as in other parts of Tropical Africa—he is subject to a system of law and discipline which he understands, the law is not one which we have invented, or are inventing; he has inherited it. All the sanctions, punitive and civil, which instinctively rule his conduct are based on his own native law and customs.
>
> If the tribal organization is broken up, the discipline and authority under which the native lived disappears and he becomes merely an individual in the community in the same way if he were a coolie brought here from India or China.
>
> The State would at the same time become a State organized entirely in accordance with European methods, and the discipline and authority of the tribal system would be replaced by the discipline and authority of a system of European law.
>
> Under conditions such as these, future generations of natives would become merely members, and servile members, of a State organized on

European principles, and severed from all their own traditions and customs, from their own system of life and law, just as if they had been sent across the sea; they would occupy in the community very much the same place as the slaves occupied in the Southern States of America after they were emancipated.

Apart from other reasons, a community lodged in a European environment, with European ideas and principles and nothing else constantly set before its eyes, cannot always remain in a servile state. A portion of it will have acquired a European education and it will eventually, whether it takes one century, or two or three, for this development, claim a share, and a large share, in the administration of the country under the only system which would then exist, that is a system of Government based on European methods. Let us reflect here for a moment on the fact that the natives will always largely outnumber the Europeans in a country like Tanganyika.

I admit that my arguments are largely fallacious if my statement is incorrect that the natives cannot for all time be kept as a servile race.

On the other hand, if we preserve the tribal authority, gradually purging native law and customs of all that offends against justice and morality, building up a system for the administration of the affairs of the tribe by its hereditary rulers, with their advisors according to native custom, we immediately give the natives a share in the government of the country, and that, moreover, on lines which they themselves understand and can appreciate.

The position given to the Chiefs in this way will be jealously guarded by them and their people, especially against the assaults which may in the course of time be made against it by Europeanized natives seeking to obtain political control of the country and to govern it entirely on European lines. We are not only giving the natives a share in the administration of the country but we are at the same time building up a bulwark against political agitators.

At the same time a discipline and authority by the Chiefs which the people understand will be preserved and we shall avert the social chaos which would ensue if every native could do exactly as he pleased so long as he did not come into conflict with the law.

The Chiefs are much better equipped to punish their tribesmen than we are under a system of British laws and we have given them their own Courts for that purpose.

To break down the only form of discipline and authority that the natives know and then to cry out that they are rapidly becoming more and more ill-disciplined is merely to admit failure, and to admit it without realizing the causes that underlie that failure.

There is no doubt at all in my mind that the economic progress of the country must be set back if a condition of affairs arises in which the influence that we can bring to bear through the natural rulers of the people disappears and the native can do as he pleases.

I can exhort the people, through their Chiefs, as I have repeatedly done, not to idle but to take up some form of work, and the Chiefs as a rule will keep this precept before their people; it would be quite useless for me to speak in this way to a number of individuals.

In many districts the existence of the people is seriously threatened by the invasion of the tsetse fly and they are in danger of losing their cattle. The Chiefs can (and do) induce their tribesmen to come out and fight their own battle against the fly, but this would not be possible if the tribal instinct no longer existed.

Again, strong pressure can be brought to bear through the Chiefs in our efforts to improve the health and sanitary conditions of the people; it would be impossible for us to exert the same influence on a community of mere individuals.

In many other ways the influence which we can exert now for the good of the people themselves would be totally destroyed with the disappearance of the tribal organization.

It is quite clear that it will disappear if we do nothing to build up and maintain the authority of the people's hereditary rulers, and we assert that this can be done only by the methods of native administration that have been established in this Territory. (Colonial Office, 1926, pp. 7-9)

In the same year Cameron wrote the following passages which discuss the implications of indirect rule for the political structure of the nation as a whole:

It is to be observed that the problem confronting this Government arises from a recognition of the fact that races other than African have become, and will remain, a permanent element in the population of this Territory. The European and the Asiatic have come to stay, and the problem therefore is not "is the native desirable?" but "how can the interests of all races best be reconciled and their relations adjusted so as to provide for all alike favourable conditions for the development along such lines as economic and social forces may make possible for them?"

In facing that problem certain factors must be recognized: in the first place a state of affairs in which the African tribes will not very greatly outnumber all other races is inconceivable in this Territory.

At present there are roughly 3,000 Europeans, 15,000 Asiastics and four and one half million natives: the numbers will vary, but it is extremely unlikely that any appreciable increase in the proportions of the first two classes to the last will occur at any time: the 3,000 Europeans may become 6,000, the 15,000 Asiatics may become 30,000; but the four and one half million Africans will in all probability have become five, five and a half or even six millions at the same time, and the question therefore is "how can this vastly preponderating mass of Africans be incorporated in a State composed of such diverse elements?"

Care is needed lest false analogies be drawn from countries, such as, for example, South Africa, where conditions are entirely different. If the South African natives (who only outnumber the Europeans by 5 to 1) ceased to exist there would result a great economic upheaval and a period of serious financial difficulty; but that is not all. The existence and activities of the European race would not be imperilled, and that race would adapt itself to the new conditions created by the elimination of the African labourer as an economic factor. But in Tanganyika there is no form of industry of any importance under European or Asiatic direction which could exist at all without native labour; the native is essential to the continued existence of the other races, and the contact between the races must therefore be close and constant.

Recognizing this and being convinced that it is neither just nor possible to deny permanently to the natives of the Territory any part in the government of the country, the Government of this Territory has adopted the policy of Native Administration, a policy which aims at the elimination of race friction by the provision within the limits of their own Native Administrations of legitimate scope for the political interests of Africans both educated and uneducated, so making it possible for them to evolve, in accordance with their traditions and their most deeply rooted instincts, as an organized and disciplined community within the State, within a State which by reason of the widely divergent degrees of civilization and wealth of its component races, does not admit of political evolution analogous to that of homogeneous nations in Europe and elsewhere in the world.

Not only is this policy not inimical to the interest of other races, it is their strongest safeguard, the surest and safest foundation upon which their existence in the Territory can be built, for it enlists upon the side of law, order and good government all responsible elements in native society, and it aims at preserving that society intact and at protecting it from disintegration into an undisciplined rabble of leaderless and ignorant individuals; moreover it makes it possible for other races occupying the Territory to pursue steadily and in security their lawful occupations, and to organize their industry in such a manner as to enable them to enlist, by favourable treatment and attraction of good and regular wages, that sufficiency of African labour without which their existence in the Territory would cease to be profitable, and would therefore come to an end. (Colonial Office, 1926, pp. 8-11)

The introduction of the principle of indirect rule was hailed as a radical departure from the previous system in which an African official know as an *akida* was brought in, usually from the coast, to govern tribal groups in the interior as an agent of the German regime. In many cases, however, the inauguration of the new policy did not bring about any spectacular change because often only the identity of the highest chief was changed, and in some cases even this did not occur; the titles of the chiefs were merely translated from Swahili to the local language, the people holding the chieftainships remaining the same.

The fundamental idea of indirect rule was quite a simple one, namely that indigenous political institutions should be taken over or, where they had been destroyed by the Germans, revived. These could then be utilized for purposes of modern administration. Ideas such as public finance, the responsibility of local government to develop economic potentials of their areas, promote education, etc., were to be introduced into these traditional structures. In the course of time it would be possible to transform these political institutions into ones bearing a closer resemblance to European models. A basic feature of the plan was that the British administration should work through traditional leaders who would have the backing of their people. Implicit in the minds of the administrators who put this policy into operation was a theory of African political systems which had as one of its basic premises that from time immemorial each tribe had been ruled by its own chief. In actual fact, it would appear that only in a few cases did such a situation exist at the time when the Germans assumed control of the country. In the most prominent case, that of the Hehe, such centralization under a paramount chief occurred only in the nineteenth century. In many cases the Germans created tribal chiefs. With the Iraqw of the Northern Province, for example, a tribe with no chiefs and no political unity, the Germans appointed a paramount chief and placed under him a number of subchiefs arranged in a two-level hierarchy. The British administration utilized this German-created system. In other instances, where it was realized that the tribe had never been amalgamated into one unit, a series of small chiefdoms was recognized. Thus, down to the present time, the Gogo, who number more than a quarter of a million, are divided into a large number of small independent chiefdoms, each of which contains only a few thousand people.

Each chief has his hierarchy of subchiefs and headmen, and all those recognized by the government receive salaries. The chief, the major executive of the tribe, also serves as a judge. In all of the larger chiefdoms certain subchiefs also have courts where they render decisions, aided by a group of elders. Other than the government administrative officials who supervise and ultimately control the operation of the chiefdoms, no Europeans are involved. Appeals from the courts of the subchiefs are made to that of the chief and from his court to the district court in which the judge is a European. Chiefs and their agents have no authority over those living on land in their area owned by European farmers. Neither a European settler nor an Indian trader who lives in a tribal area can be charged in the native courts. On the other hand, the European farmer or the Asian trader has no right to interfere in the political affairs of the chiefdom.

There has been a constant tendency to amalgamate chiefdoms so that an entire tribe is brought under one centralized political administration. Notable is the case of the Sukuma, where a tribal federation has been established. Elsewhere, a number of small chiefdoms have been combined into one large chiefdom. The outstanding example is that of the Chagga, who live on the slopes of Kilimanjaro and who, since the war, have been combined into one chiefdom under Thomas Marealle, perhaps the best-known traditional leader in the territory. While amalgamations of this sort depart from the strict principles of indirect rule, it is argued that this is precisely the sort of change which it was originally intended for the future. It is further argued that the administration has merely brought to completion a process of tribal political consolidation already under way in aboriginal days.

It is apparent that the European administrators would look favorably upon any move towards amalgamation of small chiefdoms into larger units since such development simplifies organizational problems by reducing the span of control. Such bureaucratic motivations are most clearly apparent in the case of the native treasuries. While in 1929 there were about 120 native treasuries in existence (Colonial Office, 1929, p. 98), by 1957 the number had been reduced to 56 (Colonial Office, 1957, p. 17). What has usually happened is that all of the separate native treasuries in a district have been combined into one central treasury. Not only is it much easier for administrative officers to oversee the operation of one native treasury rather than three or four, but treasury consolidation also allows planning to take place on a district-wide basis, the district being the unit with which the European officials are concerned, irrespective of the tribal complexity of the area. In many areas it is difficult to find Africans with sufficient skill to operate one such fiscal unit, let alone a multiplicity of them. In those cases in which petty chiefdoms were amalgamated to form a council, the tribal entity was usually respected, but in treasury matters this principle has been abandoned. For example, in Mbulu District, with one Bantu, two Kushitic, and one Nilo-Hamitic tribe, each tribe has its own political organization, but all of them now participate in the operation of a common treasury. Amalgamation on the fiscal level has far outstripped any development or sentiments of unity on the part of the four tribes in question. It can be argued that this radical departure from the principles of indirect rule is justified since cooperation within the context of a single treasury is a way of achieving a sense of interdependence. This, in turn, may result in a feeling of loyalty to a larger political entity, the district.

The consolidation of smaller local treasuries into larger, district-wide units is congruent with the postwar emphasis on the expansion of local government activities. Local African treasuries have been given vastly increased responsibilities for the provision of all sorts of services—educational, medical, veterinary, etc. Very great sums, at least by prewar standards, are now in their hands. In the political sphere this policy has meant a shift of emphasis in terms of standards by which chiefs are evaluated. Administrative efficiency is given greater weight than traditional right when the claims of rival candidates to a chieftainship are being considered. Another important trend has been the creation of representative councils.

There is great variation from one district to another in the degree to which the powers and accompanying responsibilities granted to local government bodies are actually exercised by Africans. In some places plans are formulated and executed largely by Africans, while in others the decisions made in the name of local African political bodies really emanate from the District Commissioner's office.

Large numbers of people are now employed by the local African governments. In addition to chiefs and clerical workers, government employees supervise cattle and produce markets, provide veterinary services, teach in schools operated by the native authorities, etc. The people so employed are usually members of the local tribe. More important, perhaps, is the growing number of African civil servants employed by the central government. These men can be posted anywhere in the territory and like the European officers, they are frequently transferred from one place to another. As a result, they acquire a knowledge of conditions in different parts of the territory, as well as the ability to see problems in terms of Tanganyika as a whole. They associate with colleagues who may have different tribal backgrounds but with whom they share a common educational experience, a common way of life, and common problems. Since the war, the government has organized a large number of specialized training schools for those who wish to enter public service. The Medical Department, for example, maintains centers at which special courses are given to train people for the following positions: medical assistants, laboratory assistants, pharmaceutical assistants, rural medical aids, nurses, midwives, assistant health inspectors, health nurses, health orderlies, and malaria assistants. Most of these training programs admit students who have completed two years of secondary school, although at least one requires a full secondary school training and some admit students who have completed only eight years of schooling. In 1938 the African civil service numbered under 7,000 (Colonial Office, 1938, p. 187); the total had risen to 11,000 in 1950 and over 19,000 in 1955. The training schools produced over 2,000 graduates in 1957 and in 1958 they were expected to have over 4,000 students enrolled (Colonial Office, 1958, p. 17).

It would appear that before the war there was general satisfaction with the political system which had been developed in the first decade of British rule. Most officials and others who gave any thought to the question seem to have been of the opinion that any great alteration in the system was many decades away. However, the situation altered radically after the war, and it was soon clear that independence would be granted in the not-too-distant future. Difficulties were caused by the fact that wealth, managerial ability, and technical skill were concentrated in the hands of the immigrant groups even though they formed only an infinitesimal proportion of the population. Under these circumstances the government tried to implement a policy of multi-racialism, which meant in effect the sharing of power equally between the three principal groups: Europeans, Indians, and Africans. This policy failed, however, and it was clear by 1960 that independent Tanganyika would be an African-controlled state.

Until then the government, as far as African political affairs are concerned, was preoccupied with government at the local level and little attention was given to the problem of stimulating a sense of national consciousness among the African population. The creation of an African civil service was probably the most important single, although unintended, contribution of the government along this line.

Africans, as has been mentioned, were not appointed to seats in the Legislative Council until 1945. The principle of indirect rule inhibited effective representation of the African population at the national level. African Council members could only serve, by the extension of this principle to the new situation, as spokesmen for their own tribal groups and not for the African population as a whole. Further difficulties were caused by the question of what sort of African to select. Educated Africans, who were outside the formal system of native administration, were not considered fit spokesmen because only the chiefs were recognized as leaders of the people. The chiefs, on the other hand, were selected on the basis of traditionalistic criteria and were, for the most part, lacking in education. When two Africans were finally nominated to the Council, both were chiefs. And since then leaders of a newer type have been appointed. In July, 1959, three African elected members of the Legislative Council were appointed as government ministers.

The results of missionary activity as far as the present problem is concerned are not clear-cut. Through conversion Africans have become members of organizations transcending local boundaries which put emphasis upon the importance of church membership as opposed to tribal affiliation. However, the fact that there are a number of competing missionary societies means that new principles of division have been introduced into the African population. Education, which has been largely in the hands of the missions, has done a certain amount to foster feelings of Tanganyika national identity. But attitudes of this sort which have arisen out of the educational experience are probably due less to the content of the schooling, as such, than to the fact that most education above the level of Standard IV has taken place in boarding schools which usually bring together children from different tribes.

National consciousness has arisen to some extent through contact among laborers on estates who find themselves treated as African laborers rather than as members of particular tribes. Far more important here are the populations living in the towns, populations which have grown up more or less spontaneously outside the framework of government policy. These people, who are referred to as "detribalized," are in a sense the first true Tanganyikans. This is because in many instances they have cut themselves off from their tribal backgrounds, sharing a way of life and participating in a type of social structure found in all of the towns.

The most important event in recent years in the development of African national consciousness has been the formation of the Tanganyika African National Union or TANU, as it is known. This party, which came into being in 1954, is led by Julius Nyerere, a relatively young man of Christian background who was educated in the United Kingdom and was formerly a school tecaher. It is significant that his tribal affiliations are with the Zanaki, a very small tribe in the Lake Province, since this facilitates his attempt to minimize tribal differences between his followers. TANU has opened branches in all parts of the country. TANU has pressed constantly for an early transfer of power and has opposed the policy of multiracialism. Its activities are viewed with open alarm by the European settlers and the bulk of the Indian population. Most officials look upon it with suspicion. Of necessity, local TANU chapters have had a good deal of autonomy and often local leaders have advocated policies in conflict with those developed at the national headquarters in Dar-es-Salaam. In some instances, local chapters have come into direct conflict with the local administration and they have been proscribed. A case in point is that of the chapter in Iringa District which was accused of formenting opposition to a government scheme for dipping native cattle in an effort to eradicate certain tick-borne diseases, although Nyerere himself supported the scheme. As yet, the party commands the enthusiastic support of only a small minority of the population. It draws its support from the educated, i.e., those who have had eight or more years of school, and from town Africans of all types. The African population of Dar-es-Salaam is solidly behind the party. Some of the strongest supporters of TANU are in the civil service but they are officially debarred from participation in political activities. TANU has difficulty getting leaders and organizers who have the requisite skills because such a very large proportion of the educated public is in the civil service.

THE MISSIONS

Missions have played a very important role in the life of the country. In fact, missions may be more important agents of social change than the government itself. Missionary activity in East Africa preceded European political control of the region. In Uganda, in particular, the fact that the missionaries established themselves so strongly at an early date and had strong and influential backing in Europe was one of the major reasons that the British government finally felt obliged to assume a protectorate over the country. In Tanganyika, both Catholics and Protestants have been at work for almost a century. The Holy Ghost Fathers established a mission station at Bagamoyo on the coast opposite Zanzibar in 1863. In the following year Bishop Tozzer of the Universities Mission to Central Africa made Zanzibar his headquarters and work on the mainland itself began in 1868 in the Usambaras in northern Tanganyika. In addition, the missionaries who intended to work in Buganda entered this kingdom from the south through what is today Tanganyika. This led to the establishment of a number of stations along the route into the interior. Later when the German government assumed control over the area, German missionary interest was aroused and within a few years five German missionary societies were at work.

In 1957 there were thirty-five missionary societies established in Tanganyika, ten of them Roman Catholic and the remainder Protestant. There were 2,359 Europeans engaged in missionary activity, which means that, without counting the wives and children of the Protestants, missionaries composed more than 10 per cent of the total European population. Almost two-thirds of the missionaries are Roman Catholic and it would seem that the number of Catholic as opposed to Protestant converts is roughly in proportion to these figures (Oliver, 1952, p. 239). In terms of nationality, British missionaries are the most numerous, closely followed by the Germans, Dutch, and Americans, in that order. In 1957 the missions claimed that 1,362,000 Africans, or almost a sixth of the total population, were members of their churches (all figures: Colonial Office, 1957, p. 57).

The missions, of course, have as their goal the radical transformation of the African population. Although their primary interest lies in changing the religious ideas and practices of the local people, the accompanying moral code involves changes in a number of spheres, particularly in the fields of kinship and family life. Furthermore, the missionary effort usually extends far beyond the purely religious and moral aspects of the life of their converts. Although it is not always so, the missionaries usually have, with the exception of certain government officials, more personal contact with the African population than any other Europeans. In Tanganyika there are no small European traders as there are in Oceania and certain other parts of the world. The owners and other Europeans employed on the sisal and coffee estates have very restricted contacts with their African workers and neighbors and they are usually profoundly ignorant of most aspects of African life. In contrast to the government officials who seldom remain very long in one place, missionaries often spend many years in one locality. During this time they often learn to speak the local language and acquire considerable knowledge of their converts, their families, their ways of life, and their problems.

Some of the earliest mission stations began as centers for freed slaves. This meant that the missions became completely responsible economically and politically, as well as spiritually, for the Africans attached to them. For this and other reasons, a system of Christian mission plantations came into being. The Africans were allowed to build on land which had been alienated to the mission by the government. Here they either worked for wages on land planted by the mission or else they cultivated plots assigned to them on a tenant basis (Oliver, 1952, pp. 52-65). Later when the missions were dealing with free tribal people in the interior there were many who thought that the same system should be applied. It had the advantage of isolating those who had been converted so that they could lead Christian lives in the setting of a Christian community. It was argued that the individual Christian living in a pagan community would be under constant social pressure to revert to pagan ways. However, this system could only be an initial stage in the long-run process of mass conversion and it was never utilized on a large scale.

Many of the missionaries believed that they should do what they could to improve the economic lot of the African population and some of the missionaries were pioneers in introducing new crops and agricultural techniques to the local population. Certain groups, in particular the Catholic societies, placed considerable stress on teaching Africans useful crafts, such as carpentry and masonry. Among the Protestants, the Moravians were the ones who were most interested in this aspect of their work. To quote the historian Oliver,

> Of the German societies, the Moravians, working to the north of Lake Nyasa, were also traditional believers in economic as well as spiritual rebirth. Their object had never been to convert whole nations, but rather to gather within each nation communities of elect souls, self-supporting and in other ways self-sufficient unto themselves. Hundreds of Africans were employed in the building of substantial villages and the laying out of plantations, which gave excellent opportunities for language study, for gaining confidence and also for the first missionary contacts. Only Christians were allowed to settle permanently at the stations while all catechumens were obliged to do so at least during the period of instruction. As one village filled up another was founded, a native council of elders being in each to supervise the agricultural work, to maintain law and order and to make contact with intending settlers. The Moravians further insisted that commerce was an essential ingredient of all lasting mission work. "If you seek economic improvement you must either give or trade." Rather than allow their converts to make dangerous contacts with Indian or Swahili merchants, they set up a wharf and warehouse at Kyimbila on Lake Nyasa and appointed two missionaries to conduct the import and export business of the whole area. (pp. 173-74)

The missions have also been responsible for bringing modern medical care to many parts of Tanganyika. Even today they provide a very large proportion of the medical services of the territory. There are seventy-five missionary European physicians in the territory as against seventy-three European physicians employed by the government (Colonial Office, 1957, p. 169), although the latter, it should be added, employs an additional twenty-five Asian and five African general medical practitioners. The missions operate thirty-five general hospitals in various parts of the territory, as against forty-seven by the government (Colonial Office, 1958, pp. 173, 176). Very often the mission hospitals are located in rural areas whereas most of the government hospitals are in towns or administrative centers.

EDUCATION

The system of education which has evolved in Tanganyika is of immense importance in changing the Africans' conceptions of themselves and the world in which they live, in defining new goals for the individual, and equipping him with new skills with which he can find a place in the modern world. Here, too, the missions have led the way. They continue to dominate the educational field even though they have never had the near monopoly of education that they have had in Uganda. The Germans organized about a hundred government schools for 6,000 pupils, primarily with the aim of developing a cadre of Africans able to occupy subordinate positions in their administrative system. But they were overshadowed by some 1,800 mission schools (Colonial Office, 1920, pp. 40, 41), even though most of the latter were undoubtedly so-called bush schools mainly concerned with imparting religious instruction and attempting no more than to give the pupils a bare knowledge of reading and writing.

The missionaries entered the educational realm for a variety of reasons. Most missionaries have believed in the value of imparting to their converts certain aspects of Western culture in addition to making them Christians. The provision of educational (and medical) facilities brought Africans to the mission stations of their own accord, thus affording opportunities for conversion. To a large extent, it would seem that it is the provision of these services which has accounted for the success which the Christian missions have attained in competition with Islam in the interior of the territory. Through the schools, missions convert the children of pagan parents, something which otherwise would not take place on any large scale.

Tanganyika's schools are of three types: (1) primary schools for the first four years, (2) middle schools for Standards V through VIII, and (3) secondary schools where the last four years of education are given. The primary schools are day schools attended by children who live within walking distance. Both the middle and secondary schools are usually boarding schools drawing their pupils from wide areas. In 1957 there were the following government-aided schools in the territory (Colonial Office, 1957, p. 188):

	Mission	Government	Other	Total
Primary	1,814	721	29	2,564
Middle [a]	313	99	—	412
Secondary	16	10	—	26

[a] Not all of these were full middle schools. Many had only two grade levels.

The government schools include both those run by the central government and those operated by the local native authorities. Most of the primary schools are organized locally, but all of the secondary schools are operated by the central government. At the present time, it is hoped that in the foreseeable future all children will be able to take the four-year primary course. From the middle school, pupils can go to teacher training schools run by both the government and the missions, trade schools, or to certain government schools which will fit them for lower ranking civil service positions. It is hoped that a large proportion of those who complete the secondary course can be sent elsewhere for university training. Makerere College in Uganda serves Tanganyika as well as Uganda and Kenya. A student going to Makarere is expected to pay £ 40 out of a total of £ 873, the rest of which is paid by the government. However, if he is unable to do so, the government pays the total amount and gives him £ 17 pocket money as well (Hill and Moffett, 1955, p. 66). These costs which refer to 1952 have since gone up substantially. However, very few Africans complete the secondary course and go on to Makerere. Most boys are forced to leave secondary school after the first two years and go into one or another of the various schools run by government departments, where they receive training which fits them for work in the civil service.

Language is a difficult problem in the educational system. Swahili is used in the primary schools (and it is becoming increasingly necessary for Africans to have a command of Swahili even if they live in a rural area). However, except for those children who live on the coast or in the towns, the language of the home is not Swahili and it must be taught as a foreign language. Fortunately, for the children of Bantu-speaking tribes, who make up the bulk of the population, it is very easy to learn. English is introduced in the middle school and becomes the medium of instruction at least by Standard VIII. This means that a great deal of time must be spent learning languages.

In recent years the educational system has developed at a very rapid rate. In this the government has played a very important role, for although most of the schools remain in the hands of the missions, the missions themselves are becoming increasingly dependent upon government financial aid. All of this is quite clearly shown by a comparison of the situation in 1938 with that in 1957.

In 1938 the government gave the missionary societies £ 24,000 to support schools run by them for the African population (Colonial Office, 1938, p. 124). It is of interest to note that in that same year the government spent over £ 35,000 on European education (p. 131). At that time the missions operated some 220 schools which met the standards required by the government. Approximately 25,000 children attended schools of this type. The missions also ran an additional 674 schools, most of them primary schools which were not eligible for state aid and which had another 26,000 students. In addition, the government itself operated almost a hundred schools with 10,000 pupils. In 1957 it is estimated the missionary societies received over £ 1,338,925 in support of their schools (Colonial Office, 1957, p. 127).

Both the Catholics and the Protestants (the latter represented by the Christian Council of Tanganyika) maintain Educational Secretaries at the capital. At the local district level there is a local education committee on which both groups are represented and at this level competition for new school sites and for funds is often intense.

In 1957 almost 400,000 pupils were enrolled in school. However, about half of these were in the first two grades. From the following figures it can be seen how rapidly the numbers decrease the further one goes up the educational ladder (Colonial Office, 1957, pp. 193, 195):

Standard I	110,000
Standard IV	70,000
Standard V	10,000
Standard VIII	6,000
Standard IX	1,480
Standard XII	150

In addition, there were 180 students from Tanganyika at Makerere College (p. 76), plus a larger but unknown number at overseas colleges.

The decreases at the different levels are due to a variety of causes. Of all the children who complete the primary course only a portion chosen by examination are permitted to go on to middle school. Large numbers also drop out or are withdrawn by their parents since in many tribes children are of considerable value in the household economy. Many parents who themselves have received little or no education believe that bare literacy is all that a child needs to equip him for life. An important factor is that school fees are charged at all levels. In the primary schools, fees may run as high as fifteen shillings a year per child. In a government middle or secondary school, they are 250 shillings a year. All of these fees are high when one considers the cash income of a rural African. It must also be remembered that a family may have more than one child of school age so that even the primary school fees can be a heavy burden.

Of particular significance are the small numbers enrolled, not only in universities, but in secondary schools as well. As can be seen above, less than 1,500 students entered secondary school in 1957. It was largely upon this group that the responsibility for running the country would rest when Tanganyika attained independence with an African-controlled government. It is of interest that the Indians who formed only a minute proportion of the population had twice as many children (6,000) in secondary school as did the entire African population (Colonial Office, 1957, p. 191).

THE ECONOMY

Under aboriginal conditions the bulk of the African population was engaged in a subsistence economy based in most cases upon some combination of agriculture and livestock management. While hunting was practiced in most areas, it was not an important source of food, nor was fishing except for those people living directly on the sea coast or on the shores of the great lakes. Usually, the individual household had a very high degree of self-sufficiency. The exchanges of goods which did take place tended to be very localized and on a personal basis. Markets such as existed elsewhere in Africa, particularly on the west coast, were conspicuous by their absence. With the exception of a few favored groups living in regions enjoying high and reliable rainfall, most groups experienced periodic droughts which resulted in famine. Aboriginally, transportation facilities were severely limited since the only methods of transport were headloads and donkeys, wheeled vehicles being unknown in the interior. Due to the lack of good transportation and organized markets, it was not possible for those in famine areas to obtain any quantity of grain from other areas which enjoyed good harvests.

For the Germans, the first problem was the pacification of the country and the establishment of an administrative system which would provide and enforce a territorial system of law and order. This was a precondition for the attainment of the second goal, economic development.

Previously, the chief exports had been slaves and ivory. Here, as elsewhere in Africa, development meant finding and exploiting mineral deposits and stimulating the production of crops which could be exported and sold on the world market. Mineral production has played a decisive role in most of the countries in Africa south of the Sahara (Frankel, 1938, p. 212). One advantage of mining is that Western techniques can be applied directly with little or no adaptation to local conditions. In the case of gold and diamonds, which are very valuable in proportion to their weight, transportation poses no serious problems. The stimulation of agricultural production for export is by contrast a much more complicated problem. Suitable crops have to be found and this requires a great deal of time-consuming experimentation. Once such crops have been identified people must be found who will grow them. At the end of the last century, there seemed to be two choices: the encouragement of European settlement, leading to large-scale production on estates employing locally recruited wage laborers; or the stimulation of production by Africans on small plots. In Tanganyika, both approaches were utilized and the two forms of production have continued to exist and expand down to the present day.

Under the German regime prospecting was carried out vigorously but with no great success. It is estimated that in the entire German period the total value of the minerals produced (for the most part gold and mica) came to only about half a million pounds (Hill and Moffett, 1955, p. 686). During the British period the situation improved. In the twenties, diamonds became the principal mineral export, totaling £ 101,000 in the best year, 1927. Diamond production dwindled to almost nothing in the thirties, but in 1940 the famous Mwadui field in northwestern Tanganyika was discovered by the Canadian geologist Williamson, and since the war diamonds have regained their former position. In the thirties, gold dominated the mining scene. At one time about 20,000 Africans were employed in the Lupa goldfields alone. During the postwar period gold has been second in importance although in 1957 lead replaced it. In 1957 the total mineral production was valued at £ 5,463,000, of which diamonds contributed £ 3,287 (Colonial Office, 1957, p. 140). Some 16,000 Africans as well as over 600 Europeans were employed in the mining industry (p. 142). However, even now when mineral exports have reached quite a high level, the export trade continues to be dominated by agricultural produce which is many times more valuable.

Transportation

Tanganyika lacks navigable rivers which would have permitted ready access to the interior and the rapid development of an inexpensive system of transport by boat. This meant that the production of bulky cash crops was limited to the coast and the immediate hinterland because transport by means of headloads was prohibitively expensive. If economic development of the territory based upon agriculture was desired, it meant that a railway system had to be constructed. As Frankel has said, "A railway train of average capacity and engine power will do the work of from 15,000 to 20,000 carriers for one-fifth to one-tenth of the cost" (1938, p. 32).

The Germans constructed two railway lines. The first line was begun in the north in 1893 from the port of Tanga, with the object, which was never attained, of reaching Lake Victoria. The route selected was a sensible choice since it ran through great stretches of country suitable for the production of sisal and since it made accessible the highland areas of the Usambaras, the Pares, Mt. Kilimanjaro and Mt. Meru, all of which are suitable for the production of high rainfall crops such as coffee. A second line was begun from Dar-es-Salaam towards Kigoma on Lake Tanganyika. This line was a much less attractive economic proposition because much of it traversed some of the driest and least promising country in the territory. The construction of these railways proceeded at a slow pace. The Tanga Line did not reach Moshi, 219 miles from the coast, until 1911, almost twenty years after the start of construction. The Central Line was built at a more rapid pace. Rails were first laid in Dar-es-Salaam in 1905 and nine years later the railway reached Lake Tanganyika, nearly 800 miles away. But the railways did not pay for themselves (Economist, 1955, p. 32), so, even though construction was begun under commercial auspices, the German government was forced to assume financial responsibility (Hill and Moffett, 1955, p. 148).

The desire to put the railways on a paying basis was one of the main reasons which led the German government to do all it could to encourage the growth of European estates, particularly along the Tanga Line. In this way the foundations were solidly laid for the great sisal industry in the northwestern stretch from Tanga on the coast to Korogwe and beyond. Large sisal areas were also developed along the Central Line in the Morogoro and Kilosa regions, while the northern highland areas such as the Usambaras and the Moshi-Arusha region saw the development of estates with coffee as the main crop. Some 400 estates were in operation at the end of the German period, many of them owned by large corporations (Frankel, 1938, p. 164). These areas remain the principal European-occupied areas. The British extended the railway system in the twenties by building a branch line from Tabora to Mwanza on Lake Victoria. This line tapped an area which has become an important center for African production and it established a link with steamer service on the lake. The Tanga Line was extended another fifty miles to Arusha. With the exception of a couple of small branch

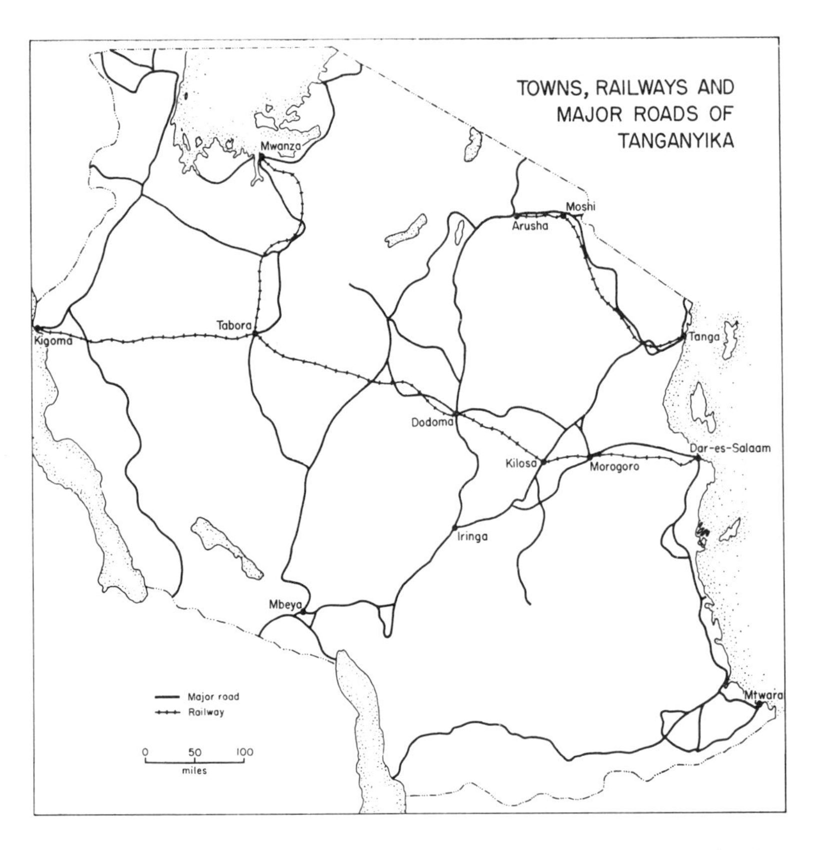

lines no other railway development took place until after the last war when a line was begun from the port of Mtwara into the interior of the Southern Province. This line, which was begun in connection with the groundnut scheme, extends only a short distance into the hinterland.

It was inevitable that a European power, wishing to open a territory such as Tanganyika to the outside world at the turn of the century, should, in the absence of navigable waterways, attempt to gain access to the interior by the construction of a railway system rather than a network of roads. However, as time went by, a road system became increasingly desirable and necessary. Today, such a system exists but it is still far from satisfactory. Great obstacles have always beset its construction and expansion.

Roads

Tanganyika is an enormous country and major long-distance roads have to traverse very rough country and pass through almost uninhabited areas. It is unfortunate that the best agricultural areas and those carrying the densest populations are widely scattered. Funds for road construction were always short, particularly after the onset of the Depression. For these and other reasons the development of a network of roads has proceeded at a very slow pace. Since the Germans were preoccupied with the railway system, the British found practically no motor roads outside the towns when they arrived (Hill and Moffett, 1955, p. 126). In the period between the wars, roads were laid out with the emphasis on feeder routes for the railway and on north-south routes (the railways all run east-west). These roads were of a very poor standard and were traversible only during the dry season. As has happened elsewhere in Africa where railways have been constructed which have run into financial difficulty, there has been a great reluctance to build roads which would parallel them and bring the railways into competition with trucks. One of the writers remembers traveling in 1950 along the road which connects Mombasa and Nairobi, the two main cities of neighboring Kenya. In places the road was little better than a track with high grass growing in the center. During the thirties the policy of protecting the railroad was carried so far in Tanganyika that tolls were levied on trucks using the primitive roads which ran along the rail lines.

Today, after forty years of British occupation and despite the large amount of road work which has been undertaken since the war, an enormous amount of new construction and upgrading of already existing roads needs to be done. The first hard surface road in the country, a road which connects Arusha and Moshi with the Kenya border, was begun in 1949. Another hard surface road from Dar-es-Salaam to Iringa was nearing completion in 1958. All other roads are merely earth or earth and gravel. There is no through road connecting the capital with Lakes Tanganyika or Victoria. The Southern Province can be entered from the rest of the country by only two routes and these are open for only a few months of the year. The western entrance has a forty-mile stretch where logs are laid across the road on the hills to contain the shifting sands, so that the effect is that of driving up a flight of stairs. The eastern coast route is also said to have disadvantages. Despite these conditions, in 1951 some 19,000 motor vehicles were operating in the territory.

The Role of the Indian Trader

While the road and rail networks constructed by the government have contributed much towards the introduction of a cash economy, the stimulation of the production and marketing of cash crops owes much to the efforts of the Indian traders. In the interior of Tanganyika much of the country appears uninhabited. Often this is actually the case. In many instances, the country is able to support only a very light population and those homesteads which exist are located away from the roads. But, even in densely areas, one does not see anything which might be dignified by the term village, for the predominate settlement pattern of the African population in the interior is a dispersed one. Each homestead stands on its own, separated by fields from its neighbors. Apart from the few widely separated towns and the odd mission station the only settlements one encounters are the trading centers consisting of small clusters of shops, perhaps only three or four or perhaps a dozen or more in number. Although occasionally owned by Arabs, Somalis, or Sikhs, these shops usually belong to Gujerati-speaking Indians. In older trading centers the buildings are strung out in a line along the road. The newer ones planned by the government are built around an open square. In the middle of the square is an open-sided building where produce is sold. Each building, which is constructed with sun-dried bricks or perhaps merely with mud and wattle topped by a corrugated iron roof, serves as shop, warehouse, and home for the trader and his family. The front portion is the shop, where goods of all sorts are displayed. A sewing machine is standard equipment. In the back, which has a yard surrounded by a high wall, are the living quarters and storerooms. Unless the trader is very poor, he has at least one truck. The shops are open from early morning until sunset, when all of the doors are tightly bolted and the settlement appears deserted. During the season when the local cash crop is being harvested and sold at the trading settlement, the shops are scenes of lively animation. The rest of the year things are very quiet indeed; a small shopkeeper may sell only ten or twenty shillings worth of goods a day, if that.

The traders perform three types of services: (1) They sell manufactured goods, in most areas principally cloth, to the people of the surrounding countryside; (2) They purchase the produce which the Africans bring to the buying point; (3) They transport it to nearest railway station.

The Indians operate under a number of restrictions. They can buy produce only at government-supervised buying points; they are forbidden to buy crops in the fields or at the homes of African producers. They are allowed to build only in places designated by the government as trading centers. Such centers may be demarcated at the instigation of a local administrative officer, as the result of pressure from Indian traders who believe that a certain place offers commercial possibilities, or by agitation on the part of local Africans who would like to have shops more conveniently located. A plan is drawn for the settlement and building plots are allocated to those who apply for them. The successful applicants must pay an initial fee and thereafter a small annual rent to the government for the use of the land. Certain minimum standards of building and sanitation are enforced. The settlements are usually provided with a piped water supply, all of the shopkeepers drawing their water from a communal tap.

The African trader suffers none of the restrictions which are imposed upon his Indian competitor. Once he has his trading license, which is less expensive than the one which an Indian must obtain, an African is free to open a shop wherever he desires and the building need not conform to any standards. But despite these advantages, the African trader seldom thrives or offers any real competition to the Indian. His shop is usually very poorly capitalized and it is not uncommon to find one which has a total of only fifty shillings worth of goods.

It has already been mentioned that the Indians stand outside the local political system, which is purely African. Other regulations ensure that the Indian does not penetrate into the African social structure. The Indians are not only prevented from building anywhere but in the trading center, but they are also prohibited from purchasing land from Africans for any other purpose. Indebtedness on the part of the rural population to the traders is prevented by the law that an Indian cannot sue an African for the recovery of a debt. The only people exempted from these provisions are Africans holding trading licenses. Such Africans can be held responsible for the repayment of debts they have incurred in the course of their operations, but even in these cases, if the African is a farmer as well, his land cannot be taken from him to settle a debt.

Cash Crops

The present status of the cash sector of the agricultural economy can be seen in the accompanying table; the figures are broken down to show the respective contributions made by large-scale production on estates, principally owned by Europeans (although some Indians are involved as well), and by African production. It can be seen that while some crops are grown under both systems there has been a tendency for most crops to be grown under one or the other. Of the three major crops, sisal is almost entirely estate produced, while cotton is a crop chiefly grown by Africans on small holdings. Cotton was formerly grown on estates, but it was grown on land which is also suitable for sisal and the latter appears to give a better return. Only coffee is now grown under both systems.

The total production of the three principal crops is exported. Most of the other crops are exported as well. The principal exceptions are rice, sugar, and maize. Rice is the staple foodstuff of the Indians, who consume the bulk of it although it is now coming into favor with many Africans as well. Rice is much more expensive than maize, which is purchased in the form of flour by the town-dwelling Africans. Maize flour is also the staple foodstuff of the workers on the estates. Modern processed sugar, all of which is produced on one large estate owned by a Danish firm, is also consumed locally.

In addition, certain crops are sold for cash outside of the new government-sponsored marketing system. Tobacco and sugarcane are two examples of such crops which are locally important. Most of this produce is sold by itinerant African traders or is carried to an area where African buyers can be found and it can be sold in small quantities by the producer himself. Various grains are also marketed in this manner, as is honey, an important commodity in certain parts of the territory.

Some figures are available showing a breakdown between native and non-native production (Colonial Office, 1957, p. 134). (In some cases, such as that of castor seed, we have arbitrarily allocated the total production to the native category in the absence of any information about non-native production, which is known to be very small.)

Crop	Estate	African	Total
sisal	£9,534,000	£ 106,000	£9,640,000
coffee	1,300,000	7,100,000	8,400,000
seed cotton	—	7,300,000	7,300,000
cashew nuts	—	1,500,000	1,500,000
groundnuts	—	1,100,000	1,100,000
oil seeds (other than castor, e.g., sunflowers)	—	1,100,000	1,100,000
sugar	1,000,000	—	1,000,000
castor seed	—	900,000	900,000
tea	773,000	—	773,000
tobacco	461,000	188,000	649,000
copra [a]	100,000	400,000	500,000
pyrethrum	210,000	—	210,000
wheat [a]	180,000	20,000	200,000

[a] Our breakdown.

Maize and rice are two other crops which are of considerable importance in terms of the cash economy. It is said that 45,000 tons of maize are necessary to feed the wage farming population in a normal year. However, as much as another 60,000 tons may have to be purchased to feed rural people in famine areas in a bad year. The main areas of production are the Northern Province and the area between the Wami River and Kilosa District in the Eastern Province with Handeni and Mara Districts as subsidiary centers. This crop is grown both by Europeans and Africans. From the last figures which are available (1952) it would seem that the crop was worth at least £ 800,000 (Hill and Moffett, 1955, pp. 378-79). It might be noted that in twelve of the fifteen years preceding 1952 maize had to be imported into Tanganyika (Hill and Moffett, 1955, p. 549).

Rice is grown entirely by African small holders and the bulk of it in the Eastern Province. It is eaten by the coastal people and by an increasing number of other Africans. In 1952, some 20,000 tons of rice, worth about £ 750,000, was bought from the producers (Hill and Moffett, 1955, p. 551).

Bees have long been kept by the African population in hollow-log hives suspended from the branches of trees. A fair amount is also collected in certain areas from hives discovered by bee-hunters. It is estimated that in 1952 honey worth approximately £ 750,000 was gathered, and £ 210,000 worth of beeswax was produced for export. Beeswax as a cash crop is particularly important in the Western and Central Provinces, and to a lesser degree in the Southern Province. Some of the honey enters the local markets, but most of it is either consumed by the honey-gatherer and his family or is made into beer.

The Non-African Estates

From the earliest years of the German occupation, land in Tanganyika has been alienated, i.e., transferred to the control of non-African individuals (usually Europeans) or corporations. This process is still under way and large amounts of land have been disposed of in this fashion since the last war.

The German government granted large tracts of land to Europeans, particularly in what are now the Tanga and Northern Provinces. Much of this land was granted under conditions of freehold tenure. An official British source charges that "the European system of land tenure was introduced by the late German Government and large grants were made to individuals and companies, often with little or no consideration for the rights and requirements of the native population" (Colonial Office, 1920, p. 70). The German government finally put a stop to this by decreeing "that no more Crown land should be alienated in the district of Tanga, in the districts of Pangani and Wilhelmstal (Lushoto) north of the Pangani River or in the cultivated area of the Moshi and Arusha districts, around Kilimanjaro and Meru Mountains" (Colonial Office, 1920, p. 57).

Some 400 holdings outside urban areas totaling almost half a million acres are held under freehold tenure by virtue of grants made during the German period.

The bulk of the land alienated under British administration has been in areas either completely unoccupied or very sparsely inhabited by local tribes. In some cases, though, land has been alienated which would otherwise have been utilized by a tribe for expansion. An example is the large block of land at Oldeani, which was alienated in the early thirties and which could have been used in recent years by the rapidly expanding Iraqw on a small-holding basis. It should be pointed out, however, that this was land to which the Iraqw had no traditional claims. In recent years a well-publicized dispute over land finally reached the United Nations. This arose from the dispossession of a group of Meru, who were compensated with land elsewhere, in order to open an area for European occupation. Such disputes have been rare, the entire situation regarding alienation having been eased a great deal by the fact that sisal, the principal estate-grown crop, is grown in areas which are marginal for African cultivation.

By the end of World War II the British had alienated a thousand additional holdings, comprising some three-quarters of a million acres under long-term lease, usually ninety-nine years.

The government's postwar policy regarding the acquisition of land by people other than Africans is summarized in the following quotation:

> The essence of this land policy is accordingly that, while African interests in the land are to be carefully safeguarded, and while adequate allowance is to be made for the natural increase in population over the years so that overcrowding does not result through lack of adequate land, the economic development of the territory must be advanced by the allocation of more land for agriculture and enterprise generally. . . . As a further increase in population occurs it is virtually certain that only a proportion of the increase will be reflected in the increased use of land for agriculture, and the remainder will be absorbed in the increasing calls of industrialization and the growing opportunities for paid employment on the land as the territory develops. The ability of Tanganyika to feed

itself depends upon great efforts being made to increase production, and its economic development will be stifled if large sums have to be spent every year on importing foodstuffs. This increase of production can come only from greatly increased effort from agriculture working with modern mechanical means, and backed up by indigenous agriculture with the improved methods which are being gradually introduced. It is now generally accepted that the health, wealth and general interests of the African are not best served by leaving him in isolation, surrounded by great tracts of undeveloped land which may be needed by his anticipated progeny. On the contrary the development of the territory depends on the combined efforts of all communities working and thriving in mutual interest and assistance towards a common goal of prosperity. In considering therefore, the matter of availability of land in the area the criterion which is applied, once it has been decided that the land is not essential for the natural increase of the indigenous population, is the best use to which that land can be put in the interests of the territory as a whole. (Hill and Moffett, 1955, pp. 219-20)

Since the war an additional million acres divided into about 450 new holdings have been leased. More than half of this has been allocated to public or semi-public bodies such as the Tanganyika Agricultural Corporation, a government-owned corporation which has received 486,000 acres, most of it land at one time used by the groundnut scheme. Some 70,000 acres have been granted to Tanganyika Packers, a beef-packing concern in which the government holds a controlling interest, and some 44,000 are held by the Colonial Development Corporation.

The land thus far alienated comes to somewhat less than 3,000,000 acres, which is slightly less than 1 per cent of the total land surface of the territory.

	Acreage
Alienated and private	
Freehold	471,309
Long lease	1,779,556
Subtotal	2,250,865
Public or semi-public	609,913
Total	2,860,778

During the German regime most of the land was granted to German settlers and corporations. This land was confiscated and reallocated after the war. In addition to British settlers, much of it was taken up by Greeks and Indians. In the twenties and thirties a certain number of Germans again took up land in the territory, but their holdings were confiscated once more during the Second World War. In 1957, of just over 1,600 long-term rights of occupancy for which figures are available, 262—totaling only 16,555 acres—were held by missions. Of the remaining 1,356 rights, the leading nationalities represented were as follows (all figures: Colonial Office, 1957, p. 133):

	No. of Holdings	*Acreage*
British	461	1,390,577
Indian	286	235,855
Greek	268	336,233
South African	107	184,543

It is of particular significance that the British have only 461 holdings as compared with 915 in the hands of people of other nationalities.

The Sisal Industry

The sisal industry deserves particular attention because for several decades sisal has been not only the principal crop grown on alienated estates, but it has also been the most valuable single item exported from the territory.

The Germans experimented with a large number of possible crops. In the course of their research they introduced practically all of the crops which are of commercial importance today. Among them was sisal which was brought from Florida in 1892. Its cultivation was taken up by German estates along the coast and thereafter large acreages were devoted to it along the newly opened railway lines, particularly the Tanga Line. By 1913, 20,000 tons a year were being exported, worth almost as much as all other exports together (Economist, 1955, p. 32).

The war disrupted the industry and it was not until 1926 that production again reached the prewar figure. Since then there has been a steady rise in production decade after decade, as the following figures indicate (1958 figure: Colonial Office, 1958, p. 298):

	Tons
1926	25,000
1938	101,000
1948	121,000
1958	197,567

By 1956 Tanganyika was by far the most important sisal-producing country in the world. Its exports accounted for 38 per cent of the world production.

The steady rise in the quantity produced has not been reflected directly in the value of the crop, which has fluctuated wildly. In 1913 the crop was worth just over half a million pounds. In 1929 the figure rose to a million and a half but thereafter declined sharply and it was not until 1936 that it regained its former value (Economist, 1955, p. 35). After the war the price shot up astronomically with the result that in 1951, the peak year, the crop was sold for £ 23,500,000. Since then the price has declined. In 1956 less than £ 11,000,000 were received for the crop despite the fact that 186,000 tons were produced, as compared with 124,000 tons in 1951. In 1957 the amount produced remained about the same, 182,000 tons, yet the value sank still lower, realizing less than £ 9,500,000, the lowest figure since 1948 (Colonial Office, 1957, p. 130).

During the period between the wars, sisal accounted for between a third and a quarter of the total exports in any given year (Economist, 1955, p. 35). Since World War II sisal's role in the export economy has varied over a greater range. In 1951 sisal accounted for 60 per cent of the value of all the exports; in 1957 it fell to less than 25 per cent.

In 1956, 644,000 acres were under sisal (Guillibaud, n.d., p. 130). It was being produced on 169 estates, the average yield being something over a thousand tons, but there was great variation in the amount produced on different estates. Twelve estates produced more than 3,000 tons; between them they provided almost a quarter of the total (Guillibaud, n.d., p. 130). At the other end of the scale, there were thirty-one estates which produced less than 250 tons and between them they accounted for only about 1.5 per cent of the territorial total. The Greeks produced the most sisal, 32 per cent, followed by the British with 31 per cent, and the Indians with 24 per cent.

An economist who has recently studied the industry estimates that the total capital invested in sisal is in the neighborhood of £ 20,000,000. He is of the opinion that most of this has been invested by ploughing back profits rather than by obtaining new capital from outside (Guillibaud, n.d., p. 57). Entry into the industry is now restricted either to corporations or very wealthy individuals for it is estimated that a capital outlay of £ 50,000 is required to start a new sisal estate of an economic size capable of producing a thousand tons a year (Guillibaud, n.d., p. 56).

Estate Labor

In recent years the sisal estates have employed over two-thirds of the Africans working in non-native agricultural enterprises and about one-quarter of the number of all the Africans working for wages in the entire territory. There has been little fluctuation in the figures: in most years the number employed has been between 125,000 and 150,000. A remarkable, but not entirely explicable, feature of the labor situation is that a substantial expansion in output has taken place in recent years with very little rise in the number employed.

Year	*Tons Produced*	*Total No. Workers*	*Workers per Ton*
1948	118,000	122,500	1.04
1956	186,000	125,600	.68

While a sisal estate requires a considerable amount of water, obtained either from streams, wells, or ponds, for use in the factory where the fiber is processed, the sisal itself thrives under quite dry conditions. Therefore the bulk of the crop is grown on land which is not very suitable for traditional African subsistence farming. This means that relatively few Africans were dispossessed by the establishment of the sisal estates. Looking at it from another point of view, this also means that the sisal growers did not have a readily available source of labor in the form of a subsistence population which had suddenly had its land expropriated and found itself a landless proletariat. In many cases, even the adjoining areas were not densely populated.

As a result the sisal growers were forced from a very early period to rely upon labor brought from distant places. Through the years, however, local supplies of labor have been built up. Certain workers have decided not to return home but to settle in the sisal areas. These men obtain plots on nearby land which has not been alienated or they settle as squatters on parts of the estates which, for one reason or another, are not under cultivation. Here they build their own houses and cultivate their own small holdings, growing subsistence crops and often cotton or maize as cash crops. These people now supply 60 per cent of the labor force (Gullibaud, n.d., p. 80). However, the other 40 per cent must still be obtained from distant areas.

The recruitment of this labor is in the hands of a central organization known as "Silabu" which is a part of the Sisal Growers'

Fig. 19. The early Arab settlement of Tanganyika was concentrated on the coast, and Dar-es-Salaam remains the capital. This photograph shows an administrative center built by the Germans, who once controlled Tanganyika.

Fig. 20. Residence of senior colonial official in Dar-es-Salaam. *Photo courtesy of J. C. Ramsey.*

Fig. 21. Among many modern institutions in Dar-es-Salaam is this government technical school.

Fig. 22. Home of a wealthy Indian in Dar-es-Salaam. Indians in East Africa attained considerable economic status but were socially segregated.

Fig. 23. At the foot of Mt. Kilimanjaro in the town of Moshi is the coffee cooperative controlled by the Chagga tribe. Coffee, produced in some of the higher, rainier areas of Tanganyika, has become the basic cash crop of certain tribes.

Fig. 24. Sisal plantations in the more arid areas are, like this one near Kilosa not far from Kaguru territory, owned by Europeans. They provide cash income to men who work seasonally by contract.

Fig. 25. Sisal production requires relatively little skilled labor. Leaves are shredded into fibers which are then dried in the sun.

Fig. 26. Near Morogoro, the Catholics maintain a teachers' training school.

Fig. 27. African housing in an administrative trading center in remote areas of Tanganyika is not comparable to the modern buildings of Dar-es-Salaam.

Fig. 28. Members of the Arusha tribe buy beads at an Indian shop in northern Tanganyika. In all but the small shops in restricted native land, Indians are the principal merchants.

Fig. 29. Sir Richard Turnbull, the last British Governor of Tanganyika, visits the Gogo tribe in central Tanganyika. By their system of indirect rule, the British normally left local affairs to African courts, administrative officials, and chiefs whom they appointed in the absence of traditional chiefs.

Association. The worker contracts to fulfill twelve cards (the meaning of these cards is explained below). He is then transported, with his family if he so desires, free of charge to a sisal-growing area where he is allocated to a particular estate. There, he receives housing, wages, food, medical attention, etc. When his contract is fulfilled he is repatriated at the expense of the employer. Many other workers make their way to the sisal areas on their own.

Of the workers who come from distant areas about a fifth come from outside Tanganyika, from Portuguese East Africa and from Belgian-administered Ruanda-Urundi. While these men form only a small proportion of the total working force, they are of critical importance since they are recruited mainly as cutters, the work of cutter being considered the most undesirable. On a sisal estate about a quarter of the workers are employed in the fields cutting the leaves. Another quarter are employed in the factory, while the rest carry out various tasks, such as removing the old plants, clearing new lands, cultivating, tending the nurseries, etc.

A worker who has been brought from a long distance and settled on a particular estate can easily leave the job if he finds it unsatisfactory and can find a position on another estate. In this respect it must be kept in mind that in the sisal-growing areas the roads run for miles past one estate after another. Thus it is simple matter to get from one estate to another and, if necessary, a worker can change his name. The sisal industry, like any other, has its own terminology. A worker who leaves a particular estate before he has fulfilled the terms of his contract is referred to as a "deserter." At the plantation next door where he appears seeking work he is termed a "volunteer." On any given plantation the distance workers are classified as recruited labor and volunteers. For the industry as a whole, the labor supply is not affected by the breaking of contracts, but the estate which loses a deserter has had to bear the expenses involved in the individual's recruitment and transportation to the sisal area, while the estate which acquires his services has evaded these charges. The worker, of course, loses his rights to be repatriated when he breaks his contract, but usually the second estate offers to do this if he works for a certain period of time. The possibility of such movement puts pressure upon the managers of the estates to treat their workers as well as possible, and leads to the provision of facilities above the minimum required by government regulations and by contract. It also exerts an upward pressure upon the wage structure. Local labor does not have quite the same mobility. Due to the transport problem, the local

African finds it difficult to work on any estate other than the one nearest his home.

The actual system of labor utilization is of considerable interest. Only the men in the factory, who are under constant supervision, work regular daily shifts, which, at the present, depending upon the estate, vary from about six and a half hours to eight hours a day. Here the whole organization of the work force and the pace of work is dictated to a large extent by the decorticating machine, which converts the sisal from leaf into fiber, the only complicated machine in use. By contrast, the worker outside the factory has no set hours but instead carries out a task which is defined as "a day's work." This system is known throughout East Africa by the Swahili term *kipande*. *Kipande* means a small piece of anything, and it is now used to refer to the card on which the daily work is recorded.

A worker is usually said to earn so much a month but what is actually meant is the amount which he earns per card. The estate "month" has only a loose relation to the calendrical month. A "month" or a card means thirty days' work. In theory, a man could complete a "month's" work—or in other words, fill his card—in fifteen days.

The job of a cutter may be used to illustrate how the system works. Each day he works in a certain part of the estate, cutting those leaves which are ready for harvest and leaving the rest of the plant intact. The most common definition of a day's work or task is seventy bundles, each consisting of thirty leaves. The man works by himself cutting the leaves, putting them together into bundles, and then carrying them to a place where they can be picked up and carried to the factory either by a truck or by a miniature railway car. When the seventy bundles have been deposited at the collection point the task is completed. The work is carried out at the cutter's own pace, but usually the time spent in the field varies from about three to five hours per day. Generally, cutters begin their work early in the morning so they are usually finished by eleven o'clock at the latest. If he desires, the cutter can undertake another task. For this second task he has the option of being credited with another day's work on his card or receiving an immediate cash payment. On any given day, only about a fifth of the workers undertake a second task (Guillibaud, n.d., p. 93).

While a worker could complete his card in fifteen days, the estate tries to get him to do it within forty-two days. If he completes his card within that period, he is given a substantial bonus. With the standard wage for a cutter being twenty-seven shillings per card, he is given a bonus of twelve shillings. The major reason for offering such an incentive is that the worker costs the employer money even while he is idle. In addition to the estate housing which he may be occupying, he is given a weekly food ration. The ration is based upon maize supplemented by beans, groundnuts, meat, sugar, salt, vegetable oil, and fresh vegetables or fruit. By government regulation this should not be less than 3,500 calories a day (Guillibaud, n.d., p. 95). In 1956 meeting these requirements is said to have cost the estates in the Tanga area about twenty-three shillings per card or almost as much as the wage before the bonus (Guillibaud, n.d., p. 96). If he wishes, the worker may receive a cash equivalent in lieu of a ration. In 1956, this was paid at a rate of fifteen shillings per card.

The estate "month" is actually equivalent to six weeks. With six Sundays this means that a man can complete his card in the required length of time if he takes no more than six days off during the period. In effect this works out to a five-day week. This may not seem too odd although most people are accustomed to think that a five-day working week is only a feature of the most highly industrialized and wealthiest countries. What is rather astonishing is that the number of hours worked per week varies from about fifteen to twenty-five. This deserves comment since the estates are thought of as trying to wring the last bit of work out of their employees. Furthermore, many African workers are described as "target workers," i.e., people who are trying to earn a certain sum of money for one reason or another, say to buy a bicycle or pay bridewealth, and who, once they have passed it, return home.

The *kipande* system has a number of advantages. It reduces the cost of supervision to a minimum, and this is important in a country such as Tanganyika where it is relatively easy to obtain unskilled workers but difficult to find men who can be entrusted with jobs equivalent to that of foreman. On an estate of great size with a very small European staff, perhaps two or three men, this problem becomes critical. The *kipande* system permits the African worker to choose his own days and time of work and it allows him to carry out the task at his own pace. It minimizes the conflicts and antagonisms which are apt to arise in a situation in which a group of workers are closely supervised and constantly exhorted to greater efforts. Conflicts of this sort are particularly likely to arise when the people involved have different cultural backgrounds. This is of particular importance with a pre-industrial population unaccustomed to having their working hours dictated by a factory whistle. A certain number of men are absent from work on any given day, but in the sisal industry where work is carried out on a year-round basis this presents few difficulties. With a large labor force the number of absentees averages out and the amount of leaf coming into the factory remains fairly constant.

All of this does not explain the short working hours. Here the reason seems to lie not in the characteristics of the labor force but rather in the nature of the competition between the estates for labor. A particular estate can attempt to hold its own labor force or to increase it by gaining workers from other nearby estates in two ways (neglecting, for the sake of the argument, such fringe benefits as better rations or better housing). One way is to raise the wage per card and the other is to decrease the amount of work required per card. Whether or not African workers are more responsive to decreasing the tasks demanded of them than they are to wage increases is an open question. What does appear to be quite clear is that task reduction is a more subtle form of competition for labor than is wage manipulation. It must be remembered that the people in charge of the sisal estates are members of a very small community in which they depend upon each other to a very high degree for companionship and aid in other ways. The man who raises wages incurs the hostility of his neighbors who may be the only friends he has. In such a situation reduction in the size of the task demanded from the worker is socially the most innocuous form of competition. Evidence that this form of competition in this type of labor market is not peculiar to Tanganyika or the sisal industry in particular is furnished from Uganda. There it is said that in the twenties workers on European estates were able to finish their daily tasks by nine in the morning (Powesland, 1957, p. 31).

AFRICAN METHODS OF ADAPTATION TO THE NEW CASH ECONOMY

In the rural areas, individual households are still to a very high degree self-sufficient. Most families attempt to grow enough of the staple foodstuffs—maize, sorghum, or plantains—and except in bad years most of them succeed. Superimposed upon this older type of economy is a new one involving cash and oriented towards the market. With the exception of a few people, such as the Hadza of the Eyasi Basin who continue to practice a hunting and gathering way of life, all of the Africans in the territory are involved in the modern cash economy. Here, as in other parts of Africa, one of the first acts of the European administration was to levy a tax upon the local population. This tax has fallen upon the able-bodied adult men, although for the first few decades the tax was actually levied upon the house rather than the individual. This taxation policy forced the African population to find means of raising cash. Nowadays, getting enough money to pay the annual tax is still an important matter, but it has been greatly overshadowed by other motivations. Africans buy considerable quantities of manufactured goods, particularly cloth; and money is required for such things as church contributions and school fees. Cash has also entered into traditional spheres. It is often used in bridewealth transactions, sometimes directly, sometimes indirectly, as when a man earns money to buy the livestock he presents to his future wife's father. But, the most important item today is the purchase of home brewed beer. Although a certain proportion of it is given by the brewer to guests on ceremonial occasions or is used to reward people who have come to help him in his fields, most beer is sold on an ordinary commercial basis.

Broadly speaking, there are three main ways now open to Africans seeking cash: (1) They can find wage opportunities such as are available on the sisal estates; (2) They can grow a cash crop; (3) They can sell some of their own property, livestock being the best example. From one point of view, the major breakdown is into wage labor and local production for the market. However, there are important differences between the sale of cash crops and that of livestock which make this a significant distinction. Other methods of acquiring money, such as commerce and manufacturing (with one exception to be noted below), are of minor importance.

In attempting to present a broad picture many details and complications must, of necessity, be neglected. For example, in a tribe in which the major form of adaptation is wage labor, some men may obtain sufficient cash by selling livestock. Moreover, a given individual may respond in all three ways to the situation, e.g., a chief may receive a salary, grow a certain amount of cotton, and sell an ox from time to time. Furthermore, the form of adaptation may be greatly influenced by age. Younger men may go out to work while their elders, who control the herds, make their livelihood from the sale of livestock.

With these reservations in mind, one can say that various groups have made characteristic adjustments to the situation. The major determinants are: (1) the traditional way of life of the people,

(2) the potentialities of the area in which they live, and (3) their relation to the transportation network.

The influence of the first factor is most obvious in the case of the purely pastoral peoples, such as the Barabaig and the Masai. Here there was never any question of producing cash crops even, which is admittedly not the case, if the areas occupied by them were suitable. Furthermore, they are quite opposed to going out and looking for manual labor. Fortunately, their wealth in livestock has provided them with sufficient cash to make this unnecessary.

The potentialities of the local environment are of great importance. Unfortunately, in most of the territory the environment does not offer wide opportunities to the African entering a cash economy, but instead imposes the most severe limitations. The primary factor here is the low rainfall which prevails over most of the territory and which, especially in view of the limited potentialities for irrigation, makes enormous areas completely unsuited to the production of any crop. In addition, huge tracts of country which are unsuitable for cash cropping but which could be utilized for livestock production are rendered useless for this purpose by the tsetse fly. Of these two problems, lack of water is by far the more intractable because, given enough manpower, large areas can be freed of the fly by felling the bush, as has been demonstrated in Mbulu District and other areas.

The third aspect to be discussed is the communications network. As far as cash crops are concerned, since most of them are exported, the question becomes one of transport costs to the ports: Tanga or Mombasa in the north, Dar-es-Salaam for most of the country, and Mtwara for the extreme southern region. It is not so much the distance from the ports which is important as it is the distance from the nearest railhead. Most crops can stand the cost of transport by rail even from those parts of the territory which are farthest inland, but costs mount very quickly when it becomes necessary to transport a crop by truck from the areas in which it is grown to the railway line. Some of the areas in the south of the country which enjoy relatively favorable rainfall are so far from the railway that it is extremely difficult to find a crop which has such a high value, particularly in relation to its weight, that it can bear the costs of transport.

The tribes in which it has now become customary for a large portion of the adult men to be away working as wage laborers are those, such as the Nyamwezi, Nyaturu, Gogo, Ha, Ngoni, Yao, etc., who live either in poor environments in terms of the modern cash economy or who are situated unfavorably as far as the transportation system is concerned. In some cases both factors are operative.

With this broad picture in mind, we can proceed to discuss wage labor, cash crop production, and livestock sales. In each case, following some general remarks, a tribal group which has responded in a characteristic manner to the modern situation will be described: the Ngoni who leave their homeland in search of employment, the Chagga who grow a valuable cash crop, and the Iraqw who sell livestock.

Employment

When discussing wage employment, a distinction has to be drawn between unskilled laborers and those engaged in occupations such as that of clerk, teacher, etc., which require a certain amount of education. The unskilled laborers are drawn principally from those tribes which are at a disadvantage in terms of the modern economy. The recruitment of skilled workers, including white collar workers, is a more complex matter. It appears that in earlier years when education was almost entirely in the hands of the missions, the people who later were able to fill responsible positions were those whose parents happened to live near mission stations providing educational facilities. The location of these mission stations had little connection with the factors determining the modern economic prosperity of the various tribal areas. For example, although both areas are among the most remote in the territory, Songea and Ufipa Districts have witnessed very heavy missionary commitments in education, medical aid, etc. In recent years, however, as government bodies, particularly the local native authorities, have provided more money for education, there has been an increasing correlation between economic prosperity and educational facilities. The Chagga are an example of this. They have achieved wealth in the modern world through the cultivation of coffee. As a result they have been able to invest a good deal of money in schools and a higher proportion of Chagga parents have been able to pay school fees than is the case with other tribes less advantageously situated. Thus while practically no Chagga goes elsewhere in search of work as an unskilled laborer, many Chagga, who are trained in medical work, veterinary practice, teaching, etc., are forced to go outside their local area because their homeland does not provide enough opportunities for employment.

In 1957 a considerable proportion of the adult male African population was employed. The census of that year reported a total of 2,246,598 males sixteen years or older (Colonial Office, 1957, p. 98). In that same year some 430,000 people were employed. This figure does contain a certain proportion of women and juveniles, but since the labor census does not include all categories of employees, the figure above probably gives a good idea of the proportion of men employed.

Let us first consider the breakdown for the total African wage-earning force (Colonial Office, 1957, p. 156):

Agriculture (including forestry, hunting, and fishing)	211,000
Public services (including railways)	94,000
Domestic servants	40,000
Manufacturing	19,000
Mining	13,000
Services	13,000
Construction	11,000
Commerce	10,000
Transport and communication (not including railways)	8,000
Other employment	11,000
Total	430,000

The first thing to note is the importance of agriculture (the numbers employed in forestry, hunting, and fishing are very small) and public service, which includes the railways. The majority of those working in agriculture are employed in the sisal industry. These two categories, agriculture and the public services, account for about three-quarters of the total number employed. Manufacturing claims less than 5 per cent, less than one-half the number employed as domestic servants. All of these wage earners work for European or Indians.

When we look at the employment figures decade by decade there is a steady increase (first three figures: Hill and Moffett, 1955, p. 278; last figure: Colonial Office, 1957, p. 156):

1925	127,000
1936	244,000
1947	346,000
1957	430,000

In recent years, however, the numbers of those engaged in employment for wages has failed to rise. This has been so despite a steadily increasing population and conditions of prosperity. (Figures through 1951: Hill and Moffett, 1955, p. 278. Other figures: Colonial Office, 1952, p. 318; 1953, p. 172; 1954, p. 200; 1955, p. 256; 1956, p. 146; 1957, p. 156).

1947	346,000
1949	474,107
1951	455,398
1952	433,597
1953	448,271
1954	439,094
1955	413,100
1956	424,209
1957	430,470

In the postwar years trade unions have come into existence. Particularly noteworthy has been the successful organization of the dockworkers. Strenuous efforts are being made to organize the estate workers, particularly the sisal workers. The unions share with the nationalist party the distinction of being purely African-controlled and against the currently established order. The connection between the two is close and any African who considers himself a union man fully supports the aspirations of the nationalist movement.

THE NGONI: MIGRATORY LABORERS [2]

The Ngoni are an example of a people who have a long tradition of furnishing migratory workers to the modern, alien-organized economic organizations, particularly the sisal estates.

The Ngoni practice an almost entirely agricultural economy. They are situated in the interior in the most remote district of the Southern Province some 400 miles from the sea. This means that they are at a great disadvantage in terms of the modern economy since a cash crop must be able to stand the costs of truck transport on the long trip to the coast. The government believes it has found such a crop in tobacco, but despite years of effort it has not succeeded in convincing the Ngoni that they should cultivate it on a large scale. According to Gulliver, the Ngoni leave their area to seek work "because they cannot (in their opinion) obtain adequate money at home, or alternatively, because they feel that it is much easier to earn a given sum abroad" (1955, p. 22).

[2] This account is based upon the investigations made by P. H. Gulliver as reported in his monograph (1955).

There are some 130,000 Ngoni (including Ndendeuli) and at any given time about a third of the adult men are away at work. Two-thirds of these obtain work on sisal estates, 40 per cent in the Kilosa area alone.

To the Ngoni seeking work, the recruiting organization of the sisal growers offers free transportation for themselves and their wives and children to the sisal-growing areas, as well as free food en route. If a man signs a contract, he is given cooking pots, a blanket, and clothing and cloth for the other members of his family. Despite this, three-quarters of the men reach the Kilosa area by their own devices and a large number of them walk the full 300 miles. The fact that they do so testifies to their suspicion of the recruiting organization. This suspicion probably has its roots in the wartime conscription of labor for work on these same estates.

Before the war married men invariably left their wives behind, but now about a third take their wives with them. Children, however, are seldom taken. They are either left behind with their mothers or, if the woman accompanies her husband, they remain in the care of close relatives. It must be borne in mind that the man must feed his wife and children out of his own pocket. While he himself is issued a food ration, there is no such provision for his dependents.

Although there are many variations on the pattern, men tend to leave the Ngoni country after the harvest and perhaps after having prepared the fields for the next year. They are then absent during the subsequent wet season (December to April), which is the growing season, and return towards the end of the following dry season (September to December). Some men stay away for a second year. If they fail to return at the end of that period, it is presumed that they have settled where they have gone in search of wage labor. It is difficult to estimate the rate of this permanent emigration, but Gulliver found that 10 per cent of the men about whom he was to make inquiries had been away for seven or more years.

It is very difficult to find an Ngoni man who is thirty years old and who has not been away from home at least once. Usually a man leaves for the first time before he reaches the age of twenty-five. It is very rare for a man over forty-five to make another trip. It would appear that most men make at least two trips during their working life and a good proportion make four or more journeys. Gulliver says that 10 per cent make four or more trips, but the proportion is obviously much higher than this since the bulk of his sample is composed of men who are still of working age and who may make additional trips. In particular, his sample includes a large number of men in the late teens and early twenties who have not had time to make more than one or perhaps two trips. While we can assume a much larger proportion of men, perhaps 20 per cent or more, make four or more trips, we can accept Gulliver's statement that the most common pattern is for a man to make two trips during his life. A man usually goes away for the first time when he is about twenty and makes an additional trip when he is about thirty. After that, he settles down at home.

A migrant who works for nine to eighteen months brings back an average of about seventy-five shillings in cash and about fifty shillings worth of goods. There are, of course, wide variations here. Men often bring back a wooden box filled with extra clothing which they have purchased for themselves and cloth for their wives, children, and other relatives. Men who have been away for a longer time do not seem to bring back appreciably more cash than those who have been away for a shorter period. The explanation appears to be that when they first start working on an estate, men spend money rather freely on such things as beer and they continue to do so until they decide to go home. They then begin saving for a period of from four to six months.

Concerning the effect of the migratory labor system upon the family and the household economy, it is worth quoting Gulliver at some length because he believes that the disintegrative effects of this pattern are usually overstated. His remarks apply to the families of men who are away for short periods, not those who are away for a long period. In these latter cases the men may have deserted their wives and families.

> One of the most common objections to labour migration which is made by Government officials and missionaries is that it leads to severe hardships for the wife and children who are left at home by the labourer. It may be clear, however, that an Ngoni wife is less dependent upon her husband than her European counterpart, and . . . she is able with relatively little difficulty to maintain the food supply of her home in his temporary absence. She is able to continue her relations and mutual assistance with her female kin and neighbours and by the nature of the economy and low demand, she and her children can comfortably continue with little or no money income. She may suffer from a break in normal married sexual relations, but even this should not be over-emphasized for it is the custom that a man and wife do not cohabit for two or more years after a baby is born. If the man is away during that period (as many young husbands are) no special hardship is experienced.
>
> Because of the network of kinship ties, the wife left at home has a num-

ber of both men and women to whom she can look for support and assistance as of right. Her husband's brother, cousin or father who lives in the same hamlet or nearby will expect to come to her aid, to help (for example) to arrange agricultural working parties for her, to sell her produce, to repair the house or to look after the goats and in general to give her that male support which she may require from time to time because of her inferiority as a woman. Within this kinship network no one person is so indispensible as in the isolated European family system. Most certainly the majority of migrants make arrangements before they leave so that a brother or uncle shall be responsible in particular for helping his wife. Many a man has told me that he cannot himself go away to work abroad until his brother (or some other kinsmen) comes back in order that their wives shall not be left without close male support. . . . (1955, p. 37)

African Production of Export Crops for Cash

Coffee and cotton are by far the most important cash crops grown by the African population. In 1957 the coffee and cotton crops were each worth more than £ 7,000,000. The third most important crop, cashew nuts, was worth only £ 1,500,000. Coffee gives the individual producer by far the greatest return. Unfortunately, it can only be grown in very restricted areas where soil and rainfall conditions are favorable. Cotton can be grown in areas which receive much less rainfall and thus, although the value of cotton crop is about the same as that of the coffee crop, it is grown more extensively, particularly in the Lake and Eastern Provinces, and several times as many people are engaged in its production. Unfortunately, conditions are not favorable for its growth in large parts of the territory and some areas where it could be grown successfully are so far from the railhead that the crop cannot bear the transport charges. Where cotton cannot be grown it is usually difficult to find a marketable crop. Cashew nuts are suitable crop for the particular conditions found in much of the Southern Province and in recent years the government has encouraged its production. Elsewhere, particularly in the drier areas, the production of oil seeds such as sunflowers and castor has been feasible. However, an enormous proportion of the territory is of little agricultural value at the present time and the prospects of finding cash crops which will grow under local conditions and return a satisfactory income to the producers are not very good.

PRODUCERS OF A CASH CROP: THE CHAGGA

The Chagga live on the slopes of Mt. Kilimanjaro. Kilimanjaro has fertile volcanic soil and its high rainfall and its streams provide water for extensive irrigation systems. It rises like a huge green oasis out of the surrounding desert-like plateau which is occupied by only small numbers of pastoral, transhumant Masai. The mountain is densely populated. In 1957 the Chagga formed the fifth largest tribe in the territory with more than 300,000 people.

The Chagga began to grow coffee with the encouragement of the German government before the First World War. In the twenties the British government urged them to take up coffee growing on a large scale; of particular importance were the efforts made by Sir Charles Dundas (later Governor of Uganda) when he was the District Commissioner of Moshi District. In 1925 the Chagga growers formed a cooperative society. "It was started . . . largely as a response to European planters' opposition to native coffee growing based on the fear that badly managed native *shambas* would harbour some of the bugs and pests that delight in fastening on the species arabica, and that have been known to wipe out trees over whole regions and even whole countries as happened in Ceylon" (Huxley, 1951, p. 85). Later this cooperative society was reconstituted under the name of Kilimanjaro Native Cooperative Union or KNCU. For fifteen years this venture was under the direction of a European, Mr. Bennett, to whom much of its success is due. It is now managed completely by a group of Chagga officers. The cooperative was strongly backed by the government and membership in it was made compulsory (Huxley, 1951, p. 86). In the past it had a great number of difficulties and at times a large proportion of the Chagga opposed it. At one point its buildings were burned (Huxley, 1951, p. 86). Now the cooperative movement has the general support of the Chagga and the KNCU has built the most imposing building in Moshi, the local town. One difficulty faced by the KNCU in its earlier years was the slump in coffee prices during the thirties. Since the war, however, the price of coffee has risen astronomically, as the following figures illustrate (Hill and Moffett, 1955, p. 772):

Season	No. Growers	Tons of Coffee	Total Payments to Growers	Average per Grower		
			£	£	*s.*	*cts.*
1932–33	12,529	1,072	39,152	2	16	55
1937–38	25,226	1,472	40,695	1	6	33
1942–43	27,572	3,103	163,221	5	5	46
1947–48	31,674	4,235	463,124	11	18	66
1951–52	33,151	4,642	1,396,382	34	0	45

While the amount of coffee produced rose by almost half from the early to the late thirties, the total value of the crop actually declined and the amount received per grower was sharply reduced. A few years later, during the war, though the number of producers increased only slightly, the value of the crop increased fourfold. This upward trend continued in the postwar period. In the 1951-52 season the number of growers increased by only a third. In comparison with the period before the war the amount produced had tripled, yet the sum received from its sale had increased more than thirtyfold.

As a result of the development of the coffee industry, the Chagga enjoy an unparalleled standard of living among the tribes of the territory. At the present time a large portion of them are Christian and they place a great emphasis upon education. The mountainside is dotted with schools. This has been done through contributions both to the local native administration and to the local churches, Lutheran and Catholic. Now one finds Chagga in all parts of the territory as school teachers and government servants.

Internal Marketing of Traditional Forms of Wealth: The Livestock Industry

The livestock industry differs from the production of such cash crops as sisal, coffee, and cotton in that it came into being in response to local, as opposed to foreign, demand. Its growth has been made possible by the political unification of the country, the development of a diversified economy, and the rise of the towns. Among other things, it permits people who live in areas which are too dry to grow cash crops, or who are too far from the railway to market them profitably, to participate in the modern cash economy without having to leave their tribal areas in search of employment.

Most of the tribes in Tanganyika, with the exception of those living on the coastal plain, traditionally maintained herds of livestock. In addition to their role in the subsistence economy, livestock have been integrated into the social structure by means of bridewealth transactions and by the part which they play in the system of prestige, the man with a large herd being accorded respect and deference.

In 1957 the government estimated that there were more than 7,000,000 head of cattle, over 4,000,000 goats, 3,000,000 sheep, and over 150,000 donkeys in the territory (Colonial Office, 1957, p. 135).

In recent decades the number of livestock in the territory has increased tremendously. Although, in some places, cattle have been introduced into societies which were formerly purely agricultural, much more important have been the almost complete cessation of cattle raids, particularly by the Masai, and the work of the Veterinary Department in all branches of livestock management, especially in the control of epidemics. Herds have increased to such an extent that a large proportion of the best pastoral land in some areas is seriously overgrazed and soil erosion is well underway.

There have been complaints from government officers and others that the attitudes of the Africans towards their cattle preclude the development of a rationalized livestock industry. It is alleged that the African is reluctant to sell his beasts and that he places more importance upon numbers than quality. While there is a certain amount of truth in these remarks, the position has been overstated. The fact that Africans will sell their cattle has been shown for many years by the vast numbers sold at the markets. The truth of the matter is that they are not reluctant to sell stock, they are merely reluctant to sell female breeding stock and this makes very good sense (see Schneider, 1957, pp. 278-301). The practice of communal grazing also leads to a higher ratio of beasts per acre than would be the case were the individual owner grazing his cattle on his own enclosure.

The livestock industry is now of considerable importance in the economy of the country. It is almost entirely in the hands of the African population with the exception of a few small dairies run by the government and some Indians to supply milk to the immigrant communities living in the towns. Although in recent years the government has attempted to stimulate the development of European ranching, as yet this type of endeavor has not reached any large proportions.

At the present time, the dairy industry is of very little importance among African cattle owners. The government has, however, stimulated the production of ghee (clarified butter), which is used by the Indians. In 1952 some 76,000 tins of ghee, each weighing some thirty-six pounds, were produced. This amount was worth a quarter of a million pounds.

Of far greater importance is the sale of hides and skins and the slaughter of stock sold on the hoof. Formerly, hides and skins were used for bedding, mats, and clothing. They have been almost completely replaced by manufactured textiles, blankets, and cotton piece goods with the result that today when an animal is slaughtered at home or when it dies, its skin is dried and sold to the local Indian trader. The hides and skins purchased in this manner and exported give quite a good basis for the estimation of the number of livestock slaughtered. In recent years it has been estimated that about a million head of cattle die or are slaughtered in the territory each year, in addition to 1,800,000 goats and sheep (Hill and Moffett, 1955, p. 606). In 1957 the value of the hides and skins exported came to £ 1,223,000 (Colonial Office, 1957, p. 130).

In contrast to hides and skins, slaughter stock are purchased from the herdsmen primarily for consumption within Tanganyika, although it is true that in some years considerable numbers have been sent to Kenya and recently a packing company has been exporting a certain amount of tinned meat. Through the years, the demand for meat has steadily increased as more and more people have entered paid employment. Sisal estates and mines are required to include a certain amount of meat in the rations supplied to their workers, and consumers are found also among the immigrant communities, particularly the Europeans, as well as among the increasingly large number of African town dwellers. A further important development is the purchase of meat by rural Africans. The most striking example of this is offered by the Chagga, who keep cattle themselves but not in sufficient numbers to meet their present demands. They use some of the money obtained from the sale of coffee to buy meat from cattle obtained in Masailand and Mbulu District. In 1951, out of the 2,100 licensed butchers in the territory, 350 were carrying on business in the Chagga area.

At first, livestock was bought by itinerant traders, mostly Arabs and Somalis. In the early twenties an auction system was organized and government-supervised markets were opened in most of the main stock-raising areas. As of 1951, there were 150 regular livestock markets, usually consisting of holding pens and an enclosed ring, often built of stone, where the animals are led in one by one to be auctioned off to buyers who sit on the wall. The auction is conducted by a government-employed African auctioneer. The livestock trade is the only type of business in which Indians do not participate. Instead, it is dominated by Somalis and Arabs although some local Africans are involved. A few years after the war, an organization known as Tanganyika Packers, Ltd. was set up. The government owns 51 per cent of the capital, while the rest is in the hands of a British meat-packing concern. Two factories were built, one in Arusha and the other, the larger of the two, in Dar-es-Salaam. The Dar-es-Salaam factory cans beef using cattle brought chiefly from the Lake and Western Provinces by train. The Arusha factory depends mainly upon cattle purchased in the Northern Province and was designed to supply frozen beef to the local European estates and the sisal estates along the Tanga Railway Line. In 1952, the only year for which figures are available, the Dar-es-Salaam factory processed 53,000 head of cattle (Hill and Moffett, 1955, p. 634). At that time its output, which was valued at £ 876,000, was purchased by the Ministry of Food in the United Kingdom.

Some indication of the growth of the livestock industry is given by the following figures:

Year	*No. Cattle Purchased*	*Average Price per Head*	*Total Amount Paid*
		s.	£
1938	72,153	27	97,406
1952	255,922	138	1,765,851

LIVESTOCK PRODUCERS: THE IRAQW

The Iraqw, who live in the Mbulu District of the Northern Province and who now number about 130,000, are a group of people who have adapted to the new economy primarily through the sale of livestock. Their traditional economy has been a mixed one in that each household containing an elementary family carried out both agricultural and pastoral pursuits. Their subsistence economy is based upon grains: maize, sorghum, and millets. This is supplemented by milk and a certain amount of meat.

In most parts of Iraqw country, almost all of the cash which comes into the hands of the local people is derived either directly or indirectly from the sale of livestock. A certain number of men work on the European-owned estate at Oldeani on the northern borders of the Iraqw country; and a certain amount of agricultural produce consisting principally of wheat, onion, and beans is grown by the Iraqw for sale. But with the exception of one newly developed area in the extreme north, the amount of cash realized by produce sales is of minor importance.

In 1957 the Iraqw sold over 14,000 head of cattle, over 11,000 goats, and slightly more than 1,000 sheep for a total of more than £ 150,000. All of this money was received by the stock owners and while every house has stock attached to it, ownership is not so widely diffused. Men who do not own livestock manage to acquire animals by means of a system of loans, but ultimate control lies in the hands of the owners, who can decide to sell the animals at will and who receive the entire sale price. The principal mechanism whereby the non-stock-owning population acquires cash is through the sale of beer made from sorghum. On the basis of the number of brewing permits issued in 1957, it is estimated that at least £ 50,000 worth of beer was sold in that year.

The transition from a subsistence economy to one which includes the sale of livestock for cash is a relatively easy matter. Unlike wage employment, such an economy does not require an individual to travel to strange places and carry out unfamiliar tasks under novel living conditions. Furthermore, since adult men do not have to leave home, family organization is not affected. It also lacks certain of the complications attendant upon the development of a system of cash cropping. When cash cropping is superimposed upon the subsistence economy more land is placed under cultivation and more labor is required. In some cases, this has meant an alteration in the traditional division of labor between the sexes with accompanying changes in the organization of the family. The sale of livestock instead of a cash crop would seem to have fewer implications for the social structure in other ways as well. In many societies in the interior of East Africa prestige and social status have accompanied the ownership of cattle. When money is obtained by the sale of cattle, the high status of the sellers is reinforced rather than threatened or destroyed. Traditionally in Tanganyika, great respect has been paid to older men by younger men. In a society in which cash cropping or, more particularly, wage labor is the chief form of adaptation, it is possible for a young man to acquire a much larger income than an older man, causing an alteration in the system of power and prestige. Among the Iraqw, however, ownership of cattle is concentrated in the hands of the older man so their sale reinforces the traditional social system by putting money in the hands of the elderly. Although other factors are probably at work, this aspect of their economic adaptation does much to explain why tribes such as the Masai and the Barabaig (whose sole source of cash is through the sale of livestock) and those such as the Iraqw (among whom such sales are the chief source of monetary income) should be considered by government officials and missionaries to be extremely conservative and resistant to change, in comparison to other tribes.

NATIONAL INCOME

Estimates of the national income became available for the first time only recently. The Royal Commission prepared the first such estimates during the course of its investigation. These were published in 1958. Later, two British economists, Peacock and Dosser, prepared estimates at the invitation of the Tanganyika government. These figures, also published in 1958, were followed in the same year by similar accounts calculated by the East African Statistical Department. The calculation of national income, or the gross domestic product as it is technically known, is beset with a number of difficulties in a country such as Tanganyika. For one thing, the government does not collect figures concerning many economic activities. Another serious difficulty is that the African subsistence factor plays a major role in the total economy. Experts differ as to whether or not this sector should be included in the calculations and, if so, what value should be imputed to it.

The accompanying table shows the income generated in the various areas of activity. It is broken down into two parts to show the relationship between the monetary and the subsistence sectors of the economy.

TABLE 1. NATIONAL INCOME (in Thousands of £)[a]

Sector	Monetary	Subsistence	Total
Agriculture	£32,580	£43,887	£76,467
Livestock products	3,945	11,700	15,645
Forest products	3,670	2,700	6,000
Hunting and fishing	147	1,960	2,107
Mining	5,015	—	5,015
Manufacturing	5,167	5,380	11,047
Construction	4,415	4,847	9,795
Public utilities	974	—	974
Transport, storage, and communications	10,049	—	10,049
Distribution	7,800	—	7,800
Ownership of dwelling	3,065	—	3,065
Public administration and defense	10,893	—	10,893
Misc. services	4,539	—	4,539
Total	£92,259	£70,174	£162,433

[a] 1958 was the first year in which the Tanganyika government published estimates of the national income or the gross domestic product. These covered the years from 1954 through 1957 (Budget Survey, 1958-59, p. 34). We have added the figures which they have given in a supplementary table to those they have produced for the subsistence sector of the economy since their estimates of the value of African subsistence agriculture appear no more reliable than their estimates of such things as the value of firewood and African beer, which are included in the supplementary table. In fact, the former may be less trustworthy.

Of considerable interest are some figures prepared by the Royal Commission, showing the amounts received by the African population from the crops and livestock and from wages. They also permit comparison to be made with neighboring Kenya and Uganda.

Although it is the largest both in area and in population, Tanganyika is the poorest of the three territories comprising British East

Africa. In its overall economic structure Tanganyika bears much more resemblance to Kenya than it does to Uganda. Although in all three countries the minute immigrant communities (including companies based overseas) receive cash incomes which are astronomical in relation to their size, in Uganda the economy is dominated by the Africans whose total income is three times that of the immigrant communities, while in Kenya and Tanganyika, by contrast, the immigrant communities receive the lion's share of the income which is generated. In Tanganyika the immigrant communities receive almost twice the cash income of the total African population, while in Kenya the immigrant communities receive almost four times as much as the total African population. This is consistent with the fact that there are almost twice as many Europeans and Indians in Kenya as there are in Tanganyika, and that they, particularly the Europeans, have far more power in the former country. In both Kenya and Tanganyika the African population acquires more money through wages than it does through the sale of produce in the rural areas, but this is much more marked in the case of Kenya. This reflects the fact that so much of the best land in the territory is in the hands of the Europeans and that urbanization has proceeded further in Kenya. In Tanganyika, the African earns much more from the sale of produce than he would in Kenya. But even this level of production bears no comparison with Uganda, where a similar African population receives five times as much.

TABLE 2. NATIONAL INCOMES FOR BRITISH EAST AFRICA: KENYA, TANGANYIKA, AND UGANDA (in Thousands of £)[a]

	Kenya	Tanganyika	Uganda
Total net geographical (money) product	£80,800	£62,000	£81,200
Net money product of agricultural, commercial, trading and other enterprises of indigenous economies	4,700	10,000	51,100
Wages earned outside indigenous economies, including values of rations, housing, etc.	13,200	12,800	9,300
Total money product of commercialized activities of indigenous economies	17,900	22,800	60,400
Total money product of immigrants	£62,900	£49,200	£20,800

[a] Kenya figures for 1951, Tanganyika figures for 1952. East African Royal Commission, 1953-55, pp. 478-79.

TABLE 3. 1953 POPULATION FIGURES FOR BRITISH EAST AFRICA: KENYA, TANGANYIKA, AND UGANDA (in 1,000)[a]

	Kenya	Tanganyika	Uganda
Total	5,851	8,069	5,343
African	5,644	7,965	5,286
European	42	20	7
Indian (and other Asians)	131	65	47
Total immigrants	173	85	54
Percentage of Indian immigrants to total population	3%	1.4%	1%

[a] East African Royal Commission, 1953-55, p. 457.

In Uganda there are few alien-owned estates. In recent years, particularly, the whole focus of attention has been upon African production. In Tanganyika the modern sectors of the economy have been in the hands of the immigrant communities, although as far as agriculture is concerned, the policy has been to encourage both alien-owned estate production and African production. On the face of it, it would seem that the policy pursued in Uganda has been a much better one from the point of view of the African population. However, it must be remembered that Uganda is a much smaller country where the development of transportation facilities has been much easier. Its arid areas lie on the periphery of the country and not in the center, as in Tanganyika. Furthermore, a much larger proportion of Uganda is suitable for the production of cash crops.

Leaving aside the political aspect of the question, in Tanganyika the problem is whether the African population would be any wealthier if there were no European estates. In such a case, Africans would lose a good deal of the cash income which they now receive from their work on these estates. While small-scale African cultivators could derive sizable incomes from working some of the estates, particularly those growing coffee, this would not be the case with sisal, for the African population still does not possess an adequate number of people with managerial and technical skills to run large-scale enterprises of this sort.

GOVERNMENT FINANCE

During the period between the wars the attitude of the British government was that Tanganyika should lift itself by its own bootstraps. The basic policy was that the British Treasury should not have to pay for the operating costs of the Tanganyika government, which should raise its own funds locally. It was impossible to put this policy into operation immediately because, when the civil administration took over in 1919, the country was in a chaotic state as a result of the war. The government did not achieve a firm financial position until 1926. However, the British Treasury only granted it subsidies until 1921. For the next few years, although aid was granted to Tanganyika, such grants took the form of loans and not outright subsidies. After 1926 the Treasury limited itself to granting loans to Tanganyika and underwriting other loans obtained from the public. By 1929 Tanganyika had a national debt of £ 8,750,000, of which a little over £ 3,000,000 was owed to the British Treasury. The rest was raised on the open market in London. Five million of this was borrowed to develop and maintain the railway system. In the thirties this rigid policy was relaxed somewhat and modest development grants were made as gifts from the British government. However, by 1939 such grants had only reached the very small total of half a million pounds.

For the most part, except for these loans, the Tanganyika government was dependent upon the sums which it could raise internally. During the entire twenty-one-year period from 1919 to 1939, the total revenue of the country totaled £ 33,000,000. In no year did the revenue raised by the government amount to as much as £ 2,500,000.

The budget for 1939 is a typical prewar budget. In that year revenue was £ 2,160,000 and the expenditure £ 2,280,000, the budget being balanced by a development grant from the United Kingdom of £ 120,000.

In 1939 about one-third of the budget was used for the direct or indirect costs of administration, broken down into the following categories:

Provincial administration	£ 210,000
Defense	160,000
Police	110,000
Pensions and gratuities	110,000
Prisons	40,000
Local government	30,000
Total	£ 660,000

Another £ 150,000 was allocated to repayment of the public debt. Relatively small amounts were therefore left over for development projects. The Public Works Department received only £ 150,000, a large proportion of which was undoubtedly spent on the upkeep of roads already in existence and on such things as the construction of offices and houses utilized by the administration. The Department of Agriculture, which is responsible together with the administration for the development of African cash crops, received only £ 70,000. The Veterinary Department, which concerns itself not only with the health of livestock but with all problems of stock raising, such as pasture management, livestock marketing, etc., received a mere £ 40,000.

With sums of this magnitude available to it from internal sources and with practically no help from the British government, what is remarkable is not so much that Tanganyika did not make more notable strides in economic development, but that in fact so much was accomplished. Added to the difficulties of Tanganyika in the thirties was the reluctance of private capital to invest in a country of this sort during the Depression.

The situation in the twenties and the thirties can be viewed as one in which Great Britain took responsibility for Tanganyika on the international scene and sent out men to administer the country and to staff the various branches of the government, such as the Medical, Veterinary, and Public Works departments. Looking at it one way, it can be said that Great Britain, as an experienced colonial power, sold administrative and technical services to the people of Tanganyika who were expected to pay the salaries of the men sent out to supply these services, and to support the plans which they devised.

If we examine the revenue received by the government in 1939, we find an extraordinary situation, particularly when we bear in mind the distribution of monetary income as analyzed by the Royal Commission. Almost one-third of the total revenue (£ 650,000) came from a head tax levied upon the African population. The only direct tax levied upon the European and Indian communities was the Non-Native Poll Tax, which amounted to only £ 50,000 in all. In addition to the head tax the other large source of revenue was the duty imposed upon imports. These duties produced another third of the total revenue (£ 650,000). It is impossible to assess the incidence of this tax. The basic rate for a long time was fixed at 22 per cent. The Europeans and Asians imported large quantities of goods, but it should be noted that such items as trucks and agricultural machinery, which were purchased almost entirely by the immigrant communities, were duty-free. There was no income tax, although in 1937 an inquiry was made concerning the advisability of instituting such a levy. Those responsible for the inquiry came to the quite remarkable conclusion that there were very few people with high incomes in the territory and that the yield from an income tax might well be less than the yield from the Non-Native Poll Tax (Moffett, 1958, p. 115).

Since the war the situation has altered radically and the whole climate of opinion has changed. The government has made a determined effort to speed up the pace of economic development. A special part of the budget has been set aside for development programs and a great deal of money has been spent on extending the network of roads and making available new water supplies. Departments, such as Agriculture and Veterinary, which are directly concerned with economic progress in the rural areas have been greatly strengthened. The government has made itself responsible for a greatly accelerated program of social services in the fields of medicine and, in particular, education.

In 1956-57 about ten times as much was spent on medical services as had been spent in 1939: £ 2,139,000 as against £ 210,000. The amount spent on education has risen more than thirty times from £ 110,000 in 1939 to £ 3,806,000 in 1957 (for 1939 figures, see Moffett, 1958, p. 344; for the 1956-57 figures, see the Budget Survey, 1958-59, p. 29). Far more is now being spent on education alone than was spent by all branches of the government in the prewar period.

The British government no longer feels that it can be content to send out administrative and technical officers and then cheer from the sidelines. The current view is that the metropolitan country has an obligation to aid the development of Tanganyika in a material sense. For example, in the fiscal year of 1956-57 the United Kingdom's Colonial Development and Welfare Fund allocated almost a million pounds to Tanganyika (Colonial Office, 1957, p. 110).

The government budget has been rising from year to year with the result that now the amount spent in a single year is beginning to approach the total amount spent in the entire period between the wars. In 1956-57 the central government's budget came to almost £ 23,500,000.[3] In addition, the African local treasuries have developed a great deal in terms of the range of activities in which they now engage and in terms of their financial responsibility and power. In 1957 the fifty-four local treasuries had a combined revenue of more than £ 3,000,000, derived mainly from graduated taxes levied upon the adult male population and from taxes levied upon produce

[3] While these sums are very large in terms of the previous history of Tanganyika, some sense of proportion can be gained if we realize that the budget of Tanganyika and that of the University of Illinois have been about the same in recent years.

sold at the markets. These bodies spent about three-quarters of a million pounds on social services alone (Colonial Office, 1957, p. 113).

The funds to support the vastly increased government expenditures in recent years have been obtained in various ways. Greatly increased revenue has been received from some of the traditional sources and new taxes have been introduced. Aid has been received from the outside, particularly from the United Kingdom but also from the United States under the Marshall Plan. In addition, loans have been raised both in England and in Tanganyika itself. In 1956-57, for example, the government received approximately £ 17,500,000 from recurrent sources. Three and a quarter million were raised through loans and the United Kingdom contributed almost a million pounds (Budget Survey, 1958-59, pp. 25, 26).

In the postwar period there has been a considerable change in the burden of taxation. A few years ago the Native Poll Tax was abolished and its place has been taken by the Personal Tax which is levied upon Africans, Europeans, and Indians alike. It is graded according to income level and ranges from twelve shillings a year for those with incomes of less than £ 100 to a maximum of 180 shillings for those earning over £ 600. In practice this is levied only on adult African men who, except for those in the civil service and other salaried positions, pay only twelve shillings (Colonial Office, 1957, p. 120). In 1956-57 this tax raised some £ 1,096,000 in revenues, of which it is estimated the African population contributed about £ 800,000 (Colonial Office, 1957, p. 112). While import duties held first place in 1956-57, it was estimated that in the following year the income tax would replace it as the single most important source of revenue (Colonial Office, 1957, p. 112). During the war an income tax was introduced as an emergency measure despite the protests of the European settlers. While in theory it was applicable to all inhabitants of the territory, in practice it was levied almost exclusively upon the European and Indian populations. In 1938 the Europeans and Indians paid only about one-thirteenth as much as the Africans in direct taxation. In 1956-57 the former groups paid more than four times as much as did the Africans.

With this survey of government financial policy, we have completed our remarks about Tanganyika as a whole. We can now turn to the specific conditions to be found in one part of the country and see how one group of people with a distinctive way of life has been influenced and reacted to the various forces which have emanated from the wider society in which it now finds itself a part.

Part II. Ukaguru: The Local Level

PHYSICAL SETTING

Ukaguru is located in east central Tanganyika about 150 miles from the coast. It lies in the central portion of a great 9-shaped chain of mountains which extends from the southwest to the northeast of the territory. Two-thirds of Ukaguru is located in the northern portion of Kilosa District (Eastern Province), and the remainder to the west in the northwestern portion of Mpwapwa District (Central Province).

This part of Tanganyika is occupied by several very different African peoples. First of all, there are a group of highland Bantu peoples who are matrilineal and who share many common cultural and linguistic traits. The Kaguru belong to this group, as do the Sagara and Vidunda to the south and the Luguru, Nguu, and Zigua to the east. In the past, the Zigua and Nguu as well as the coastal Zaramo, who came into contact with the Arabs at an early date, tended to prey upon their neighbors to the west and south, but some peaceful intertribal relations were maintained among all these groups.

To the north and west of these Bantu peoples are the Nilo-Hamitic Masai. A related group, the Baraguyu (Kwavi), have settled in the Ukaguru area. To the west of Ukaguru is a vast area settled by the Gogo, one of the largest tribes in Tanganyika. The Gogo are a Bantu people practicing a mixed agricultural and pastoral economy. Culturally they differ considerably from the Bantu people to the east of them.

Kilosa District, in which most of our investigations took place,

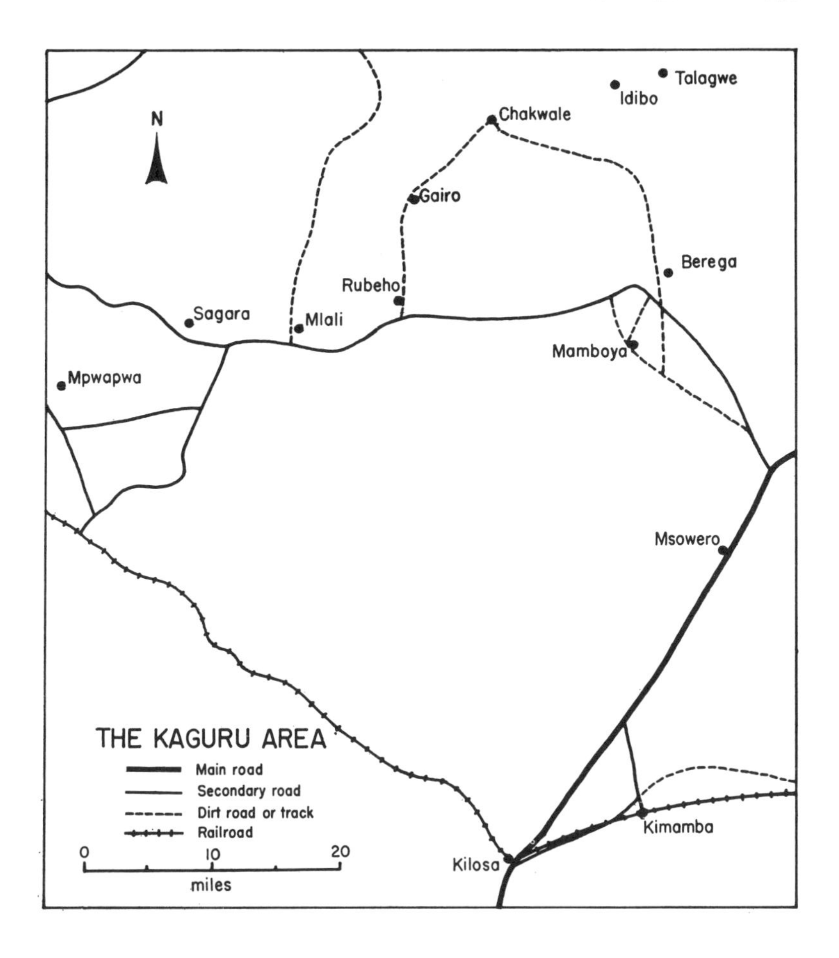

is a relatively small administrative district about the size of Connecticut and Rhode Island combined, the Ukaguru section of the district being about the size of Rhode Island. The district contains about 300 Europeans of both sexes and all ages; over half of them are Greeks and most of them live on the sisal estates. A large proportion of the English are connected with the government. Other non-indigenous people are the Indians (about 1,000), the Arabs (about 400), and the Somalis (less than 100), all engaged in trade.

The African population of the district may be divided into two broad categories: (1) those living on the estates and in the towns of Kilosa and Kimamba—most of these people have come from elsewhere in the territory—and (2) the local, indigenous tribes which form the bulk of the district's African population and live for the most part in the uplands. A third of the indigenous people are Kaguru who form the largest tribe in the district. The Sagara, who number about 18,000, are the only other important tribe in the district and comprise about one-eighth of the population. In addition to the 50,000 Kaguru in Kilosa District, there are another 30,000 in adjoining Mpwapwa District, as well as about 5,000 more in other areas of the territory. Almost none of these reside in towns.

In Kilosa District there are also about 2,000 Kamba (see Beidelman, 1961b), about 2,000 Nguu, and about 1,800 Baraguyu (Kwavi) (see Beidelman, 1960), most of whom live in Ukaguru. The Kamba and Nguu practice agriculture and herding and live in small hamlets alongside the Kaguru. They tend to be somewhat more prosperous than the Kaguru and are more frequently engaged in petty trading. The Baraguyu are purely pastoral, living in small temporary camps completely apart from the other tribal groups.

Kilosa District is economically dominated by the large sisal estates which run the length of the eastern portion of the district. The administrative center is at Kilosa town through which the Central Railway Line runs. However, most of the motor traffic in the area runs through the northern portion of the district rather than through Kilosa town. The main east-west road of Tanganyika runs directly through Ukaguru, connecting the communication centers and provincial capitals of Dodoma and Morogoro. This road tends to link Ukaguru more closely economically with these two centers rather than with the district administrative center to the south.

Kilosa town has a population of over 3,050 Europeans, 400 Indians, and about 3,000 Africans. It is the government headquarters for the district and here are to be found the offices of the British officials, a hospital, a jail, a police station, etc. Kilosa town also has two small Greek-owned hotels, a European club, a post office, a large train station, a Catholic and a Protestant church, an Indian-owned cinema, several Greek and Indian shops catering to Europeans, many bars both for Africans and others, Indian and African schools, a Jamat Khana, and an African social center building. It is still an important center for the sisal estates surrounding the town, although much of this sisal trade goes through the rail station of Kimamba town nine miles east and Morogoro, the provincial capital some fifty miles east by rail. Kimamba town is less than half the size of Kilosa and acts chiefly as the center for the surrounding sisal estates. Its European community is exclusively Greek. It has a Greek club and an imposing Greek-owned hotel.

Morogoro town is one of the major commercial and communications centers of Tanganyika. It is located in Morogoro District, which lies east of Kilosa District. It is the center of the Eastern Province sisal estate area as well as a collection point for the food crops which are grown in the nearby Uluguru Mountains and sent by rail down to Dar-es-Salaam. As a provincial capital, it has all the amenities to be found in the most modern Tanganyika communities, although these are somewhat less extensive than one might expect from the town's size since the town is relatively near Dar-es-Salaam. Morogoro has a population of over 12,000, of which 200 are Europeans and 1,500 Asians.

Most of Ukaguru lies within the Kaguru or Itumba Mountains which separate the Great Central Plateau in the west from the lower Mkata Plain in the east, although the eastern edge of Ukaguru extends into the Mkata Plain itself. Flat and covered with scrub and grasslands, this plain is watered by a few rivers from the mountains to the west. This low area is subject to considerable destructive flooding during the rainy season.

On the plain there are numerous small plots cultivated by laborers on the estates and by local Africans, but most of the land is devoted to vast Greek and British sisal estates. Very little of this land was utilized previous to European contact because much of it is too dry for food crops and because the area was vulnerable to raids by marauding Masai, Baraguyu, Kamba, and others. In this area roadside settlements containing shops and markets provide services to all alien estate laborers and to the local Africans. Many local tribesmen live in small hamlets in this area, but most of the estate workers live in huge housing compounds located on the estates themselves.

The Kaguru Mountains form a precipitous highland which is very difficult to traverse. It is characterized by many fantastic peaks of great beauty. The mountains range from 4,000 to 8,000 feet in elevation. The southern portion of this highland has the highest, most rugged peaks and consequently the most inaccessible areas. Some of the mountains are completely wooded and forests are to be found in many of the valleys as well. The forests vary from parklike woods to thick rain forests which occur at the higher elevations. Many of the mountain slopes, however, are grassy pasture lands and parts of these are sometimes cultivated. There are innumerable small mountain valleys with rushing streams which provide plentiful water even during the height of the dry season. In these valleys one finds small pockets of arable land. The mountain grasslands provide grazing for herds of cattle, sheep, and goats. This southern area is one of irregular and light settlement, of small clusters of low, long, fortlike *tembe*[1] houses with each settlement situated atop its own ridge and rather isolated from its neighbors. During the rains it is an area of penetrating cold and dampness and thus it is disliked by the majority of the Kaguru who prefer the lower valleys. This area is almost completely isolated during the worst of the rains.

In the north central portion of the Kaguru Mountains the land is far less rugged. Large peaks are scattered five to ten miles apart and the intervening low hills are cut by a series of rather wide river valleys leading eastward down into the Mkata Plain. Most of the land is wooded parkland suitable for light grazing but insufficiently watered and too rocky for cultivation.

The valleys watered by small streams are cleared and cultivated in irregular patches. The broader river valleys, however, present an almost continuous patchwork of fields extending as far as the eye can see. The drier, less fertile land above these valleys is more irregularly cleared and cultivated. This higher land has been subject to many years of slash and burn agriculture and in place of parkland forest one finds scrub or thorn thicket with only scattered trees.

The rivers of this portion of Ukaguru vary strikingly with the season. During the rains they are broad and often impassable, while during the dry season they shrink to mere trickles. During the last months of the dry season they appear to be broad expanses of sand. However, water is always available if holes are dug a few feet into the sandy beds.

In this central portion of Ukaguru, and in the north as well, the population is relatively dense, especially along the rivers. Here too one finds a number of small settlements with shops and other facilities. The southernmost of the valleys of central Ukaguru holds Mamboya, an old caravan center and the present capital of the Kaguru's paramount chief. North of Mamboya is the mission center at Berega. In the extreme north of Ukaguru are the market centers of Iyogwe, Talagwe, and Idibo, the latter being the major settlement in northern Ukaguru. To the west are the important trading centers of Chakwale and Gairo. These centers service an irregular but almost continuous network of river valleys which contain the bulk of the Kaguru population. They are the scenes of the most lively social activity and it is here that social change is most apparent. At these settlements are located the markets, the

[1] The *tembe* is a low, rectangular, flat-roofed house built of wood and earth.

Fig. 30. Much of the Kaguru territory is cut by rugged mountains. Prior to pacification by the British, the Kaguru lived in such country where they could defend themselves, rather than in the fertile lowland valleys.

Fig. 31. Modern Kaguru cultivation is practiced in fertile places, as along this seasonally dry stream bed.

Fig. 32. A remote Kaguru hamlet in the Idibo area is built on the hill slope near cultivated plots watered by a stream in the valley. *Photo by J. H. Steward.*

Fig. 33. Traditional Kaguru huts with Mount Idibo in the background. *Photo by J. H. Steward.*

Figs. 34 and 35. The typical Kaguru show few influences of modernization except the manufactured cloth used for garments.

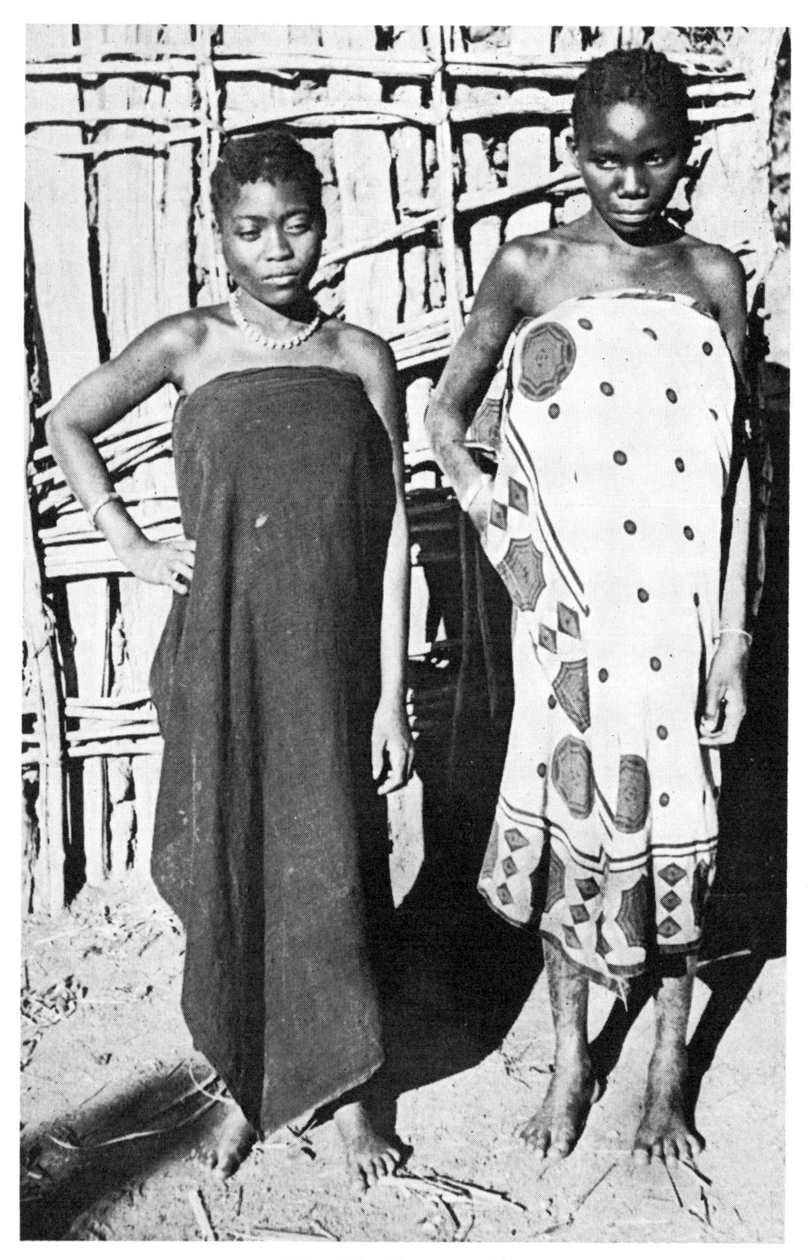

Fig. 36. Kaguru girls.

Asian shops, the courts, the schools, the churches, and the beer clubs.

Each settlement has a unique character. For example, Chakwale is centered about the cattle market and the veterinary station. It bustles with life for two days every month, the days when the cattle auction takes place. Then the shops are open, as many as eight or nine trucks and cars visit the market and over a thousand Africans, mostly Baraguyu from Kilosa and neighboring districts, jam the trading center and auction place. It is a hubbub of vendors, traders, and people drinking beer and visiting with one another. It is perhaps the single most colorful event in Ukaguru. The day after market many of the shops close and Chakwale resumes its somnolence for another month. Settlements such as Idibo and Mamboya which have African courts are busy on court days, twice a week, with Saturday being an important market day as well.

There are but few Kaguru who have to walk for more than an hour or two to reach one of these centers. While such settlements are focal points for commercial, social, and political life and while their shops, dispensaries, and other government buildings are visited by large numbers of people from the surrounding countryside, they are not Kaguru communities in any real sense of the word. The permanent dwellers in these settlements are for the most part Asians and Somalis, together with a few Africans from elsewhere who work for the merchants or the government. Even Kaguru who are employed in the settlements tend to live outside them, often a mile or two away.

The western portion of Ukaguru resembles the central area in its topography except that it gradually slopes off from the mountains into the Great Central Plateau of Ugogo, a vast, semi-arid plain of thornbush scrub, scattered baobab trees, and grassland. In this western area the Kaguru live side by side with the Gogo and dwell in Gogo *tembe*-type homesteads widely dispersed over the landscape. The major settlements west of Gairo are Mlali and Sagara in Mpwapwa District.

Only in the far west of Ukaguru, at Gairo and in the Kaguru-occupied section of Mpwapwa District, is there any shortage of water and even there the shortage does not approach the problem presented in areas such as most of Ugogo or Masailand. In contrast to such areas, Ukaguru is abundantly supplied with water. There is never any severe shortage of water for human or livestock needs —only an occasional shortage for crops.

HISTORY [2]

In the past, Ukaguru was an area of important concern to the Arabs and later the Germans. It was of strategic importance to the Arabs who journeyed from Zanzibar and the coastal ports to the region of the great lakes, and to the Europeans who followed them. Ukaguru lay astride the safest route to the interior. To the south of Ukaguru were the Hehe, to the north the Masai. These two warlike tribes discouraged most attempts to penetrate their areas.

To the caravans this mountainous area was a pleasant contrast to the humid, unhealthy coast and the stark desert-like plains of the interior. Ukaguru was the place where supplies of food and water could be replenished.

The caravan route ran from the Arab dhow ports of Sadani and Bagamoyo west across the coastal hills and savannah to the Mkata Plain. Beyond this point there were two routes, one north through the heart of Ukaguru, and one which took a more southerly course passing near the present sites of Morogoro and Kilosa town and thence through northeast Usagara and southwest Ukaguru to Mpwapwa. The southern route through the Mukondokwa Valley to Mpwapwa was the more convenient in terms of terrain but by far the more dangerous. It was subject to raids by Hehe who were extending northward during the 1880's. The Baraguyu (Kwavi) and Masai also raided this area (see: Last, 1882, 1883a, b; Burton, 1860, Vol. I, pp. 198-238). For this reason much traffic preferred the more mountainous but safer route through central Ukaguru. Both routes converged at Mpwapwa, which was the major caravan station on the journey to the interior. Mpwapwa owed its prominence to the fact that it was the last place before Ugogo where food and water could be obtained at any season.

In the mid-nineteenth century Arabs from Zanzibar set up caravan stations along both these routes through Ukaguru: one at Kondoa (just to the east of Kilosa town), serving the southern route, and the other at Mamboya, the present capital of Ukaguru, serving the northern route.

After these stations were established, the Arabs themselves did not attempt to enslave the Kaguru because stable conditions in this area were important to them from the point of view of obtaining supplies. However, coastal Africans using arms obtained from the Arabs sometimes raided the area for slaves. For instance, about 1860, African coastal raiders ravaged the Mamboya area taking

[2] For a more detailed historical account as well as an historical bibliography, see Beidelman, 1962.

many slaves (Last, 1883a). Furthermore, the Nguu and Zigua also sometimes sold Kaguru to coastal Africans and Arabs.

The first European explorers who reached the vicinity of Ukaguru were Burton and Speke, who passed through the southern part of the area in 1857 en route to their great discoveries in the region of the central lakes. Burton, who used the Mukondokwa River Valley route, commented on the difficulty of the terrain, on the great unrest and disorder due to intertribal raiding, and on the danger from Baraguyu raids.

Undoubtedly, the most famous visitor was H. M. Stanley, who passed through Ukaguru first in 1871 and on several later occasions. In 1874 Stanley took the route through central Ukaguru. He was deeply impressed by the area: "Grand and impressive scenery meets the eye. Peaks and knolls rise in all directions, for we are now ascending the eastern front of the Kaguru mountains . . . remarkable peaks or mountain crests break the sky line on every side. Indeed, some parts of this great mountain range abound in scenery, both picturesque and sublime" (Stanley, 1879, Vol. I, p. 91).

In 1876 the Church Missionary Society of London, representing the Anglican church, sent a group to Uganda which took the customary route through central Tanganyika and thence north from Tabora to Lake Victoria. These missionaries passed through central Ukaguru and were so impressed with the area as a possible place for work that they founded a station at Mpwapwa that same year and a second station at Mamboya in 1880. Berega and Itumba (Uponela) were added in 1900, Kongwa in 1904. These sites were located on the trade route partly for convenience but also as a means of agitating against the slave caravans passing through.

In 1879, as European penetration increased, Sultan Bargash of Zanzibar garrisoned Mamboya, probably to strengthen his own territorial claims. When they first entered an area, the Arabs usually allied themselves with one of the local chiefs or leaders. Ukaguru provides an excellent example of this technique. A local Kaguru had become powerful in the Mamboya Valley. However this leader, Senyagwa Chimola, was not recognized by Kaguru outside this narrow area. Senyagwa previously had bolstered his power by making blood brotherhood with the raiding Baraguyu. He showed himself more than willing to cooperate with the Arabs, providing local labor, housing materials, and food for them. He is said to have greeted the armed men of the Sultan with gifts of ivory and with laborers to build a stockade. In turn he was given beads, cloth, guns and gunpowder—and recognition as chief of all Ukaguru. He thus became ruler, at least in name, not of a small valley but of all of Ukaguru, an area of over 3,600 square miles. In deference to his "friend," the Sultan, Senyagwa became Sultan Saidi, and Mamboya became a small but important caravan station. Many aliens, especially Nyamwezi, were brought in as slaves or came independently and these people carried on intensive cultivation of a type unknown to the local Kaguru. Even today many Nyamwezi remain in this area.

During this same period European interest in Africa grew immensely. The race for African colonies began and in the events which secured much of East Africa for Germany, Ukaguru played a key part. In 1884 the Society for German Colonization sent out an expedition led by Dr. Carl Peters, a man of enormous energy and personal ambition. In November of that year he, the politician Count Von Pfeil, and two other Germans traveled incognito to Zanzibar. They landed on the coast in April of the following year and set out from Sadani following the Arab trade route used by Stanley. Peters saw only the borders of Ukaguru, but he was deeply impressed with the area, especially the district mountains to the west, and put it first on the list of places for future German settlement. He conjured up dreams of a great white highlands populated by German planters and worked by African labor.[3] Peters traveled through the coastal highland collecting the marks of various African chiefs on treaties signing over their lands to the protection of Germany and his company. His methods have been described as follows:

> Before arriving at the village of a chief or ruler, Peters sent ahead a messenger with presents and a request for permission to camp at the village. Having arrived, he then sent an invitation to the chief to dine with him. During the dinner the chief was plied with drinks and after dinner with more presents. Then Peters asked him whether he would sign a document recording his friendship with the German Empire. The chief could hardly refuse. Dr. Juehlke then read out a document, written in German and therefore unintelligible to the chief. The African signed his name and Germany had acquired a new "Protectorate." Dr. Peters shook his victim by the hand, ran up the German flag and fired a salute. More drink fol-

[3] Meyer notes (we translate from the German): "No other East African mountain area has been so glowingly praised by so many travellers as Usagara [he refers here to Ukaguru]. A good deal of this is due to the fact that no other mountain land in East Africa must be traversed by the great inland caravans, and that every traveler after the exhausting march through the hot plains experiences with doubled delight the revitalizing freshness of the mountain air and the running water, the satisfying green of the bushes and mountain meadows and the beautiful lines and colors of the mountain peaks" (1908, Vol. I, p. 19. See also Peters, 1895, pp. 246, 251-52).

lowed and sometimes in honour of the occasion Dr. Peters and the Sultan took a bath together. The expedition then hurried off to perform the same ceremony with some other Sultan. (Woolf, 1920, p. 237)

Here is an example of a treaty obtained in this manner, that of Msowero, in what is now eastern Ukaguru:

. . . the Sultan Mangungo hereby cedes all the territory of Msovero (southeastern Ukaguru) belonging to him by inheritance or otherwise for all time, to Dr. Karl Peters, making over to him at the same time all his rights. Dr. Peters, in the name of the Society for German Colonisation, undertakes to give special attention to Msovero when colonising Usagara. . . . the Sultan on direct inquiry having declared that he was not in any way dependent upon the Sultan of Zanzibar, and that he did not even know of the existence of the latter. (Lewin, n.d., p. 173. For the German, see von Koschitzky, 1888, p. 252.)

The treaties not only served to support German territorial claims against those of other European powers, but against the Arabs of Zanzibar as well.

Once the Germans were established in this part of East Africa, they applied stringent measures against the Arab slave trade and attempted to divert interior trade to German merchants and away from the Arabs of Zanzibar—all with very little military support. These policies seem to have been among the major causes of a bloody rebellion in 1888-89. This was led by an Arab named Bushiri who was defeated on the coast and fled to Ukaguru, where he successfully stormed the German outpost of Mpwapwa.

The German trading company was unable to cope with these disorders. In addition, it had encountered difficulties in carrying out many of its other aims. As a result, in 1891 the German government took over the administration of the area as an imperial German colony.

This new political status led to the first attempts to incorporate Ukaguru into a colonial administrative system. Ukaguru was divided into two districts, the bulk of it falling within the boundaries of Mpwapwa (later named Dodoma) District. Up until shortly before World War I, the administrative center for this district was located at the old caravan station of Mpwapwa. The eastern fringe of Ukaguru was assigned to Morogoro District and was administered from the German fort at Morogoro and from an auxiliary outpost at Kilosa. German Mpwapwa District was an enormous area of about 40,000 square miles, including all of Ugogo, most of Ukaguru and extending north into the southern portion of Mbulu and much of the Masai Steppe.[4] This huge area was admin-

[4] German districts such as Mpwapwa (or Dodoma) and Morogoro did not have the same boundaries as those of the present districts with these names. The German districts were very much larger.

istered by very few Europeans and transport was extremely difficult, so that only a semblance of colonial order existed over most of this domain.[5] Most local control was carried out through *akidas*, African officials appointed by the Germans. The agents were usually coastal Africans with little or no ties to the local Africans whom they supervised. They were often arbitrary, harsh, and corrupt. In Ukaguru, there were two such *akidas*, one at Mamboya and one in the lowlands at Mvumi.

The Church Missionary Society of London had preceded the Germans into Ukaguru by five years in Mamboya and ten in Mpwapwa. When the first Germans arrived, the missionaries are said to have urged the Kaguru Sultan to receive the Germans cordially. It is said that Saidi Chimola gave the Germans twenty cows and thirty goats to show his loyalty. During these early years the Sultan was able to maintain relations with the Germans much as those he had previously had with the Arabs. However, occasional difficulties arose for the Germans were more demanding in their needs for forced labor. Saidi's successor was jailed and displaced for his inability to fulfill these needs. The Germans required labor not only for roads, the railway, the construction of buildings, and as porters, but also they used Kaguru to clear a few fields for cotton in the plains below Ukaguru.

The Germans continued to recognize the same opportunistic Kaguru leaders who had been supported by the Arabs. In fact, these leaders' positions were consolidated and their numbers increased as leaders farther from the trade route sought European recognition and support. It was through these men that taxes in foodstuffs were collected and labor secured. If one of these leaders failed to comply, he risked replacement by a more cooperative and realistic leader of a rival Kaguru faction in the same locality. When they encountered any strong opposition, the Germans used the garrison of German and African coastal troops stationed at Mpwapa.

The first Germans in Ukaguru were concerned chiefly with the protection of the caravan routes. The route running through the south had been frequently raided by the Hehe. By 1894 Hehe raids had become a considerable threat to the commercial life and order of the colony. An all-out campaign was launched and the Hehe were defeated in 1898.

In 1905 the famous Maji Maji Rebellion broke out in the Liwale

[5] Even at the outbreak of the First World War, German reports list a total of only thirty-eight Europeans residing in this entire area. This apparently included all types of people, from officials to missionaries (Meyer, 1908, p. 81).

District in the southern portion of the colony. While this revolt did not directly involve the Kaguru, some of them were forced to serve as porters in the campaign, and Africans from the south went into hiding in the Kaguru Mountains. However, most of the Europeans in all parts of the colony were deeply alarmed and those living in more isolated areas fled to places protected by troops. The missionaries from the Church Missionary Society in Ukaguru fled to the vicinity of the German garrison at Mpwapwa. All educational, religious, and medical work ceased in Ukaguru for several years.

German control rapidly and deeply affected Kaguru life. The order and relative peace guaranteed by the German garrison at Mpwapwa permitted great changes in Kaguru settlement patterns and in the economy. The cessation of the slave trade and the raids of the Baraguyu, Masai, and Hehe opened to occupation extensive riverine areas previously only sparsely settled because of their indefensibility. Furthermore, the Kaguru could again keep herds of livestock with little fear of raids. The German government encouraged missionary efforts in the fields of education and medicine whereas their predecessors, the Arabs, had if anything opposed the work of the missions, especially in the field of education.

The Germans quickly organized the estates which now dominate the district's economy. Peters' dream of vast plantations in Ukaguru itself proved to be unrealistic, but the adjoining lowlands were soon utilized. In the early 1900's Germans and Greeks began to clear land in the Kilosa-Kimamba area. At first cotton was the major crop but later the estates concentrated more and more heavily upon sisal.

To encourage this development and to facilitate administration, the Germans made plans for a cross-country railway. Work was begun in 1905 and the line was operating between Dar-es-Salaam and Morogoro by 1907. It reached Kilosa in 1909 and Mpwapwa in 1910. The 800 miles of track from the coast to the lake was completed on the eve of the First World War. Most of the laborers for the railway came from the western portion of the colony, but many men from Ukaguru worked on the stretch between Kilosa and Mpwapwa.

The First World War had severe effects upon German East Africa, and Ukaguru was no exception. The schools and dispensaries were closed and the English missionaries were interned as enemy aliens. Kaguru were drafted as porters and some food supplies were commandeered for the troops. As the Germans were driven southward by the British and Belgians they destroyed their installations and records. The mission stations in Ukaguru at Mamboya and Berega were damaged and the government records in Kilosa destroyed. Most of the railway bridges and water stations on the track between Dar-es-Salaam and Dodoma were wrecked.

The British took over a colony in which most of the commercial facilities were destroyed, the railway partially crippled, government services and administration in chaos, and local native government in confusion. On top of all of this, there was a disastrous crop failure in the area west of Ukaguru. Many deaths were caused by the influenza epidemic which swept most of the territory. While there was no real famine in Ukaguru, the food shortages and the epidemic put considerable pressure upon the resources of the area due to the arrival of people fleeing from the stricken area. The gravity of the situation was intensified locally by the absence of many of the prewar missionary medical facilities.

KAGURU SOCIAL STRUCTURE

The social structure of the Kaguru is based upon matrilineal principles. In view of the notorious complexity of African matrilineal societies, it will be appreciated that the following remarks give only a very generalized picture of the situation. For present purposes, attention will be devoted to four types of groups: clans, lineages, hamlets, and localities.

All of the Kaguru claim membership in one or another of the approximately hundred matriclans (*ikungugo*). The most probable explanation of the present situation is that the various clans owe their origin to groups which arrived in Ukaguru at different times. However, many Kaguru maintain that all of their ancestors came into Ukaguru as a single group which then dispersed, the various clans occupying separate localities. The name of any particular clan is usually derived from the legendary event which occasioned its separation from the others.

All the members of a clan are said to be descended from a common ancestress but this can never be established by precise genealogical reckoning. While rights and obligations between those who are related matrilineally are stated in terms of clan membership, it is actually only within the component lineages of the clan that the privileges and responsibilities of membership in a descent group are felt to be truly binding. Lineages have a shallow genealogical depth because even the elders are unable to trace their ancestry back more than three generations. A lineage, for which the Kaguru term is *nyumba* (literally, house), consists of all of those claiming descent through women from a common ancestress said to have lived two or three generations before her oldest living descendants. Within a lineage, groupings of lesser span, each claiming descent from one of the daughters of the founding ancestress are ranked in terms of seniority. Although senior branches are said to have authority over junior branches, there is no indication of this in practice. However, certain descent groups which will be discussed later occupy special positions within the territorial organization.

Some matrilineages have slave origins. In the past, wealthy men often acquired female slaves. The children of such women could not be integrated into the Kaguru system except through membership in the clans of their fathers. People who are descended from a slave consider the fact to be shameful and they are insulted if it is recalled in their presence by others. The accusation by members of one lineage that another lineage of the same clan has slave origins is a serious matter but one which is nevertheless a common feature of interlineage disputes.

It is said that in the past all the members of a lineage lived in the same locality, something which would have been possible, despite the rule of lineage (and clan) exogamy, due to the multilineality of the local groups. Whether or not this was ever the case, it is not so today when one often finds members of the same lineage dispersed over a very wide area. This dispersion is itself sufficient to prevent lineages from serving as social units in the ordinary routine of agriculture, marketing, and other everyday affairs. Lineages come to the fore only in such matters as legal cases, the accumulation and distribution of bridewealth, raising funds in emergencies, etc.

An individual is primarily concerned with two descent groups, that of his mother—which is also, of course, his own—and that of his father, although groups to which he is tied more remotely such as that of his father's father may be taken into account when it appears useful to do so. Even in the past, when most property rights were transmitted matrilineally, that is, from maternal uncles to their nephews, an individual depended for support upon his father's group as well. This is symbolized by the fact that at most of the rituals carried out in order to promote the welfare of an individual, it is necessary for the father's group to be represented as well as the person's own group.

Before the European era, the fear of enemy raids prevented

people from establishing isolated homesteads. Instead, they lived together in large nucleated settlements situated with an eye to their defensibility. Today, with warfare a thing of the past, the settlement pattern is very different. The bulk of the population is now to be found in the river valleys. The adjacent uplands are sparsely populated and wooded hills far from water are utterly uninhabited. In the valleys, individual houses and small clusters of them are usually visible in all directions. In certain fertile areas, habitations are found every few hundred yards.[6]

While settlements containing twenty or more huts are still to be found, and although in certain areas groups of at least ten houses can be found every two or three miles, most clusters do not have more than five houses and single houses are not uncommon. We use the term hamlet when referring to any discrete settlement whether it contains but one hut or twenty.

Although some hamlets contain a sizable number of people, a stranger to the area is apt to obtain an exaggerated impression of the population of most hamlets if he bases it upon the number of buildings which are visible. The Kaguru have an unusually large number of houses in proportion to the population. This results from the rule that people of opposite sex beyond the age of puberty may not share a house unless they are married. Thus, for example, a Kaguru couple with two adolescent children, a son and a daughter, must have three huts.

There is a great deal of variation in the social composition of hamlets. At one end of the scale are lone houses inhabited by a nuclear family or even by a widow and her children while at the other extreme one finds very complex networks of relationships. Perhaps the most common pattern is a group consisting of a man and his wife and their married sons, plus the wives and unmarried children of the latter. Although many men continue to live in the same hamlet with their fathers after marriage, there is no rule regarding this. It is considered desirable for a man to live somewhere near his parents but he need not do so. On the other hand, despite his freedom to live where he chooses, it is advisable for a man to establish his home in the vicinity of someone with whom he can claim a fairly close relationship of one sort or another.

A number of hamlets are grouped together to form a locality. Localities, which have precise boundaries to which there is general

[6] In this and the following paragraphs we describe the situation in eastern and central Ukaguru. In western Ukaguru, where the large flat-roofed *tembe* is found, each building stands by itself. However, the internal composition of these long houses is the same as the hamlet in other areas.

agreement, vary greatly from one another in terms of their area and population. Some localities contain over 4,000 people while very small ones may have less than 200 inhabitants.

In each locality one clan is dominant. The dominance of a particular clan within a given locality does not mean, at least at the present time, that it occupies a position of numerical superiority. Its ascendancy is based, instead, upon political and ritual rights held by virtue of the fact that its members are supposed to have been the first settlers in the locality. In some cases the clan which is now dominant is said to have acquired its rights from another previously dominant clan in return for some favor such as aid in warfare. It is held, in theory, that members of other clans who reside in the locality do so only because of the good will of the dominant clan. In actual fact though, today, as in the past, a locally dominant clan depends upon the support of factions from many other clans which are locally resident in order to maintain its security both within its own area and against its neighbors.

A particular clan may be dominant in several localities but in each locality one lineage is considered to have seniority. It is upon this lineage and in particular upon its senior resident member that the primary responsibility lies for the initiation of the rainmaking and cleansing rituals which are considered necessary for the fertility and well-being of the locality and its inhabitants. The rituals themselves, it might be noted, are usually carried out, not by members of the lineage, but by rainmakers and other ritual specialists.

As far as political power is concerned, although leadership within a locality was restricted to members of the dominant clan, leaders gained their positions not as the result of any system of inheritance but rather as a result of their personal capabilities. It was always possible for a new and vigorous leader to gain power by a few strokes of luck.

In the days when warfare was a constant threat, a locality's strength was determined by the number of men who could aid in its defense. Thus leaders welcomed newcomers to their localities. Furthermore, while they exercised considerable power, they could not afford to be too autocratic for fear that people would migrate to other localities. Leaders also attempted to strengthen their localities and their own positions as well by allying themselves with more warlike groups which coexisted with the Kaguru in the same area. The alien groups so utilized were principally the Baraguyu and the Kamba.

EFFECTS OF COLONIAL RULE UPON THE SOCIAL STRUCTURE

The arrival of Europeans and the imposition of a system of colonial administration had a number of important consequences for the social structure. We already have had occasion to note the disappearance of large villages on defensible elevations and their replacement by small hamlets situated for the most part in the valleys. People moved down to lower sites in order to be nearer water and their fields. Settlements increased in size because social divisions previously suppressed by the need for cooperation against hostile neighbors now came to the fore.

In the European period there has been increasing conflict and confusion over the obligations toward matrilineal relatives. Matrilineal groups have lost some of their traditional ritual sanctions. More important, there are now fewer occasions when the members of a lineage need cooperate. The intrusion of Western, Christian values has encouraged the questioning of lineage obligations, as has the introduction of sources of wealth (by employment and cash sale of crops) outside the traditional system. All of these factors in turn have emphasized the nuclear family rather than the lineage whose interests cut across those of any individual household. In short, rights of spouses and children have gained in emphasis at the expense of rights towards lineage relatives. The father-child relationship in particular has gained new importance at the expense of children's previous primary obligations towards their mother's brothers.

Although clan and lineage relations are weakening in some of the social situations in which they operate, at present no new social units exist which could replace them. The nuclear family is frequently a battleground where the conflicting obligations of the traditional matrilineal and the new patrilateral emphases compete. Sometimes the conflict is phrased in terms of Christian versus pagan values, sometimes in terms of whether the greater share of some expense or benefit should be assigned to the father or to the child's lineage relatives; sometimes a woman's husband and her lineage relatives will dispute over her conduct or that of her children.

Individuals seek from time to time to gain their own ends even at the expense of their lineage relatives. On the other hand, the Kaguru seek to utilize all their available kinship connections, ideally balancing the father's lineage against their own in order to gain the fullest advantages from each. The wise Kaguru keeps on fair terms with both groups and tries not to be wholly dependent nor wholly opposed to either. However much he may wish to do so, no Kaguru would dare for long to reject all obligations to local clan relatives. Sooner or later such rebellious individuals are brought into line by the difficulties of Kaguru life. This is because almost no Kaguru has sufficient resources by himself to continue to meet the many problems which he faces, e.g., payment of bride-price, fines, school fees, medical costs, and other unforeseen expenses. That clans and lineages have not lost more of their traditional importance may be partly explained by the relatively low level of individual production and cash income and the lack of pressures which would force Kaguru out of their local areas or which would motivate them to create social units of a new type, such as cooperatives.

In contrast to this general picture, a few matrilineal groups seem to have gained a new and stronger sense of cohesion in recent decades as a result of the fact that they have been formally invested with political power by the European administrations. The matrilineal group of the paramount chief is the outstanding example. The British have fostered this process by recognizing the claims of various clans to hereditary headmanship.

The Kaguru who practice polygyny contract marriage through the payment of bridewealth, which is divided between the lineages of both the girl's parents. In the past such payments were usually quite low, a hoe, a few beads, and two or three goats. Furthermore, sometimes bride service could be substituted. In recent decades, though, brideprice has risen drastically and today accumulating sufficient bridewealth presents one of the greatest problems confronting a man. Since 1957 the chiefs and headmen have attempted to limit such payments to a maximum of 360 shillings or about $52. Payments beyond this amount can only be made secretly and are rarely returnable. Before this ceiling was set, brideprice had been known to reach almost double the current maximum, especially in the case of school teachers and other salaried Kaguru.

The rise in brideprice may be explained by several new conditions. For one thing, with peace and better communication, neighboring tribes such as the Gogo, Nguu, and Kamba, who had more cattle than the Kaguru, were able to compete in the Kaguru bride market. Furthermore, the influx of cash from wages and the sale of produce drove up the price. Perhaps most important of all, the mission preached that divorce was contrary to Christianity. Christian Kaguru were not allowed to obtain divorces. With divorce no longer possible in certain cases, the Kaguru took the view that some of the powers previously held by the lineage over its married women were being lost. Thus the woman's relatives demanded full payment of a higher brideprice before marriage took place. While only a minority of the Kaguru are Christian, it is precisely those with salaries and education who are able to pay more and who are invariably, at least nominally, Christian.

The modern tendency to place family interests above those of the lineage is reflected in the current reversal of the traditional distribution of brideprice for women and the collection of brideprice funds for use by boys. It is said that previously the bride's lineage was allotted about two-thirds of the sum, the father's lineage, one-third. At present, the father receives two-thirds and the mother's lineage one-third. Such an allotment is now sanctioned by the Kaguru Native Courts.

THE KAGURU POLITICAL SYSTEM AND COLONIAL ADMINISTRATION

In previous sections we have dealt with the traditional political system of the Kaguru and with the impact upon it of the Arabs and the Germans. It will be recalled that originally the Kaguru were organized in terms of localities. Each locality, which was organized around a dominant clan, acted as an independent political unit. The Arabs gave special recognition to the leaders of certain localities but while they gave such leaders some arms and ammunition, they did not actively aid them in making their claims to wide political power a reality. Unlike the Arabs, who were interested only in establishing stable and friendly African political units in the immediate vicinity of their caravan routes, the Germans who supplanted them were interested in the control and administration of the entire land.

Due to the lack of European personnel, the Germans had to rely to a very large extent upon *akidas*, administrative agents recruited from among the coastal Swahili-speaking population. The *akidas* exercised control over officially recognized leaders of the indigenous population. In most of Tanganyika, where a strongly organized local political system was already in existence, it was utilized by the Germans. Where it was weak it was consolidated and where, as in Ukaguru, its traditional legitimacy and its popular support were in question, it was fostered. One local leader was recognized as the paramount chief of the Kaguru and a number of others were given the status of headman in charge of the various outlying areas.

The first German-levied taxes were collected in the form of maize. Later the yearly tax had to be paid in cash. Cash payment of taxes forced a number of Kaguru to seek employment with the

Germans and drove many others to sell part of their food crop or some of their livestock. Some Kaguru carried foodstuffs to the lowland areas, sometimes as far as the coast. Most, however, were content to receive the lower prices offered by the Arab and Indian traders in Ukaguru itself.

After the First World War, German rule was replaced by British. To most Kaguru this merely meant the replacement of one group of authoritative Europeans by another. However, the new administrative districts set up by the British did introduce a very considerable reorientation within the tribe. Whereas the German district of Mpwapwa (later called Dodoma) included almost all of Ukaguru under one administration, the new boundaries divided it. The eastern two-thirds formed part of Kilosa District, Eastern Province; the western one-third formed part of Mpwapwa District, Central Province. Thus not only was Ukaguru divided by district boundaries but by provincial ones as well.

The Kaguru of Kilosa District constitute the largest tribe in the district and have their own Native Authority which is autonomous of other tribes except in finance.

The European administration is headed by the District Commissioner, who has from one to three District Officers under him. During the brief periods when only one such assistant officer is present the burden of administration is exceedingly heavy. The senior District Officer is customarily assigned the duty of overseeing the Ukaguru area in addition to many duties at the district level. No European officer is permanently resident in Ukaguru itself, but the District Commissioner and the District Officer in charge of Ukaguru make frequent and extended visits to the area.

The Kilosa Native Authority, while headed and staffed by Africans, is ultimately responsible to the District Commissioner and his assistant officers. All policy decisions and expenditures are subject to their approval. In actual fact, due to the especially low level of training and education of the chief and subchiefs of this area, most policies are initiated by the European administrators.

Various government departments—Medical, Agriculture, Labor, Roads and Public Works, Police, etc.—are represented in Kilosa District. Usually each department has one European officer who supervises the work of a staff of Indians and Africans. Some, such as the Veterinary Officer and Labor Officer, oversee areas far larger than Kilosa District.

While none of these European technical officers are resident in Ukaguru itself, a number of African employees of the various departments do live there. These Africans implement departmental policies at the local level. The three most important departments operating in Ukaguru are the Medical, Agricultural, and Veterinary departments, the latter devoting most of its attention to the problem of the cattle-keeping Baraguyu. The Medical Department in particular employs a large number (about fifteen) of trained people, African medical assistants, dispensers, dressers, and midwives who work at the various dispensaries in the area. While most of the lower posts in all of the departments are held by Kaguru, almost all of those requiring higher technical training are held by members of other tribes.

A few of the Africans who are engaged in providing government services in Ukaguru operate completely outside the scope of the Native Authority, since they work directly under European officials and are paid by the territorial treasury. Most of the government services, however, are made possible by funds provided by the Native Authority. These funds are not controlled locally in Ukaguru. Instead, they are handled by the Kilosa Native Treasury which operates on a district-wide basis. The Africans employed by the government have especially weak ties to the Kaguru chiefdom due to the fact that although they should take cognizance of the local leaders, the chief, and subchiefs, they are actually responsible for the conduct of their duties to the various departmental officers in Kilosa.

AFRICAN ADMINISTRATION

The Kilosa Native Authority is composed of the tribal Native Authorities of the Sagara, Vidunda, and the numerically predominant Kaguru. The chief and the subchiefs of these various Native Authorities meet in the Kilosa District Council. This is a legislative body with formal control of the Native Treasury and as such assists the European administration in forming local government policy.

The Native Authority provides a number of services: courts, medical facilities, schools, agricultural aid, livestock dips, local roads, transport, etc. Some idea of the size of its operations may be gained by examination of the 1956 Native Treasury Revenue.[7]

[7] Unfortunately figures were only available for all of Kilosa District Native Treasury rather than Ukaguru alone since the Native Treasury is organized on a district rather than a tribal level.

The figures on liquor licenses are now far higher than these since in 1958 the district administration allowed brewing throughout the year rather than only after harvest. The former rule had almost no effect on control of brewing as it was hoped, but did keep considerable potential tax from the government as such activities were concealed.

Share of taxes	£12,751
Court revenue	1,226
Liquor licenses	6,229
Market receipts	5,014
Produce cesses	3,046
Cattle rate	1,515
Sundries	2,294
Total	£32,075

In Ukaguru a number of Africans serve as court clerks. Since the chief and three of the four Kaguru subchiefs and many of the headmen are illiterate, these clerks often play a semi-administrative role in interpreting procedure and policy for their "superiors." Over half of these clerks are not Kaguru.

The Kaguru section of the Native Authority is headed by the paramount chief at Mamboya. He is chosen by his fellow dominant clan members of Mamboya, subject to approval by the District Commissioner. He heads the Mamboya Court, which, in addition to hearing cases in the Mamboya chieftainship area, serves as an appellate court for the four courts of the Kaguru subchiefs.

Beneath the chief are the four subchiefs and beneath them, the numerous local headmen. With the inception of the policy of indirect rule in Tanganyika, the administration made an effort in Ukaguru to recognize legitimate rulers. The chief and his kin produced genealogies and histories to substantiate their claim to traditional power. A British administrator toured the area asking the people who should be their local headmen. These headmen (*jumbe*) were chosen with a fair degree of local agreement since they represented a system of dominant clan rule of localities which was indigenous to the Kaguru. However, while some dominant clans are populous and claim control of rather large areas, others have very few members and their localities may measure as little as one or two square miles. Since one of the aims of the British administration in granting official recognition to headmen was to facilitate local administration, it may have been felt that the recognition of all of these tiny groups would have defeated one of the purposes of the reorganization. At any rate, some of the lesser of these numerous dominant clans were not recognized. In Ukaguru there are only fifty-three headmen representing thirty-seven of the approximately 100 Kaguru clans. Some clans have several different areas in which their dominance is officially recognized and thus may have as many as four or five headmen, one in charge of each area. Thus, almost two-thirds of the clans are not represented officially in this scheme.

Since the paramount chief (*mundewa*) could not supervise such a large number of headmen, the administration arbitrarily created the four subchiefs who, of course, had no traditional authority. Each subchief was given charge of a court. The Mamboya area has no subchief, the chief ruling that area directly. Whatever clan had been officially recognized as dominant at the site of the new subchief's court was allowed to select the subchief as well as the headman of that area. The Kaguru themselves speak of the good fortune of some clans and the misfortune of others in regard to the original organization of the present Native Authority.

In actual practice the chief has little administrative power in the four other subchieftainships. Although theoretically he can remove a subchief or headman if sufficient grounds can be shown, to our knowledge this has never been done despite the continual disregard of his wishes by his official subordinates. The chief rarely visits the subchiefdoms and Kaguru in these areas often speak of their own subchiefs as the "real leaders." In addition to the problem of transportation, lack of traditional sanctions for his position, and considerable local feeling on the part of Kaguru in the various outlying areas, the paramount chief is severely limited by his illiteracy and by his great reluctance to see any changes made in his area.

Most instructions given by the European administrative officers in Kilosa which concern the particular subchiefdoms are transmitted not through the chief, but to the subchiefs directly. These instructions may be received verbally when the administrative officer is touring the area or they may be received at the subchief's office in the form of a letter. In the usual case such letters can only be read by the clerk who alone is literate. In his turn a subchief has very little direct contact in his administrative capacity with the people whom he rules. Instructions received by a subchief are passed on to the headmen who actually see that they are carried out. The headmen for their part are responsible for submitting taxes, school fees, and various reports to the subchief at his headquarters. Much of the power of the subchiefs lies in the fact that they are court holders.

In his judicial capacity the subchief exerts considerable power and comes into frequent contact with his subjects, although never without the presence of the headmen involved. Officially a headman is not allowed to settle disputes, exact fines, impose corporal punishment, or imprisonment. A headman is officially obligated to bring all disputes and infractions of the law to the court of his subchief. A Kaguru dissatisfied with the conduct of his headman may also bring his headman to the court and accuse him of some wrong he is alleged to have committed. Thus it is primarily as a judge that a subchief controls policy in his area and disciplines the headmen beneath him. A subchief has several counsellors (some on Native Authority salary and some merely holding the subchief's favor) who assist him in arriving at judgments. Losers of cases pay a fee to the court, and the amount of the fine varies according to the judge's decision as to the severity of the wrong involved.

Direct contact between the Kaguru people and the government is made by the Kaguru headmen (*jumbe*). Selected by and from the officially recognized dominant clan of a locality, they are responsible for the enactment of policy in their areas, the collection of taxes and school fees, and they must report all offenses against the law, unusual matters, etc. Each is the official spokesman of a locality's dominant clan and as such theoretically controls the allocation of land and must approve the entry of any householder into the locality as well.

Although officially headmen are not allowed to hear cases, in actual fact headmen serve as arbitrators in most local disputes. While they are often biased and prone to bribery, most headmen make a real effort to settle a dispute submitted to them for judgment. Since the officially recognized courts are also sometimes corrupt, since court fees must be paid, and since it is often inconvenient to attend hearings, many people prefer to settle their disputes outside the official courts. In such cases a headman receives gifts in compensation for his efforts. Even in cases brought to court, many Kaguru consider it wise to pay gifts to a headman to ensure his sympathetic testimony. Headmen gain authority not only from their position as representatives of a locally dominant clan and as enforcers of government law but as skilled manipulators of local factions. Many Kaguru see such headmen as more understanding and sensitive to the local scene (in which the headmen must live) than the subchiefs, the chief, or the Europeans.

Headmen may occasionally take advantage of some of their subjects, especially poorer men who are not of the locally dominant clan—but headmen rarely defy the majority of their own clan fellows or the more affluent or educated local men regardless of their clan affiliations.

It was hoped that through the Native Authority under European guidance the Kaguru would gain experience in governing themselves. What has occurred has not always been satisfactory to either the European administrators or to the Kaguru. From the point of view of the Europeans, the Native Authority might be far more efficient if its leaders were educated and if its personnel were appointed on the basis of ability rather than chosen by the dominant clans of the various localities. Unfortunately, those who are best able to manipulate the members of the various lineages are often those least interested in fostering education or other features which might undermine the traditional system. Furthermore, Native Authority posts offer salaries equivalent to those of artisans. In 1958 the subchief of Idibo, who has jurisdiction over about 14,000 Kaguru, received 120 shillings (£17) monthly. One of his headmen, who had political control over about 2,000 Kaguru, received 31 shillings monthly. Many headmen receive far less than this. By comparison, truck drivers and school teachers may receive from two to three times the salary of the Idibo subchief. The low salaries encourage the acceptance of bribes and at times very irresponsible attitudes. Furthermore, these salaries do not attract the few educated Kaguru even when, as is rarely the case, they are offered such posts.

The number of Europeans engaged locally in administrative work has always been so small that close supervision of the activities of the Kaguru Native Authority has been impossible. This allows many Kaguru leaders to pursue their own personal interests in the name of the government. Many abuses and injustices which a Kaguru leader will blame upon the person immediately above him in the hierarchy or upon the European administration are actually abuses stemming from the corrupt and often highly illegal actions he himself pursues for his own personal gain. For example, fines may be collected for acts which are not illegal by district law; cases may be heard in court and biased judgments or questionable testimony not registered in court records; the same offense usually merits a light punishment for a friend of a leader and a heavy punishment for a personal enemy; the court may delay cases in the hope of receiving bribes, etc.

The chief and his subordinates are caught between the European administration and their own people. While ostensibly representing their own people and their traditional laws, Kaguru leaders must not support Kaguru opposition to government policy. Conversely, while they must follow government policy, even when it is unpopular with local Kaguru, they must retain some local loyalty if they wish to carry out any kind of effective local administration of these policies.

The Kaguru see the chief, the subchiefs, and headmen as intermediaries between themselves and the Europeans. Kaguru have no really strong check upon their leaders since the powers of these men and the rules they enforce are derived far more from the Europeans than from the Kaguru themselves. Thus there is a system of power with no strong checks from below, only from above and outside.

NATIONALISM AND TRIBALISM

There are three political movements active in Ukaguru. These are USA (Ukaguru Students' Association), *Umwano* (meaning "war cry" in the Kaguru language), a vigilante-type, tribalistic group, and TANU (Tanganyika African National Union).

USA is an organization formed to encourage the preservation of Kaguru traditions and to urge the adoption of means for the material improvement of Ukaguru, chiefly through various cooperative activities. It was originally composed of Kaguru students, but it has been expanded to include any Kaguru willing to pay membership fees. It entered Kilosa District politics by criticizing local administrative policy in Ukaguru and by criticizing the chief and demanding his dismissal. As a result USA was declared a political organization and as such no Native Authority employee is allowed to be a member.

USA condemns Kaguru localism and emphasizes the tribal unity of all Kaguru. It tries to encourage a feeling of pride in Kaguru customs, often conducting meetings in the Kaguru language and mimeographing a propaganda leaflet partly in that language which makes use of many traditional motifs. USA has tried to foster cooperative transport and marketing groups, but it has failed because of lack of capital and because of the great distrust, intense self-interest, and localism of individual Kaguru.

USA is a symptom of the frustration of young men who have little voice in local political or economic affairs. The traditional system, as supported by the government, affords few openings for such youths. Ironically, Kaguru who have the skills necessary to become clerks, dispensers, market masters, etc., are often not eager to work in Ukaguru as long as the traditional leaders are in control. Furthermore, they dislike many of the economic demands made upon them by their relatives and they feel more keenly the pressure of clan politics than do outsiders.

USA is tribalistic in name but its ultimate aims are more closely linked to the aims of the nationalists than to those of tribal conservatives; nevertheless, it has no formal relationship with TANU. Considering the Kaguru's pre-colonial localism and lack of unity, we might think of USA's efforts toward tribal consciousness as a step towards modern unification. Like nationalism, USA is a movement oriented against the current political status quo (i.e., both the colonial administration and the Native Authority) and is recuited chiefly from dissatisfied younger people. But unlike TANU, USA's statements utilize strong Christian and aboriginal motifs in addition to advocating modern, materialistic improvements and self-government.

Umwano is a conservative, tribalistic organization formed specifically to combat the Baraguyu and to prevent livestock murders. *Umwano* was given an organizational permit, apparently with the administration's mistaken hope that this might foster intertribal order. Significantly, this group was severely reprimanded by the government in 1959 because intertribal conflict had not abated and several Kaguru headmen and subchiefs had committed a number of illegal acts in merging *Umwano* and government policies in the local courts. *Umwano* was far more localistic than USA and was formed merely to secure Kaguru unity vis-à-vis the Baraguyu. *Umwano* membership involved the payment of membership fees, taking oaths, and good tribal medicines. Its adherents held feasts and beer parties and paraded with bows and arrows to the accompaniment of war horns.

Umwano persists in order to combat cattle thefts and as a means by which men can meet to drink, feast, talk, and gain recognition. It is an extremely popular movement in the traditional areas adjoining Masailand, which are also the areas where Kaguru own cattle which compete with Baraguyu cattle for pasture and water. *Umwano* is less popular in central Ukaguru where many Baraguyu have settled but where virtually no Kaguru own cattle.

TANU, the nationalist party, has a district headquarters in Kilosa town. It occasionally sends representatives to Ukaguru to collect membership fees. Sizable sums have reputedly been collected on this basis, especially among the more educated Africans, such as the teachers and Native Authority employees (although government employees as civil servants are not legally allowed to join). Embezzlement of local funds by Kaguru TANU secretaries in the past had given the organization a rather bad name locally.

TANU very strongly condemns any intertribal dispute or conflict. It insists that these must be forgotten if political and social progress is to be made. In practice this position is extremely distasteful to most Kaguru. Ukaguru is occupied by five tribal groups and while the Kaguru are in the majority, the members of the minority tribes are often more prosperous and more aggressive. Kaguru history is filled with episodes of violence between these groups, which have not refrained from trying to force TANU to take sides in some of these issues.

TANU strenuously opposes any controversial government policy which is protested by local Africans. It strives to be considered the spokesman and defender of the Africans whose rights are, they claim, abused by Asians and Europeans. For example, the year TANU established a branch in Kilosa town, it strongly opposed government efforts to alienate land for cotton ginneries. It later opposed the removal of Baraguyu from the government ranch at Mkata. Since then it is said to have criticized the abuses and corruption of the Kaguru Native Authority.

TANU has come into conflict with local Kaguru leaders when it has attempted to hold meetings in the vicinity of the Native Authority courts. TANU has not formally declared itself against these traditional leaders, but it is clear to the shrewdest of them that the aims of TANU and their own are not the same. Kaguru tribal leaders feel that their power will be destroyed if TANU should gain control in Tanganyika. Conflicts of this type are widespread throughout the country, but the issue is particularly sharp in Ukaguru where there is such a wide gulf between the uneducated, conservative traditional leaders and the educated younger men.

TANU's influence increased immeasurably in Ukaguru when the first general elections in Tanganyika were held in 1958. This election greatly impressed the Kaguru intelligentsia (Standard V through Standard X). Mr. Nyerere, the leader of TANU, spoke in several parts of Ukaguru. Previously Kaguru felt they were considered too remote to merit such attention. In this campaign Mr. Nyerere was a candidate for the Legislative Council from the Eastern Province of which the Kilosa section of Ukaguru is a part. His chief opposition on the ballot came from a Luguru subchief from Morogoro. To many Kaguru and other Africans this contest epitomized the conflict between those representing the political status quo based upon the policy of indirect rule and those who are educated and skilled but without a voice in the traditional structure of local affairs.

It is increasingly true that Kaguru young men are considering politics as a means for power and recognition. Employment by the missions and government provides only limited scope for advancement, and the local political system is almost completely closed to them. As a result, many go to the towns such as Morogoro and Dar-es-Salaam. If Kaguru will one day have leaders of a new type, they will come from this currently dissatisfied group of young men.

THE MISSIONS AND CHRISTIANITY

Today in Ukaguru, which was the scene of some of the earliest missionary endeavors in the whole of East Africa, the Anglican church occupies a very prominent place. As an agent of social change the mission rivals the territorial government itself in importance. The prominent role played by the Church Missionary Society, or the CMS, as it is usually called, is due to several factors. CMS missionaries were the first local European residents and even today more than half of the handful of Europeans living in Ukaguru are missionaries or members of their families. For this reason, a large proportion of what the Kaguru regard as typical European behavior derives from their observations of the missionaries. Furthermore, the mission offers the Kaguru a set of values and a code of behavior which they are encouraged to believe will enable them to approach the status of Europeans. In the past all of the schools, the gateways to the modern world, were operated by the mission and although the Native Authority has opened its own schools, more than half are still in the hands of the mission. A further consideration is the fact that the mission is, next to the Native Authority, the largest employer in Ukaguru.

History of the Mission

Anglican missionaries worked in Ukaguru for a number of years before the establishment of European political control in what is now Tanganyika. The CMS first established a station in Ukaguru at Mamboya along the Arab caravan route in 1880, four years after a station had been founded at the important caravan center of Mpwapwa in nearby Ugogo. Later the station was moved a few miles from Mamboya to Berega, its present site.

In the beginning, progress was extremely slow; the first conversion was not made until 1886 (Church Missionary Society records, Berega). During subsequent years sometimes only two or three conversions took place in any given year. In this early period the strongest motivating force towards conversion appears to have been the faith which many had in the missionaries' power to treat the sick. The missionaries took advantage of this and often made special trips to areas suffering from epidemics in order to conduct vigorous campaigns on behalf of Christianity.

Widespread interest in Christianity did not occur until the arrival of the Germans. At that time, some of the Kaguru began to appreciate the importance of the educational facilities offered by the missionaries in obtaining posts in the new colonial system. The Germans themselves played an active role in this sphere, forcing the sons and nephews of important leaders to attend mission schools where they existed. Nevertheless, although the rate of conversion increased somewhat for this and other reasons, progress remained exceedingly slow by comparison with other areas, a state of affairs which continued throughout the entire German era. The situation was so discouraging that in 1908, for this reason as well as others, the CMS seriously considered abandoning Ukaguru.

Berega in Ukaguru was an outpost of the CMS and in the attempt to maintain it, the mission found that it had overextended itself. In addition to the difficulties presented by the terrain and the living conditions, there was a chronic shortage of funds and often a lack of sufficient European and African personnel to staff the station properly. Having embarked upon its campaign in Ukaguru, the CMS desired to continue its work there despite the difficulties which it constantly encountered, partly due to a reluctance to admit defeat and partly to the fear that if they left the area the Kaguru would come under the influence either of Islam or the Catholic church.

The Anglican missionaries were interned by the Germans during the First World War and this set back their work a great deal, although some of the African members of the mission continued to work without salaries during this trying period. Considerable damage was done to the mission buildings, and after the war the mission was faced with enormous tasks of reorganization and rebuilding. Their obstacles were augmented further by the influenza epidemic and a famine. Later the Depression severely reduced the funds which the mission had been accustomed to receive from Europe and Australia.

Despite the many difficulties faced in the past and although many years will elapse before Ukaguru can be called a Christian country, the local church organization is a strong and expanding one and a considerable proportion of the Kaguru have been converted to Christianity. At the present time, if we include nominal Christians, i.e., those who disregard most of the mission prohibitions in regard to drinking, dancing, polygamy, etc., there are probably some 20,000 Christians among the Kaguru, or a quarter of the total population. This includes those who live in Mpwapwa as well as those in Kilosa District. The proportion of Christians varies tremendously from one area to another. For example, when the government conducted a sample census in a few small areas, in one area almost 80 per cent of the people reported themselves as Christians, whereas in another only 3 per cent did so. These differences are directly related, as one might expect, to such things as the distance of the area in question from a church and the presence or absence of a school in the neighborhood. Christians also tend to be strongly represented in the vicinity of the modern trading centers.

The Present-Day Mission

Berega Mission is the center of church activity for the whole of Ukaguru. It occupies an extensive tract of land on both sides of a stream. Here are a church, a hospital, houses for many members of the staff, both European and African, a primary school, and a middle school with dormitories for the boarding students. A great deal of land not occupied by building or utilized as playing fields is under cultivation. Some of this land is being used for gardens attached to the schools while other plots are cultivated by Africans employed by the mission. There is also a mission-owned shop, which sells items, such as photographic film, which are otherwise unobtainable locally. The same building also serves as the post office for all of Ukaguru. To the outsider the Berega station appears rather unimpressive in terms of its buildings by comparison with other mission stations in Tanganyika, particularly some of the Roman Catholic centers. Elsewhere in Ukaguru the mission has a half-dozen parish churches and a dozen primary schools.

The Anglican church in Ukaguru is part of the Diocese of Central Tanganyika, whose headquarters are in Dodoma, in Ugogo. This diocese has been assigned to the Australian branch of the CMS and as a result most of the European members of the mission, including the Bishop, are Australians.

In Ukaguru itself at the time of our study, there was one European clergyman. The other European members of the staff were a physician and two nurses attached to the hospital. An African clergyman was in charge of each of the parish churches. These clergymen were responsible to the Archdeacon, himself an African, who resides at Berega.

Local church policy in Ukaguru is formulated by a Ruridecanal Committee. This is composed of all the Europeans living at Berega all of the African pastors, all the catechists of whom there are about forty, the headmaster of the middle school, as well as many of the other teachers attached to the mission schools, and one lay Christian (who is often a local headman) from each parish. The committee meets at least twice a year to discuss the use of local church funds, policy towards the congregation, and local moral and religious affairs in general. The committee controls funds which amount to about 5,000 shillings.

Today the European clergyman and even the African pastors make but little effort to convert the pagans living in their areas. They devote themselves almost exclusively to the affairs of the church and of the Christian community. The work of proselytization is almost entirely in the hands of the catechists and evangelists. Cathechists are people who have had some formal religious training and who receive small salaries for their work, although this has not always been true in the past. Evangelists, by contrast, seldom have had any formal training and instead claim to be moved to eloquence by the Holy Ghost. They receive no salaries. Catechists and evangelists are both in constant contact with their pagan neighbors whom they try to convert. Once a pagan has shown an interest in becoming converted, he is urged to attend the small classes which are given by the local catechist who attempts to impart the rudiments of reading and writing. There are some forty catechists at work in Ukaguru and a similar but fluctuating number of evangelists. The catechists and evangelists, particularly the former, act as the principal assistants of the pastor in each parish.

Berega, as the religious center of the area, is the scene of far more formal religious activity than is the case with the outlying parishes. In addition to the Sunday service, there is also a daily service held just before the mission employees go to work for the day. Bible classes are held once a week and should be attended by all converts but, in fact, less than half the number of people who attend church on Sunday appear at these classes. Bi-weekly classes are held at Berega for those who aspire to baptism and confirmation.

On these occasions instruction is given concerning the Bible, the Book of Common Prayer, conduct in church, etc. At the end of the period of instruction, oral examinations are given by the pastor and the catechist. As previously mentioned, instruction is givin in reading and writing and it is expected that all Christians should be literate, but one can find many Christians who are unable to read or write. This is due partly to lower standards prevailing in the past and partly to the fact that many Kaguru soon forget these arts through disuse. The Sunday service, the best attended religious event of the week, usually draws from 150 to 200 people. By contrast, at an outlying parish church, such as the one at Idibo, the congregation on Sunday seldom numbers more than fifty.

Social Services: Medicine

The mission is not merely a religious organization offering the Kaguru a set of beliefs and practices as alternatives to their traditional religious beliefs and rituals; it is also a major source of modern social services, in particular medical and educational services. Modern medical practice is one of the most important aspects of Western culture impinging upon the Kaguru. The mission brought the first medical facilities to Ukaguru shortly after its establishment in the area, and today the only qualified physician resident in Ukaguru itself is the one stationed at Berega in charge of the mission hospital. At the present time, few Kaguru are willing to rely solely upon European treatment to the exclusion of aboriginal measures. However, most are willing and eager to receive treatment at a dispensary or a hospital and many Kaguru would experience a great sense of deprivation were the mission medical facilities to be withdrawn. Concerning the use of traditional remedies, Christians who bear marks on their skin which indicate that they have resorted to aboriginal treatment may in some cases avoid the mission hospital for fear of criticism, but pagans are not embarrassed by this and some, in fact, continue to take native medicines while they are in the hospital itself.

The European physician is assisted by two European nurses and by a staff of Africans. The hospital has four wards including one for maternity cases and an operating theater. There is usually a fairly extensive supply of drugs on hand. In the past the mission attempted to maintain outlying dispensaries, but now it concentrates its energies upon the hospital, leaving the organization of rural dispensaries in the hands of the Native Authority and the Medical Department of the government.

While the provision of the best type of medical treatment, given the circumstances, is the primary aim of the hospital staff, the mission views pagan patients as potential converts. However, such patients are subjected to only the mildest forms of persuasion as they lie in bed. The effect of the hospital from a purely religious standpoint is rather difficult to gauge. Certainly its presence has attracted a great number of people to the mission station who otherwise would never have appeared there. Also it has created a great amount of good will towards the mission on the part of a significant portion of the population. Nevertheless, there are some who resent the fact

Fig. 37. Kongwa, which was the headquarters for the unsuccessful attempt by the British to develop peanut cultivation, is now an administrative center and a place of Indian merchants.

Fig. 38. Highway maintenance affords the Kaguru one of the few sources of cash income.

Fig. 39. Catholic mission church in Iringa.

Fig. 40. This Kaguru headman's house is one of the few to be built in European style.

Fig. 41. Even at Idibo, in a remote part of Kaguru territory, colonial law was represented by a native court.

Fig. 42. In the absence of a courthouse, court hearings might be held in the open air.

that the mission hospital charges for its services unlike the government dispensaries where treatment is free.[8] Also, a considerable proportion of the pagans who present themselves for treatment are the Baraguyu, who would appear to be incorrigible pagans interested in few aspects of Western culture other than medicine itself.

Education

The CMS organized the first schools in Ukaguru and, until recently, if a man wanted his children to obtain an education locally, he had to send them to a mission school. Today the Native Authority has schools of its own, but even in these schools the traditional connection between Christianity and education has not disappeared because the teachers in the government schools are invariably Christians and the CMS is permitted to give religious instruction in conjunction with the new schools. In the mission schools, in particular, very strong informal pressure is placed upon pagan pupils to become Christians, although since the schools now receive subsidies from the government, a pupil cannot be refused admission or the right to continue if he is a staunch pagan or Muslim. For this reason, while some of the most sophisticated Kaguru who have lived outside the local area and who have had extensive experience in em-

[8] Shortly before we left the field, mission medical services also became free.

ployment of various types will on occasion criticize the Christian churches, it is virtually impossible to find anyone who has an education at the level of Standard IV or beyond who does not claim to be a Christian.

Today there are some eighteen primary schools in the Kaguru chiefdom, some of which are located on the plains in the vicinity of the sisal estates. Of these, a dozen are operated by the mission while the rest are under the control of the Native Authority. Other than the strong religious tone of the mission schools, there is little to differentiate the mission and government schools because both are supervised by the Education Department of the Tanganyika government and must adhere to its standards.

Each of the primary schools, both Native Authority and mission, has about 150 pupils, of whom about two-thirds are boys. The pupils, following a government syllabus, are taught Swahili, arithmetic, general knowledge concerning Tanganyika, geography, and crafts. For the first three years students attend school on a half-day basis. The fourth year curriculum is taught on a full-time schedule. Most of these schools have only two teachers although a few of them have staffs of three. A large proportion of the students' time is spent in outdoor activities, in games and manual labor around the school, particularly in the gardens. At least one garden is maintained by each school, the avowed purpose being to give the pupils agricultural instruction. It would seem that the type of agricultural instruction given has little bearing upon the problems faced by local Kaguru cultivators: the methods of labor are not appropriate to local conditions, and in some cases the crops cultivated at the schools are not those best suited to the area. At the middle and primary schools at Berega, for instance, cotton—which is not well suited to local conditions—is cultivated in preference to tobacco, a crop with considerable potentiality in Ukaguru, because of the mission's objections to tobacco on moral grounds.

Parents of boys must pay fees of ten shillings a year at both the mission and Native Authority schools. In order to induce parents to send their daughters to school, the CMS charges only five shillings for a girl, while the Native Authority schools admit girls free of charge. While these fees may seem rather low, the cost of primary education places a great burden upon many Kaguru, particularly those with more than one child of school age.

The boys' middle school at Berega is the only school of its type in all Ukaguru. However, another middle school, also for boys, run by the Native Authority is located near Kilosa town. The nearest

CMS girls' middle school is at Mvumi in Ugogo, over 150 miles away.

The middle school at Berega, which has been in operation for only a few years, was built with government funds, the mission having supervised its actual construction. It has four classrooms, five dormitories, a workshop, mess, storage building, and houses for three school masters and their families. Over 100 acres of land are attached to the school, and much of that not occupied by buildings or used for playing fields is under cultivation.

In 1958, 140 students attended the school, which had a staff of six teachers. The headmaster had graduated from Standard XII before entering a teachers' training school; the other teachers, in addition to their training as teachers, had Standard X educations. None of the teachers had been trained in a government school; all were trained by the CMS or other Protestant groups. Only two of the six teachers were Kaguru; the others came from elsewhere in Tanganyika.

The subjects taught in the school are Swahili, English, geography, general science, arithmetic, agriculture and livestock management, crafts, and religion. All of the advanced courses are taught exclusively in English. The students are regularly marched to and from the church to attend services.

The middle school fees are more than 250 shillings a year and in addition there is the cost of school uniforms, pencils, paper, soap, blankets, etc. One of the reasons why the fees, which cover only a part of the expense of running the school, are so high is that this school, like almost all those above the primary in the territory, is a boarding school. Some understanding of the burden imposed by fees of this magnitude can be gained if we bear in mind that in the course of a year most households in the Berega area produce crops worth between 300 and 600 shillings, the portion used for subsistence purposes being included in these totals.

One of the methods utilized by the mission to reduce operating expenses is to have the students do a good deal of work. Unfortunately, this often interferes with their opportunities for study. Usually every student spends from one to one and one-half hours a day on school chores or working for the teachers. In addition to this, the students also work in the fields attached to the school. During certain periods, such as harvest time or when intensive cultivation is required, the students may spend half the day in the fields. In this way, however, a considerable portion of the food required for the students during the year is obtained.

Since the school fees are high, some otherwise eligible students are unable to go beyond the primary level. Their parents cannot afford to support them. Despite this fact, there is considerable competition among candidates for the places available in the middle school. The expense of a middle school education is also to a large degree responsible for the fact that on an average the students are three to four years older than they would be had they entered primary school at the earliest opportunity and then entered the middle school four years later. The age of those beginning Standard V varies from eleven to eighteen years. It often takes a student and his family some time to accumulate funds to pay his tuition at the boarding school after he has completed his primary education. The government will pay part of the tuition if a student can prove himself in need, but in actual practice such financial aid seldom exceeds half of the cost of tuition and it is available to only a few of the very best students.

The graduates of the middle school are mainly from what may be termed the educated class among the Kaguru. Their goals and view of the world differ markedly from the illiterate mass of the population. A young man of this type usually aspires to a position of responsibility and prestige. Furthermore, he has desires which can only be satisfied by an income considerably above that of the average Kaguru. At the present time, however, a graduate of a middle school who fails to continue his education is in a rather unenviable position. In recent years, in an effort to upgrade the civil service, the government has required that Standard X be completed before a student can be admitted to most of the special government schools at which training (without the payment of tuition fees, incidentally) is given, leading to well-paid, prestige-conferring positions. Graduates of Standard VIII are forced to accept inferior positions. As a result of this situation, there is naturally a great desire on the part of boys who are in their last year at the middle school to go on to secondary school. Since there is no secondary school in Kilosa District, the boys at Berega must seek admission to a school elsewhere, usually either at the government secondary school at Morogoro or the CMS secondary school at Dodoma in Ugogo. The facilities of these and other schools are very limited and many boys who have graduated from middle school with satisfactory grades are unable to obtain admittance to a secondary school. To date, only a few Kaguru have attended secondary school and a Kaguru has yet to reach the college level, although the mission recently sent a Kaguru to Australia for religious training.

The fact that few Kaguru have been able to obtain the necessary educational qualifications is the major reason why most of the positions in Ukaguru which have high prestige in the modern scheme of values are held by people who are not Kaguru. However, this is not the entire explanation, because those few Kaguru who do qualify for such posts usually prefer to work in other areas, in order to escape the diffuse obligations of a Kaguru to his relatives, the local headman, and the mission.

ISLAM, CATHOLICISM, AND THE ANGLICAN MISSION

When the CMS first began working in Ukaguru, some of the local Kaguru leaders were sympathetic to Islam as a result of the support which they received from the Arabs. Later many of the German government's African employees stationed in the area were Muslims from the coast and the CMS feared that the connection between Islam and positions of power in the new regime would lend additional support to the Muslim cause. But, the fears of the missionaries regarding Muslim influence would seem to have been unnecessary, because Islam has remained singularly unpopular with the great bulk of the Kaguru. This is perhaps partly due to the fact that Islam has always been strongly associated in their minds with the slave trade. Whether its fears were justified or not, the mission countered this possible threat by establishing schools where children were offered the opportunity to acquire the basic skills needed by those who wished to obtain the posts in the new bureaucracy. Furthermore, the mission eagerly supported the German policy of educating the sons and nephews of Kaguru in positions of power.

Roman Catholicism was a much more serious threat to the CMS and this continues to be the case today. In the 1880's, Ukaguru and Ugogo to the west were essentially CMS areas, while Catholic missionaries were at work in the areas to the east and the south. Shortly before the First World War, the Benedictines entered Ugogo and soon after the war the Holy Ghost Fathers attempted to extend their activities westward from Morogoro and northward from Usagara into Ukaguru. Some idea of the feelings which these moves aroused among the members of the CMS can be gathered from the following quotation from a CMS publication: "Another foe to Protestant Missions besides Islam has lately come to the fore in Ukaguru and Ugogo, viz. Roman Catholicism, and in 1912 the aggressiveness of its representatives became more pronounced. . . . The Rev. T. B. R. Westgate says that 'marshalling and organizing all the forces of knavery, an art in which they are thoroughly accomplished, they seem to have deliberately set themselves to the task of checkmating our every effort'" (Church Missionary Society, 1912-13, p. 53). In the records of Kilosa District there are frequent references to stormy complaints to the government in regard to benefits granted one group or the other. In European colonial society, the Roman Catholics are at a disadvantage because they are continental Europeans and members of a faith which is not that of the great majority of the officials. The advantages which the CMS workers have in these respects are, however, more than counterbalanced by their strong condemnation of such things as alcohol, tobacco, cards, and dancing.

In recent decades the Protestant-Catholic conflict has centered around the school system. While both missions are in opposition to the continual expansion of the government's system of Native Authority schools, they are also bitterly opposed to one another's expansion programs. The government holds the purse strings through its power to give or withhold financial aid to the mission schools. It attempts to establish new schools, those under government and mission auspices alike, in such a way that the maximum population can be served with the resources available. The government will not allow rival missions to construct schools near one another. In Ukaguru this policy has given the CMS a great advantage because, up to the present, the Catholics have never been given permission to build a school in the area. The failure of the Catholics to establish a school system has greatly hampered their efforts even in the peripheral area of Ukaguru where they have established a mission station, at Talagwe in the north, where two African priests reside.

The Impact of the Mission

The mission has affected the lives of all the Kaguru, whether Christian or pagan, either directly or indirectly and whether the people concerned are aware of the influence or not. Those who have been most strongly influenced are, of course, the members of the active Christian community who as yet form only a minority of the total population. The core of the Christian group consists of those actually employed by the church and in particular the highly educated (by local standards), strongly Westernized elite. The vast majority who are not employed by the mission run the gamut: some have gone through the ceremony of baptism in the past but are otherwise indistinguishable, either in behavior or in their ideas, from the avowed pagans; others are fervent believers who take an active part in church affairs. Particularly noticeable are those who have participated in the revival movement.

Effect upon Traditional Customs

The mission is strongly opposed to certain traditional customs and members of the church are forbidden to practice them. The mission has achieved a widely varying degree of success, depending upon the particular custom in question. Ceremonies for ritually cleansing the land, for instance, which were carried out on a local basis, seem to have disappeared in most areas, even in localities where the population is almost entirely pagan. Other pagan religious ceremonies, such as those for rain, continue to flourish. Although Christians rarely participate in them openly, many of them do lend support to these and similar ceremonies by contributing to the expenses involved. Often a Christian can give beer, a fowl, or a sheep to an older pagan relative who then actually performs the ceremony from which the Christian expects to benefit. By this procedure the Christian does not have the fact that he has participated in a pagan ceremony weighing upon his conscience and there is little chance that his Christian neighbors will learn of his involvement in the matter. Finally, at the other extreme, are certain customs, especially female circumcision, which are still adhered to as strongly by the Christians as by the pagans despite the strong condemnation of the mission.

In many events of life the ordinary Christian, as opposed to a member of the mission staff, utilizes both Christian and traditional patterns. A wedding furnishes a good example of this. Before the marriage banns are read in church, bridewealth is paid at the village of the bride's family. The etiquette of this payment, the previous discussion of clan ties, the ritual of anointing the participants with oil, the subsequent dance and beer party, all affirm Kaguru traditions. On the wedding day the bridewealth is registered in a book at the mission by the pastor who then lectures the couple concerning the moral obligations of husband and wife. The church ceremony itself involves the bride's being given away by a member of her father's matriclan. At this ceremony the participants wear clothing of a European type, and if possible they are photographed. The entire party then marches from the church, singing to the beat of a drum, towards the bride's village. If it is many miles distant and if the people have the money, an Indian or Arab truck is hired for the occasion. Away from the mission, the group sings Kaguru songs as well as hymns and once in the village, Kaguru dances are begun and beer is served.

In an affair of this sort, few Christian Kaguru, whatever their personal preferences, would dare to offend their relatives (many of whom are invariably pagans, and whose support is vital in making the bridewealth payment) by omitting ceremonial features held in esteem by the pagans.

The missionaries at work in Ukaguru always have been extremely puritanical and they have long condemned practices which are not prohibited by other missions, in particular the Roman Catholics. The local mission is strongly opposed to dancing, beer drinking, and the use of tobacco. The following gives a rather clear view of the mission's attitude towards dancing: "In some quarters heathenism is still strongly entrenched and licentious dances are indulged in by all the youth of the district, even young lads and girls frequent these horrible orgies. In such places there is no desire for the gospel message" (Church Missionary Society, 1922-23, p. 15).

Dancing and beer are essential for most traditional Kaguru ceremonies, especially those concerned with marriage, circumcision, and initiation, while the brewing of beer is an important and in some cases major source of cash for many people. Beer drinking and dancing serve as emotional outlets and are the only cheap forms of entertainment and pleasure locally available. Together with church meetings, beer gatherings and dancing are the major occasions when young men can form liaisons with young women. In view of all this, it is not surprising that there is considerable resistance in these matters to the mission's prohibitions. In so far as the drinking of beer is concerned, most of the local Christian men would have to be classified as sinners.

The generalizations made above do not apply to those who have participated in the revival movement nor to the great majority of the employees of the mission. Both of these groups, although there is a certain amount of overlap between them, deserve separate consideration.

The "Saved"

The most spectacular and best attended religious services in Ukaguru at present are the special revival meetings which are held from time to time. Sometimes such meetings are attended by as many as 400 or 500 people. This movement began to play an important role in the life of the local Christian community only after the last war. It has been strongly supported by the European members of the mission. Recently, several meetings have been held each year, the leaders often coming from outside Ukaguru. The necessity of feeding the guests causes much activity and the expectation of large crowds creates an air of excitement. These meetings, which are usually too large for the church, are held in the open air. They are characterized by singing, preaching, confessions, dedications to Christ, and occasionally by plays given by students and others. A person who takes an active part in such a meeting refers to himself as a *mwongofu*, i.e., one who is "directed, instructed, put in the right way." In English such people refer to themselves as the "saved." Anyone attending one of these meetings may feel the Holy Ghost descend upon him and stand up and deliver a speech. Very often such people describe in considerable detail mystical religious experiences which they have had. Often in the course of such speeches they strongly condemn those who have not been saved. The most spectacular feature of many of these speeches is the confession of sins. Occasionally, the person confessing his sins may take one or more items representing his sinful past and publicly destroy them. For example, a woman confessing to adultery may destroy a piece of clothing or an ornament which made her alluring or which she received as a present from her lover. Although they are rather rare, the most sensational events occur when people confess to having practiced sorcery and then proceed to destroy the medicines which they used.

The identity of those who have been saved is an extremely interesting but complicated question. Many of the men who take an active part in the movement are relatively young men attached to the mission who are seeking recognition and who are desirous of improving their economic and social status but who have not been conspicuously successful, either in the mission itself or in Kaguru society as a whole. Certain other people who have been dismissed from mission employment as a result of non-Christian behavior secure readmission to the church and re-employment as a result of such public confessions.

The "saved" are extremely puritanical and strongly opposed to traditional Kaguru practices. Furthermore, they are very militant in the presentation of their views.

African Mission Personnel

In the pursuit of its primary aim, the total conversion of the Kaguru and the establishment of a self-sufficient native church, and in its attempts to provide certain social services, the CMS has brought into being a rather elaborate bureaucratic organization. It is a profoundly European type of organization which is much closer in many ways to the colonial government than it is to any indigenous organization of which the Kaguru have had any experience.

The local mission employs over 100 Africans in various capacities. The largest single group is composed of the catechists, of whom there are about forty. Next in numerical order are the teachers, of whom there are about twenty-five. Almost all of those who are directly attached to the mission are dedicated Christians, this being particularly the case, of course, with the clergymen. As has been previously noted, of the seven clergymen in Ukaguru all but one are Africans. African employees of the mission are expected to participate actively in the religious life of the mission and to assume additional duties. This is true even in the case of teachers or dressers in the hospital, whose duties are primarily secular in nature. Thus, for example, a European missionary's cook may be found acting as a prayer leader.

The group composed by the African members of the mission is hierarchically arranged. At the top are those who occupy positions of responsibility, positions for which they have qualified by relatively long periods of training. Among this group are to be numbered the clergymen, the school teachers, and those holding responsible positions in the hospital. At the other end of the scale are those employed to do manual work in the hospital and elsewhere. These variations in status are not merely a matter of the amount of prestige which a particular post confers. There are also tremendous differentials in salary. A middle school teacher, for example, earns several hundred shillings a month, more than twenty times as much as a servant for one of the Europeans, who may earn only twenty or thirty shillings in the same period.

Africans attached to the mission have very practical reasons, of course, for adhering to the code of conduct introduced by the Europeans, for they may lose their jobs if they deviate from it. However, it is clear that many of them, in particular the members of the elite, have internalized this code. Often they are more severe in their judgments, more harsh and unbending towards their fellow Africans than are the Europeans. Frequently the impetus towards discharging a local mission employee comes from members of this group, this being the case even when jealousy is not a plausible motive. One finds them advocating stronger measures against sinners than the Europeans would contemplate. For example, some members of this group advocated the introduction of a rule which would compel a pregnant but unmarried woman to divulge the name of her lover.

The elite members of the missionary staff typify an emergent group in Tanganyika as a whole whose outlook upon life and mode of living diverge very strikingly from those of the mass of the local population, whether Christian or pagan. In most respects they are similar to their counterparts in Roman Catholic missions and to those occupying positions of responsibility in the government service from whom they differ chiefly in their attitudes towards such matters as drinking and sexual behavior. Members of the mission elite live in houses of European style built by the mission. They use European-type furniture, drink from glasses, make use of European-introduced sanitary arrangements, etc. They dress in European manner and like European middle class parents, they attempt to give their children the best education they can afford. They read newspapers when they are available and they often have wireless sets with which they follow events on the national and international scene.

While they are to a large extent living embodiments of the fulfillment of the goals of missionary endeavor, the members of this group have in the course of attaining this position brought new problems into being. By adopting so many Western patterns of life this group has largely alienated itself from the mass of the people, with whom they have but little in common. In some cases the problems confronted by these people in attempting to communicate with and to understand the local population are little less than in the case of the European missionaries. In Ukaguru this general problem is aggravated by the fact that a large proportion of this elite are members of other tribes, Nguu, Gogo, etc. Thus these people are seen as being doubly alien by the local Kaguru.

"Materialism"

While still engaged in their battle against many aspects of traditional life, the European missionaries see a new danger arising: ". . . the subtle modern forces of materialism and bitter nationalism impose a new kind of bondage on the heart and minds of the African. As another missionary put it: 'Our battle today is not with the bad old things but with the bad new things'" (Church Missionary Society, 1947-48, p. 11). Africans for their part, members of the general public and mission employees alike, often express very similar complaints against the missionaries. These complaints on both sides are particularly disruptive of the relationships between the Europeans and the new African mission elite.

While the salaries of the Europeans are paid from funds received from overseas and while partial support for certain activities derives from the same source, the mission is largely dependent upon local sources of revenue for its operation. The Tanganyika government, while it does not, of course, contribute financially to the purely religious work of the mission, does give fiscal support to the mission in its program of social services. For instance, the salaries of the teachers in the mission schools are paid, not by the CMS, but by the government. However, much of the financial burden falls upon the Kaguru themselves. As we have seen, they pay school fees for their children—fees which, at least in the case of the middle school, are extremely high. Likewise, patients who present themselves for treatment at the mission hospital are required to pay for the services rendered although the charges are minute by American standards. The Kaguru must pay the salaries of their pastors and catechists and must pay for the physical maintenance of their churches. In order to meet these latter expenses, the mission attempts to collect six shillings a year from every adult Christian, both men and women. In addition to paying rent for their quarters, mission employees are expected to contribute a portion of their salary to the church every year. In the past, for example, teachers were expected to contribute 10 per cent of their salaries. Although a certain amount of moral pressure is still exerted upon them to contribute at this rate, after a number of protests by the teachers this is no longer obligatory and in most cases the misson has to be content with contributions which average about 5 per cent of the income received. The mission, as we have noted, operates a shop on the grounds of the station at Berega. While the mission admittedly hopes to make a profit on its operation, or at least meet its costs, the Europeans see the shop as primarily a service to the Westernized Africans in the area as well as to themselves. Many Africans, however, see the shop as merely an additional means by which the Europeans extract money from their pockets. To give a final example, when European members of the mission travel in the church vehicle, they usually take Africans with them only on payment of a fare. While the missionaries do this in order to help defray the expenses involved in the upkeep of the automobile, the Kaguru contrast this behavior with that of other Europeans, such as those in government service, who if they do allow Africans to ride with them, expect no payment for the favor. The local African finds the mission frequently demanding money from him and it is not surprising that he often sees the Europeans as money conscious and grasping.

The Europeans missionaries on their part see the spirit of materialism in many Africans but particularly among their own employees, who constantly desire higher salaries and who, as we have seen in the case of the teachers, are unwilling to contribute even 10 per cent of their salaries to the church. We can understand the distaste and discouragement felt by the Europeans in the face of such attitudes and actions on the part of the Africans only when we appreciate the notions of service and sacrifice which play such an important role in the lives of the missionaries. The strength of these ideals can be seen, for example, in the case of a mission physician who earns a mere fraction of the amount he would earn at home, or, for that matter, in Tanganyika itself if he were in the government medical service. As a result of the low salaries which they receive, financial questions are a continual source of anxiety to most European missionaries, particularly to those who are married and who are faced with problems such as clothing and educating their children. By contrast, they see the upper echelons of the African employees of the mission occupying positions of great prestige in their own society and enjoying incomes which are fantastically high in comparison with the mass of the local population. From the European point of view, the Europeans engaged in missionary work are leading a life of poverty and sacrifice while the Africans who work for the church—far from sacrificing anything—are gaining wealth and enjoying previously unknown amenities.

While the Europeans view these matters in a comparative context, the Africans view them against an absolute scale. To the African clergyman or school teacher, the most obvious fact is that the standard of living and salary of the European missionary are higher than his own. The European missionaries at Berega live in superior houses which are better furnished, etc., and they have the use of an automobile. While many people in America or in Australia, for that matter, would be extremely loath to exchange their lot with an Australian missionary in Tanganyika, it must be remembered that for many Kaguru the standard of living now enjoyed by the missionaries remains the ultimate goal to be achieved either in their lifetime or that of their children.

While it is perhaps almost inevitable that certain Kaguru should aspire to the goals mentioned above without any stimulation other than the mere comparison of their own way of life with that of the missionaries, it must be said that religious and moral aspects of Christianity have been linked by the missionaries themselves with many secular and, to use their own term, materialistic aspects of Western life. The missionaries have tended to present European dress, methods of sanitation, etc., as morally superior. From the

Kaguru point of view, concrete aspects of Western life as well as less intangible ones, such as European forms of etiquette, are seen as having been presented to them together with new religious ideas in one cultural bundle. Thus if one is to be a proper Christian then one must also adopt many non-religious patterns of European origin. Many Kaguru interpret this linkage of material and religious traits in such a way that the assumption of European dress, modes of housing, possession of radios, etc., are seen as being important symbols of the acquisition of Christian status. In fact, in this almost Calvinistic juxtaposition of secular and religious traits, many Kaguru Christians feel themselves provided with the chief recipe for their entrance into modern life.

It is, of course, precisely those Africans who form the elite among the mission employees who have most thoroughly accepted this definition of the situation and who desire most strongly to become full-fledged Christians. The adoption of Western patterns, however, requires money and the more Western the style of life becomes, the more cash that is required. Thus, although the salaries of certain of the mission employees are very high by local African standards, nevertheless, they are low by European standards and do not permit the African receiving them to live in the style of the European missionaries. Therefore, there is constant pressure for higher salaries. This is seen by the Europeans as a rejection upon the part of the Africans of the mission tradition of sacrifice.

For a number of reasons the church assumes an attitude of neutrality towards modern African political movements. Nevertheless, as the quotation at the beginning of the section would indicate, the Europeans tend to view organizations such as TANU and USA with disfavor. USA is particularly unpopular because it organized a student strike at the CMS secondary school near Dodoma. African mission employees are discouraged from participating in African movements, but despite this, Africans attached to the mission have been extremely sympathetic to both TANU and USA. As a result of this, church facilities, for example, were utilized for the USA general meeting in 1957 at which the policy of the government in Kilosa District was sharply criticized. African members of the mission staff circulate the *Voice of Ukaguru*, the journal published by USA.

USA's periodicals and programs are strongly Christian in tone. Constant reference is made to God being on the side of the Kaguru as opposed to the government. It is often stated that members of USA are children of God and that to join the movement automatically ensures God's blessing and aid. The fact that an organization of a modern type such as USA is so strongly Christian in its orientation testifies to the very strong imprint which the mission has made upon those who are attempting to develop Kaguru society in new directions.

THE ECONOMY

Pre-Contact Economy

Before they came into contact with Arabs and Europeans, the Kaguru were mountain-dwelling cultivators, maize being their staple crop. Maize, together with other New World crops such as tobacco and groundnuts, was introduced no earlier than the seventeenth century. It enabled the Kaguru to occupy rainier mountain areas where millet and sorghum, the principal grains previously available, do not thrive. Despite continuous efforts to increase the size of their herds, most Kaguru had relatively few cattle or livestock of any type, chiefly as a result of the raids of neighboring predatory tribes, the Masai, Baragugu, and Hehe in particular. The fear of these raids as well as raids from other quarters for slaves prevented any extensive use by the Kaguru of the more fertile but indefensible river valleys. As a result of the vagaries of the rainfall, crop failures were experienced on an average of once every three or four years. Inadequate methods of storage made it difficult for the Kaguru to utilize the grain harvested in good years to tide them over the lean years.

A certain amount of intertribal trade took place during this period. The Kaguru grew tobacco for which there was a demand on the part of the people to the north and west, the Baraguyu, Masai, and Gogo. They also worked small iron deposits in the mountains of southern Ukaguru. These deposits which appear to have been controlled by local leaders were used for the production of weapons and tools which were exchanged with the Gogo, and probably the Baraguyu and Masai as well, for livestock.

The arrival of the first Arab caravans disturbed the equilibrium of this economy and set in motion a series of changes which have continued to the present day. The early caravans stimulated a desire for European- and Asian-manufactured jewelry and clothing which, it would appear, began to displace their traditional counterparts as early as the middle of the last century. Today there is a demand on the part of the Kaguru for a range of manufactured goods, principally textiles and metal goods, and an increasing desire for new services, especially those of an educational and medical nature. Although, in the beginning, the Kaguru were able to obtain these new goods by barter, trade soon began to take place in terms of cash. This process was greatly accelerated after the Germans introduced a system of taxation.

The caravans not only created a demand for a new range of goods but they also created a market for agricultural produce and thus provided the Kaguru with a means by which they could obtain some of the things which they now desired, at first directly by barter, and later by the acquisition of cash. Subsequently the new towns, and in particular the nearby European-owned estates with their large labor forces, replaced the caravans as the source of demand for agricultural produce grown in Ukaguru.

The new conditions made it desirable for the Kaguru to produce crops in excess of their immediate subsistence needs. Their ability to produce surpluses in this sense was made possible on a substantial scale once political stability had been achieved, a process which began in the Arab period and which reached completion after the advent of the Germans. In this new political climate, the Kaguru were able to occupy the river valleys where they were able to cultivate more extensively on more fertile land. The new situation also permitted them to augment their meagre herds of livestock.

Alien traders established themselves in Ukaguru and today all of the major shops are owned by Indians, Arabs, or Somalis. These merchants also buy the produce grown by the Kaguru and arrange for its transport out of the area. While the Indians dominate the local mercantile scene, the Arabs are also strongly represented. In this respect Ukaguru is unlike many areas of Tanganyika where Arabs are few in number or totally absent. This may be the result of the Arabs' long and generally amicable contact with this area.

Present-Day Economy

Today, as in the aboriginal period, the vast majority of the Kaguru make their living from the land. Opportunities for employment in positions providing regular monthly wages are few in number and are limited almost entirely to the government or mission services. Those who hold such positions, with the exception of a few bachelors, attempt to cultivate as well so that even they do not constitute a class of people divorced from the soil.

Despite the continued primacy of agricultural pursuits, the economy has undergone a drastic transformation. While barter with other tribes was formerly of peripheral importance, the Kaguru are now firmly integrated in the larger economy of Tanganyika and the world. As in the past, each household today attempts to be self-sustaining in terms of its primary requirements for grain and other foodstuffs. However, it also requires at least a minimal amount of cash each year in order to meet certain obligations, such as the government-imposed tax, and to purchase certain manufactured goods, such as cloth. In an economy of this sort, the system by which access to land is gained is obviously crucial and it is to this aspect of the local situation that we will first devote attention.

Land Tenure

In central Ukaguru, in the area near Berega, most households cultivate about three acres of land of all types. In the west, however, where the rainfall is lower, where the returns per acre are less, and where repeated weedings are unncessary, some households cultivate as much as six acres.

Most householders cultivate one or two small plots in the immediate vicinity of their houses, one or more plots in a river valley, and in addition a certain amount of land on higher ground.

All of the land in a given area is thought of as "belonging" in some ultimate sense to the locally dominant clan. Members of other clans who invariably form the great bulk of the local population obtain land utilization rights from the dominant clan, usually in the person of the local leaders. The dominant clan has revisionary rights. In practice the rules regarding land tenure are of vital concern only in the case of the fertile and scarce riverine plots.

Any individual who is permitted to dwell in a given locality is assumed to have tacit permission to cultivate a small plot or two near his home. Such plots, which are seldom larger than vegetable gardens in an American suburb, are used for food required on short notice when guests appear unexpectedly and for the things which are utilized as supplements to the regular diet or to season it.

The use of outlying fields on higher ground is readily acquired although an individual must obtain the explicit permission of the local leader before he clears a particular plot. Land of this type, which is covered with trees, scrub growth, and grass, requires a great deal of labor before it is ready for cultivation. Once cleared the plot can be cultivated for three to five years. Then it must be allowed to remain fallow for about ten years before it can be used again. At this time, of course, the arduous task of clearing must again be faced.

By contrast, riverine plots require little preparation. They are far more fertile and as a result give much greater yields. The Kaguru land usage practices are not in accord with modern principles of soil conservation and erosion often results. Most of the riverine plots, however, are replenished each year by fresh deposits of soil and therefore can be cultivated for at least twenty years, if not longer. Another obvious advantage of riverine plots is that crops planted here are far less vulnerable to drought than are crops grown on higher land. Along the length of every river in Ukaguru there is a continuous patchwork of holdings under cultivation. The size of the individual plots varies tremendously, running from minute scraps of land less than ten square yards in extent to large plots of three acres, with the average being two-thirds of an acre.

Riverine land is scarce. If the average Kaguru has two or more plots of this type, he is apt to have them in widely separated places. Furthermore, the same individual cultivates land on high ground in the bush perhaps a mile or two from his home. Many people are therefore forced to spend considerable amounts of time going to and from their fields and from one field to another. The dispersal of an individual's holdings is one factor inhibiting the introduction of the ox and plow. This situation also makes it difficult for a household to protect the crops from the depredations of wild animals, in particular monkeys and baboons. One advantage obtained, however, is that the individual is better protected against the total destruction of his crop as the result of some catastrophe —a flood, the raid of wild animals, or trespass by cattle.

Much of the power of the local leaders is dependent upon their ability to allocate riverine land. Once an individual has permission to use a plot of this type, he is secure in his tenure, but should he fail to cultivate the land for three years in succession, his rights lapse. Otherwise he cannot be evicted unless he is expelled from the community for suspicion of witchcraft or some flagrant violation of the norms. If a local leader wishes to evict a man, a case must be brought against him in the local court, an extreme and rarely successful procedure. But while he is relatively secure in his tenure, the occupier of such land is severely restricted in regard to its further disposition. A plot holder does not have the right to sell, rent, or otherwise dispose of the land in his charge. Furthermore, his relatives, his sons, his nephews, or others, do not inherit his rights. At a man's death his land rights revert to the local clan which can dispose of them as it sees fit. This is the theory. In actual practice the situation is much more complex. Men often lend land to which they have rights to friends or neighbors. Such arrangements are always made in order to help the other person with the unspoken understanding that the latter will reciprocate by rendering the same favor or another one in the future. Likewise, a man's sons may utilize their father's plots after his death if they have not already been doing so, as is often the case. From time to time, though, the locally dominant clan does exercise its powers or is enabled to utilize them by default, e.g., when a man dies without any children or without any children who are locally resident. In the same way, when a man moves to another locality (and quite a bit of movement of this type takes place), the dominant clan has an opportunity to redistribute the plots which the emigrant has abandoned. Thus the local clan, with the local leader acting as its surrogate, has the power to allocate riverine plots from time to time as they become available. Since most Kaguru want to extend their holdings of such valuable land, it is incumbent upon them to remain on good terms with certain dominant clansmen and to accord them a certain amount of deference if they hope to acquire rights to such plots.

Crops

A variety of crops are grown by the Kaguru, but wherever conditions are suitable, maize is the main crop. Pounded into flour, it forms the basis of the diet and is the chief cash crop as well. It may even be made into beer. Each household attempts to grow enough maize to remain supplied with grain throughout the year, and in addition, to produce a surplus which can be sold to the Asian traders. While the amount set aside for subsistence purposes is relatively constant, the amount of maize which is brought to the market varies tremendously from one year to another. These fluctuations are almost entirely reflections of the yearly variations of rainfall. The accompanying table shows the quantities of maize sold at the government-supervised markets in all of Kilosa District (separate figures for Ukaguru were not available).

Year	*Tons*	*Year*	*Tons*
1947	2,601	1952	1,570
1949	169	1953	20
1950	3,980	1954	1,407
1951	3,468	1955	4,373

These figures illustrate the extent of the fluctuations and show that every third or fourth year a poor harvest is obtained, permitting only small quantities to be sold. In fact, in bad years, such as 1949 and in particular 1953, many households did not have enough to carry them through the year.

As far as food crops are concerned, the maize diet is supplemented chiefly by sweet potatoes, beans, groundnuts, marrow, and bananas, the latter being grown in small quantities in suitable areas.

Subsidiary cash crops are sunflowers and castor. Of the two major cash crops produced by Africans in Tanganyika as a whole, cotton and coffee, cotton is produced only by a few Kaguru who live in the lowlands in the extreme eastern portion of the Ukaguru in the areas adjacent to the sisal estates, and coffee is not produced at all, although parts of the area are suitable for it. Recently the Native Authority established some experimental plots near Mamboya but, as yet, only a few Kaguru have shown any interest in the project. The areas most suitable for coffee production lie high in the mountains and the Kaguru dislike such places for climatic reasons. Furthermore, these areas are at present almost inaccessible by modern means of transport. These same areas offer excellent conditions for the growing of vegetables for the urban market. While crops of this type may be produced in the future, the possibilities of such a development are inhibited at the present time by the same factors which inhibit the production of coffee, although the lack of transport facilities is an even more critical consideration.

Certain other crops, while they do not pass through the official markets, are of considerable importance in the modern cash economy. Millet is grown almost exclusively for brewing beer. It is the second most important grain crop after maize in terms of the acreage devoted to it. Kaguru also grow small quantities of tobacco which they sell among themselves and to neighboring peoples. Tobacco is sold in the form of small cakes. In proportion to its weight, it brings the highest price for any crop grown in Ukaguru, the price being about a shilling a pound. Despite its high market value, tobacco is not grown on a large scale. The government estimates that in 1953 only ten tons were produced in the entire district of Kilosa. The main reason why it is not a more popular cash crop would seem to be the great amount of work required for its cultivation and preparation for sale.

While the above remarks apply to most of Ukaguru, in the west the situation is quite different. The area is too dry for maize, and its place is taken in the subsistence sector of the economy by millet and sorghum. Cash is obtained by the extensive cultivation of castor. Castor plants grow very rapidly and soon develop into small trees, often over ten feet high. This makes it very difficult to harvest the pods which must then be dried and shelled by hand. Thus its preparation for the market is much more time consuming than is the case with maize. Castor also has the disadvantage that, unlike maize, it cannot be used as a foodstuff or for brewing.

AGRICULTURAL TECHNIQUES AND LABOR UTILIZATION

Despite the involvement of the Kaguru in a modern cash economy and despite the fact that for many years an Agricultural Officer has been stationed in Kilosa District carrying out extension work among them, their agricultural techniques probably have been less affected by contact with the Western world than have most other aspects of their lives. The hoe remains the primary agricultural implement and no land is plowed with the use either of tractors or oxen.

The Kaguru possess considerable knowledge of the agricultural potentialities of the local terrain and of the requirements of the range of crops which they cultivate. Nevertheless, their system of agriculture is by no means a perfect one, given local conditions. For instance, yields could be increased considerably by spacing plants differently and by more frequent weedings. Maize is usually interplanted with other crops such as castor, pumpkins, and sunflowers, despite government advice against this. Cattle manure is never utilized as a fertilizer although it is available in certain areas. A considerable amount of erosion occurs every year which could be prevented in large part by the adoption of some rather simple procedures. But despite continual propaganda on the part of government officials and, in some instances, the enactment of rules by the Native Authority, few Kaguru have adopted improved techniques.

As far as cultivation is concerned, with the exception of some of the heavy work of clearing new plots on high land which is done by men, the various tasks are shared equally between the sexes, men and women planting, weeding, and harvesting together. The Kaguru are thus unlike some East African societies where the burden of this type of work falls almost entirely upon the women. Despite this, Kaguru women do work much harder than the men because, in addition to their agricultural tasks, they must gather firewood, fetch water, wash clothing, pound flour, cook meals, and take care of the children. Furthermore, while a man's work is largely seasonal, a woman has to work continuously. Of all the additional tasks for which women are responsible, that of preparing flour is the most arduous and time consuming. We estimate that between two and three times as much labor is required to prepare maize into flour as is required to cultivate and harvest it. Grinding grain by mechanical means is the major way in which the work load of the women could be reduced in the foreseeable future. At the present time there is, in fact, a flour mill at Berega which is owned by an ex-clerk and an African clergyman. Funds for its establishment were obtained by means of a government loan. However, only a few households feel that they can afford to have their maize milled on a regular basis.

Agricultural work is done on a household basis. A man may brew beer and invite his kinsmen and neighbors to assist him in the fields on the day of the beer party, but the use of this device for obtaining additional labor is rather rare. Beer parties of this type are given more frequently to obtain a number of workers for the final stages of housebuilding. Men do not hire other Kaguru to work in their fields for cash wages.

The Agricultural Year

In a few places in the mountains it is possible to cultivate throughout the year and in those areas where streams flow perpetually a few plots are utilized on a continuous basis by means of small-scale irrigation systems. With these minor exceptions, agricultural activity is controlled by the seasonal rains. The rains usually begin in late November or early December. In late October and throughout November the people prepare their fields for the coming agricultural year by clearing away the debris of the previous year's crop and burning it. This work can be carried out at a leisurely pace. Once the rains start, however, a considerable amount of work is required in the fields and this remains the case until the rains cease in June, although the peak demand upon labor resources comes at the beginning of the rainy season during the period of planting and initial weeding.

It is always advantageous to get maize into the ground as soon as possible in order to ensure an early harvest. Grain supplies are almost always running short by the time the first maize is ready to be harvested. If the previous year has been a disastrous one, grain may already be in short supply at the beginning of the rainy season and it will be necessary to supplement these stores by green maize eaten on the cob as soon as it is ready. Even if the previous year has been a good one, the householder may have miscalculated and sold more maize on the market than was wise with the result that, if his maize does not mature soon enough, he will be forced to buy grain from the Asian traders at a very high price. Finally, even if the previous year has been a good one and a household has sufficient stores of grain, a cultivator will be anxious for an early harvest because the first maize on the market will fetch a much higher price than that harvested later in the year. Millet, too, should be planted as early as possible because it requires a long growing season. If a Kaguru is pressed for time, he may plant millet or, in extreme cases, even maize, in closely set order in a small plot and then transplant the young plants to a larger field when he has more time. Once the basic grain crops are in the ground, other subsidiary crops such as groundnuts, sweet potatoes, and beans, all of which require deeper and more intensive cultivation, are planted. Weeding is done at least twice and in some cases more often.

With the exception of maize in the riverine plots, where an early crop may be harvested in the middle of the rains and a second crop of beans or vegetables planted, harvest takes place during the dry season from June to September and October. Unlike the planting season when speed is of overriding importance, the harvest can be carried out in a relatively leisurely manner because at this time of the year the Kaguru can be certain of a succession of dry sunny days. The most time-consuming chore connected with the harvest is that of transporting the produce from the fields to the houses because pack animals are not used and because, as it will be recalled, the fields are often at considerable distances from the homesteads.

In contrast with the rainy season, the dry season is one of intense social activity. September and October in particular are the months when the most drinking, dancing, and ritual activity take place.

Produce Markets and Shops

The Kaguru bring their cash crops, maize, or, in the west, castor, to the markets in small amounts of from five to forty or fifty pounds. The principal reason for this is that the produce must be carried by headload, often for considerable distances.

The bulk of the produce is purchased by Indian traders, although Arabs and Somalis are active on a smaller scale. As is the case elsewhere in Tanganyika, Asian traders are unable to open shops except in those places such as Mamboya, Chakwale, and Gairo where land has been set aside by the government for this purpose. By government regulation, all produce must be purchased at government-supervised marketing points which are located at these trading centers. An African clerk employed by the Native Authority is in charge of the operation of the market. He is responsible for the accuracy of the scales which are in his charge; he regulates the bidding and supervises the payment of cash to the sellers; he enters each individual sale by weight and price in a book. His primary purpose is that of safeguarding the interests of the producers, most of whom are illiterate and unable to read the scales. However, it is not unknown for such men to accept bribes from the Asian traders.

Most of the Asian traders possess trucks which they use to transport the produce out of Ukaguru and bring back the manufactured goods which are stocked in the shops. Would-be Kaguru traders find it almost impossible to compete with the Asians because, among other things, they lack the capital to purchase a truck which is vital if one is to participate in the produce business. Furthermore, they lack the ramifying ties of kinship and friendship which the Asian traders have with other merchants in the area and in the towns. Local Africans do have an advantage over the Asians in that they are not restricted to locating their shops in certain places. However, this advantage is largely nullified by the fact that almost all major purchases are made at the trading centers where the produce markets are located. For these and other reasons there are but few African-operated shops in Ukaguru and most of them hardly deserve the name, for they often have only thirty or forty shillings worth of stock in all. The few which are of any importance, having a few hundred shillings worth of goods, often prove upon closer examination to be owned by Indians but registered in the names of Africans in order to evade the rules regarding the location of Asian shops.

Livestock

We estimate that the Kaguru in Kilosa District possess some 18,000 goats and 6,000 sheep, in addition to some 15,000 head of cattle. Extensive holding of cattle dates only from the beginning of the European period. The cattle are not distributed evenly throughout Ukaguru. Most of them are found in western and northern Ukaguru, while in some places, for example Berega, there are virtually no cattle in Kaguru hands, although the purely pastoral Baraguyu maintain large herds in these same areas.

The Kaguru are not skilled herdsmen and their efforts in this direction are considered rather ludicrous by the Baraguyu. It is noteworthy too that the Baraguyu, once they have been convinced of the usefulness of a drug or other measure introduced by the

Veterinary Department, make use of it eagerly, while the Kaguru herdsmen remain suspicious and uncooperative.

At the present time, it would seem that there is little scope for the expansion of the Kaguru herds, for such an expansion would have to be made at the expense of the Baraguyu. Nevertheless, there is considerable opportunity for increasing the returns received from the present sized herds by the use of dips, rearrangements of milking schedules, refraining from scarring the hides, etc.

Livestock are relatively unimportant in supplementing the almost purely vegetarian diet of the Kaguru, except for the favored few who have herds large enough to ensure them a regular supply of milk. Although the Kaguru do derive a certain amount of cash from the sale of hides and animals on the hoof, the amount so obtained is minor compared with the income derived from the sale of agricultural produce. While the ownership of livestock confers prestige, livestock are probably principally important as a means by which an individual, who by one means or another amasses a certain amount of money, can profitably invest it. Opportunities for investment of money are relatively few unless we include the payment of school fees for children. A few Kaguru purchase sewing machines but this means the acquisition of a new skill as well. Obtaining a beer license is another opportunity, but for most people the alternatives are limited to the payment of bridewealth for another wife or the acquisition of livestock.

Beer

Some people make woven mats, baskets, winnowing trays, etc., which they sell, principally to the Gogo and Baraguyu, but by far the most important home industry is the brewing of beer made from millet, store-purchased sugar, or sugarcane. Although a man, or rather his wife, can brew beer for distribution at the homestead to people who have helped in the construction of a house, or to guests at a wedding, etc., all beer which is offered for sale is required by government regulation to be sold on licensed premises. The holder of the license may brew the beer or it may be brewed by others and sold to the licensee who in turn sells it to the general public. The local headmen are the people who are primarily responsible for seeing that people do not sell beer illegally in their homes. The diligence or lack of it displayed by the headman can have considerable effect upon the sales of beer at the local "Klubu." Many headmen, although they are not permitted to hold licenses themselves, do in fact own beer clubs which are registered in the name of someone else, usually a close relative. Again, other headmen participate in the profits by means of bribes.

Beer clubs are, of course, particularly active in those months when the Kaguru are selling their produce and thus have money to spend. During large parts of the year in some parts of Ukaguru, the backbone of the clientele consists of the Baraguyu who have money to spend at all times since they sell their livestock on a year-round basis. Some of the Baraguyu, who it must be remembered have little desire to spend their money on Western-type goods, drink prodigious quantities of the local brew. The sale of beer is in fact the principal method by which a substantial portion of the money which the Baraguyu obtain from the sale of their livestock reaches the hands of the Kaguru.

CONCLUSION

In the Kaguru we see a group of former subistence cultivators, among whom trade with other adjacent peoples was formerly of minor importance, who have adapted themselves to changing conditions and have taken their place in the modern economy of Tanganyika. Now in most years, they produce a marketable surplus of agricultural produce while continuing to provide themselves with the basic means of subsistence. They have managed to do this with little alteration in their traditional productive techniques. Except in the drier western areas where they now produce castor (a crop previously known to them but not cultivated on any scale), they continue to grow the same range of crops. Maize maintains its central position, its importance merely being augmented by its utilization as a cash crop as well as a subsistence crop. The Kaguru's situation in an area close to the sisal estates which employ thousands of workers is advantageous for the production of a crop such as maize which brings a relatively low price in terms of its weight and which as a result is not profitable when long distances and correspondingly high transport costs are involved. The fact that the Kaguru have been able to exploit the opportunities presented to them by their geographical situation has been due in large part to their freedom to occupy the riverine areas as a result of the new political stability introduced by the European colonial regime.

The relative success of this subsistence-plus-cash economy can be judged from one point of view by the fact that the Kaguru do not find it desirable or necessary to seek employment on the European estates in the neighboring lowlands. Thus the local social structure has not been forced to adjust itself to a situation in which a large proportion of the younger adult men are away from their homes for long periods. We estimate that in a reasonably good year, such as 1958, in the Berega area most households produced crops worth from 300 to 600 shillings, including both the produce sold and that consumed by the members of the household. By contrast a worker on a sisal estate who completed each of his "cards" within the allotted time and thus received his bonus and who also took cash in lieu of his rations, would have earned about 470 shillings during the year. On the other hand, since they grow a crop which fetches a relatively low price, the Kaguru are unable to obtain incomes of the magnitude received by those people in other parts of Tanganyika who produce crops of much higher value. The Chagga, as has been noted earlier, in the year 1951-52 received on an average 680 shillings for their coffee, this, of course, being augmented to a considerable but unknown amount by the value of their subsistence crops. This disparity not only prevents the Kaguru from acquiring a greater amount of consumer goods but it is one of the reasons why a lower proportion of their children have received educations beyond the primary level in comparison with the Chagga.

From a broad comparative point of view, it is not surprising that changes have occurred in the way of life of the Kaguru as the result of the superimposition of a market-oriented productive system upon the foundations of the old subsistence economy. What is striking is that no fundamentally new types of social relationships have come into being as a direct result of the new use made of the agricultural potential of the region. Thus there are no Kaguru today who derive their incomes in whole or in part from the rent of tenants working their land. Not only are there no tenants but neither is there a class of landless agricultural laborers. A few Kaguru have noted the wealth acquired by the Europeans on their estates through the use of hired labor and would like to emulate them and expand the scope of their household operations by employing other Kaguru to work for them. But such a system has shown no signs of coming into being. Furthermore, there is little likelihood of its development in the near future. Only one Kaguru, an ex-soldier, has tried to farm in this manner and he has had little success. He attempts to cultivate some fifteen acres but his labor force is very unreliable and consists for the most part of youths. Attempts to farm in this manner are doomed to failure not only because of the previously mentioned lack of a landless labor force, but also because those men who might be willing to enter into employment locally, at least part of the time, are busy in their own fields at precisely those times when a potential employer might want to make use of their services.

Underlying the failure of forms of social organization characteristic of market-oriented economies in many other parts of the world to develop in Ukaguru is the fact that the system of land tenure remains outside the cash nexus. Land is not a marketable commodity and it can neither be rented nor can it be bought and sold. The government insulates the operation of this system from developments in the wider territorial economy by preventing members of alien groups, Indians, and Europeans, from acquiring land, either by outright grant or purchase. Furthermore, the Africans cannot use their land as security in raising loans from outsiders, such as the Indians, thus losing their land in this manner or letting it fall under the control of members of these groups. If in recent decades the Kaguru had been able to rent or sell the plots to which they had access, there is little doubt that many Kaguru would have lost their holdings and would have been forced to work for others for wages or been forced to live as tenants on the land of others. This would have been especially likely in years characterized by the partial failure of the rains when cash or, in extreme cases, grain for subsistence purposes were in short supply. Kaguru obtain rights to the use of land, not because they can afford to pay for them, but rather, because they have ties of kinship or friendship with a man who has power to allocate land or because a local leader wishes to enlist support or for other reasons only remotely, if at all, related to the cash economy. Once a man has the right to cultivate a piece of land he has very strong rights to it. In some ways their rights are deeper than freehold rights because as the situation now stands a man cannot be deprived of his rights because of financial reverses, unwise loans, etc.

Today we find in Ukaguru a system of land tenure which developed within the framework of a subsistence economy. This system continues to exist within a modern cash-oriented economy, its persistence being explicable in terms of certain political and social rather than economic forces. The continued operation of this system of land tenure accounts for the fact that the new economic forces now operating in Ukaguru have not produced new types of social organization for the exploitation of the agricultural resources of the area. It also accounts for the failure of hierarchically arranged social statuses to emerge as the result of differential relationships to the land.

Sources Cited

Beidelman, T. O.

1960 "The Baraguyu," *Tanganyika Notes and Records*, Vol. LV, pp. 245-78.

1961a "Beer-drinking and Cattle-theft in Ukaguru: Intertribal Relations in a Tanganyika Chiefdom," *American Anthropologist*, Vol. LIII, pp. 534-49.

1961b "A Note on the Kamba of Kilosa District," *Tanganyika Notes and Records*, Vol. LVII, pp. 181-94.

1962 "A History of Ukaguru; Kilosa District: 1857-1916," *Tanganyika Notes and Records*, Vols. LVIII-LIX, pp. 11-39.

Budget Survey

1958–59 Dar-es-Salaam, 1958.

Burton, R.

1860 *The Lake Region of Central Africa*, London.

Church Missionary Society

1912–13

1922–23 *Proceedings*, London.

1947–48

East African Royal Commission

1953–55 *Report of the Royal Commission on Land and Population in East Africa*, London, 1955.

The Economist

1955 *The Economy of East Africa*, London.

Frankel, S. H.

1938 *Capital Investment in Africa*, London.

Colonial Office, Great Britain

1920–58 Annual *Reports on Tanganyika . . . to the League of Nations . . . to the United Nations*, London, 1921-59.

Guillibaud, C.

n.d. *Economic Survey of the Sisal Industry of Tanganyika*, Arusha.

Gulliver, P.
1955 *Labour Migration in a Rural Economy*, East African Institute of Social Research, Kampala.

Hill, J., and J. Moffett
1955 *Tanganyika: A Review of Its Resources and Their Development*, Dar-es-Salaam.

Hollingsworth, L.
1960 *The Asians of East Africa*, London.

Huxley, Elspeth
1951 *The Sorcerer's Apprentice*, London.

Koschitzky, M. von
1888 *Deutsche Kolonialgeschichte*, Leipzig.

Last, J. T.
1882 "A Journey to the Nguru Country . . . ," *Proceedings of the Royal Geographical Society*, Vol. IV, pp. 148-57.
1883a "A Journey to the Wa-itumba Ironworkers . . . ," *Proceedings of the Royal Geographical Society*, Vol. V, pp. 581-92.
1883b "A Visit to the Masai People . . . ," *Proceedings of the Royal Geographical Society*, Vol. V, pp. 517-44.

Lewin, E.
n.d. *The Germans and Africa*, New York.

Martin, C.
1953 "A Demographic Study of an Immigrant Community," *Population Studies*, Vol. VI, pp. 233-47.

Meyer, H.
1908 *Das Deutsche Kolonialreich*, 2 vols., Bibliographical Institute, Leipzig and Vienna.

Moffett, J.
1958 *Handbook of Tanganyika*, Dar-es-Salaam.

Morris, S.
1956 "Indians in East Africa: A Study in a Plural Society," *British Journal of Sociology*, Vol. VII, pp. 194-211.

Oliver, R.
1952 *The Missionary Factor in East Africa*, London.

Peters, C.
1895 *Das Deutsch Ostafrikanische Schutzgebiet*, Munich.

Powesland, P. G.
1957 *Economic Policy and Labour*, East African Institute of Social Research, Kampala.

Schneider, H. K.
1957 "The Subsistence Role of Cattle Among the Pakot . . . ," *American Anthropologist*, Vol. LIX, pp. 278-306.

Stanley, H. M.
1879 *Through Darkest Africa*, New York.

Woolf, L.
1920 (?) *Empire and Commerce in Africa*, London.

The Kipsigis of Kenya: Culture Change in a "Model" East African Tribe

ROBERT A. MANNERS

Part I Introduction

THE FIELD WORK

The field research on which this study is largely based was conducted in two periods. The first of these ran from September, 1957, through August, 1958, with research funds provided by the University of Illinois, supplemented by a grant from the Samuel Rubin Fund, Brandeis University. The second field period extended from October, 1961, through April, 1962, and was financed by a grant from the National Science Foundation.

In the initial plans for field assignments (see Steward's introduction, for a detailed discussion of the background, methods, hypotheses, etc. of these Studies of Cultural Regularities of which he was director) it was decided that I would carry on my research somewhere in East Africa, preferably Kenya or Tanganyika. Choice of the particular group with which I was to work was left for later decision, after I had had a chance to survey the situation in the field. My family and I made our temporary headquarters in Nairobi, Kenya, from early August until the first week in October. During that period I had several meetings with the then Government Sociologist of Kenya, Mr. Gordon Wilson, and with the then Government

NOTE: Several passages in this essay have appeared in three short papers published earlier: "Colonialism and Native Land Tenure: A Case Study in Ordained Accommodation," *Process and Pattern in Culture* (ed. Manners), pp. 266-80, Chicago, 1964; "Land Use, Labor, and the Growth of Market Economy in Kipsigis Country," *Markets in Africa* (eds. Bohannan and Dalton), pp. 493-519, Evanston, Ill., 1962 (republished as "The Kipsigis—Change with Alacrity," *Markets in Africa* [eds. Bohannan and Dalton], pp. 214-49, New York, 1965); and "The New Tribalism in Kenya," *Africa Today*, Vol. IX, pp. 8-10, 14 (October, 1962).

Sociologist of Tanganyika in Arusha, Dr. P. H. Gulliver. I also spent some time working in the files and library of the East African Institute of Social Research in Kampala and discussing with its director, Dr. Aidan W. Southall, the problem of tribal selection as it related to the overall interests of our project.

During the two months while I was officially headquartered in Nairobi I had an opportunity to examine the materials in the excellent African collection of the McMillan Library and the materials on file in the government's African Affairs Department. With the assistance of various government personnel in Tanganyika and Kenya I arranged a series of meetings with provincial and district commissioners of the territory and the colony to discuss the criteria for tribal selection. By the beginning of September I had narrowed my choice down to Kenya, and in Kenya down to Nyanza Province in the western part of the colony. I had been forced to eliminate Tanganyika from consideration because the more promising tribes —promising from the point of view of the kinds of change I considered most useful in the context of the project's purposes—like the Arusha, Meru, and Chagga (which had figured most prominently in my library and archival surveys in the International African Institute in London as well as in the Nairobi repositories) were either preempted by other investigators then in the field or were considered areas of political sensitivity. Moreover, since Drs. Winter and Beidelman had already decided on an area in central Tanganyika for their own research, it seemed more desirable from the point of country or national diversity to locate my own studies in Kenya if possible.

Although we had assumed in our initial stateside discussions that the Mau Mau Emergency, whose active phase had only terminated in 1956 (the Emergency remained officially in force until 1960), might have produced a formal prohibition on anthropological research in Kenya, I discovered in my talks with Nairobi officials that this was not the case. At least it was not the case as far as Nyanza Province was concerned. It was made quite clear to me from the outset that research among the Kenya Meru, the Embu, and especially the Kikuyu was out of the question at that time. Finally, however, after further consulting the personnel and the files in the African Affairs Department, and after conferring at some length with the Provincial Commissioner and District Commissioners of Nyanza Province, I hit upon the Kipsigis as the very best possible choice for my researches. Not only had they been labeled the "show tribe" of Kenya for the speed with which they had embraced important technological and cultural changes during the preceding two decades, but with J. Peristiany's *Social Institutions of the Kipsigis* and Ian Q. Orchardson's detailed and illuminating manuscript on the Kipsigis which came into my hands in September, 1957, I had two very useful ethnographies of that tribe compiled before 1940. Orchardson had come to Kericho in 1910 where "he closely associated himself with the Kipsigis people and in many respects became a member of the tribe, to whom he was known as *Chemosusu*, 'the man who does anything and everything.' He spoke fluent Kipsigis and wrote an authoritative grammar of the language . . ." (Matson, 1961). Although Matson does not mention it, Orchardson was married to two Kipsigis women, had several children by them, and did indeed "in many respects [become] a member of the tribe." He completed the first draft of his manuscript on the Kipsigis in 1929 and produced the final revision upon which Matson's abridged version is based in 1937. Peristiany did his field work on the Kipsigis in the late 1930's and published his book in 1939.

According to my reckoning, this meant that both manuscripts were completed just prior to the period of very rapid cultural change which characterized the 1940's and 1950's. In short, these studies combine fresh reconstructed data on the aboriginal cultures with first-hand observations on the consequences of European contact from almost the very first years of that contact to the period just preceding the eruptions of the past two decades. Thus, the two vital base lines—Kipsigis culture before European contact and Kipsigis culture before World War II—as represented in these two works, enhanced the opportunities for comparison with the present in a way that was not matched by any of the other tribes it might have been possible for me to study.

As soon as I had settled upon the Kipsigis as the tribe with which I should be working, I accepted the offer of the District Commissioner to help me find a location in the Kericho District which would place me as close to Reserve and settled areas as possible. We soon found a place in Sotik a small village some 35 miles from district headquarters in Kericho, which combined the features I was looking for at the same time that it provided adequate shelter for my wife, two older children, and the new baby born in Nairobi early in September. Our house was surrounded by Reserve, settled area, and the village. Our front door opened on the village soccer field. This location made it possible for me to carry on a part of my field work using my house as "the ethnographer's tent in the field." For the rest I went on safaris of up to several weeks at a time to various parts of the Reserve and to areas in Masai territory outside the Reserve where Kipsigis had taken up residence. My eldest son, who was then twelve, made good use of the soccer field and the supply of soccer balls we had brought with us to establish friendships with the Kipsigis boys of his age. These relationships deepened until he was spending almost all of his time playing with his friends, staying with them while they cared for their animals, hunting, hiking, and even attending school with them. This contact proved very useful in at least two ways. In the first place, Kipsigis of all ages were most favorably disposed towards the father and the family of a European child who assumed to such a marked degree the identity of a Kipsigis. And in the second place, my son proved an invaluable source of information to me on the culture of pre-initiate boys and girls.

For most of the 1957-58 period in the field I had the services of an interpreter and assistant, Richard arap Koech. For the 1961-62 stint I did not use an interpreter. During both field trips I made extensive use of data in the files of the District Commissioner in Kericho, as well as the records of the District Agricultural Officer, the District Education Officer, and others. I was also fortunate in having access to the notes and research materials of Mr. A. T. Matson of Kapsabet and to unpublished materials on Kipsigis grammar and culture compiled by the Hon. Taita arap Towett, Minister of Labour and Housing in the coalition government of Kenya in 1961-62. Mr. Matson, Mr. Towett, and members of the District team were not only generous in providing me with the written materials and notes in their possession, but all gave most generously of their time in consultations with me and shared safaris with me to all parts of the Reserve.

The 1961-62 period in the field was spent filling some of the gaps in the earlier material and analyzing some of the more important changes which had taken place in the intervening three years. This time we lived in the town of Kericho itself, since a good deal of my time was spent in the government offices and with government, tea, and union officials administratively involved in the procedural and structural changes which had transpired since 1958.

THE SETTING

The Kipsigis Reserve lies within Nyanza Province in the southwestern corner of Kenya. The westernmost portion of the Reserve's 1,001 square miles is barely 12 miles from the Gulf of Kavirondo, the eastern arm of Lake Victoria. Except for that small part of the

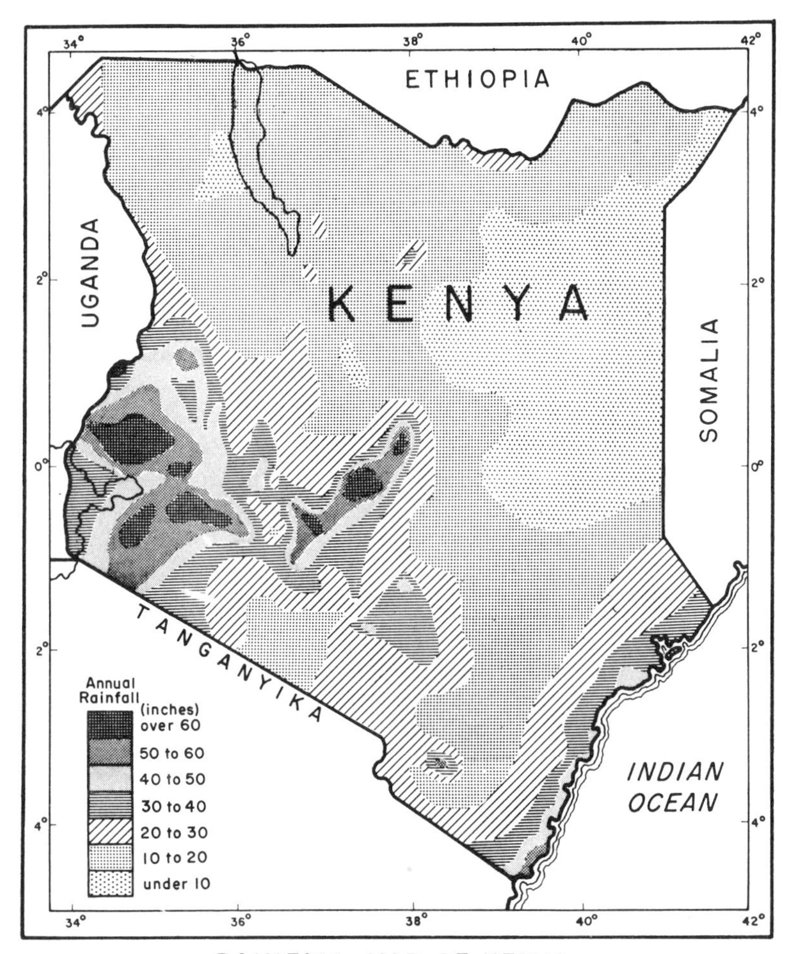

RAINFALL MAP OF KENYA

Reserve which slopes and sometimes pitches down the escarpment to the Great Kano Plain, most of it lies at an elevation of between 5,000 and 7,000 feet; and all of the Reserve is embraced within 1° south of the equator. On the north and the northeast the Kipsigis are bounded by lands alienated to European settlement. And on the southwest is another area of European farms, a segment of which intrudes like a crooked finger into the Reserve itself, almost cutting off the southern portion from the rest of Kipsigis territory. Native peoples of other tribes make up the remaining contiguous populations; the Kisii and the Luo to the west, and the Masai to the southeast and the south (see maps, pp. 278 and 284, *infra*).

In the drier parts of the Reserve rainfall averages around 40 inches, but in the high areas adjacent to the Mau Forest there is as much as 70-75 inches of rain a year. Much of the rain falls during the two periods known locally as the "long rains" and the "short rains," namely, April-June and October-December, but precipitation is not confined to those periods. Thus, in contrast with some other tropical areas where dry and wet seasons are rather sharply demarcated, there is likely to be some rainfall in all parts of the Reserve during every month of the year. And while January and February are generally the warmest months and August the coolest, the differential is very slight, and the important temperature changes are diurnal, these ranging from an average high somewhere in the low 80's to an average low in the high 40's.

Although one might assume from the equatorial position of the Kipsigis Reserve and the annual distribution of rainfall that this is an area in which two or three crops a year could easily be harvested, this is not generally the case. The great daily range in temperature modifies the effects of a fairly well-distributed rainfall and proximity to the equator. Cool nights and mornings—when, at the highest altitudes, a touch of frost may occasionally be detected—inhibit the rate of growth so that a crop which might be harvested in four months along the coast often takes six to eight months to mature in the Reserve Highlands. For example, in the Koiwa and Kimulot areas bordering the Mau Forest a crop of maize takes up to eight months to mature. Consequently it is the rare Kipsigis farmer who harvests more than one crop a year in the same field. While the possibility of producing two annual crops may be relatively unimportant in areas where land is abundant and free for the taking, it is a crucial factor in confined regions where the amount of land per capita decreases with the growth of the population. Such is the situation of the Kipsigis, surrounded and cut off from expansion to the south, southwest, north, and east by fences or their symbolic equivalents; and in the west by the even more densely populated reserves of the Luo and the Kisii.

Today (1962) some 200,000 Kipsigis share the 1,001 square miles of the Reserve. Were it possible to distribute the land—arable, grazing, scrub, and forest—equitably among the entire population this would mean about 3.4 acres for each Kipsigis, or approximately 16-20 acres per nuclear family. Compared with their Kisii and Luo neighbors to the east of them—especially the latter—this would appear to allow for an economy of relative abundance. Unfortunately, however, not all of the land is suitable for cultivation, and some areas are even inadequate for grazing, while a fairly sizable piece—parts of the Chebalungu Forest in the south—is virtually closed to use and occupation by anyone. In effect, then, there is a real or potential land hunger in certain sections of the Reserve. The areas that are lower and drier or those with impeded drainage require larger family farm units than the more favored areas at upper elevations. But the haphazard patterns of land tenure and acquisition which have developed over the past twenty to twenty-five years have nowhere been related to the realities of productive or carrying capacity. Thus, some of the larger farms are to be found in the better areas, some of the smaller ones in the desiccated and overgrazed regions adjacent to Masai country.

As a consequence of these inequalities, both of size and fertility, several hundred Kipsigis families, especially within the past six or seven years, have been impelled to leave the Reserve to seek land elsewhere. Scattered small settlements of these may be found living in Masai country to the south, and two relatively large groups of Kipsigis have established major settlements at Ngata Baragoi and Njibiship in Masailand. Other Kipsigis may be observed virtually hovering in the vicinity of the five-strand barbed wire fence that separates them from this ancient enemy, waiting for the opportunity to cross over with their families and their stock to make a new home for themselves "where there is grass upon which the cattle may feed so that they will give milk for ourselves and our children and land upon which we may plant a little maize and some millet."

That the colonial administration has been aware of the growing land-shortage problems which confront their "exemplary" tribe is made clear in at least two ways. In the first place they have arranged for the legal migration of limited numbers of Kipsigis to pre-selected locations in the Masai Reserve; and second, they are considering the possibility of an organized redistribution of Reserve lands to reduce the inequalities which are the product of the rapid and anarchic shift within the past twenty to twenty-five years from free tribal lands to the present pattern of individual ownership. The two controlled development schemes which were launched within the Reserve during the 1950's are a striking demonstration of contrasting land productivity within Kipsigis country and of the government's recognition of this and its efforts to point up a solution by example. The Kimulot scheme was located in high, fertile country where rainfall averages over 70 inches a year and where the soils are generally well-drained. The Itembe scheme, on the other hand, was in lower country where rainfall averages some 40-50 inches a year and where the shallow "black cotton" soils (gramosilic) and the dark brown clays with light-textured topsoil (planosilic) are featured by an undulating and almost impervious murram base. Such soils hold little moisture in times of low rainfall and tend to become waterlogged during the heavier rains, thus handicapping cultivation and making the lands of the scheme most suitable, by and large, for grazing (Survey of Kenya, 1959, p. 16). Allotments to individual families in Itembe averaged 30 acres. In Kimulot they ran around 20 acres. But there is more to it. For while there was never any serious talk of reducing the size of farms in the Itembe scheme, there was early administration planning for reduction at Kimulot. "If this size [20 acres] proves to be well above the minimum economic holding, subdivisions, perhaps to seven acres, may be permitted among a farmer's heirs" (Ministry of Agriculture . . . , 1956, p. 166). In point of fact, within two years after settlement was completed in 1955, twenty-two farms at Kimulot had been cut in half by the administration. By the end of 1960 both schemes had "ended," and conditions of land use and tenure became virtually the same as those prevailing in the rest of the Reserve.

In Nairobi and in administrative and non-administrative quarters throughout the colony, the Kipsigis have been described as: "one of our most progressive tribes," "a forward-looking people," "the tribal showcase of Nyanza Province if not of the entire Colony," "the Africans who are moving most rapidly and most surely out of a primitive past into a civilized future." Important visitors from outside are almost sure to find a trip to Kipsigis country on their itinerary. And nobody comes away from the Reserve without either saying or hearing it said that the Kipsigis Reserve "looks like a bit of rural England." Elspeth Huxley remarked, "Kipsigis looks like Somerset without the trees" (Huxley, 1960, p. 81). Live fences of Mauritius thorn, euphorbia, or aloes dissect much of the countryside into a pattern of rectangular fields, paddocks, and gardens. If the Kipsigis could somehow contrive to export the next generation or to reduce their population by 30 or 40,000 and then keep it at that level, it is likely that an orderly, uncrowded, and relatively rapid development would take place—a development unhampered by land pressure, fragmentation, erosion, and excessive human poverty. And the administration's goal of balanced, mixed farming for all families throughout the Reserve might be realized. But the population is sure to expand in coming years, and the expansion to make itself felt in pressures on the land and the search for alternative means of survival. It is unlikely that the Kipsigis will achieve a continuously rising standard of living on an agrarian base whose emphasis is subsistence or production for consumption. Expanded cash crop production and employment for wages seem to be essential requirements if the tribe is to be allowed to improve its condition individually and collectively, if it is not to become stagnant or to regress to lower levels of consumption as the inevitable fragmentation of a fixed quantity of land proceeds.

The Kipsigis are Kenya's tribal showcase because they have come so far so fast. But the distance they have traveled is only far relative to what they *were*. It is not so far in relation either to the standards and practices of the Europeans who surround them or to their own expectations and desires. And under the terms which have until very recently been imposed upon them by the administration, by their environment and by their technological facilities for its exploitation, they could not go very much farther. The technological as well as the administrative terms will have to be changed if the Kipsigis are ever to realize the standards they have set for themselves or even the more modest goals which have been set for them by some of their well-wishers. For it is unlikely that the environmental impositions—and advantages—may be altered or removed for them as a tribe in the near future.

In sum, then, the natural habitat—climate, topography, rainfall, soils, fauna and flora, other available resources—is an essential part of the picture that one must view in evaluating or assessing the kind and direction of change that the Kipsigis are likely to undergo in the coming period. But it is only one of the features that needs to be understood. We must know something of tribal history—especially recent history—and a great deal about various features of the existing culture. But, perhaps above all, we must pay careful attention to those aspects of Kipsigis life which are affected by events, decisions, and developments which originate outside the Reserve. For it is obviously these forces and factors which account for and explain many of the historical changes—as well as the future course of developments—which we shall record in the pages that follow.

The character of Kipsigis culture today is different from what it was before 1900 because features of the industrial, European world intruded clearly and directly on the older tribal patterns. The Kipsigis, like other primitive people, have never been wholly insulated from contact with non-Kipsigis peoples (Lesser, 1959, p. 11), but the processes of internal development generated by contact with other primitives were of a different order than those which have occurred under pressure from the whites during the past sixty years. Thus the context in which we shall view the changes in content and structure of Kipsigis culture includes more than the natural habitat and the desultory and/or organized contact with other adjacent African societies. It includes what Gluckman, Fortes, and others have referred to as the social field, or the area of human and institutional influences which—regardless of their locale—exert pressures upon the people and the culture of the geographically delimited tribe in its own lands (Gluckman, 1949; Fortes, 1936).

The tea estates and the settled farms which surround the Kipsigis are in many ways as much a part of their lives as the open salt lick or the native market. The District Commissioner, the District Officers, the Agricultural Officer, and the other numerous personnel (European at the top) generally referred to as "the Administration" are instruments of a system which affects their daily lives and determines the course of Kipsigis cultural change and accommodation perhaps even more profoundly than the bonds of kinship or the ties of age-set and neighborhood social group or hamlet (*kokwet*). Climate, topography, and soils may impose limits or define alternatives in the course of the Kipsigis' increasing involvement in the world of cash; but external commerce, conditions of the local market, the activities of remote competitors, and the functions of European administration will, in the final analysis, dominate the direction, speed, and intensity of this involvement. Thus cultural change for the Kipsigis, as for virtually all people in the world today, represents something far different from a synthesis between the old and the new. Contact between Western industrial civilization and indigenous Kipsigis forms and practices is producing a cultural and social transformation. The Highland equatorial setting is one of the important factors determining the content of this change. The new forms that are emerging and, most important, the factors which engender this change are being transmitted from a world which lies outside the tribal boundaries, outside the Highlands, and outside Kenya and East Africa itself.

A number of people from that world laid a railway across Kenya from Mombasa to Kisumu at the turn of the century. Compatriots of theirs took up the lands which lay adjacent to parts of this new railway in order that the expense of its construction might be justified in terms even more practical than "access to the wealth of the country around Lake Victoria," and "an end to the barbarous slave trade." In the process they "discovered" that much of the land which had appeared unoccupied or only sparsely occupied was often essential to the subsistence of the shifting cultivators or the pastoral peoples who wandered over it in search of pasture for their herds and flocks.[1] So subsequently they entered into "treaties" with some of these people and made arrangements with others whom they had displaced or diverted with their fences, and their herds, and their cultivation. And later still they stipulated clearly which lands were to be reserved for their own use and which lands were to be assigned to the original inhabitants as their own reserves.

Within a relatively few years a mere handful of visitors from the outside world had altered not only the patterns of warfare and the paths of nomadism and shifting cultivation of hundreds of thousands or even millions of Kenya's native population, but they had confined them often to small parts of the land over which they had once roamed freely. They had removed them from some of the most fertile areas, imposed unaccustomed taxes on them, brought an unaccustomed peace, and involved them in corvée and work for wages. With these changes came a complex set of administrative controls which, on the one hand, opened the door to the native peoples for their plunge into the ambience of Western industrial civilization, and on the other hand, precipitated them unprepared and often unwilling into its complexities as a disadvantaged majority whose work and deprivations laid the foundations for the creation of a society which they could not join and a prosperity in which they could rarely share.

[1] Salvadori points out that the railroad threatened to become a serious economic drain without extensive economic development. Thus: "*L'attention du Haut-Commissaire se tourna vers les hauts-plateaux non occupés ou qu'on prétendait être non occupés . . .*" (1938, p. 61).

Part II. Pre-Contact History

The Kipsigis belong to the so-called Nilo-Hamitic cluster of East African tribes.[1] Among such linguistically related tribes as the Nandi, Tirik, Sabei, Marakwet, Keiyo (Elgeyo), Tugen (Kamasia), and West Suk—the Kalenjin group—the Kipsigis have closest relations with the Nandi to the north, who are separated from the Kipsigis by a wedge of European farms and estates. It is generally considered that the Nandi and Kipsigis were originally one group which split during a time of drought and famine. Although the time and the place of their separation are not known—and estimates vary from 100-150 years to 800 years (Anderson, n.d.; Orchardson, 1937; Towett, 1956; Peristiany, 1939)—it is commonly assumed that they came from the north, possibly from the vicinity of Lake Baringo which lies some sixty miles north of the present reserve. Other estimates would place them farther north in a mythical place called Burgei. Since the word *burgei* means warm, this tells us nothing. Some old men insist that Burgei is southern Egypt (Misiri); others that Burgei was a stopping place on the way south from Misiri; still others that To, a place vaguely to the south of vague Burgei, was the place of origin.

Whatever the more remote northerly origins of the Kipsigis may have been, I believe it is unlikely that they have lived in the present area for more than around 300 years. Until that time they appear

[1] Cf. Greenberg's revision of the linguistic map of Africa (1955, p. 62). His more reasonable nomenclature would leave undisturbed many of the earlier postulated relations of Kipsigis to other tribes in the area, even while it points up the dubious character of Hamitic connections. Greenberg refers to an Eastern Sudanic family within which there is a subfamily of the Great Lakes languages to which Kipsigis-Nandi, Tugen, Suk, Masai, and others belong.

to have been one with the Nandi and referred to themselves collectively as Miot. After the separation, the Kipsigis drifted south and southwest, while the Nandi settled in the high areas to the west and north of the Kano Plain.

In the early years of their arrival in this part of the country, the Kipsigis seem to have concentrated in the lower areas, particularly in parts of the plain adjacent to what is now called the Nandi Hills. They lived mainly around Kedowa, Lumbwa, Fort Ternan, Kibigori, and Muhoroni. But there was reputedly another supposed branch of the Kipsigis, the Mang'orori, whose movements took them in an easterly direction to a place called Tegat (bamboo). This is said to be in the Kericho area and to the east in the forests of the Mau. It is here that they are alleged to have met the Ndorobo, called by them Okiek. Some sort of fusion must have taken place, because the term Okiek is today used generally not to designate a people different from themselves but more usually to refer to those Kipsigis who made their homes in the forest. In any case, some of the forest-dwelling Ndorobo or Kipsigis-Ndorobo have undoubtedly been absorbed into Kipsigis, while others retained a somewhat distinctive forest adaptation which, until fairly recent times, seems to have marked them off from the rest of the tribe.[2]

Kipsigis settlement of the area occupied by them when the British arrived around the turn of the century had not been accomplished without additional difficulties and intermittent struggles with the people whom they chose to supplant. Kisii were the enemy in the western and southwestern portions of the area, while the Kipsigis fought and appear to have ousted the Masai from northern, eastern, and southern parts of the land they came to occupy. Although it is not likely that intermarriage and fusion on a very large scale took place between Kipsigis and Masai, the evidence for intermixture with the Kisii is clear. Many people now living in the Sotik area and in parts of Bureti are believed to be descendants of Kisii-Kipsigis unions. And some of the Kisii clan names, such as Mabasik, Mataborik, Bakuserek, Baswetek, Narachek, Kimeitek, and Kamagoi are found among Kipsigis in the Sotik area today (Towett, 1956). Thus, while relations between Kipsigis and Masai were overwhelmingly hostile, this is not true to the same degree of Kipsigis' relations with the Kisii. In this connection it is well to

[2] Some clan names of the Kipsigis are alleged to be Ndorobo in origin, e.g., Kipcheromek and Kipsamaek.

remember that the Kisii are a Bantu people and agriculturalists while the Masai were more purely pastoral-nomadic than the Kipsigis themselves. Consequently, when the Kipsigis had finally driven the Kisii from the lands they wished to use for their own grazing, they seem to have turned—especially during periods of drought, famine, and other difficulties—to these farming peoples for assistance. The celebrated *rupet ap Kosobek*, or the famine of Kisii (*sic*), which occurred in the latter part of the nineteenth century, was such an occasion.

At that time the Kipsigis were in such grave straits that they sold many of their children to the Kisii in exchange for finger millet and possibly even sheep and goats. One hundred pounds of husked millet was exchanged for a child of eight to ten years old. Although the peace that marked this period was not permanent, it at once reflected and accentuated the ties between the two tribes. For while desultory and even large-scale cattle raids were resumed after this and other periods of peaceful relations between the tribes, the patterns of intermixture and interdependence seem to have been facilitated. Many Kisii came voluntarily to live with the Kipsigis, and after formal adoption they and their descendants became an indistinguishable part of the Kipsigis tribe. It would be too much to say that the Kipsigis have turned increasingly to soil tillage during recent years solely as a result of their close contact with the Kisii or, to a lesser extent, with the adjacent Nilotic and farming Luo, with whom relations appear always to have been more remote. For as far as we know the Kipsigis have cultivated finger millet or eleusine [3] for a very long time and have names for at least ten distinct varieties of this grain. While it is possible that finger millet, sorghum, calabashes, and the few garden vegetables cultivated by the Kipsigis have come to them only since the migration into their present homeland, all of the Kipsigis whom I have questioned on the matter believe that they brought cultivation with them and that they themselves gradually perfected some of the several varieties of millet which they now use.

And so it is that although the Kipsigis probably did not learn cultivation from the Kisii, it is very likely that contact with them, in the context of the favorable environmental circumstances in which they lived, may have given some stimulus to the growing emphasis on food cultivation as an adjunct to animal husbandry.

[3] Although eleusine or finger millet is sometimes referred to by botanists as a "false millet," I shall use the term millet throughout this report as shorthand for these terms. The Kipsigis word for eleusine is *bek*, but sometimes the more familiar Swahili term, *wimbi*, may be used.

As we shall see later on, there are signs that cultivation may soon provide the Kipsigis with an overwhelming proportion of their total subsistence and cash income.

Kipsigis relations with non-Africans may have begun as early as the middle of the nineteenth century when an occasional Arab caravan followed a route that took them through central or southern Kipsigis country on their way to Lake Victoria. But such contacts appear to have been infrequent, for most of the Arab traders took a more southerly route from the coast through Masai country to the lake (Matson, personal communication). Two of the very oldest men of the tribe with whom I talked agreed that they had heard of Arab trading expeditions which had passed through lower Bureti and upper Sot. On one of these occasions, it was told to me, several Kipsigis warriors had been humiliated by members of the caravan who had rubbed corn meal into the Kipsigis' coiffures (at that time the Kipsigis warriors generally did up their hair in curls with liberal amounts of fat and red ochre, in the manner of the Masai of today). In retaliation, a large group of warriors (*murenik ap luget*) attacked the caravan at nightfall and killed every member of the party but two who escaped. This may have been one of the last Arab caravans to have passed through the country. It is placed sometime in the 1870's or 1880's, and it allows us to infer that trade goods did not reach the Kipsigis on an important scale until sometime later when the first whites and the first East Indians appeared in that part of the country which lies on the plateau between the two Rifts and east of the great Kavirondo Plain. Beads, metal objects, and even some cloth of European origin reached the Kipsigis long before the turn of the century, but these were apparently obtained in relatively small amounts and were acquired primarily by way of trade with other African peoples—such as the Luo, Masai, or the Kikuyu—who themselves either raided upon or traded with Arab slaving and trading parties. Because the Arabs generally favored the northerly return route through Lake Baringo and the ivory-rich areas of the Turkana, Suk, and Tugen, the Kipsigis themselves must have seen relatively few of these Arab-Swahili expeditions.

Matson (1958) tells us that the so-called Sotik-Lumbwa or southern route through Kipsigis country was favored by "many of the caravans" on their way west to the lake. They returned by the northerly route through Elgon and Baringo to the country of the Kikuyu and the Kamba "where slaves could be obtained to carry the ivory to the coast." The way through Kipsigis country must certainly have been familiar to the Arabs shortly after their first sight of Victoria in 1852, for Thomas Wakefield, a missionary in Zanzibar, had known enough of this area by the year 1870 to provide us, Matson says, "with circumstantial details of the country, peoples, established camps, distances, water, and so on." Information I have obtained would suggest, however, that few caravans actually did traverse Kipsigis country through fear of difficulties they might encounter either with the Masai or with the Kipsigis. In any case, whatever the incidence of contact with Arab-Swahili caravans may have been from mid-nineteenth century onwards, it neither involved the Kipsigis directly in the slave trade nor does it appear to have had more than the most superficial effect upon their economy or trading activities. For the massive and turbulent influences which were to unleash forces of culture change in depth, the Kipsigis people had to await the railroad and the coming of the Europeans. Nothing that came before seems to have affected either the content or the structure of their culture in a way to alter seriously the ancient patterns. Everything that came afterwards either foreshadowed or contributed directly to those profound transformations which have increasingly marked the transition from aboriginal to modern lifeways of the Kipsigis.

As nearly as we can determine, the Kipsigis of the early 1890's lived much as their ancestors of a hundred and more years before had lived. A few years later, after the "twin rails of civilization" had traversed their terrain and the political cloak of the Pax Britannica had been stretched to embrace them, the Kipsigis entered into a way of life new and different from anything they had known. The direct impact of these and other forces of change has not touched all Kipsigis equally or in the same ways, but all have been affected in some way. Now—that is, in 1962 when this study was completed—many Kipsigis are rushing as rapidly as their talents and circumstances will allow into the new way of life. It is not so much that they are striving to erase the ancient but generally superficial distinctions among themselves which have been accentuated in recent years as it is a desire to obliterate the distinctions *between* themselves and the Europeans around them who have provided the material image of a life they would like to share. For while the Europeans have created new goals and transformed ancient aspirations among the Kipsigis, they have simultaneously placed impediments in the way of their achievement. In something less than sixty years a whole new world has burst upon the Kipsigis, and already most of them seem eager to discard the old for this new one—or even for as much of the new as they may be allowed to grasp. No strong tribal or individual resistance to change is evident in this striving. On the contrary, there is good evidence, especially in the last twenty to twenty-five years, of a strong opposition to the Europeans who seem to be standing in the way of the Kipsigis' embracing of that change. Thus, the most significant historical marker between the old and the new in Kipsigis is clear. It is signaled by the appearance of the first Europeans.

It is likely that the earliest of these Europeans was Dr. Fischer who came into present Kipsigis country from the south in the year 1886. We do not know very much about his visit, and it is unlikely that he saw or was seen by many of the Kipsigis. Frederick Jackson, who came through in 1889, not only saw something of the country of the Kipsigis but managed as well to establish close relationships with some influential members of the tribe on behalf of the Imperial British East Africa Company, his employer. In 1891, another employee of the IBEA, Major Smith, traversed the extreme southern portions of Kipsigis country without any difficulty. But his companion, A. H. Neumann, who was sent back to examine the route more carefully in that same year did not fare so well. With a group of some ninety men, Neumann made camp in Kipsigis country one night. The Kipsigis attacked the party and killed thirty-two of their number, Neumann and the others escaping through the forest to Naivasha. The IBEA then decided to persist with the northern or Baringo route and sent no more caravans through the Kipsigis country (Matson, 1958).

In May, 1892, Pringle led a railway survey large enough to discourage predation and looked into the possibility of a southern route through Kipsigis country. Although the party avoided any serious trouble by reason of the implied threat of their force and a judicious use of such devices as rockets and searchlights, they discovered on their arrival at Mumias, a town some 40 miles northwest of Kisumu, that their superiors had decided to use the route through Uasin Gishu (Matson, 1958). This ended the immediate utility of further explorations of the southern route through Kipsigis country. A few Germans, including Oscar Neumann in 1894, and Schoeller and Kaiser in 1896, passed through Kipsigis country, but their impact was apparently negligible.

It was not until the railroad construction gang approached the Nyando Valley area that the serious and significant contact with Europeans and Asians which was to mark Kipsigis development during the next sixty years really began. We cannot be certain of the extent to which Kipsigis collaborated with the Nandi in the latter's "wars" on the Europeans between 1895—the year in which the Kipsigis made "peace" with the British by cutting a dog in half at Kipkelyon, thereafter called Lumbwa (from *mbwa,* Swahili for dog)—and 1905. A number of old men still living stated that Kipsigis from Sotik and from the northern areas became involved at least in minor ways in these struggles. There is no doubt, moreover, that the Nandi turned many of their cattle over to Kipsigis for safekeeping during this period. There is evidence also that Kipsigis attacks on the Luo had grown so serious by 1897 that the British were concerned lest their food supply from the latter be cut off. By 1900, however, the efforts of Ternan and Gorges in pacifying the Kipsigis in the vicinity of the Fort (Ternan) seem to have borne fruit. In this year a group of 500 Kipsigis warriors from Sotik were dissuaded by their northern kindred from joining the Nandi in further action against the British (Matson, 1958).

In April, 1902, there occurred what was, so far as I can determine, the final incident of strife between Kipsigis and railroad construction crews. On this occasion some Indian laborers had been involved in a dispute with a young Kipsigis girl and some Kipsigis shepherds. The Indians had tried to take an ornament from the girl and had driven off some sheep. In retaliation, 500 warriors raided the construction camp, drove off some small stock, killed one of the Indians and wounded half a dozen others. The attack was no more than a reprisal for the particular molestation, and no further raids or difficulties followed. However, the British were moved by the incident to speed the erection of a permanent post in Kipsigis territory as a means of keeping better watch on affairs and facilitating their control of tribal activities through closer contact with tribal leaders. Consequently, two months later Gorges began to lay roads and to put up buildings on the present site of Kericho, the largest town in the Kipsigis area. This development of Kericho appears to have been an important factor in determining continued Kipsigis neutrality through the campaigns of 1903 and 1905-6 against the Nandi (Matson, 1958). From that time on relations between the Kipsigis and the European and Asian communities have been generally peaceful.

Part III. Pre-Contact Culture

SUBSISTENCE AND RELATED ACTIVITIES

While it is impossible to know for certain just what was the condition of the Kipsigis in remote aboriginal times, it seems reasonably safe to assume that they have always been a people primarily dependent upon their herds and flocks for subsistence and survival. Even if we accept an estimate of 400 years during which they have done some cultivating, I think we should have to agree that this was largely confined to the growing of millet. Several varieties of wild spinach or related grasses are known, and a few others (*isagek, inderemek, mborochik, moobek,* etc.) are actually planted today by the women of the tribe. But it is generally asserted by the older people with whom I have discussed the matter that neither these grasses nor the calabashes which were occasionally planted in the millet fields were either important or ancient in the life of the Kipsigis. Some of the old men insist that the original importance of millet itself comes from its use in the manufacture of beer and that it came only later, and as an accidental concomitant of its use in beer-making, to be used as a food. Certainly its logistical advantages must have become apparent quite early to a predatory people whose forays in search of cattle may have carried them fairly great distances and kept them for extended periods away from their homes. For when men describe campaign and cattle-stealing experiences of their own or of their fathers and grandfathers, they will generally remark on the tight discipline of the march and how this was reflected in the measured consumption of the small grain rations that each warrior carried with him. However, one could not judge from the use of millet in making beer or as military rations either its antiquity or its general significance in the diet of the tribe. Nor could one even be certain whether the crop itself was cultivated anciently by the Kipsigis or obtained more commonly in barter from other people—although I would suggest that there is no evidence for the latter.

In short, we can only know that prior to the coming of the Europeans the Kipsigis cultivated millet, that it was essential in the manufacture of beer, and that it was undoubtedly an element in their diet. It is even likely that millet and the other cultivated and wild vegetables, plus the occasional game animal and pot of honey —obtained by placing a hollowed section of log in a tree to attract the bees (Dobbs, 1924, p. 14)—were important staples, especially in the diet of those Kipsigis who were poor in cattle, sheep, and goats. Although the origin of the term Lumbwa, formerly applied to the Kipsigis, is somewhat in dispute, it is generally reckoned a derogatory term of rather ancient vintage applied to the Kipsigis by the Masai who held them in contempt because they tilled the soil. I have also been told that it was not only the occasional plague, or drought, or other misfortune that drove the Kipsigis into a greater dependence upon vegetable foods, but that even in times of relative plenty there were many families who had too few animals to support themselves or even to cover the essential bride-price payments. In short, while milk, blood, and meat may always have been the preferred staples of Kipsigis consumption, there is little doubt that the Kipsigis, unlike the purely pastoral segments of the Masai with whom they were in frequent contact, used wild and cultivated vegetable foods as important supplements—or even staples—of their diet long before the Europeans arrived. This, however, should in no way be understood as an attempt to diminish the importance, both symbolic and actual, of milk and cattle in the lives of the Kipsigis. For milk, preferably soured and flavored with wood ash (*iteet*) from a branch of the *senetwet* or some other bush, is and was apparently prized above all other foods.

It is said that in the past the milk of sheep and goats, as well as that of cows, was drunk by the Kipsigis (Orchardson, 1937). Neither of the former appears to have been an important source of supply, and today it is only rarely that one encounters goat's milk in the home of a Kipsigis. I have never met anyone who milked his sheep, although I have been told that the practice may still be encountered on occasion and when other alternatives are not available.

In addition to soured milk, the Kipsigis drank fresh milk. While the taboo against consuming milk and meat on the same day was apparently much stronger in the past than it is today, this restriction did not apply to milk mixed with blood drawn from one of the large veins in the neck of a calf, an ox, a heifer, or a goat. For the Kipsigis make a distinction between *blood* from a living animal and the *meat* that is obtained through the slaughter or death of an animal. Sometimes the freshly drawn blood is eaten with a stew made of cooked vegetables or one of cooked vegetables and bits of meat. Almost always, too, it is not the whole blood which is eaten but only what remains after the coagulants have been removed by twirling a twig rapidly back and forth between the palms, the forked end of which is immersed in the blood. Usually the coagulant itself is eaten directly by the young boys, what remains going into the milk or into the vegetable stew.

The method used for extracting the blood from the animal is the same as that described for the Masai. A rope is tied around the animal's neck and tightened like a tourniquet until a suitable vein becomes distended. Several assistants hold the animal, while one man kneels to one side with a short venisection bow (*kirerto*) and special blocked arrow (*loinik*) whose point is embedded in a heavy-ended shaft so that it may not penetrate too deeply into the vein. The tip of the arrow is held about four or five inches from the vein and the arrow is released from that distance. When enough blood has been withdrawn—usually a quart or so from larger animals, somewhat less from a heifer or a calf—and caught in a kind of pot or container called a *kipkorotit* or *tabet*, the tourniquet is removed. The same animal will not be bled again for at least several weeks.

Although the Kipsigis made butter for ceremonial usage and, more rarely, as a general lubricant for the skin, they did not use it as a food. Nor have they ever, so far as I know, made cheese from the milk of their animals. Millet is boiled in water and consumed either in the form of a thin gruel or as a more solid mass (*kimnyet*) from which pieces are removed with the fingers and pressed into bite size by rolling them between the palm and fingers of one hand.

While the care of sheep and goats was usually assigned to women and children, cattle were formerly tended only by males. Young boys generally supervised the movement of the animals when there was no danger from enemy raiders, warriors assisting or taking over if the grazing area was considered to be in threatened territory. The normal pattern of animal care often involved the separation of men and boys from their womenfolk and the older men for periods of weeks at a time. Thus, the women, very young children, girls, and older men would remain in the permanent residence (*mossop*), tending the patch of millet in the field which was always close to the house and taking care of the sheep and goats. Occasionally, as well, a few cattle might have been kept near the house if this was in an area where no raids were expected and if there was need for an immediate supply of fresh milk for a young child or a nursing mother. Generally, however, most of a man's cattle were to be found several miles from his permanent home where richer grazing was available. This temporary cattle camp (*kaptich*) was moved from time to time both to find fresh grass and to make location by the enemy more difficult. Older, but pre-circumcision, boys were responsible for taking the cattle to and from the night cattle pen (*boma*), watering places, and grazing areas, while the warriors usually posted themselves as guards around the periphery of the area in use. There appears to have been no set procedure about milking. Cows which had freshened recently were milked twice daily, others were generally milked only once a day. Milking time both now and in the past seems to vary. Sometimes the cows will be milked around noon or even at one or two o'clock in the afternoon. Evening milking may come as late as nine o'clock. If the cattle have long distances to go for pasture and water, the first milking might be at about seven and the last in the evening at about eight o'clock. Formerly women were never allowed to milk the cows, and a menstruating woman had to be especially careful not to go near the cattle.

Unrestricted communal grazing—i.e., grazing in which the animals of all herds mingle freely in the pasture—seems to have been uncommon. Each herdboy was expected to keep the cattle of his charge away from all others, even though many households used the same grazing area and the fighting strength of the warriors was pooled in collective guard duty. Sometimes the boys were discovered playing together while their herds mingled at the watering place or in the pasture. For this behavior they were usually beaten by any adult male who discovered the lapse. It was not that the Kipsigis feared such intermingling might lead to confusion about ownership of the animals, for, like other cattle people, the Kipsigis always knew their own animals, giving to each a name descriptive of some particular historical circumstance, some anatomical or physiological feature. They seemed to be more concerned about the breeding bulls and any harm that might come to them through fighting with the bulls of other herds or even, as one elderly man told me, that the bulls might dissipate their "ngufu" (force, or strength) on some of the cows in heat among the other herds.

Since a good part of each household's food ordinarily came from their cattle, and most of these were usually pastured in areas remote from the permanent home, women and children used to make trips to the pasture areas (*soin*) to bring millet to and get milk, blood, and sometimes meat from the distant herds. On these occasions an unmarried and uncircumcised girl might stay several days in the camp of her lover, spending the nights sleeping with him and the days gathering wood and water or performing other household tasks until she was ready to return home with her calabashes of milk.

With the Kipsigis, as among other East African peoples whose cattle provide them with the bulk of their subsistence, cattle played an important part in their ceremonial life as well. Cattle were the only real measure of a man's wealth; they bestowed prestige; and they were the indisputable key to many of the social distinctions which were apparently prevalent in pre-contact times. It is impossible to know the exact size of some of the individual herds in aboriginal times, but they seem to have been much smaller than those usually attributed to the Masai. A man with as many as eighty to one hundred cattle would have been considered very wealthy indeed. Although there may have been some with larger herds, the vast majority of Kipsigis appear to have got along with far fewer cattle than this. Some poorer men had only a few or none at all. However, almost every household seems to have had some goats or sheep. And sometimes a number of these could be exchanged for a bull or a heifer. But the more ordinary road to acquisition of cattle—whether one had none or many—was through raiding the adjacent Masai, Kisii, or Luo, a practice which continues—although sometimes in a curiously altered form (see p. 308, *infra*)—until today.

It is often stated, when referring to the Kipsigis or to any of the other people of the so-called East African cattle complex, that one can assess the significance of cattle to these tribes by noting, among other things, that cattle are bride-price or the means through which marriages are made and new families are created. They are the means through which the group is, in effect, perpetuated. While there is no reason to question the importance of cattle to the people in these areas, there is also no doubt that a profound mystique has sometimes been attached to this importance.[1] Thus, it is occasionally made to appear as though marriage itself were somehow a by-product of cattle-centeredness. Without cattle, it is said, a man could never have a wife. Cattle, marriage, and group survival are thus inextricably bound together as though there were no natural order or precedence among the elements.

Cattle are—and apparently have been for a long time—extremely important in the Kipsigis scheme of things. As with many others in the East African cattle complex area, their beasts have provided them with much of their subsistence and clothing (Herskovits, 1926). A man who had ample cattle found survival relatively simple; one with few or no cattle always wavered on the brink of starvation. It is easy, under the circumstances, to comprehend the concern for cattle and the preoccupation with increasing the size of one's herd. Cattle were wealth, the only form of wealth. Even the number of wives a man had was a direct reflection of the size of his cattle holdings. The wives were an expression of the real wealth which had made their acquisition possible. The land belonged to everyone, while cattle were the personal property of an individual. Because they were the tangible evidence of his prosperity and his freedom from want now and in the future they bestowed upon their owner a special status and a prestige which elevated him above those who did not have a like wealth of cattle. He used his wealth to confirm and to validate his status. For he was expected to fete his guests and to be generous with those who came to him in honest need.

But important as cattle may have been to the Kipsigis—both in the subsistence and the contingent symbolic sense—their value seems to have been measured with a very practical eye. One does not get, from an inquiry into the uses of cattle and the attitudes about them in the past, any impression that the care devoted to them was excessive in terms of the genuine importance of the animals to the people in their daily lives. One lavished a certain amount of attention upon them because without proper care there might have been less food. One named cattle because one spent a great deal of time with them and came to know them as individual beasts. One used them to cement the ties of marriage because these ties

[1] See Huntingford, 1933; Colson, 1951, for a discussion of the "practicality" aspects. And for a somewhat different emphasis, see: Evans-Pritchard, 1953; H. C. Jackson, 1923; Westermann, Introduction to Huffman, 1931, p. vii; Wilson, in Gleichen (ed.), 1905, p. 140; and Seligman, 1932.

were of preeminent importance to the group and no more practical symbol of its importance could be found than cattle, the measure of all wealth. One raided and risked one's life in the doing, or fought to protect one's own cattle from the raids of others, largely as one always fights to protect one's livelihood and not, I think, because of any deep or involved mystical relationship between cattle and man. This is not to say, of course, that there was no affective side to the Kipsigis' relations with his cattle. In the context of their importance to the people such emotional accretions could hardly have failed to develop. But I believe it can be demonstrated for the Kipsigis that these attitudes were dependent, superstructural, or epiphenomenal. If they had a life of their own, I would guess that it was a tenuous thing, one that hung by a slender thread to the source of its own vitality—i.e., cattle as the major means of subsistence. In short, while the acquisition of cattle for their own sake most certainly existed as a Kipsigis value, even the acquisitive practices had their base in the living benefits to be derived from the ownership of cattle. Speaking of the Nandi, Huntingford ascribes the practical importance of cattle to the fact that they "are at present the only form of personal property the Nandi have, and till quite recently formed their sole industry, their main support, and their only stimulus to action—[raiding]" (1933, p. 251).

Those who have postulated a deeper, a more intransigent relationship between men and cattle in East Africa suggest that the attachment is so profound that it continues to operate when objective circumstances dictate severance of the tie and the adoption of a more practical means to survival. This may be true for other tribes in the area. I do not think it holds very well for the Kipsigis. In part this may be due to the fact that they have known for a long time how to cultivate the soil and have grown at least a portion of their subsistence requirements, but I do not think this is a full explanation. For even the type-tribe of the East African cattle complex, the Masai—most of whom have not yet taken to cultivation—have demonstrated recently that they are not so devoted to cattle for cattle's sake as to cling relentlessly to increasingly uneconomic herds in the face of other practical alternatives. For example: a single auction yard at Lasit on the Tanganyika border shows Masai cattle sales of 8,766 animals between July 12, 1955, and December of the same year. No more recent data are available to me. But there is evidence from other parts of the Masai Reserve (Narok) that they, too, are selling their cattle with increasing regularity at auctions (Ministry of Agriculture, 1956, pp. 66-79).

If there is indeed a "cattle complex" (in the psychopathological sense as well as the cultural-pattern sense) in East Africa, and if it involves a non-rational persistence of the idea, or the passion, or the affect long after practical impediments to change have been removed and/or alternative incentives and devices have been made available, I would suggest that there is negative evidence for this among the Kipsigis. I would suggest further that where persistence is encountered and can be demonstrated to fly in the face of practicality in stock control, that motives other than persistence per se —or some equivalent mystique—be explored. I believe there is mounting evidence to indicate that where fear and distrust can be removed while education and demonstration of the *ultimate subsistence and cash values to the individual or the tribe* advance, stock controls and voluntary range management will improve. I am not convinced that a mystical attachment to cattle or an equally mystical "resistance to culture change" explains the unwillingness of a group of primitive pastoralists to accept stock reduction and range improvement plans. In the absence of greater understanding, and in the presence of generally long histories of disappointment and duplicity, it is no wonder that many pastoralists—in the New World as well as the Old—react strongly against any suggestion that they curtail the only sure means of survival known to them, and merely because the people of whom they have good reason to be suspicious say that the move will be a good one for them. "The conservative force of tradition is never proof against the attraction of economic advantage, provided that the advantage is sufficient and is clearly recognized. . . . The classic case of African conservatism—the reluctance of the stock owner to reduce the numbers of his stock and to improve their quality—is also explained in terms of the emotional and religious attitudes towards them that is so marked a feature of many African societies. But here too it may be that the emphasis should be laid on inadequate incentive rather than on conservatism as such" (Mair, 1948, p. 189. See also Tax, 1952; Beals, 1954; Gerschenkron, 1952; Lamb, 1952; Erasmus, 1954; Barnett, 1953; Linton, 1952; Manners, 1956 and 1961).

I shall show later how Kipsigis attitudes towards their cattle have remained flexible, and how they have accommodated to altered conditions, particularly within the last decade or so. For the present I should like to point out that even before contact the Kipsigis seem to have resisted a mechanical attachment to customary cattle usage when that threatened their survival as a group, or even when it might have meant group disturbances of lesser impact. Periodically, in the past, outbreaks of rinderpest or other cattle diseases have wiped out whole herds or seriously reduced the cattle population of the tribe. Such an outbreak in the 1890's reportedly destroyed almost all of the cattle over much of the area then occupied by the Kipsigis. Some sheep, goats, wild animals, vegetables, fruits and berries, and small amounts of cultivated grain and garden produce were all they had to keep them alive. During this time, and in the aftermath while they were building their herds again through raiding or trade with itinerant Somalis, the marriage rate reportedly did not decline. And bride-price was paid in the then-current coin of survival: grain, goats, sheep, pots of honey, or even, I have been assured, in the promise of these or other edible commodities. As for poor men, men who have had few or no cattle of their own at any time; men whose kindred have also been too poor to make the loan of cattle to cover the bride-price; men whose raids brought them no animals or who were themselves the victims of raids in which they lost their own cattle—these too have immemorially existed and have immemorially married and paid bride-price without cattle. Many such cases were reported to me by informants, some from among their own families. Several have told me that their own fathers paid bride-price in honey and grain for their mothers. And there seemed to be no sense of shame in the telling. For how can a man pay bride-price in cattle when neither he nor his father nor his brothers have any to give? And how can a man live without a wife?

Several times in the course of the preceding discussion I have indicated that among the Kipsigis there were always some people so poor that they owned no cattle. The statement is true as far as it goes, but the tragic implications of such a condition were seldom realized in practice. For there was a custom among the Kipsigis—one which persists in a radically modified form even today, as I shall point out later—as among certain other pastoral peoples in East Africa, a custom of lending out cattle (*kimanagen*) for care to friends, age-mates, or kinsmen. There were some ostensibly curious features of this practice of cattle-lending which should be noted. For while one might expect the "rich man," the owner of a large herd of cattle, to lend cattle to those among his kin and friends who seemed most in need of animals, the practice, in point of fact, was not confined to them alone. The poorer man, the possessor of only four or five beasts might also be expected to have one or two or more of these out on loan to a friend or kinsman. Even when the rich man loaned out some of his oxen or heifers he was almost invariably the recipient of cattle which had been loaned to him by his friends or kinsmen.

Thus, the herd cared for by a man and his sons, whether it was large or small, usually included not only those cattle he called his own but others which had been lent to him for safekeeping. Naturally the blood and milk taken from these animals belonged to the man who was caring for them. And the truly poor man who claimed no beasts of his own often managed to survive and to care for his family with cattle which had been loaned to him by others. In this manner, I have been told, very few families (except in time of pestilence) were denied the use of cattle, although relatively large numbers of men at any one time might have no animals of their own.

There are certain obvious practical benefits to this system of cattle-lending found among the Kipsigis. They involve in part a kind of reluctance to place all of one's eggs in the same basket. For an outbreak of rinderpest or east coast cattle fever or some other disease might easily wipe out all of the cattle in a single herd or *boma* or in a series of *bomas* in a given area. Moreover, the ever-present threat of a raid, particularly by the Masai, could mean the theft of a man's entire herd if he pastured them together. Under the custom of cattle-lending, however, either of these calamities would not leave a man destitute. For afterwards he could make the rounds of those to whom he had loaned cattle and ask—politely and with proper explanation—for the return of the animal(s) and, if it had been a cow or a heifer, for all or part of the increase which had accrued from the time of the lending, which might have been several years before.

Apart from the practical advantages of cattle-lending already cited, there were other associated benefits less tangible in nature but significant nevertheless. Since possession of cattle bestowed prestige upon the owner, even the appearance of possession, i.e., a well-stocked *boma*, reflected a measure of glory on the man in whose *boma* the cattle were seen. It did not matter that everyone knew precisely which cattle belonged to the man and which were on loan. In either case, the milk and blood were the property of the man who had accepted the loan of cattle. Occasionally, if the loan (*kimanaktaet*) was of long duration, the owner might make a gift of one or more of the progeny to the caretaker. For the giver too there was payment in the form of enhanced esteem. Certain rich men might have large numbers of their cattle out on extended loan, some of these going to men of equivalent affluence, others to those more acutely in need of the blood and the milk which the animals would provide. These rich men were usually looked upon as good and generous men by the community even, I am told, while it was recognized that the lending imposed no special hardships on them and may even have involved some potential benefits. The judgment is akin in some respects to the feeling shared by many people in our own country for the philanthropist who is known to be "spreading his largesse" partly to acquire honor and partly to "dodge" taxes. The motives may be understood, but the action is itself often reckoned laudable.

In any case, cattle-lending was formerly universal among the Kipsigis, and it served the multiple functions of insurance, status enhancement, and a general cementing of cordial relationships among those involved in the exchange, and hence a widening—or at least a deepening—of the network of friendships and interdependencies which go so far in strengthening ties among a tribal population living in such a dispersed pattern of settlement as that of the Kipsigis. Moreover—and I would reckon this among the most important functions and consequences of the exchange— it supported and made possible the only feasible pattern of herd ownership under the circumstances, i.e., individual rather than communal possession of animals. Were it not for this system of exchange under the circumstances of what looks like an inescapable pattern of individual tenure in cattle, it is difficult to see how the tribe, as such, might have survived. Such radical inequalities in ownership of the primary source of subsistence would have inevitably led to internal strife were it not for the presence of some corrective like this system of exchange which, in many cases, permitted a cattleless individual to live and to bring up his family with "borrowed" animals. One might even view this device for social cohesion as another of the variant forms of hospitality found elsewhere in the primitive world of pastoralists and collectors. For in essence this is a kind of hospitality which involves not only those who have but those who have not, serving not only to cement relations between equals but to convert the potential discontent of unequals into its opposite.

Thus we find that a generous man, a man who loaned his cattle freely (perhaps eagerly) to others could count on their support in times of trouble. When the warning cries and the shouts of the women announcing the presence of a party of raiders went reverberating from hill to hill and from *kokwet* to *kokwet*, the poor men are alleged to have rushed first to defend the cattle of the generous man, leaving their own—or borrowed—beasts temporarily to the care of the old men, the women, and the children.

I have dwelled rather long on the role played by cattle in the lives of the Kipsigis, for I believe it was a most important one, and because I plan later to show how this allegedly fixed cornerstone upon which rested the weight of much of the Kipsigis cultural edifice is even now in process of removal, gradually to be replaced by another, upon which in turn will rest an altered structure, a new way of life for the Kipsigis in which cattle play a far different part —practically and affectively—than the one played by them through several centuries of pre-contact pastoralism. The life of the Kipsigis *was* closely involved with their cattle because these were the principle means of their survival in the pre-contact and earliest contact periods. As their material importance has diminished and dependence upon them lessened, the older attitudes towards cattle have changed, so that before too long only remnants of these will remain. It is precisely in the decline of this devotion that we may, I think, detect clearly the rational roots of its origins and its earlier persistence. If the patterns of interest in and care for cattle seemed extravagant in the past when life, as it were, depended upon them, then it should be no wonder to us that these patterns are being seriously altered in the present when life need not depend upon cattle, when other means for survival are available or somewhere to be sought.

SETTLEMENT PATTERNS

The Kipsigis house—formerly always round with a gentle to sharply peaked thatched roof over mud and dung walls on a firm framework of bound branches, saplings, and tree limbs—is usually located on the side or brow of a slope, or on some other well-drained spot, which is not too close to water or the "cold" of a swamp. The houses are not clustered in villages but scattered over the countryside in individual household units. Each unit includes—in addition to the area on which stands the main house or houses for each wife, the granaries, and the occasional smaller houses for children who are too old to sleep in the same dwelling with their parents—a plot of land for the garden and sometimes a rudely fenced night *boma* for the cattle. More often today, however, there is no special pen for the cattle. They are pastured in one of the several thorn-fenced paddocks or enclosures into which a man's land is divided. Before the turn of the century, and before large parts of land at the higher elevations were alienated to European use, many of these "permanent" homes were located in the high country (*embwen*) and were occupied continuously by the females, the young children, and the older males. The pre-initiate boys and the warriors spent much of their time with the bulk of the cattle in the lower pasture areas (*soin*), living in the smaller, more temporary huts of the *kaptich* (the place or home of the cattle). The latter were moved from time to time as the grazing areas shifted. In some of the drier and less desirable parts of the Kipsigis range the separation between permanent house and pasture areas was not so clearly marked, and the two often merged in a general area so that the herdsman and his animals returned each night, and the members of the household saw each other daily.

In a limited area in the extreme southern and southeastern portion of the present Reserve there developed a slightly different pattern of settlement than those just described. Here, where parts of the land are characterized by shallow soils over an undulating murram base which is fairly impervious to water (see p. 214, *supra*), the Kipsigis built their homes on the flatlands below the gentle hills and then located their gardens in parallel horizontal strips from just above the base of the hill to as close to the top as possible. Cattle were pastured on the flats and in the adjacent savannah areas. This alteration of the more usual pattern was due apparently to the Kipsigis' observation that while the impeded drainage in the flatland below the hills caused the soils either to dry out too rapidly or to rot the seeds and the seedlings in the ground, the natural drainage on the slopes did not produce these effects. Hence they reserved these places exclusively for cultivation and built their houses on the more abundant but less fertile areas below.

The other, and prevailing, pattern which involved placement of the dwelling near or at the top of the slope or ridge was accompanied by a different distribution of cultivated plots. Here the usual practice was to cultivate the land below the house. In the practice of shifting cultivation employed by the Kipsigis in their growing of millet this generally meant that succeeding years would see the garden dropping down the slope in a line from the house to the stream or river in the valley below. Hence all the land below a man's house for the width of a normal garden plot (some 200 feet) was generally left to his use. This gave him easy access to water and allowed him to pasture his sheep and goats on fallow land bush close to his home. Thus, each man's garden plots ran vertically up and down the slope in contrast with those of the impeded drainage

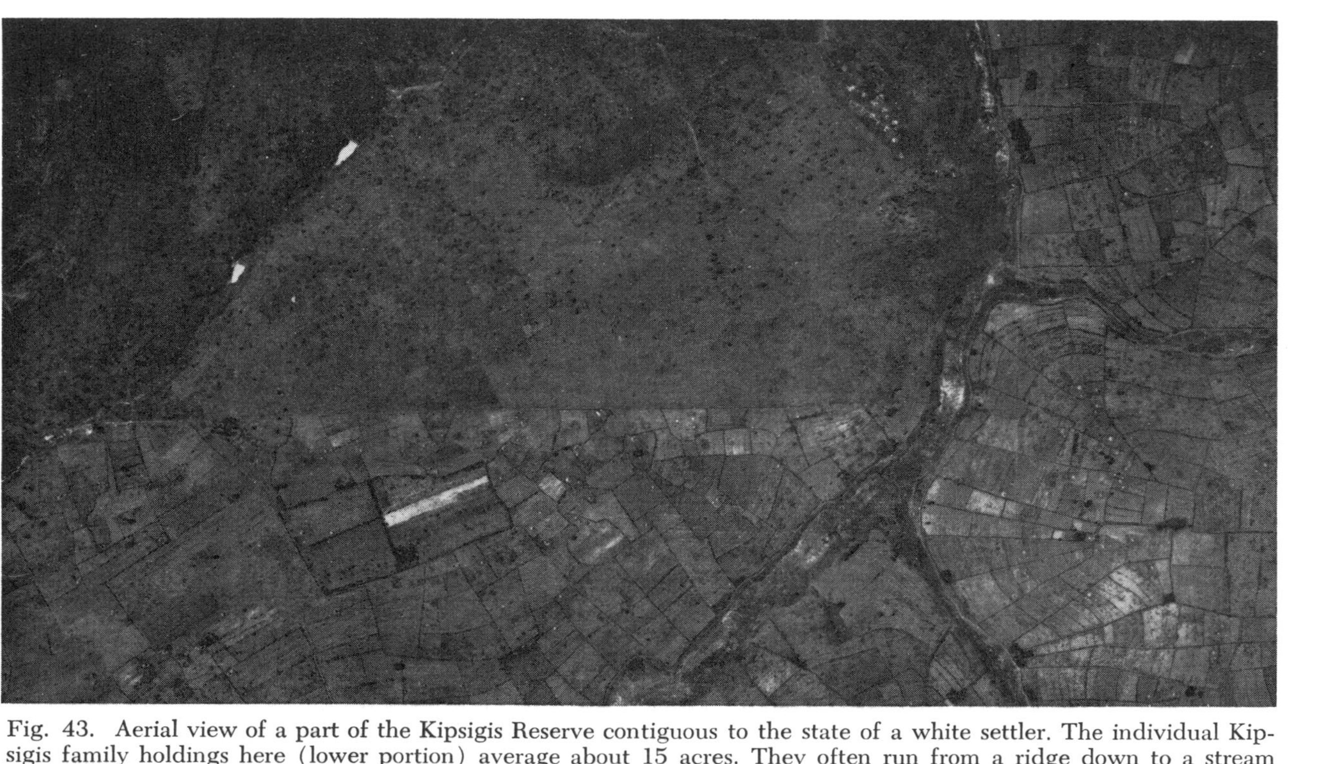

Fig. 43. Aerial view of a part of the Kipsigis Reserve contiguous to the state of a white settler. The individual Kipsigis family holdings here (lower portion) average about 15 acres. They often run from a ridge down to a stream and are divided into plots for rotational cropping and grazing. A settler's farm in this area (upper half) may comprise several thousand acres, much of it unused either for crops or pasture. *Photo courtesy of Dept. of Information, Nairobi.*

Fig. 44. A portion of the 28,000-acre Brooke Bond Tea Plantation which adjoins the Kipsigis Reserve. The plantation buildings are next to a settlement of resident workers who generally come from land-poor areas of other tribes. White spots in the fields are ancient sites of native huts. *Photo courtesy of Jeffrey Taylor.*

Fig. 45. The Kipsigis farm is usually surrounded and subdivided by thorn hedges. In aboriginal times hedges kept livestock out of the small farm plots. Today they serve especially to keep animals in the plots and to demark ownership boundaries. *Photo courtesy of Dept. of Information, Nairobi.*

Fig. 46. Close-up view of an aloes hedge which is very effective in the absence of wire. *Photo courtesy of Dept. of Information, Nairobi.*

Fig. 47. Kipsigis man with distended ear lobes, but wearing modern felt hat and cloth garment. Recently some Kipsigis have had the extended ear lobe amputated. *Photo courtesy of Jeffrey Taylor.*

Fig. 48. Most modern Kipsigis women wear European dress of manufactured cloth. The traditional leather dress, like the one shown in the photograph below, is rarely seen.

Fig. 49. Where millet, the traditional food staple, is planted, sod is burned to fertilize the field. Maize, first grown for the European market, is now replacing millet in the native diet. *Photo courtesy of Dept. of Information, Nairobi.*

regions where all dwellings were located closer to water and the cultivated lands climbed the hills in horizontal strips, *one man's plot above another's.*

By 1962 land enclosure was so nearly complete in all parts of the Reserve that land-tenure patterns in the areas of impeded drainage came to resemble those of the more "normal" Kipsigis areas. Although dwellings still remain largely on the flatlands or in the valleys, the cultivated fields belonging to an individual have been consolidated by informal exchange so that a series of contiguous plots moving up a hillside now belong to the same person and not, as in the past, to different Kipsigis.

It is apparent that the early process of accommodation to internal differences in Kipsigis environment could have had very little significance in times when land was relatively plentiful, when individuals and families were free to move and settle any place they liked within customary Kipsigis territory. But this is now changed, and the consequences of these varied adaptations have been making themselves felt in recent years under the impact of a shrinking land base, i.e., a growing population, and new concepts of private property in land. When *pasture* was all-important, the areas of impeded drainage were altogether suitable for Kipsigis settlement. But as *cultivation* became increasingly significant in the lives of the Kipsigis, it is clear that these areas, with their sharply defined and limited patches of tillable soil, gave rise to special problems. It is here that overcrowding sometimes becomes acute. And it is no wonder that a rather large percentage of Kipsigis migrants—either to Masai country or to the farms and estates of the Europeans—comes from some of these centers of impeded drainage.

THE *KOKWET*

Whatever the pattern of settlement and the distribution of cultivated lands may have been in the past, there was always a minimal corporate entity which regulated in some measure the day-today affairs and activities of the people. This unit is called a *kokwet.* It has been referred to variously as a neighborhood, a parish, a ward, a hamlet, and—by Ian Orchardson—somewhat vaguely as a "social unit." The land encompassed by the members of the *kokwet*—or, less commonly, of two or three adjacent *kokwotinwek*—has another name, *koret.* Hence there is some justification for Orchardson's insistence that the *kokwet* is not a geographical unit. In any case, the members of a *kokwet* are people who occupy a certain area which is usually demarcated by such natural features as a stream or river, a stretch of bush or forest, etc. Typically the members of the *kokwet* community share certain natural resources such as water, pasture, firewood, salt licks if there are any, and so on. Until fairly recent times many of these economic assets were utilized in true communal fashion by members of the *kokwet*. However, the concept of private property in land has altered these usages in recent years.

Included within the *kokwet* may be people of different families, clans, and *boriosiek* (regiments is the usual translation; possibly phratries would be better). The area covered by the *koret* may be as little as a half square mile or as much as two or three miles square. As few as ten or fifteen households or as many as a hundred or more may be included. Members of the *kokwet* ordinarily cooperated in a number of routine activities, and in case of need an individual could virtually demand the help of other members of his *kokwet*. A council of *kokwet* elders, also called *kokwet*, supervised routine activities and adjudicated most disputes arising within the *kokwet*. Huntingford's concise description of *kokwet* (council) functions among the Nandi applies as well to the Kipsigis. He tells us: "A *kokwet* is held whenever necessary, and not at any fixed interval; and the subjects it deals with include murder cases, punishment of crime and compensation for private delicts, and what action should be taken to deal with calamities like cattle disease, drought, locusts and taxation. Questions of inheritance and the settling of disputes may also be brought before the *kokwet*. There is often no formal verdict, but a state of agreement is reached, and it is then left to the people concerned to act in accordance with that agreement." He adds that the *kokwet* decisions have the power of law, and that "the public opinion" which backs them "is strong enough to insure that the decision of the *kokwet* is obeyed" (Huntingford, 1944, p. 6).

When the members of the council of elders were unable to reach a decision, the matter in hand was usually referred to an outside judge (*kiruogindet*) or judges (*kiruogik*) acceptable to the litigants. Their decision, delivered in council, was final and binding, solemnified by the slaughter of an ox, a ram, or a male goat. For all practical purposes, however, the *kokwotinwek* (pl. form of *kokwet*) were the non-kin social units within which most of an individual's activities took place. A man could generally move very freely from one *kokwet* to another unless he had a reputation for being a troublemaker. Approval of the *kokwet* elders was necessary before a family would be allowed to settle in a particular *koret* area, but this was usually given quite routinely. Thus, membership in a *kokwet* was flexible, involving people from different lineages, clans, phratries, and age-sets, and this social unit was an important structural element for forging and maintaining unity within a tribal population prompted to dispersal by its particular herding-plus-cultivation patterns.

THE CLAN

No two lists of Kipsigis clans which I have seen or myself been able to collect are in complete agreement. The best estimate is that there are at present some forty to seventy patrilineal clans (*ortinwek*; sing., *oret*), with the certainty that, whatever the number, it is far larger than the sixteen reputedly in existence around the turn of the century. Towett remarks that "an attempt to analyse . . . Kipsigis clans is [like] analyzing a bucketful of sand." He reckons that the total number today cannot be known (Towett, 1956). The clans are named, non-local, faintly totemic, and exogamous. They are generally identified with an animal, but other objects, such as edible fungus, may serve as a "totem."

Sometimes several clans share the same "totemic" animal, but since their names differ this is not a source of confusion. As far as I have been able to discover there do not—at least in the last sixty or seventy years—seem to have been any important ritual or ceremonial practices or activities connected with the totem animal. And there is in general a rather casual air about the whole matter of clan and clanship, a casualness which appears to be so well established that I am not powerfully inclined to doubt the accuracy of my informants when they tell me that it was "always" the same. Few people even know the clan of some of their close friends.

It is only within the past few years that there has been a revived interest in clans and in *boriosiek* (regiments or phratries) in certain parts of the Reserve. This interest stems from the political activities of a particular chief who has chosen to use these social groupings, readapted to contemporary purposes, for enhancing his personal prestige and power. I shall discuss later the implications of this phenomenon as a modern device for extending one's influence outside *kokwet* and local areas.

The exogamous functions of the clans seem to have persisted in what must have been their aboriginal force fairly unchanged until today. It sometimes happens, however, that in the greater haste of these times a marriage will take place between a man and woman of the same clan, an occurrence which is not remarkable considering the generally relaxed feeling about clan identity that prevails. Thus, the couple may or may not have been aware of this in advance. In any case, when the situation is discovered, all that needs be done is for the man to allow himself to be adopted into another clan. His children will be identified with that clan.

One other function of the clan which was formerly of great importance, but seems now to be diminishing under the influence of certain cash considerations, is that of collective responsibility for the actions of any clan individual. A homicide within the tribe (or one involving another of the Kalenjin-speaking peoples with whom the Kipsigis are friendly, e.g., the Nandi) demands compensation (*moget*) in the form of cattle—a specified number for a man, or woman or child. It is the responsibility of the clan of the man who committed the crime to make restitution to the clan of the victim. Distribution of the blood cattle is then made by the clan of the murdered man with most of the cattle going to his male relatives or to his widow to be held in trust for present or subsequent male heirs.[2]

Nowadays the clan members, who are widely scattered throughout the Reserve and outside, try to avoid their responsibility and shift the burden to the family of the culprit if this is possible. Another interesting modification of the practice of paying *wergild* as compensation for the killing of a tribesman was instituted by the colonial government several years ago with the establishment of Border Committees to settle cattle-stealing disputes between the Kipsigis and their Masai, Luo, and Kisii neighbors.

Government representatives meet with each of these tribes several times a year to try to secure an accounting and to extract payment for animals that have been stolen by members of both tribes. Usually the individual is billed for the theft. In the case of the Kipsigis, if a man fails to make good, his *kokwet* will be held responsible. The *kokwet* elders will, in turn, try to extract the money from the man's clan. But this, I am told, is always a most difficult proposition, and pressures are therefore more commonly applied to the man's father or *closest* male relatives. Finally, there is an occasional homicide committed in the course of these sporadic raids. Compensation for the killing of a man—either a member of the raiding party or of the tribe which is being victimized—has been set by the government at 2,000 shillings. Clan responsibility is assumed, but the backlog of unpaid compensation is testimony to the general ineffective-

[2] A form of the levirate is practiced in which all subsequent children of the widow and her late husband's brother continue to identify the deceased husband of their mother as their father.

ness of this "traditional" responsibility in the present—or at least in the altered context of the responsibility. The payment of compensation to such traditional enemies as the Masai, Luo, and Kisii is a striking departure from custom and an enforced alteration of one of the major criteria by which we have often identified the primitive tribal unit (Evans-Pritchard, 1940a, p. 278). By government edict, and as an act implementing the Pax Britannica, tribal distinctions are showing signs of becoming blurred. I shall have more to say later on about the import of these changing relationships between ancient enemies.

THE *BORIET*

Every member of the Kipsigis tribe belongs also to one of four *boriosiek* referred to earlier (p. 244, *supra*). I have suggested that these units might be called phratries rather than regiments, as they are usually designated. However, since phratries are generally defined as units of linked clans, it may be difficult to justify the use of this word, but I believe it is more appropriate than regiments, and I prefer it to the sib or clan designation used by Pilgrim (1959) and Towett (1956). There is some historical support for the belief that each *boriet* was actually once a single clan, then a localized group of linked clans before it became what it is today. To refer to these *boriosiek* as clans or sibs today and to what I have called clans as subclans or subsibs seems to me somewhat confusing. For the *boriet* has neither the totemic nor even the minimal marriage-regulating features which we commonly if not universally associate with clans. Nor is it involved in *wergild* payments. In short, it shows few features of clanship in the present or in the late pre-contact period. Since most clans *tend* even now to be identified with one or another *boriet*, the term phratry, with all its shortcomings, seems preferable to clan and even to regiment, for each *boriet* also had certain ritual functions of a non-military nature which it performed as a unit on such occasions as the annual ceremonial of public worship (*kapkoros*).

The *boriosiek* are neither endogamous nor exogamous, and not only their origin but their functioning in the remote past is shrouded in uncertainty. It is alleged in one of the stories most favored by Kipsigis with whom I have discussed the matter that the four phratries, Ng'etunyo, Kebeni, Kipkaige, and Kasanet, were established by four brothers "very long ago." It is uncertain whether they were originally exogamous and later endogamous or not, but as time passed they grew so large that the descendents of each of the founders began to refer to themselves by the name of an ancestor less remote than he. In this manner, it is believed, were established the subdivisions which ultimately became recognized as clans. Originally, then, and until fairly recent times most clans were identified with a particular *boriet*. But intermarriage among the *boriosiek* has become so common that members of all clans may now be found in each of them. A woman who marries a man from a different *boriet* than her own automatically becomes a member of her husband's *boriet*, and even "after death her spirit belongs to her husband's line of descent."

Sometimes the four *boriosiek* are regrouped into two moieties, one being known as the "fortunates" and the other as the "unfortunates." Kipkaige and Ng'etunyo form one of these moieties and Kebeni and Kasanet the other. Since their functions in the past became largely military, the designation of fortunate or unfortunate applies to the frequency with which fortune favored or failed to favor the paired regiments on their raiding and military missions. Members of both moieties have regaled me with stories of the treachery of the other, and there is even now a residue of animosity and ill-feeling sometimes discernible between them. I believe this potential for conflict of interest is presently being exploited and revived under the influence of the chief referred to earlier. I would guess that the conflict may sharpen in the immediate future and that it will have certain divisive effects within the tribe; but that it will in the longer run—and this is only a seeming paradox—produce forces, groupings, and leaders of these groupings which will serve to advance the Kipsigis in sophistication and understanding and to sharpen the political weapons which will make the tribe *as a whole* much more effective in its efforts to wrest concessions from the departing colonial administration and to play its part in African politics in independent Kenya. In 1960, the Kalenjin Political Association, a union of most of the Kalenjin-speaking tribes of Kenya, was formed, partly under the aegis and through the influence of a few Kipsigis leaders, one of whom is this chief. The alliance holds a leading place in the Kenya African Democratic Union which is presently (January, 1962) the party of the government in Kenya.

There is general agreement among the Kipsigis that the regiments were originally associated with geographical areas, with the Kasanet-Kebeni people forming the bulk of the population to the north and northwest, while Ng'etunyo-Kipkaige were those who settled to the south in the area called Sot. In any case, the regiments, before pacification, went into battle in separate files (a *kwanet*) so that there might be no dispute over the spoils. Peristiany tells us that a severe defeat of Kipsigis by the Kisii at the battle of Ngoino led to a re-examination of the practice and it was thenceforth decided that each *kwanet* must contain elements from all four of the regiments or phratries (1939, pp. 163-64). On ceremonial occasions, however, the *boriosiek* still retained their separation.

AUTHORITY PATTERNS

Before the coming of the British the Kipsigis had no chiefs. The closest approximation to chiefs were the military leaders (*kiptainik*) whose functions were limited to activities in warfare and raiding. Naturally these military leaders were men of some stature in the community, but their powers outside of battle were completely *ad hoc* and without any formal sanctions, involving only the giving of advice. In this regard their opinions in everyday problems and disputes are of far less importance than those of the *boyosiek*, or elderly leaders, and the *kiruogik*, or so-called judges of the *kokwotinwek*.

In short, while there were "judges" who performed their functions within a group of adjacent *kokwotinwek*, and while some of the elders were also sought for their opinions in disputes, there appears never to have been any overall binding political organization which embraced the Kipsigis as a whole or which subjected them to some centralized individual or council authority. The only occasions on which tribal organization seems to have appeared was in the *kapkoros* ceremony and in the prosection of offensive raids and war against other tribes. Even here we cannot be altogether sure that all or almost all of the Kipsigis warriors were ever involved in a single engagement. In any case, the organization was fleeting and disappeared with the end of the military venture, the authority of those who had been in control of the activity (the *kiptainik*) terminating with the return from the foray and the division of the spoils.

There was one man who served as an important military leader (*kiptaet*) among the Ng'etunyo shortly before the arrival of the British, and who was referred to by two of the old men with whom I talked as a "chief of the Kipsigis." His name was arap Kisiara,[3] and he is alleged to have been instrumental in forging a temporary peace with the Masai (which was shortly violated by some ambi-

[3] Matson (personal communication) suggests that Kisiara—or Kisharia—is probably the Menyakishavia with whom Jackson signed a treaty (African Affairs Library documents, Nairobi) and made blood brotherhood in Kipsigis country on October 13, 1889 (Jackson, 1930, p. 211).

tious Kipsigis warriors, much to the embarrassment of Kisiara). It was said by these old men that Kisiara was a chief because, before the incident which discredited him, no warriors would have raided enemy territory without first receiving permission from Kisiara. When questioned more closely on this point, however, my informants agreed that Kipsigis warriors living in areas contiguous to Masai, Luo, or Kisii would, in all probability, not have delayed an inspiration to conduct a raid while they sought Kisiara's permission.

It seems likely, then, that even when Kisiara was at the height of his power, the older-type cattle forays continued under the sanction and guidance of purely local leaders. On the other hand, a new pattern of military organization may actually have come into existence—or been revived—during the last two or three decades of the nineteenth century. This may have involved much larger groups of warriors and more highly centralized control under a single leader. We know, for example, that the disastrous defeat and slaughter of the Kipsigis that took place in Kisii country during this period involved many hundreds—some say thousands—of Kipsigis warriors in a truly major military operation. If small raids rather than massed warfare were the pattern before this, as all of the information available suggests, then we must look to other late pre-European circumstances for an explanation of this postulated development in military behavior. It is suggested by Matson (personal communication) that while the number of Arab caravans passing through Kipsigis country may never have been large, it was during this period that the traffic reached its peak. These incursions may very well have produced a sharp increase in aggressions from both the Arab and the Kipsigis sides. Patterns of warfare appropriate to the traditional intertribal cattle raids might have proved inadequate in the new circumstances which could have demanded more highly centralized controls.

Many interesting parallels of this kind—the emergence of new and more complex forms of military and social organization under the pressure of unaccustomed hostile or other intervention—are reported not only for other areas in Africa but from the New World as well. Formerly dispersed settlements, lineages, and villages have been welded into large bands, tribes, or nations under a centralized military and sometimes civil authority. Often this has resulted from threats to territory and subsistence posed by an intrusive power (e.g., Ndebele); sometimes by the competition with other aboriginal groups for new areas to exploit in response to the trading demands of the intruder (e.g., Iroquois); and sometimes, as may have been the case with the Kipsigis, in an effort to provide a more effective structure for defense and predation vis-à-vis the intruders (e.g., Northern Paiute or Apache). Naturally these "response-activities" are not always distinct from each other. Defense, offense, predation, and new forms of exploitation usually are intermingled in the behavior of formerly segmented communities as they unite in various ways when confronted by the challenge of Western interventionists. Often, too, they fail to unite, or having been united, they sometimes have disintegrated under these pressures. But in the case of the Kipsigis, the evidence available suggests that for at least a brief period they may have increased the size of their tactical military force even if there was not time for the emergence of a parallel civil structure. With defensive and offensive behavior channeled into somewhat different lines by the appearance of Arab traders in their territory, it is conceivable that a local military leader with a special talent for leadership might come to exercise temporary control over the military activities of larger numbers of warriors and over a much wider area than had been customary. In this way, Kisiara or someone like him could have gained such reknown in the period just before the coming of the railroad that to some Kipsigis his image conformed with the idea of tribal chief as one now thinks of the term.

However, there is no evidence that he was in fact a chief of all the Kipsigis in all parts of the territory, or that there was even remotely the kind of political structure within Kipsigis society which could have made such chieftanship possible, especially in affairs of a non-military nature. It is possible that a political hierarchy based on the emergence of a dominant phratry or moiety or some other segment of Kipsigis society might ultimately have developed in the absence of white encroachment and in response to increasing pressures from enemies outside. And it is possible further that such a structure might have been dominated by a chief with strong powers in matters of both a military and non-military nature. But it is certain that this had not developed among the Kipsigis prior to the turn of the century, and that there was no machinery either of communication or control which could have made it possible for one man to direct the destinies of the Kipsigis in war and in peace. I think we must dismiss Kisiara as a possible pre-contact candidate for chieftanship, while we admit that he must have been a person of considerable stature and personal charisma to have left the image —with even a few people—that he was truly a chief of *all* the Kipsigis.

I have suggested earlier that the minimum effective political unit among the Kipsigis was the *kokwet* or neighborhood group and that leadership within these *kokwotinwek* was exercised ad hoc by a council of elders. Among these was usually one outstanding elder to whom others might often defer and who, in the absence of a full council meeting, served most often as informal advisor in disputes. For most peaceful purposes, indeed, it may be said that the *kokwet* was not only the minimal but the maximal effective political unit, although clans, phratries, and moieties appear to have exercised sporadic regulatory and guiding functions chiefly in the ways in which I have already specified.

LINEAGE

Before turning to a brief discussion of the family I should like to insert a few comments about the lineage among the Kipsigis. I would say that the lineage—maximal, minimal, segmentary, or otherwise —does not seem to have exercised any corporate functions whatsoever. The various activities and responsibilities assigned to lineages of all kinds in other parts of the continent were distributed, in Kipsigis, among the age-set, *kokwet*, *boriet*, clan, and family.

Neither Towett (1956), Anderson (n.d.), nor Orchardson (1937 and Matson, 1961), in their discussions of social forms and organization, describes a corporate entity which could properly be labeled a lineage. Lineages, in a purely mechanical or descriptive sense, can, of course, be found among the Kipsigis. But they can not be identified in the several functional senses in which they have been found and described elsewhere by anthropologists. I believe that the combination of frequent and essential neolocality after marriage, plus the contingent judicial powers of the *kokwet* elders and the obligations of age-set membership, in combination, tended to inhibit the appearance of strong clan or lineage attachments. It is possible— even while it seems a paradox—that the functions of the lineage, *qua* lineage, were much more significant in former times when the Kipsigis were more mobile and nomadic, more fully dependent upon their flocks and herds than they are today. In the present, however, and in the memory of living informants, there is no evidence that the term lineage, as applied to the Kipsigis, has any particular analytic significance.

For example, Orchardson (Matson, 1961, p. 10), in his discussion of "the various institutions and groupings which go to make up Kipsigis society," outlines them as follows: "The groupings in order of magnitude, though by no means in order of importance, are: (1) the *puriet* (pl. *puriosiek*) [*boriet* and *boriosiek*] or army group; (2) the *ipinda* (pl. *ipinwek*) or age set; (3) the *oret* (pl. *ortinwek*) or clan; (4) the *kokwet* (pl. *kokwotinwek*) or social group; and (5) the family. These groups all overlap and cross-cut each other; e.g., a member of any clan may be a member of any *puriet*, or age set, or *kokwet*. Even members of the same family may be of different *puriosiek*, different age sets and different *kokwotinwek*. Even different clans are brought together by the groupings, as the wife's relations must be of a different clan from that of the husband, although her relations form a part of the family group. All sections of the tribe are held together by this interweaving."

While it is possible that Orchardson would have been familiar with the term "lineage," it is quite clear from the discussion which follows these comments, and particularly from his analysis of the family's functions, that the form of the Kipsigis lineage was not accompanied by any of the varied regulatory functions usually assigned to it. Finally, it should be noted that Evans-Pritchard (1940b), drawing largely upon Peristiany's published (1939) and unpublished materials, concludes: "Neither the Kipsigis clan nor the Kipsigis subclan was a lineage. . . . The clans of the . . . Kipsigis . . . were not, nor were any of their segments, co-ordinated with local groups . . . they had not a lineage structure, but a different form of segmentation" (pp. 259, 265-66). Bernardi goes further than this for the Nilo-Hamitic societies as a group: "Kinship, lineage, and clan have practically no political importance" (1952, pp. 331-32).

THE FAMILY

Undoubtedly more significant to the Kipsigis in his daily life than any of the other social groupings of which he was a part were his patrilineal families of orientation and procreation. These could be either monogamous or polygynous. As far as I can determine, postmarital residence was often patrilocal, although full neolocality, initial neolocality, and even matrilocality occurred. There were no rigid rules governing residence. The sometimes changing composition of the *kokwet*, the grazing requirements of the sheep, goats, and home-based cattle, the patterns of shifting cultivation, and the common practice of moving one's residence after some calamity or series of hardships—all of these, plus the relative plenty of unsettled or unused land, combined to foster flexibility in family residence.

Decisions about residence, as about most other matters, were in the hands of the male. Apart from the fact that there must be a separate house for each wife there were no requirements governing how the man disposed his time among his wives. The favorite wife —and she need not be the first—was known as the *kerotyet* or best loved. The number of wives a man had depended strictly upon his capacity for paying a bride-price for each and his contingent ability to support them with the animals belonging to him or remaining to his dependable use. Although polygynous marriages are not at all uncommon today, they were apparently more common in aboriginal times and before pacification tended to offset the imbalance between males and females in the tribal population. In certain areas of the Reserve the number of plural marriages is said to average almost half of the total. Where I have been able to check into the matter I have myself encountered an average of about 35 to 40 per cent plural marriages for a group of males in two contiguous *kokwotinwek*. Whatever the true figures may be—and estimates given me by a series of informants range pretty widely—there is general agreement that the custom is on the decline. This owes, I believe, not only to the influence of the missions but to a combination of other factors as well, including land pressure, interest in education (which costs money), and the not insignificant force of emulation of European patterns of formal monogamy.

Cattle for the bride-price were formerly accumulated by the young warrior in raids on other tribes or with occasional assistance from his father or older brothers, and always with the help of bride-price cattle which had been paid to his father for his own sisters. In fact these latter cattle were unequivocally reserved for this purpose and could be withheld by the father only under the most extreme circumstances of want, and then for just a limited time.

Each wife had her own patch of land which was devoted to the cultivation of millet—sometimes mixed with sorghum—and a plot close to the house where she might grow some of the spinach-like vegetables and some calabashes. If the land was virgin land or land occupied by heavy brush or trees, it was the job of the husband to clear it. Grass, light brush, and grazed or cropped land needed no preliminary clearing, and it was then the woman's job to prepare the field for planting by turning the sods with her hoe. These were later piled, and when dry enough were fired, the ashes being subsequently scattered over the field. This is a method of preparation still used for the planting of millet only. The soil for maize is almost invariably prepared by plowing, and the sods are never burned.

In the preparation of the field and in the harvest, a woman could usually depend upon the help of other women from her *kokwet*. She, in turn, assisted them in the preparation of their fields. Girls and young children would always help with the weeding (*waet*), but this was often a household or family affair and did not depend upon cooperative labor. I will return later to the matter of cooperative labor itself and associated activities in the present, indicating some of the changes that have taken place and the presumed reasons therefor.

Care of the family's goats and the sheep, which almost invariably outnumbered the cattle owned by any individual, was assigned to the young boys and, less often, to the girls. The cattle that were pastured in the vicinity of the house (*mossop*) rather than some distance from the house in the common grazing area (*kaptich*) were also supervised by very young boys and old men. Formerly, no woman was allowed to milk the cows; menstruating women were not even supposed to go near cattle.

A young father might accompany his own cattle to the grazing areas. As he got older and as his sons grew up, he would generally remain at home and they would be sent to these areas to care for and to guard the cattle. Sometimes if a man were rich he would engage other young warriors who had few or no cattle of their own to care for his cattle in the common grazing grounds. His own sons, if he had any, might then remain at home. Or, if a man had several sons these might rotate in their guard duties away from home. In any case, distinctions of privilege in terms of wealth seem to have an ancient background among the Kipsigis, for it is alleged that there were always young warriors available whose own poverty made them more than willing to take on the job of minding another man's cattle. They were paid off with an ample supply of milk from the cows under their care and sometimes with the gift of a heifer or two and possibly a young bull with which they might start their own herd.

The head of the family (or families) whose wealth and/or grown sons made his own presence in the remote pasture area superfluous had very little work to perform at home. He might take a hand in the harvesting of his wives' millet, and he would help in the heavier jobs of clearing. Sometimes he would visit the grazing areas to see how his cattle were doing. But much of the rest of his time was spent in the company of other men similarly situated in his own or adjacent *kokwotinwek*. They would sit around the beer pot talking and sucking beer through their six- to ten-foot tubes (*rogorosiek*) until it was time to go home. The young men who were not serving their stints in the grazing areas were sometimes allowed to attend these "beer parties" too, but they were expected to remain discreetly in the background during the discussions.

The beer parties still exist today, although they are not so frequent nor so widespread as they once were. The young men must still be restrained in the presence of the old men (*boyosiek*). But they are no longer so restricted in their social activities by this exclusion. For a good many of them now drink their beer out of bottles in the company of other young men who also have acquired the cash, by one means or another, with which to buy European beer, in bars and shops throughout the Reserve. Moreover, at their beer parties, these young men talk about different matters from those which generally occupied their parents or grandparents.

The beer parties of the past were ritualized activities through which the heads of families affirmed their status, and, directly or indirectly, asserted the significance of traditional tribal values. To the extent that these activities persist they continue to support the same values and to serve the same functions. They are still a considerable conservative force in Kipsigis society. But the young unmarried sons and the newly married who have now been relieved of their guarding and raiding functions by the Pax Britannica and other influences which both attract and employ them are no longer outsiders or peripheral elements in the social activities from which change may be encouraged or impeded. These drinkers of the new beer—who may still be excluded from or shunted aside in the old beer parties—dedicate their ritual parties not to adoration of the past but to exploration of ideas for the future, not to the preservation of what they have (or, as they put it, what they have not) but to its destruction and replacement with something—many things—else. These young men have not only been freed of the cattle-nursing activities which consumed all of the time of their ancestral counterparts, but they have been given a forum from which to discuss the ideas which the liberation and the new education have revealed to them in the context of their changing world. It would have mattered very little if the young men of the past had been permitted greater freedom of discussion in the beer parties of their day. For there would have been little or nothing in the world of which they were a part to stimulate them to thoughts of far-reaching change. More raids, more cattle, more leisure, more beer. These were the things the heads of families talked about, and they would have been the things the young men would themselves have approved had they been allowed to. The pattern of affirmation was generally well fixed in these gatherings, and remains largely so even today. Generally speaking, then, the old beer parties do not provide an atmosphere conducive to talk of change or revolt against conditions and the assumed or real authors of these conditions.

Certainly the young men, educated, liberated, and confronted by an amazing new world would, in the absence of beer and beer shops, have found other places and other means of expressing their wonder, their plans and their prospects in this changing world. For young men caught up in this phenomenon in other places in Africa and elsewhere in the less developed parts of the world are finding things to talk and think about and ways of doing both, sometimes without the beer. But for the Kipsigis and some of these others there is at once an aptness and a cultural impropriety in the drinking of beer and the animated talk of change which so often dominates the conversation at these new rituals. It is, one may say, a kind of new wine in old bottles, except that in the case of the Kipsigis even the bottles are brand new. And they have set aside forever the slow, sucking tube.

THE AGE-SET

There is at least one other social grouping, the age-set, whose importance, especially in the past, has been stressed by Peristiany (1939), and Orchardson (1937 and Matson, 1961) for the Kipsigis; by Huntingford (1953a, b, c), and Hollis (1909) for the Nandi; by Prins (1953) for the Kipsigis, Kikuyu, and Galla; by Gulliver (1952 and 1958), Bernardi (1952), and others for these and different tribes. In fact, though a great deal has been written about these groupings in Africa, there are certain differences among them, even within the Kalenjin-speaking groups, which make it difficult to generalize about their functions. Moreover, they seem to have been altered under the impact of generally changing conditions so that it is difficult to reconstruct their true aboriginal nature. Briefly, however, there is among the Kipsigis a cycle of seven age-sets (*ipinwek*) which succeed each other in regular order. According to Peristiany and Huntingford (for the Nandi) each *ipinda* or age-set lasts for fifteen years. Hollis (1909) suggests seven and a half years for the Nandi. Orchardson sets the duration for the Kipsigis and the Nandi at twenty-one years. My own inquiries, I must confess, yielded some further confusion and led me to the belief that the figure probably has a great deal more flexibility than has previously been suggested; in short, that an age-set may last fifteen years or may go on for something over twenty. In any case, I consider the matter of no overwhelming importance so far as traditional and contemporary functioning of the institution is concerned.

Each of the age-sets is further divided into subsets which apparently had some significance formerly but are now rarely referred to. Age-sets seem to have functioned most importantly in the regulation of marriage (i.e., a man could only marry the daughter of a man of the age-set above him or the one below him, never the daughter of a man of his own age-set) and in determining the main membership of the warrior class. For while it is sometimes asserted that the warriors were all of one age-set among Kalenjin-speaking peoples, this was not the case with the Kipsigis. Naturally the larger part of any military expedition would normally consist of individuals from a single age-set because they composed the bulk of the active adult male population. But men of an older generation usually went along—especially on important campaigns—and these might often serve as the *kiptainik* or leaders of these expeditions, for seniority itself bestows privileges and powers among the Kipsigis. And younger men of the technically non-warrior age-set also accompanied these excursions.

Normally, too, relations between members of the same age-set would be much closer than those between members of adjacent age-sets or others further removed. A man could count on hospitalities from the members of his own age-set which he could not expect from those in others. These were the formal ways in which the internal bonds of the age-set were strengthened. And it is certain that the links among members were strong, persisting and making themselves felt clearly in ordinary social relationships even today. But if one recollects the expanse of years that embraced a single age-set —and here I believe we must reckon with a minimum of fifteen— one can see very readily that sometimes there might be considerable difficulty in maintaining close social ties between members at either extreme of a given age-set. In point of fact, I have been assured that these mechanical distinctions in set affiliation were often overridden in the conduct of daily life. This is not to say that regulations of hospitality, marriage, and the forms of behavior appropriate to members of one's own or an age-set different from one's own were lightly set aside in favor of the facts of chronological contiguity. This is not so. The more important forms were maintained, but they did not come incongruously to dominate all events in the daily social round.

We must, I think, remember always the importance of the elders in *kokwet* and supra-*kokwet* activities. For even if the warrior age-set had great status it did not dominate tribal affairs nor did it, in effect, have the same voice in decision-making as that of the age-sets senior to it. In fact, as I have implied above in my discussion of beer-drinking, in all matters not involving the direct conduct of raids or warfare, the warriors were expected to remain discreetly in the background and, in general, to be deferential in their attitude towards their elders.

One can see persistences of this behavior in Kipsigis even today. But new elements of assertion—sometimes in conflict, sometimes in harmony—have arisen in recent years, and new patterns of behavior appropriate to the new situations seem rapidly to be replacing the older and more restrained forms of dialogue between the warrior group and their elders under certain conditions.

On the traditional side, I had the good fortune to be an involved witness to a couple of events which illustrate the prestige and the power of the elders—at least as they are still exercised in certain matters of a non-secular nature. Shortly after I had arrived in Kipsigis country on my first field trip, it was time for the annual initiation and circumcision ceremonies for the boys to begin. I asked my warrior-age assistant to intervene on my behalf with the members of his *kokwet* so that I might be permitted to see these ceremonies. He arranged for a *baraza* (Kiswahili for a meeting, discussion) to be held at the home of the father of one of the initiates, a close friend of my interpreter. Some forty men finally gathered and we sat on the ground in a circle. I spoke a few halting words, introducing myself and stating why I wanted to witness the ceremonies and adding how appreciative I would be of the honor and trust bestowed upon me if I should have my request granted. Then my assistant stood up and in very eloquent terms, and for some fifteen minutes, stated the case for allowing me to watch and record the ceremonies. After he sat down two old men talked briefly—and negatively—(I won't repeat the arguments used on either side for they are not relevant here), my interpreter offered a brief but calm rebuttal, and then we waited for someone else to get up. The father of the boy had invited me and wanted me to be allowed to attend, but he said nothing. After a while my assistant said there was no point in hoping any longer for expressions of support, so I stood up and went into the nearby hut to join the men in their beer-drinking. Some time later we left and were on the way back to the road when we were joined by a group of young men (in their twenties and early thirties) who had been present at the meeting. They assured us that they had wanted to intervene on my behalf but had been deterred by the strong stand of the old men and the fear of supernatural consequences if they crossed them in this important ritual matter.

A few days later, and still in pursuit of the privilege of witnessing the ceremonies, I enlisted the aid of the senior chief of the Kipsigis who had by this time "adopted" me into his clan. He is himself an elderly man, and I accepted his assurances that he would be able to help me witness an initiation ceremony in a *kokwet* near his home. But when he called in the elders of the *kokwet*—in my presence—and asked their permission they were adamant. Despite all his pleas and the added persuasion of his son (at that time a president of one of the District African courts in the Reserve) the old men remained firm. Finally the chief drew me aside, and with not a small sense of humiliation, confessed himself powerless to override the wishes of the elders in a matter of this kind.

One of the curious features of both occasions was the lack of any real dispute or argumentation. My backers stated the case, listened attentively to the denials and the explanations of the old men, and then tried to restate the case in somewhat different words. There was never any attempt to browbeat or to suggest that the unusual nature of the request ought not to be treated with a routine denial. In short, there was no sign that anyone questioned the right of the old men to make the decision or that force could or would be applied to obtain a reversal. My supporters only asked in my behalf that a favor be granted out of the elders' generosity of heart.

The other side of the coin, however, may be seen in the increasing frequency with which matters of a secular nature become subjects for open debate at *barazas* between the elders and members of the warrior age-set. Under the relatively static conditions which prevailed in pre-contact times, the range of subjects about which there might conceivably have been some dispute must have been fairly narrow. Today, under the impact of changing conditions and the demands and needs nurtured by money and the products of industrial civilization, the areas of potential disagreement between young and old are far greater. And the formal and informal occasions for dispute have consequently multiplied. Moreover, while the authority of the elders, the *kiptainik*, or military leaders, and the *kiruogik*, or judges, has declined sharply under the combined assault of an expanding material universe and the constrictions of British administration, the voice of the younger and educated—those who are better equipped to understand and to deal with the new—has grown louder, firmer, and more insistent than ever before.

Formerly, the old men knew virtually everything there was to know and, in an unchanging cultural environment, had lived through the phases which those younger than themselves were passing. This is no longer true. It is the young men now growing up who understand much more about the new, changing world than their elders. Whole realms of experience and knowledge are opening up to these young men while their elders generally remain without the tools of understanding required to face and to deal with the problems raised by the new experience and the new knowledge.

Thus, I have witnessed *barazas* dealing with a wide range of topics, from the plans for student gardens in an intermediate school to the virtues of communal cattle dips and the dangers of allowing a mission station to construct a hydroelectric system for generating limited amounts of power for its hospital and school. In most of these it is always the young men who speak up, the young men who are articulate in support or criticism while the elders sit, for the most part, and learn from them what are the issues in this bewildering new world. One such *baraza*—the one dealing with the mission's attempt to convert water power into electricity—was a prime example of the power of the young men to make decisions that involved the welfare of large parts of the tribe. I won't go into the details of the particular case, for it has a complicated history. But the gist of its significance for the issue under examination lies in the fact that many of the benefits of the scheme would presumably have fallen to the Kipsigis in the form of lower hospital charges, etc. In the discussion, young and old alike played on the theme of deceit: time and again in the past when the tribe had "agreed" to certain measures proposed and supported by the administration, the results had proved either catastrophic or at least contrary to their best interests as they conceived these. In rejoinder, European spokesmen for the government admitted that there may have been past disappointments, and the missionaries confessed that there may have been cause in the past to question the good faith of the Europeans or whites (*chumbek*). But they offered every opportunity to the tribe and its representatives to prepare a contract which would guarantee no loss to themselves (the tribe) and would pave the way for an inexpensive transfer of control of the system to the Kipsigis whenever they could pay off the actual costs of construction. Naturally there were many reservations—voiced and implied—in the attitude of the Kipsigis speakers and the spectators. But, generally speaking, I detected, as the discussion developed, a growing disposition on the part of the Kipsigis in attendance to think the matter over, until one of the young warriors made an eloquent plea for denial of the mission request on the grounds that if the project was a good one for generating electric power inexpensively, the tribe itself should undertake the expense of construction of the system and then sell the power to the mission station—and, as an afterthought, anyone else who wanted to buy it.

The old men and the partisans of the mission cause retreated in disorder, for there was no satisfactory way to rebut the appeal to a tribal scheme for making money. "It will not be long," the speaker said, "before we have our own trained Kipsigis engineers [4] who will build and run such a scheme for us. Why should we give this opportunity for making money to the mission?" This pecuniary pie in the sky, as it were, has an unanswerable appeal in the present, for money is the means to acquisition of many desirable things. It is the young men who know about this matter, hence it is far better to listen to their advice than that of the "old men of the beer and the *rogoret*" (sucking tube), for what can they—the old men—know of such things?

One has only to attend the periodic sessions of the Kipsigis African District Council (the part-elected, part-appointed "legislative" body for the tribe) to see the new strength of the young men exercised in council with elders whom they would not heretofore have dared to oppose, in order to understand the significance of the shift that has been taking place in the locus of authority. Here, among the twenty-four members are representatives of several age-sets, but it is the younger men who set the tone of discussion, the younger men who dominate the decision-making in a way which would have been incomprehensible thirty or forty years ago. Knowledge—however imperfect and limited, however hampered by inadequate understandings and insufficient access to information—knowledge, or better, assumed knowledge of the new and its processes is the key which explains the increasing ascendancy of the young Kipsigis over the old in the secularized universe of the 1960's.

LAIBON OR HEREDITARY SORCERERS

I stated earlier that the Kipsigis probably never had chiefs or "kings." But there was for a time in their history a class of individuals, the *orgoik*, who had considerable status and who acquired great power over the Kipsigis in a variety of ways. I have reserved

[4] One Kipsigis in a population of over 200,000 has a university degree, and he earned this by correspondence from South Africa.

mention of these for the concluding paragraphs of this section on social forms not only because this group appears to have come on the scene in fairly recent times,[5] but because the source of their power was purely supernatural and because its exercise was desultory, unstructured, and operative in ways and in realms somewhat different from those to which we are accustomed when we think of the activities and the functions of secular and/or sacred rulers. These *orgoik* or *laibon* were, in effect, witches or sorcerers who came to be known by the Kipsigis as "the owners of the country" because they could make extraordinary demands upon individual Kipsigis and expect that these would be met for fear that failure to comply would result in death, disease, disaster, or that the *orgoyot* (sing.) would devour them. Although each of these sorcerers exercised a kind of dominion over a particular geographic area, he did not perform those functions of organization and control which we customarily subsume under political or governmental activities. No sorcerer was ruler of the others, although all of them originally belonged to a single clan, Talai. Since sorcerers were customarily polygynous, and since the status was inherited by all male descendants, the number of these in Kipsigis country was considerable and continued to increase until the time of their removal to Gwassi in 1934-36.

Although the matter is surrounded with considerable uncertainty, it is generally believed that the *laibon* originated with the Masai and ultimately came to the Nandi. As a consequence of mounting suspicion, envy, and a series of difficulties within the Nandi tribe, it is said that they drove most of the *laibon* out and that some of these settled among the Kipsigis. This may have happened sometime in the last two or three decades of the nineteenth century, certainly no earlier than that. It appears also that this was a most propitious moment for their acceptance by the Kipsigis, for there had been a series of military reverses, and the elders and the leaders of the regiments had decided that these misfortunes were due to the generally anarchic nature of raiding activities which prevailed at that time. They recommended that the autonomy of each regiment be limited in the interest of the whole and that in future any proposed military action be undertaken on a cooperative basis only. But the formal instrumentality for forging these links among the different segments did not exist. Consequently the decision of the elders and the regimental commanders effectively weakened the power of the latter

[5] Orchardson (1935) says the *orgoik* may have existed earlier, but believes they were less significant before the Talai clan "from Nandi and Masai" came to Kipsigis in the "1880 decade."

without substituting an instrument to implement the projected cooperative efforts.[6] A kind of general power vacuum was thus created, and, it is alleged, the *laibon* who appeared on the scene at that moment stepped into the breach.

By degrees, and as these sorcerers grew in number and influence, they began to function as advisers, prophets, and petty tyrants of a kind. They predicted the coming of natural catastrophes, defeat or success in battle, feast or famine, and so on. From prediction it was not always an impossible step to the creation and control of some of these events or happenings. Consequently the people came to fear the power of the *laibon* in all matters. The latter, in turn, used their powers to improve their material and marital circumstances. They were feted royally whenever they appeared as guests in a man's house; and often they departed with a gift of the finest heifer in the host's herd.

The sorcerers also extracted their portion of the millet harvest from each family in their domain. It was this tribute which was converted into beer to provide drink for their many beer parties. They also took tribute from the warriors after a successful cattle raid, for they had not only given their blessing to the raiders but had predicted the success of the enterprise and forecast a description of some of the cattle that would be taken. The cattle which conformed to this description were then turned over to them as their share of the loot.

Polygyny was simplified for the *laibon*, too, because a Kipsigis father was afraid to deny his daughter to the *laibon* who requested her. It is also alleged that no one would think of demanding a bride-price (*kanyook*) of cattle or sheep from a *laibon* in exchange for his daughter. The *laibon*'s messengers (*maotik*) were an important instrumentality aiding the *laibon* in their contact with, control over, or exploitation of the Kipsigis. It is significant that Towett (1956) sees the work of these messengers as comparable to that of the chiefs in contemporary Kipsigis society, for they are the link between the administrators and the people. They told the people what the *laibon* expected of them, and they reported back to the *laibon* on the behavior and the reactions of the people.

When the British first came to Kipsigis country, and for a time afterwards, they did not attempt to remove the sorcerers but, on the contrary, invited them to participate in *barazas* along with the

[6] See pp. 249-50, *supra*, for a discussion of the role of Kisiara, who may actually have forged some kind of more effective military cooperation, at least for a time.

newly appointed chiefs. In time, however, it became apparent that the *laibon* could not be utilized to unify the Kipsigis under British dominion but that they were a potent force for disruption, that they not only opposed and sabotaged government efforts but that they were preaching and predicting a kind of nativistic resurgence—a day when the Europeans would leave the country to the Kipsigis. To this end they gathered firearms and urged people to make many bows and arrows. It is not known whether they expected to be able to defeat the Europeans on the day of reckoning or whether, as I have been told, they preached simply that the Europeans would leave Kenya and that the Kipsigis must be prepared to defend themselves against the other tribes when the Pax Britannica ended. In any case they proved a constant trial to the administration and were in large part responsible for the heavy turnover in appointed chiefs during those years. Finally, in 1934-36, after a great many homes of anti-*laibon*, or "Christianized" Kipsigis, had been burned, the government rounded up all of the *laibon* and sent them off to Gwassi in South Nyanza. By 1962 all but a tiny handful of hard-core sorcerers had been returned to the District, where they were issued special passes and kept under very close surveillance. The condition of many of them now living in Kericho township is described as deplorable by some members of the Kipsigis African District Council. My own observations support these comments, since many of the returnees are without funds, without jobs, and without land.

It is conceivable that the *laibon*'s growth and influence, had they been allowed to develop unchecked by the arrival of the British, might have eventuated in centralization of power and political controls in the hands of the Talai clan and that this, in time, could have yielded a hereditary ruling group over all of the Kipsigis. Certainly the instruments for consolidation of the power of this hereditary elite already existed in the supernatural capacities which were attributed to them and in the corps of lesser and greater messengers which they had developed over the years. It is noteworthy that the efforts of the British at centralization of control were constantly thwarted by the *laibon* and that the former only achieved the degree of bureaucratic efficiency which they now have after the strength and the organization of the *laibon* had been shattered. I am not insisting that these moves by the British stifled for all time the possibilities of nativistic revivals. Certainly not, for the *Dini ya Mboja* and Kipsigis Central Association which developed as parallels of the Kikuyu Central Association in 1947 and continued until the start of the Mau Mau Emergency were clearly this kind of phenomenon (Corfield, 1960, pp. 212-13). With the coming of national independence it is certain that tribal difficulties will no longer produce the same forms of nativistic reaction. It is now clear that while the power of the *laibon* was shattered forever, the governmental machinery imposed by the British has given the Kipsigis, and all other tribes in Kenya, new channels for response to frustrations, new and old.

The tribal coherence and political controls that might ultimately have developed under the *laibon* are now being achieved under different auspices and with different goals. But it comes too late for a long life in its present form, for it comes as a stepping stone to the creation of a polity of even larger dimensions—one which will embrace all of the tribes of Kenya in a single, generally cooperative structure. This appears to be an inescapable consequence of unavoidable outside controls. The British have had to forge the political devices which the Africans are now adapting to dispose of them. Creation of chiefs, destruction of the *laibon*, establishment of the Kipsigis African District Council—these are the instruments and the "insights," among many others, which have been loaned to the Kipsigis. The tribe means to hold on to them for a while, even if they are prepared to reshape them for new battles, new raids, and a new future.

LAND TENURE AND LAND USE

Until the first British settlers arrived in the area—around 1906—the Kipsigis had no conception of private and permanent ownership of land. There were no clan lands, no exclusive regimental domains, and even the *kokwet* took just a casual interest in the distribution of land among its members, intervening only in cases of altercation about a particular plot of land. Even this was unlikely while land remained plentiful and there for the taking. Generally, such a rare dispute about land might revert to the *kokwet* elders for disposition only after a man had spent a great deal of time and effort in clearing a particular patch and then had, for one reason or another, left the area. In these cases, kinfolk within the *kokwet* were likely to have first call on the land, provided they were prepared to use it. Sometimes, too, the *kokwet* would assume collective responsibility for designating areas to be cleared and cultivated when it had been agreed that communal clearing efforts were desirable. But the amount of land cultivated by a family was a matter of their own choice, for there was plenty of land to be had. Grazing areas were open to all, and a man might graze his animals anywhere so long as they did not damage the gardens of his neighbors or become inconveniently mixed with the herds and flocks of other Kipsigis. "Every man may build where and when he likes and may graze his flocks and herds from one end of the country to the other" (Orchardson, 1931, p. 471).

Unlike most of the Masai or the Turkana, the Kipsigis have not—at least for the last hundred years or more—been completely nomadic pastoralists. Cultivation of millet and a few garden vegetables has implied a more or less permanent home for each family. The main herds might be pastured relatively far from this home and would inevitably have to move from place to place as pasture became exhausted, but the homesite itself would be changed infrequently.

A man who cleared a piece of land for his use could lay claim to that land as long as he used it or for as long as he indicated an intention of returning to it. In that sense only was the land considered *his*. He had, as they say, "put a lot of sweat into the land," and others could not casually appropriate this product of his labor while he had any further use for it. In no sense could the claim to such land be made permanent as the claim to one's cattle and their progeny, or the claim to one's skins and weapons, or one's house and harvest.

With a population density only a fraction of that prevailing today, and with a personal demand for land limited to an amount required for each year's millet and vegetable crops, there would have been no point to the development of a system of private ownership in land had the idea even occurred to the Kipsigis.

The Kipsigis knew that millet planted on land recently cultivated did not thrive as well as millet planted on fresh ground or ground that had lain fallow for four or five years, for the weeds grow thicker on recently cultivated land and the yield is lighter. Consequently millet was, and still is, planted each year on a fresh plot. When uncultivated land in the vicinity of the house has been exhausted, fields farther away may be prepared and planted, or one may return to a plot which has lain fallow long enough.

This pattern of shifting cultivation was at once advantageous agriculturally and feasible in terms of land availability until the coming of the settlers restricted freedom of movement, and until concomitant pacification and the introduction of medical and veterinary services brought about an increase in the human and stock populations. In practice it meant that no man claimed more land than he could use at any particular time (or in a cycle of several years), and, just as important, it meant that there was no pattern of inheritance in land. The primary importance of land was for the pasture it afforded the animals, and for this purpose no one could be denied access to grazing lands, for these belonged not to individuals or even to *kokwotinwek* but to all of the people who needed them.

For cultivation of millet the heavy clearing, if necessary, was the job of the men. The women were responsible for turning the sods, drying them, piling, burning, and later scattering the ash over the field. The millet was sowed broadcast and hoed lightly into the topsoil. This was followed by breaking the lumps of earth by hand (*burburenet*), and this by the first weeding (*waet*) during which the remaining dried grass and earliest weeds were removed. When the millet was about six inches high, another weeding took place (*butisyet*), and this generally concluded the work on the crop until it was time for harvesting. The several weedings were performed either by the women and children of the household or by cooperation among a number of women and children in the *kokwet*. The earlier work of turning over the sods was almost invariably performed by women working in groups. The work of each member of the group was carefully measured and she was then owed an equivalent amount of work on her own field. The harvest was a communal activity involving other members of the *kokwet* on each household plot in turn. Men, women, and children participated and the activity was attended by the drinking of beer and feasting.

I should like to point out one other fact in connection with the matter of claims to land in pre-contact times which is of some importance in relation to the patterns which have emerged more recently under increasing land pressures and the growing importance of cash and cash crops. It was on land immediately adjacent to a man's house (or houses if he had several wives) that the wife living in the hut planted her small vegetable garden. And it was often from the ridge or slope on which the house rested, on a line down to the bottom of the slope that the successive fields of millet were located. Sheep and goats were grazed and browsed on the unused areas of this vertical strip. Although there were variations on this pattern of cultivation and grazing, it was fairly general throughout most parts of Kipsigis country with the exception of the areas of impeded drainage in the extreme south of the present Reserve. The garden plot was usually enclosed by a rough, temporary fence of sticks and brush and the plot of millet—measuring perhaps an acre, more or less—was always fenced in to protect it not only from one's own animals but from the depredations of neighbors' animals as well.

Thus patterns of use-expectation as well as patterns of enclosing one's own plot have a respectable antiquity in Kipsigis customs of land use. Knowing this helps us to understand some of the possible means by which the recent and dramatic changes in land tenure were implemented in the process of transition of this society from one of complete subsistence to one of increasing cash orientation. Later on I shall discuss some of these changes in detail.

THE SUPERNATURAL

In the foregoing rather broad sampling of elements of the pre-contact culture of the Kipsigis I have discussed briefly social forms or structure, land tenure and land-use practices, and a few other features of the economic and social life of the people. Before turning to an examination of the changes wrought in these cultural provinces by the intrusion of certain features of Western industrial culture as conveyed by the British, I want to add a few comments about supernatural beliefs and practices of the Kipsigis as they may be reconstructed for the pre-contact period, so that we may assess the extent of change brought about in this part of the tribal culture as well.

Earlier I discussed the hereditary sorcerers (*laibon* or *orgoik*) in terms of their social-control activities, real and potential. It should now be re-emphasized that the sources of their power lay in their control over supernatural forces, their capacity for foretelling the future and for bringing punishment upon Kipsigis who refused to comply with their demands and their wishes. There were also several classes of witches and shamans among the Kipsigis. The *boonik* (sing., *bonindet*) are those who practice evil witchcraft, and these may be either men or women. Another special group of women called *chebusurenik* (sing., *chebusuryot*) were the practitioners of contagious magic, those who caused illness primarily through the use of a person's "dirt." Practitioners of white or healing magic, called *chepsogeinik,* often combined their activities with the function of curer. This does not signify that there was a failure to distinguish between illnesses caused by the intervention of witchcraft and those having other (but ill-defined) causes. Some such distinction was apparently recognized. But the *chepsogeinik* were invoked when there was suspicion of witchcraft or sorcery and also when familial herbal remedies proved ineffective in cases where witchcraft or sorcery were *not* suspected. In this sense they appear to have served at times in a more clearly supernatural fashion, at others as superior technicians in the manipulation of curative devices.

It is generally believed that Kipsigis theology was essentially monotheistic and that the one god to whom appeals might be made was somehow closely related to the sun. The word for this god is Asis or Asista, sometimes translated as sun, perhaps better interpreted as the power or light *of* the sun. Although the profusion of names which has come to be attached to this god may give the impression that the Kipsigis recognized a variety or even a hierarchy of gods, it is, I think, much more likely that each of these many names (Chepteleel, Chepopkoiyo, Chepoomoni, Ngolo, Chepomircho, etc.) referred to a particular form, activity, or function of Asis. In any case, there is no evidence that there was a great deal of ceremonialism or ritual associated with this deity beyond the so-called *kapkoros* ceremony which seems to have been held routinely only once a year, but irregularly and infrequently on other crisis occasions when it seemed desirable. At the *kapkoros* (roughly, altar or place of sacrifice) the people would appeal, after appropriate ritual activities, for assistance in making the tribe prosperous, in defeating its enemies, increasing the fertility of the cattle and the women, improving pastures, and so on. From our point of view, however, one of the more significant features of the *kapkoros* ceremony was that it may have brought together peoples from different parts of the Kipsigis country and from all four sections (*boriosiek*) of the tribe. Orchardson says only that "several *kokwotinwek* joined together for the ceremony and a large concourse of people gathered for the occasion. The ceremony has not been held this century and the old organization has been largely forgotten" (Matson, 1961, p. 21).[7] My own informants say they were told that the *kapkoros* involved Kipsigis "from all over." If my information on this point is correct, and I am not at all certain that it is, one could say that these periodic functions involved the tribe, as tribe, more completely than even the late pre-contact large-scale raiding or war activities ever did. Men, women, and children are said to have participated, and it is apparent that some form of communal agreement to decisions more centrally derived would have had to precede the voluntary assembling of such relatively large numbers as are

[7] However, in an article published in 1933, Orchardson says that the last *kapkoros* ceremony was held "about 1903" (1933, p. 155).

reported. However, the incidence does not argue either for autocratic control or centralized authority, for we are told that the *kapkoros* arrangements were generally made by the elders of *kokwotinwek* in the neighborhood of the ceremonial area, and the other groups participating were informed by runners or messengers. There seems to have been no compulsion to attendance at all. There was no theocratic or secular body capable of enforcing everyone's attendance, and it would have been impracticable in view of the manpower demands involved in care of the herds and flocks which could not be brought en masse to the *kapkoros* grounds.

One might, a priori, expect that an apparently monotheistic people like the Kipsigis would take more readily to missionization at the hands of the Christian churches than a polytheistic people. In any case, this point has been suggested before. Later on I shall deal with some of the probably indirect effects of missionizing on the Kipsigis, but in the matter of conversion itself, the testimony of the missionaries suggests nothing phenomenal about its rate or incidence. However, since the statistical data are inadequate and confusing in the case of the Kipsigis, and since it is, moreover, not my intention to attempt a comparative survey of rates of acceptance of Christianity among mono- and polytheistic peoples under contact, I shall not dwell on this particular point. Nor am I convinced that a significant index of the ease and depth of acceptance of the Christian god is reflected in the tendency among Kipsigis to use the Swahili word Mungu (God) or the word Jehoba more commonly than Asis. After all, when they do use these terms they are indeed referring to the God of the Christians. And since all the evidence I have gathered on the matter suggests to me that religion in general sat rather lightly on the shoulders of the Kipsigis, I am not at all surprised to find that the references in daily life to any deity are infrequent and that these occur more casually in the context of new but shallowly implanted Christian values.

A number of Kipsigis whom I know are apparently devout Christians. But these represent only a fraction of the total. Many of the remainder who have taken over easy reference to the Christian god in their conversation seem to have done so either carelessly or in tacit recognition of the pervasive power of *anything* European. I would thus not argue that their aboriginal "monotheism" had prepared them for a more rapid acceptance of the core and inner meaning of Christian monotheism than would have been the case had they been complexly polytheistic. One cannot really know.

If, as a number of elderly informants assured me, people did not in the old days give much thought to Asis or to matters of "religion" generally, I would say that the same is true today, whether the deity in question be the same Asis or Jehoba, or Mungu. The Christian god comes along as part of the general cultural baggage brought to the Kipsigis by the Europeans. For the majority he has neither transformed nor very directly affected them one way or the other. They seem to be willing to wait and see, while they reach for those remaining features of the same European baggage which show some clear relevance to them in their daily lives.

Ancestor worship in patterns familiar to us from other places and tribes in Africa does not form an important part of Kipsigis traffic with the supernatural. True, it is believed that a man's spirit is transmitted to one of his sons, and then in turn transmitted to one of the grandsons, and so on, but the veneration in ritual and ceremony encountered elsewhere does not appear to have been a part of Kipsigis practice. Nor is the land itself ever referred to as the abode or resting place of ancestral spirits and therefore hallowed ground. The corpse of the dead man is quickly disposed of by his eldest son, burial usually taking place in the remote bush. This is followed by purification rites and the distribution of cattle. The grave is unmarked and the ground is unhallowed. It is hoped that the spirit of the departed will be kindly and that it will return only to do good to the living, particularly to offspring who bear the dead man's name. Spirits descend in the paternal line only, and they can do neither good nor harm to those outside this direct line.

Part IV. Recent Changes in Kipsigis Culture

The preceding chapters of this work have sketched in very abbreviated form some of the features of pre-contact (pre-1900) life and organization among the Kipsigis so far as I have been able to discover them, touching occasionally on their persistent or altered forms in the present. In what follows I shall try to give some evidence for additional cultural-institutional consequences which followed contact and to suggest why the changes have taken certain forms, where they appear to be heading, and why. I shall not have the space here for detailed treatment of all of the changes which I have been able to record in the course of my research. This will be reserved for a later monograph on the subject. For the present I shall outline in a fairly rough way some features of present Kipsigis culture as these may be contrasted with the aboriginal features touched upon in the earlier chapters.

I shall be assuming, of course, that present cultural patterns among the Kipsigis, in so far as these differ from the period before 1900, have come to differ as a consequence of the particular kind of European contact they have experienced; that this contact was itself shaped in large part by certain needs, demands, and resources of the mother country in its position as a leading industrial and imperial power with limited land, resources, and "acceptable" investment opportunities at home; and that the forms and devices employed in settlement, in exploitation of the land and the people, were themselves limited by the resources encountered in the colony, and dictated by the local potentialities as these related not only to the direct needs of the mother country but to world needs expressed in terms of an export market. In short, Kipsigis culture of 1960 would certainly have been more like Kipsigis culture of 1900 had the British—or any other modern industrial entity—never appeared. The general character of the changes that have taken place, as well as the flavor that foretells the future direction of change, belongs preeminently to the Kipsigis' (and Kenya's) involvement in production for the local and world markets and in a general cash nexus. The special features which distinguish Kipsigis patterns of change from those of, let us say, the Luo, the Kisii, or the Kikuyu—or other peoples in other underdeveloped areas elsewhere in Africa or in the world—may be attributed to their different historical development and circumstances, to contacts with other peoples, and to ecological processes.

A cross-cultural *content* or *trait* analysis of Kipsigis, Luo, Kikuyu, or any other culture in the process of involvement—either by colonization and/or imperialism and investment in any of its forms—may reveal distinguishing features of each imported and each precontact cultural trait as it became adapted to the old and the new influences and pressures, to local conditions, circumstances, and history.

And a cross-cultural *formal* or *structural* analysis of these cultures will show that pre-existing features are often transformed under the pressures of massive contact, or that, if they retain their ancient institutional outlines, they are almost invariably and profoundly altered in function.

I have tried in this account of the Kipsigis to deal, both descriptively and analytically, with each kind of change, the content-trait and the formal-functional, in order to provide data for comparison with the other essays in these volumes. The cross-cultural presentation clearly illustrates a trend towards convergence or increasing similarities in form-function as well as content, despite the very dissimilar histories, environments, and types of imposed controls under which changes in the societies studied emerged and developed.

LABOR, LAND USE, AND LAND TENURE

Although the first serious contact between whites and Kipsigis took place during the construction of the railroad from Mombasa to Kisumu around the turn of the century, the true impact of this contact did not make itself felt until the earliest European settlers came into the area in 1906-7. They settled first just to the north of Kericho where they took over land just as rapidly as the government surveyors provided the markers. Most of the early settlers got anywhere from 500 to 5,000 acres each, sometimes in freehold, more often on long lease, or a combination of the two. The distinction was not very important, however, for leasehold land was granted for ninety-nine years and this was subsequently extended in many cases to 999 years (Crown Lands Ordinance, 1915). The freehold sold for as little as "ha'penny" an acre, and the terms for leasing were comparably generous. Shortly after the first settlements were assigned, the government opened more freehold land to the Europeans in the Sotik area. All farms were 5,000 acres in size, and the maintenance of freehold title was formally contingent upon development. When the freeholder failed to develop adequately, the government merely converted the units to leasehold titles—under similarly generous terms.

It has been asserted repeatedly by apologists for British colonization in Kenya that most of the land taken over by the Europeans in the White Highlands was either completely unoccupied or occupied only in passing by pastoral nomads. This may be true for some of the Highland areas, but the assertion would most certainly not hold for the Kipsigis, since they were found to be settled in their semi-permanent habitations on all of the farms that were turned over to the British either as leasehold or freehold lands. In those cases where the Kipsigis were not actually evacuated from the alienated lands, each of the European settlers was at liberty to make whatever arrangements he chose with the natives he found in occupation of "his land." In the majority of cases, the settlers preferred the Kipsigis to remain on the land; and the latter "happily" reciprocated by staying where they were.

In return for the privilege of continuing to graze their animals and cultivate their small gardens on the lands newly alienated to their landlords, the Kipsigis tenants were expected to provide labor as this was needed—for a wage—and sometimes a small grazing fee of something like one pint of milk a day was paid to the landlord from every family owning fewer than twenty cattle, and two pints a day from those owning more. Those who did not choose to work were free to leave, and some did. The others were expected to work a minimum of seventy days a year to maintain their legal squatter rights. Various schemes of work days and days off were improvised by the settlers, but the basic rate of pay during the years before the end of World War I ranged around 8 to 12 shillings for each thirty days' work completed.

Some settlers placed limits on the number of cattle that could be owned by any one squatter family—perhaps thirty or forty. There was usually no limit to the number of goats or sheep. Many of the European farmers began their activities with the ranching of native cattle, since this enterprise could be carried on with minimal clearing of land, and since cattle were a cash crop which did not demand the construction of roads for transportation to market or railhead. Simultaneously, however, they began the clearing and plowing of land for cultivation of other crops, among which maize was of first importance.

Upbreeding of cattle was initiated with the importation of European strains like the Holstein-Friesan, Jersey, Ayreshire, and so on. At least one early settler near Kericho concentrated on the raising of pigs for sale to the Uplands Bacon Company. But when the price of feed skyrocketed he was forced to slaughter all of his animals.

In general, it may be said that the first few years of settlement were characterized by concentration on activities with minimal labor requirements. For the settlers could not be altogether sure that they could muster the devices and the attractions that would bind together a dependable labor force, although the passage of the 1900 Tax Regulations by the government had opened the way to a solution. In the slightly longer run, however, the hut and poll tax provisions encouraged the settlers to focus their attention on activities which involved the use of the plentiful labor potential which surrounded them and squatted on their lands. These taxes had to be paid, and the government sent collectors around to insure that they would be paid. For a brief time the collectors were permitted to accept payment of taxes in labor or by taking a goat which could then be placed for sale; but this not only entailed more difficulty than it was worth, it threatened to defeat one of the principle objectives of the tax program itself. Collectors were "urged" to insist on payment in cash (Fearn, 1961, p. 66). Some of the Kipsigis were willing to sell one of their animals to pay the tax, but the majority retained the traditional attachment to the animal, for it represented the only kind of starvation insurance they knew. Thus they would rather go to work for the white man, keep their goat, and pay their taxes in the coins which had as yet little exchange value and no other significance for them.

With a relatively secure and assured labor force, the new settlers soon began vigorous clearing of the land and expanded the cultivation of maize, peas, beans, and other crops which were then in demand in other parts of the colony. Many of the squatters in the northern and eastern parts of the district were initially Kikuyu who were imported as labor in those areas where Kipsigis left the alienated lands or were not numerous enough to supply all labor requirements. In time, more Kipsigis were incorporated into the labor force.

The start of World War I in 1914 precipitated a heavy demand for flax, and virtually all of the settlers turned promptly and concentratedly to its cultivation. During the next four years prices for flax continued to climb until they reached a peak of £240 per ton. Encouraged by the prosperity this represented, and aided by generous grants of land from the Crown, a relatively large number of settlers crowded into the area under the BEADOC scheme immediately after the war. (These were veterans of the British East Africa Disabled Officers' Corps who accepted farms of 5,000 acres, generally in the Kericho area, since Sotik was some thirty miles farther from the railroad at Lumbwa.) They, too, turned enthusiastically to the cultivation of flax, but the price immediately dropped back to £40 a ton, and with their dreams of quick and easy wealth shattered, many of the BEADOC settlers returned bankrupt to England.

Meanwhile, all of the land alienation and settlement had not gone too smoothly. For there were certain sections of Kipsigis country where native occupation was relatively dense, as in the area to the west of the Kipsonoi River, now known as North Sotik (see map), and here it was considered advisable to remove all of the Kipsigis after the land had been surveyed and to leave the region unoccupied. It was assumed that as the settlers arrived they would make their own arrangements for squatter labor and recall as many of these as they considered essential to the operation of their farms. It appears that density of settlement was one of the factors in this particular solution, for in most other areas it was not considered necessary during this early period (it was in fact considered undesirable) to remove the Kipsigis. But another element may have been involved in the decision to clear the Kipsigis completely from that land. For this was the area immediately adjacent to the Kisii, and it is believed now that the District Commissioner who ordered and supervised the removal of the Kipsigis from here around 1908-9 feared that the prospective European settlers might be caught up unhappily in the ongoing cattle conflict between members of the two tribes. In fact, this point came in later years—but with a somewhat different rationale—to be emphasized in the idea of a "buffer zone" in which West Sotik, and somewhat illogically, Central and East Sotik as well were included. These latter areas were allegedly

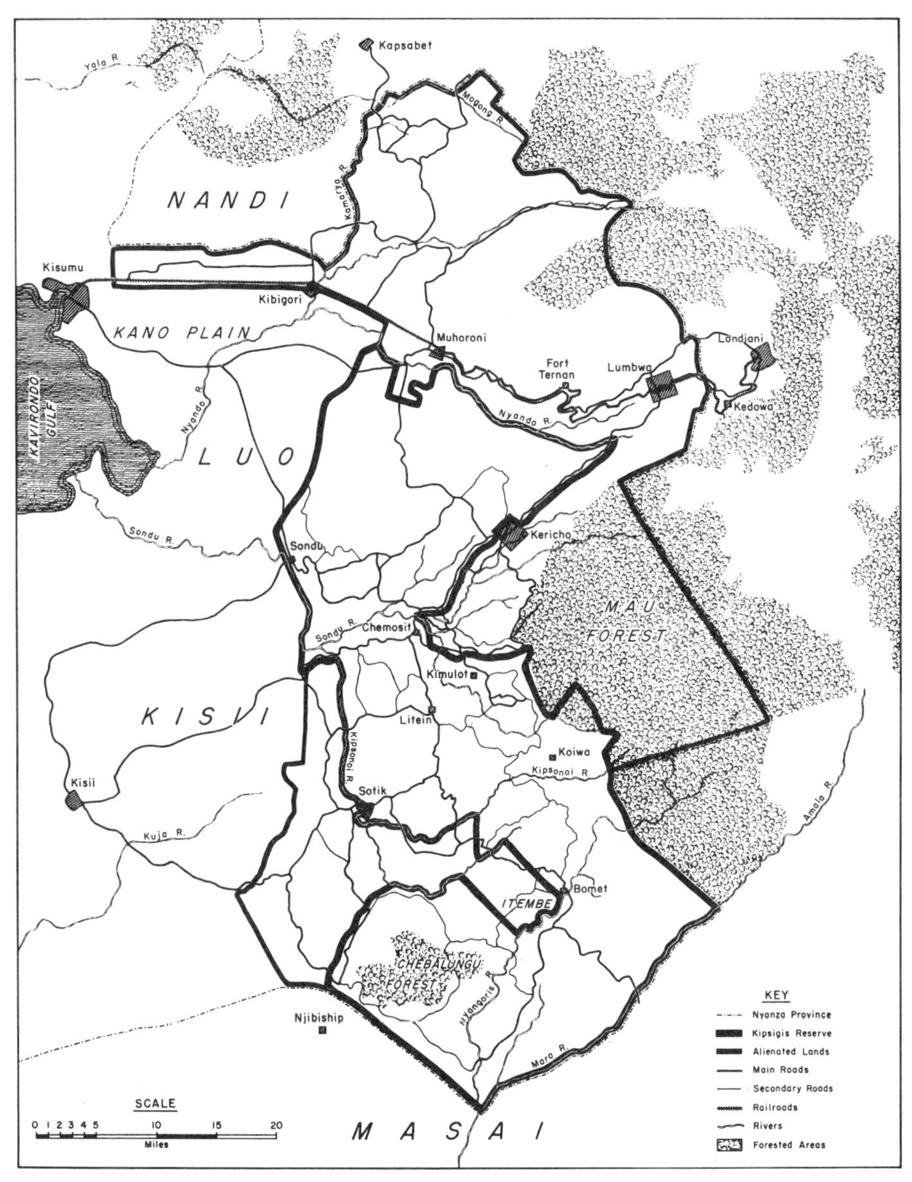

KERICHO DISTRICT AND ENVIRONS

designed to throw a wall of European farms between the Kipsigis on the one hand and the Kisii and Masai on the other in order to keep the tribes from raiding each other for cattle. The Kipsigis found it hard to accept this explanation, charging that it was merely an excuse for taking more good land from them and giving it to the Europeans.

In any case, since many of the Kipsigis refused to remove themselves peaceably to the eastern side of the Kipsonoi River as District Commissioner Partington—or Capt. Monckton—had requested, he used a more direct device to get them out of the area, a device employed again several times and in several places during the next fifty years when the Kipsigis seemed unwilling to relinquish lands they occupied to the Europeans: their huts were burned (Carter, 1934b, Vol. III, p. 2441). There seems to have been no organized Kipsigis resistance to this act. The people simply moved across the river, built new huts, and re-established their *kokwotinwek*. A number of years elapsed before the European settlers began to take up their claims, and during that period the land remained unoccupied and most of it unused as well. When the Europeans finally arrived—sometime around 1912, but in greater force after the First World War—they recruited their workers on a day basis from among those Kipsigis across the river who either refused to sell a goat to pay their tax, who had none to spare for this purpose, or who saw some other use to which they could put the cash they earned through their labor. Soon a number of the day laborers were invited to return with their families and to take up permanent squatter residence on the side of the river from which they had been expelled. They were allowed to bring their animals with them and to till as much soil as they needed for their own consumption purposes. Apparently many Kipsigis were eager to take advantage of this offer, for grazing land was in increasingly short supply as a result of the sudden overcrowding caused by their enforced occupation of the eastern areas, and what pasture there was was seriously overstocked.

At the same time they were accepting squatter labor on their farms in North Sotik, the European settlers allowed other Kipsigis to bring their cattle across the river and to graze them on their lands in return for a daily payment of milk. Meanwhile the flocks and the herds of the squatters grew inordinately, for each squatter accepted the care of some of the animals of his friends and kinfolk across the river who were short of pasture. Sometimes a poverty-stricken Kipsigis from the eastern side of the Kipsonoi would turn up as a squatter on one of the western estates, bringing a large herd of beasts in tow. These were, of course, the cattle of other Kipsigis. Although the new squatter had to work to maintain his rights to "squat," he drew benefits from the herd, and the real owners could claim a share of the milk and all of the herd's increase.

Ultimately the effectiveness of these devices as a means to find grazing land for the Kipsigis' animals was weakened, for the Europeans began placing informal limits on the size of the herds a squatter might possess, and, later, formal regulations were instituted by the administration which reduced these limits still further.

The pattern which was to become accentutated in later years had been established. *Kodi* (taxes) had forced a certain number of Kipsigis to accept employment with the whites. Manufactured products from a Western industrialized society had been introduced, and these served as further bait and incentive to keep the Kipsigis working. Now pressures on a forcibly contracted land base were combined with these devices to compel even more wage labor on the farms of the European settlers. As time passed taxes became the least important element among these three in bringing Kipsigis into the labor market. The demand for manufactured goods which could only be met by the sale of one's animals or one's labor power increased and continues to increase in importance.

For a time, the understandable reluctance to sell one's cattle to obtain money with which to buy Western manufactured products drove those Kipsigis who wanted these commodities to work for wages. More recently the reluctance has diminished, not only because the demand for Western goods has grown stronger, but because the contraction of the land and the gradual elimination of squatter grazing rights (really both parts of the same process) has made it impossible for a man to let his herds grow without restriction or limit. Moreover, cattle themselves are no longer essential to bride-price. The money one earns as wages working for the white men will usually do just as well.

Perhaps more important than all of this, however, is the fact that wage work—which began as a device for getting the wherewithal to pay taxes; and continued in order to allow the purchase of blankets, baubles, and trinkets; and expanded in order to provide pasture for cattle and living space for their owners—has now become only one of several means of satisfying the growing drive for cash accumulation.

Work for wages has its place—and an important place it is, too —in the developing keenness for money shown by the Kipsigis. But it is not exclusively as a wage worker that the cash-hungry Kipsigis sees himself. He has learned that it is not necessary to work for the Europeans in order to survive, to pay taxes, to send one's children to school, and to buy the many things one wants. He has even discovered that one may live better, *mirabile dictu*, with few cattle than with many. And he knows that some of the many cattle may be sold for the cash that opens the door to "better living."

He has discovered too that there is yet another way to wealth—other than wage work or the sale of one's animals—and that is in the cultivation and sale of cash crops: maize, coffee, and, best of all, tea. But whether he sells his labor power, or his animals, or the crops grown on his soil, the Kipsigis has become increasingly devoted to cash itself. He is no longer satisfied with just enough money to pay his taxes, or with the opportunity of having access to grazing land for some of his animals. He wants cash not only to buy some of the many things he sees in the shops, but to enable him, perhaps, to buy the land and even the labor that will yield more cash. Cash, like cattle, has the power of reproducing itself if properly cared for. And so increasing numbers of Kipsigis have been turning hopefully towards those activities which have made the Europeans and the Asians around them "wealthy" men. The cultivation of maize, wattle, and other crops for sale is one of the ways by which the man with land may prosper. Ownership of a bus, truck, or tractor for hire; or running a shop in one of the new marketplaces in the Reserve—these are other ways to acquire cash, especially if a man has too little land for cash cropping.

This is not to say that all, or even a majority, of Kipsigis are engaged in one or more of these cash ventures. The majority are still living lives patterned largely on subsistence farming with little or no surplus left for sale. But every Kipsigis family has some need for cash beyond the payment of taxes. Salt, tea, sugar, metal utensils, cloth, and other items have become indispensable commodities, and these may be bought only with money. For most, the money that provides these commodities comes from the regular or desultory wage work of one or more members of the household or some close kinsman. And even the small, poorly stocked shops scattered in fixed marketplaces throughout the Reserve have other things to buy, things which increasingly tempt the Kipsigis who has no money as well as the one who has.

Although the shift to at least a partial dependence upon cash is relatively recent, it has profoundly affected some basic Kipsigis institutions. I believe the Kipsigis are adapting to the new conditions which have been thrust upon them in virtually the only way possible if they are to survive. Once the old patterns were destroyed or severely altered by imposed controls and administration, there was nothing left for the tribe but to accommodate in the several ways they have done. For while certain features of the adjustment were open to choice, the most massive changes had to follow along the general lines laid down by the nature of the contact under the particular historical and ecological circumstances prevailing during the past sixty years. In short, once colonization had begun, and given the aims under which it was launched and developed and the methods employed by the British in carrying it through, the effects upon the Kipsigis and upon their pre-contact institutions were bound to have been profound. The precise manner in which these changed was, of course, dependent upon certain antecedent and continuing conditions and circumstances, upon Kipsigis resources, alternatives, and culture. But these effects were neither completely unpredictable nor whimsical. And there are apparent in this specific accommodation reflections of a process of change and reorganization, a general dynamism, which has marked the transition of many peoples in different parts of the world who have come or are now coming under the influence of Western industrial civilization.

LAND PRESSURES AND THE EUROPEANS

The British pattern of development, colonization, and exploitation of Kenya was featured by many important elements which distinguished it from the methods and devices employed, for example, in West Africa. I am not here referring to direct vs. indirect rule (Lugard, 1893, Vol. II, pp. 649 ff. See also Perham, 1934) as the chief differentiating character, for it is now clear that these differences are sometimes more apparent than real. What is perhaps more important is that penetration into the interior of the colony was effected within a few years of annexation. The building of a railroad which traversed Kenya from east to west was accomplished within a few more years. In 1902, one year after the railway from Mombasa to Lake Victoria was completed, the British administration, expanding on the precedent established with the taking of a mile-wide strip on either side of the railroad, implemented another in the series of ordinances which culminated in the designation of all land in the colony as "Crown Lands."

Meanwhile large tracts within the Highland region were assigned for alienation to Europeans on long-term lease (ninety-nine to 999 years) and for freehold purchase. The railroad had been conceived and built partly as a means for facilitating access to the wealth of eastern Uganda and the region around Lake Victoria, and partly, it was said, to provide the means for ending the slave trade through better control over the interior. But some, like Lord Delamere, were alert to the possibilities of land utilization and exploitation much nearer to the coast—and close to the newly completed railroad. Hence, beginning early in 1903, Delamere launched his celebrated agricultural experiments on the first of a series of huge Highland estates gradually acquired by him over the years. He was followed by other Europeans (Huxley, 1935).

Until 1961 the amount of land in Kenya held by Europeans or available for purchase or lease exclusively by them totaled something over 13,000 square miles as compared with some 52,000 square miles in native areas. Kenya's total area is some 225,000 square miles. This includes in addition to the above: crown forests, townships, government reserves, royal national parks, other unsurveyed crown lands which were considered partially "suitable for alienation," open water, and 114,317 square miles of northern frontier territory, generally asserted to be useless desert. According to the Ministry of Agriculture, about 40,760 square miles of "land of high potential" (good soils and more than 30 inches of rain a year) are to be found in Kenya. Of this, 32,300 square miles are in African areas, while 8,460 square miles are in the hands of Europeans. This means that more than 20 per cent of Kenya's best lands are under the control of less than 1 per cent of its population (Huxley, 1960, p. 260).

The Kipsigis are one among those Highland tribes which have lost some of their better lands to the Europeans. In his handing-over report for 1934, Kericho's District Commissioner describes the Kipsigis' feelings about the land they had lost through alienation: "The members of the Local Native Council [Kipsigis] have a definite land complex, but this is not surprising, when a glance at the map will show you how much of their land has been alienated, and when it is realized that much of this land was their best grazing." The District Commissioner's report for 1946 says: "Certainly no tribe has lost more land than the unfortunate Kipsigis."

The problem has also been very acute for the Kikuyu people in the vicinity of Nairobi, but no tribes in the arable regions of Kenya have been completely unaffected, either directly or indirectly, by the land pressures which resulted from the patterns of white occupancy. From Delamere's time until the present it has been apparent that whatever wealth is extractable from Kenya must almost surely come from agriculture and related activities. While it is conceivable that some peasant form of native cash cropping might have been

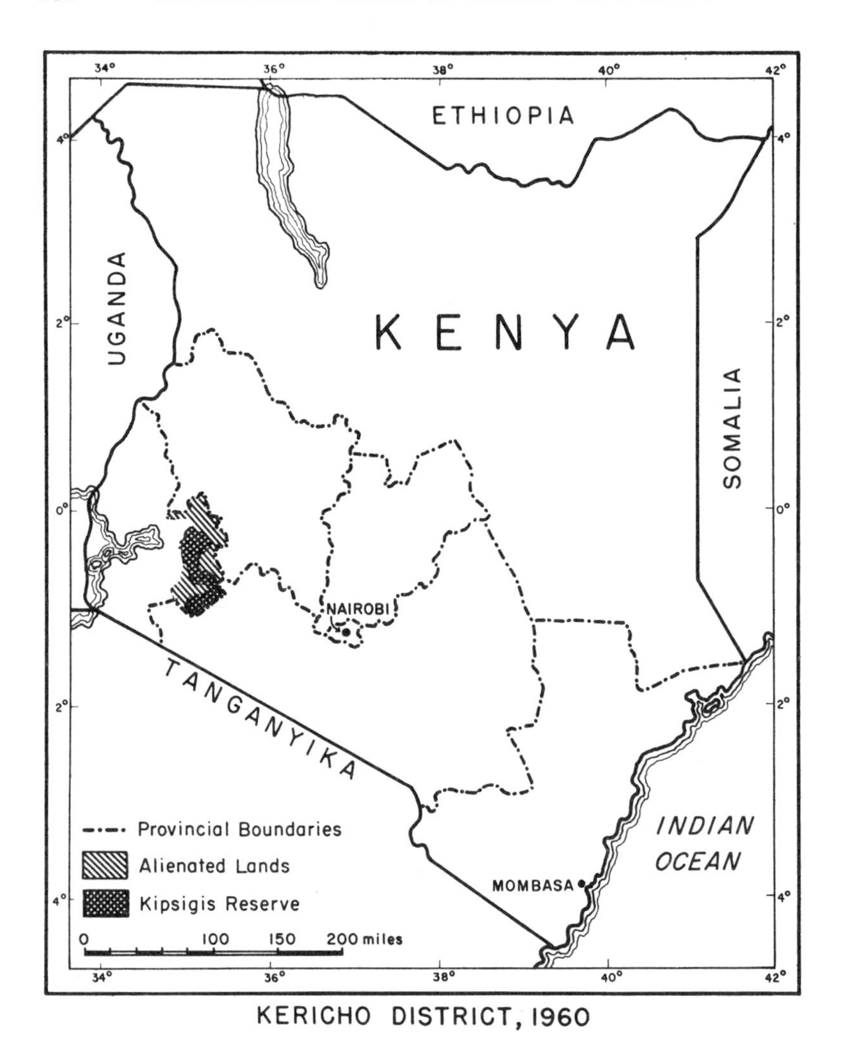

KERICHO DISTRICT, 1960

worked out over the years to facilitate the process of "extracting," as it was, for example, in most of Uganda and in West Africa,[1] the pure agricultural development of the Highland areas has probably gone forward much faster under an estate system than would have been the case had the government attempted seriously to introduce peasant cultivation of cash crops from the beginning.

[1] C. C. Wrigley (*The Development of Economic Agriculture in Uganda*, London, 1952, p. 1, cited in Fearn, 1961, p. 81) states that but for "the collapse of the world commodity markets in the latter part of 1920," just as plantation agriculture was getting its start in Uganda, that country would have followed Kenya's pattern of estate cultivation.

Lord Delamere and other propagandists for a plantation-type development of the Kenya Highlands emphasized the distinction between these areas and the hotter, wetter regions of tropical Africa to the west. This was a place suitable not only for investment but for investment with colonization. Most of the tribes in this part of the world were organizationally and militarily unequipped to offer more than token resistance. Thus, the Nandi Wars which ended in 1906 were the most serious opposition to their colonization encountered by the British until the Mau Mau Emergency of 1952. And the former hardly proved anything more than annoying.

Much of the area coveted by the Europeans was fairly well-watered parkland awaiting only the steel plow to release its fertility. Days were warm but never hot, and the nights were often cool enough to make a fire in the fireplace a welcome thing. Labor would certainly appear as the need for it grew. In short, there was plenty of gold to be mined from the red soils of Highland Kenya, even if the base substances of the settler-alchemist's equipment were the plow, his cattle, sheep, wheat, maize, coffee, and, above all, the hands of black Africans.

When the European settlers came to the country of the Kipsigis and moved to the lands on which many of the tribe had pastured their flocks and herds and had grown their few vegetables and their modest crops of finger millet, a series of changes was precipitated which came to affect not only those Kipsigis who were embraced by the leasehold, or those who were forced to leave for other parts, but the entire tribe. For as the penetration of European nations into Africa itself demanded an institutional apparatus for effective functioning, and as the application of the controls and instruments of this apparatus ultimately affected most Africans in varying ways and in differing degrees, so did the activities and the devices that accompanied the Sotik and Kericho settlers quickly reach out to change the lives of the people who lived in this segment of the Kenya Highlands.

In the beginning, most of the Kipsigis who were driven off the land to make room for the new white landlord, and those Kipsigis who could have remained but did not want to, simply moved to another part of the country which was familiar to them or to a place where they had friends, age-mates, or kin and were absorbed by existing *kokwotinwek*. Some thought to escape the vicinity of administration more surely by joining Kipsigis who had been living near Kilgoris or in other southerly regions where the Masai came to graze their great herds and flocks. These lived in fairly peaceful relations with each other, and occasionally a Masai warrior would take a Kipsigis girl for a wife—legally, and with full payment of bride-price.

As the prodding of the administration was intensified, and as the hut and poll tax became burdensome, other Kipsigis emigrated to what was now gazetted Masai country and established small settlements in the midst of their ancient enemies. Paradoxically, however, there were those who took refuge from administrative controls precisely by remaining as squatters on the estates of the European settlers. For the administration and its constantly expanding corps of functionaries, white and African, did not trouble the settlers very much. The tax was collected by the farmer, but all the other little annoyances to which Kipsigis in the Reserve were being subjected under chiefs they had never known before, the magistrates, the sometimes officious headmen—these did not reach them on the estates where the word of the settler was virtual law. Here, too, there was usually ample grazing land and the chance to earn a little cash.

Eventually, however, the administration began to restrict and finally to curtail completely the right of the squatters to keep cattle. Those settlers who could count upon a dependable supply of squatter labor without cattle were pleased to comply with the new regulations. Others who saw their laborers drifting off to greener pastures if they were not allowed to have their own cattle resisted the efforts of the European administrators to get rid of the squatter cattle. Those dispossessed Kipsigis who tried to take their cattle back into the Reserve encountered difficulties because by now—the late forties and the fifties—pasture and even house space was in increasingly short supply. Many of them were forced to find their living space outside the Reserve. Thus, this late crop of migrants has been motivated not nearly so much by the desire to escape the interminable efforts of the agricultural officers to get them to plant more maize or to cull out their herds and flocks, but by an acute and growing land hunger.

This is certainly the case with the two largest Kipsigis settlements in Masai, Njibiship and Ngata Baragoi, where I spent some time. The Kipsigis in these communities ridicule the assumption that they may have left their own Reserve in order to escape the prickings of the administration, the meddling of chiefs, or the pressures to cultivate rather than herd. "How can one get away from the *chumbek* (European) officials any place?" they ask. "We have come here because there is land. Our Reserve is too small for us."

Many of these Kipsigis-dwellers-in-Masai are legal "acceptees," having been approved and sponsored by Masai elders with the stipulation that they would "live as Masai and not as Kipsigis." The whole plan was developed and sanctioned by the European administrators in charge of the Masai and Kipsigis areas as a device to take some of the pressure off Kipsigis lands. But the migrants have already shown their contempt for the stipulations under which they were accepted. Not only are they plowing the land and planting crops in profusion, despite the protests of the Masai who have tried to have them removed for thus violating the agreements, but the elders have told me that the pasture which is now communally grazed in these areas will soon be enclosed in private holdings. Already, for example, the 114 families of Ngata Baragoi know exactly the boundaries of the land each will claim as its own when "the time is ripe." In short they have not, as some government officials suggested to me, run away from Kipsigis country to escape the pressures of administration. They have run away because land they would have liked for their own has already been taken, because there is no more unclaimed land on their own Reserve. And they have brought with them into the open grazing lands of the Masai the concept of individual ownership of land which completely dominates today on the Kipsigis Reserve.

CHANGING CONCEPTS OF LAND TENURE

This pattern of land ownership which is applauded by the Kenya government has developed within the past twenty or twenty-five years, although it had its first foreshadowings in the early thirties. I do not think it is possible to assign to any single factor the explanation for the change from tribal usufruct and communal grazing to individual ownership. But certainly the introduction of the steel plow and the encouragement of maize cultivation for cash sale in the local market must be reckoned among those factors which have helped to bring about this crucial change in Kipsigis culture.

Maize had reached the Kipsigis as early as 1906-7, and despite a good deal of initial resistance to its cultivation some Kipsigis planted it in small patches, using the harvest, in the beginning at least, largely in the manufacture of beer.

My informants insist, with almost complete unanimity, that resistance to the introduction of maize, or of wattle, or of a good many other European-sponsored innovations came not so much from a veneration for entrenched patterns or even from a "natural conservatism" as from a suspicion that the product would be appropriated by the Europeans. In this sense, they seem to have related government sponsorship to corvée labor. If the product of the latter passed over to the government, the product of the former might do so also. Naturally, there may also have been other factors involved in the resistance to maize, such as the *laibon*'s instructions to boil the government seed before planting in order to insure that it would not germinate. But the opposition of the *laibon* might have been in part determined by the same general suspicions as well as by a more likely anxiety about the threats posed to their control by the British.

In addition to the maize that was used to make beer, some was eaten, and some was sold to Asian merchants in the period before the First World War. The war itself gave a new impetus to its production, so that by 1921 the District Commissioner states in his annual report that "owing to the plentiful supply of maize very low prices were obtainable, not more than one rupee per load being paid to the natives for maize." By this time also, it should be noted, the Kipsigis were engaged in the sale of other commodities such as hides, skins, honey, the "indispensable" cattle (888 were disposed of at *official* trading centers in 1921), and sheep and goats (1,573 of these in the same year).

Only one Kipsigis, arap Bargochat of Belgut, was using a plow in 1921 to prepare the field for his maize. By 1927 the number of plows in use by Kipsigis had grown to 65, and there were 33 Kipsigis-owned flour mills! Just two years later, in 1929, the District Commissioner reports 249 ploughs and 62 flour mills. Maize for cash had unquestionably caught on.

During the post–World War I period there was a sharp increase in the sale of other locally produced items, including finger millet. Numbers of Kipsigis were employed on farms within the District as well as in the more remote settled areas of the Rift Valley. While only a small percentage of the approximately 12,000 employees on the burgeoning tea estates in 1930 were Kipsigis, several thousand were earning some wages—and getting pasture for their animals—on other farms in the District. The number of shops available for purchase of manufactured goods in and on the Reserve appears to have been in excess of fifty. Money was becoming increasingly important. Work for wages was one of the slower means of accumulating the desirable cash. Stealing cattle, however, was unquestionably profitable, and a handsome return could be realized quickly on their sale. Thus the third and fourth decades of this century witnessed a sharp rise in cattle thefts from Kisii and Luo in particular. The pattern was one of small parties and quick raids. But the government became more alert, and the risks grew greater.

However, there was always a ready market for maize. The Asian shopkeepers and traders would buy whatever one had to sell. Then the tea estates and the farms of the settlers needed maize for distribution to their laborers as rations. A man with a plow and two to eight oxen could plant a good-sized field of maize from the sale of which he might realize a good return. There was nothing to stop him, for there were no customary limits to the size of the field he might plant for his own use—even if his own use should no longer mean subsistence exclusively.

In 1931 the District Commissioner remarks in his annual report that there may be some cause for alarm in the situation which is developing on the land of the Kipsigis. He notes that "natives, chiefly mission, have denied their responsibility established by custom, to fence their cultivation." He does not pursue the implications further. In 1934 another District Commissioner notes with some alarm another aspect of the growing emphasis on the cultivation of maize. "A situation is arising in the South Lumbwa District [Kericho District] which may well prove a matter for anxiety in a year or two. A number of the more advanced Kipsigis are plough owners, and as the tribe has no system of land tenure, other than as a community, these plough owners tend to cultivate very large areas indeed, thus reducing the available amount of grazing. If at any time the squatters are removed from the Sotik farms, and have to return with their cattle to the Reserve, the overstocking question may arise here." In the same year, the Carter Commission observed: "It is apparent that the tribe has not nearly reached the stage when individual ownership of land can emerge" (1934a, p. 305).

The District Commissioner was properly concerned about the threat to grazing areas posed by the use of the plow, by increased cultivation of maize, and by the already apparent contraction of squatter privileges in the settled areas. Perhaps he did not see, for he does not mention it, the more profound implications for a complete change in patterns of land tenure among the Kipsigis. The plow might have been brought to the Kipsigis and remained an implement of only minor importance, despite its apparent advantages over the hoe, had there not been such a ready local market for maize, or had new pasture lands been provided to take care of growing herds of cattle. (See Schapera, 1928, p. 181, for a discussion of the introduction of the plow by the missionaries in South Africa, encouragement of its use by the administration, and the way in which the plow opens the door to trade.)

From its feeble beginnings in 1906-7 under the urging of District Commissioner Partington—who required grain to provide for the expanding numbers of police, military, and other agriculturally non-productive administrative personnel—the production of maize for sale in the local market grew. Especially after World War I, and with the opening of the tea estates, the demand for maize sky-rocketed. It was apparent to increasing numbers of Kipsigis that this local market would be a dependable source of cash income to them if they should be able to produce the grain required by the Kericho estates to feed their thousands of workers. Shops, markets, and itinerant traders with their alluring stocks of manufactured items made the cash to be earned from the sale of maize immediately attractive. Lumbwa, Kericho, Bomet, and Litein were lively centers of trade. By 1925-26 the first Kipsigis-owned shop was opened at Chemosit, adding to the large number of Asian and the smaller number of European shops already in existence, and forecasting a trend which was to eventuate, by 1962, in more than sixty marketplaces and almost six hundred Kipsigis shops in the Reserve alone.

In the year 1930 there were more than 8,000 regular and 3,000 casual laborers working on the tea estates that border the Kipsigis Reserve. Adult males were earning 14 shillings per 30-day work period. The District Commissioner estimates that in 1930 the expenditures of the tea companies alone in wages, transport, and *food* amounted to about £ 200,000. In 1932, District Commissioner Tomkinson remarks of the Kipsigis: "Few tribes can be so well situated to dispose of their produce, since the tea companies do not grow maize to any appreciable extent, but require the crops of nearly 9,000 acres to feed their labour force . . ." (Carter, 1934b, Vol. III, p. 2455).

Though 1921 is the first year in which a Kipsigis is reported as owning a plow, the interest in maize cultivation came earlier. As I have noted (p. 288, *supra*), the District Commissioner's report for 1921 states that the supply of maize is so plentiful that "the natives" are getting only one rupee a load for their product. But the low prices did not seem to deter "the natives" in their early scramble for cash. In the towns and centers alone, 20,119 loads were sold that year. In 1923, "a large amount of maize was sold to Indians and Europeans." In 1925, it is reported that "the area under maize has increased enormously in the last few years." In 1927, "the maize acreage in Belgut [one of the Reserve's locations] . . . [is] considerably more than ever before." In 1928, there is an "encouraging increase in the acreage under maize. . . . Some natives . . . are paying a European to use his tractor for breaking land in the Reserve." Significantly, the District Commissioner fears that the Kipsigis may be "growing themselves out" of the labor market. And by 1930 the annual report tells us: "The fact that comparatively few Lumbwas [Kipsigis] were employed on the Tea Estates is a good indication that the tribe as a whole was not hard hit financially." It also confirms pretty clearly that the tribe was "not hard hit financially" because it had discovered through maize, and probably through the sale of cattle as well, other means than wage labor for the acquisition of cash.

The Kipsigis had thus not only learned about the "joys of money," but they found that for them, unlike many of the other tribes in Kenya, there was a handy market-way to the accumulation of this cash. A combination of historical circumstances had placed the Kipsigis in an area which was considered suitable for tea cultivation by experts from the metropolis. The Kipsigis learned quickly to emphasize cash crops which would satisfy the local consumption needs of the non-food-producing work force engaged in the production of that tea. All that remained to complete their conversion into a true peasantry (see: Kroeber, 1948, p. 284; Firth, 1951, pp. 87-89; Redfield, 1956, pp. 35-66, for various definitions of peasantry and the role played by these sociocultural segments in relation to other societal groupings) was a chance to exercise a more dependable control over the lands they devoted to the cultivation of their maize than was allowed by traditional land communalism. And that step lay just around the corner.

We have seen, on the one hand, that cultivated fields seem to be growing larger, and, on the other, that there is a reluctance on the part of some tillers of these large fields to fence their plots. What is the connection between these practices—still in the 1931-34 framework of community or tribal land tenure—and the drive towards conversion of these holdings into the first private property in land among the Kipsigis?

I drew attention earlier to the Kipsigis pattern of land use of contiguous plots usually adjacent to the house, or running in a series from ridge to valley. The ordinary plot size for millet was about an acre or less, and it was always fenced to protect the crop from sheep, cattle, and goats. The alert Kipsigis of the early thirties who anticipated—and helped to bring about—the trend towards private ownership of land made use of one feature of the traditional pattern in furthering their enterprise while abandoning another. They plowed lands adjacent to their houses—starting with a plot as much as six or eight acres in extent—but they did not fence the cultivated area. The particular Kipsigis who appears to have been a leader in all of this, and whose method was quickly copied by others, described it to me as follows:

I plowed as much land with my first two oxen as I could [this was in 1930]. The land I plowed was between my house here on the hill and the house I built for my mother on the slope below me (about five acres). I planted the plot to maize and did not put a fence around it. [Cf. District Commissioner's Report for 1931, p. 289, *supra*. When I asked him whether he had neglected to fence the plot because it was too large for easy fencing, he shrugged.] No, I had another reason for this.

When the animals of my neighbors started to come into my field to molest the young maize, I ran to them and told them that they must keep them out of the maize or I would take them to court [the local African tribunal] and collect damages from them. They answered that I must build a fence as we Kipsigis have always done or they would not be responsible. But they were really afraid and they tried hard to keep their animals out of my maize.

Then I said to them that if they really wished to avoid trouble why did they not plant their own fields of millet right up to the edge of my fields of maize. Then the fence that they erected to protect their millet would also discourage their animals from coming into my maize.

Apparently his neighbors agreed to the proposal, for they instructed their wives to follow the suggestion. Then, this man continued, since millet was never planted two years running in the same field, he extended his plowing in the following season to take in all of the contiguous plots which had been devoted to millet. Because there was no serious fertility problem about the repeated cultivation of maize on the same plot—for at least four or five years—he used this technique in successive years for expanding the area of his original cultivation from the center out. When it came time to leave the central areas fallow, he solidified his claim to them by grazing his own cattle there and *fencing in the paddock area.* In time the fenced paddock areas became fenced cultivation areas, and the process of land accumulation on the part of this man was only stopped when his own neighbors undertook the cultivation of maize and defended themselves against further encroachment by this means and by the erection of paddock fences.

It should be noted, at least in passing, that in areas of the Reserve which lie adjacent to European farms, many of the latter have had substantial amounts of their land cleared free of charge by employing a slight variant of this device. They have invited land-hungry Kipsigis to cultivate a patch of millet on their land. In order to do this, the Kipsigis must first clear the land of brush and sods. After the millet is harvested the Kipsigis are invited to consider another patch for the following planting. The European farmer then uses the ex-millet plot either for pasture or for his own maize. Some Kipsigis refer to these Europeans as "good men." Others find different ways of describing this particular kind of altruism.

While fences have a respectable antiquity among the Kipsigis, their use for anything besides protection of areas of cultivation and for night *bomas* was unknown before the 1930's. By adroitly combining initially unfenced maize plots with fenced pasture land, my informant and those who followed him seem to have launched the Kipsigis on the road to private ownership of land. Initially this particular mission-trained Kipsigis—who told me that he learned the virtues of individual care, responsibility, and ownership of land from his American teachers at the African Inland Mission (Protestant)—met with considerable resistance from his neighbors, and the *kokwet* elders were called in to remonstrate with him over his failure to fence in his maize and later again when he undertook the fencing of his pastures. But it was a relatively simple matter—as I confirmed in further inquiries among his neighbors and with some of the elders—for him to defend his actions. Traditionally there had never been any limits to the size of a plot a man could claim for cultivation, because it was always assumed that he would only cultivate as much land as he needed for subsistence. To have planted a larger plot and produced a surplus beyond his subsistence needs would have been foolish and unnecessary. What could one have done with the surplus? So when this man asserted to the protesting elders that he had a use for any grain that he cultivated in excess of his own requirements for food and beer they could not dispute his right to the land. He had carefully refrained, in the first place, from taking land to which another Kipsigis might lay claim, and as he expanded his cultivation area he did so by moving into plots on which millet had just been harvested. Everyone knew that such land was useless or, like other fallow areas, useful only for free grazing. And there was still, generally speaking, enough of that around in the 1930's to vitiate complaints on that score.

As for the later fencing of his pastures, he pointed out that this practice was also unassailable, for was it not acceptable Kipsigis practice for a man to indicate land which he intended to cultivate by erecting a fence around that land (either before or after clearing it)? And did he not return on occasion to the cultivation of that enclosed pasture after the animals had cropped it for a proper time (and added to its fertility in the process)? His neighbors envied and despised him for what he did. But even as they protested his untraditional behavior, they made their own plans to do as he had done. (See Mair, 1948, p. 187, for a discussion of the effects of a cash economy on communal patterns of landholding.)

So while 1921 is the first year in which we find a Kipsigis owning a plow, less than a dozen years later that tool had been made the instrumentality for the ultimate destruction of ancient practices of land use and land tenure and their replacement by practices closely related to those of the people who had taken over much of their land. It must, however, be re-emphasized that the plow would not, unaided, have been enough to effect this transformation. Among the many other elements that were involved, we must certainly recognize the following: the increasing inclination on the part of local and colony-wide administration to favor private ownership of land; the relative ease with which traditional patterns of land utilization were convertible to private tenure; the example of firmly-fenced, no trespassing, no-nonsense private lands all around them in the hands of the Europeans by whom they had been dispossessed; the urging of certain missionaries who saw land-use improvement contingent upon private ownership—so that a man might not visit the sins of his malpractices on others or be forced to inherit the product of others' malpractices; the growing numbers of small shops and Indian *dukas* in and around the Reserve, each with its expanding array of useful and not-so-useful items to be purchased with money if one had any; the limited and inelastic areas suitable for pasturing animals; the realization that hitherto unusable grain surpluses were now valuable because they could be sold to the surrounding tea estates with their large labor forces whose supplies were rationed; and the further realization that the cash earned from the sale of maize and cattle, of skins and hides, had a marvelous and durable quality of its own which made many of the tempting materials of the new life available to the producer-seller.

Surplus was good now, and the accumulation of a surplus in grain was made much simpler with the use of the plow than it would have been with the traditional tool of cultivation, the hoe. Nevertheless, surpluses could be realized only if there were enough tillable land so that expanding cultivation did not threaten to reduce grazing areas below tribal requirements, *or* if the cultivator could somehow contrive to exercise continuous control over his land *despite* the grazing needs of the tribe. Ironically enough, traditional patterns of Kipsigis land use had paved the way for such control, and the final transition from this to outright possession with the right of disposal by sale (to another Kipsigis) was a small and subtle step which, with proper hindsight, seems to have been inevitable in the *total* climate of British colonization in Kenya. From the moment disputes over land boundaries had arisen and been adjudicated by *kokwet* elders (as in aboriginal times), and then by the new native courts, and once these decisions had been upheld by District Officers and the District Commissioner, there was, it seems, no turning back.

It is conceivable that the administration might have taken a hand to halt the movement towards private possession of land once it became aware of the trend. Or it might have insisted that the practice be restricted to the few areas in which it had begun. But it did not want to reverse the trend or to invalidate the *ad hoc* determinations which had inaugurated the process and which had their basis in ancient and customary tribal law. The agricultural program depended for its development on the conversion to individual ownership of some kind; and this in turn involved the building of paddock fences for rotational grazing and natural fertilization of fields. The only way the government could have halted the entire program of conversion once it got under way would have been to order the destruction of the very fences which it considered essential to the development of its improvement schemes. However, I would guess that even if they had been willing to do this, or to forbid further claims, the process would have gone on because it had immemorial sanction in land-use customs, further support in the forms of herd ownership, and no workable scheme existed—during this period at least—of communal efforts towards the desired goals of cash accumulation. As a matter of fact, a few efforts at communal dairying and farming ventures which were launched during the 1940's failed.

Except for a few isolated hillocks where thatching grass grows, some swampland, cattle tracks, roads, gazetted markets, school sites, rivers and river banks, and a few insignificant and submarginal patches still open to free grazing in the most undesirable parts of the Reserve, all land is now claimed by individual Kipsigis. While the number of court cases and appeals involving land disputes in the Reserve shows some fluctuation during the last fifteen years, the trend in the areas where individual ownership was begun is down very sharply in the past five or six years. Even in those areas in which clearing is only now getting under way the number of court cases is clearly down. One may predict that litigation over original claims will continue to decline in all areas, and will, within a very few years, come almost completely to an end throughout the Reserve.

Figures from the files of the African courts in the Reserve are reproduced in the following tables. The Ndanai court is in Location Six, one of the more recently developing areas; Sosiot and Ainamoi courts deal with cases in Locations One and Two which show some internal differences in rate of enclosure (until 1956 there was no court in Ainamoi, hence the figures given through 1955 relate only to Sosiot and from 1956 to both courts combined); the Kapkatet court is in Location Three where Kipsigis land enclosure began; Silibwet court is in Location Five, one of the drier areas where the rate of enclosure has been erratic; and Longisa court is in Location Four where enclosure began relatively late.

It should be noted that land-grabbing and "speculation" have been a part of the transition, and that many inequities in the distribution of Reserve lands among the Kipsigis have become a by-product of the transformation. Some Kipsigis are completely without land and others have claims to land in several parts of the Reserve. In its concern over the inequities and the resultant growing discontent of those who are either landless or nearly so, the District administration in 1958 appointed a Working Party on African Land Tenure, consisting of Kipsigis and Europeans, to try to bring some sort of order out of the chaotic land situation which now prevails and which promises to become more serious as the pressures of a growing population on limited land increase. They are presently (1962) in the process of drawing up a series of recommendations which they hope to have enacted into by-laws by the Kipsigis African District Council. Since there is neither the wish nor intention of nullifying all existing holdings and starting from scratch, the best the Working Party may expect is a reduction in some of the more blatant abuses precipitated by land-grabbing. They must proceed with the recognition that *de facto* private tenure exists and that there is no retreating from this condition. Those claimants who cannot support their claims with evidence of use and/or improvement may lose some land. But the vast majority—even those who grabbed large chunks of forest and scrub during the last fifteen

Year	No. of Cases Filed	Year	No. of Cases Filed
	NDANAI		
1949	4	1956	405
1950	17	1957	259
1951	65	1958	142
1952	66	1959	126
1953	73	1960	69
1954	136	1961	17
1955	331		
	SOSIOT AND AINAMOI		
Sosiot only:			
1945	5	1951	367
1946	9	1952	515
1947	18	1953	479
1948	24	1954	336
1949	64	1955	294
1950	217		
Sosiot and Ainamoi:			
1956	358	1959	129
1957	307	1960	90
1958	157	1961	85
	KAPKATET		
1945	7	1954	155
1946	73	1955	160
1947	124	1956	92
1948	71	1957	62
1949	120	1958	50
1950	185	1959	49
1951	155	1960	51
1952	151	1961	60
1953	145		
	SILIBWET AND LONGISA		
Silibwet:			
1948	12	1955	207
1949	58	1956	251
1950	131	1957	185
1951	223	1958	146
1952	330	1959	55
1953[a]	173	1960	74
1954	225	1961[b]	48
Longisa:			
1953	192	1957	193
1954	212	1958	114
1955	214	1959	107
1956	232	1960	42

[a] Longisa established.

[b] Longisa closed down; cases transferred back to Silibwet.

years—will not have their land confiscated. For there is a ready market for land at anywhere from a couple of hundred to a couple of thousand shillings per acre. And the threat to dispossess non-using owners may only, it seems to me, stimulate more rapid sale of those lands which might come under question if and when the projected by-laws have been fully implemented.

In the preceding pages I have dealt at some length with the problem of land tenure and the relation of changes in traditional patterns of tenure to the overall matter of Kipsigis involvement in a cash economy which was brought to them from the outside. This cash orientation did not merely replace a prior economy of barter, but initiated the ongoing transformation of the Kipsigis from a condition of near self-sufficiency to one in which trade, with cash as the medium of exchange, is indispensable for survival. Many other changes have taken place in the lifeways of the Kipsigis as a result of their invasion by the Europeans, as a result of their existence within the Kenya Colony and of its position in the British Empire.

In his study of the economic development of Nyanza Province of Kenya from 1903-53, Fearn remarks: "The diverse pattern of the present-day economy of Nyanza [of which Kericho District is a part] has been moulded by four principle influences. These have been the non-African or world influence, the metropolitan influence, the 'Nairobi' influence, and the varied 'local' influences. From the conflicts of these influences during the past fifty years the Nyanza economy of today has emerged. . . . By the very fact of being part of Kenya Colony the Nyanza economy could not escape the consequences of colonial policy as this had been determined from time to time in the metropolitan capital of London" (1961, pp. 221, 222).

Subsequently I shall sketch some of the cultural changes—other than those in land tenure—which have taken place under British sovereignty, for they reveal, it seems to me, a kind of patterned inevitability. This is not to say that things could not have been different if the soils and climate of the Kericho area had been different; if circumstances in the Metropolis and the trade- and war-involved world of which the Metropolis was a part had been different; if the Kipsigis had been pure pastoralists at the time of initial contact; and if a number of other circumstances and conditions had not been what they were. One could, indeed, go on almost endlessly enumerating all of the circumstances which did and do exist and then conclude that in the absence of these or any one of them, things would have been different. Perhaps. But that is not the

point. The crucial point is that the Kipsigis, like many
all over the underdeveloped world were caught up in
of empires, in the scramble for colonies which characte
nineteenth and early twentieth century struggles of
industrial powers. Survival for each demanded expanding supplies of raw materials, markets for the disposal of manufactured products, and areas for the exportation of capital. The precise manner of exploitation of each area as it came under control of one or another of the imperial powers might have varied in details—in the forms of political control, in the kinds of crops grown and/or minerals extracted. These features were of course shaped by local conditions as well as by the power, and the material and ideological resources of the intruding nation.

In no two places in the world were the circumstances of contact and further development exactly alike. Nevertheless the results in all areas reveal such striking similarities of form and content that one can only describe the processes of change as convergent, as moving in the direction of sameness or at least towards a continual diminution of differences. Although a few of the observed changes which are recorded here bear a peculiarly Kipsigis-like flavor, many are virtually identical to the kinds of end-products which have been observed elsewhere and are revealed in the other essays of these volumes. Even those which appear to be unique outcomes of the contact often have close affinity in form with content-distinct features from other parts of the world.

POST-MARITAL RESIDENCE

It has been generally asserted for the Nandi-Kipsigis people that patrilocality prevailed. My own researches suggest, and Towett (1956) confirms, that while patrilocality may have been the preferred or most common form of post-marital settlement, it was by no means either uniform or rigidly prescribed. Matrilocality or neolocality, after an initial period of patrilocality, was not uncommon before contact, and the latter particularly so in the early adjustment to the invaders. When the drive for individual holdings erupted in the late thirties and the forties—and even down into the fifties—neolocal residence became widespread. But now within the last few years, and since free land for settlement has disappeared, there is already a noticeable trend towards patrilocality, which is bound to become accentuated at least until fragmentation of present holdings by inheritance (a problem with which the Working

Party on African Land Tenure is wrestling) makes the units completely uneconomic. I would expect, however, that as individual holdings shrink through fragmentation part of the answer will be furnished by increased peasant production of tea and by the tea estates and other large employers of African labor who will begin to drain off ever greater numbers of Kipsigis. Thus, between the time I completed my first field trip in 1958 and the time I left at the end of my second stint in 1962, there had been an increase in the number of Kipsigis employed on the tea estates of the two largest growers in Kenya, the African Highlands Produce Company and the Kenya Tea Company, from an estimated 10 per cent of the total to an estimated 20 per cent. This is true despite the fact that inheritance fragmentation can not have gone very far in the three and one-half years since the original research was completed. Higher wages, following the invasion of the tea estates by the Tea Plantation Workers Union of the Kenya Federation of Labour in 1959, may be a far more potent factor in the present movement of Kipsigis to the tea estates.

Those Kipsigis employees who are attracted to this labor market by the wages, or are compelled into it by land hunger, will, if they have them, continue to hold their homestead sites in the Reserve, but these may be inadequate to provide them with the major portion of their living needs. Right now one can see the foreshadowings of this process at work in some of the drier areas of Belgut which are adjacent to the tea estates of the Kenya Tea Company and the African Highlands Produce Company. Numbers of Kipsigis in this area are reluctant to put in the amount of labor that would be required to maximize returns from their poor lands. So while they generally make some minimal use of the land for grazing, they have not yet pushed forward with the earnestness of many other Kipsigis who are settled in more suitable parts of the Reserve where rainfall and soils can be depended upon to yield better returns in crops and in pasture. Kipsigis in the drier areas can be found in increasing numbers as casual labor on the tea estates. I shall have more to say about this later on when I discuss the position of the tea estates in the local culture and especially in the economic aspects of life in the Kericho District.

CATTLE

In pre-contact times cattle provided the Kipsigis with the major part of their subsistence and other needs. On the basis of statistics provided by local administration it would appear that this is still the case. For example, the District Commissioner's annual reports inform us that in 1957 the "sale of cattle through sale yards" yielded £182,585 ($511,238); in 1958 the figure was £204,384 ($572,275); and in 1959 it was £138,240 ($387,072). The income from the sale of maize through approved channels is given as £27,191 ($76,134) in 1957; £48,062 ($134,573) in 1958; and £76,240 ($213,472) in 1959.

Thus, even while the income from the sale of maize is increasing very rapidly it has *apparently* not equaled income from the sale of cattle. If we add to the figures for the sale of cattle the *estimated* value of the milk sold by Kipsigis producers it would appear that the cash value of their cattle is greater still. No figures on the internal sale of milk by Kipsigis are available, but the District Agricultural Officer estimated that in 1957 alone (the only year for which I could get such estimates) the Kipsigis earned somewhere near £10,000 ($28,000) through the sale of milk to other Kipsigis. Incidentally, this figure should be compared with the recorded figure of £13,500 ($37,800) paid to European dairymen by Kipsigis consumers for milk purchased at the Kenya Cooperative Creameries in Sotik in 1957. Now, if we add to the cattle and milk sales figures and estimates the money realized from the sale of hides—£16,109 ($45,105) in 1957; £6,171 ($17,278) in 1958; and £27,973 ($78,324) in 1959—we have, even with all of the probable inaccuracies of these figures, a seemingly convincing demonstration of the great cash value to the Kipsigis of their cattle.

There are, however, several unrecorded facts which render the maize-cattle comparison on the basis of official sales figures highly questionable. The first of these is that while large numbers of cattle are sold outside the auction lots maintained by the Kipsigis African District Council, the cattle sale figures given unquestionably represent a considerable amount of duplication and even triplication. For the same animal may often be sold in two or three yards before he finally passes to the ultimate owner, the butcher, or to a purchaser outside of the Reserve. As for maize, it is the unanimous opinion of those members of the administration who are involved with the matter, as well as the opinion of all of the Kipsigis informants questioned by me on the subject, that the total cash value of the maize crop to the Kipsigis is at least two or three times as great as the official figures suggest. One arrives at this conclusion by adding an estimate of the value of maize sold directly to the tea estate workers [2] and resident labor on many of the European farms, to the estimated value of the tremendous amounts of maize sold "over the border" to the Luo and the Masai, to the considerable internal sale among Kipsigis, and to other "illegal" sales made by the Kipsigis in order to realize a better price than that fixed for them by Produce Control.

On the basis of their knowledge of unrecorded as well as recorded sales of cattle and maize, there is no question in the minds of the agricultural staff, the marketing personnel, and the many Kipsigis with whom I have discussed the matter that maize is presently the number one money crop of the Kipsigis despite the *apparent* position of first importance given to cattle and cattle products by the official figures.

None of this means that the Kipsigis are indifferent to increasing the income to be derived from their cattle. Rather, they are intensely interested in improving the milk yields of their animals. To this end they conducted a running warfare with the administration for the right to own European grade cattle. Many of the Kipsigis with whom I talked during my first tour were resentful of the cash being drained from the Reserve by the purchase of milk from the Europeans, and they felt that they could tap this market if they were allowed to purchase grade cattle and gradually to get rid of the low milk-producing native animals. Since they work as milkers on most of the European farms whose milk goes to the Kenya Cooperative Creameries they felt that they had an opportunity to evaluate the relative merits of grade and native cattle.

But the Provincial Commissioner had issued orders that Kipsigis might not own these cattle, that they must stay with the native variety or upgrade by breeding their animals with Sahiwal, a superior humped cattle. To this end the government set up stations where cows could be served for a nominal rate; and from time to time it placed for sale large numbers of cross-bred cattle. The Kipsigis were generally uninterested in the superior meat and draught features of Sahiwal. They were determined that they should have cows that give more *milk*. Consequently a few hundred up-

[2] Rationing of workers on the tea estates was abandoned in 1959. This resulted in a sizable, but unrecorded, jump in the local Kipsigis sale of maize. Formerly the tea estates had contracted with large European growers and Maize and Produce Control for some of their maize ration requirements. The remainder, for rations and extra family requirements, was supplied by Kipsigis growers. Other Kipsigis maize (and millet) ended up on the estates in the form of beer brewed by the Kipsigis and sold to the tea laborers. With rationing ended, the laborers now buy almost all of their *posho* (maize meal) in the shops, markets, and barter markets of the Reserve where Kipsigis-grown maize provides the bulk of the meal sold.

Fig. 50. Cattle were formerly so highly esteemed and regarded with such affection that the first man who used them to plow a little over a generation ago did so at considerable risk to his welfare and status in the community. Today cattle have substantial commercial value and plows are used throughout the Reserve.

Fig. 51. The modern commercial value of cattle is evidenced by periodic auctions in various places in the Reserve. These auctions are carried on under tribal auspices and the sales are carefully recorded.

Fig. 52. One of the various government services to the farmers is the construction of water tanks, some of which are built to prevent the cattle from muddying up the water which is also used for human consumption. *Photo courtesy of Dept. of Information, Nairobi.*

Fig. 53. In a few places the government has piped water to centrally located faucets which relieves women of the need to carry five-gallon cans of water up steep hills from the streams. In this photograph a woman in traditional leather garments draws water into a native clay pot. *Photo courtesy of Dept. of Information, Nairobi.*

Fig. 54. In the town of Sotik, government institutions are mediated to the Kipsigis through the police headquarters, the post office, the infirmary, and the resident farm specialists; while stores, gas stations, garages, and other non-governmental services are in the hands of Indians, and the once-weekly banking activities (Barclay's) are conducted by Europeans.

Fig. 55. Within the Kipsigis Reserve commerce and trade are largely restricted to the Africans, although several trading centers, like those at Bomet, Litein, and a few other towns, are still dominated by Indians even though they are inside the Reserve. Markets are held at scheduled intervals. The buildings house shops which sometimes specialize in different commodities, while individual traders may lay their wares out on the ground.

Fig. 56. A major government service is to check tsetse flies, the bearers of sleeping sickness. Inspection may involve a blanket, as in this photograph, automobiles, or anything else that is suspect. *Photo courtesy of Dept. of Information, Nairobi.*

graded (native mixed with European) or pure grade cattle came, more-or-less illegally, into the hands of individual Kipsigis before 1960. Periodically, the government threatened to confiscate all of those animals for which specific permission had not been given. (A few Kipsigis were allowed to keep animals of this kind that they acquired, and the government kept a record of these.)

In a series of meetings that I attended in 1958, and which were held by the District Agricultural Officer and his staff at each location within the Reserve, the principal item under dispute was this one of the cattle. Numbers of Kipsigis had been fined for failure to get rid of their grade or upgraded cattle, but the protests mounted. The administration says that they insisted on native cattle or upgrading with Sahiwal because the Kipsigis were not prepared to give grade cattle the care they need; because native or native-with-Sahiwal do much better on the inferior kind of care the Kipsigis would give; because indiscriminate use of grade cattle would produce all kinds of undesirable hybrid strains in the Reserve; because many European farmers would take advantage of the Kipsigis by unloading their inferior grade stock on them at unreasonable prices; because the most serious of the sterility diseases, epivaginitis, causes only a fleeting infection to native cattle while European grade cattle never recover from the infection; because two lesser diseases of infertility, vibriosis and trichomoniasis, affect European cattle but do not seem to bother the native animals; and because the tick-borne east coast cattle fever, to which most of the native cattle seem immune, is often fatal to the European grade cattle.

To all of these admonitions the Kipsigis were indifferent. If the administration warned them that they would be victimized by unscrupulous European farmers anxious to unload inferior or diseased stock, the Kipsigis said calmly, "We, too, know a little bit about cattle." Or they replied, as did one man in one of the Locational Council meetings, "We are accustomed to disease and to death. Let us decide this matter for ourselves." Moreover, they were convinced that they had been forbidden to own grade cattle because the European administration supported the European farmers and wanted to insure that the latter would have a ready market for all of their milk; that the government, in short, did not want to permit the Kipsigis to compete with the European farmers for this lucrative market. And, they asked, if native cattle or native-with-Sahiwal are so wonderful why are the Europeans not building their own herds from this kind of breeding? They asserted, also, that the government wished to maintain the visual distinctions (conformation and color) because they feared that obliteration of these would make cattle theft from the Europeans a much easier matter.

As for the European farmers themselves, opinion among them was divided. On the one hand, many of them felt they could do pretty well if they were allowed to sell off their excess stock to the avid Kipsigis. This would certainly be a good and dependable market for some time to come. On the other hand, many feared thefts and the practical consequences of increased competition from the Kipsigis if the latter should develop herds of heavy milk-yielding animals. In this connection, the Kipsigis pointed to one of the European farmers in the Sotik area who, beginning in June, 1958, sent a daily truckload of milk to the small markets in the Reserve. This man was given special permission by the Provincial Commissioner of Nyanza Province to carry on this trade within the Reserve, and in six months sold 36,000 gallons of whole milk and 2,000 gallons of skim milk to Kipsigis consumers. "You know," said one young Kipsigis who had trouble with the administration over some four of his own beasts which were part "European," "this is the same Provincial Commissioner who told us we might not have European cattle ourselves. He does not seem to mind that we buy milk from these European cattle, only that we shall not own the cattle which would enable us to sell milk to our own people."

In the summer of 1960 the Kipsigis won their battle with the administration and are now allowed to own European grade cattle. A few of the local administration (European) claim the results have been disastrous in terms of loss through east coast cattle fever. However, the District Commissioner's report for 1960 states that "there is no reason why Grade cattle should not be a success." And many other members of the administration admit that after an initial period of difficulty, the Kipsigis are proving themselves capable of "coping with these more delicate animals" without experiencing undue losses.

The large and growing sale of cattle has another purpose and another function besides bringing in needed cash. It enables the increasingly sophisticated Kipsigis farmer to cull out his stock and simultaneously to reduce the dangers of overgrazing on restricted pasturage. The majority of Kipsigis feel that they will do even better with fewer cattle than they have now, provided these cattle are heavy milk-producers like the European grades. This trend is especially significant in the light of the many comments and assertions that have been made in the past about the reluctance of "Nilo-Hamites" or any "cattle complex" Africans to follow a program of voluntary reduction of their herds.[3]

It is interesting to note that while government precautions and defenses against cattle-stealing from other tribes improved over the years, and while the penalties for apprehension are severe, the practice has not died out. In fact, during the past thirty years, there have been periods of heightened activity of this kind. Today there exists an elaborate "underground railroad" for the rapid disposal of stolen cattle from Masai, Luo, and Kisii areas. That the practice has become a very lucrative business is attested by the fact, as reported to me by European police officers as well as by Kipsigis informants, of intertribal cooperation in the thefts—something unthinkable before pacification. The business not only involves Luo selling to Kisii and Kisii selling to Kipsigis, etc., but Luo who steal from Luo, Kisii who steal from other Kisii, and Kipsigis who steal from Kipsigis. The thieves and the authorized station-masters along the route all come in for their share of the loot. Sometimes the "hot"

[3] Early in 1962, the District Agricultural Officer told me that parts of Location Three (Buret), the most advanced of the Reserve's present nine locations, are now *understocked*. He reckons that more good cattle should be added here to maximize the cash potential of the land and to maintain good grass cover and high manuring.

cattle are sold directly and smuggled out of the district. Sometimes they are traded for "unhot" animals which may be added to the herds of the businessmen involved but are more often sold at leisure at a local auction.

Information from the District Commissioner's files reveals dismay at the heavy traffic in stolen animals. In the earlier reports, as well as in data supplied me by Kipsigis informants, it is apparent that many young Kipsigis warriors measured the year of work time (at 8 to 15 shillings a month until fairly recent times) required to save up enough to buy a heifer against the risks of going into Luo, Kisii, or Masai country to steal one. One informant told me he worked eighteen months on a farm in the Rift Valley in the late thirties, and with the money he earned he bought a heifer. Just one week after he got the animal home she died. "I was sad that I had worked so long for nothing," he said. With cattle easily convertible into the more magical medium of exchange represented by shillings, it is no wonder that the authorities have found it difficult to put a stop to cattle thefts, even while the grazing land shrinks.

OTHER CASH CROPS

Apart from maize and wage labor, animals and their products bring more money to the Kipsigis than anything else. However, there is no doubt that tea cultivation will soon supersede all of these in importance as a source of cash. Temperatures, soil, and rainfall combine over large areas of the Kericho District and parts of the adjacent country to make a situation ideal for the cultivation of tea. One of the special virtues of the crop at this latitude and these altitudes is that there is no particular harvest time for tea. It is plucked throughout the year. During the months which have less rainfall each plant may be plucked every fourteen or fifteen days. During the wetter and more rapid growth periods, each plant is likely to be plucked every eight to twelve days. This kind of harvesting—all done by hand—requires a dependable supply of labor all year round. In the Kericho District alone in 1958 there were more than 26,000 employees engaged in the various stages of tea cultivation and manufacture, almost 25,000 of these employed by the two largest companies: Kenya Tea Company (affiliate of Brooke Bond Company) and the African Highlands Produce Company (a James Finlay Company subsidiary). By 1962, due to certain improvements in methods of cultivation and processing, the number had declined by about 1,500 to approximately 24,500 for a slightly larger acreage of tea.

The first one and one-half acres of tea were planted in Kericho in the year 1912, but it was not until 1924 that the first small factory for its processing was erected. The ideal natural circumstances for its cultivation, coupled with the existence of a large and growing labor supply, a friendly colonial administration, and an expanding local and world market for the consumption of tea combined to encourage the rapid growth of the tea industry in the Kericho District during the past thirty-five to forty years.

Despite the rather sharp increase, between 1958-62, in the proportion of Kipsigis employed on the tea estates, only about 20 per cent of tea labor is Kipsigis, although the lands of this tribe edge the boundaries of the tea producers. Most of the labor is provided by Luo and Kisii tribesmen (resident on the estates), with a sprinkling of people from other and more remote reserves. This seemingly illogical minority status of the Kipsigis labor force has customarily been explained in the past as owing to three factors: (1) the reluctance of Kipsigis males, as compared with the agricultural Luo and Kisii, to engage in work with the hoe, since this kind of labor was the usual province of women, (2) the relative abundance of Kipsigis Reserve lands as compared with those of the more hard-pressed Kisii and especially the Luo, and (3) the presence, *in these very tea estates*, of a handy market for the sale of large quantities of Kipsigis-grown maize.

One might expect further changes in these proportions as the land base of the Kipsigis shrinks and the demands for cash continue to grow. For there are few opportunities outside of agriculture in which sizable numbers of Kipsigis might be employed.

Were it not for some other elements in the situation, one could, I think, predict with confidence that the growing land pressures on the Kipsigis and the tendency to be less finicky about hoe work than they were in the past might even lead to a reversal of the tribal proportions now found—especially on the estates of the largest companies—even while many Kipsigis continued to produce maize for sale to estate workers. However, there are at least two or three other factors which may inhibit the trend. One of these is simply that as pressures on Kipsigis land grow more severe, those on the more densely populated lands of the Luo and the Kisii also intensify. As the surplus population of these other tribes pours into the labor market it is natural that many will gravitate towards the tea estates where they may find jobs alongside friends or kin. In the second place, long years of experience with Kipsigis labor have turned many estate managers against them, for, as several of them complained to me, they often have trouble shifting a Kipsigis from a work he finds congenial, like pruning, to one he does not want to perform, such as hoe cultivation. Since the manager is understandably unwilling to saddle himself with a large staff of specialists whom he cannot shift around as the need arises, he is reluctant to employ Kipsigis. Moreover, since less than one-third of the Kipsigis live on the estates when employed, they are as a group not so dependable as the Kisii and the Luo, virtually all of whom live in company housing on the estates. Casual labor, like that of the majority of the Kipsigis, can become pretty risky in a tea situation where a dependable force of pluckers and processors is essential if the tea is to survive and the factory to be kept running.

A third element in the situation which may tend to retard the rate of Kipsigis employment in European tea-producing activities is one that has arisen since 1957, when each of 106 Kipsigis farmers was allowed to plant one-third of an acre of tea on his own farm. Since then many more have been brought into the scheme, and current plans call for a total of slightly over 1,200 acres of peasant tea production by 1965. At the moment this would mean roughly 1,200 producers, because the present prospectus calls for limiting each grower to one acre of tea. By the end of 1961 the number of Kipsigis engaged in tea cultivation had risen to 945; and while the government envisages the limit cited, there is no question that political realities and impending independence for Kenya have already rendered these estimates obsolete.

The passion for tea-growing may be seen all over the Reserve, even in those areas where natural conditions of rainfall and soil seem to make it impractical. Many more than 1,200 Kipsigis see themselves in the role of peasant tea grower, and a good many of these who had been reluctant to undertake wage work on someone else's tea were bouyed up by the hope that they might soon be working on their own tea.

In 1959, the Kenya Federation of Labour launched a drive to unionize workers on the tea estates in Kericho. At the time, the tea companies threatened to drop or seriously to curtail their extensive welfare activities if the drive succeeded. They said they might install mechanical pluckers (presently in use in Russian Georgia and Japan, but frowned upon by the teatasters because they tend to get much undesirable leaf). Finally they hinted that they might find it necessary to dispose of some of their tealands. The workers showed some interest but not much concern over the threats to curtail welfare activities and to introduce mechanical harvesting. But most of those with whom I discussed the matter in 1958, when the unionization rumors were just starting, ridiculed the idea that the tea companies would voluntarily diminish their holdings of cultivated land. Such a step, they implied, would offer no compensating economies and could only reduce further the profits that might be affected by enforced payment of higher wages. Moreover, it should be added, processing efficiency depends upon a crop geared to the optimal capacity of the factories. Reducing the size of the holdings would mean reducing the leaf to a point where processing would be conducted below an economically efficient level.

The companies have enormous investments tied up in land, tea bushes, and processing equipment. Plantation rather than peasant cultivation seems much more desirable under present circumstances. For not only do the factories represent an enormous investment whose economic functioning depends upon careful control of the crop—it costs about half a million dollars to put up a factory with an annual capacity of one million pounds of made tea—but the quality of the leaf must be dependably good. This is something which, the companies say, is easier to control on large estates than on hundreds of scattered peasant holdings. Finally, plucking schedules must be controlled and geared carefully to factory capacities.

So when the union did succeed, without any apparent difficulty, in overcoming the organized resistance of the Kenya Tea Growers' Association as well as the tribal differences and the assumed tribal hostilities of the labor force, the companies capitulated. A strike called in September, 1960, shut down completely all tea cultivating, harvesting, and processing activities for two weeks, and resulted in an increase of the basic wage from 72 shillings to 90 shillings ($10.08 to $12.60) per month. The large producers retaliated with some slight reduction in welfare activities. But it was not until January 25, 1962, that curtailment of welfare benefits took a form which was genuinely upsetting to resident labor. For on that date the Kenya Tea Company and the African Highlands Produce Company terminated their free primary education program for the children of resident workers. Before this, the companies' schools had provided the only organized free education in the District. From that point on, their schools charged the same fees as all others.

New wage negotiations were launched in 1961. The conciliation board's compromise failed to satisfy the union, and as this is being written (early 1962) they have threatened another strike if their demand for an 8 per cent increase "across the board" is not met.

While the tea companies are apparently in favor, right now, of limiting the amount of peasant-produced tea to a small fraction of the total (509 acres of African compared with about 25,000 acres of European-grown tea in 1961)—and have even agreed to process Kipsigis leaf for several years, or until they can get their own factory—they may in the long run count on certain advantages from expanded peasant cultivation. Labor costs are a tremendous factor in tea production, averaging for the most efficient producers about 0.9 worker per acre per year and, for the less efficient, 1.0 worker per acre per year. This is probably higher than most other important cash crops. The growers, who are now processors and sometimes distributors as well, might some day find it more attractive to try to dispense with these heavy labor charges—and the other risks of cultivation—by concentrating on processing and marketing and passing the labor costs of production and the risks of cultivation entirely on to the peasant cultivators.

But I do not think the Kenya Tea Growers' Association will, for the present, elect this particular response to unionization and periodic wage hikes. With annual profits for at least one of the major producers, Kenya Tea Company, ranging somewhere between a low of 14 per cent and a high of 40 per cent in the thirty-five years of their operation (McWilliam, 1957), they have a handy cushion to absorb some of the shock of higher wages for some time to come. Moreover, they may be able to economize with further cuts in their welfare program. And always there is the possibility that growing pressures from the overcrowded African areas may some day weaken the bargaining position of the union or destroy its effectiveness completely.

In any case, I would predict that more and more Kipsigis will accept employment on the big tea estates, even while others grow their own tea and/or grow maize for sale to tea workers. I would also guess that the cultivation of tea, of the less popular coffee, and of the newer cash crops of pyrethrum, groundnuts, garlic, and cotton, which have been pushed by the district administration with encouraging signs of success since 1960, may lead to even greater internal disparities in the size of holdings within the Kipsigis Reserve than now exist. For with land purchase legitimized, and with the real and potential value of tea and some of the other cash crops established, there will be a means available to astute and fortunate Kipsigis to acquire more land. Even if, as is most unlikely, the government is able to enforce acreage limitations on an individual producer, I do not see how the restriction could be applied effectively to purchasers of land where the crop already exists.

The Kipsigis have themselves raised the question of constructing a tea factory on a cooperative basis so that they would not be at the mercy of the European processors. However, getting a factory presents not only the problem of finding the $400,000-$600,000 (depending on capacity) with which to build it, but of providing also the roads and transportation equipment required to insure that delivery of the leaf to the factory will not drag out beyond the maximum time allowable between plucking and the start of processing —a matter of hours.

In 1960, the Kenya government negotiated a loan of £900,000 ($2,520,000) from the Colonial Development Corporation for the development of peasant tea cultivation. The bulk of these funds will go into the construction of six 1,000-acre capacity factories, one of which will be erected at Litein in the Kipsigis Reserve. This plant should be able to take care of most of the green leaf produced by Africans in the District provided the present proposed limit of 1,205 acres is not exceeded. An additional maximum of £60,000 ($168,000) has been promised by the Kenya government to make necessary improvements in the road network from tea farms to factories. The Kipsigis are, in general, pleased with these developments, although they are unhappy about the high carrying charge of the loan (7¼ per cent) and the heavy cess imposed on their leaf by interest and operations costs. And since they are looking beyond the 1,205-acre limitation, they have already begun to wonder how they may be able to meet future obstacles to the creation of a large peasant crop of tea in the District. With independence expected late in 1963, many of Kenya's politicians—including those in the Kericho District—are anticipating a strong influx of capital in the form of grants and loans, part of which, they hope, will find its way into the construction of more tea factories and a network of dependable roads. Whether or not heavy loans, investment, and grants are forthcoming—and there is every reason to believe that some help for peasant tea as well as other agricultural activities will come to Kenya with independence—I feel certain that ever-increasing amounts of Kipsigis labor will be found on the existing tea estates, and on the larger farms of other Kipsigis who have themselves been able to develop a respectable acreage of tea which cannot be handled with family labor alone.

The tea companies appear to be hung on the horns of a dilemma: If they hold on to their present acreage, they will need a dependable supply of about 20,000-25,000 laborers (unless they turn to mechanical plucking, which is not impossible even though most "tea men" apparently abhor the idea), and this labor may be in a position to present wage demands which would cut seriously into the present large margin of profits; if they abandon or sell their present fields to small European farmers or to Africans, they run the risk of deterioration in quality, difficulties of controlled plucking schedules, and, ultimately, the possible competition of cooperatively run factories. But the difficulties are less real than apparent. While there will be an increasing amount of peasant-produced tea in the next few years, the most important production—barring an unlikely expropriation of the tea companies soon after independence—will be on the corporate plantations with their own factories. And the combination of peasant and plantation production may turn out, in some ways, to be the most likely device for the preservation of the large companies, especially since virtually all blending and marketing operations involving East African tea are controlled by Brooke Bond Company, the parent organization of Kericho's second largest tea grower, the Kenya Tea Company.

Like tea, coffee is a new crop for the Kipsigis—so new that the first harvest was in 1960. Coffee presents fewer problems of labor and processing than tea, since it may even be sold in the red berry form (*buni*) in which it is plucked, and it need not be rushed from bush to processing plant in a matter of hours. However, some kind of processing is desirable, and there are relatively inexpensive pulpers and other equipment which might be used by the Kipsigis if several growers combine to purchase them. All gazetted growers in the Reserve are members of a single cooperative launched in 1959. It is expected that sometime during 1962-63 a loan will be made available to this group for construction of a pulping and drying plant.

Because coffee is a much chancier crop than tea, the Kipsigis are, generally speaking, not too keen on its cultivation. In Kenya, coffee is subject to coffee berry disease and crinkle-leaf, particularly at elevations over 5,000 feet; and the price fluctuations on the world market have been much more radical than those of tea. Besides, the Kipsigis know that many of the once prosperous European farms in the Sotik area invested heavily in coffee and went bankrupt in the early thirties when the bottom dropped out of the market. Very few of these farmers persisted with their coffee after that. They turned instead to dairying, maize, and ranching. Only a few of the old timers are once again trying coffee. The Kipsigis will tell you that no such calamity ever visited the Europeans who grow tea.

Under pressure from the District Agricultural Officer, however, we may expect to see coffee assume some importance as a cooperatively processed and marketed cash crop in certain parts of the Reserve during the next decade or so. Certainly, the neighboring Kisii have been busy during the past ten or fifteen years in the development of their peasant-cooperative coffee enterprise. And the crop is bringing them more substantial returns than it did before membership in the cooperative marketing and initial processing societies was made compulsory.

Earlier I discussed the importance of maize as a cash crop. I wish to add briefly here the reminder that there was some resistance to its cultivation in the first decade of contact, and that this resistance appears at least in part to have grown out of the activities of the sorcerers (*laibon*) who attempted to thwart most European administrative moves that seemed to challenge their control and power. Another reason for resistance to maize in the early period was that it was considered inferior as a food to finger millet. Finally there was the fear that since the government was handing out the seed and urging its cultivation, the Kipsigis could expect that they would reap the harvest and even seize the land. This last suspicion interfered somewhat later with the government's plans to encourage the planting of black wattle trees for firewood, soil conservation, and for cash from the sale of the bark which is processed for use as a tanning agent. The Kipsigis had watched them plant seeds in government nurseries, and from this many of them deduced that when the trees matured the government would come and take them and the land they occupied as well.

Although there is some fluctuation in the amount of maize sold from year to year—or at least in the amount which appears in the regular and supervised marketing channels—the trend is clearly upward for it is a favored crop with the Kipsigis. Even more than milk it makes up the largest single item in their diet, long ago supplanting the more nutritious millet. Maize is, for the Kipsigis, an ideal cash-plus-subsistence crop, while millet is produced in much smaller quantities and geared primarily to home consumption as beer. I think it is worth emphasizing, also, that the basic dietary shift from millet to maize took relatively few years, but that the change was unquestionably facilitated by the cash virtue of maize. For in the earliest years of contact there were already a number of fixed and some itinerant Asian traders who would buy all the

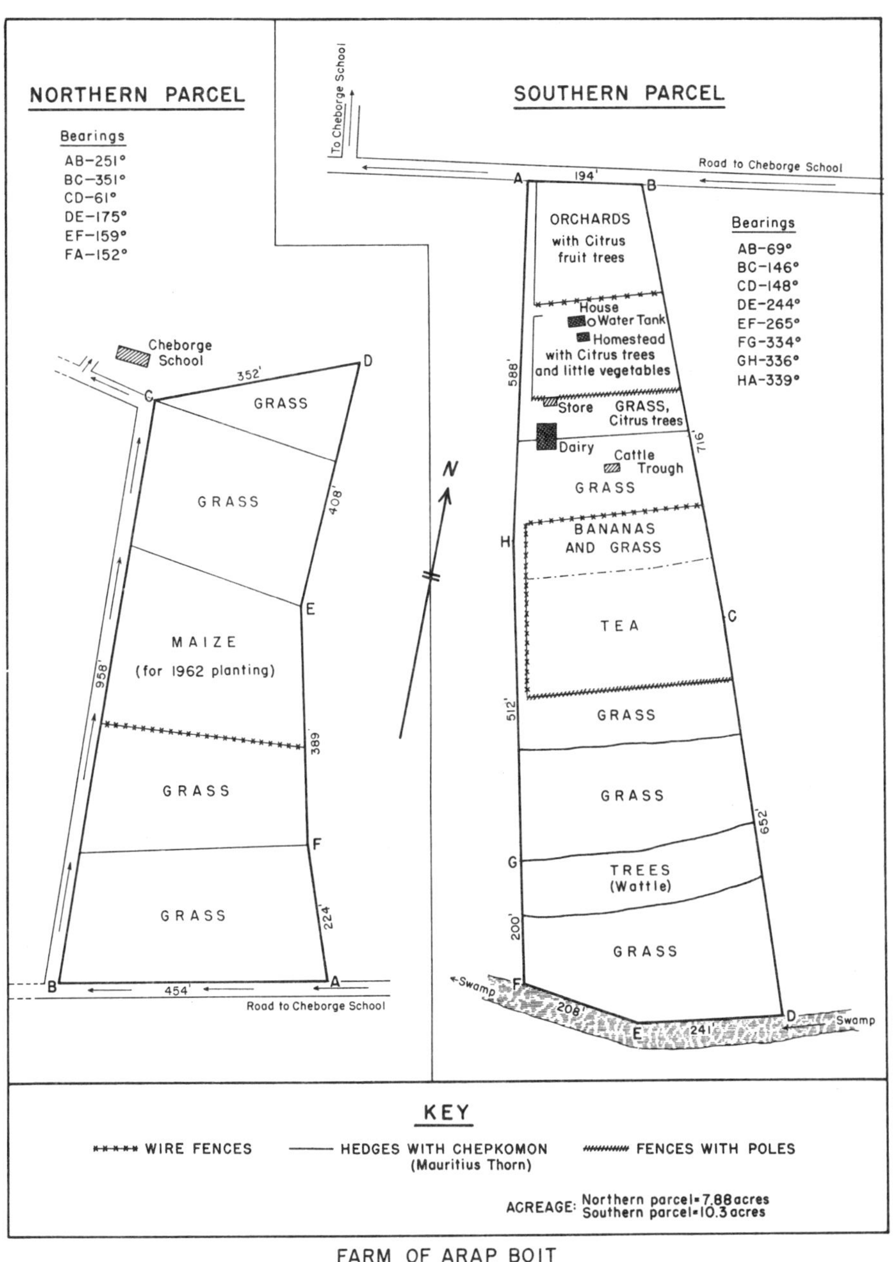

FARM OF ARAP BOIT

maize that was brought to them. Despite a very sharp decline in maize prices elsewhere in Africa during the past few years, the Kenya government, through the agency of Maize and Produce Control, has pegged local prices at a level high enough to encourage African producers to concentrate on maize. The Kipsigis producer had always had the added incentive of the adjacent tea estate laborers and their families for whom he grew maize. Now this market has been expanded even further since the tea companies terminated maize-meal rationing in 1959-60.

Other crops such as potatoes, onions, beans, cassava, wheat, black wattle, castor seed, and, more recently, pyrethrum, groundnuts, and cotton are produced and sold somewhat sporadically by the Kipsigis, but these do not loom nearly so large in agricultural income as maize and cattle. Some of the progressive Kipsigis farmers who follow closely the suggestions of the European agricultural staff have shown themselves eager to experiment with any variety of crops so long as these give a prospect of bringing in some money. The majority of Kipsigis, however, have tended to stay with maize and animals, and to use these for whatever cash requirements they have.

COMMUNAL LABOR AND WAGE LABOR

Some of the communal *kokwet* labor which is associated with the cultivation of millet may still be found in most parts of the Reserve. As in the past, this is confined only to the single crop, and the labor is usually repaid in exact amounts, or in the case of harvesting or fencing, with a beer party and a feast. It is interesting to note that communal activities were never applied in the cultivation of maize, for here a man appears to reckon his labor time in terms of the potential cash value of the crop and he would, I have been told, rather apply this time to the growing of his own maize (or potatoes, or beans, etc.) than to that of his neighbor or kinsman from whom he might indeed expect beer or meat, but never any of the cash realized from the sale of the maize.

An intriguing readaptation of communal labor with a modern cash twist came to my attention at one point. It was the time for digging up the sods, preparatory to drying and then piling them in heaps for burning. The *kokwet* bordered the farm of a European settler. Six women of this *kokwet* were involved in a communal labor exchange covering the digging of the sod on the plot of each. As was usual in these cases, each participant was responsible for a measured strip of the total field, an amount exactly comparable to the amount she would assign in turn to each of her companions when they came to her own field. Five fields were cleared in this manner and five women owed the remaining one an amount of clearing equivalent to what she had done on each of the others' fields. But instead of taking them to her field to work, the sixth member of the communal work party marched them over to the farm of the European settler, chatted briefly with him, and then led her squad to a field on which the European had himself wanted to plant some millet. When the team finished its job, the entrepreneur collected her fee—in cash—from the European, marched back to her own plot and began the single-handed clearing of the sods, a job which she finished unaided a few days later. But she had converted the communal labor into cash, getting it done quickly enough to satisfy her employer.

When I discussed this incident with some of my informants later, I was told that it was not at all uncommon for a group of women from a *kokwet* to hire themselves out as a working team for cash, thus retaining the virtues and the advantages of group work while converting the product into cash instead of crops. Within recent years some Kipsigis have begun to hire themselves out for wages to other Kipsigis. They are generally engaged in such work as plowing, fence-building, or milking and care of cattle. But by far the largest number of workers employed by Kipsigis with relatively large holdings are Kisii and Luo, with Watende, Kikuyu, or other tribesmen occasionally used. These may be employed in a variety of ways, but invariably their work will be tied to some cash-producing activity of their employer as, for example, weeding and thinning a maize crop, chopping of trees and manufacture of charcoal, pit-sawing timbers into planks, and, more recently, the plucking of tea. The wage generally runs between 50 and 75 shillings a month, with rations of ground maize-meal, salt, some milk, sugar, and, occasionally, meat. This compares with starting wages paid by the large tea companies of 78 shillings (90 after 3 months) for 30 days' work for adult male workers. Before 1959-60, rations were furnished on the tea estates if desired and reckoned at 23 shillings per month, this amount being deducted from the former minimum wage of 61 shillings for adult males. Adult females were paid 27 shillings per month with rations, and juveniles 17 shillings per month with rations. Even before rationing was completely abandoned by the tea companies, the trend had been sharply in the direction of demanding cash in lieu of subsistence. This was uniformly true of the majority of the Kipsigis, for these were casual rather than resident laborers. Resident laborers, on the other hand, who were accompanied by their families often found it more economical to accept the rations, which, according to the calculation of one of the largest companies, averaged over 26 shillings or three shillings more than cash payment.

Rationing was a holdover from former times when there were fewer outlets for the spending of cash. The big companies were pleased to see it end, for they have been expanding their own marketing activities with generally well-stocked shops, butcheries, and tailoring establishments on their estates. They have also instituted the sale of tea, bread, and bottled beer in their recreation halls. The margin of profit on items sold in these halls and the estate shops may be somewhat lower than that of outside shops, but the arrangement does serve to keep the cash circulating within the estate. And the distribution of rations was itself a costly and time-consuming operation.

SOME NEW SOCIAL FORMS

When the British arrived in Kenya and found no chiefs among most of the tribes with whom they had dealings they were impelled to resolve the complications this presented by appointing chiefs. Circumstances would not allow the kind of indirect rule Lugard and others had advocated on the basis of experiences in northern Nigeria and in parts of Uganda (Lugard, 1922). Furnivall reminds us, for Asia, that practical considerations usually dictate the choice between direct and indirect rule. "Colonial relations are primarily economic and, although pronouncements on colonial policy will be framed in terms congenial to national traditions, colonial practice is conditioned by the economic environment, and it is this, rather than any national philosophy of empire, which determines the choice between direct and indirect rule" (1948, p. 277). To this one might add that such a "choice" suggests the specious nature of the differences in function between the direct and indirect varieties of rule. But the fiction of indirect rule might be maintained if one seemed to be administering through a hierarchy of chiefs, subchiefs, and headmen who were the "natural leaders" of a society in which an entrenched political apparatus with centralized controls had never been established.

In their understandable haste to get things organized among the Kipsigis, the British sought these natural leaders by inquiry among the people. It is an ironic circumstance that while certain forms of natural leadership in the presence of the military leaders (*kiptainik*) or the judges (*kiruogik*), or the sorcerers (*laibon*) and their messengers did indeed exist at the time of initial contact, it was *not* these men, who were accustomed to positions of leadership among their people, who were chosen to be the transmission belts through whom government policies, directives, and plans might be put into operation. Most often lesser-known and even obscure individuals were appointed by the British. However, it was not a matter of British administrative policy that led to the selection of chiefs from among the ranks of undistinguished Kipsigis. For with the clear exception of the *laibon*—whose power presented a threat to British administration which greatly overbalanced any possible advantages that might have accrued through their utilization as a corps of leaders or chiefs —the intruders would probably have preferred to exercise their control through the Kipsigis' "natural leaders." But in practice the job of "chiefing" the different parts of the Reserve fell largely to men who had exercised no leadership functions in the past. In effect, these lesser men were chosen by the Kipsigis themselves, for they made it a policy in those earliest days to steer the British away from their own most competent people. Since they could not be sure of what would happen to the men whom the British were appointing they decided to offer them not their most desirable leaders but lesser people. If anything bad were to happen to these new British servants, they did not want it happening to their best people. These were to be held in unencumbered reserve so that the Kipsigis might have them to turn to for advice, help, and leadership in times of need.

Since proper administration of the tribe could not have been conducted without a political hierarchy which was both responsible to British aims and capable of reaching down through the most remote and smallest *kokwet*, the British superimposed upon this traditionally segmented tribal structure a centralized system of control whose apparent authority rested in the hands of the appointed chiefs and headmen. These were, of course, responsible in all matters to their creators.

At this time clan and phratry loyalties and obligations were not powerful enough to exert divisive pressures on the newly centralizing efforts of the British administration. Since the method of control was naturally enough directed through geographical units (called locations), and these crosscut phratry lines and invariably embraced people from a number of clans, there would have been impediments to any Kipsigis attempts to revive these social units as foci of opposition. Nor, under these circumstances, could clan and phratry have been made the instrumentalities of British administration. The superimposition of a new social structure left phratry, clan, *kokwet*, and family—monogamous or polygynous—temporarily undisturbed in form. The function of these accommodated and altered in time with pacification and the application of increasing amounts of governmental controls. But, just as significantly, their functions changed in response to economic pressures: land shortage; wage labor, first for taxes, then for the manufactured commodities of the industrial world, then for the purchase of land; cash crops; and, latterly, such money-making activities as building and renting of shops or running of same. Kipsigis men left their families to work on distant farms where they could not ordinarily be visited as they may have been in the old days when they cared for their cattle in far-off pastures. The phratry ceased to function as a military unit, but in recent days has blossomed as a kind of political club in at least one important sector of the Reserve. The clan, too, has begun recently to take over some of these same functions while declining in importance as the unit of collective responsibility for the actions of individual members. Nowadays, for example, clan members will often refuse outright to make cash restitution for obligations contracted by one of their group. When the family of an individual receives such restitution it is much more likely to be distributed among themselves than to go, as formerly, to clansmen.

With wergild and bride-price paid increasingly in cash rather than animals, there is a growing disinclination to shoulder the extensive collective responsibilities, as in former times. In defence of this process of individualization, the Kipsigis will often say that since things are not as they were in the old days, and since the government runs their lives and holds each Kipsigis individually accountable for his actions, it no longer makes sense for them to try to perpetuate the ancient patterns. "Who will pay my taxes if I am unable? My clan?"

In 1957 and 1958 it began to appear that while the military and collective responsibility features of the larger social units among the Kipsigis had either disappeared or were sharply on the decline, their newer political club usages might soon become a force for constructive internal conflict—constructive in the sense of furthering political action within the *tribe*, increasing the general level of political sophistication, and binding the parts in a struggle with each other into a more effective unity over time. In short, the creative and unifying functions of conflict and opposition (see Simmel, 1955; Gluckman, 1955; Coser, 1956) seemed then on the way to being realized in the emerging political functions of clan and *boriet*.

RECENT POLITICAL DEVELOPMENTS

But the African revolution ushered in by Ghanaian independence in March of 1957 was to hinder this line of political development so that internal unity and higher levels of political sophistication among the Kipsigis did not come out of clan and *boriet* conflict but in response to the continental "winds of change" and the worldwide forces of the post–World War II period which had stirred up the breezes in the first place.

Perhaps few things illustrate so well the structural involvement of the Kipsigis with this world outside their Reserve as do the political events which transpired between 1958 and 1962. The social field, the "system," or the structure of which the Kipsigis tribe is a part is, in one sense at least, the entire world. Whatever the creative role or functions of clan and *boriet* conflict *might* have become in a system better insulated from outside contact or pressures, these never got a chance to prove themselves.

Before 1958 a modicum of Kipsigis political education and action had been provided through the Kipsigis African District Council (KADC), a group of "elected" and nominated members whose functions, under the control of the District Commissioner, were largely advisory and administrative rather than policy-making. The KADC forum might serve occasionally to air some features of the European-African conflict. But its very structure insured that it could not function as an effective instrument of opposition to the European administration whose purpose, it was generally assumed, was to further the interests of the settlers at the expense of the Kipsigis. Besides KADC, the Locational Councils—as I have indicated elsewhere in discussing the arguments over cash crops and grade cattle—have proved an occasional forum for political expression. But apart from these and the clandestine activities of one of the oath-taking groups which functioned briefly and ineffectually among the Kipsigis in the early fifties, political activity and expression among the Kipsigis before 1957-58 appears to have been desultory, largely unorganized, and generally limited to a few "malcontents and troublemakers" who saw the source of most difficulties—and especially of the restricted pace of Kipsigis African economic development—in a repressive British administration. Since that time, however, large numbers of Kipsigis have become politically minded.

More than a score of African independencies have emerged between 1957 and 1962, and virtually all Kenya Africans are now looking forward to their own independence before the end of 1963. Thus, much recent political fire in Kenya has been directed against the colonial power and the residual injustices and frustrations of colonial rule. But for the Kipsigis and their Kalenjin congeners tribal loyalties seem for the present to be dominant over the apparent political need to submerge tribal differences in the interest of unity for independence and the fabrication of a nation. The threat, real or imagined, that an independent Kenya may be dominated by a coalition of Kikuyu and Luo, and that such a coalition of the land-hungry would exercise its political powers under independence to appropriate for themselves some of the land which the Kalenjins consider their own, has triggered a counterassertion among the Kipsigis which, for the moment at least, cements tribal feeling and centralizes tribal political efforts on the job of defending "tribal lands" against the potential raids of the outsiders. A generalized indifference to the fate of Kipsigis in other parts of the Reserve has been replaced by the feeling, as one elderly Kipsigis put it, that "if we do not put aside our envy of each other and fight together to hold our lands, we shall lose everything to the Kikuyu when the British have gone." Thus, a kind of modern politics has come alive for the Kipsigis, but with an ironic twist. The old enemy—the British—are still the enemy. But they are, for most Kipsigis, a far lesser evil than those African tribes allegedly poised and waiting to seize Kipsigis land when the British protector has gone.

Strange new alliances have been forged under the threat of independence and its aftermath. Thus, the organizing secretary for the Kalenjin Political Alliance headquartered in Kericho is a Luo. And, despite periodic ups and downs during the summer of 1962, the Luo and the Kikuyu have cooperated splendidly in their constitution-building activities and in their agitation for immediate independence. The Masai, ancient enemies of the Kipsigis and the Nandi, are now embraced within the same political party; while the Wakamba, Kikuyu, and Kisii find a new common cause with the Luo in the rival African party.

Since the summer of 1960, Kenya Africans have been divided into two political parties: the Kenya African Democratic Union (KADU) which includes the Kipsigis and other Kalenjin-speakers, the Masai, many of the Abaluhya, some coastal tribes, etc., on the one hand, and, on the other, the Kenya African National Union (KANU) consisting of the Kikuyu, Luo, most of the Wakamba, Kisii, etc. From the beginning, both parties have found some adherents in virtually all of the tribes. But the Kipsigis offered near-unanimous support to KADU which has emphasized what it calls regional "sovereignty over certain matters." The party has indicated Switzerland, the United States, the United Kingdom, Australia, and several other countries as examples of the "federalism" towards which it aims. KANU's leaders, until now (fall, 1962) have refrained from specifying particular models but have hinted strongly that they find Tanganyika's "one-party democracy" under strong central control an interesting East African development. Nevertheless, it has been remarked that in the present struggle for adherents KADU "stands foursquare for strong regional government" with a central government in control of defense, foreign relations, currency, higher education, etc. And KANU "stands foursquare for a strongly centralized or unitary government" and for the devolution to localities, districts, regions, counties, or whatnot of certain administrative and policy matters. In short, while both parties storm at each other for allegedly profound ideological and policy differences, each clearly recognizes the need for a central government apparatus with the power to give unity to the tribes and regions which make up Kenya; and each party agrees that the governing of a new nation, like that of an old one, requires the reservation of certain functions and powers to communities or parts of the whole. It need not be surprising, however, to one familiar with the sources of conflict that the issue of regionalism has emerged and become solidified as a hub around which deep anxieties and suspicions may be created and rallied.

About two years before the official split occurred, the African members of the Kenya Legislative Council had grouped themselves roughly along tribal lines. Even after the split was formalized in August of 1960—when the government had agreed to allow formation of African parties on a *national* basis—no issue of substance or policy separated the two parties. Both declared for immediate self-government and tandem independence. Both demanded the immediate release of Jomo Kenyatta. There was *no* discussion of post-independence regionalism or anything of the kind. KADU stated simply that they had been "forced" to create their party because African leaders like Mboya and Odinga (Luo), and Kiano and Gichuru (Kikuyu) gave every sign that they would take land from the "more fortunate minority tribes" after independence and give it to the "less fortunate" and land-hungry Kikuyu, Luo, and Wakamba.

Just prior to the birth of KADU, and while national African parties were still *verboten*, local leaders, including Towett, Ngala, Lemomo, Keen, and others had established tribal and linked-tribal associations like the Kalenjin Political Alliance, a union of the Kipsigis, Nandi, Elgeyo-Marakwet and other Kalenjin-speaking peoples; the Masai United Front; the Coast African Political Union, and others. Of these, probably the strongest and best-disciplined is Towett's Kalenjin Political Alliance. Towett is a Kipsigis, the first of his tribe with a university degree, and the first Kipsigis to be elected to the country's Legislative Council where he now serves as Minister of Labour and Housing. In the February, 1961, election Towett, running on the KADU ticket, polled 56,445 votes against a combined total of 158 votes for his two KANU opponents. (On a national basis KANU received 67.4 per cent of the popular vote against 16.4 per cent for KADU.) His overwhelming popularity among the Kipsigis may be attributed to the happy coincidence that the tribe is relatively well off with regard to the quality and per capita distribution of its land and the proximity of excellent European settled areas to which the Kipsigis wish to lay exclusive tribal claim as these may "come up for grabs" after independence. Towett has capitalized this land anxiety as a major source of his political strength by repeated reminders at rallies and *barazas* and in newspaper interviews that the tribe must be prepared to defend its lands against seizure by "enemy" tribes. So far as I know, no single event or combination of events in the post- or late pre-contact history of the Kipsigis has so united them as the "threat" of independence—as this has been emphasized and amplified by Towett and others.

For example, in a KADU rally held at Kapkatet in the Kipsigis Reserve on December 30, 1961, the organizing secretary of the party exhorted an enthusiastic audience to hold out for "regionalism or death." And on the same day at a mass meeting held in the Rift Valley town of Nakuru, the party's Executive Officer announced that "there is no freedom without regionalism." Thousands of Luo and Kikuyu living and working on European farms and estates in the Kericho District were warned at another rally that they had better leave before they were forcibly expelled. And some Luo students attending secondary school in the Kericho District have several times been forced back onto their own Reserve when they attempted to return to classes after a holiday.

In the fall of 1961 the Member of the Legislative Council (MLC) of the Kalenjin Elgeyo (KADU) told his constituents that "Jomo Kenyatta [leader of KANU] knows that the Kalenjin Area is not Kikuyu Country. If he attempts to spread KANU in our area he will be inviting war." At the same meeting a Nandi MLC warned that "if the Colonial Office gives power to KANU then it must make sure that it has sufficient forces in the country because we will resist." And a Masai spokesman instructed an audience of Kipsigis to stifle political action by Luo tea workers in the area. "If you see anyone opposing our policy of regionalism you should remove him from the area."

On another occasion during the winter of 1961-62 the irrepressible MLC from Elgeyo (KADU) told a Kalenjin audience: "If the British government refuses to give us *majimbo* [regionalism] I shall tell my people to sharpen their spears and poison their arrows so that we shall fight. . . . I will lead the war myself."

And the elected leader of the Kipsigis, Towett, announced to his tribespeople during a 1961 rally: "If the Kikuyu continue taking oaths there is no doubt that there *will* be a Congo in Kenya. And if they start anything we are prepared to wipe them out."

All of this agitation and incitement to violence have had their expected effect on the normally fragmented Kipsigis. In the light of the largely imaginery threats—fanned, it must be said, at least in part by the personal ambitions of KADU politicians who see their present favored status evaporating in future elections—the Kipsigis seem to have put aside ancient intratribal differences and indifferences and become united against African outsiders. It is an irony of recent history that all of the injustices (real and imaginary) suffered by the Kipsigis at the hands of the British settlers and administrators never served to unite them against the Europeans as a tribe in active protection of their group interests. Yet the fostered fear of *other Africans* has brought about that internal unity, and it has done so in an era when nation-building in Africa has made tribalism anachronistic.

Late one afternoon in October of 1961, an old Kipsigis woman climbed to the top of a hill some two hundred yards above her hut. Facing south, she uttered a short, loud cry, repeating it until it was picked up by another woman on a hill about a quarter of a mile away who, in turn, faced south and aimed the same cry at a hill almost half a mile from where she stood.

Before morning, the ancient war-cry of the Kipsigis had traveled 75 miles from Lumbwa on the northern edge of the Reserve to Kapkimolwa on the south. Before nightfall, ten thousand warriors were massed at several hundred points on roads and tracks throughout the Reserve. Many of them carried shields and spears and had their faces daubed with paint, others had only a bow and poisoned arrows, a short sword, or a club. Except for a few Kipsigis who lived near to the place where the cry had originated, none knew what had caused the alarm. But the warriors stayed and milled around, speculating excitedly about whether "the day" had come, until the tribal police explained that a young European farmer had fired his gun "in the air" in order to encourage some Kipsigis to get off his land, and that one of the men seemed to have been wounded slightly in the shoulder. This was not the news they had expected (in fact, a rumor had already begun to go around to the effect that some Kikuyu laborers had burned down fourteen Kipsigis huts). When it came they revealed a mixture of relief and disappointment as they broke up and returned to their homes.

This was the first time since the Pax Britannica that the war-cry had rocketed from one end of Kipsigis country to the other. In fact, it was the first time since 1936—when the theft of a few cattle led to a small, localized mobilization against the Luo in the border village of Sondu—that the cry had been heard at all. Yet ten thousand men, many of them born after the Sondu incident, rushed out of their homes prepared to defend themselves or to attack an unknown enemy.

Two weeks later a dog chased the goat of a Kipsigis on to the plot of a Luo laborer. Later, when the owner went looking for his goat, he saw it grazing peacefully near the Luo's hut and mistakenly assumed that it had been stolen. In a few minutes the war-cry was heard again. Inside of an hour hundreds of armed Kipsigis had once more assembled—only to disperse when they learned the cause of the alarm. Three more times during the winter of 1961-62 the war cry was heard and warriors gathered.

Most people who know the Kipsigis assert that five or six years before—or even five or six months before—none of these mobilizations could have occurred. Most *kokwotinwek* and sublocations on the Reserve concerned themselves with their own problems and paid little attention to the lives and problems of other Kipsigis. And though they have a central governing body in the form of the Kipsigis African District Council, the mass of the tribe have tended until very recent times to think more in parochial than in tribal terms.

In short, the spirit of tribalism demonstrated by these incidents and by the enormous increase in the clandestine manufacture of bows, arrows, and poison throughout the Reserve, reflects not so much a revival and accentuation of ancient loyalties as an accommodation to events and pressures of the very recent past. The significance of Kipsigis behavior in these battle-ready assemblages lies in the fact that several incidents which would have gone virtually unnoticed some months before became cause for full mobilization.

A dog chases a goat into the garden of a Luo; and a Kipsigis is alleged to have been wounded by a European. Thousands of warriors mobilize—not because they *know* that a Luo is supposed to have stolen a goat or that a European may have wounded a Kipsigis, but because they, like a good many other Africans in Kenya, were led to believe that they were in danger of losing land to some of their badly overcrowded neighbors if the "wrong" political party came to power. They had been warned often in the preceding few months to stand ready against this threat. As a result they came to think of themselves less as part of a country on the verge of independence and nationhood than as a tribe which might have to defend its substance against predatory tribes who will use independence or the prospect of independence to take over land claimed by the Kipsigis.

Taken by themselves, however, these incidents do not signify the triumph of tribalism over nationalism in Kenya. They could be just isolated examples of the not uncommon phenomenon of a revived provincialism or tribalism going hand-in-hand with an upsurge of nationalism. Evidence of these two ostensibly conflicting tendencies is reported from many parts of the "developing" world: from Southeast Asia, from various parts of Africa, from the West Indies. Unfortunately, however, in the opinion of those who see a better chance of peaceful development towards economic and political stability in a strongly centralized government than in a polity in which regionalism and tribalism could be the pattern, the behavior of the Kipsigis is not unique to them.

So alarming did the general situation become that District Commissioners and police officers in the widely affected areas held repeated public meetings, exhorting the people to remain calm and to avoid the rekindling of ancient animosities and the creation of new tribal enmities. The Minister of Defense made personal visits to several of the more explosive areas to confer with European officials and with tribal leaders. On one such visit to Kericho he pleaded once again for an end to tribal threats. He deplored the "inflammable statements" of politicians and asserted that "tribalism . . . is being fostered entirely by the African politicians themselves.

. . . They are insulting rival tribal leaders and abusing them by saying such things as 'we don't want foreigners in our area' and 'look out for chaps over the border.' "

It is not true to say that another Congo is impossible in Kenya, but at the same time it makes no sense in the present circumstances to cite Mau Mau as evidence for the fact it *can* happen here. Mau Mau was not a movement of tribe against tribe. If violence and bloodshed should come to Kenya now it would not derive from the violence that was Mau Mau but from today's fabricated fears of "foreign" tribes. In the late winter of 1961-62 two Kipsigis watchmen on an isolated tea estate in Kericho were attacked by a "gang of ten Africans." One of the watchmen escaped, the other was beaten to death. Four days later another Kipsigis watchman on a tea estate was attacked by "unknown African assailants." Both of his hands were cut off. On the same day six "Africans attacked two Luo walking along a road" in Luo country not far from the Kipsigis Reserve. One of the Luo escaped and the other was beaten and stabbed to death. It is impossible to know whether any of these or other similar incidents had anything to do with the politically fomented increase in antagonism between Luo and Kipsigis. But this type of occurrence has been uncommon enough in the past to warrant some concern. In any case, it is apparent that given the intense sense of tribalism that appeared under careless nurturing during the political campaigns of 1961-62, a wandering goat, an insult, a chance political remark in the wrong place might easily have precipiated a far more serious incident.

Internal opposition to KADU and to the charisma of Towett have been slow to appear among the Kipsigis. The handful of those who have been alarmed by the prospects of regionalism are fearful of taking an open stand in favor of the political program of KANU. Instead a group known as the Kericho Africa Club (KAC) was formed in October, 1961, and served in a very small way as a local avenue of expression for KANU-type views on the issue of a strong central government. Ostensibly, those who joined the KAC were not KANU but individuals interested in "studying" some of the developing political issues of the day. Membership was solicited from *all* tribes and all racial communities in the area. Two public dances, one celebrating Tanganyika's independence and the other celebrating Christmas, were held. These were well attended by Kipsigis and by a few members of non-Kipsigis tribes. No Asians and no Europeans, with the exception of myself, came to either dance.

A series of public debates and meetings was also held for the purpose of discussing regionalism, Africanization, the problems of independence, etc. These were attended almost exclusively by local Kipsigis and myself. The organizer and leader of the Kericho Africa Club, Theophilus arap Koske, is Secretary of the Kipsigis African District Council and generally believed to be sympathetic to KANU and the idea of a strong central government, although he has been careful in the prevailing climate of opinion to deny formal association with KANU.

Whatever the political interest and activities of the Kipsigis, as a tribe, may turn out to be between this writing and independence—and after—it is fairly clear now that this pre-independence period has involved them with "national" issues in ways in which they have never before been involved. Further, it is my guess that the alarming strength of tribal feeling and the monolithic support for Towett and KADU which now feature their expanding political consciousness will, before very long, tend to dimish. For with the coming of independence and the almost certain accompanying political growth and dominance of KANU, I would expect increasing numbers of young Kipsigis males to declare themselves openly in support of KANU. A strong opposition to Towett's domination of the political scene should then emerge.

Although the social field of which the Kipsigis are a part has included their European "neighbors" and administrators for the past 60 years, it was possible for many Kipsigis largely to overlook or to underestimate the significance of their ties with extra-familial, extra-*kokwet* or extra-tribal groups. However, events of the last few years have probably altered that naive sense of isolation for all time. Thus, the fierce increase in Kipsigis anxiety about their "tribal lands" is less a manifestation of the tribal wish to be left alone than it is a perverse sign of their recognition that they will never again *be* left alone.

MARKETS AND MARKETING

The growth of markets among a people who had never known them before contact with Western industrial society is at once a manifestation of that contact and an indispensable agent of its intensification. If one is willing for the moment to pass over the missionizing and the anti-slaving purposes of British intervention in East Africa—even while admitting that these elements have been present in the whole fabric of imperial relationships—one must admit that Kenya (and Uganda, and India, and etc.) was occupied and developed by the British with the aim of extracting wealth, either in the form of agricultural produce or raw materials for sale in a world market, or as a place for the sale of home-manufactured commodities and the investment of metropolis-owned capital. If export commodities were to be produced, they would require the use of indigenous labor. And if the labor was technically free or unforced it must have had either incentives or the absence of alternative modes of survival available to it before it would do the work that creates or makes possible the production of items for market sale. (See Ross, 1927, pp. 92 ff., and Weston, 1920, for a discussion of the devices and abuses practiced to bring the Africans into the labor market and hold them there.)

A long heritage of intertribal hostilities was one of the factors that limited the possibility of migration of the Kipsigis—and other groups in Kenya—in sizable numbers to areas where they might escape the new administration which came to them around the turn of the century. Another element tending to keep emigration rates for the Kipsigis relatively low was the fact that the land they had finally come to occupy after a century or more of conflict was, by and large, good land with good pasture and adequate rainfall, far better than many of the lands around them to which they might have essayed migration. And a third—if not the final—feature was the Kipsigis' familiarity with the land and an unwillingness to leave it unless the outside threat became so formidable that there would be no choice but to leave or to die if they remained. The vast majority of Kipsigis has apparently never felt the British to be such a threat.

In short, apart from those Kipsigis who were forcibly evacuated to make room for Europeans, the overwhelming majority remained because they saw no struggle for survival impending as a result of the loss of some of their lands. Those Kipsigis who did not find themselves suddenly embraced as squatters on land which was formerly theirs might have persisted indefinitely in the old subsistence ways—eked out by minimal barter for metal spears and hoes or a few other essentials which they ordinarily did not themselves produce. Those who, as it were, awoke one day to find themselves squatters [4] had the choice of remaining and going to work for the new white

[4] Smith (1950, p. 92) reports an "old petty chief" from the Transvaal saying, "My grandfather went to sleep one night in his own Kraal. Next morning he awoke and found a white man there who said, 'You are living on my farm. You must work for me.'"

owner of the land or moving to unalienated lands among their friends and kinfolk.

Thus, while the new white settlers required labor in order to make their own investment and that of the mother country pay off, they found in Kipsigis a people who might, at least in the beginning, survive in their accustomed ways without going to work for the white man. Even the hut tax and the later poll tax could not alone be counted on to produce the growing labor supply required by the settlers. For if the resistance to this kind of labor were stronger than the fear of losing a small portion of one's subsistence to the tax collector, the Kipsigis could have paid their taxes from the sale of animals. But the resistance to working for the white man was in general *not* strong enough to prompt the sale of a goat or a sheep for tax money. Many sold hides and skins and, later, maize to itinerant Asian traders, but the majority went to work in order to earn money. Soon the itinerant or other traders settled down at Litein, Bomet, and Kipsonoi in the Reserve as well as in the main towns of Kericho and Lumbwa. They not only bought the hides and skins, and the maize that was beginning to come in, too, but they had commodities for sale. Cloth, beads, knives, axes, *pangas* (machetes), salt, sugar, and other items soon crowded the shelves of the Indian traders, and the Kipsigis bought more and more of these things as time went on and as they began to acquire more cash. On some of the estates the European owner himself set up a small shop in which he offered goods for sale to his squatters. But by 1962 the main volume of trade had become concentrated in two towns, four major trading centers (where the shops were owned chiefly by Asians), and in sixty African market centers (with more than 500 shops) scattered through 1,001 square miles of Reserve. In addition, almost all of the approximately fifty tea estates and many of the private farms that ring the Reserve still have their own shops.

It is impossible to get any accurate information on the volume of trade conducted in the towns, trading centers, markets, company stores, and the huge open markets of Kericho and Sondu—not to mention the once- or twice-weekly open barter market [5] held at each of the Reserve's African market centers. But it is considerable. There is little question that government support and encourage-

[5] So-called. The only barter I have ever encountered at any of these or other markets in the Reserve involves the exchange of maize for clay cooking vessels. The latter are made by the Luo and transported to the Kipsigis Reserve. The hawker will usually accept in lieu of money as much maize seed as is required to fill the pot. All other transactions almost invariably involve cash.

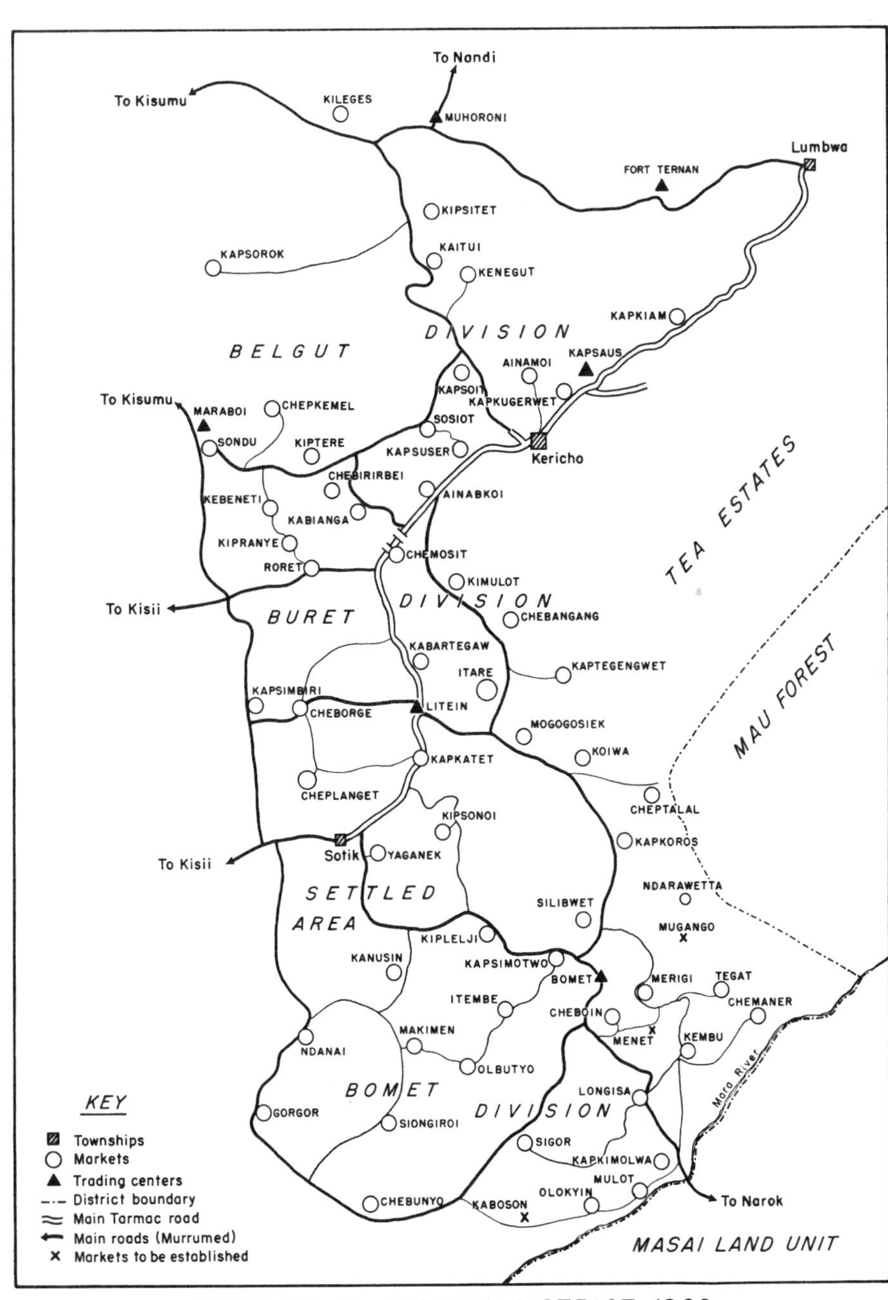

MARKETS IN KERICHO DISTRICT, 1960

ment of formal marketing played an important part in advancing wage work among the Kipsigis even before Nyamburugi arap Rotich set up the first Kipsigis-owned shop at Chemosit in the year 1925 or 1926. Leys remarks: "For a tribe to be content with its own produce is referred to almost as if it was wicked. To increase the wants of Africans was the universally approved object to be pursued . . . the object aimed at was to induce Africans to become wage-earners." "Formerly wealth could only take the form of more wives, more sheep, more beer. Now there are innumerable ways of spending money delightfully: On European food, clothing and furniture, in cinemas, on gramophones, sewing machines, cigarettes" (1924, pp. 201, 261).

Trade and market centers have proliferated so rapidly in the years since arap Rotich opened his shop that the commerce carried on in these centers has become an important source of wealth for increasing numbers of Kipsigis. For example, in 1957, 450 traders licenses and 23 stock traders licenses were issued in the District. In 1958 the numbers rose, respectively, to 832 and 38. And by 1961 the number of traders licenses issued reached 1,304 and those for stock traders 49.

In 1949, Kenya's Registrar of Cooperatives assisted 183 shopkeepers to launch the Kipsigis Traders Cooperative (KTC) to help them with the purchase of stock. Shares are 500 shillings ($71) each, and no member may hold more than three shares. This enterprise has faltered several times in the course of its existence and been rescued with loans issued by the central government and the Kipsigis African District Council. In 1958-59 the United Africa Company, Limited took over as managing agents but gave up in 1961 when management was assumed by Dalgety and Company, a firm whose East African headquarters are in Nairobi. The Cooperative is still under the nominal ownership of its Kipsigis shareholders, but management of its affairs is in the hands of Dalgety's own highly trained personnel. Despite all the official effort expended on its behalf, it is estimated by officials of the KTC that only 20 per cent of all goods and supplies currently purchased by Kipsigis shopkeepers, including members of the Cooperative, comes from the Kipsigis Traders Cooperative. The remainder is supplied by two Asian traders in Kericho whose vans visit each of the sixty markets in the Reserve at least once a week. Until 1960 they—and the occasional bootleg trader—were in the habit of extending short-term credit to some shopkeepers in the Reserve. But losses tended to run fairly high, so the two merchants agreed—in the absence of any other severe competition—that they would sell only for cash. They have adhered to this policy ever since and say that they are more than pleased with the results.

In general, competition is confined to the Asian merchants themselves, for the products handled by them are bulk food items, bottled beverages, canned goods, etc., while the Cooperative concentrates on a different set of commodities. There is no evidence at present that Dalgety plans to "move in" on the range of items peddled by the Asians. They seem to feel that with the total volume of trade expanding as rapidly as it has during the past few years, even 20-25 per cent of the market will justify their efforts.

CREDIT

Sources of credit for African shopkeepers are limited, especially since the two chief Asian traders discontinued short-term credit in 1960. Official government sources are hedged around with very serious restrictions and carry an interest rate of 5½ per cent. Among the several impediments to securing one of these loans from the Kericho Joint Loans Board (African Traders) is the stipulation that the borrower must be using the money for expansion or development only and not for the replenishing of stock. Moreover, before an application is finally approved, the applicant must attend a six-week course—at government expense—in bookkeeping, stock management, etc. Attendance at such a course presupposes literacy, so no Kipsigis who cannot read or write may even apply for one of these restricted loans. In Kapsuser, one of the largest and most prosperous markets in the Reserve, only three applicants out of approximately twelve were approved for loans. In other markets the average is considerably lower. The Board was established in 1953-54 with a revolving fund of 200,000 shillings ($28,570), provided half by the central government and half by the Kipsigis African District Council. Since that time there has been no increase in the capital funds, and only fifty-three loans totaling 288,000 shillings ($41,143) have been approved. In terms of the size of the fund itself, the figures appear quite satisfactory. But in terms of capital requirements and the number of loans vs. the number of refusals, the amounts are considerably below current and expanding demands. For example, in 1959 only ten loans were approved for a total of 21,500 shillings ($3,071); in 1960, twelve loans totaling 28,970 shillings ($4,138) were granted; and in 1961 the number of loans dropped to five and the amount to 16,000 shillings ($2,285).

A small number of the African shopkeepers, particularly in a large trading center like Litein, may get loans from their more prosperous Asian competitors in the center. Although the interest rates are allegedly much higher than those charged by government, the Asians insist that they offer the service with considerable reluctance for, as they point out, it means support for their competitors. They add that they do not have much choice, for the refusal of a prosperous Asian shopkeeper to lend money to a struggling Kipsigis shopkeeper might hurt his own business. With racial feelings exacerbated during 1961-62 by the imminence of independence and the appeals of the Kenya African Democratic Union (KADU) to tribal loyalties, Asian shopkeepers have become even more sensitive to the threats of an unofficial boycott of their premises if they do not lean over backwards to accommodate their Kipsigis competitors when they are able to do so.

In general, then, we must conclude that there are as yet few sources of long-term credit available to the Kipsigis. A small number of loans has been made to Kipsigis who are certified as "better farmers" and who want to improve their domestic water supply by building a house with a corrugated iron roof and gutters leading to a water storage tank. Thirty-year mortgages covering 90 per cent of the cost of purchase are being offered during 1962 to 109 farmers selected for occupancy of the first Land Settlement scheme in the Kericho District. This scheme has been subsidized in part by Great Britain and in part with funds provided by the World Bank. The Kenya government has already purchased a number of farms in various parts of the White Highlands. These are being divided into individual holdings on a freehold basis. A Sotik farm of 3,300 acres was bought from its European owner and carved up into 109 farms ranging in size from an average of 24 to an average of 38 acres. Three thousand, five hundred and forty-five Kipsigis applied for these 109 farms in 1962. Roughly 300 additional family-sized farms are scheduled to be made available from further purchase of European lands in the East Sotik area. In 1963-64, 500 more farms will be opened to the Kipsigis with the freeing of 18,000 acres out of 25,000 now held in the Chebalungu Forest Reserve by the Kipsigis African District Council under instructions from the administration. It is said that the 500 Chebalungu and the 300 East Sotik farms will be "presented" to landless Kipsigis without charge, hence without mortgages and without the need for that form of credit.

With the exception of funds recently made available for the purchase of tea stumps (seedlings) and coffee seedlings on a long-term basis, there is little credit for the purchase of seed, or of fertilizers, farm machinery, insecticides, and so on. When the loan program was instituted in the early fifties, some grants for the purchase of oxen and plows were made, but that was soon discontinued. The borrower's cattle are formally pledged as collateral on the loan, but the government admits that it would be very difficult to collect these from a defaulter, for they would be almost sure to disappear before the creditor came to claim them.

With the general encouragement to some cash cropping which followed the introduction of tea and the lifting of restrictions on the purchase of European grade cattle in 1960, the situation began to improve somewhat, and small loans were given towards the purchase of grade stock. However, it should be noted that, apart from credit extended for the purchase of tea and coffee seedlings, the entire amount available for loans of all kinds to Kipsigis farmers in 1961 was something under £ 5,000 ($14,000). Consequently, many Kipsigis could still be found insisting that the meagerness of the all-important farm-capitalization loan funds reflected the government's "genuine feelings" about the encouragement of peasant cash crop production. The administration's answer to these complaints is that they are now "encouraging" the planting of coffee, pyrethrum, cotton, groundnuts, and other cash crops. And the present tea planting program has been made possible only through grants, first by the Kenya government and, since September, 1960, through a long-term Colonial Development Corporation loan of £ 900,000 (at 7¼ per cent per annum), administered by the newly established Special Crops Development Authority (see p. 314, *supra*). The program not only supports time-purchase of tea stumps but provides funds (reimbursed through a cess on every pound of green tea turned in by the grower) for collecting, processing, and marketing of the tea, as well as for the construction of six factories, and the creation and support of tea nurseries. The Authority has set a goal of 1,205 acres of peasant tea for the Kericho District by 1965 (Special Crops Development Authority, 1962).

One other type of government loan was made available to the Kipsigis in the 1950's. This, too, was a water loan and allowed for the construction of rams and pumps—usually expensive projects in which a number of borrowers might be involved. Up to January, 1962, the government had made several such loans, with preference going to Locational Councils rather than individuals.

Fig. 57. The traditional type of Kipsigis house was well known among the tribes of western Kenya for its superior construction.

Fig. 58. This European-type house was built with money earned by a Kipsigis who pioneered in the move to cash cropping and private ownership of land. He claimed some 200 acres and became very wealthy.

Fig. 59. One of the "model" Kipsigis farms is owned by a school teacher. He built a modern house for his wife and children but his mother lives in the traditional-type house, the inside of which is blackened by smoke which can escape only through the thatched roof. The layout of this farm is diagrammed on p. 317, *supra*.

Fig. 60. In some of the primary and most of the intermediate schools, classes in farm improvement are offered along with more conventional subjects. See p. 348, *infra*, for an example of an intermediate school farm plan. *Photo courtesy of Dept. of Information, Nairobi.*

Fig. 61. The girls' initiation ceremony involves traditional rites concerned with circumcision but has also included use of Western dress and even spectacles by certain participants during observances the night before. *Photo courtesy of Jeffrey Taylor.*

Fig. 62. A group of female initiates in traditional leather garments and masks. *Photo courtesy of Jeffrey Taylor.*

Fig. 63. Tribal elders gather to suck native beer through long tubes and to talk. *Photo courtesy of Jeffrey Taylor.*

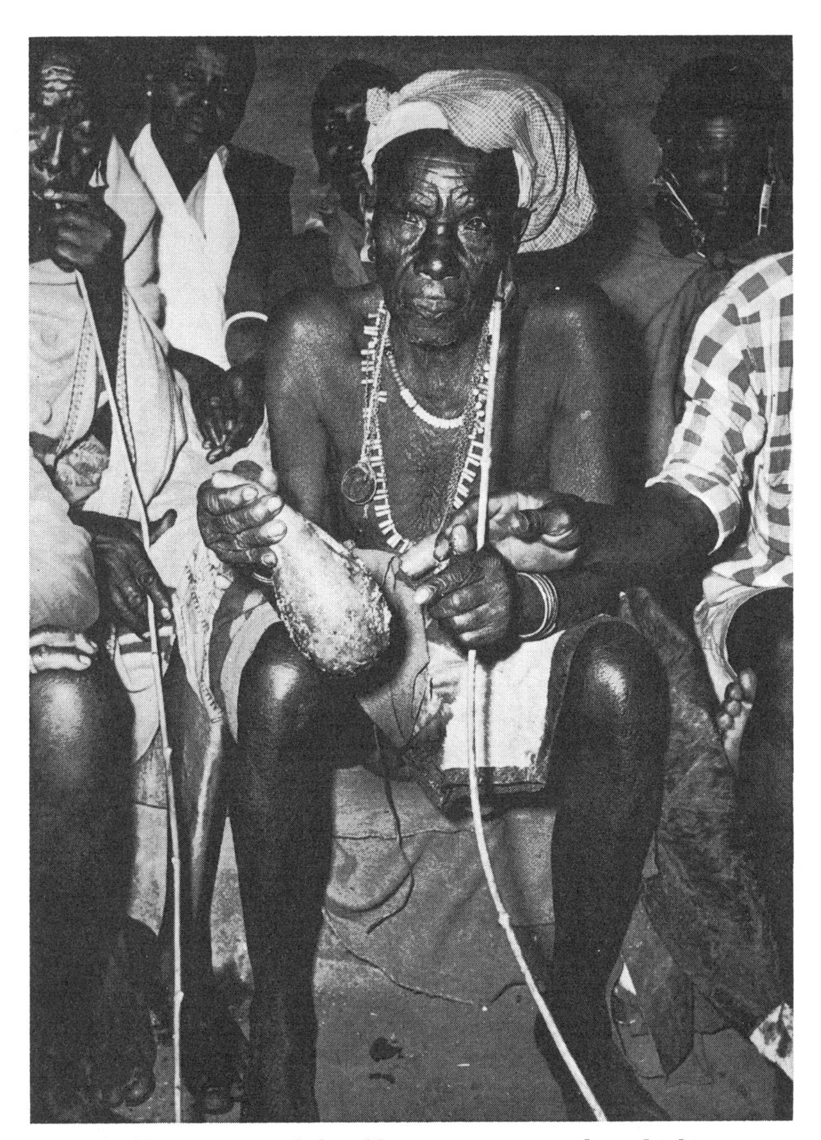

Fig. 64. Kipsigis man of the older generation at a beer-drinking party. *Photo courtesy of Jeffrey Taylor.*

Of the short-term individual improvement loans mentioned earlier, there were 177 made up to January, 1959, from Kipsigis African District Council, African Land Development, and Joint Water Board funds. The total amount approved from this revolving fund to that date was 278,400 shillings ($38,976). Overdue installments on this sum came only to 16,630 shillings ($2,328). Toward the end of 1959, the administration proposed that "the granting of loans should be restricted to enterprises which were likely to increase the farmer's profit sufficiently to enable the loans and interest to be repaid with some profit for the farmers." However, this new emphasis has had little practical effect on cash cropping in the District, since only 15 loans totaling 29,600 shillings ($4,144) were approved during the year, and most of these went for water improvement (District Agricultural Officer's Annual Report, 1959). In 1960, the number of loans issued by the Kipsigis Joint Loans Board rose encouragingly to 63 and the amount to 69,480 shillings ($9,727) (District Agricultural Officer's Annual Report, 1960). Again most of the loans were made for improving water supplies and were limited, with few exceptions, to a maximum of 2,000 shillings per borrower. In 1961 the Board, still emphasizing water development but now making a few loans for construction of cattle-cleansing facilities as well as for the purchase of grade cattle, granted 91 loans totaling 79,280 shillings ($11,099).

If one discounts the time-purchase of tractors, buses, and trucks by companies of Kipsigis (sometimes as many as twenty or thirty men will be partners in the ownership of a tractor, bus, or truck), there are no other significant ways beyond those already mentioned in which a Kipsigis may borrow money. Loans from kinfolk, friends, or age-mates are uncommon, primarily because savings are generally low or nonexistent. The general assumption of the people at this stage of their involvement in the money economy seems to be that of subsistence-habituated peoples elsewhere: "If you haven't got it, can't get it from the *serikali* [vaguely, the government], or can't make it out of your own *akile* [shrewdness or skills] and resources, you must try to be content with getting along as you have in the past."

I think it would be safe to predict that when and if the present landholding arrangements in the Reserve are converted by registration into formal freehold or fee-simple property, the sources of credit will blossom. For then it will be feasible to pledge one's land as collateral for a loan, provided, of course, that land registration goes hand-in-hand with expansion of cash cropping. Thus, the land will serve, on the one hand, as security for the loan, and, on the other, as productive capital earning money to repay it. The creditor will see more clearly the justification for making a loan which is to be applied to capital investment rather than to consumption. Under present circumstances, it is obviously impossible to secure a loan against land from the banks, and there are few Kipsigis with enough resources to lend large amounts of money. Besides, there is always the possibility that the *kokwet* elders or the courts might refuse to approve occupation or possession to a Kipsigis who acquired a piece of land from another as the result of debt defaulting.

MIGRATION

Apart from the relatively permanent out-migration of Kipsigis to certain settlements in Masai country, there is, as yet, comparatively little movement of Kipsigis out of the District. Land hunger is not the important factor here that it is among such tribes as the Kikuyu and the Luo. The tea estates of Kericho and Sotik can usually absorb a good proportion of those Kipsigis who want extra cash, who are without any land, or who must find work to eke out an inadequate landholding. Although it is impossible to get accurate data on the movement of Kipsigis into the larger towns like Nairobi, Kisumu, Mombasa, and Nakuru, it is reckoned by local officials—and supported by my own observations and inquiries—that not many Kipsigis have transferred to urban centers. In the first place, Nairobi, which is Kenya's largest and most important city, virtually impinges on the Kikuyu Reserve, and the Kikuyu have been far more severely hit by land hunger than the Kipsigis. Consequently most of the relatively few jobs available in this lightly industrialized city went, before the 1952-56 Emergency, to Kikuyu. Kisumu is surrounded by Luo, Abaluhya, and other tribes whose reserves are also more densely populated than that of the Kipsigis and who, therefore, have been in the job market there and elsewhere for a much longer time. Mombasa has work on the docks and the railroad yards for limited numbers of Africans, but most of these jobs have long been preempted by Luo, Wakamba, and other tribesmen.

During the twenties and the thirties, and again during the Second World War, numbers of Kipsigis did go to work on European farms in the Rift Valley and elsewhere in the Highlands where they served as herdsmen and milkers, jobs which they prefer. Even this trend seems never to have been very great nor the numbers involved very large. Some of the men who migrated in this manner took their families, others did not. The vast majority of them have apparently come back, and it is unlikely that more than a few thousand Kipsigis in all (including some 250 in the colonial police force and the army, and an indeterminate but probably sizable number of prostitutes) are employed outside of the Kericho District. Consequently the volume of outside money coming back into the Reserve is not nearly as great as it might be were there more cities and more industrial activity to provide jobs in Kenya. In fact, one of the compelling difficulties in the Kenya situation—which affects the Kipsigis far less at the moment than it does many other peoples—is the absence of an industrial community, of important mining, transportation networks, and other laboring activities to absorb the increasingly large numbers of reserve-bound Africans who are being forced off the land as the population grows.

HEALTH, EDUCATION, AND THE MISSIONS

The three most important missionary groups in the Reserve are the Mill Hill Roman Catholic Mission with three stations and six missionaries, in addition to a staff of European nurses and a doctor; the African Inland Mission with one major station and seven missionaries; and the World Gospel Mission with about twenty-eight missionaries and three major stations, including a hospital and doctor. The Seventh Day Adventists have come into the District recently, but it is too soon to judge the progress they have made. The Roman Catholic Mission has been functioning in Kericho only since 1946, the WGM and the AIM trace their origins through a series of other designations back to the end of the first or the beginning of the second decade of this century.

While it is difficult to assess the full impact of these missions on the Kipsigis—even in terms of conversion—I am convinced that they have had a far greater influence on the Kipsigis in ways that are not formally religious than they have on their attitudes towards the supernatural.

In a charmingly frank autobiography, Willis R. Hotchkiss, the first missionary to settle in Kipsigis country (he came in 1905), has emphasized one of the extra-curricular or adjunct advantages of missionizing. His remarks were calculated to pacify those skeptics in the mother country who may have had qualms about spending "all that money just to bring the Word to a bunch of ignorant—and certainly unappreciative—savages." .Rev. Hotchkiss says: "Trade always follows the missionary. . . . It seems incredible, therefore, that any intelligent man can fail to be interested in Christian missions, when every pagan brought to Christ becomes in the very nature of the case an asset in the economic structure instead of a liability. These very Kipsigis, who but a few years ago were a drain on the British taxpayer, are now buying everything, from needles to automobiles. By every consideration of good business sense, therefore, Christian men ought to get back of the missionary enterprise instead of leaving it to the women, as they have done hitherto" (1937, p. 101).

While I have been furnished figures on conversions and baptisms, I am quite ready to accept the word of the missionaries who themselves gave me the data that these figures may be so wide of the mark as far as indicating the Christianizing of those who are enumerated that they are not very useful.

In the secular sense, however, there is little doubt that the missions have had considerable influence on the lives of the Kipsigis. For education was almost entirely under their supervision until very recently; many of the medical facilities from field dispensary to hospital are provided by the missionaries; and the source of a good deal of the early impetus towards cash crops, construction of mills for grinding maize, as well as the drive towards individual land acquisition appears to have been some of these same missionaries.

The Mill Hill Roman Catholic Mission has its headquarters in London, and the fathers are themselves from England and the continent. The World Gospel Mission and the African Inland Mission are American-supported, multi-sect, Protestant fundamentalist in character. The latter two condemn most dancing, all smoking and drinking, the cinema, polygyny, female circumcision, all "pagan ritual," and unsupervised communication between boys and girls. The more relaxed attitude of the Catholic missionaries towards most of the items on this list has won them greater support from many Kipsigis while simultaneously earning for them a reputation among the American missionaries of opportunism, syncretism, and downright paganism.

While most of the costs of education are born by the Kenya government and the Kipsigis African District Council, and subsidized in part by tuition fees,[6] the formal administration of the majority

[6] In 1958 fees in the four primary years for each student were 20 shillings a year and in the intermediate school's four years, 45 shillings. Costs for the primary student were computed at slightly more than 63 shillings and for the intermediate student at 171 shillings. In 1960 tuition went up to 25 shillings and 55 shillings a year, respectively.

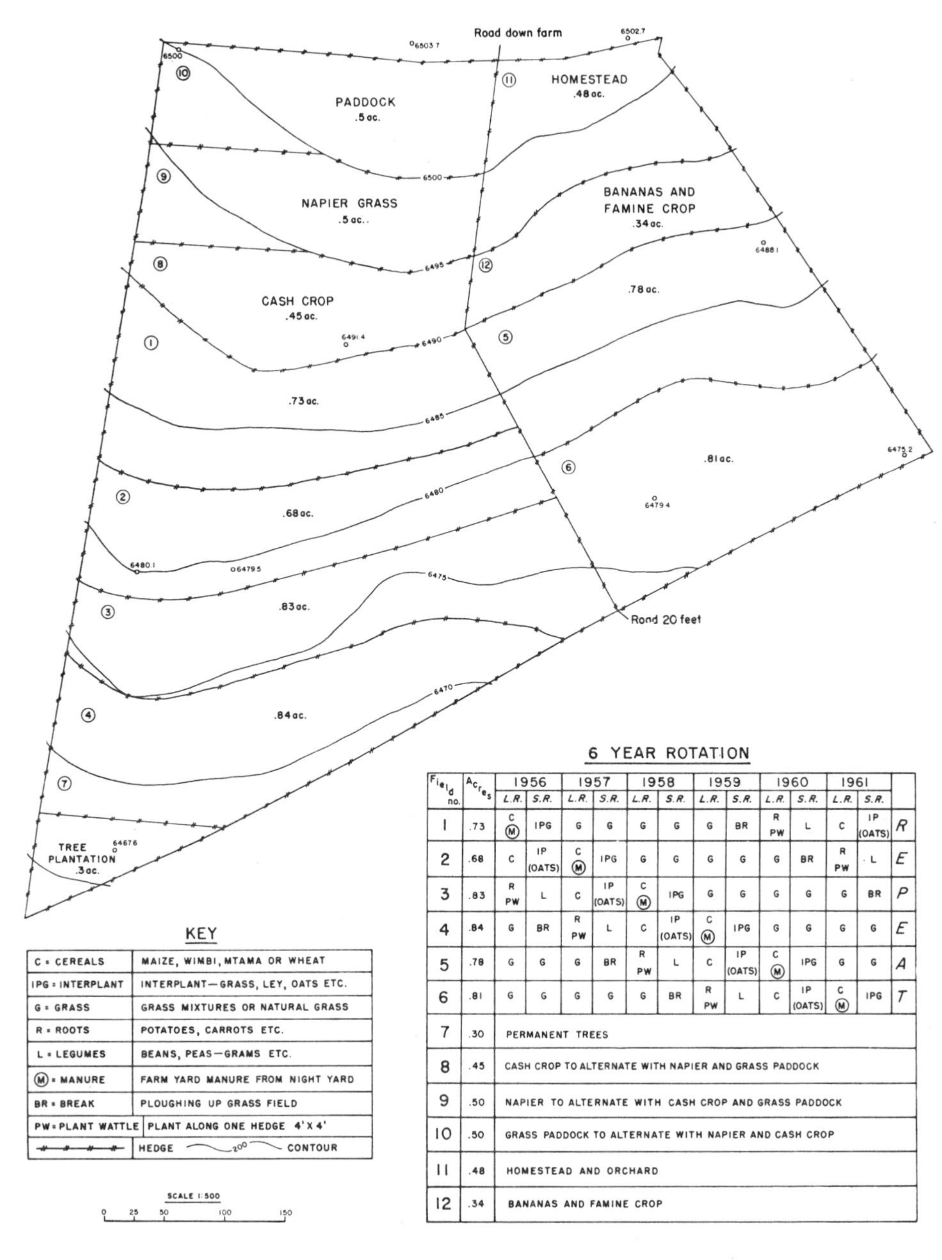

6 YEAR ROTATION

Field no.	Acres	1956		1957		1958		1959		1960		1961		
		L.R.	S.R.	L.R.	S.R.	L.R.	S.R.	L.R.	S.R.	L.R.	S.R.	L.R.	S.R.	
1	.73	C (M)	IPG	G	G	G	G	G	BR	R PW	L	C	IP (OATS)	R
2	.68	C	IP (OATS)	C (M)	IPG	G	G	G	G	G	BR	R PW	L	E
3	.83	R PW	L	C	IP (OATS)	C (M)	IPG	G	G	G	G	G	BR	P
4	.84	G	BR	R PW	L	C	IP (OATS)	C (M)	IPG	G	G	G	G	E
5	.78	G	G	G	BR	R PW	L	C	IP (OATS)	C (M)	IPG	G	G	A
6	.81	G	G	G	G	G	BR	R PW	L	C	IP (OATS)	C (M)	IPG	T
7	.30	PERMANENT TREES												
8	.45	CASH CROP TO ALTERNATE WITH NAPIER AND GRASS PADDOCK												
9	.50	NAPIER TO ALTERNATE WITH CASH CROP AND GRASS PADDOCK												
10	.50	GRASS PADDOCK TO ALTERNATE WITH NAPIER AND CASH CROP												
11	.48	HOMESTEAD AND ORCHARD												
12	.34	BANANAS AND FAMINE CROP												

KEY

C = CEREALS	MAIZE, WIMBI, MTAMA OR WHEAT
IPG = INTERPLANT	INTERPLANT—GRASS, LEY, OATS ETC.
G = GRASS	GRASS MIXTURES OR NATURAL GRASS
R = ROOTS	POTATOES, CARROTS ETC.
L = LEGUMES	BEANS, PEAS—GRAMS ETC.
(M) = MANURE	FARM YARD MANURE FROM NIGHT YARD
BR = BREAK	PLOUGHING UP GRASS FIELD
PW = PLANT WATTLE	PLANT ALONG ONE HEDGE 4' X 4'
—#—#—#—	HEDGE ~~200~~ CONTOUR

SITOTWET A.I.M. SCHOOL FARM
LOCATION 2 KERICHO
(7.24 ACRES)

of these schools is still in the hands of one or another of the three leading missions within the District, although their autonomy in educational matters has now been drastically curtailed. The curricula are prescribed by the District and Provincial Education Boards as part of the Kenya education system which is, in turn, tied in to the Commonwealth system (at the conclusion of secondary school or the twelfth year) by the Cambridge Overseas School Certificate.

Although the administration opened four new intermediate schools (Standards V through VIII) in 1958, and five in 1959, only 38 per cent of those students applying to the intermediate schools in 1958 were accepted, and 34 per cent in 1959.

Before I returned to Kenya in 1961, I had almost been persuaded by these and other discouraging figures that unless the central government were prepared to make massive contributions to school construction and teacher training (of a total of 497 teachers in the District at the end of 1959, 299 were listed as "trained," 198 as "untrained"—which means that they had not completed intermediate school), the eagerness of the Kipsigis children and their parents for education would continue to outstrip the administration's capacity for coping with it. Even now most schools are built with voluntary contributions of cash and labor by the members of the *kokwotinwek* which are to be served. The increase in enrollments within the three-year period from 1957-59 not only reflected the value being placed on education as a device for upward mobility in the new cash-oriented world of the Kipsigis, but carried the threat that funds and staff would be unable to keep pace with the demand. In 1957 there were 15,551 children enrolled in the four primary grades in the District, of whom approximately 2,800 were girls. In 1958 these figures rose to 16,603 including 3,224 girls, and in 1959 the number was 18,500 with 4,015 girls.

However, by the time I had completed my second field trip I became convinced that primary and intermediate education (now combined into a single seven-year program) would soon be available to almost every Kipsigis child whose parents were able to afford the fees and the loss of labor or income implied by the child's attendance at school. For I discovered that the addition of eight new intermediate schools in 1960 allowed 65 per cent of the students who applied in that year to be accommodated. And by the end of 1961 *all* Standard IV children were given places in Standard V for 1962. Meanwhile, the enrollment in all primary schools in the District had risen to 22,352 at the end of 1961, of whom 23 per cent or 5,959 were girls. At the intermediate level there were 5,960 students enrolled in the District of whom 17 per cent or 813 were girls. The facilities for teacher-training have been expanded in Kenya, and there is every expectation that independence will see an accelerated training program and an expansion of the seven-year primary program. A number of new secondary schools have been opened in Kenya during the last three to four years, and increasing numbers of students for whom there would have been no accommodation in the past may now count on admission to this higher curriculum.

Many of the parents who send their children to school today do so at considerable sacrifice, for tuition and other expenditures may represent a significant portion of the family's total income. But wherever I went in Kipsigis country, and no matter whom I talked with about the matter there was the same enthusiastic agreement that education was the prerequisite to accomplishment in the present world and that it was worth any sacrifice to insure that the children would be well equipped to cope with a new world in which it was not enough that one should know how to care for cattle or to plant a field of millet. One must know as well how to read and to write and to figure. Many Kipsigis parents have expressed to me, sometimes with almost poetical fervor, the importance of education for their children. Most of them seem clearly unconvinced that the old way of life can come back or that it should come back. "The tools of success in today's world are no longer the spear and the knife but the pencil and the book." When the government in the past failed to provide enough schools and teachers, Kipsigis looked upon this as a conscious ruse to keep the Kipsigis illiterate and non-competitive—an ample and continuing supply of unskilled labor to take care of the needs of the European farms and estates in the District.

There is little question that the efforts of the missionaries have made some slight inroads on the practice of female circumcision and polygyny. But still the overwhelming majority of girls—even many of those who have been to mission schools—submit to circumcision and the protracted initiation ceremonies and rituals associated therewith. While the missionaries might prefer to take complete credit for what appears to be a small decline in plural marriages—particularly in areas close to their headquarters—I would speculate that pacification (bringing the sexes into a better numerical balance), developing land shortages, and the growing shift from cattle to cash as bride-price are also factors which have played a part in whatever decline has taken place. In partial support of the missions' asserted effectiveness in this matter, however, I must point out that my own investigations revealed a larger proportion of polygynous marriages in the more remote and underdeveloped parts of the Reserve than in those areas where enclosure, cash cropping, and other signs of the shift from "pure" subsistence to cash-plus-subsistence are more numerous. And these are developments in which the missions have played their own small part, however guided, defined, or limited by forces outside their particular jurisdiction.

Because selection of teachers rests ultimately with the supervising mission body, the missionaries have in general tried to staff their schools with avowed adherents of their own church. Since adherence means, among other things, compliance with the restrictions on smoking, drinking, and so on, the teachers in Protestant-supervised schools are subject to suspension or dismissal for violation of the injunctions against this kind of behavior. Caution and cynicism are the uniform response. It was alleged by many of my young friends—some of whom were themselves teachers—that they could not live in strict accordance with the regulations laid down for them. Virtually all of the young men and some of the young women teachers as well either smoked or drank or did both when they were safe from detection. They resented deeply the infringement on their personal rights. But, as they pointed out, hypocrisy was not a choice but a necessity. Their employment depended upon outward conformity, and they needed their jobs.

In the realm of health, the missionaries and their medical services have made important contributions to the welfare of the Kipsigis. Increasing numbers of women go to the mission hospitals to have their children. Mission, government, and Kipsigis African District Council dispensaries treat large numbers of people daily. And the two mission doctors on the Reserve have, through their efforts and their achievements, impressed large numbers of Kipsigis with the efficacy of European methods of curing and controlling disease. A number of native "doctors" function within the Reserve, and these are still utilized by many Kipsigis. But it is a curious and interesting fact that where, in former times, most Kipsigis would seek European medical assistance almost only when they were *in extremis*, today they often turn to the tribal practitioner only after the medicines of the white man have proved ineffective.

In general, the pattern in health as well as in education is the familiar one which appears over and over as the underdeveloped areas of the world come under the influence of Western industrial society. Community agencies take over many of the functions which were formerly the province of the family, clan, or a local part-time shaman. For it is apparent to most Kipsigis that in matters of health (as well as of education) the older social forms which served them before contact are not as effective as the new ones. Understandably enough, the Kipsigis, like many other people, are indeed much concerned with effectiveness—more concerned with it, in fact, than with the preservation of traditional forms and norms merely for the sake of their preservation.

Part V. Conclusions

In something less than sixty years the Kipsigis of Kenya, having come under the control of a highly industrialized Western state, have undergone a series of profound changes in their traditional lifeways. But the changes of the next twenty-five years will carry them forward at a far greater rate than the preceding sixty. For once the enforced institutional alterations had been made, they took on a life of their own. The changes set in motion by British intervention in Kenya gathered momentum from the very nature of the society and the world that had implanted them. While it is certainly no accident that Kenya became a colony—in the sense of an area of settlement for people from the mother country—this fact has certainly had enormous significance for the patterns of development in the past and the possibilities of the future. Had Kenya, like Nigeria or the Gold Coast, been looked upon as an area unsuitable for this kind of colonization, it is certain that the history of its development would have been something different than it has been. But that is self-evident. The important point to be made here, it seems to me, is that while Kenya does indeed present certain special problems, partly of a racial nature, which distinguish it from Nigeria or Ghana, and which distinguish it especially in these "years of resolution," it also reflects profound similarities to these countries in development, in the forms of emergent institutions, and in the patterns of problem-solving innovations and devices employed to deal with the social consequences of closer involvement with the economies, the polities, and the cultures of the Western world.

The Kenya Highlands greeted the first European settlers with the promise of great wealth, a wealth that was there for the taking if one could only turn the many pairs of black hands living in and around the area to the job of extracting it. When, in the very beginning, it appeared as though it might be difficult to draw these hands into "purposeless" labor on behalf of the white man, the settlers were encouraged to try ranching, because that was an activity that did not require a large corps of workers—and the grants and leases had been exceedingly generous. However, it soon became clear that there might be ways of getting the Africans to work for them, and the profits to be made in these alternative enterprises looked even more promising.

The Foreign Office first and then the Colonial Office in Great Britain were charged with supervision over the administration and development of Kenya. Inevitably, their support and programs were shaped to the assumed needs of the metropolis and to the demands of the growing body of white settlers. Occasionally there was conflict between the wishes of the settlers and the plans and purposes of the home government. But in general the aim of colonial development in Kenya was clear. It called for the encouragement of agriculture, Kenya's major or only apparent source of wealth. Under pressures imposed by the powerful settler minority, this encouragement was given—for obvious reasons—to a plantation, estate, or hacienda pattern of exploitation rather than a peasant pattern. Automatically such an intrusion on the land and assumption of control involved more direct forms of administration than were essential to or feasible under forms of peasant cultivation. This was not a situation in which the middleman-processor-distributor could pass on the risks of production to others but one in which he would have to assume them himself. If the primary producers were to be enticed into participation at all, then government would have to reduce those initial risks to a point where production itself showed potential promise. Some form of more direct rule than that applied in Nigeria and Uganda had to be applied as part of this insurance. For, in effect, it was the seizure of large tracts of land for alienation to the Europeans which, more than the absence of developed native political institutions, demanded the stricter controls and supervision of this kind of direct rule. Note, for example, that segmentary polities and/or the proliferation of tribes in Tanganyika was no impediment to the institution in that territory of certain forms of indirect rule akin to those of Nigeria and Uganda after World War I (Cohen, 1959).

Then there was the railroad. Finished by 1901, it lay ready to transport the produce of the white settlers who would come to develop the country. Finally, to these enticements and guarantees the government, by 1906, added a completely pacified and large potential supply of African labor. I have described earlier some of the devices which were first used to bring these laborers into the fields of the white settlers. And the body of this work has been concerned with a discussion of the ways in which the natural consequences of population growth in newly delimited Reserve areas have helped to fulfil the implicit promise of government to the white settlers; how the gadgetry, the skills, and the education of the Western world are coming to be a part of the world of the Kipsigis; how they have contrived—and continue to contrive—means of acquiring these things for themselves; how this effort not only brought them to the service of the settlers but simultaneously opened doors to devices which will very soon reduce or altogether terminate these services.

The political sophistication, the education, and the power that the Kipsigis—and other tribes of Kenya—will require to advance the process of Westernization upon which they have now been launched are as yet only poorly developed. But the Africans have been provided with the means of acquiring these forces, and those who launched them—for their *own* purposes—had small choice in the direction they would take.

The Kipsigis are only one of a number of tribes in Kenya which have felt the effects of outside contact and undergone the inevitable development and changes which flowed from that contact. These tribes have all grown in wisdom and experience together. Together they are on the verge of realizing still greater changes. One may hope that when these changes do come there will be few impediments to the tribes' cooperation as linked elements in the independent and developing nation of Kenya. For one hopes also that during the long and sometimes painful period of tutelage under the British the Kipsigis, and all other tribes in Kenya, have learned (with the rest of us) the increasing inevitability of interdependence—tribal, national, continental, and global—and will therefore strive in their new status to promote its benefits while minimizing its difficulties and dangers.

Sources Cited

Anderson, Rev.
n.d. *The Kipsigis of Kenya* (mimeographed).

Barnett, H. G.
1953 *Innovation: The Basis of Cultural Change*, New York.

Beals, Ralph
1954 "The Village in an Industrial World," *Scientific Monthly*, Vol. LXXVII, pp. 65-75.

Bernardi, B.
1952 "The Age-System of the Nilo-Hamitic Peoples," *Africa*, Vol. XXII, pp. 316-32.

Carter, Morris
1934a *Report of the Kenya Land Commission, September 1933*, London.
1934b *The Evidence*, 3 vols., London.

Cohen, Sir Andrew
1959 *British Policy in Changing Africa*, London.

Colson, E.
1951 "The Role of Cattle Among the Plateau Tonga," *Human Problems in British Central Africa*, Rhodes-Livingstone Journal No. 11, pp. 10-46, Manchester.

Corfield, F. D.
1960 *The Origins and Growth of Mau Mau*, Sessional Paper No. 5, 1959-60, Nairobi.

Coser, Lewis A.
1956 *The Functions of Social Conflict*, London.

Dobbs, C. M.
1924 "A Few Notes on Bees in Lumbwa District," *Journal of East Africa and Uganda Natural History Society*, No. 19, p. 14.

Erasmus, Charles J.
1954 "An Anthropologist Views Technical Assistance," *Scientific Monthly*, Vol. LXXVIII, pp. 147-58.

Evans-Pritchard, E. E.
1940a "The Nuer of the Southern Sudan," *African Political Systems* (eds. Fortes and Evans-Pritchard), pp. 272-96, Oxford.
1940b "The Political Structure of the Nandi-Speaking Peoples of Kenya," *Africa*, Vol. XIII, pp. 250-67.
1953 "The Sacrificial Role of Cattle Among the Nuer," *Africa*, Vol. XXIII, pp. 181-98.
Fearn, Hugh
1961 *An African Economy: A Study of the Economic Development of the Nyanza Province of Kenya, 1903-1953*, Oxford.
Firth, Raymond
1951 *Elements of Social Organization*, London.
Fortes, M.
1936 "Culture Contact as a Dynamic Process," *Africa*, Vol. IX, pp. 24-56.
Furnivall, J. S.
1948 *Colonial Policy and Practice: A Comparative Study of Burma and Netherlands India*, Cambridge.
Gerschenkron, Alexander
1952 "Economic Backwardness in Historical Perspective," *Progress of Underdeveloped Areas* (ed. Hoselitz), pp. 3-29, Chicago.
Gleichen, Lt. Col. Count (ed.)
1905 *The Anglo-Egyptian Sudan*, Vol. I, London.
Gluckman, Max
1949 *An Analysis of the Sociological Theories of Bronislaw Malinowski*, Rhodes-Livingstone Papers No. 16, Oxford.
1955 *Custom and Conflict in Africa*, Oxford.
Greenberg, Joseph H.
1955 *Studies in African Linguistic Classification*, New Haven.
Gulliver, P. H.
1952 "The Karamajong Cluster," *Africa*, Vol. XXII, pp. 1-22.
1958 *East African Age Group Systems: Some Preliminary Considerations* (mimeographed), East African Institute of Social Research, Kampala.
Herskovits, Melville
1926 "The Cattle Complex in East Africa," *American Anthropologist*, Vol. XXVIII, pp. 230-72, 361-80, 494-528, 633-44.
Hollis, A. C.
1909 *The Nandi, Their Language and Folklore*, Oxford.
Hotchkiss, W. R.
1937 *Then and Now in Kenya Colony*, London.
Huffman, Ray
1931 *Nuer Customs and Folk-Lore*, London.
Huntingford, G. W. B.
1933 "Some Aspects of Nandi Stock-Raising," *Journal of East Africa and Uganda Natural History Society*, Nos. 49 and 50, pp. 250-62.
1944 *The Nandi*, Nairobi.
1953a *The Nandi of Kenya: Tribal Control in a Pastoral Society*, London.

1953b *The Northern Nilo-Hamites,* International African Institute, London.
1953c *The Southern Nilo-Hamites,* International African Institute, London.

Huxley, Elspeth
1935 *White Man's Country,* Vols. I and II, London.
1960 *A New Earth: An Experiment in Colonialism,* London.

Jackson, Sir Frederick
1930 *Early Days in East Africa,* London.

Jackson, H. C.
1923 "The Nuer of the Upper Nile Province," *Sudan Notes and Records,* Vol. VI, pp. 94, 96.

Kericho District Agricultural Officer
1948–61 *Annual Reports,* Kericho.

Kericho District Commissioner
1921–61 *Annual Reports,* Kericho.

Kroeber, A. L.
1948 *Anthropology,* New York.

Lamb, Robert K.
1952 "Political Elites and the Process of Economic Development," *Progress of Underdeveloped Areas* (ed. Hoselitz), pp. 3-53, Chicago.

Lesser, Alexander
1959 "Some Comments on the Concept of the Intermediate Society," *Intermediate Societies, Social Mobility and Communication* (ed. Ray), pp. 11-13, Seattle.

Leys, Norman
1924 *Kenya,* London.

Linton, Ralph
1952 "Cultural and Personal Factors Affecting Economic Growth," *Progress of Underdeveloped Areas* (ed. Hoselitz), pp. 73-88, Chicago.

Lugard, Lord F. J. D.
1893 *The Rise of Our East African Empire,* Vols. I and II, London.
1922 *The Dual Mandate in British Tropical Africa,* Edinburgh and London.

McWilliam, M. D.
1957 *The East African Tea Industry 1920-1956: A Case Study in the Development of a Plantation Industry,* Oxford.

Mair, L. P.
1948 "Modern Developments in African Land Tenure: An Aspect of Culture Change," *Africa,* Vol. XVIII, pp. 184-89.

Manners, Robert A.
1956 "Functionalism, Realpolitik and Anthropology in Underdeveloped Areas," *América Indígena,* Vol. XVI, pp. 7-33.
1961 "Anthropology and Community Development," *Social Service Review,* Vol. XXXV, pp. 268-77.

Matson, A. T.
1958 "The Founding of Kericho," *Kenya Weekly News,* October 31, 1958, pp. 40, 62.

1961 (ed.) *The Kipsigis* (of I. Q. Orchardson), Nairobi.
Ministry of Agriculture, Animal Husbandry and Water Resources
1956 *African Land Development in Kenya, 1946-1955*, Nairobi.
Orchardson, I. Q.
1931 "Some Traits of the Kipsigis in Relation to Their Contact with Europeans," *Africa*, Vol. IV, pp. 466-74.
1932–33 "Religious Beliefs and Practices of the Kipsigis," *Journal of East Africa and Uganda Natural History Society*, Nos. 47-48, pp. 154-62.
1935 "The African Explains Witchcraft: Kipsigis," *Africa*, Vol. VIII, pp. 509-15.
1929–37 *The Kipsigis* (MS), Kericho.
Perham, Margery
1934 "A Restatement of Indirect Rule," *Africa*, Vol. VII, pp. 321-34.
Peristiany, J.
1939 *Social Institutions of the Kipsigis*, Oxford.
Pilgrim, John
1959 *Land Ownership in the Kipsigis Reserve* (mimeographed), East African Institute of Social Research, Kampala.
Prins, A. H. J.
1953 *East African Age-Class Systems: An Inquiry into the Social Order of Galla, Kipsigis, and Kikuyu*, Groningen and Jakarta.
Redfield, Robert
1956 *Peasant Society and Culture*, Chicago.
Ross, W. McGregor
1927 *Kenya from Within: A Short Political History*, London.
Salvadori, Max
1938 *La Colonisation Européenne au Kenya*, Paris.
Schapera, I.
1928 "Economic Changes in South African Native Life," *Africa*, Vol. I, pp. 170-88.
Seligman, C. G.
1932 *Pagan Tribes of the Nilotic Sudan*, London.
Simmel, Georg
1955 *Conflict* (trans. Kurt H. Wolff), Glencoe, Ill.
Smith, Edwin W.
1950 *The Blessed Missionaries*, Oxford.
Special Crops Development Authority, East Africa
1962 *First Annual Report*, Nairobi.
Survey of Kenya
1959 *Atlas of Kenya*, Nairobi.
Tax, Sol (ed.)
1952 *Heritage of Conquest*, Glencoe, Ill.
Towett, Taita arap
1956 *Traditional History of the Kipsigis* (MS), Kericho.
Weston, Frank (Bishop of Zanzibar)
1920 *The Serfs of Great Britain*, London.

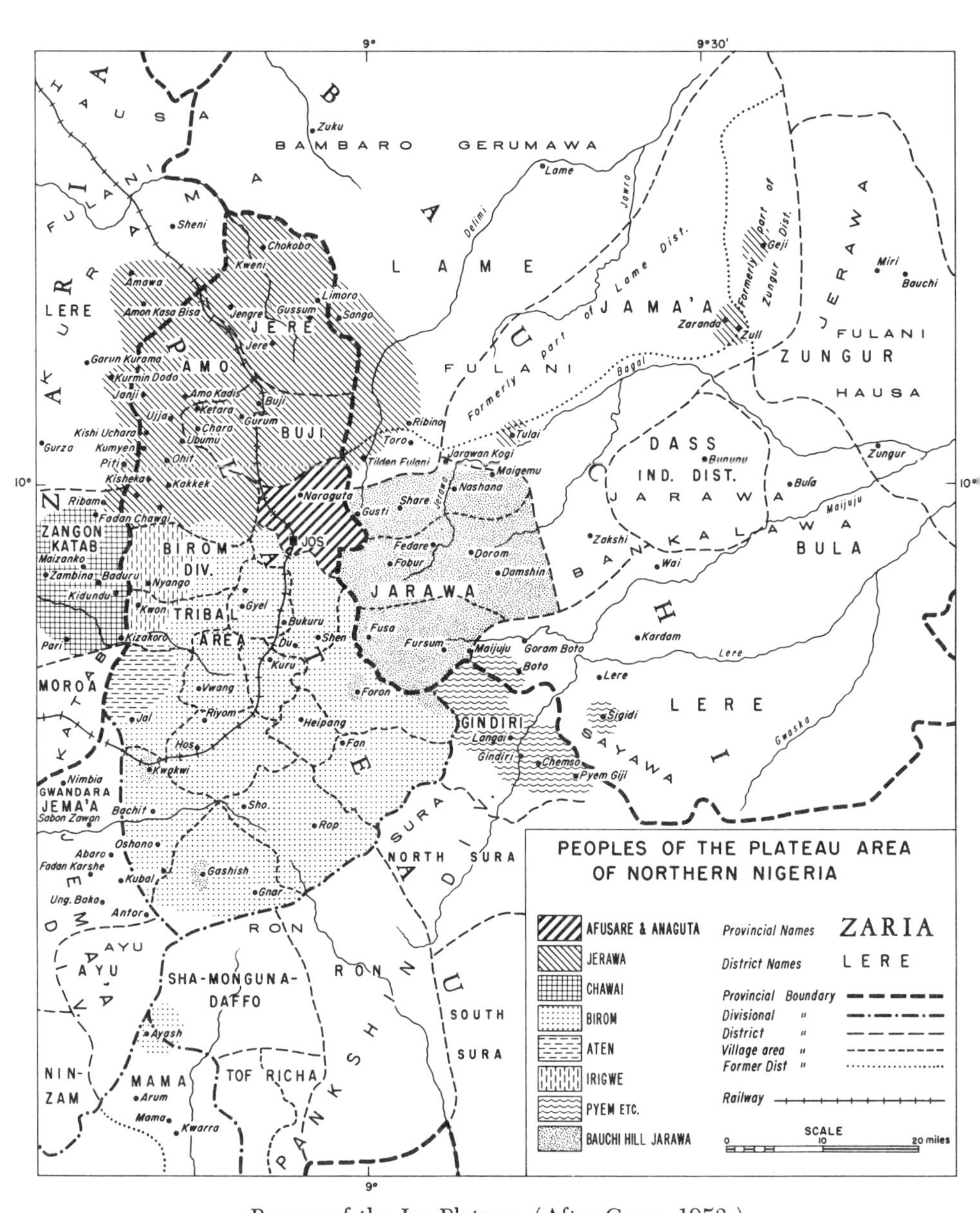

Pagans of the Jos Plateau. (After Gunn, 1953.)

The Anaguta of Nigeria: Suburban Primitives

STANLEY DIAMOND

Anaguta mini ma gheri.
The Anaguta are a basket of water. (Anaguta proverb)

. . . Africans of the indigenous tribes of the Province—and the same may apply possibly to others as well—often become ill and die in the minimum of time for no other reason than that they have apparently given up the will to live. . . .
(Ames, 1934, p. 319)

Hello there, man, you little two-legged plucked cock! It's true!—Never mind what people say—the sun won't rise in the morning unless you crow—
(Nikos Kazantzakis)

Part I. The Problem

A VANISHING CULTURE

The Anaguta are a virtually unknown Nigerian people, whose culture is vanishing. There is an obvious distinction between the condition of such a culture, disintegrating, blowing away like smoke on the wind of African change, and one that is being transformed, absorbed, acculturated, or assimilated. In the former instance, authentically transitional or perhaps new, more or less viable forms are not created. The phenomena of decay predominate; rituals lapse, social institutions wither away, even the pursuit of subsistence falters. Life becomes a round of insubstantial forms, stubbornly followed, without hope but, strangely—at least it seems strange in our New World perspective—without despair. A minimum of temporary, substitute, merely expedient cultural patterns may materialize overnight, as it were, like mushrooms, but they merely serve the most elementary need of keeping the group functioning a little longer. They have no historic depth, their connections with antecedent forms may be logically reconstructed, but they are disjointed; the organic, felt continuity has been ruptured.

When we say that a culture is vanishing, we mean that it is passing out of history, out of the consciousness of men. In the case of a

NOTE: All statistics and social facts, whether relevant to the Anaguta in particular, or Nigeria in general, hold through the late 1950's, that is, the immediate pre-independence period, unless otherwise noted.

The larger portion of my notes were stolen in October, 1960. Where statistical and technical materials presented here may be imprecise, I have indicated uncertainty by the appropriate qualifying adjective. However, I am confident that the core of the Anaguta cultural predicament is accurately exposed.

primitive, unrecorded and unrecording culture, the disappearance is, practically speaking, total. The impact of the Anaguta on adjoining peoples may be remembered a short time, although such groups themselves are changing rapidly, in the direction of a certain kind of survival, as we shall see. But that impact can hardly be understood or interpreted once the interacting groups are gone, each in its own way. Even the promise of some sort of distinctive archeological survival for the Anaguta is small. Their artifacts are almost indistinguishable from those of adjacent peoples; they lack a memorable graphic or plastic art in a durable medium—and the rituals, proverbs, tales, and myths of non-literates either leave no trace behind or the authorship and origin remain unknown. Moreover, conditions on the High or Jos Plateau of Northern Nigeria are not conducive to the preservation of whatever cultural debris of clay, wood, stone, and iron may escape natural erosion. Modern roads, utilities, forest preserves, and the junk heaps of civilization will inexorably roll over and further obliterate the few remaining square miles left to the Anaguta.

How could an archeologist, even today, were the Anaguta to become extinct on the instant, sort out and give a cultural name and habitation to the bicycles, padlocks, potsherds, chunks of melted down, unworked iron, ceramic pots, bows and arrows, medicine bundles, firedrills, match covers, shillings, shells, razor blades, stone shrines, and so on, that would lie mixed together on or near the surface of the hard, thin, stony, eroding earth? This culture, so little known in life, so difficult to delineate against the shifting background of Plateau Pagan [1] society, would utterly disappear in death. Their nearness to us increases their distance, for the civilizing process, in this case, overwhelms as it destroys. If *we* survive, we shall, I believe, know more, 100 years from now, of the Upper Paleolithic inhabitants of southern France or northern Persia than we do today of the Anaguta. There may remain a few moldering and inaccurate official tax records, census figures, court reports, which will sooner or later be destroyed to make room for more solvent archives of the state. And several fragmentary ethnographic references, of a speculative character, along with administrative notes will endure for a while, the latter perishing with colonialism and further governmental change, the former entombed in a few libraries, where, in a generation or so, the name Anaguta will make little sense and be of less interest to even the most specialized scholars.

[1] The term "Pagan" is generally used in Nigeria to designate non-Christian, non-Islamic tribal peoples. It is adopted here as a convenience.

The Meaning of Cultural Extinction

Cultural extinction is not in the same dimension
change. Perhaps this requires a further word in explic
eval Europe no longer exists, nor do the Roman Empire, Periclean Athens, Byzantine Ravenna, Mogul India, Dynastic Thebes, the buffalo-hunting Crow, or Classic Ife. But they survive in the memories of men, historians dispute their social and cultural characters and try to trace the transformation of their institutions through time. Their impact on contemporaries and their *place* in history are examined—how they came to be what they were, and how they changed, paving the way for what came after are matters of continuing concern. They no longer exist in the transient sense, fleeting for all of us, that their creators are no longer alive, but they maintain their status as historical phenomena; they led to something. But the Anaguta will, in a little while, I believe, cease to exist historically; their culture is coming to a stop; nothing is emerging out of it; it is not mingling with the dynamic, multi-faceted fabric which is, hopefully, expanding into a polity called Nigeria. It is not assimilating natively, nor acculturating to Euro-American patterns. It is not even leaving anything useful behind.

The Demographic Profile; an Hypothesis

Moreover, the Anaguta seem to be dying out literally, physically. A few individuals may escape into the nearby city, Jos, or, conceivably, to other areas of the country, and, by ridding themselves of Anaguta attitudes and identity, manage to become solitary Nigerians. It is unlikely that their grandchildren will know or care about their antecedents. Memories, transvalued values, and adaptive forms are held and developed by immigrants en masse, particularly when a physical nucleus survives, even while shifting culturally in the place of origin, as history, by its very nature, illustrates. For history, at the very least, is the process of man's physical survival, intermingling, migration, cultural expansion, the putting forth of shoots into the future. The young solitary Anaguta refugee, having been abruptly deracinated at home, can hardly be expected to celebrate a society that has become a cemetery; he does not have the forms at hand and he probably would not even mourn.

In 1934 (Ames, 1934, p. 347) the population of the Anaguta was estimated at 5,780, having been revised upward from a figure of 3,000 by the same authority before his *Gazeteer* was published. A decade later, in 1944 (Davies), the number had apparently shrunk to 2,580. These are the only known counts, presumably from other than tax and census records, in the literature, except for my own, which shall be indicated below. If these data, collected by Ames and Davies, two colonial officers with an ethnographic flair, are taken at their face value, it means that within a ten-year period, the Anaguta had been reduced by more than half. In an originally small population, such a decline would certainly be perceived as, and could have been the gross result of, a natural or social catastrophe —an obliterating disease, famine, war. No such event appears on the record and the Anaguta do not refer to any concentrated disaster. Still, for reasons that I shall note, so dramatic a reduction in population could have occurred. But, it is more likely that the Anaguta have experienced a steady diminution as the result of a more chronic catastrophe extending over the past half-century. This depopulation is not, it should be emphasized, the result of significant migration, for which there is no evidence and which Anaguta deny, but is an endogenous process. It seems certain that as Jos expanded, the Anaguta contracted territorially and culturally; finally they began to die off. And it may well be that the decade 1934-44—the "middle period" between initial European contact in 1904 and the present —was the most traumatic for them, since the impact of the expanding town and the shrinking of their horizons may have, at that time, become suddenly evident in a variety of ways.

Statistics are, in this instance, no more than an impressionistic guide. The opinion of the Anaguta, who, as a small group, may be assumed to be aware of their own gross demographic situation, is more reliable. They cannot analyze specific causes; indeed, our own efforts must be speculative. They have no traffic with numbers; counting people still seems absurd to them and even dangerous because of its association with the collection of taxes. They have no sense of the total number of Anaguta; in the old days, it was enough, now it is not enough. Even the number of people in one's compound is not known—they are not added up—people are identified concretely by their individual names and characteristics, and severally by the needs of specific group functions, as in composing a work party. But mere numbers serve no social purpose and are, moreover, too abstract to bother with. Concretely, the Anaguta claim that they are declining. There are not enough young men to cultivate the fields, nor girls to marry the men who are available, nor babies who survive childbirth, nor women who become pregnant. The causes are complicated and obscure; the demographic process and structure are bizarre, but the Anaguta insist on the social facts.

Apart from the non-specific, unenumerated certainty of the Anaguta, there are two sets of figures that may be consulted in an effort to understand the demographic profile—census data and ethnographic materials. The census data are probably the more unreliable, since they are related to tax assessments, which are notoriously inadequate among primitive, non-politically organized peoples. In 1921 (Meek, 1925, p. 185) the official number of Anaguta was reckoned at 3,282, categorized as follows:

Adult males	986
Adult females	1,066
Non-adult males	989
Non-adult females	241

The figure for non-adult females is almost certainly under-reported, but tax evasion can hardly be the reason since women and children were not taxed. Possibly, it was the fear of the (young) women fleeing as a result of being counted (*Census of Nigeria*, 1931, p. 12) or of their being abducted, probably reflecting an old suspicion of political techniques, either historically or logically. Such fears, if they existed, would have been singularly confined to the socially immature females, but of the many tribes reported in the census, none displayed such a discrepancy.[2]

Taken as a whole, the proportion of non-adults to adults is 38 per cent. Generally speaking, 40 per cent is considered to be the proper ratio in a healthy population, that is, one which does not reveal a morbidly low fertility or high mortality rate. But the further question that arises here is the cut-off age between "adults" and "non-adults." If it is as high as 17 or 18, then the indication of a slightly abnormal population is sound; if the cut-off age is 15 or less, the disproportion may not be meaningful.

In 1931 (*Census of Nigeria*, 1931, p. 68) the census figures claimed a total of 3,798 Anaguta, divided as follows:

Adult males	1,117
Adult females	1,353
Non-adult males	673
Non-adult females	655

Here, again, the figure for non-adult females is less, but probably within the normal expectation of the proportion between the sexes in childhood, since males outnumber females at birth by a ratio of about 105 to 100.[3] Moreover, women marry earlier and tend to mature socially more rapidly than males, so that non-adult males are

[2] This discrepancy could also be the result of miscalculation and/or the deliberate or mistaken skewing of the cut-off age.

[3] In Euro-American populations; more precise African ratios have not been determined, but are roughly the same.

more visible. Conversely, the greater number of adult females is also unexceptional, particularly since males, in most human populations, have a higher death rate. However, the sequence of figures for females from 1921 to 1931 is, on the face of it, absurd. Yet, if a significant disproportion of females in fact existed between 1921 and 1931, then it is possible that the "normal" number a decade later was the result of Anaguta men purchasing Birom (a neighboring Pagan people) women in marriage, that is, a form of in-migration. The proportion of non-adults to adults here is 35 per cent, which is a reasonable indication of a declining population, again, if the cut-off age for non-adults is above 15. The cut-off age is also pertinent to the evaluation of the male predominance over females among non-adults. The higher it is, the older the children are, and the odder the population profile. But, even if the cut-off age is low, that is, about 15, the greater number of males is an unusual entry among the dozens of tribes enumerated. Be that as it may, a gross increase in population of over 500 is indicated between 1921 and 1931, which, given the detailed breakdown, contradicts the data as a whole. However, the 35 per cent proportion of non-adults to adults for 1931 may be meaningful and makes, at least, a theoretically neat sequence from the 38 per cent in 1921, if we assume that the figure for adult females in 1931 is inflated by the presence of Birom women.

Unfortunately, no effort at a detailed tribal listing was made in the 1952 census of the Northern Region. The Anaguta are not even mentioned, although the Birom are numbered at 116,000, a grossly exaggerated figure, which can only have been arrived at by assimilating many of the smaller Pagan groups to Birom identity for political convenience.

The 1960 census, taken after independence, may list the tribes in detail, but the results have never been and shall not be published because of reciprocal charges of miscounting in the Eastern and Northern Regions. This was the first census to be attempted after Nigeria attained independence and was particularly important because the results could have shifted the balance of power in the national coalition government in successive elections. Interestingly enough, the attempts of the citizenry to avoid the census, because of its obvious association under colonialism with taxation and other forms of civil imposition, have persisted, requiring the national government to use every means of communication to assure the nation —as Western governments are still conventionally obliged to do— that no ulterior motive was intended and that the enumeration was for the benefit of all the people. Given the Nigerian political situation, population counts in the foreseeable future shall, almost certainly, be of little use for a more refined and specific demographic inquiry.

Neither Ames nor Davies indicate the sources of their Anaguta figures, nor are they subdivided into sex and age categories. But we must assume that Ames (1934) can distinguish Anaguta from Jarawa or other Pagans, since he is consistent in doing so throughout his text and, therefore, would not revise 3,000 to 5,780 because of confusing one people with another. It would seem that he means us to take the Anaguta figure, along with others that were revised, as definitive, and to ignore his previous estimates, but he gives neither sources nor reasons. Davies' (1944) figure of 2,580, ten years later, is equally unelaborated, but it is also likely that Davies, who collected a brief Anaguta vocabulary, was aware of the identity of the people he was attempting to count. If Ames's maximal figure is accepted in comparison with Davies' (and there is no other source for the generation 1934-59), then an attempt must be made to account for so drastic a decline in the absence of out-migration. There is one outstanding possibility—venereal disease.[4]

As we shall see in the discussion of the growth of Jos, by the early 1930's the town had a sizable alien African population, drawn from all over Nigeria, either working in the tin mines or in the facilities that developed under the stimulus of mining. During this period more extensive contact between Anaguta and venereal-ridden natives in the town was probably established, in part, through Birom and Jarawa women. Either sex could have contracted the infection—the women, through casual liaisons with Jos Africans, on the occasion of their going to market; the men, through marriage to Birom women, or through contacts with prostitutes in Jos or the native suburbs. Like all mining towns, Jos had, and still has, to a lesser extent, a disproportion of males to females and, given the character of the population, a more than usual lack of prophylaxis. Once the infection was contracted, it would have spread with unusual speed among people such as the Anaguta because of their involved and "promiscuous" sexual arrangements before and after marriage. Today, gonorrhea is pandemic among the Anaguta; it is dreaded and causes much suffering. There is every indication that it (and possibly syphilis) are new afflictions and, therefore, may have taken an unusually heavy toll in the decade following intimate contact with the city.

[4] Predominantly gonorrhea, but there may have been a significant incidence of syphilis.

The fact that the Anaguta do not speak of any catastrophe between 1934 and 1944 is puzzling, since a decrease of over 2,000 people, at a rate of more than 200 a year, should certainly be felt even more specifically than is indicated in the general certainty that Anaguta express about their decline. Still, they are profoundly afraid of venereal disease, and have no idea of how it is communicated. Gonorrhea (and possibly syphilis), has, undoubtedly, lowered the fertility rate, increased the infant mortality rate, and shortened the life span, a trinity of decline encountered elsewhere in Africa (Romaniuk, 1961).

If we ignore Ames's (1934) figure of 5,780, there is a decrease of approximately 500 in the decade 1934-44. It is difficult to diagnose this, but the same factor could have been operating, even if more mildly. However, it must be noted that in the absence of more detailed demographic data, and on the basis of this more conservative sequence, it is probably unwarranted to characterize the Anaguta as a declining population during that period.

If Davies' figure of 2,580 in 1944 is correct, then the Anaguta had become relatively stabilized during the ensuing fifteen years, since my count in 1959 came to just under 2,500. A factor in this "stability" could have been the clinic which functioned in the local courthouse in the 1940's, and was notorious for "giving injections," presumably of penicillin. Alternatively, after the first traumatic effects of venereal disease, the population could have attained a temporary equilibrium.

However, the population profile in 1959 seems to reveal the symptoms of decline. The proportion of non-adults to adults is about 33 per cent. While the cut-off in age distribution can only be roughly described as "adolescence," and could, conceivably, range anywhere from 13 to 18, a reasonable mean age might be 16-17, excluding a few married individuals who may have been younger, and including several others who may have been older. The presumption of decline is, as noted, supported by the Anaguta, and ascribed by them to female sterility and a very high infant mortality rate, including stillbirths, tendencies evident in other African populations (Crocquevielle, 1953; Culwick, 1938-39; Boelaert, 1947; Mission Socio-Economique Centre-Oubangui, 1960). Anaguta claim that in any given sequence of ten efforts at birth, half to the total may die. Although there is no way of checking these assumptions, an infant mortality rate exceeding 50 per cent is not unknown in Africa, but it is ordinarily balanced by a high fertility rate. Venereal disease may account for the relative sterility of Anaguta women and would compound the difficulties of pregnancy and increase the rate of stillbirths.

Another possible cause in the apparently high percentage of neonatal deaths may be the deterioration of midwifery techniques. Anaguta women complain frankly about the pain and hazards of childbirth. Assisted births are the rule, but there are few women practiced in the traditional procedures. On the other hand, Anaguta women do not call upon medical doctors or make any effort to enter hospitals in order to bear their children. Thus, it may be that many infants die in the breach between deterioration of traditional techniques and the refusal to resort to new ones.

Hunger may be another element in the morbidity rate among children. Customarily, Anaguta young are nursed until the age of two and a half or three years. The milk of the mother or mother-surrogate is the predominant source of food during the first 12 to 18 months of life; one frequently encounters infants, even children of three or four, at the withered breasts of old women. No regular, adequate alternative diet has been established,[5] and should a mother be ill or undernourished, as is frequently the case today, the infant is likely to sicken and die. Anaguta report that many children under the age of four die of very severe diarrhea, which could be the result of inadequate, improvised feeding, and/or lowered resistance to chronic, or newly introduced, gastro-intestinal infections.

Kwashiorkor is probably implicated here. It is endemic among the Anaguta as it is wherever people do not have enough meat, fish, fowl, eggs, milk, beans, or other protein-rich food in their diet. Since milk is the infant's normal source of protein, if that is deficient or lacking, even a "successful" switch to starchy foods, such as maize, bananas, manioc, etc., will not prevent him from becoming ill before his second birthday. Moreover, the child's inability to handle coarse or bulky foods in his immature digestive system deprives him of even the small amount of protein which may be present in his diet (Burger, 1963, p. 5). The result with a substantial number of Anaguta infants seems to be debilitation and death during the most critical phase, the first five years, of tissue and bone building.

Chronic marital instability and divorce, pandemic among the Anaguta, have also been identified as obvious factors depressing fertility (Dorjahn, 1959, p. 110). Moreover, demographic and other social forces, to be considered below, lead to a high incidence of chronologically odd pairings—between young women and old men, or old women and young men—which also lower fertility.

[5] Sour milk (*nono*), purchased from the Fulani, is sometimes used when available, but this has not become a regular practice.

Conscious or unwitting contraceptive and abortive methods of a mechanical type could also increase the sterility and mortality rates, and generally decrease birth rates, but no information is available. However, the conventional taboo on intercourse between the parents from childbirth to weaning, at about the age of 3, could be a factor minimizing the numbers of pregnancies per female. More remote possibilities that warrant only the barest mention are: first, true sister exchange marriage, if pursued beyond an initial generation, leads to double cross cousin and more intricately related matings among descendants of the originally pairing families; the genetic viability of infants and the fertility of parents could be adversely affected. Second, the sexuality of a culturally (and perhaps psychologically) depressed population may become inhibited, resulting in fewer, and/or less psycho-physiologically fruitful matings.

If the Anaguta are declining as a whole, the females seem to be decreasing even more rapidly.[6] The proportion of males to females is about 55 per cent, that is, 1,375 males to 1,125 females, the ratio being roughly the same among adults and non-adults. If these figures are tenable, and I emphasize that the Anaguta insist that they suffer a shortage of females, then there are two possible explanations. The first is a high mortality rate among women in childbirth, which could overbalance the anticipated greater vulnerability of men to disease and other hazards in later life. The second is female infanticide, increasing the natural percentage of males over females at birth in any standard population. Thus, males would outnumber females during childhood, and at maturity, when the disproportion might tend to level out because of differential effects of disease, the females would be further reduced by childbirth. A third possibility—that there is a genetic skewing in the Anaguta population, leading to a consistently higher proportion of male over female births than is ordinarily the case—is too tenuous to consider.

The problem in assuming female infanticide is that Anaguta do not admit the practice. But infanticide need not be a systematically planned or customary act; certain infants may be subtly neglected, accidentally smothered, and so on, without compromising the affection directed toward the survivors. It is even possible that Anaguta certainty about the dwindling number of females may be a means of indirectly communicating the existence of a pattern of informal

[6] Oosterwal (1961) reports a parallel demographic pattern in Tor Territory, Northern Netherlands New Guinea, where females are in the minority; but the presumed cause, a grossly uneven birth rate, more obvious now that males are no longer killed in intertribal feuding, is different. Similar phenomena have been reported from India, Pakistan, and Ceylon, but in these cases the high maternal mortality rate seems to be the issue.

infanticide; the reasons may lie in the new ecological and subsistence pressures to which they are now being subjected.

Symptoms of Withdrawal

As it is, the Anaguta seem to have made a series of critical choices, adding up to a single conscious decision not to make an effort to adapt to the new world growing up around them. With insignificant exception, they refuse to migrate from their dwindling lands, do not convert to Christianity or Islam, do not encourage their children to go to school, do not send vanguard groups to settle in the town and search out new possibilities of livelihood. They are disinterested in agricultural resettlement schemes; do not work for Europeans; and like most Plateau Pagans, they shun the tin mines. They are not even interested in Nigeria; some do not understand what the term denotes, most cannot conceptualize it. The majority have been no further than 10 or 12 miles from their native hamlets; they have heard of Kuru, but not of Ibadan. Planes fly over their hills, dotted with tiny beehive huts; once they were frightened, now they are unconcerned. Electricity, the cinema, trucks, automobiles, the artifacts of white civilization, do not arouse their curiosity. They retreat and retreat, physically and culturally, pursuing the fragments of ancient usages. Yet no nativistic idea or messianic tremor compensates for their flight. But we must understand this response in the perspective of the Anaguta. They believe their native territory is at the "center of the world" (Diamond, 1960, p. 33), where space and time intersect, and that, for them, is "equivalent to living as close as possible to the Gods" (Eliade, 1960, p. 91). Eliade has expressed the meaning of primitive attachment to a homeland as well as anyone:

> to settle in a territory is in the last analysis equivalent to consecrating it. When settlement is not temporary, as among the Nomads, but permanent as among sedentary peoples, it implies a vital decision that involves the existence of the entire community. Establishment in a particular place, organizing it, inhabiting it, are acts that presuppose an existential choice —the choice of the universe that one is prepared to assume by "creating" it. Now, this universe is always the replica of the paradigmatic universe created and inhabited by the gods; hence it shows the sanctity of the gods' work. (p. 34)

The Anaguta are faintly inquisitive but not fascinated by white men, whom they formally regard as spirits, *andoogubishee*,[7] in one aspect ancestral, in another local, the inhabitants of their sacred groves, to be used, placated, and prayed to by their Priest Chiefs.

[7] The term for spirit is *undoogubishee* (pl., *andoogubishee*).

Having categorized white men, they have named the nameless, and somehow having conquered it, can relate to it. But this does not exhaust their perceptions of white men—it merely conceptualizes them in a useful way. White men are, in a certain sense, *andoogubishee*, but *andoogubishee* are not merely white men. This kind of logic is not at all Western. The assumption is not classically syllogistic: the individual Anaguta is not saying that some, but not all, *andoogubishee* would, therefore, be white men. Rather, he is claiming that white men are a form which *andoogubishee* may take, without fully projecting the being of either.

The Anaguta accept things as they are, immerse themselves in surfaces, grasp them with all the senses, and are not embarrassed by changes of shape, form, or emphasis. They even have a tale that places the whites in natural history. Whites, they say, came from the bottom of lakes and rivers, where they were like fish. Then they climbed onto the land, and from the land up into the trees, and only recently descended, just having lost their tails, which is why they look so much like monkeys. They do not dislike these occult monkeys, but they need not be awed by them—they have found a place for them in Anaguta lore, perhaps by adapting a Hausa folk version of a well-known European theory. As they can be pragmatic about the supernatural, so they accept the presence of whites, or rather, to the Anaguta, everything that exists is natural; there is no need to be alarmed. It is even possible for them unconcernedly to accept the white man as a fully human being, despite the partial classification as an *undoogubishee*, or as a recently evolved animal.

The Anaguta remember their victories. A century and a half ago, they kept the Fulani horsemen, seeking tribute, from driving up to the Plateau and into their central valley. It is a battle that they ritually re-enact, in sacred surroundings, with hundreds of participants. The cap of the conquered Fulani chief—it may have been taken with his head—is still hidden in a special hut. Fifty years ago, they say, they drove an English tin prospector out of their central valley, and none has ever returned. When the British, supported by weapons that the Anaguta knew were insuperable, for tales had preceded their arrival, asked to see their chief in 1904, they sent an ordinary elder—of junior status, not a priest—for they had no political chiefs and learned to match indirect rule with indirect subjection. They remember their victories, direct and indirect; and as the outside world closes in on them, they practice, or if they cannot practice, they re-enact within a narrowing circle, they ritualize the tactics that made them possible, choosing to go under rather than change.

Such nostalgia

> may appear intolerable and humiliating to modern eyes. . . . [It] inevitably leads to the continual repetition of a limited number of gestures and patterns of behavior. From one point of view it may even be said that religious man—especially the religious man of primitive societies—is above all a man paralyzed by the myth of the eternal return. A modern psychologist would be tempted to interpret such an attitude as anxiety before the danger of the new, refusal to assume responsibility for a genuine historical existence. . . .
>
> . . . [this] implies the problem of the opposition between pre-modern and modern man. Let us rather say that it would be wrong to believe that the religious man of primitive and archaic societies refuses to assume the responsibility for a genuine existence. On the contrary, . . . he courageously assumes immense responsibilities—for example, that of collaborating in the creation of the cosmos, or of creating his own world, or of ensuring the life of plants and animals, and so on. But it is a different kind of responsibility from those that, to us moderns, appear to be the only genuine and valid responsibilities. It is *a responsibility on the cosmic plane,* in contradistinction to the moral, social, or historical responsibilities that are alone regarded as valid in modern civilizations.
>
> . . . existentially, the primitive always puts himself in a cosmic context . . . this experience finds expression in the certainty that life can be periodically begun over again with a maximum of good fortune. Indeed, it is not only an optimistic vision of existence, but a total cleaving to being. By all his behavior, religious man proclaims that he believes only in being, and that his participation in being is assured him by the primordial revelation of which he is the guardian. The sum total of primordial revelations is constituted by his myths.
>
> [The Primitive's] personal experience lacks neither genuineness nor depth; but the fact that it is expressed in a language unfamiliar to us makes it appear spurious or infantile to modern eyes. (Eliade, 1961, pp. 93-95)

Today Jos grows out to meet them, and they recoil, seeking invisibility. Indeed, the greatest gift with which a man may be endowed is the capacity to become invisible. He cannot will, or fake it; it is the proof of his strength; it comes upon him in moments of crisis, and he is saved. I knew such a man; he was one of my informants and there were said to be eyewitnesses to his first seizure. There are many claimants to the cherished gift; they are tolerated by being ignored, but they are seen and heard. The Anaguta have made a blessing out of invisibility; this is an old belief, serving a contemporary need so literally that it seems fantastic.

Surrounding people are aware that "the Anaguta are a basket of water." Other Pagans say that they are very hard to understand; they do nothing for themselves. The only British Assistant District Officer who seemed to have known a bit about them was exasperated by their capacity to withdraw; he felt that they were the most dilapidated and moribund of all the Pagan groups. No white man speaks their language, and I encountered only a handful of neighboring Africans with a fragmentary knowledge of it. Why bother to learn Eguta?

Yet the Anaguta have made their decision and reacted to their circumstances with dignity. If the way we meet and understand our fate defines our freedom, the Anaguta are free. The elders know what is happening to their culture, and probably to their people; they see no more desirable alternative. They were willing to discuss the matter with me, thanked me gravely, and agreed with my conclusions, but did not share my concern.

In a generation or less, the culture and the language will have vanished, deprived of any historical continuity whatever; a greater or lesser number of refugees will have dispersed to other parts of the country. And the Anaguta will have achieved a peculiar kind of moral victory, denied them in fact. What they could not defeat, they refused to join and support.

Existential, Historical, and Scientific Importance of the Anaguta

The fate of this obscure people is important for three related reasons. First, it is significant in itself. The death of a culture and a language is a cause for mourning. A human possibility is in the process of being erased, not merely changed or transformed. We are not so culturally rich and diverse in the contemporary world that we can afford this process of obliteration. At least, if we do not ignore it, as exemplified in the Anaguta, it will add something to our humanity, but that, of course, will not effect the actual condition of the Anaguta, which must be respected in itself.

Second, it is important historically. We live at a time of such accelerated and momentous change, the gulf between the present and the past widens so immensely, the quality of contemporary experience is so unprecedented, that we are threatened with the loss of our sense of history. History becomes an academic exercise, no longer felt. That is to say, the respect for and recourse to tradition disappears from the everyday life of people everywhere engaged, or wishing to be engaged, in the new technology, in order to survive, if for no other reason. Tradition becomes another subject for the expert, something to be studied rather than lived. We are leaving history behind, and man's sense of himself is becoming merely current, amnesiac, and opportunistic. This discontinuity is ominous; it leads to the expedient tautology, not of the jungle but of civilization, that what survives is good and necessary, therefore necessarily good merely because it survives. The Anaguta do not share this style of reasoning; for this alone they deserve another look. They have been, perhaps, fatally slow in accepting the simplest assumptions of the modern world, and they incarnate an historic phase of our common humanity which will soon cease to be represented anywhere on earth. To stop a moment our flight into outer space, to explore more fully our inner selves, to care about a powerless culture and a brave and dignified people is to come face to face with our own history and its ever-renewed contemporary meanings. To question where we have been and where we are going, to respect the accumulated experience of mankind is to exercise the sense of history, shake our deterministic faith in progress, and provide us with another way of looking at ourselves.

In the words of one authority,

> All of these Pagans are conservative by nature and their outlook is backwards, maintenance of contact with the past being of more importance, apparently, than speculation about the future. . . . Living in their own villages and preferring their own company, they are still largely spectators of the approach of civilization. But just as in the past Tribes have sometimes adopted a custom from a neighboring Tribe, so in recent years many of them have shown an increasing tendency to avail themselves of the amenities of civilization where they see a distinct advantage to be gained. (Ames, 1934, p. 16)

But it is just here that the Anaguta are, even in the context of Plateau Pagan society, extreme. They have adopted very few of the "amenities of civilization," and these, unsystematically. Belief in their basic usages remains unshaken, even though the functions have been crippled.

There is another, more pragmatic sense in which the Anaguta are significant historically. If their response to the challenge of the modern world, or rather to the way in which the modern world has confronted them and they have perceived it, is at all symptomatic, even if extreme, then that will certainly affect the nature of the province, the region, the nation, the continent, and the world of which they are a part. And to the degree that aboriginal peoples in other places have responded similarly, the effects on modern civilization already have been and shall continue to be incalculable. That is, we experience one kind of history rather than another because of the way aboriginal peoples have adapted or failed to adapt to Western-derived institutions and techniques since the achievement of the commercial and industrial revolutions. Western agents have shown little effective concern with the cultures that were being so thoroughly replaced or destroyed, and this has given and shall give us one kind of world rather than another. It is, I believe, merely ethnocentric to assume that there have been and shall be no alternative possibilities of change.

Finally, the Anaguta are important scientifically. Cultural deterioration is a process, like any other, worthy of examination in the hope that certain generalizations, applicable beyond the specific case, may be constructed. It is primarily toward this latter point that the balance of this study is directed.

Part II. Habitat, Identity, Formative Historical Conditions

THE MIDDLE BELT IN THE CONTEXT OF NIGERIA

Geographical Definition

Nigeria is the most populous country in Africa, the largest of the ex-British territories on the continent, and potentially the most politically significant. The Northern Region of Nigeria comprises three-fourths (280,000 sq. miles) of the land area of the country, and just over half the total population. The Middle Belt makes up the southern half of the Northern Region and is a distinctive and critical area. Its population is perhaps seven million, one-third of the region as a whole, and about one-sixth of the country at large. The Middle Belt is composed of six provinces—Illorin, Kabba, Benue, Niger, Adamawa, and Plateau—which span the center of the country across the Niger and Benue valleys, and project into the adjacent uplands. But this area of some 140,000 square miles, nearly twice that of the Eastern and Western Regions combined, is a heterogeneous, thinly populated territory; its ecological, social, and historical character, although transitional between the regions in some respects, is unique in others, and the mélange has led to its being recognized as a separate area. This is, however, an unofficial status; the Middle Belt is not a governmental region, although a political movement with that end in view has been generated in recent years. Should Middle Belt identity within the federation be achieved, the Northern Region would no longer dominate Nigerian politics, and the consequences for both the nation and West Africa would be profound (Diamond, 1962a).

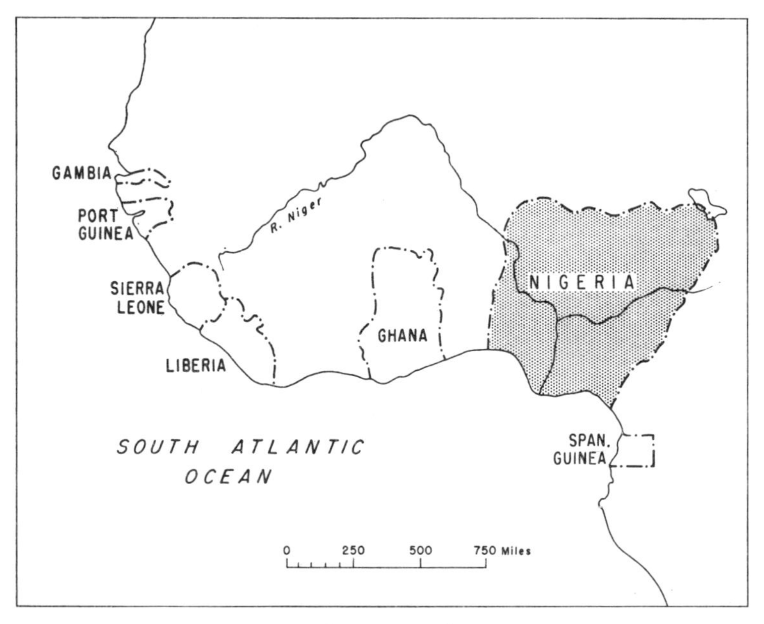

Nigeria on the West African coast.

Ecological Definition

Each of the major sectors of Nigeria, other than the Middle Belt, is distinguished by the fact that it is dominated by a particular tribal or linguistic group, has a certain historical continuity, and is knitted together in a production-distribution network by dependence on a major cash crop, grown by small-holder peasants, primarily, but not exclusively, for export. The Sudan Provinces, north of the Middle Belt, comprised the historical Hausaland and the major arena of the Fulani Jihad, excepting Bornu, which is, nevertheless, traditionally Moslem; they are the centers of groundnut and cotton production. Cocoa is the major export crop of the Western Region, which is primarily Yoruba in ethnic composition. The East is dominated by the Ibo, who are the major producers of palm oil and kernels. These correlations, which have potent political and economic consequences, are paralleled by other factors that delineate the Sudanic North from the South in general. The indigenous food crops of the former area are grains, primarily Guinea corn and millet; of the latter area, root crops, particularly yams and cassava. The South is tropical, with typical rain forest conditions. The Far North is a sudan savannah, fading to semi-desert. With reference to subsistence crops and climate, the Middle Belt is transitional between North and South.

Comparison of the three major regions of Nigeria.

More significantly, the Middle Belt is marked by certain discontinuities within the Nigerian context. It is not dominated by a single cash crop; an insignificant amount of cotton is grown; benniseed, of minor export importance, is cultivated in Benue Province by the Tiv; groundnut production is negligible, and cocoa and palm products practically nonexistent. This relative lack of export cash cropping is the major reason for the scanty transportation and communication facilities, and the greater emphasis on subsistence production than is evident in the Far North, East, and West. Correlatively, only two towns of any consequence have developed in the area—Illorin (in Illorin Province), fundamentally Yoruba in its traditional "urban" pattern, a center for the internal exchange economy, supplying produce to the "food-deficit" areas of the cocoa belt; and Jos, the European-structured entrepôt in Plateau Province, which grew out of a tin miners' settlement.

Ethnic Composition

Approximately half the population of the Middle Belt is of Hausa, Fulani, Nupe, Yoruba, or Tiv origin; all, except the Nupe, are rela-

tively recent migrants. The remainder are members of at least a hundred lesser known groups, provenience largely unknown, ranging in size from less than a thousand (the Pakara) to several hundred thousand people (the Idoma). Although the Fulani Jihad, at the turn of the nineteenth century, had penetrated most of the Middle Belt, thus making it plausibly a sector of the North in later colonial perspective, the impact was superficially political and tributary. Mohammedanism remains a minority religion through most of the area; if Hausa influence was at all significant prior to the Jihad, it was not of a religious, i.e., Islamic, nature, but was, more likely, politically transient and also tributary. Christianity has made small inroads in Illorin, Kabba, and Plateau provinces, but the original agreement between the British and the Fulani Emirs to prohibit missions in the North helped inhibit its spread. The multifarious peoples of the Middle Belt, many of whom have not yet been adequately identified, and the majority never properly counted, are fundamentally pagan, in contrast with the basically Hausa-Fulani-Kanuri population of the Sudan Provinces, which is nine-tenths Mohammedan, at least by formal affiliation.

The Middle Belt, then, is the most idiosyncratic area in Nigeria. It is the least known, least developed, most subsistence oriented, sparsely populated, tribally heterogeneous, and least integrated sector of the country. Its continuity lies, so to speak, in its relative, and recent, historical discontinuity with the major regions, and it is marked, at present, by the absence of internally unifying characteristics of any socioeconomic consequence. It comprises a unit by exclusion and is, as it were, an historical "leftover."

Historical Definition—Migration, Conquest States, and the Slave Trade

The designation "Middle Belt" is a convenience—arbitrary and retrospective; a more rational integrity may or may not develop after the fact of "recognition by exclusion," based on modern technological and political possibilities. Middle Belt identity may expand to meet its physical boundaries, and thus impose a retroactive unity on its history as, say, in the cases of Texas or Pennsylvania, or any other modern political integer of consequence. But that depends on what the people decide to make of their resources and specific histories.

Whatever the remote past of most groups presumed to be native and found within recent times in the Middle Belt may have been, there seem to be two major reasons for the miscellaneous character of this broad central sector of Nigeria. First, it was probably populated by a continuous series of migrations caused directly and indirectly by ecological factors and the growth, for over a thousand years, of conquest states in adjacent West African areas. Further synthesis and exposure of archeological, ethnological, and linguistic evidence may eventually enable us more fully to understand the continuities and discontinuities within the Belt, and between it and other areas, but the prospects are not sanguine. The building of utilities, roads, new settlements, industries, and systems of agriculture—which must proceed if underdeveloped, but no longer primitive nor even archaic, peoples are merely to survive in the modern world that has engulfed them—shrink ethnological time and archeological space. These new artifacts, which they must create in order to survive, create, in turn, the new conditions for their existence. But only Africans themselves, by maintaining a passion for their own past, and cultivating the most excruciating discipline needed to record it in its many dimensions, while they are in the very act of changing what they record, can keep their continent from sinking under the tide of historylessness that accompanies massive, sudden commercial-industrial processes.

Second, the slave trade that had built up for more than a thousand years as both a stimulus and result of archaic state formation in the Western Sudan reached its peak under the Fulani conquest. Whatever the complexity of its intention (Hodgkin, 1960, pp. 38 ff.), the Jihad had from the beginning the effect of being, and finally, openly became, a huge, theocratically inspired slave raid, which further depopulated and redistributed the societies of the Middle Belt. As Sir Alan Burns (1955, p. 192), quondam Governor of Nigeria, put it, "The Fulani were aliens ruling over a subject people whom they had antagonized by decades of slave-raiding and injustice." The surplus of this traffic fed the human markets of North Africa and the Near East, but domestic slavery was reputed to be relatively mild; in most local areas slaves could be adopted into the families of their masters, inherit property, and marry freemen. This latter type of local, probably indigenous African slavery developed as an elaboration on, or adaptation to, aboriginal kin usage; the fruits of labor and induction into the normal web of social relationships were hardly denied local slaves once they had settled into a community. However, the slaves of the civil authorities, pressed into specialized labor or military service, or sold across the Sahara by Arab middlemen, were outright chattels. But it was, of course, the demand of the European factors on the Guinea coast, steadily mounting from the sixteenth to the middle of the nineteenth century, that turned West Africa into a vast, commercial slave market, with social, cultural, psychological, and demographic repercussions that have hardly been explored and are, perhaps, beyond calculation.

The peoples of West Africa were then caught as in a vise between Arab markets in the North, and the Europeans on the coast. Native states, with all the attendant bureaucratic apparatus, geared to regularized and politicized war, rose and foundered on the basis of the slave trade; their paramount chiefs and kings were both procurers of slaves and middlemen in the trade. Cheap European goods—notably cloth, guns, spirits—flooded West Africa. Many native crafts, including pottery and metal working, withered "or even died out" (Fage, 1956, p. 61) in competition with the swifter rewards of trade for which slaving provided the prototype. Cultures were vul-

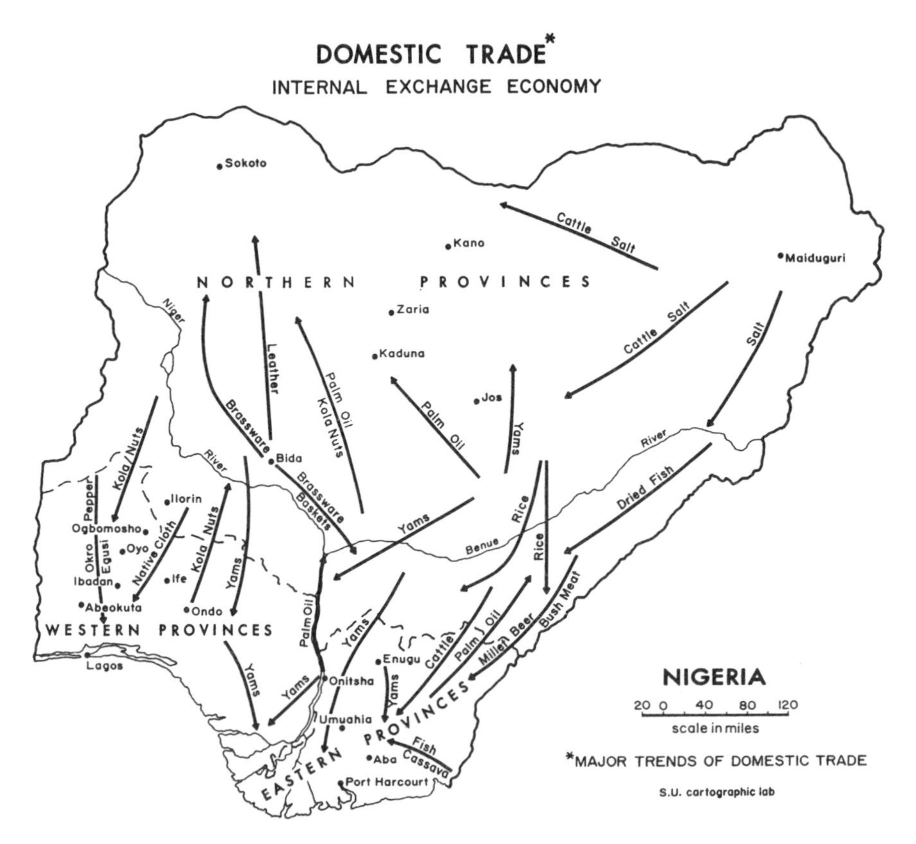

garized, exchanging their human and material resources, their skills, for the products of mercantile Europe, while being preadapted to more systematic dependence on commodities salable abroad. Certain peoples, e.g., in Dahomey, even neglected subsistence technics. The whole pattern of cash cropping, the correlated hunger for imported materials beyond the technical capacity of native cultures, and thus overvalued, the passive-aggressive dependence on Europe, and the overwhelming orientation toward trade of any type and degree which dominated the broken, archaic societies of West Africa during the pre-colonial and colonial periods, and which are only now being challenged, have their origin in the aims and impact of slavery.

The metropolitan, especially British, apologia (Hodgkin, 1960, p. 51) that nineteenth-century penetration of West Africa was intended to spread Christian civilization, develop education, and halt the slave trade (Burns, 1955, p. 294) must be viewed in a fuller, less culturally screened perspective. The British government did not build the infra-structure of education; the missions did. In Southeastern Nigeria, for example, the Catholic missions are prominent, and they do not even represent the established English church.

So far as Christian civilization is concerned, Northern Nigeria, the anchor of British control and the most heavily populated single region in West Africa, was not only closed to missions, but the alliance with Islam was actively pursued.

The slave trade was halted and gradually abandoned by the more commercial European nations, in conflict with the more feudal and agrarian, because (1) it had begun to interfere with other, more lucrative sources of trade, such as palm oil (Stapleton, 1958, p. 177), and (2) the slave market had been glutted, and the growth of manufacturing was making the institution obsolete. The loss of the American colonies probably also accounted, in part, for Britain's disinterest in maintaining the slave trade. Slavery was as immoral, as un-Christian, in the sixteenth century as in the nineteenth; the ethos had not changed. *That* was a constant, the *variable* factor was the shift in the needs of the metropolitan nations.

Thus, the dynamic of West Africa is not only that of colonialism, for which parallels exist elsewhere, but of colonialism in the aftermath of large-scale, systematized, commercialized slavery, and it is this that gives West Africa its peculiar historical character. Under the polar stimuli of Europe and the Arab countries, a huge convulsion, lasting 300 years, shook the length and breadth of the region, catalyzing a relatively mild native institution into a ferocious, self-destroying force. In certain internally marginal areas, populations lacking the "protection" provided by native political structures, which (sometimes) drew a circle around their subjects while preying on outside people, were decimated. Such an area was the Nigerian Middle Belt, a rich slaving ground almost equally accessible (or inaccessible) from the Sahara and the Atlantic. There, under the spur of their own socioeconomic needs, the major raiders for at least half a century following the Jihad (1802) were the Fulani Emirs—primary suppliers to the Arab and European markets. Indeed, slaves were widely used as currency in the Emirates and were a pillar of the ruling class. Therefore, we find that "ruthless slave raiding, continuing in many areas until the late nineteenth century, decimated the population of much of the Middle Belt, and drove the survivors to seek refuge in the remote and topographically difficult areas" (Buchanan and Pugh, 1955, p. 62).

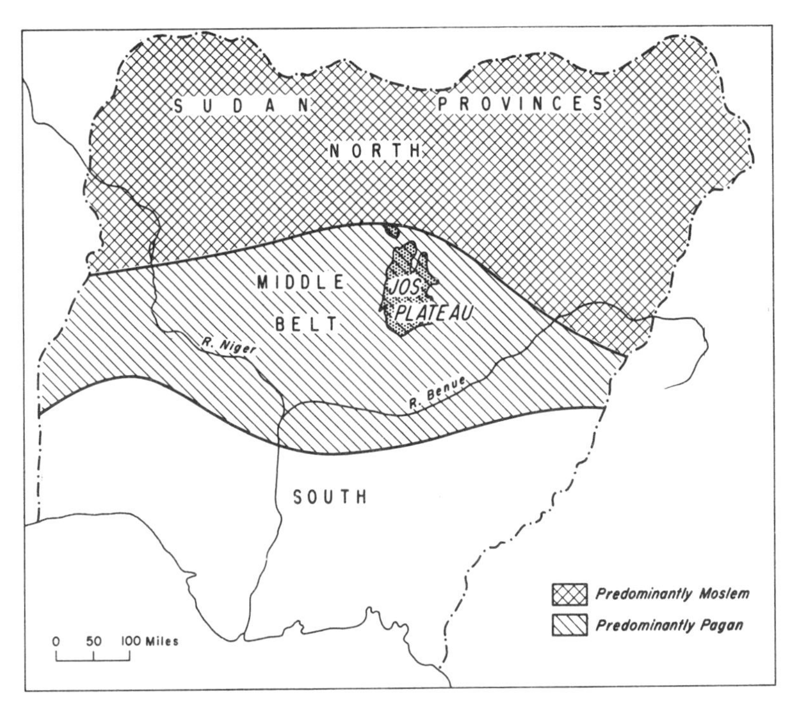

The Middle Belt in the context of Northern and Southern Nigeria.

THE PLATEAU PAGANS

Peoples and Cultures

Pagan peoples, on the periphery of the Moslem North, decentralized, primitive, and thus relatively defenseless, fled for their lives and cultural integrity. Many are found today in Plateau Province, the smallest of the Northern Provinces, about 10,000 square miles in area, and bounded on the northwest by Zaria Province, on the southwest and south by Benue, on the east by Adamawa, and on the northeast by Bauchi. Thus, Plateau Province lies at the very heart of the Middle Belt, and its people are certainly related to those in surrounding areas, from which they must have originally migrated.

There are approximately forty aboriginal peoples, speaking as many languages, grouped into a few major subfamilies (e.g., Bantoid, Chadic), and still functioning, to one degree or another, in the province. These Plateau Pagans, as they are called, number about half a million, and are probably the least known group of peoples in contemporary Africa. They share a series of complexly overlapping cultural, linguistic, and social traits which sometimes make it difficult to define objectively the extent of any given "tribe" once the borders of the immediate local unit—a hamlet or village—are passed. However, the subjective sense of individual group identity is strong; the people, as we would expect, are quite capable of defining themselves as Rukuba, Pakara, Jarawa, and so on, amid the welter of intertribal associations. Yet dialectic and other cultural variations penetrate to the village level, and hamlets may act autonomously when their inhabitants feel constrained by a political or social occasion.

The province at large gives the impression of being a culture area of considerable time depth, with randomly distributed and uniquely combined traits in specific locales. But this is not to claim a continuous or ancient peopling of the province by the present tribes; the traits and combinations of traits probably crystallized in adjacent sectors of the Middle Belt and were further intensified or diffused in the course of successive migrations. Correlatively, Plateau Province is a linguistic shatter-belt, and refined analysis of the relations among languages and between dialects, which will be most significant culturally, remains to be done if and when the data are available.

The High Plateau

The underlying ethnological character of the population as a whole is most sharply outlined on the High Plateau, after which the province is named. The High (Jos) Plateau consists of Jos Division, and most of Pankshin, two of the five major administrative units into which the province is divided. It is a relatively "treeless downland, studded with rugged hills," similar to the South African veldt. This area of 1,800 square miles lies at an average height of 4,000 feet, and is difficult of access from the surrounding plains. Thus, it provided refuge for almost half the Pagan population of the province at large—that is, some twenty tribes, consisting of about 200,000 people, are found there today. Since the Fulani were never able to occupy the area nor subdue its peoples, the political and cultural decentralization, random complexity of voluntary associations, and spirit of independence had been even more evident among them than elsewhere in the province. Although the Fulani had been held at bay, the British, urged on by the Mining Department of the Royal Niger Company and attracted by tin and rumors of tin, could not be avoided. By 1905, the High Plateau had been occupied and, within a few years, pacified. The remainder of the province, save for some sporadic outbreaks lasting through the

1930's was subdued at approximately the same time. The original purpose was to secure the company trade routes that ran north from the depots at Lokoja, at the Niger-Benue confluence, and Ibi on the Benue, skirting the province to the east and west. This, of course, is in the classic pattern of colonial intention in British West Africa: pacification and administration in the interests of trade. Mary Kingsley, intrepid and acute, had suggested the pattern independently of Lugard. She had, invited by Joseph Chamberlain, Colonial Secretary since 1895,

> worked out a system under which the traders should have the chief responsibility for administering West African territories, for the trader knew the African as no one else could know him; the Chambers of Commerce in Liverpool and Manchester and other great cities should be the seat of power, not Whitehall. Side by side with areas administered by the traders, the African should be encouraged to administer his own territory by his own laws, purged by British influence from such abuses as human sacrifice and slave-trading. *Trade was, or should be, England's only respectable reason for being in Africa at all.* (Middleton, 1964, p. 106)

It is one of the minor ironies of history that the peoples of the inaccessible High Plateau, including the Anaguta, should have found a place from which to stand off the Fulani and preceding conquerors, only to have occupied an area peculiarly rich in tinstone, and thus attractive to a more highly evolved civilization with which they could not possibly cope. Still, as late as 1934, the Resident of Plateau Province was moved to write, "Perhaps the most striking feature about the indigenous population of the Plateau province is the almost negligible effect that a quarter of a century's close contact with Western civilization and the alien mining community has had apparently on their manners, customs, religion, and more noticeably, on their dress" (Ames, 1934, p. 3).

It would seem, then, that the past generation has been decisive; during this period the Pagans have begun actively to formulate their fates out of the historical conditions, created by a superior power, with which they were confronted, and to which they were obliged, in one way or another, to accommodate themselves. In order to understand the specific position of the Anaguta in this adaptive process it is first necessary to discuss the significance of Jos.

JOS

Mineral Wealth—Distribution and Structure

Nigeria ranks sixth in the production of cassiterite, i.e., tin ore, (5 per cent of the world total) and first in columbite (95 per cent of the total), these two deposits being found in geological association, notably in the alluvial granites of the High Plateau, where columbite has been a relatively recent by-product of tin mining. The province, as a whole, produces about 85 per cent of Nigeria's tin, and 70 per cent of the columbite.

The uses of tin are familiar; columbium, obtained from columbite ore, is a highly heat-resistant, strategic metal used in the manufacture of steel alloys, particularly in lining gas turbines and jet engines. Cassiterite and columbite account for 99 per cent of Nigeria's mineral exports, exceeding, in 1954, a value of $30 million. The production of these and associated "rare" minerals, such as tantalite and wolfram, are almost entirely the business of expatriate companies. And all tin concentrates are shipped to the United Kingdom since there are no smelters in Nigeria.

Some sixty-two limited liability companies mine tin and related minerals in Nigeria, accounting for about 90 per cent of total production. Companies incorporated in the United Kingdom had twenty times the authorized capital of those incorporated in Nigeria, although the latter are also foreign owned. However, one expatriate combine dominates the tin field, producing about 50 per cent of the ore; a total of four company groups account for 80 per cent; and similar corporate proportions obtain in the extraction of columbite. Although the volume and value of production in Nigeria's mineral export industry have not been high, representing, in a peak year, about one-ninth of major export cash crop values and only a fraction of gross domestic product, profit margins have been substantial. Moreover, this sector of the economy "attracts more new private investment by companies than does any other single activity" (Blankenheimer, 1957, p. 57). More than two-fifths, (£4,652,000) of the total expended for capital improvements for 1954-55 went into mining, a statistic which helps elucidate both the primacy of trade in the economy and the low cost of maintaining trade circulation and installations. Still, in the early 1950's, and for an indeterminate period before that, mining revenues constituted the Northern Region's principal source of funds, indicating the economic importance of Plateau Province to the regional government. This, in turn, helps clarify the nature of the economic bond between the Northern Region and the British, to whom the province had also been of critical importance.

Unlike export cash cropping of cocoa, palm products, and groundnuts—which is pursued on a small-holder basis, with fractionated per capita returns to the peasant proprietors—the mineral industry, the deposits of which yield a variety of products, is concentrated in a few expatriate companies, in a circumscribed geographic area, where, it should be noted, hydroelectric power has been readily available since the Plateau is a hydrographic center. Moreover, African labor is cheap, whether directly employed or utilized as "tributors" [1] who sell ore at fixed prices per pound to the companies, the leases of which they work. In the latter instance, there is a curious analogy with small-holder cash cropping; it is as if an industry had tried to adopt the trading company pattern, thus attenuating its connection with, and responsibility to, the primary producers.

Conversely, mechanization of the open-cast mines that indent the Jos Plateau is initially quite expensive, but has proven to be cheaper in the long run, and otherwise more efficient, than continued dependence on hand labor. Mechanization, one factor leading to increased consolidation of the larger operators, has been speeded by the international tin quota of 1956, a response to the relative "oversupply" of tin on the world market in the postwar years. This has had the local effect of discouraging smaller enterprises, since each country's production is fixed at a particular level. During the first half of the 1950's, Nigeria, along with other primary producers, was protected against the results of postwar deflation in the value of tin and columbite by massive American military-industrial stockpiling of both minerals, but this prop has been removed.

However, the basic problem faced by the major mining companies that dominate the High Plateau is the depletion of tin reserves. It is estimated that the richest ores have already been tapped, and what remains must be reached through a heavy overburden. Within a decade the tinstone will probably have been worked out. And the prospect for columbite is not much brighter. Primary deposits seem plentiful but are expensive to work, their mineral content is low, the demand for columbite is limited, alternative materials are available, and high price levels must be maintained to make operations commercially feasible. Furthermore, the mechanization, and exhaustion of the mines lead to increasing unemployment of the alien workers, which, in turn, compounds political and economic problems on the Plateau.

Thus we find that the Nigerian export mineral industry has run a classic course. It is extractive only, and exemplifies primary production within an economically colonial structure. Smelting is done

[1] In 1955 it was estimated at one-third of the labor force, today about 10 per cent.

abroad and no finished products are fabricated in the country of origin. Corporate control is oligopolistic and, of course, wholly expatriate; the Nigerian government, after independence, as before, receives its due in the form of royalties. Moreover, the major mineral is being rapidly worked out, so that Nigeria at large cannot be said to have benefited from her own resources, in her own way.

Certainly the people of the High Plateau have not benefited. With minor exception, the Pagans have refused work in the tin fields, and migrant laborers from more "sophisticated" groups throughout Nigeria and West Africa have been employed; during the Second World War they were imported. By the mid-1950's, approximately 40,000 Africans, alien to the province, were working the mines and had long since turned Jos into an entrepôt. Furthermore, the system of open-cast mining has led to extensive destruction of topsoil, and has, directly and indirectly, narrowed the living space and cultivable land of the Pagans throughout the Plateau. Conservation measures, even if in some degree successful, cannot significantly reverse the damage already done. The Pagans, then, in the memory of their elders, have had their lands colonized by the British, in whose wake followed their ancient antagonists, the Hausa and Fulani, as traders, pastoralists, and political superiors; and the latter were joined, in turn, by thousands of workers—Tiv, Yoruba, Ibo, Ijaw, Ibibio, Kanuri, Ewe, Idoma, Igala, Nupe, and Beriberi are a few of the peoples encountered. As civilized amenities developed, Europeans turned the Plateau into a leave center, adding still another note to the cultural antiphony. In little more than a single generation, a remote and inaccessible area had become a part of the Northern Region, of Nigeria at large, and of the modern world.

Contrast with Colonialization of British West Africa

It was a forced occupation of a peculiar character. In other areas of British West Africa, indeed in the major regions of Nigeria, the bulk of the population were drawn into the colonizing process both economically and politically. Slavery, with the cooperation of native chiefs, as indicated, had given way to trade based upon the growing of cash crops for export, and just enough British control had been exerted, wherever possible through pre-existent native authorities (the functions of which were thereby changed), to stabilize the area, collect taxes in support of the new administration, and develop necessary communication and transportation facilities through local resources and metropolitan loans.

Indirect rule was the political instrument of colonial penetration by trade. "Most of the trade of Nigeria is in the hands of large firms and combines, mainly British, the head offices of which are in England. . . . For this reason it is the Chambers of Commerce of London, Liverpool, and Manchester that control Nigerian trade, rather than the Chambers of Lagos, Calabar, Port Harcourt, and Kano" (Burns, 1955, p. 288). Investments of manpower and resources for other purposes in British West Africa were inconsequential. Vocational education, for example, was directed to the training of clerks in order to staff administration and business. On a higher level, barristers were produced, but technical training was almost entirely neglected.

According to one source, foreign (mostly British) capital investment in Nigeria during the period 1870-1936 totaled £71,500,000, almost equally divided between public investment in railways and harbors, and private holding in trade and distributive organizations (Frankel, 1938, pp. 156 ff.). In 1954, the Bank of England reported the nominal value of all British *private* capital in West Africa at £ 42,000,000; presumably about half of this sum was invested in Nigeria (Blankenheimer, 1957, p. 19). Even if "nominal" value is assumed to be well under prevailing net asset valuations, and much less than market value, the sum is still startlingly small. The relative volume and pattern of governmental and private investment are clear enough. Britain could have "freed" the colony long before the official date of independence, with its trading profits assured and a minimum of capital investment at stake. But the converse does not hold. Nigeria could hardly have afforded to sever its ties with Britain. Indeed, the dispatch with which the Metropole formally disengaged itself from Nigeria may be attributed, in part, to its reluctance and incapacity to grant or lend the huge sums and technical facilities necessary to modernize the native economy and change its dependent structure. The further point is that in the non-settlers' colonies of British West Africa, the major metropolitan purpose, which seems to have developed pragmatically, was to extract as heavy a load of primary products as possible, build the infra-structure necessary for that, and sell finished goods back into the same trading company networks out of which export flowed, through an infinitude of African middlemen and retailers.

So far as settlers are concerned, even if they had found the area congenial, they would have upset the administrative procedures and frustrated related economic motives to a critical extent, while developing their own interests divergently from those of the Metropole, a familiar enough process in the history of colonies. And it is in this context that the "no settlers" policy of British West Africa needs to be examined.

The remarkable system of colonial remote control, once installed by political and military means, does not require the continued political subjection of the dependent territory. It can persist through self-government and formal independence; only a complementary socioeconomic, or "neo-colonial," relationship need be maintained (Diamond, 1963d). Even Africanization of expatriate organizations does not necessarily run counter to metropolitan aims. For, in the first instance, "it is unlikely that commercial firms, with an eye to profits, would have employed expensive European staffs if a sufficient number of capable Africans had been available locally" (Burns, 1955, p. 273). But the system of "remote control" does, of course, require leverage for its initial establishment—administratively, from cooperative native authorities, and economically, by engaging the people in dependent market relations which enables them, in turn, to pay taxes in partial support of the new colonial structure, thereby further wedding them to the market. And to keep the wheels in motion, the stimulus of European goods is, as noted, effective and useful.

The Classic Case of Northern Nigeria

Northern Nigeria had lent itself ideally, through the tribute-based Fulani Emirates, to a superimposed administration that actually strengthened and extended their power, while consolidating the archaic burden of imposts into a proper system of taxation. No one could have put the case better than Lugard (Commission of Inquiry, 1952, p. 10), in addressing the Court at Sokoto, on March 21, 1903, with his usual masculine candor:

> The old treaties are dead, you have killed them. Now these are the words which I, the High Commissioner, have to say for the future. *The Fulani in old times under Dan Fodio conquered this country. They took the right to rule over it, to levy taxes, to depose kings and to create kings. They in turn have by defeat lost their rule which has come into the hands of the British.* All these things which I have said the Fulani by conquest took the right to do now pass to the British. Every Sultan and Emir and the principal officers of State will be appointed by the High Commissioner throughout all this country. The High Commissioner will be guided by the usual laws of succession and the wishes of the people and chiefs, but will set them aside if he desires for good cause to do so. *The Emirs and Chiefs who are appointed will rule over the people as of old time and take such taxes as are approved by the High Commissioner*, but they will obey the laws of the Governor and will act in accordance with the advice of the Resident. . . .[2]

[2] Italics added.

The Government will in future hold the rights in land which the Fulani took by conquest from the people, and if Government require land it will take it for any purpose. The Government hold the right of taxation, and will tell the Emirs and Chiefs what taxes they may levy, and what part of them must be paid to Government. The Government will have the right to all minerals, but the people may dig for iron and work in it subject to the approval of the High Commissioner, and may take salt and other minerals subject to any excise imposed by law. Traders will not be taxed by Chiefs, but only by Government. The coinage of the British will be accepted as legal tender and a rate of exchange for cowries fixed, in consultation with Chiefs and they will enforce it.

Before colonial conquest, as Lugard (1918, p. 73) indicates,

every form of handicraft had its special tax—smiths, dyers, weavers, leather-makers, salt makers, canoe men. hunters, fishermen, ferry men, etc. In some places a liquor tax was imposed, in others each date-palm or beehive paid its toll. Prostitutes, dancing-girls, gamblers, were taxed by one or another chief. Sellers in the market had for the most part to pay royalties on the wares they sold. Traders paid toll at every town which they passed. To all these and many other taxes were added the *gaisua*, or present, which every man had to bring when he came to see his immediate superior, more especially at the periodical festivals, together with arbitrary levies in cash or kind, irregular fines without trial, and forced labour for building the city walls or the houses of the Chiefs.

Political appointments were bought and sold, and the peasants were exploited in the most arbitrary fashion. However, as Lord Hailey (1950) estimates, the actual revenues collected under the more regularized system of colonial taxation were greater than under the Fulani. And Burns (1955, p. 296) is careful to point out that as the general position of paramount chiefs, under indirect rule, "was more assured and their incomes more certain . . . [they] had little to complain of."

A colonial report (Commission of Inquiry, 1952, p. 7) elaborates the point as follows: "The comparatively high state of political organisation reached by protected Mohammedan Emirates has rendered possible a maintenance of their existing institutions to a remarkable degree, and the suzerian [British] power has confined its activities to supervision and control. Alien rule was no new conception as the people had been accustomed for centuries to the theory and fact of subordination, whether of race by race or class by class. Any opposition to British rule was originally and largely religious and was assuaged by a religious policy which was tolerant from the first."

The Emirates had been rotten with slavery (Lugard, 1905, p. 404) when the British government took over in 1900 from the Royal Niger Company, its chartered instrument since 1886, but within the decade the British-Fulani alliance had been tested, strengthened, and extended beyond the limited de facto control of the company (around the Niger and Benue confluence) through most of the Northern Region. By 1900, the company's military, diplomatic, and economic functions had ramified to the point where government control had become necessary and desirable. The ensuing sixty years, culminating in formal independence in 1960, constituted the period of frank political colonialism, but pre-colonial and post-colonial phases had and have their own types of socioeconomic subjection. It is pertinent that Sir George Goldie, the Governor of the company, was also known as the founder of Nigeria, and preceded Lugard as a theorist of indirect rule (Flint, 1960). Indeed, Lugard had first served in Nigeria in 1894 under company auspices in order to secure the western boundary of its territory against the French; and he had returned in 1897 as General of the West African Frontier Force, which finally stabilized the western borders of the developing colony, Nigeria emerging, in fact, as a lucrative enclave in an area that was developing into French West Africa.

In the North, the colonial intention was further realized as groundnuts developed into a major export crop during the twenty-five years following the transferral of authority from the company to the government. By 1950, at least 60 per cent of the peasants of the Sudan Provinces were engaged in the groundnut market.

Comparison with Colonialization in Eastern and Western Nigeria

A similar combination of administrative means (the paramount chiefs) and economic ends (cocoa) subdued and further transformed the Western Region. In the East, palm products provided the major leverage, but there were certain complications arising from the virtual absence of centralized native authorities, and the fact that palm oil was an important local food, unlike cocoa and groundnuts. Only the surplus was exported, and neither Ibo ecology, social organization, division of labor, nor the British administrative pattern could have generated a large-scale plantation economy. These factors made it difficult for the British to grasp the region as firmly as they did the North and West, and accounted, in part, for the keen Ibo sense of self-determination. Nevertheless, palm products are Nigeria's leading cash crop, and had been the country's primary export item, following slavery. A *modus vivendi* was eventually worked out, after the Aba riots of 1929, with the multitudinous clan and village heads, the natural rulers, who then replaced the warrant chiefs, the latter having been directly appointed by the British. Thus the peoples of the Eastern Region, along with those of the North and West, were, by the end of the nineteenth century, shaped to a colonial social economy.

As the United Africa Company (modern heir of the Niger Company and subsidiary of Unilever), which alone accounts for 50 per cent [3] of Nigeria's import trade, states the case: "Towards the end of the nineteenth century, export of palm oil and cocoa, and a few years later of palm kernels and groundnuts, began to expand; and the volume of the merchandise trade grew likewise" (United Africa Company, 1950, p. 2).

The company goes on to explain:

> By what means was this growth of trade in the nineteenth century made possible? As we have shown, early trading ventures consisted of a single voyage: the trade in those days must have been spasmodic. Apart from the Coastal forts erected by the rival trading nations in the Gold Coast in and after the seventeenth century, there were few permanent trading points. Friendly relations with the Africans had not yet been established. Means had to be found, nevertheless, for establishing resident traders if trade was to be conducted continuously. The first step was the system of working pairs of sailing vessels in relays; the second was the system of trading from hulks moored in the rivers and creeks of Nigeria. As the confidence of the Africans was gained, these hulks were replaced by permanent shore establishments, and by the 1870's, with few exceptions, the trade was being conducted from shore stations. *Thus, by the time the West African trade began its great expansion—in the 1890's—the means and machinery for supporting a continuous flow of trade in both directions were already in existence.* (United Africa Company, 1950, p. 4)

[3] This figure happens to be identical with the proportion of Nigerian imports from the United Kingdom. While Nigeria exports two-thirds of its primary products to Great Britain, the United Africa Company purchases only about one-fifth of the total, mostly as an agent for the Regional Marketing Boards (set up in 1947-50), at fixed fees; this has reduced company risk in crops subject to wide price fluctuations, but does not hinder the flow of goods to England. Investment of marketing board surpluses in British banks have also been useful to the Metropole, while helping to stabilize raw product prices to the peasant by enforced savings in good price years. But the marketing boards have, by the same token, depressed the purchasing power of the peasant, which could be a basic factor in initiating an upward spiral of national growth in favorable years, and, so to speak, banked that potential purchasing power at the center for future use at the discretion of welfare-oriented government. The results of this policy could not fairly be tested under colonialism; only now, with political independence, can its integrity and wisdom be explored fully. It should be remembered that the position of the peasant, who is historically a member of an *exploited* rather than *exploiting* class, has been a major problem in those underdeveloped areas where planned, rationalized, and stimulated growth have been attempted. For, in such programs, peasants are forced into a new national role, that of controlled, intensified, and specialized production, which may run contrary to both their own traditions and expectations of "freedom."

By 1919 Lugard was able to write: "Nigeria affords an immense field for British trade, and though it has developed at an extraordinary rate, it is capable of indefinite expansion" (1919, p. 29).

Position of the Pagans Under Colonialization

But the British found no administrative or economic leverage among the Pagans of the High Plateau. The aboriginals had fled from the areas of commercialized slavery; they grew no crops that could be drawn into the export market; they were, indeed, subsistence cultivators unacquainted with, and uninterested in, a money economy. Their most significant native authorities were sacred, nonpolitical figures who were reluctant to deal with outsiders, and decision-making was local, democratic, and decentralized. The British had no interest in the Pagans, beyond pacification, and the Pagans had no need of the British. The colonial business on the Plateau was tin, and that, it turned out, could be extracted by an alien labor force working for European companies, on land leased according to regulations laid down by the Metropole.

It should be re-emphasized that the High Plateau was not under Fulani suzereinty when the British arrived; "The primitive pagan races held their own in the inaccessible fastnesses in the mountainous districts of the plateau . . ." (Commission of Inquiry, 1952, p. 6). Indeed, the province itself was not organized until 1926; prior to that time, but following British formal occupation of the North in 1900, the territory had formed part of Bauchi, Muri, and Nasarawa provinces. Under Fulani administration, the Emirates at Bauchi and Zaria had sporadically attempted to subdue the outlying areas of what was later to emerge as Plateau Province. But the majority of people inhabiting the interior were never subject to the Fulani. Indeed, even those groups that were claimed as subjects, e.g., the Ankwe of Shendam Division, and certain Angas villages in Pankshin, had a problematical status; at most, Fulani control was nominal to the point of occasional token tribute. Interestingly enough, the Sardauna of Sokoto, who became Premier of the Northern Region and was a direct descendant of Othman Dan Fodio —the leader of the Fulani Jihad at the turn of the nineteenth century—implicitly acknowledges this in his biography by indicating on a map of the old empire that the current area of Plateau Province did not lie within the Fulani fold (Bello, 1962, p. 118). The point is that the tin fields of the High Plateau were directly expropriated by the British. Throughout the Jos area, and most of the province, there were no superordinate authorities, no native conquest states, whose prior colonization of the territory could be recognized and adapted to the uses of a new political power. As K. W. J. Post has properly noted, "In . . . societies which traditionally lacked centralized authority there appeared to be a greater ability to assume a unified aspect when faced by what was thought of as a challenge from outside." [4]

On every count, then, indirect rule had no substance on the Plateau, resulting in a situation idiosyncratic in British West Africa. That is to say, direct exploitation of a native resource developed under resident European managers. European prospectors were permitted into the territory and the aboriginal population, proving economically and administratively useless, was, to its apparent satisfaction, largely ignored. A handful of dedicated and curious District Officers indicated interest in the Pagans and left a few records behind, but government anthropologists were, for the most part, busy with more urgent problems involving people of greater importance to the Colonial Office. Colonial authorities typically dismissed the Pagans as intractably savage, after the fashion of Sir Alan Burns (1955, p. 193); and this was also the standard attitude of the Fulani, Hausa, and other prominent African peoples.

Lugard (1922, p. 58) commented about such Pagans: "In one case I received a reply that they had eaten every kind of man except a white man, and they invited me to come that they might see what I tasted like." But Ames (1934, p. 36), the sole historian of the province, and a District Officer in the early 1930's, writes, ". . . we should perhaps mention the bravery of the tribesmen and their inherent sense of *sportsmanship*, which made them observe the rules of their own methods of warfare, and we can then ask the forgiveness of their living descendants for somewhat airily dismissing their wars as being of no great importance." The fact is that the primitive peoples of the Plateau area were neither organized for, nor interested in, large-scale war or conquest, from which they had fled. Their little battles, along with attendant usages, such as the cannibalism and head-hunting practiced by certain groups, had a profound and complex ritual, in a sense, a sacramental character—to discover what the enemy "tasted" like, to absorb his qualities, simultaneously to honor and humiliate him, but always to acknowledge the concreteness of his humanity. These primitive

[4] Post then states that this cannot be explained "until much more work has been done by anthropologists and sociologists on the behavior of different societies in a modern political context" (Post, 1963, p. 380). Perhaps this monograph will contribute an explanation. See also Diamond, 1951.

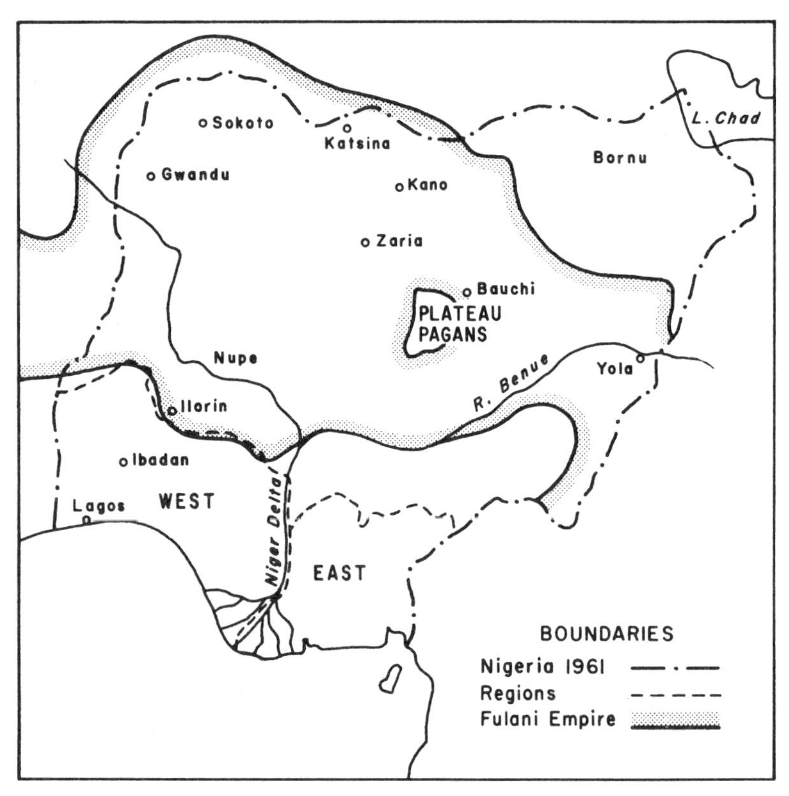

The *formal* borders of Fulani sovereignty (1809-1900).

wars were self-limiting, few people were killed, or permanently subjected. It is a paradox that the destructive potential and actuality of war, its increasingly acquisitive and abstract ideological nature, its literally *unsportsmanlike* character, has developed along with the "refinement" of civilized sensibilities.

Thus, the "militarily weak and defenseless savages" were ignored. They moved in another dimension. Even when they shared the same physical space with Europeans or sophisticated Africans, these incarnations of radically different modes of culture and distinct levels of history literally looked past each other, without acknowledgement or recognition. And the contrast remains striking today when, for example, a naked Pagan woman bearing a thirty-pound load of firewood on her headtray disinterestedly steps aside for a ten-ton truck on a bituminized road leading to a minefield.

Such contrasts are most evident in the immediate neighborhood and in the city of Jos, which constituted part of the aboriginal territory of the Anaguta and the nucleus of colonial conquest. While the Pagans tried to go about their customary business with undiminished dignity, ringing ". . . the changes of the seasons with their sowing, farming, reaping, beer-drinking, dancing, and hunting," commercial-industrial processes to which they were utterly alien were completely transforming the basic conditions of their existence. To them, this new growth must have had the character of a vast, uncontrollable natural phenomenon. Like the peasants at the base of Etna, they simply had to assume that it was not there. It is an assumption that the Anaguta have never surrendered.

Indeed, it is possible to climb to the peak of a hill in the heart of their territory and look down on the white roofs of Jos, a few miles to the south; if it is late afternoon in the rainy season and a mist diffuses the air, the city, insubstantial, shimmers in and out of view. Or even on blazing afternoons, from the sudden perspective of a mountain trail, its bulk contracts and it appears as just another bright patch on an endless, ancient landscape. The Anaguta play with these perspectives, from the heights they command they know every visage of the city, in each season and hour; but the city is not an optical illusion, however illusory may be the purposes that established it, or the ends it pursues. As the Anaguta conjure with the invisibility of individuals, so they conjure with the invisibility of Jos. But the city is there.

British Establishment on the High Plateau

As already noted, the Niger Company was responsible for first "confirming," in 1902 (two years after the surrender of the charter), the existence of a tin field in the province. Native smelted and hammered "straw tin," thin bars used in trading, had been recognized in the North as early as 1885 by Europeans, but the ultimate local source remained unknown. The attention of the company had finally been attracted to the province because of the "amount of tin being purchased from native traders" (Ames, 1934, p. 39) at Ibi, on the Benue, its northernmost depot. As we have seen, by 1905, the Jos tin fields had been discovered, and the British military had followed the company lead up to the Plateau. In the interim, the company had abandoned actual prospecting, but a prior agreement with the government entitled it to a 50 per cent share in all mineral royalties accruing from most of the Northern Region. In 1949, before the columbite boom, but after the tin reserves were known to be reaching exhaustion, this right was sold back to the Nigerian government for the flat sum of one million pounds. In the years prior to 1949,

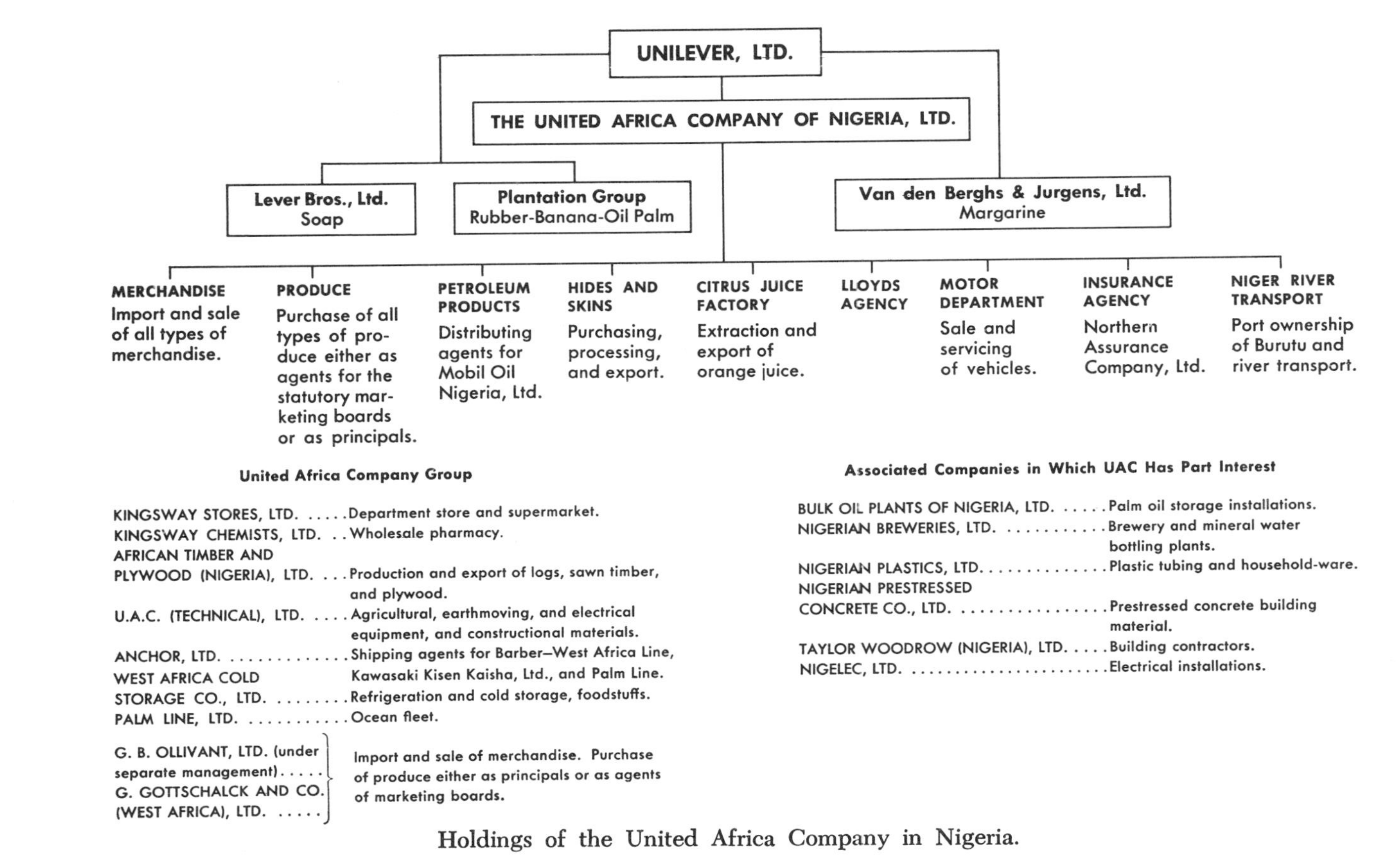

Holdings of the United Africa Company in Nigeria.

the company half-share "had amounted to as much as £250,000 per annum" (Buchanan and Pugh, 1955, p. 79), on the basis of "discovering" lands which only the Pagans traditionally owned. The company had never engaged in any productive work in the Plateau tin fields.

Prior to 1910, Jos Township, the contemporary headquarters of the province, was "unoccupied farmland," and the adjoining Native Town consisted of only a "few houses" (Ames, 1934, p. 32). But mines in the immediate vicinity were already being worked, and by 1911, the Niger Company had put up its storehouses, symbolically enough, the oldest buildings in the township. The local seat of government, for what was then called "Naraguta Division" (a unit of Bauchi Province), was the village of Naraguta. This deserves a brief explanation.

The Naraguta Problem

Naraguta is the Hausa rendering of "Anaguta." Following the Hausa, most Africans and Europeans refer to the Anaguta as "Naraguta," and some connection between the people and village of that name is assumed. Indeed, current recognition of the Anaguta usually originates in misidentification of the people with the village. Today, Naraguta, which lies about five miles northeast of Jos, on the edge of Anaguta occupied land, is a small, but typical Hausa village, quite different in layout, house type, and cultural atmosphere from Anaguta settlements. There is no evidence that the village itself was Anaguta in origin, despite the confusion in colonial records, e.g., the remarks in Temple (1919, p. 8). Gunn is unable to discern the relationship between the place Naraguta and the people Anaguta, although he states, "It is only certain that Naraguta was earlier regarded as the chief settlement of these people" (1953, p. 61). Naraguta, however, was probably founded by Hausa traders, who followed the British up to the Plateau, perhaps as early as 1905, and clustered near the initial center of government, from which a track ran to what seems to have been the first tin mine, operated by the Jos Tin Areas Limited. The earliest "prospecting base" had been established, in 1903, at the site of the present Fulani-Hausa village of Tilden Fulani, about ten miles northeast of Naraguta; shortly afterwards contact was made with the Anaguta in the vicinity of Naraguta. But no Anaguta hamlet of that name exists; nor is there any indication that one ever existed; the Anaguta deny the association. As indicated, Anaguta (Hausa, "Naraguta") is, in the aboriginal context, a peoples' name for itself. It seems, therefore, that the British expedition had contacted initially those Anaguta whose compounds were scattered along the northern slopes of their traditionally occupied hills, above and, perhaps, adjacent to lands adjoining the present site of Naraguta, and had simply named the whole area, including the hills, after the Hausa term for the people who owned the land. Certainly the Hausa and Fulani of Zaria and Bauchi Emirates knew of the territory, and the British must have adopted the general designation from them, perhaps before mounting the Plateau. But the village itself was, undoubtedly, the result of colonial occupation; thus the British and Hausa themselves conjured up an entity which has confused the few people who have tried their hand at the history of the area, and also helped to misidentify the Anaguta.

Be that as it may, Naraguta, founded on Anaguta land, was the primary locus of government on the Plateau. Jos was, as noted, also established on land claimed by the Anaguta, a claim acknowledged by the various aboriginal groups in the immediate area, notably the Jarawa and the Nyango, and also confirmed by the only knowledgeable British authority in the city. Indeed, the Jarawa (Afusare) of the several villages scattered in and through the hills north of Jos, and those Nyango who had settled in a new native suburb northwest of the town, sought, in 1959, to utilize Anaguta priority in the area in order to break off from what they felt was the British-Hausa–influenced and Birom-dominated Native Authority, headquartered in Jos, under a Birom paramount chief. The purpose was to set up a new amalgamated Jos native authority under the nominal leadership of the Anaguta chief, who already held the position of Chief of Gwong, which, geographically, but not juridicially, includes the city of Jos. Characteristically, the Anaguta were not interested in this historically justifiable maneuver, and the effort failed.

Birom primacy had been recognized by the British. With a population of about 50,000, they were the largest group on the Plateau; moreover, their territory, lying south of the city, proved richest in tinstone and, after 1910, became the focus of the mining industry. This constructed political primacy also has ethnographic implications. British Colonial Officers tended to regard adjacent peoples as a sort of "illegitimate" Birom, just as they were inclined to use the entity "Hausa" in order to identify assorted cultural and linguistic traits throughout the Northern Region. This political distortion of ethnography must be routine in colonial areas, and surely bears further investigation.

The Growth of Jos

Naraguta remained the government center until 1921 by which time the population of Jos had reached 720 and the transferral of authority began. New public offices—Provincial, Mines, Survey, and Treasury—neatly indicating the British *raison d'être* on the Plateau, were opened in Jos in 1927; the shift was completed by 1929, two years after the formation of Plateau Province. In the interim, mining had its primary boom in Birom territory, probably accounting for the shift of government south to Jos—closer to the major tin field—from the less economically significant area of Naraguta. In those days, a few miles either way meant pounds and shillings in terms of labor, time, and transportation facilities.

By 1912, eighty-two companies were mining on the Plateau, with a total capital of £3,792,000 (Blankenheimer, 1957, p. 58). Three years later, the number had consolidated to sixty-eight, but capital had increased to £6,360,000; in 1915, 6,910 tons of tin were extracted, at an export value of £773,700 (Cook, 1943). The 1915 tonnage was already more than half that achieved in the early fifties, but represented a much smaller fraction of the 17,000-ton maximum reached for several years during the Second World War, when "the best deposits were used up" (Blankenheimer, 1957, p. 58).

It is worth noting that officially encouraged speculation by a variety of companies, followed by government-sponsored or regulated consolidation, leading to oligopoly and greatly increased profits, has been the pattern of commercial development in British West Africa, initiated in trading, and followed by the extractive and light manufacturing enterprises. This, of course, reflected, more extremely, a similar pattern at home, the domestic and foreign shibboleths of free trade notwithstanding. Indeed, the major trading company has been complexly involved in all three types of undertaking. Free trade, under the banner of which the charter of the Royal Niger Company had been revoked, has meant, in fact, the freedom of the commercial-industrial centers of the world to dominate, by "natural" market mechanisms, the areas of primary production, as Myrdal (1957) has indicated. Colonialism has been, and is, only an aspect of this process, for which no better historical model than British West Africa exists. And the Jos Plateau, although culturally idiosyncratic, is a good index of the results.

By 1915, the tin business was well established, and the Bauchi Light (narrow gauge) Railway had been completed. This 133-mile link from Zaria to Jos had been built specifically to serve the "booming mining industry," and was, because of the gradients that had to be overcome, a signal engineering feat in the cause of commerce. It fed into the main Kano-Lagos Line, completed in 1912, and was for thirteen years the sole rail link to the mines, transporting "all the machinery originally required for the industry" (Buchanan and Pugh, 1955, p. 209). In 1927, another main line from Port Harcourt on the Bonny, a shorter and easier haul, had been extended through Kafanchan to Jos, and the Light Railway gradually fell into disuse. Its track and rolling stock stand like toys in the Native Town today.

The tin industry was, of course, one of the major factors in the growth of the "export biased" Nigerian railway system, which would have "moved slowly," on the basis of "the political penetration of the country" alone (Blankenheimer, 1955, p. 71). As one authority put it rather mildly, "such lines [limited to the] prospects of developing good freight traffic . . . do not necessarily provide a colony with a complete system of communications" (Hawkins, 1958, p. 8).

Indeed, "the Nigerian national economy is a product of the road and rail systems which have successfully created a national market over what is a very large area. . . . In the North . . . the principal function of road transport is the delivery of groundnuts to the railheads, and the distribution of imports brought from the Coast by the railway" (Hawkins, 1958, p. 17). But we find that, as late as 1956, only 13 per cent of the area of the Northern Region, three-quarters of the country, was within one square mile of any kind of vehicular road. This was apparently sufficient for the uses of trade.

The accident of tin, then, turned Jos, within a generation, into a major rail and road junction. By 1927, a fifty-line telephone exchange had been installed in the town, the first through boat train had arrived, and two Royal Air Force planes had landed in the area. As its cosmopolitan population grew, supplying goods, services, and labor typical of mining centers, Jos also became an important trading depot. Roads branched northwest to the Chad basin, south to Enugu in the Eastern Region, and northeast to the regional capital, Kaduna, and the export crop areas around Zaria and Kano.

By the beginning of the Second World War, the town itself had expanded into a small city, dense with feeder roads from the major arteries of trade and industry. The city's outer shape had been determined by an arbitrary pattern of mining leases, many of which are worked out and unrestored, thus inhibiting further growth;

Fig. 65. The traditional Anaguta compounds overlooking the Sabon Gari.

Fig. 66. Jos, a town of 50,000 persons of whom only 2 or 3 per cent are European, has exerted comparatively little influence on the Anaguta. The Kingsway store, a retail outlet of the United Africa Company, sells groceries, household supplies, hardware, and clothing.

Fig. 67. A trading company store in Jos sells hardware and materials for the mining industry as well as tires. Note anachronistic name.

Fig. 68. A traditional Anaguta hill compound.

Fig. 69. Fulani chief in Gwong Native Court; note Moslem influence in his robe and turban. The Anaguta remain pagan, having escaped significant Moslem or Christian influence.

Fig. 70. A Fulani beauty. Her crown of twisted cloth is for carrying calabashes of milk.

Fig. 71. Anaguta woman with a headboard carved by her husband, a skilled woodworker, who stands by her side.

Fig. 72. A classic Anaguta type.

others are merely restrictive legally, giving Jos a roughly oblong contour. The core of Jos is commercial-administrative, also reflecting fundamental colonial purposes, unlike the archaic urban areas of indigenous Africa. European-stimulated installations are "grafted on" to the residential-marketing centers of native towns, whether Islamic (Kano) or Yoruba (Ibadan). Conversely, the inner commercial-administrative zone of Jos embraces banks, insurance companies, specialty shops, mission headquarters, bookstores, government offices, food stores, automobile agencies, pharmacies, garages, a cinema—all the typical signs and substances of modern civilization—but no residences.

Around this nucleus, the city divides into three residential areas: the northern quarter, predominantly Hausa; the southern, composed primarily of Ibo, Yoruba, and Kalabari elements, along with Levantine residents; and the more segregated European section. Each area has a cultural and architectural style of its own, but the bustling, polyglot life of the town, from teeming native market to staid Kingsway supermarket, spills over everywhere during the course of the business day. To the south, just beyond the limits of the town, in the direction of the major minefields, are the airport, the European hospital, race course, clubs, and Rest House. To the north is the *sabon gari,* or new town, a native suburb made up of poorer, more recent, mostly Southern residents; a similar suburb, composed of "acculturating" Pagans, is forming to the northwest.

Despite the disproportion of the African population (about 50,000) to the European (about 1,200), Jos has the atmosphere of a settlers' enclave, an idiosyncratic colony within a colony. The physically European pattern of the city itself is one reason for this, but other factors are equally significant. The expatriate population, numerically small, although second only to Lagos and relatively higher, is stable, residential, and culturally dominant. Europeans tend to settle with their families in long-range executive jobs created directly or indirectly by the mining industry. They find the climate tolerable, and Jos is also a local leave center, which refreshes the population and multiplies the amenities necessary to cater to civilized needs. Mission headquarters are clustered in the area, which had no indigenous Islamic tradition, and there is a school serving the children of Protestant missionaries throughout West Africa. A representative list of European organizations in the city includes: Boy Scouts and Girl Guides Associations, British Council, British Empire Society for the Blind, British Red Cross Society, Church Missionary Society, Electricity Corporation of Ni-

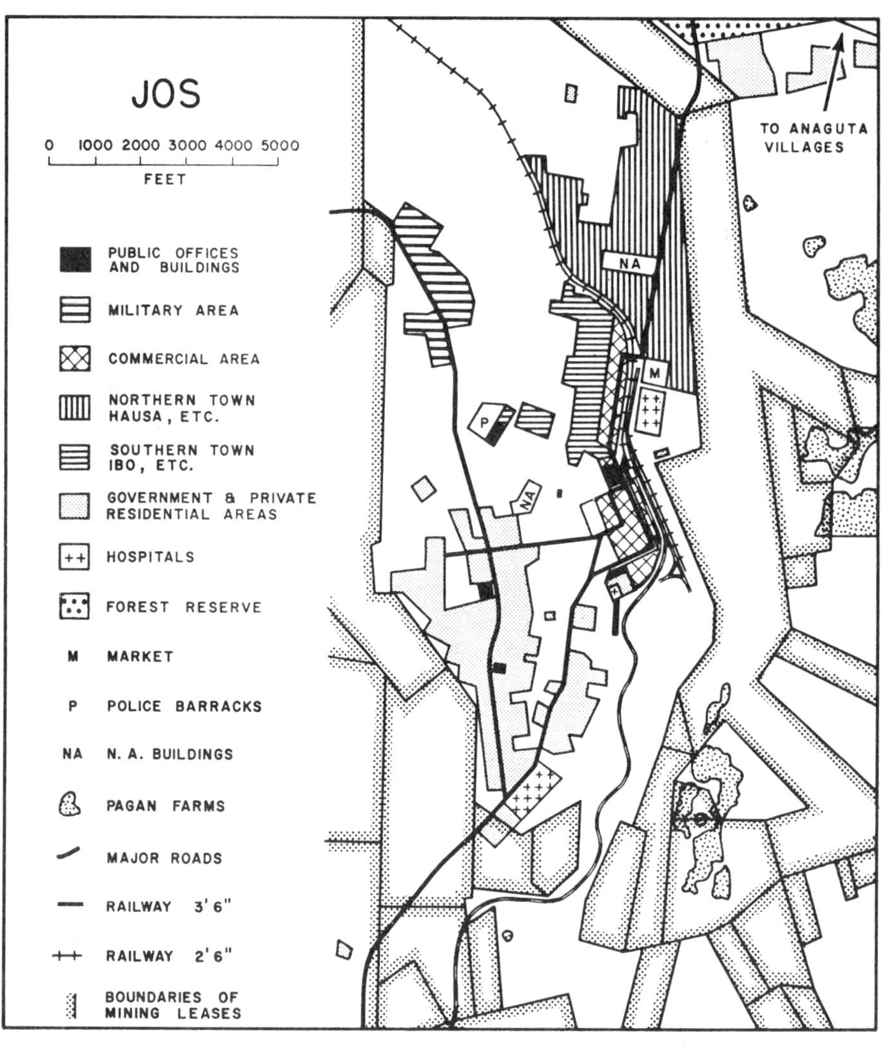

The city of Jos. (After Buchanan and Pugh, 1955.)

geria, Methodist Mission, Nigerian Chamber of Mines, Nigerian Electricity Supply Corporation, Nigerian Railway Corporation, Roman Catholic Mission, Sudan Interior Mission, Sudan United Mission, and the West African Airways Corporation.

But apart from the predictable variety of European residences and institutions distributed in and around Jos, there is an overriding sociopsychological factor at work generating the European aura. The African population is, with trivial exception, also alien or "expatriate." The Africans from other parts of Nigeria live in the European-established city on capital created, accumulated, and distributed by Europeans. They are not directly displaced peasants, but traders, manual laborers, servants, artisans, clerks, chauffeurs, shopkeepers—all of whom have migrated to Jos seeking employment. No African considers Jos his real home—he hails from Sokoto, Ibadan, Onitsha, Maiduguri, Fort Lamy, and one day he plans to return to the place where most of his extended family remains. The Africans are at least as transient as the Europeans in Jos; they, also, are pursuing profit; the city has no African center.

The European is master in Jos and he meets few Africans of the traditional or modern elite character with whom he would be likely to rub shoulders in Lagos, Kaduna, or Ibadan. Class and occupational differences compound racial distinctions, and we find that the clubs are informally segregated; moreover, this exclusivity penetrates into the European society which folds back on itself, creating a hierarchy of trivial statuses and an electric circuit of tension and rumor.

But there are displaced persons, and they are, of course, the Pagans. Unseen in their hills and hidden valleys, they drift like shadows even down and through the center of the city. Neither alien African nor European recognizes the reality of their priority. They are an impertinence. Between modern African and European, the Pagan presence silently intervenes. The African is embarrassed by them; to the European, they *are* the African in his aboriginal condition, and, all prejudices reinforced, there can be no communication.

The tiny, euphorbia-hedged compounds are, then, the fourth "quarter," the outermost primitive suburban ring, which pierces the mining leases, around the civilized city of Jos.

THE ANAGUTA

The Problem of Birom Affiliation

Nothing definitive is known of the more remote origins of the Anaguta. Ames (1934, p. 25) speculates that they are one of the three branches of the Birom "which moved northeast," from forest country south of Plateau Province, and "settled on the Naraguta hills where they joined others (probably Jarawa) and became the Anaguta tribe." The occasion for the Birom migration from "somewhere down towards the Benue," may have been the expansion of the Jukun conquest state in the seventeenth century, driving the "politically weak and defenseless peoples" in their path onto the High Plateau, a pattern of migration which peopled the area. Although one Anaguta elder stated that the Anaguta had, at one time, lived in Kabong (a Birom village area), and elders of Kabong have a similar tradition, the Anaguta do not recognize any generic connection with the Birom. As Ames points out, the Anaguta may once have lived at Kabong with Birom from Udu (Du), an adjacent area, but Udu spoke a Birom language, along with Eguta, while Anaguta did not speak Udu, and that, along with other incongruities, makes any immediate generic connection unlikely. Moreover, the relationship of Udu to Birom remains uncertain. All that is known is that at one time Udu became Birom, whatever their prior identity. Still, it is interesting to note the insistence of Birom speakers in Kabong, who no longer speak Eguta, that they are related to the forefathers of the Anaguta. If Udu-Birom are descendants of the Anabuze (of Buji District), as they also claim, then the Birom overlay would be recent, and, as we shall see, the supposed relation with Anaguta would become more credible.

Most Anaguta deny Birom associations. Indeed, the attitude toward the Birom is condescending and slightly contemptuous. Birom practice bride purchase, which Anaguta regard as a chattel sale. Bride wealth had never been an Anaguta tradition; they regard it as a degradation of the women, and, I discovered, find ethnographic arguments to the contrary amusing. Anaguta do purchase Birom women in marriage, however, and there is no indication that they are treated poorly, although the method of initiating the union remains a source of shame.

Anaguta also feel that the customary near nudity of the Birom, who wear a little less than themselves, is laughable. Birom men, who traditionally wore only penis sheaths, are particularly ridiculous, and Anaguta have a low opinion of them as warriors.

On the whole, little evidence exists for viewing the Anaguta as a Birom subgroup, despite certain social connections. Until recently, an annual ritual was shared (but other nearby peoples were also said to attend), intermarriage of Birom women to Anaguta men is not infrequent (but the reverse hardly ever occurs), and there are general similarities, perhaps most evident today in material culture. Birom and Eguta, although ultimately related, are distinct languages; on the other hand, standard lexico-statistical lists indicate a close connection between Eguta and the languages of the Anazele and Anabuze, of the Jerawa group, the implications of which will be noted below.

The Problem of Afusare Affiliation

The Anaguta are more often considered to be congeners of the Afusare, or Hill Jarawa of Bauchi and Plateau Provinces; occasionally the Afusare are considered a composite community, inclusive of the Anaguta (Gunn, 1953, p. 63). The dominant population of the Gwong Village Area is Anaguta and Afusare; with a single exception—that of an Afusare settlement, a ward in an Anaguta village—the villages of each people are physically and socially distinct. Elements of material culture are similar, traditional facial markings are identical, but these also share the pattern of certain Anabuze. Eguta and Jarawa today are distinctive, mutually unintelligible languages, whatever their ultimate genesis.

Afusare acknowledge the primacy of the Anaguta in Gwong, and properly regard themselves as recent immigrants from Bauchi. Despite the many significant cultural differences between the Anaguta and Afusare, particularly in social and ceremonial life, each people respects the other, and they have united successfully against common enemies in the past, most notably the Fulani. There is no question about the independent identity of each people as it exists today, and in its immediately known or traditional past. The Anaguta themselves recognize an affinity for the Afusare, but deny any generic connection. As in the administrative subordination of the Anaguta to a Birom identity, the tendency to assimilate Anaguta to Afusare seems a result of the more extensive population and distribution of the Hill Jarawa, and their more obvious significance to the pre-colonial and colonial powers. Gunn (1953, p. 60) notes that "the Anaguta of Jos Division, although entirely surrounded by Afusare and closely related to them, have retained their distinct name in the chronicles of the [Bauchi] emirate and in administrative papers, for reasons not apparent."

But the retention of the Anaguta name in Fulani and British records is quite understandable; as noted, the Anaguta never accepted Fulani sovereignty, and Naraguta was the first government mining settlement on the Plateau. In actuality, the traditional sovereignty of Anaguta in Gwong is recognized by all adjacent Pagan peoples, and their cultural identity is as clear as, if not clearer than, any other people in the area.

The Jerawa Link

On the other hand, most Anaguta elders feel closest to the Anabuze of Buji District, the people of the above-mentioned Jerawa group. *Jerawa* needs to be distinguished from *Jarawa*. The Afusare

are Hill Jarawa and are said to have no connection with the Jerawa. But this is one of the several insoluble puzzles of Plateau Pagan relationships, since a tie exists between the Anabuze and the Anaguta, who are, in turn, said to be related to the Afusare. Moreover, if the Udu-Birom are descendants of the Anabuze, then one could construct links among Afusare, Anabuze, and Birom. Pertinently, it is reported that Udu-Birom, along with Anaguta elders, have visited in Buji District for ritual purposes.

In any event, the languages (including the language of the Anazele, the dominant people of Jere district, from which *Jerawa* is derived) seem similar enough to be regarded as dialects, although variations in pitch, accent, and form make mutual understanding difficult. Furthermore, the marriage complex, centering around sister exchange, is strikingly similar, in contrast to the divergence between Afusare (marriage by "capture") and Anaguta, on the one hand, and Birom (marriage by purchase) and Anaguta, on the other. It should also be noted that Anabuze are occasionally encountered in Anaguta compounds, where they have the status of working guests.

Summary of Above Affiliations

It is evident, then, that the Anaguta are linked, in the shorter rather than the longer time perspective, linguistically with the Anabuze and Anazele (Jerawa), socially and militarily with the Afusare (Hill Jarawa), and ceremonially with the Birom. Yet, these overlapping connections do not, in any way, diminish the identity of the peoples concerned. Indeed, it would be possible, I believe, to trace a dense cultural network, further complicated by new political alignments, among all neighboring peoples, along with tantalizing signs of common descent. But the more precise generic problems, stemming from both active relationships and institutional similarities, may defy definitive solution.

Who, then, are the Anaguta? They, themselves, have no migration tales, nor elaborate legends of origin. The elders firmly believe that their forefathers emerged from holes in the ground in the vicinity of their present settlements. Their ancestors, they claim, have always lived in Gwong. But it is possible that the Anaguta claim to Gwong may indicate their concern with contemporary usurpation of their lands. The insistence on occupancy from the beginning may be a politically screened memory, or a more conscious strategy to justify their refusal to engage in resettlement or relocation schemes.

Historical Inferences—Material Culture

Several elders asserted that formerly the Anaguta had lived in caves, and had customarily used stone tools, both in Gwong and in the nearby area of Kabong, and that up to the time of their grandfathers, they had always done so. Of course, a primitive peoples' reference to grandfathers has no precise chronological significance. It is a way of telescoping the whole past, even though, in this instance, the grandfathers of the informants were in their maturity around 1820, the period of Fulani invasion, during which the Anaguta may actually have spent extended periods in their caves. There is no question that these caves had once been occupied, since hearth marks, grinding stones, potsherds, and conveniently shaped stone "implements" are found in abundance on, or just beneath, the surface. But there are no signs of long continued habitation. Most of the caves are better described as shallow rock shelters formed by the juxtaposition of huge boulders broken from the eroding surface of the Plateau, difficult of access yet no proof against the weather. It is probably safe to say that the caves were used as shelters and strongholds against Fulani raids onto the northeast sector of the Plateau, and do not represent evidence of actual, prolonged cave *dwelling.*

But it would be tempting to view certain usages as strata of a prior phase of Anaguta culture. The Priest Chiefs are restricted to wearing animal skins; meat is ritually prized, prepared, and served; the stone shrines that are found distributed throughout Anaguta territory are said originally to have been hunting shrines; and only stone tools may be used in cutting wood in the sacred groves (although no obviously manufactured implements were found for the latter purpose, hand axes, shaped by natural or crude human percussion, could have been employed). Could these be ritualized echoes of an economy in which hunting was far more prominent, practiced, perhaps, in the forests south of Plateau Province? Could the groves—tiny forests—be sanctified today as representative remnants of a prior habitat?

Historical Inferences—Physical Type

If this were the case, then the "Bantu-speaking" peoples who originated on the Nigerian Plateau at large (the Middle Belt, excluding the Niger-Benue trough)—probably in the Western Cameroons, where six of seven Macro-Bantu languages are clustered—may have, in their expansion during the past 2,000 years, driven pygmoid hunters onto the Jos Plateau. Interbreeding may have taken place in the course of this migration, or as a result of successive migrations of "Negritos" and forest Negroes. Horticultural techniques could have been borrowed from the Bantu-Malayan nucleus, or from the Sudanic complex that Murdock (1959, pp. 64 ff.) postulates; or, alternatively, could have reached them from both sources at different times. But temporal precision is impossible here. We do not know when the High Plateau was populated, or when and under what circumstances horticulture was adopted by its peoples. Further archeological research in the area is urgent; if even rough estimates of the period of Pagan residence and of the cultural character of the first migrants on the Jos Plateau can be made, some of the most significant problems in the culture history of sub-Saharan Africa may be clarified.

Although physical anthropological classification of the indigenous peoples of the High Plateau has not been undertaken, several observers have remarked the Negrito element in the native population. Buchanan and Pugh (1955, pp. 80-81) state that "the rocky recesses of the Plateau have throughout history afforded refuge to the shattered fragments of the peoples displaced from the surrounding lowlands by stronger neighbors, *while observation suggests the presence among some of the Plateau groups of the Negrito or dwarf Negro element akin to the Negrito peoples of the Congo forests.*" [5] They also note "the role of . . . the broken terrain of the Middle Belt as refuges for the . . . Negrito groups. . . ."

This accords with my observations of the physical appearance of the Anaguta. If the pygmoid element does, in fact, exist, the historical and cultural dimension in which the Plateau Pagans have moved must be even deeper than may be deduced from the Greenberg (1959, p. 20) and Murdock hypothesis of the ancient Bantu-speakers' heartland, although it does not, of course, contradict the Bantu [6] component in their identity.

The Anaguta as Archaic Bantu

Murdock (1959, pp. 90-99) regards the Plateau or Middle Belt Nigerians as "a cultural *cul de sac* characterized by a series of interesting archaic traits . . . who have preserved a number of the characteristics of original Bantu culture." If this is true of the Ni-

[5] Italics added.

[6] The term "bantu" simply denotes "human beings" (sing., "muntu"), but it is, and has been, applied to languages, cultures, even physical types. This, of course, is theoretically poor practice, but hard to avoid, particularly when one is trying to identify certain possible historical continuities. Now that "bantu" has taken on such added ethnohistorical stature, we must be very careful not to inflate it into another, if counter, "Hamitic" construct.

gerian Plateau at large, we must assume that it is even more obviously the case among those people who have migrated to the most inaccessible area within the Nigerian Plateau, namely, the Jos Highland. If the Tiv, whom Murdock includes in his geographically uneven, but culturally sensible, Plateau Nigerian category, are archaic Bantu, then people such as the Anaguta must be at least as archaic.

The original Bantu speakers remained on the Nigerian Plateau at large, or migrated to one of the internally marginal areas and, on the basis of age-area reasoning, probably maintained traits which must have marked the dispersed Bantu when they began their migrations to Central, South, and East Africa, via the Congo Basin. Marital descent and residence rules among the Bantu speakers of the Nigerian Plateau are said to be transitional to widely distributed traits found recently among Bantu throughout the rest of Africa (Murdock, 1959, pp. 271 ff.). Certainly, the Anaguta reveal generalized elements of an extremely primitive culture, whether or not transitional to more recent "Bantu characteristics." Interestingly enough, C. R. Niven (1958, pp. 1-3), in attempting to define the culture of the peoples who preceded the Yoruba south and west of the Niger, which includes part of the Middle Belt, comes remarkably close to what we would assume about the progenitors of the Anaguta, who were probably native to areas farther north and east, in the vicinity of the Benue Valley:

If we were able to go back a thousand years we would have found that the country was much as it is now—the rivers, hills and swamps would be the same as we know them—and most of it was covered with high dense forest full of wild animals. The people living there then were hunters, inhabiting very small villages. These little hamlets would be on the high land but not too far from the many streams and rivers that run through the country for most of the year. These small villages would be in clearings in the forest with small farms around them.

Through the forest there were hunters' tracks and some of them no doubt joined hamlet to hamlet, but it is not likely that the different villages had much to do with each other. The people probably wore few clothes, which were made of the skins of the animals they killed. There were, in their houses, hardly any of the articles you are accustomed to now and what were there would be of the simplest material and pattern. . . . *It is unlikely that there were many iron tools or weapons and stone implements were more common. Their arrows and spears were tipped with sharp stone and even their knives would probably also be of stone.*[7] Their huts were of bush sticks and grass and leaves; there was little corn . . . but there would be plenty of fresh meat.

You must think of the whole country being covered with trees. In the southern part there was high thick forest with few clearings and few

[7] Italics added.

tracks. In the northern part the forest was not so thick but there were far more trees than there are now, and probably here you would find more villages than to the south. The granite hills would stick out of the trees sharply and grimly then as they do now. There was at that time in those lands a great deal of game, antelopes and birds of all kinds and beasts of prey such as the leopard and the hyena. . . .

We do not know what they worshipped or how they worshipped, but it is likely that they feared and revered the spirits as so many do even now. . . .

Whether these people were the first people to be in this land or whether there were other peoples here before them we do not know, and there is no way of finding it out unless we can find their graves. If the graves of some of these old people are found we may some day know a little more. . . .

We do not know who these first people were, or how long they had lived there, nor where they had come from in the dim and distant ages when mankind was young in the world. We have no idea what kind of language these people spoke. We do not know whether they spoke the same language from one village to another or whether different areas each had its own language. . . .

Summary

The best evidence for the Bantu component in the identity of many peoples of the Nigerian Middle Belt, and its internally marginal enclaves, is linguistic (Murdock, 1959, pp. 14, 15). Since the work of Baumann and Westermann, the generally "Bantu" character of many languages found throughout the Nigerian Middle Belt has been recognized, although the term "semi-Bantu" is linguistically inadequate. More recently, Van Bulck, as quoted by Gunn (1953, p. 15), has classified many of the languages of the Jos Plateau as "sub-Bantu." But Murdock (1959, p. 15), following Greenberg (1955) and altering his terminology, substitutes "Bantoid" (the "semi-Bantu" of others) for Greenberg's central branch of the Niger Congo stock, and classifies Eguta as Bantoid (subfamily), Macro-Bantu (subdivision), and presumably, Jarawa-Mbula (branch). One assumes that the lexico-statistical evidence based on selected vocabulary lists, along with certain structural factors (in particular, concordant prefixes), is adequate for the original and subsequent formulations.

If the linguistic and other cultural historical evidence touched on above prove credible, then the formal anthropological importance of the Anaguta and related peoples would be hard to overestimate, since they become, to paraphrase Hrdlicka's comment about Rhodesian man, "a comet" of sub-Saharan African history, extending from a Negrito horizon, through the period of Bantu expansion, to contemporary industrial civilization.

Part III. Base-Line Culture and Processes of Change

It is hardly possible to reconstruct, in confident detail, an aboriginal base-line culture against which social change among the Anaguta can be evaluated. With the exception of a few random and superficial references in Meek (1925), Temple (1919), Ames (1934), Gunn (1953), Davies (1944), and assorted colonial reports, there is no ethnographic information on the Anaguta. This initial difficulty was compounded by the fact that I was the first anthropologist to undertake work among them, and the usual difficulties in communication were encountered. Although I built up a battery of informants, the older men and women were not disposed to be garrulous on usages which had either become attenuated or disappeared. In any case, since the Anaguta were a tribe in flight, almost the whole inner life of the people, that is, their traditional culture, had become a sacred secret, to be hidden away from strangers. On the other hand, it is doubtful whether dependence on even the most skilled and cooperative informant can give a reliably detailed picture of the customs of a people once these have begun to decline, since the memories of individuals are selective, and conceptions vary. This is one of the paradoxes of anthropological research, and we have learned to live with it.

Therefore, it seems that the best mode of approach, even if not the most aesthetically satisfying, is to attempt an outline of relevant cultural phenomena as encountered today on each empirically defined major level of cultural integration, and, at the same time, to indicate the processes of change which seem to be at work on and among the various levels. We may then reason back to a prior condition on the basis of what is either observable and/or indicated by informants. Of course, a more abstract delineation of an aboriginal Anaguta culture could be presented, but such efforts should, I believe, be confined to either (1) construction of models based on a wide range of cultural forms, or (2) summary discussions of processes in general. In dealing with concrete material, even if incomplete, it is necessary to pursue an inductive approach. If one were to utilize a model, the model would have to be drawn from a series of already abstracted cultural cases, and one would not be able to break through into the specific phenomena of the culture under study. The latter effort alone can supply the information for the construction of more sophisticated models of aboriginal structure and change. The starting point for the following consideration of culture change, is, then, the society as it is encountered today, and we shall project back in time, or forward, when warranted by data and/or the developmental logic of institutions. Therefore, the term "base line" must remain ambiguous.

Since the destruction of a people's identity and group continuity entails the progressive collapse—with no adequate replacement by new, internally *unifying* elements—of the various linked levels of cultural focus and integration, each level needs to be defined and the changes examined. In the case of the Anaguta, deteriorative changes ramify through the whole ascending order, embracing nuclear and extended families, clan, village, and tribe, even if not necessarily in that sequence, i.e., changes may be introduced on any level, and echo through the whole system. It is the ensemble of these changes, occurring in a certain direction, which results in the type of cultural disintegration apparent among the Anaguta. Changes which can be contained within a single level, or which involve a single vital activity, even one as basic as subsistence, do not necessarily lead to the loss of group identity and continuity, although they will surely affect their character. It should be clear, then, that I am not only referring in this study to large-scale changes involving basic lifeways of the group, nor confining myself to a causal analysis of change within a given group, where, for example, a shift in material culture may result in a reconstitution of the labor force. Rather, I am documenting the way in which a group's connective tissue, its *definition*, is destroyed through the response to external stimuli. I shall begin by considering the overall settlement pattern of the Anaguta, and then go on to outline pertinent data and process on the tribe, village, clan, extended and nuclear family levels of integration.

SETTLEMENT PATTERN

The Anaguta are found today scattered through the rugged hills and downlands of Gwong District in Jos Division, Plateau Province. Although the acknowledged borders of the district include a substantial portion of the city of Jos, the Anaguta have no administrative connection with the municipality. Their present habitat lies to the northeast, anywhere from five to fifteen miles from the town, in rough country, inaccessible except on foot. Within the approximate 100 square miles that comprise their sector of the Gwong Village Area, the more formal designation for their habitat, live about 2,500 Anaguta, and a greater number of Afusare (or Hill Jarawa). The single Afusare village of Jarawan-Jos, has, for example, a population exceeding 1,000, which is larger than any Anaguta settlement.

The Traditional Villages

The Pagan peoples native to Gwong Village Area (Anaguta and Afusare) occupy their own settlements with very little physical overlapping or intermingling. There are five Anaguta villages: Anabor (or Jigwong), Zangam (or Andoho), Rigiza, Anagahom, and Andigwong.

Anabor, the largest, and generally regarded as the most prominent of the villages since it provides the tribal-wide secular and Priest Chiefs, contains an Afusare ward, referred to as Janda; all Anaguta share what is known as an *apari* relationship with Janda-Jarawa. That is, interbreeding is regarded as incestuous and is forbidden, while cooperative and protective relations are strongly developed. The Afusare of Janda speak Jarawa, but little Eguta; communication between the two is carried on in Hausa.

Rigiza is a recently named settlement, too new to have its own recognized chiefs or village structure, and is apparently the result of the fissioning of Zangam. The other villages seem to be of long standing, and antedate the British conquest of the Plateau.

The Effects of Down-Migration and Symbiosis with Pastoral Fulani

Since the consolidation of British authority, which is said to have made the downlands safer for the Pagans, there has been a steady migration from the Anaguta hillside settlements to the central interior valley, known as Manza (the Neil's Valley). The cessation of Fulani efforts to subjugate the territory and the suspension of intertribal feuding by colonial command are cited as reasons for this movement. They may be factors, but the increasing containment of the Anaguta to a small section of Gwong because of the expansion of Jos, along with the peopling of Gwong by alien Africans, seem more pertinent. The setting aside of forest reserves on the Naraguta hills has also constricted the living area of the Anaguta, and helped force down-migration. Reserves may be necessary in order to halt further erosion, but it should be noted that the Anaguta farm efficiently on their hillside plots and, moreover, overcultivation of the hill farms was, in the first instance, the result of restricted horizontal expansion. There is ample evidence of former Anaguta occupation and cultivation of low-lying lands beyond the Naraguta hills. This, also, makes it doubtful that Anaguta migration is simply the search for a safer environment; the conditions following colonial occupation forced vertical migration, but the cultivation of level land preceded British conquest.

Thus, the Anaguta can no longer expand horizontally, fulfilling the needs of a shifting horticultural economy. In moving from the hillsides to the downlands, they use every bit of territory available to them. Although tribal-wide, routinized, intensive cultivation, technically speaking, has not developed, the use of animal fertilizer, ironically enough, as a by-product of peaceful Fulani habitation in their central valley, seems to have increased both the productivity and the longevity of a certain proportion of their fields. However, it is already apparent that fertilizer is not used with systematic effectiveness; particular plots may be overmanured or undermanured, and the overall balance between manuring, crop rotation, and fallowing is difficult to achieve. Apart from these technical factors, the need for fertilizer is locking the downland Anaguta into a symbiotic relationship with the Cattle Fulani; without fertilizer, the bottom lands would become rapidly exhausted. Anaguta cultivators must now depend upon the good will and reliability of the Fulani for their very subsistence; they do not control their own source of manure, since they own no cattle, and this, in turn, makes it even more difficult to learn, or to establish, a reliable horticultural cycle. On the other hand, the Fulani could, conceivably, find pasturage elsewhere; it is the downland Anaguta who are in the weaker position. Pertinently, Anaguta complain that the valley is too crowded, probably because they feel confined, as they are, and dependent. However, the danger of overgrazing by the increasing number of

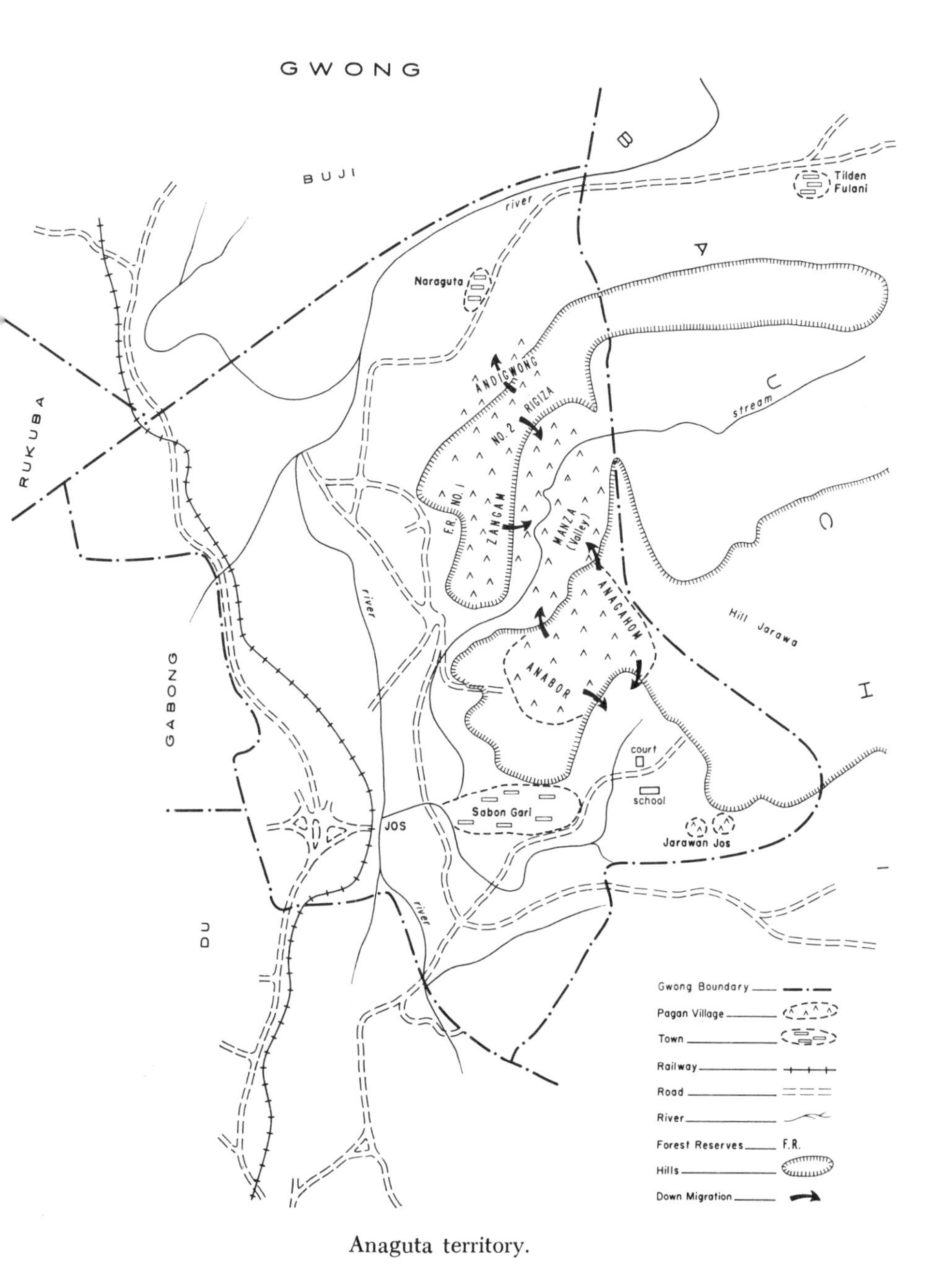

Anaguta territory.

Fulani cattle in Anaguta territory is real. Although the effort is made to keep cattle away from field crop and garden areas, an accelerated depletion of the soil can be anticipated, especially since the cycle of

Fulani semi-nomadism is becoming more restricted and the greater portion of the year is now spent in the central valley. The Anaguta are, then, caught in a further paradox: while depending upon manure to help make their new settlement pattern viable, they are also faced with the threat of overgrazed land, a situation threatening the Northern Region in general (Cronje, 1963, p. 1469).

A few dwarf cattle are today owned by the Jarawa; and the Anaguta were, at one time, supposed to keep herds, but this impression could have been the result of confusing Anaguta with Jarawa. Fulani cattle are normal sized, long-horned, and humped.

The land-population ratio, which varies from about 25 to 60 per square mile, is, in itself, not yet a serious problem. Rather, the problem lies in the fact that many Anaguta use fertilizer inefficiently, and, as noted, have not yet been able to strike a fruitful balance between manuring, crop rotation, and fallowing. Moreover, other means of subsistence—hunting, gathering, and fishing—are at the point of vanishing.

Paralleling the movement from the hillsides to Manza, that is, down the inward slopes of the hills to the valley, has been a drift down the outward slopes to adjacent lower lying land; the largest such settlement, in the vicinity of Naraguta town, is an area known as Aholl. However, these new habitations have not developed a formally recognized local identity. Thus, an extended Anaguta family may claim fields in the hills, and in the valley or lowlands. Relatively few compounds today are in the neighborhood of all fields cultivated by family members. This discontinuous settlement pattern is beginning to strain extended family, clan, and village bonds, since cooperative labor, ritual, and other customary usages are being attenuated. One frequently encounters an aged couple who has insisted on remaining in their empty compound in the hills after their children have settled in the valley. However, individuals maintain formal affiliation with the villages of their origin, and clan and family ties continue to function in ways that shall be outlined below.

The Strangers' Settlement

The New Town (strangers' settlement), or Saban Gari, of Jos, with its polyglot population drawn from the length and breadth of Nigeria, extends for about three miles from the limits of the city proper, in a narrow strip, to the borders of Anaguta country; it is the link between the city and the Pagan villages. Most Anaguta in the area use the Saban Gari as a shortcut in walking to the markets of Jos. Indeed, two or three of the younger Anaguta have set up households in the native new town, gradually abandoning their fields, while the women manufacture and sell millet beer for a livelihood. This is expedited by the fact that they have a right to occupy the Saban Gari without rent, and with a minimum of red tape, since it is on traditional Anaguta land. These people have not adapted to the life of Jos; the men have no occupation, and the households are radically disorganized, being in a state of both physical and, perhaps, social transition from their bush compounds to the ramshackle quarters in the Saban Gari. One or two family members remain behind in the bush compounds, while the remainder drift back and forth between the new town and the villages, neglecting the former mode of life and failing to pursue any alternative. Even the sale of millet beer is not a new invention, but the commercialization of a complicated, recently emergent bush pattern in a different setting. The identity of Saban Gari Anaguta is rapidly dissolving; the process of change, which is limited here to a half-dozen people, is clearly degenerative. What might be described as a tiny *lumpenproletariat* is being formed.

European Connections

There are several European residences and compounds on the borders of the village area, owned either by individual prospectors or mining companies, although no mining or prospecting takes place today in Anaguta territory. The activities of the major company are centered in Benue Province, but a nominal ground rent of a few pounds per year on administrative buildings and private dwellings is paid to the Anaguta. No Anaguta works in any of the European households or offices. Indeed, only one Anaguta boy, a primary school graduate who speaks a few words of English, is employed in Jos as a gasoline station attendant; he lives, however, either in his father's compound, or in a room provided by relatives in the Saban Gari. No Anaguta has a residence in Jos and, with the exception of a young girl who married a Birom and moved to the northern capital of Kaduna, none has migrated to any other Nigerian city. That marriage was shortlived, and the girl has subsequently returned to her family in Gwong. One Anaguta, with a fair command of English, had attended the provincial secondary school at Kuru and is a member of the only "upwardly mobile" family [1] in the tribe, but he returned home frequently and had established no permanent residence outside of Gwong. After leaving school, he worked for the Nigerian Tobacco Company in Zaria and in the office of an agricul-

[1] This family's career will be discussed below.

tural experimental station, but the employment turned out to be temporary.

In summary, then, the Anaguta, with insignificant exception, remain on their native land; patterns of migration or resettlement *within* the territory are developing, but they are unwitting and unplanned.

BASES OF TRIBAL IDENTITY

Theoretical Discussion

The Anaguta tribe consists, as indicated, of five villages, distributed through the hills, the central interior valley, and adjacent lowlands. Anaguta identity, beyond the nuclear or extended family, clan, or village is both felt subjectively and recognized in institutional affiliations. Anaguta identify themselves as a single people or "tribe," as *we* conceptualize this highest level of integration on which they function, clearly delineated from other Pagan groups, speaking a common language, and sharing certain distinctive cultural features. But shared cultural content is not viewed here as a specific binding mechanism unless actual relationships of social units on different levels and in different places are implied. Social institutions which ramify beyond the village contribute to the larger sense of cultural identity, which, in turn, prospers on the spirit of voluntary association, as we shall see.

The Priest Chief

The Anaguta, as a tribe, recognize a Priest Chief, or *Uja*, who has traditionally been a member of a particular clan within the largest and most prestigious village, Anabor (pop. *circa* 700) which, nonetheless, has no political primacy. The *Uja* is a holy figure, and has no functions which are recognized as secular. Prior to British occupation, he arbitrated disputes among clans or villages involving witchcraft, homicide, incest, or chronic feuding; the *Uja*'s justice is sacred and, except in cases of witchcraft or repeated incest, is based on the principle of compromise.

The *Uja* placates the *andoogubishee*, or ancestral spirits of the sacred groves, particularly those of Anabor, which are said to have efficacy for the whole tribe. He also personifies the *andoogubishee* in the form of a masked, materialized spirit (*Dodo* in Hausa) at certain ceremonies, one formal function of which is to frighten the women and children as a routine, but not seriously perceived part of the men's ancestral cult. He is the chief mediator between the

Anaguta and their high and single god, Uwiyang, who is equated with the sun, in the sense that the sun is an expression of God.

Apart from the more personal ceremonies of the Priest Chief, discharged in the name of the tribe, certain public rituals, or *teeshenday* (?) (sing., *reeshenday*),[2] also bind local groups into a tribal pattern. For example, an annual ceremony that takes place under a sacred tree in Manza is attended by elders from all the villages, presided over by the *Uja* and his assistants. This particular affair, a celebration of the Anaguta defeat of the Fulani, seems the most vigorously pursued and best attended tribal ritual still in existence.

Ceremonies convened in natural and social emergencies are, and have been, traditionally tribal. A bad harvest, a famine, a recurrent disease, indeed, any social, natural, or physical misfortune, or a reason for thanksgiving may become the occasion for convening a special ceremony at a public shrine, under the direction of the *Uja*. Rainmaking is his most dramatic task. But the use of the larger public shrines for these purposes seems to have atrophied.

The Secular Chief

The *Uja* is, in short, the living symbol of Anaguta identity and must be protected against contamination by white men. Therefore, when the British mounted the Plateau, a member of the *Uja*'s patrifamily was sent to greet them at their request. *This was the origin of secular chieftancy among the Anaguta.* Today, a secular chief (*Ogwomo*) from the *Uja*'s lineage at Anabor is recognized as the tribal chief by the British. The Anaguta, however, regard him merely as the tax collector and head of the native court; the *Uja* remains their traditional leader. It is also apparent that the advice of the *Uja* is sought and followed on all matters of moment, secular or religious. Pertinently, colonial officials in Jos seemed unaware of the importance or identity of the *Uja*, and were unconcerned with the internal position of the secular chief, just so long as his fiscal-judicial functions were nominally discharged. The Anaguta had thereby responded in their own indirect manner to the British technique of rule by indirection.

Intermarriage

Apart from the dual institution of chieftancy, modern and ancient, Anaguta villages and lineages are bound together through intermarriage. Females circulate, through mechanisms that shall be considered below, among and within the five villages that constitute the

[2] In Hausa, *tsafi*; a *reeshenday* is, more broadly, any sacred thing, rite, or event.

tribe, thus fixing tribal identity in a continuous series of obligations and relationships. But there are no customary channels for marriage or residence beyond the five villages; thus, marital ties are congruent with tribal borders, and help define the social content of the tribal level of integration. That is, among the Anaguta, the limits of exogomy coincide with linguistic and other cultural limits in shaping the tribe; indeed, the marital system, among this acephalous, non-politically organized people, is a primary mechanism for fixing identity beyond the local group. Therefore, stresses or breakdowns in the system are basic factors in loosening both the sense and the reality of the association.

The Cooperative Work Group and Age-Grades

Another social mechanism, functioning on the tribal level, is the cooperative work group. These groups also function within the villages and, more informally, within clans, but for particular tasks, such as the clearing or planting of a very large tract of land, young men, in numbers beyond those that could be supplied by a village, would be mustered by their local work group chiefs to discharge the tribal purpose. The age-grade also fixes tribal identity. Although centered in the village, as are the work and military groups which are aspects of the age-grading system, a man's age-grade is recognized by all Anaguta.

Contests

Dance and wrestling contests further weave the villages into a tribal pattern. Men's, women's, and mixed dancing troupes from each village perform in an informal competitive spirit throughout the dry season. Wrestling matches between the young men of various villages also take place, sometimes in association with the dances; musical instruments—flutes, reed harps, calabash guitars—are taken out of storage, and there is a general intermingling of villagers, now relieved of the tasks of the agricultural cycle, in a festive atmosphere. An annual, intervillage hunt took place in former years at this time, but with the encroachment of civilization—the withering of the bush, and the disappearance of game—it has been abandoned.

Ritual Wars

Military factors also established tribal identity. Minor, ritualized wars—that is, wars that had no political purpose, such as territorial displacement, subjugation, tribute, or large-scale slaving—were engaged in with neighboring Pagan peoples, notably, the Rukuba of the Jerawa group. The motive of such warfare was to prove courage, take an occasional head, and blood the younger men, but Anaguta testify that casualties were few and far between. Technically, the combats took the form of skirmishes or forays. However, these ritualized battles heightened the sense of Anaguta unity and also, by the very nature of the military structure, bound the villages together. The warriors were drawn from the available men of fighting age in each village, under hunting chiefs who doubled as war chiefs. The contingents were actually village contingents, with tactics and strategy worked out among the war chiefs on a tribal basis. Unlike the Rukuba, who frequently engaged in ritual internecine war, the Anaguta villages never fought each other; so internal war was not a divisive factor, even to the self-limiting degree that it may be in its ritualized forms among primitive peoples elsewhere.

Political Wars

The defensive wars against the Fulani had another character. The Fulani were political conquerors, concerned with imposing their rule. This type of political warfare threatened the social and territorial integrity of the Anaguta; it was not an arena for the achievement of ritual ends by heroic means. Anaguta fought with every means at their disposal, raining poisoned arrows and boulders down from emplacements in the hills, and hid their women and children. The tribe was united in defense, the sole purpose being to drive the Fulani off their lands. Villages worked out elaborate tactics on the tribal level; indeed, *among* tribes, as in the instance of the Anaguta joining the neighboring Hill Jarawa in their successful struggle against the Islamic horsemen.

Ritual and defensive wars, then, psychologically and structurally helped strengthen the tribal affiliation. Of course, with British occupation, wars, both ritual and defensive, ceased. But their memory is retained and ceremonialized and helps perpetuate the sense of being Anaguta.

THE TRANSFORMATION OF TRIBAL IDENTITY

Theoretical Discussion

Tribal-wide attitude and institutions thus far noted have been, with the exception of the British-stimulated secular chieftancy, traditional. Tribal unity was an aboriginal, organic condition of the Anaguta, developing through an intricate series of relationships which may be characterized as "necessary" in the historical sense of being appropriate and logical, but they were not imposed from above. The post-colonial tribal institutions were, however, so imposed. To the degree that these later institutions fulfilled their manifest functions, Anaguta society may be said to have been "reorganized." The post-colonial tribal identity began to undergo a decided change in content and is now threatened with dissolution. The content dissolves because specific usages—ritual war, preferential marriage, settlement patterns, language, religion, education, channels of authority, and subsistence techniques, among other factors—are forced to change their character or disappear. At the same time, the resistance against these changes may emerge as a new force, sustaining the identity of the people. If resistance against the arbitrary destruction of a prior mode of life finds a positive resolution, theoretically, at least, the sense of the past can be transmuted to new forms. This, however, requires a concrete sense of both the tragedies and possibilities inherent in large-scale change, which no major acculturating power has yet been able to develop or apply. The more frequent result of arbitrary change, imposed by an alien authority, is, of course, the rapid obliteration of the reduced culture and of its potential for development. In the case of the Anaguta, the resistance against direct and indirect imposed changes has been extraordinarily tough and subtle, but it is not productive of new, viable forms. It becomes a retreat, or better, a moral victory in cultural defeat. Whether this was the only path open to the Anaguta will be considered below. But neighboring peoples have not responded similarly, as will be indicated in the discussion of the Nyango-Irigwe and Afusare. If the circumstances of acculturation had been more favorable, it is, of course, possible that the Anaguta would have been less defensive and more pragmatically interested in their common future. Still, the lack of concern can hardly be put in a contemporary frame of reference. The decision to pursue their usages and to neglect our conception of their necessary development may be, under certain circumstances, easier for primitive peoples; past, present, and future are conceived of as cyclic phenomena, and the pursuit of the cycle, even when leading, objectively, to their decline, remains *subjectively* sustaining. They regard the future in a way which is difficult for us to imagine. It is not, for the people as a whole, a cumulative, progressive, and novel experience through which tomorrow is conceived to be better or, at least, "different" from today. It is, rather, the endless repetition of an established human pattern, within which individual variety flourishes without disturbing the whole; the execution of ritual and the observance of custom fix the master pattern and make life viable. Thus, the Anaguta were bent upon preserving their historical existence, not denying it, by withdrawing from civilized contact. Their customs were their life. That our sense of reality leads us to interpret the situation in other terms is irrelevant. However, as Anaguta conventions began to disintegrate, they continued to retreat from active participation in the alien culture, and it is at this point that we may regard them as having made a decision, in our sense, with a growing awareness of consequences.

Political Chieftaincy, Tax Collecting, and Judicial Power

The first tribal-wide institution indirectly imposed by the British was, as we have seen, political chieftancy. This office was the base on which the twin structure of colonial rule was reared, namely, the imposition of codified law and the collection of taxes. The new laws, first of all, established the "peace" of the colonial power, and served as an instrument for the wielding of whatever future authority would prove necessary. The payment of taxes contributed to the support of the colonial authority, and impelled the population toward a market economy and the use of a foreign or foreign-based currency as a medium of exchange. Taxes served as a tangible symbol of the new political authority, and contributed to the building of local installations which incarnated that authority; moreover, taxes paid the salaries of the native officials who, broken off from their traditional functions, came to represent the colonial power. Tax collection was also related to the taking of a census, which was, of course, useful to the occupying power in a variety of ways. Indeed, the basic, historically interrelated functions of the census-tax-conscription pattern (Diamond, 1951, pp. 34 ff.) were readily understood by the Anaguta, and other primitive people in their situation. As noted, it is precisely tax evasion which accounts for the unreliability of the census figures among the Anaguta and similar groups.

The secular chief, in combining the roles of tax collector and magistrate, embodied the relation between the two functions. Actually, he began as a messenger between the British and the tribal elders and is even today referred to as a "small boy." After the "rule" of some half-dozen secular chiefs, beginning about 1906, the position still has no prestige among the Anaguta. On the other hand, the chief, who is illiterate, as are all Anaguta elders, is not held responsible for the authority he represents. Only very young men will sometimes make a slighting reference to some decision which harmed a member of the complainant's family or to the chief's being in the pay of the administration. But the colonial authority is alert to the fiscal behavior of the chiefs; a recent incumbent was sentenced to a year in prison because of expropriation of tax money and the reported discrepancy between tax income and the number of adult males.

It should be re-emphasized that the Anaguta voluntarily supplied this messenger from their own ranks in response to a British request and, in so doing, expressed two intentions: first, they declined to challenge the British physically, apparently recognizing overwhelming physical force when they saw it; second, they began at once to probe for ways to live with this new power, with minimum cultural displacement for themselves.

The Native Court

The external political structure of the tribe, of which the political chief is both symbol and apex, is grounded in the Gwong Native Court, established between 1906 and 1910. The court seems to have evolved from the headquarters of the British District Officer, who resided in the Gwong area for a few years immediately following British occupation, communicating with the elders, and gradually transferring his authority to the messenger who, in turn, became the chief.

Since the Gwong Village Area is, today, administered as a subordinate Native Authority within the Jos Native Authority, the court had a class D status, under the magistery of the secular, colonially created chief of the Anaguta. The acknowledged Anaguta priority in the area dates back, as noted, to the original British occupation, and had been further reinforced by the existence, until 1917, of Naraguta Division, then part of Bauchi Province. The position of the secular chief as President of the Court of Gwong thus represents the continuity of colonial recognition. He has a council composed of both Anaguta and Afusare representatives, the secular chiefs of villages, along with an "at large" Fulani delegate, and this group comprises the local Native Authority, the political entity recognized by the Northern Regional and central governments.

The scribe is Afusare, since no Anaguta adult is literate in Hausa, the court's language of record. Hausa, Eguta, or Jarawa may, however, be spoken, according to the facility and convenience of the litigants. The court is empowered to try minor civil and criminal cases, levy limited fines, and impose brief jail sentences. Originally, a makeshift jail had been part of the structure, but this incomprehensible system of punishment was resented so bitterly by the Anaguta, and proved so administratively inconvenient, that the residents of Gwong were imprisoned elsewhere as soon as facilities were available. Cases involving major assault or larceny are referred to courts in Jos, to which appeals are also possible; an appeal by a Moslem Fulani or Hausa against the decision of the local Fulani chief in court is referred to a religious (Alkali) tribunal.

Most litigation at Gwong involves tax delinquency, minor assault, petty theft, an increasing number of marriage settlements, and altercations between the Fulani and the Pagan villagers concerning the sale or behavior of cattle. Charges of petty thievery, usually a failure to pay for a chicken or goat, or to reciprocate in a promised exchange of goods, and tax delinquency are the most common occasions for Anaguta adjudication. However, only one or two Anaguta, having been found guilty of assault, have been imprisoned by the court in recent years.

The court is the local treasury; taxes are counted, recorded, and banked there before being passed on to the authorities in Jos. Moreover, with its attendant Native Authority police, among whom is a single Anaguta, the court adjudicates among the various peoples now resident in Gwong, which helps strengthen its role as "protector" of the "common people" in the emergent political entity.

In the Gwong Native Court, then, local Anaguta authority is acknowledged, but it is also severely limited. The customary role of the *Uja* or *Ejagiran* (see below) in settling disputes is not officially accepted, and recourse to the court is becoming habitual.[3] But to the Anaguta, the court, with its novel instrument of police power, represents the center for alien control of their territory. It is, therefore, the target of protest against that authority; private antagonism against secular sanctions is usually directed at the court, and the

[3] Although Anaguta informants insisted that no *Uja* had ever been a secular chief, or head of court, Gunn (1953, p. 65) reports as follows: "The position of the *Uja* is defined precisely only as it relates to the judicial system. In 1927 the *Uja* insisted on delegating his authority as president of the tribal court, because, since he himself was restricted to a goat-skin, none wearing foreign garments (for example, uniformed Native Administration Police) might enter his compound; in 1932, the *Uja* agreed to advise in difficult cases, only on the condition 'that no person should . . . be brought before him in handcuffs or other sign of temporary loss of liberty.' In 1944, however, it was reported that the *Uja* had come out of 'retirement' and had been recognized as president of the Native Court."

It is possible that the British may have called the President of the Court *Uja*, since, that being the highest traditional position among them, it would have increased the nominal authority of the incumbent; and the Anaguta would have silently accepted this error in identification since it further shielded the real *Uja* from British eyes.

public demonstrations of the women take place in the courtyard.

The present court was, until several years ago, also the site of a small clinic, staffed by the personnel from a native hospital in Jos. But Anaguta depend primarily upon their medicine men, and enter the hospital only in an extremity, or when vigorously urged. Since the Anaguta were chary of visiting the place, the clinic failed to perpetuate modern ideas about medical cure and prevention, and thus served as an example of an externally imposed tribal-wide institution that failed. The failure is tragic, because the withering away of old techniques, the absence of new ones, the loosening of customary social disciplines, and the proximity to the city and new sources of infection have, as we have seen, made the Anaguta most vulnerable to disease, and disease catastrophic.

The building in which the court is located is solidly constructed of stone and cement, in contrast to the mud and thatch of the compounds that cling to the overlooking hills. The only other cement building on territory currently occupied by Anaguta is the Gwong Native School, another tribal-wide and, to a certain degree, intertribal institution constructed under British auspices. The school faces the court across a dirt road that goes nowhere, forming a social-institutional center in which Anaguta meet on non-traditional occasions, and in a new setting. The social dance competitions are now held in the convenient field adjoining the school, and even meetings on matters of tribal concern called by the elders from various villages are likely to take place under a tree in the vicinity of the court and school.

The Junior Primary School

The junior primary school, with classes through the 6th grade, was established in the early 1940's, and has never been under an Anaguta headmaster. The present principal is a Christian Rukuba, and instruction is in Hausa. The majority of pupils are Anaguta and Jarawa from the surrounding villages, along with a few Birom from the Saban Gari. When the school was first opened, it was boycotted by the Anaguta; the first family to enroll a child for instruction was ostracized and its male head severely beaten. Characteristically, Anaguta hostility toward the occupying powers has not been overtly expressed; it is the deviant Anaguta who, from time to time, has taken the brunt of the more direct resentment. Even today, most parents refuse to send their children to school; in a few cases, they plead incapacity to pay the few shillings annual tuition. But the obvious reason for the fact that only about twenty Anaguta children, ranging in age from six to thirteen, attend the school is the continuing effort of the parents to avoid participating in the new civilization.

Anaguta school children are drawn from all villages, and serve as the internal agents for tribal-wide acculturation. The continuous threat that the school poses for traditional Anaguta identity is well understood by the parents, and it is for this reason that the school is underattended. Up to the present, the effect of primary schooling has been to isolate the student, rather than to educate the parent. Thus, the students are more likely to leave Anaguta territory, one by one, in their maturity, than they are to change the direction of the people as a whole.

The Effects of Schooling—Conceptual, Practical, and Religious

At school, the children wear special uniforms, learn to speak a Hausa superior to the pidgin version current among their parents, are not encouraged to maintain the vernacular, and assimilate the outlines of a world which is wholly alien to the adults' conceptions. For example, a typical group of unschooled Anaguta had never heard of America, the Second World War, bombs, atomic or otherwise, Roosevelt, Churchill, Hitler, Stalin, the major cities of Nigeria, adjoining African countries, and so on. They had learned, however, that England was the residence of the Queen, who, they imagined, was the chief of all men, black or white; several had heard the term "Russia" in the Hausa markets, and were curious if it were a thing, place, or an event. In any case, it was known for potency. Still, the great majority were incurious; their cosmography (Diamond, 1960, pp. 31-38) and tradition realized and defined their space and time. As for their perceptions of men, the world of the tribe was various enough.

But the school children were being trained to new conceptions. We sense these in excerpts from essays written by the children on the following subjects: Our Tribe, Africa and Africans, the Europeans, School, Hausawa, Fulani, Radio, Motor Cars, Magic, God, Creation, the Court, Independence and Self-Rule, and What I Shall Do When I Grow Up.[4]

---

[4] The subjects were provided by the author and were treated as part of the regular school work by the teacher, who helped translate them from the Hausa. The students were unaware of the origin or purpose of the assignments.

Fig. 73. The Anaguta, although culturally conservative, are, like their neighbors, subject to national laws, law enforcement agents, and courts. The photograph shows two African (Jarawa) policemen in the local court at Gwong.

Fig. 74. National laws, such as the restrictions on use of the forest resources, may seriously affect the native peoples. Anaguta women gather at the Gwong courthouse to protest the ban on collecting firewood, and a rumored increase in taxes.

Fig. 75. In a portion of Jos the shops are run by Africans, but the Anaguta have little money to buy the merchandise.

Fig. 76. Cola-type drinks, like bicycles and sewing machines, are sold in all parts of the world.

Fig. 77. In a typical market in a native quarter of Jos fried cakes, cola nuts, and other foods are among the wares spread out on the ground.

Fig. 78. The Pools Office, an English version of the numbers game, is available in Jos to those who can afford it.

Fig. 79. Anaguta gather in traditional manner to drink beer. The container, however, is a metal drum.

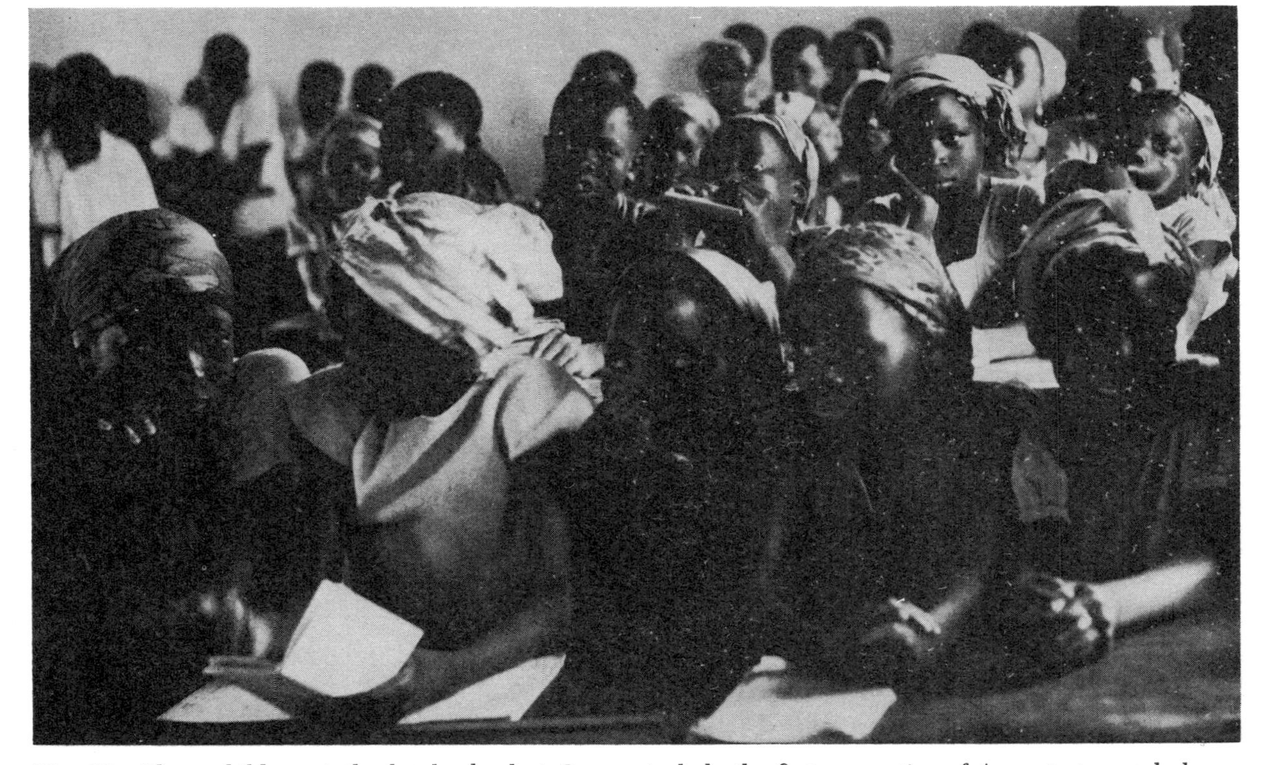

Fig. 80. These children at the local school at Gwong include the first generation of Anaguta to regularly receive instruction.

Fig. 81. Anaguta schoolboys wear khaki European-type clothes. One plays a flute made of Guinea corn stalk and leather thongs.

Fig. 82. A Birom schoolboy plays with wheeled cart which he made of scrap wire.

Our Tribe:

. . . we are very primitive.

The Anaguta live in Gwong. Their main occupation is farming. They are dancers. They farm five villages, and marry each other. They do have the custom of *apari* with some of the Jarawa people.

Some people say that the Naraguta are all the same. This is not true, for there are five kinds of Naraguta. There are people from Nabor, there are people from Andoho, Rigiza, Anagahom, and Andigwong. All these add up to make Naraguta, but the original people are the people of Nabor. We have all got the same type of marriage, that is, exchange marriage. For example, I take my sister and give her to someone in exchange for his own sister.

The Anaguta have tribal marks like the Jarawas. Girls used to wear leaves, boys used to wear skins of animals. They worship idols. Their farms are on the rocks. They keep goats.

In the beginning our people made *tsafi* [rite], and today they still do it.

Some plant pear trees near their houses. They have tall stones for *tsafi*, on which they put new crops before they taste the crop. Why they lived in rocks is because they will get caves as an easy concealment. Moreover, it is hard for their enemies to come over the rocks.

The men play flutes and drums and the girls sing. When they want to farm they wear skins, and when going to town they wrap themselves in blankets.

Anaguta people have tribal marks. They wear *gwado* [a native cloth]. Their women have the tribal marks, too. They have the tribal marks on their cheeks. Women collect dried wood, while the main occupation is farming.

The women wear leaves instead of clothes. The main food which the Anaguta eat in the afternoon is *gwate* [*acha* porridge]. I don't enjoy a day at all if I don't get that *gwate*.

We have an exchange type of marriage, i.e., one gives his sister to another man in exchange for his own sister. There is another kind of marriage called *zaga*, that is, you talk to a woman and if she agrees you marry her. But there is one thing which I hate, and that is *tsafi*.

Our women collect and sell firewood, . . . and we are very fond of *gwate*. We make a lot of *tsafi*, and a lot of hunting, too.

The boys grow very big before they are circumcised. Our people build their houses with mud, and they don't build square or rectangular houses. Young men live and farm in the bush while the old men stay at home.

Most of the Anaguta people are short and fat. They drink *gwate* day and night, in fact, *gwate* is an important food. They drink beer very much and most of their women cook beer for sale.

The Anaguta people always walk with their pipes in their mouths, in which they put tobacco. That happens day and night. The Anaguta are of medium height.

Our people marry by sending a girl to her lover's house where she spends four months, after which period she is taken away for exchange marriage.

Our people live in clans and each clan shares its *duiker* [a species of deer], and when they finishing eating they pray that God should give them some more in the future.

We are not like the Birom or the Jarawa, who wear strings on their waists. The Birom wear long leaves at the back. Our wedding lasts for seven days, during which time some of the women bring firewood from the bush, and others cook food.

Africa and Africans:

Africans were black right from creation. Their chief occupation is farming. They now use oxen in ploughing their farms. They have learned how to write and read. They have many ways of trading, mostly in the northern parts of Africa. They make canoes and many other crafts.

The Africans are black people with marks on their faces and bones in their ears. They live on mountains because there are no plains. The Africans have something called *tsafi*, and this is performed in forests very far into the rocks.

We Africans are black while Europeans are white. Europeans are wiser than the Africans. They have made a flying machine. Africans cannot make a flying machine.

Africans are wise, they like to copy the white man. They are really black in color.

We Africans are black, and we have short hairs. Most Africans speak to Europeans through a translator.

The Africans live in Africa. They do many things, their money has been changed. Africa is divided into many parts, the inhabitants of each division do different crafts. The white man came and has been buying tin. Africans have satisfied the white man and the white man has satisfied the Africans, too.

Africans differ from white men. Africans used to wear leather. Then white men invented a better way, that is why the Africans started to go to schools. This led to a great progress, for many have high education. They now earn their living by getting wages. For example, teachers.

Africa is a good land. We get many good things in Africa. For example, tin, we do also get good crops. There are many schools, many chiefs. The people pay taxes, out of which they get money to build many crafts centers.

Africa is a big continent, with Nigeria one of her countries. The people of Africa are of fair complexion, not really black. Africa is one of the important lands of the world. For example, England which is also important.

Though some Africans are blacker than others, yet we are all known as black people. Europeans are white in color. Africans are good farmers, they farm themselves while Europeans use engines. Africans are richer than Europeans.

The Europeans:

The Europeans are white people, they are very clean and their body is very soft. They are afraid of bees, wasps, etc., because these things can sting. The Europeans are very wonderful people, because they can make a man [photography], but they cannot give him life. When one goes to the canteens and he sees such men, he says, "Gudaftunu Sa," but one wouldn't hear any answer, and when one repeats, there would still be no answer. The kind of food that they eat are cabbage, fish, rice, bananas, beans, maize, groundnuts, wheat, and many others. They are very kind people because when you visit them, they must give you something, e.g., a shirt.

The Europeans were the people who stopped the slave trade and wars. They brought us civilization, they built schools and they established trades. The people who suffered to get rid of the slave trade were William Wilberforce, who took the case to the English Parliament, and David Livingstone, who came to East Africa to preach against slave trade. When he went back to England he told the House of Parliament how badly slaves were being treated, hence the English started to fight against the slave trade, and they succeeded only after 30 years. The English have helped the Africans alot because they brought us civilization, and today the North is self-governing, and we are all very glad.

The Europeans are very useful because they brought us clothes and money and we thank God that they stopped the slave trade. We are now civilized and we are living peacefully.

The Europeans are very useful because they are ruling us. But before the coming of the Europeans nobody was ruling us. The Europeans have better understanding than we people, and had it not been for them we would not have been enjoying peace among ourselves. They have taught us various kinds of trade, such as mechanic and mason.

The European is a white man. They wear trousers and shirts and shoes. Their women . . . always wear shoes, too, but they are not so fond of head ties, and most of them are tall.

The Europeans brought us motor cars, trains, and clothes. We use these motor cars, trains, and planes for traveling long distances. The Europeans like tin.

The Europeans were the first people in the world to become civilized. They developed writing and reading and arithmetic. They make money, motor cars, trains, planes, books, etc. The Europeans are white people with long hair, and they always wear shoes. We have learned how to read and write and to work arithmetic from them.

The Europeans know everything. They educated us and brought money. They make motor cars and they brought clothes and weapons for war. They build hospitals where we can go to take some medicine when we are ill.

In the olden days we had no clothing, such as shorts, shirts, etc. Had it not been for the Europeans we wouldn't have anything like money. They also stopped wars, otherwise our people would have still been fighting today. The most important thing of all is that the Europeans stopped the slave trade and they brought us civilization, so that today many people are able to read and write.

The Europeans are very useful because they brought clothes, motor cars, schools, boxes, storey buildings, dishes, and they also stopped war.

The Europeans have educated the Africans and taught them how to repair motor cars, planes, etc. A Europeans is a white man, he makes money and he rules us.

The Europeans have white skins. They were the first people to become civilized and they came to teach us so that we also could become civilized. That is why the Europeans are very useful.

The Europeans brought us a lot of help, e.g., they brought knowledge, in the olden days we were fighting wars among ourselves, but with the coming of the Europeans this was stopped. The slave trade was also stopped.

The European is a white man. The Europeans have established trade in Nigeria and they stopped the slave trade. The Europeans have long hair.

The Europeans are very helpful because they were the first people in the whole world to become civilized and they brought civilization to us. They also stopped the slave trade and wars. The Europeans have white skins and they are fond of wearing trousers and shirt and tie. The Europeans make money, motor cars, and bicycles which we use.

School:

When I grow up and become educated I would like to be a teacher where I will get a salary of fifteen pounds a month. Then I will buy a bed and a table and I will marry a beautiful clean woman. I will take my bath every day and I will buy a radio, a gramophone, a motorcycle, a bicycle, and a sewing machine.

The use of education is when someone is educated he will get a good job that can earn him a good living. Maybe become a chief. But the most important thing is for one to be really polite.

I go to school to learn reading, writing, and arithmetic. In the olden days people did not know what school was. The Arabs invented reading and writing and the rest of the world learned from them. Today anybody who does not go to school is considered a fool.

Education is a very important thing, for without it there would be no happy living in the world. Another importance of education is that if one is not physically strong but he is educated he can go to work in an office.

The name of the school is Native Authority Junior Primary School, Gwong. The use of school is one becomes educated and gets some job to do.

Education is a very important thing because educated people live much happier in the world today. The type of work that an educated man does is always very pleasant. Education can take one to other parts of the world.

Schooling is very important because we learn to be clever. We learn many kinds of trades. We learn Hygiene. Long ago we did not know Mission, we did not know Jesus.

Education is useful because you can get a job and get good pay, either weekly or monthly.

Schooling is very useful because when you go to school you can get a lot of money.

The main use of education is to look for food. Everyone is learning to be educated in order to get a good job which will earn him a good living.

Schooling is very useful, because one is educated and when one finishes one gets a job and earns money. One will not suffer like a farmer. When one is paid one can do what one likes with the money, for example, buy a bicycle. A farmer suffers before he gets any clothes to wear.

The use of education is to get a job. You then have to do as you are told. You can buy what you want to. You then feed yourself out of your salary. Schooling is very useful because whatever job you want to do today comes by some sort of education. A school boy wants to appear clean always, and he must be obedient. We do not want lazy, quarrelsome and abusive school boys.

In the school we learn reading, writing, arithmetic, and history. When one goes to school one gets enough education. A school boy is different from everyone else because he is obedient. An educated person does everything in the name of God because he has learned religion.

School is very useful, for it helps one to get a job, e.g., doctor, but a school is where you learn any kind of job. Why I come to school is to learn writing, reading, cleanliness of the house and of my body. In our school we are provided with books, pen and pencils. The school building has some doors and windows and there is a blackboard in every classroom. There are tables, benches, stove, cupboard, etc.

The use of school is for us to learn writing and reading. From learning these two things a school boy differs from everyone else. We also learn to respect and obey others. A school boy must always respect his elders, and a worthy school boy is obedient. The use of education to me is so that I can be with other people wherever I go. So that I can read and write a letter. It is not at all good for one to go about with a letter in order to give it to other people to read and tell him what the letter says.

The use of education is that one will become aware of what is happening and so escape cheating by people. Apart from this one will earn his living out of his education. Before someone can be employed he should be educated. Educated people also teach other people to become educated.

To be educated is to be able to do what other people may not be able to do. Educated people get better jobs, such as mechanics and many other works.

The use of education is to know almost everything, such as a variety of crafts, sports, current affairs about all that is going on all over the world.

Education is a very good thing because there is nothing you can enjoy in this world today without education, and in future nothing can be done without education. So that if you are not educated you cannot get any job. Therefore, may God help me so that I can do well in life.

The school that I go to is a Native Authority School at Gwong. School educates you and makes you a great man. School teaches you religion. We learn about Christ. Our school is improving greatly and may God bring us more improvements. Amen.

The Hausawa:

A Hausaman is a Moslem and he speaks Hausa very quickly.

A Hausaman doesn't like to shake hands with anybody who is not Hausa.

The Hausas are mostly black people [darker in complexion], strongly built and they speak Hausa very quickly. The Hausa man doesn't enjoy his life without *fura* [balls of cooked flour in sour milk] and they eat a lot of kola nuts. Often, one finds them dressed in big gowns and turbans, and they can abuse other people.

A Hausaman is a strongly built man, mid-height, and he wears big gowns and long trousers, and he has a lot of charms. The women put on *lalle* [henna], and both men and women are fond of eating kola nuts. The women wear clothes.

The Hausas are mostly huge people who live in clay-built houses. They are mainly Mohammedans. Both young and old men wear big gowns. A Hausa man sits and bends down properly in order to eat his food.

The Hausas live in cities. They wear big gowns and they eat a lot of kola nuts. Most of them are huge. Their girls put on *lalle*. The men live in mud houses. Their staple foods are *fura*, *nono* [sour milk] and *tuwo*.

The Fulani:

The Fulani are useful because their cows provide our farms with manure. If one goes to a Fulani's house, he gets something to eat. That is the use of the Fulani to us Pagans.

The Fulani are useful because they pay tax and this money, including the one paid by our people, is used for the building of schools and roads. We also get milk from the Fulani. The Fulani weaken our land because when they manure your farm and you don't re-manure it, the next year then you won't get any good yields.

The Fulani are very useful to us because their cows supply us with manure and the Fulani people pay *jangali* [cattle tax]. This money is used to buy our books, pencils, etc. The Fulani women sell *nono*, this is very important because when a woman gives birth to a baby, and for some reason she gets an infection in her breast so that she cannot supply the baby with milk, then this *nono* is boiled and strained—this is given to the baby instead of its mother's milk.

The Fulani cattle provide manure for our farms. They sell sour milk as well as sweet milk. If one wants to farm some tomatoes, one invites the Fulani to put some manure on the piece of land he intends to cultivate. This will hasten the growth of the tomatoes and make them produce a lot. The same thing is done on maize, spinach, and onion plots.

The use of the Fulani to us is that when our farms become old their cows often provide manure for the farms and by so doing either corn or millet can grow well.

The Fulani are useless because they call us pagans. They look upon us in the same way as they look upon dogs.

The Radio:

A radio is not like a gramophone, because when you tune your radio the speech you hear is like the speech of rich men, very interesting.

A radio is something very interesting because it can speak just like a man. You can also listen to news from places that you never knew in your life. A radio is like a box with a wire fixed onto it. If you want to listen to the radio you turn something which looks like a bottle-top cover, and you can turn to either news, prayer, or music. There are two kinds of radios—there is a big kind and there is a small kind.

A radio is a European invention. It is made of metal and wires which bring wind into the radio set, and by this means we can hear about other parts of the world. For example, news can be transmitted from Jos to other parts of the world. This news is carried by wind and the wires.

A radio is not like a gramophone because with a radio you can hear anything that is being said anywhere, unless there is no radio station at that particular place. If something is being said in England and you have your radio set you can hear it, even if you are in a cave. But before any radio can talk it must have two wires, a black one and a white one.

A radio is made of metal and it speaks just like a man does. A radio is very useful because you can hear news from England while you are sitting in your room. If you have no watch or clock you can always tell the time from your radio. A radio is made by Europeans.

A radio is a very good thing. There are two kinds of radios—there are big radios and there are small radios. The big ones have louder voices than the small ones. All kinds of radios are fitted in boxes and are capable of bringing news from any distance. Sometimes a gramophone is connected to a radio.

A radio is very useful because if news is being broadcast you can hear it sitting in your room, and you will know what is going on in the world; such as we often hear from Kaduna.

A radio is a European invention and like the gramophone, it speaks and sings. It is very interesting indeed to listen to the radio, therefore everyone should buy one.

A radio is very useful because you hear news about different parts of Nigeria, as well as other parts of the world. It is important that one gets a radio, but one doesn't have to buy a radio. There are different kinds of radios, you can get one for 8 pounds, 15 pounds, or even 200 pounds.

A radio is something which everyone likes to have except he hasn't the money to buy one.

Motor Cars:

There are three kinds of motor, there is a short kind, there is the big kind which is used for carrying stores, and there is a long beautiful one, and this is the type used by the Europeans and the Reverend Fathers.

A motor has four feet and it has a place for passengers and the driver. If you want to travel a long distance, just get some money and you can have an easy journey in a motor. A well planned road has to be constructed for the motor to run on. A motor also has glass.

A motor has four feet made of rubber, but the motor itself is made of iron and it is not a living thing. A motor is a very useful thing because it carries passengers and loads, such as bags of food and firewood. A motor has got iron tools for its repairs.

Motor is made from iron by the Europeans. A motor has an engine and when it is running it releases smoke. It has tires and one storey. It has seats. A motor uses oil which is either Mobilgas or Total.

A motor is very useful because we use it to travel very long distances. You can buy things in bulk from other towns. If you want to migrate to another place you can do so by motor.

A motor is very useful so that when you get a job you should buy a motor, which both you and your wife can use for traveling. You will just go "*Tu!*" and enjoy yourselves. Every day you can have a ride in your motor.

A motor is very useful because it helps to carry a sick person to the hospital. It carries passengers and loads for the people. You cannot get a motor without money, though it quickens your journey.

A motor cannot run without oil. A motor can kill a man if it hits him. If two motors collide they will both be damaged. A motor cannot move without an engine. A motor costs about eight and a half bags [of grain]. When it is raining there is something in the front of the motor which wipes off the rain water, otherwise the motor would fall. A big motor carries a lot of loads.

If you want to go to some place and you have some money, you can enter a motor. If you have something to sell you can take it to the market in a motor.

There are many different kinds of motors, there are big motors and there are small motors. The big motors are used for carrying loads such as firewood to other places, and they also carry bags of food and bananas to sell in other places. There is another kind called taxi. This is used to carry people to Bukuru and other places, and buses are used in this way too, and the buses have red color.

A motor is very useful because we use it for traveling to distant areas. A motor helps us in our trading activities, for all can buy certain things from one place and sell them at other places and in this way there is a lot of profit. A motor is a very important thing because it stops us from suffering.

A motor is very enjoyable, but very dangerous. A motor is very useful because if you want to go to Bukuru, Naraguta, or Bauchi you can enter a motor. Everybody likes traveling by motor now, but if a motor falls, you will hear people saying, "I will never enter a motor again, instead I'll travel by train."

Magic:

Magic is when somebody can turn into handkerchiefs or peppermint. He can then sell them two pence each. One day, one Hausa bought cigarettes and turned them into bread, so people bought the bread and gave him money. He turned a shilling into a pound. This sometimes takes place in Jos.

Magic is when someone just takes an object and turns it to money, either 5 shillings or 5 pounds.

One example of magic is when someone just cuts papers in form of currency notes. He then spits on the papers and when the papers are uncovered, you just see real currency notes. The second magic is that the magician can turn a stone into a real shirt.

There is one magician, who when he puts a mirror in his mouth, the mirror will turn into money. If he puts fire in his mouth, the fire turns into a mirror.

Magic is when you give someone a piece of paper or leaves, he will easily turn it into money, shirt, cap, or something of importance. He then tells you to give him money so that he will make you more money.

Magic is always performed by people. E.g., when a magician has a needle in his hand you will see properly, but when he throws it to you, you will find that it is no more a needle. Sometimes it will turn into money, sometimes something different. There are different kinds of magic, and there are some enjoyable ones, especially the ones of aeroplanes.

Magic means *dabo* in Hausa. Magicians are the people who do magic. A magician can turn a stone into a penny. A magician can turn rags into papers.

One can easily become a magician if only he knows the tricks by learning from other magicians. A lot of people think that magicians use medicines, but that is not true at all.

God:

God created heaven and earth, Adam and Eve, and the whole world. All the snakes and animals were created by Him.

Why I say that God is my father is that He created Heaven and earth and everything that lives. He gives life, and good health, and that is why I get the chance of coming to school. God shows our parents how they can feed us, that is why almost everybody takes religion to be very important.

Why I always say that God is my Father is because He created me, or when Jesus was in the world He always said some things about the Heavenly Father. He always prayed before He did everything.

God is our Father and He created Heaven and earth. He is the creator of living and non-living things. An example of living things is a man and an example of a non-living thing is a stone.

God is the father of my father, because He can hear us, and gives us life, food, and good health. He is the creator of the whole world and everything that is in it.

God is my father because He created me, He gives me eternal life and every bit of power I have. I must say that He gives me food and clothes too. We must worship Him because He gives us everything we ask. He is the most powerful of all beings, and can do wonderful things.

God is our father. We were created by Him. He gives us life, food and good health. He leads every creature wherever it goes. He was sent into the world to save it from sins. He created Heaven and Earth and that is why it is definite that He is our father.

God is our father because He saves us from our sins. He sent His son into the world for our sake. God always tells us to walk in the right way. If we believe in Him, we shall be His forever.

God is my father, because real father was created by Him. A man can't be compared to God at all. God made the world in six days, and on the seventh day He rested and therefore God is our father.

Though we don't see Him yet we can see what He does and He also sent His son who died because of our sins. He gives life freely.

God is our father because He is our creator, also because He is the eternal life. He takes a great care on everybody. He gives us clothes and food. He is the Saviour.

God is my real father. He created Heaven and earth, and all that is in it. It is very bad for people to say bad things about Him because that shows ignorance. It is said in the Holy Bible that we must obey Him. It is very bad for one not to obey Him.

Creation:

God created heaven, earth, and human beings. Different types of animals, two kinds of persons, the black and the white. Example of animals are leopard, squirrel, elephant, all sorts of birds and many other animals. The first persons were Adam and Eve.

Creation are all we human beings, ants, and other things created by God. We are alive, we can talk, we have wisdom, we can write and read and do some arithmetic.

God created human beings, animals, cattle, goats, chickens, snakes, scorpions, flies, mosquitoes, heaven and earth. He put on the earth ants, trees, rocks, grasses, towns. We have books and know how to read and write.

What God has created are human beings, animals and ants and also many other things. But human beings surpass everything in wisdom.

God's creations are made in different forms. Once I, the writer, was small, but now my mother cannot take me on her back. There are trees, grasses, animals, birds, and many other things. If we notice the animals we can see that they are in different forms too, for example, the ones with claws and the ones with hoofs.

God created everything, dogs, cows, ducks, snakes, illness, as smallpox. He God created Heaven and earth and all that are in the earth.

All God's creations have no knowledge of knowing God fully. Our knowledge is limited to making things such as clothes, reading and writing. We see all God's creation in mountains, in water, and things that we cannot see without the help of a microscope.

The Court:

The court is very useful because there are a lot of troubles now; and the court is where the cases are judged and settled. In the olden days there was no court. But today, if one steals one is put in prison for about four months.

The chief helps his people through the court by imprisoning whoever steals.

If there was no court people would be doing such things as fighting, arguments, stealing, murder, and etc. So the court has made people live in peace. All bad things are not much because of the presence of the court.

The purpose of the court is to help the public, because if someone is caught stealing he is judged in the court and sentenced to about six months' imprisonment. If the people fight they are taken to the court for judgment; in this way the court is very important, for otherwise people may kill each other.

In the case of some arguments the court will set right everything.

Without the court there would have been no peace among our people because there would have been a lot of fighting, hence there would not have been any free movements. With the court, even a very small child can go from here to Jos. But in the olden days this would not happen, there was a lot of robbery and plunder.

The use of a court is the punishment of outlaws, thieves, liars, and etc. If not because of the court, people will do as they like. The reason for the building of a court is to punish wrong doers.

If the case is big the person will go through a series of courts according to their importance. Finally, if the person is found guilty he will be put into the prison.

People who don't pay tax are also taken to court, so that without the court there would be no peace in the town.

The use of the court is to bring wrong doers who usually got confused. They will be judged.

The use of our court is to judge people in order to set right the wrong things. Taxes are collected through the court.

The use of a court is when someone steals he will be caught, and be judged in the court. People report in the court. The court also helps the common people.

Independence and Self-Rule:

In self-government Nigerians will do as they like to do. White man will only advise them. But when there was no independence white men have to force the African to do what they may not like to do. Now Nigerians will have a say, and will do what profits them.

The use of independence is that there will be no trouble when people say something on their right. As we have now got self-government we can set right other things and no one will cause any trouble.

The use of self-rule is that one will do things confidently. So there will be no trouble.

The use of self-government in Nigeria is that each region will rule itself. Then every town will see about its good.

It is really useful for Nigeria to become self-ruling. In the past Nigerians have suffered greatly in slavery. Now people can journey miles after miles without fear. The white man stopped the troubles. Taught the Nigerians that now they can rule themselves.

Why we are to be given self-government is to be free. In the past people used to be forced to do some kind of work. Today no one forces one to work, until somebody is willing to help. The self-government celebration took place at Kaduna. Where the Sardauna of Sokoto sits.

The use of self-rule to Nigeria is that it will urge them to learn. Also they will be happy and there will be no one to force them against their will.

The use of self-rule is some one will have the right to speak. We used to be under the English.

The main use of self-government is that white man will no longer rule over us. For they have already approved our self-rule. We shall be happy. Nigeria received her self-government in order to be as other self-governing countries. Some other countries have become self-governing for a long time now. The use of self-rule is in order to be in peace. Everyone will do what he likes, for example, you can follow whatever religion you wish to follow.

The self-rule will be useful, because in the past there used to be slavery, and work forced by the government without pay even.

The use of the self-government is that everyone should have a say. There are four parties: (1) UMBC, (2) NPC, (3) NCNC, (4) NEPU. Many other places are self-governing.

What I Shall Do When I Grow Up:

When I grow up I must build a very big house and I must marry, these are the most important things to everyone on earth.

When I grow up I will become a teacher, I will buy a radio and I will teach. I will buy all the clothing I want, and I will buy good food such as eggs, chickens, duck and cow meat, and I will marry a beautiful woman. I will buy a gramophone and a fine table for eating. I will roof my house with zinc.

I will work in an office, that is if God prolongs my life to finish my school. If God doesn't agree, then I will go to farm.

This is what I am thinking of doing when I finish my school. I would like to be either a teacher or a shop clerk, and I would marry an educated, well-mannered girl from my home town. If it all works well, and I am paid well, I would help my parents and take care of my younger brothers and sisters.

When I grow up I would like to be an Education Officer if God is willing. If this is not possible, then I will learn to farm with plough or with an engine so that I can grow enough food to help my people so that God will help me too.

When a man grows up he should live properly. Proper living means that he should believe in God. He must not steal.

When I finish my school I'll build my own house and go to work in the hospital.

When I grow up I will marry and I will get a good job which I will do every day.

When I grow up I will become a teacher and I will eat meat every day. I will buy trousers, bed and mattress, and I will build a beautiful house and roof it with zinc. When I grow up I will buy a wrist watch, chair and table and pictures. I will buy a bicycle and spoons.

When I grow up I will build my own house and I will marry. Both my wife and I will follow Jesus Christ our redeemer. When I grow I will be a doctor so that I will help people, blind men and lepers. If I cannot get this kind of job I will be a farmer using plough. Or I will become a driver. . . .

When I finish my school I would like to be manager of schools or a teacher, so that I will be slapping the children and enjoying my money. I can also become a sanitary inspector.

There are two immediately relevant points that emerge from these responses. In the first place, the culture of the school is formulated along national lines; students speak of themselves as Nigerians and Africans. They are oriented toward the future, and echo official sentiments (not without irony) about the Europeans and their contributions to Nigeria, although they agree that it is time for the white men to leave. Just as the culture taught by the teachers assumes a national form, religion becomes universalistic, a revealed faith with a doctrine suitable and necessary for all men, as opposed to the sacred and esoteric character of the tribal faith.

Second, the children imply that they, themselves, or their neighbors, travel in motor cars, visit Kaduna, possess and/or earn money, own radios or phonographs, and have jobs that no Anaguta has ever held, or for which he has been trained, and have generally benefited from the colonial undertaking in their area. But the fact is that there are no European utilities available to the Anaguta in their territory; no roads, electricity, gas mains, water or sanitation facilities; and no Anaguta has a radio, an automobile, a job of the type referred to by the students, or more than a few shillings at his disposal. Identification, then, with European tools and techniques, with the nation, and with a universal religion makes the school a primary acculturating mechanism, preparing the children for participation in a world which does not yet, in reality, exist for them. The basic training in literacy, in learning how to write Hausa (in English script), brings the children to a new level of symbolism on which ideas now seem to take on a life of their own, for they can be fixed by marks on paper. And one readily participates in the vicarious worlds revealed by picture and written word. Conceptions such as the *future, progress, civilized, the job,* within a lineal and individualistic time perspective, rapidly develop.

In this way, an abstract and conceptually realistic, a Western, broader, a *civilized* view of the world begins to replace Anaguta nominalism and existentialism (Diamond, 1963e, pp. 94 ff.). However, this is a process, not a fait accompli. The essays were presented to the students by their teacher as abstract subjects, yet the students emphasized aspects of action and use. Instead of reflecting on the court, the motor, the radio, and so on, as hypostatized ideas or things, they wrote about the *use* of the court, the *use* of the motor, even the *use* of the Fulani or the European. In short, they concretized functions in many, but not in all, cases, thus illustrating the existential tendency of their thinking.

Be that as it may, the children not only learn new possibilities of behavior in the government-established, Western-oriented school, but they have begun to conceive reality itself differently. To elaborate further, the children quickly begin to learn a technical, acquisitive, and impersonal attitude towards the human and natural environment; correlatively, they absorb the notion of becoming consumers. The school prepares them to cast off tribal identity, both culturally and psychologically. It enables them to break out of the recurring and (now) diminishing cycle of Anaguta life. Henceforth, they shall be wedded to the *idea* of a nation, to the abstractions of a religion whose spirits never materialize, to a lineal, progressive expectation of themselves, the nation, and the world, which, unlike the realization of self in sacred time and space inherent in primitive ritual, is beyond fulfillment at any given moment. Through the school, the immediacy and communality of the primitive experience, its subtle variety and repetition, becomes diffused and immaterial, hardly a memory; through the school, the students enter history. That is, they are presented with the necessity of being incorporated into the Nigerian national version of Western culture. They respond eclectically, selecting at random things that glitter or fragmentary information recently available to them as symbols of their new status. We may yearn for the communitarian being that Senghor and others celebrate in tribal Africa, but in the Anaguta school, the ontology of the junkyard, of *our* junkyard, would be a more appropriate instrument of analysis.

Although Protestant Christianity is the school's religion of orientation, and most of the students come from families that have had some exposure to Christianity, the Anaguta have never been missionized. There are, perhaps, a dozen nominal Christians among them, formally and remotely affiliated with the Sudan United Mission, an Anglican confession. The faith was introduced by an itinerant Birom preacher, who wandered through Gwong about thirty years ago. There is a single Christian family, that of the Anaguta "pastor," who holds Sunday services in an extraordinary hut in his compound in the valley, the interior of which consists of a pulpit and pews of hardened mud. Services are read in Eguta, translated verbally from a Hausa bible by the pastor, who can read, but not write, Hausa. But Christianity is of no interest to the overwhelming majority of Anaguta, and the tiny congregation is, for all practical purposes, confined to the pastor and his immediate family. However, it should be noted that the assimilation of one element in Anaguta religion—their belief in a high god—to Christian monotheism is accomplished easily by the school children and the preacher. But European religion can hardly be regarded as a new tribal integrating factor among the Anaguta. The conception of a single god is not novel, and the number of Christians is minimal.[5] Christianity is not institutionalized in the form of missions nor embodied by European clergy, and it is only among a few school children, in a European-structured environment, that its sentiments are regularly, if formally, expressed.

Hausa and English—Language as the Vehicle for Change

Language was, of course, an aboriginal bond on the tribal level. The lingua franca, Hausa, an imposed language, is of quite another character. It is identified as the speech of the conqueror and is the language of communication and government. Thus Hausa is, today, considered the "official" language of the Anaguta, and all Anaguta are bilingual, learning Hausa, along with Eguta, from the parental generation. The learning process is reinforced by contact with extra-tribal institutions. Hausa is the language of instruction in the school, the dominant spoken language, and the language of record in the court. It is the only medium through which an Anaguta can speak with adjoining peoples, and if he desires to become literate, he can only do so in Hausa. Actually, most Anaguta speak a slow, elementary, and bowdlerized Hausa, just enough for basic communication. They are aware of this, and even identify Hausawa as people who can speak Hausa very rapidly.

The results of this rapid displacement of Eguta by Hausa are various. First, the outlines of the convergent tribal-linguistic border become blurred. Hausa, flowing in from the outside, and reinforced internally by the fact that it is spoken by the parents, crosses both generational and tribal boundaries, which gradually cease to demarcate the Anaguta. Eguta is increasingly transformed into a private household or bush language, the more so since it has not been and probably never shall be written down. The ritual usages, the means and methods of tradition, lose their vehicle and thus much of their potency. This attenuation of the native language, in turn, widens the gap between the generations. The subtlety of traditional expression begins to fade; it becomes privatized, the secret preserve of fluent adults. For them, the language itself becomes a type of ritual, illuminating a fading cultural landscape. But the school chil-

[5] No Anaguta professes Islam.

dren already consider Eguta a feeble language; it has no power to move men, governments, or machines, to communicate with the new world of things and people into which they are being introduced. For them, the natural, human, or ritual referents of Eguta are rapidly becoming irrelevant.

On the other hand, the use of Hausa is regarded by the unschooled Anaguta as a necessary evil. There is no avoiding it. Even were there no school or court, the fact is that the designation of the artifacts, and many of the ideas of civilization, must be mediated through Hausa, which, in turn, may simply adapt the English word to a Hausa form, as in modern Japanese or Hebrew. Thus, Hausa becomes a medium for contemporary commercial-industrial civilization and this, also, has the effect of changing the character of Hausa itself.

The more political pull of Hausa is further evident in the use of Hausa honorifics as terms for office holders among the Anaguta. Thus, the secular chief is frequently referred to as *Sarki*, and lesser chiefs, who assist him in the collection of taxes and execution of justice, are known by a profusion of randomly bestowed and grossly inappropriate Hausa titles—*Galadima* (a principal minister), *Madaki* (in Zaria, second to the Emir), *Madauchi* (in Zaria, an important official position, held by one of the Emir's chief slaves), *Waziri* (vizier), and so on. But this entitling is purely nominal; it does not reflect the adoption of a Fulani-Hausa political structure. Only those leadership functions which have become politicized bear Hausa names, in contrast with the Priest Chiefs, compound heads, and other chiefs who represent the traditional culture. Since the Anaguta have never been under Fulani-Hausa sovereignty, it was probably the British who first named these political figures, so significant in colonial perspective, after the Hausa pattern.

Although the imposition of Hausa is both a cause and an effect of the shifting tribal and cultural identity of the Anaguta, English does not have the same impact. Only one Anaguta, a secondary school student, is moderately literate in English, and another, a primary school graduate, can speak the language tolerably. Nor is it likely that either literacy or fluency in English will increase within the Anaguta context, since the sole way of learning English is by attending secondary school. Apart from the fact that only a tiny fraction (under 1 per cent) of the population of the Northern Region may attend such schools within the next decade, those Anaguta who, by some odd chance, may be in a position to learn English during the next ten years would be doing so under circumstances and in places far removed from their traditional background. That is, learning English in the Northern Region presupposes either highly specialized training or an educational level that would, inevitably, project the individual Anaguta out of his tribal setting.

Political Parties

Political activity in the narrow sense, that is, association with political parties, supports tribal identity in a limited and contradictory way, although the great majority of Anaguta are radically disinterested in politics. They have produced only one bright young politico, who sports Hausa dress in the pursuit of his local party ambitions. Following the lead of this young man,, the Anaguta are opposed to the Northern Peoples' Congress, the dominant party of the Northern Region and of the Emirs. They favor the United Middle Belt Congress, which is antagonistic to the NPC, and agitates for an independent Middle Belt state; the former party received its initial impetus from the Action Group of the Western Region, which, for reasons both historical and contemporary, is devoted to shattering the monolithic and conservative rule of the NPC (Diamond, 1962b, c, d; 1963a, b, c). But Anaguta sentiment in favor of the UMBC is primarily symbolic. People who have never voted, and who know nothing of regional and national politics, will identify themselves as UMBC proponents because of their culturally inherited and continuously reinforced opposition to the hierarchical Fulani-Hausa structure. This strengthens the emotional sense of being Anaguta, while linking the tribe to other Pagan peoples who are also enlisted in the UMBC and Middle Belt cause; and this, in turn, intensifies Fulani-Hausa distaste for the Pagans.

However, the single Anaguta politico, who lives with one or two retainers in the Saban Gari, is becoming a minor careerist. Although serving as the link between the UMBC and the Anaguta, he quickly became disenchanted by his tribesmen's lack of pragmatic political interest. Moreover, the NPC, through threats and cajolery beyond the capacity of the UMBC, gradually won him over to the view that the North consisted of "one people, one party, one history." As he moved in the direction of the NPC, the Anaguta retained their symbolic enthusiasm for the UMBC without having any intention of putting it to practical use. Political affiliations, then, have the transient effect of bolstering Anaguta identity by opposition, but actual politics drive a wedge between the embryonic leadership and the tribesmen. In any case, the traditional tribal structure could not survive modern political activity; at most, the tribal perspective can serve to generate opposition to the more obvious forms of exploitation while stimulating a program which is closer to the cooperative and essentially decentralized spirit of the Anaguta past. This, of course, is not being done among the Anaguta. However, as shall be noted, the Nyango-Irigwe, a neighboring Pagan people, are seeking to realize themselves effectively in a modern context in terms of their own tradition.

THE BASES OF VILLAGE IDENTITY

Theoretical Discussion

The villages represent the next level of sociocultural integration among the Anaguta. But the term "village," although current, is inadequate to describe this local group. The euphorbia-hedged compounds of such a settlement are strung out for several miles and are interspersed, here and there, by small fields of grain (in the valley and lowlands) and cultivated patches on stone-girt terraces in the hillsides. A master trail winds through Anaguta territory and feeder paths, through narrow arching corridors of euphorbia, branch off to the five villages; but visiting another village remains a festive occasion.

No central paths run through the villages; there are no markets or public centers, save separate dancing areas which are set aside for men, women, and mixed groups. Compounds are distributed randomly, according to taste and the needs of cultivation; there are no neighborhoods, quarters, sections, or wards. There is, in short, no visible physical evidence of village existence. Just as the designation "tribal" is our way of objectifying the Anaguta means of linking local groups through which they consider themselves "one people," the term "village" identifies a named settlement, which is also generically designated in Eguta, consisting of a number of patriclans. This is not to imply that village functioning is simply the sum of that of the patriclans. The village has its own structure; it is a pre-colonial phenomenon, although the village organization has been used for alien purposes by the colonial power, and changes have, of course, occurred. Although the village is not the landowning body, villages have apparently fissioned in the past, by a group of patriclans, or partial patriclans, moving into adjacent territory. Thus, Rigiza has split from Zangam, but is still too new to have developed any of the formal elements of village organization—chiefs, councils, work groups, and so on—except for the name.

The Local Priest Chief

It is on the village level that the traditionally decentralized structure of the Anaguta is most strikingly evident. The inhabitants of each village customarily spoke a slightly different dialect, or subdialect, of Eguta. Vocabularies were almost identical, usages and pronunciations varied; but with the internal shifts in population and the increasing circulation of women among villages (see below), most of these distinctions are disappearing. Still, each village names the months of the Anaguta year differently, although the system of lunar calendrical reckoning is the same. Each village has its own sacred groves, the abodes of the *andoogubishee,* who, in another aspect, are the ancestral spirits of the several local patriclans. Just as the spirits in the sacred grove of Anabor, which represents that village's patriclans, can be appealed to by the *Uja* in the name of all Anaguta, so the spirits of the patriclans in each of the other villages can be solicited by the *Ejagiran* in behalf of that particular village as a whole.

The *Ejagiran,* the local Priest Chief, is the village counterpart of the *Uja.* He helps adjudicate those disputes which are not referred to the court; he is the caretaker of the sacred grove, and plays the part of the *Dodo,* the masked spirit, which seems to be both the incarnation of the grove and a collective representation of the ancestors at local ceremonies. He presides at all village rituals, most notably the *asandaka,* the harvest or first fruits festival, held in November in each village. And the *Ejagiran* also assists the paramount Priest Chief in rituals involving the tribe at large.

The Military–Work Group–Age-Grade Structure

Work groups are, most frequently, organized on a village-wide basis. Basically, the cooperative men's work group consists of the men initiated into the three-tiered system of age-grades. The mature males in the second grade, ranging from the middle twenties to the early forties, are the most skilled workers. The older men engage in light tasks, such as weeding or thatching. The younger men, from fourteen to the mid-twenties, tackle the heaviest work. The groups summoned to work in the fields of a particular patriclan are designated by the chiefs of the appropriate age-grades, at the request of one or more compound heads. The work is a ritual (blessed by the *Ejagiran*), social, and competitive occasion; men, chanting to the beat of drums, try to outdo each other in the speed and precision of their movements, stimulated by the millet beer provided by the women in the host's compound.

In former days, the same men who participated in the cooperative work groups were similarly mustered for military purposes. Thus, military units, age-grades, and work groups were simply different facets of a single village structure, which served to bind all the men of the village into a hierarchy of obligations and respect relationships that cross-cut the patriclans. The individuals in each grade usually refer to each other, and to those in the lower or higher grades, by kinship terms, such as older or younger brother, grandfather, etc. Indeed, the village-wide age-grading system can be viewed as an integrating mechanism of a quasi-kin character; its relations and functions emerge from a kin context, and are by no means civil or political. For the village, although a local group composed of kin units, was not traditionally a political structure. There were no political chiefs, no system of tax or tribute, no formal means for coercing affiliation. *Functions* that may be called political in the most abstract sense, such as the mustering of men for war, were discharged through the village organization, and within and through kin groups; but there was no specifically political apparatus.

The Critical Ritual

The ritual nucleus of the military–work group–age-grading system was the initiation of the young men, a ceremony that has not taken place for at least a decade. These ceremonies were held conjointly in each of the villages on either a seven- or fourteen-year cycle. The climax of the celebration was circumcision of the initiates, followed by several days of isolation and privation in "bush school." After initiation, the initiates moved into the first age-grade, those of the first grade moved into the second grade, and the second grade adults became recognized as elders. This was the critical ritual of the Anaguta, in which everyone participated to one degree or another. The women prepared millet beer and sang, in the company of the children, on the sidelines, while the initiates danced in a wide, slow-moving circle. The ceremony was marked by ritualized, but earnest combat between members of the higher grades, and was terminated in the sacred grove by the *Ejagiran* exhibiting heads taken in war to the initiates and their senior kin. The major effects of the ritual were to redefine the relationship between the sexes, reprime the organization of the men which undergirded the traditional village structure, and permit the expression of ambivalent feelings toward authority, as personified by the elders. The breakdown of this ritual, which Anaguta claim will be held next year, a next year that never comes, symbolizes the decay of the cultural core of the village. A remnant of the ceremony persists;

circumcision is still practiced by the Anaguta on an individual basis. But the operation is performed by itinerant Hausa surgeons.

The Organization of Women

Balancing, to a degree, the village organization of the men, each locality also has a chief of women, who is usually the most respected of the older females. She arranges for women's dances, directs the women at marital and other ceremonies, acts as advisor to the village women, and solicits and expresses their opinions on matters of concern to the village at large. She is a respected figure and, even on those occasions requiring formal segregation of the sexes, she moves with ease among the male elders. The position is a traditional one, and although symbolizing an informal female consensus, it is, in a very real sense, the counterpart of the more formal male village structure.

The Village Council

The chiefs of the patriclans compose a village council, which may act in cooperation with the *Ejagiran* and *Uja* to adjudicate disputes among members of different patriclans. They may also, in concert with other traditional chiefs, assist in resolving various village affairs. However, the council is largely informal; any elder can attend any meeting and express his own opinion or one confided to him, which may then be accepted or rejected by the group.

Other Chiefs—The Functions and Means of Appointment

Hunting, fishing, and dancing chiefs (male and female) lead the village in their respective activities. The village blacksmiths are also considered chiefs, exchanging their goods and services for goats, chickens, or grain. Medicine men are not, strictly speaking, chiefs, but have certain sacred qualities and, if successful in ministering to the sick or pregnant, they earn high status. The position of these chiefs is situational—that is, their authority is confined to particular activities in which they are skilled, in contrast to the Priest Chiefs, who are the only personages among the Anaguta who can be said to possess a *generalized* authority.

All chiefs, except the blacksmiths (and medicine men), who inherit their vocations from their fathers, are elected or appointed. Hunting, fishing, dancing, military, and work chiefs are recognized through the informal agreement of the participants in the activity. The age-grade chiefs are elected by a vote of the members of the next higher grade, and women's chiefs by a vote of all mature women and several male elders. The *Ejagiran* is appointed from a particular lineage in each village by the heads of the patriclans, with the advice of the *Uja*, but the *Ejagiran*-producing lineage may shift from time to time because of the unavailability of candidates or the appearance of an unusually promising man. Obviously, none of these mechanisms for qualified election or appointment are political or coercive, although they are binding.

The Political Chief

But each village also has a political chief. As the counterpart and representative of the secular head of the tribe (*Sarkin Anaguta*), appointed by him with the assent of the village, the functions of the local political chief are to report offenders, thus diverting an increasing amount of litigation from traditional to legal channels, and to collect taxes, for which he receives a token salary. In no case is the political chief of the village an *Ejagiran*, a blacksmith, a medicine man, an age-grade, work, hunting (military), fishing, or dancing chief. Thus, the new political structure is of a wholly subsidiary character; it neither parallels nor duplicates, nor is it identified with traditional leadership roles or statuses. It does not replace the traditional system in prestige or importance as the latter breaks down, but discharges an exclusively pragmatic function, elicited from the outside.

The Transformation of Village Identity—Theoretical Summary

Resettlement of compounds in the valleys and lowlands, the suspension of the initiation rituals, and the introduction of political factors have seriously weakened the structure and meaning of village life. Yet traditional types of chieftanship survive, along with certain institutions, such as cooperative work groups and festivals, notably those connected with the horticultural cycle. Paradoxically, the residue of village functions is one of the last echoes of corporate Anaguta identity. The reason is that, although new integrating mechanisms have been imposed on the tribal level, the villages feel their impact less directly. There are no schools or courts in the villages, no markets, no new social offices that command the respect of the people, and, of course, no emergent socioeconomic classes. The old rank and status systems are maintained, at least in rough outline. Village society is infused with an egalitarian spirit, which is not the same as the ideology of reductive equality (Diamond, 1963c, p. 84), and this lingers on even when institutions crumble.

When usages decline, they, like the lands that are disappearing into forests or under alien settlement, are not replaced.

THE PATRICLANS

Political and Economic Functions

Each Anaguta village is composed of, but not merely reducible to, four to eight named patriclans. The clan (*tibiri*) is a group localized within the village, but does not constitute a *barrio*; the patriclan does not form a neighborhood. Clusters of compounds allied to the same clan may be found in a contiguous area, but they may also be distributed randomly, in response to the needs of cultivation, throughout the village area—even, as indicated, in the valley and lowlands. Presumably, the loose distribution of clan compounds throughout the village is not a new phenomenon, since the same pattern obtains in the hill settlements.

The patriclans, specifically named after putative human ancestors and generically designated as "people of the hand," are the basic land-owning and exogomous units. Only one clan in each village has a special relationship with an animal (leopard); the flesh of the animal is tabooed. Each patriclan has the right to allocate unused land anywhere within the village area, or in the valley or lowlands, to its constituent families; conversely, no individual family is supposed to expand into new land without first getting the permission of the clan chief. The position of chief is qualifiedly elective; he must be an elder of good reputation, if possible, the oldest living male, and is installed through a consensus reached by a meeting of the male heads of the compounds constituting the patriclan. However, as in the cases of the *Ejagiran* and the *Uja*, members of particular families may succeed each other if the family has proven itself to be particularly potent. Each patriclan also provides one or more political intermediaries who collect taxes from representatives of compounds, and then pass them on to the village tax chief. These, of course, are the "office holders" in the hollow political structure, who are referred to by Hausa titles, which inflates their position beyond what it actually is among the Anaguta.

Religious Functions

A patriclan is the immediate focus for ancestor worship among the Anaguta. Just as the God-sun (*Uwiyang*) is the tribal deity mediated by the *Uja*, on a lower level the patriclans are embodied in the ancestral spirits, who, in turn, are created—as are all beings, spiritual or otherwise—by God. The clan chief acts as a priest, and may pray or sacrifice to the ancestors, according to the needs of the group. However, any mature Anaguta may call upon the ancestors for private purposes without seeking the mediation of the clan chief, just as any Anaguta elder may informally pray to the God-sun. Ancestral spirits are conventionally claimed as the cause of pregnancy; the spirit is said to have entered the womb of the woman (which may account for the conventional fear that women display to the *Dodo*), and the child is usually named after the ancestor designated. In this sense, each child is viewed as the rebirth of an ancestor; the generations are conceived to cycle endlessly. These cyclic phenomena, which are reinforced and assured by ritual, are evident also in the horticultural round, the age-grading organism, and ramify throughout traditional Anaguta life, resulting in conceptions of time and space, life and death, diametrically opposed to the linear perspective of contemporary commercial-industrial society.

The ceremonies of birth and death are the province of the patriclans, since each event is linked with the creation or re-creation of ancestors. Just as they celebrate the birth of a new child, so each patriclan has a common burial ground. Previously, the dead were buried and the long bones and skull were later exhumed and placed in large pots in the clan cemetery, where periodic rites were performed. However, the decline of the craft of pottery has resulted in the practice being abandoned.

Apari Relationships

Not only the number, but the names of patriclans vary from village to village. One village may have four, another six or eight. Names may match, in certain cases, or a name may be exclusive to a given village. Patriclans with the same names in different villages claim no relationship to each other, and in every such case intermarriage between members is permitted. On the other hand, each patriclan in each village stands in an *apari* relationship to at least one clan in every other village; moreover, a clan may have an *apari* partner in one village, but may not necessarily be *apari* to a clan that shares that partner's name in another village. As it happens, no two clans with the same name, in any of the established villages, are *apari* to each other. Thus, the clan names seem to be merely conventional, drawn from a limited number of possibilities, and reflect neither any acknowledged historical relationship, nor any specific, current connection.[6]

Sexual intercourse with a partner of an *apari* clan is considered incestuous and the penalty is sickness unto death. The *apari* tie is considered to be unusually intimate; special friendships, respect, and mutual aid bind the *apari*-linked patriclans across village boundaries, serving, so to speak, as an alternative non-marital bond within the preferential marriage system. Marriage, then, can take place among the great majority of clans in different villages; there are no specific village pairings; and there are, at this time, no designated clan marriage pairings. Village exogomy is usual, but marriages between members of different clans in the same village sometimes occur.

The Marriage System

The intratribal circulation of females is generated through the patriclans; marriage was the most vital of the traditional integrative mechanisms among the Anaguta, linking the whole hierarchy of social units from nuclear family through extended family, patriclan, village, and tribe. But the circulation of females has become increasingly anarchic.

The basic form of marriage is true, along with classificatory, sister exchange, occasionally supplemented by bride service between two men in different villages, the patriclans of which are not *apari* to each other. Such men must be "strangers"; since the Anaguta terminological system tends toward the Hawaiian, and most cousins are assimilated to siblings, the designation "stranger" excludes recognized cousins as potential marital partners. This, theoretically at least, cuts out double cross cousin marriage, involving the offspring of exchanged sisters, and generally permits a more limited choice of mates from the maternal patriclan, without invoking an absolute, general prohibition. There is suggestive evidence that, in the past, a rotating system of preferred clan intermarriages also functioned to prohibit double cross cousin unions in the presence of sister ex-

[6] However, the phenomenon of the new village of Rigiza is puzzling. By a migration that cross-cut several of the patriclans, Rigiza recently broke off from Zangam, because of land pressure occasioned by the encroachment of forest reserves in the Zangam area. Thus, clans with the same name in Zangam and Rigiza are *apari* to each other; only clans of different names in each village can intermarry, since marriage between the former would be regarded as incestuous. This may indicate that clans with the same names in other Anaguta villages also sprang from a common origin, perhaps in the beginning, from a single village, the relationship withering over time. If this were the case, then the conventional *apari* relationship between clans of *different* names would simply be fortuitous at the moment.

change, and this could have been part of a complex marriage class system, but specific information is lacking.

In the absence of a true, or acceptable classificatory sister, another female relative may be substituted, and marriages may even take place by delayed exchange, that is, a man marries a female relative of another, and pledges one of his female offspring to his wife's family. These debts and obligations are inheritable, and can ramify intricately among male members of a particular family and between families in different clans. Exchange marriage, which is arranged by either the fathers or older brothers of the respective families, has the effect of any reciprocal transaction; if a man's wife returns to her native compound, his sister is supposed to leave her husband.

Sister exchange thus may seem, and formerly must have been, a conventional means of stabilizing marriage; but today, because of the (apparent) shortage of marriageable women, their greater involvement in the market economy, and the weakening in the felt continuity of obligations, it is a major source of dispute among the clans. Efforts are made to handle these disputes in the traditional manner, by councils of elders drawn from the patriclans; but the intricately involved property rights, which now ramify politically because of the new social context in which they are contested, drive an increasing number of cases into court. Thus, the problematical nature of sister exchange, today, strains the relations among the clans and begins to have a disintegrative effect on the society as a whole.

Among the Anaguta, a woman usually does not get married until she is pregnant. The biological paternity of the child is of little social importance; a girl may have several affairs, or spend several months living with a paramour, customarily from another clan in her own village, and then, following pregnancy, will be married off via the pre-arranged exchange route, at an elaborate ceremony, which formally "compensates" for the actual looseness of the system. But children conceived before marriage become members of her husband's clan. The seeming scarcity of marriageable women and the low birth rate, which Anaguta recognize and complain of, may be factors in reinforcing the differentiation between lovers and husbands, and encouraging post-pregnancy marriage; for proof of the fertility of the woman is of primary concern to the husband's family. They may also be factors in encouraging older men to permit access to their wives and sisters in exchange for resident labor by younger, informal lovers.

THE COMPOUND—LOCUS OF LABOR

General Description

After marriage to her legitimate, or primary, husband, the woman joins him in his compound, the next social unit to be considered. The Anaguta compound consists of a series of tiny beehive huts, with thatched roofs and walls of dried mud. Sleeping huts are at the center and can be entered through several adjoining huts in the tightly clustered group. Grain storage huts are on the periphery, and the whole is usually surrounded by a euphorbia hedge with a single entrance. The compound is designed as the residence of an extended family, which may consist of a man, his wife, perhaps a married son and his children, unmarried daughters, and one or more younger brothers, and their families; that is, a nucleus of patrilineally related males. Of course, the specific personnel and size of compounds shift relative to each other over the years, as family members marry, establish their own dwellings, or migrate to another area. Each wife has her own hut in the polygynous compound, but settled polygyny, although culturally sanctioned, is rarely encountered today. Here again, we find that the (apparent) shortage of women and their economic primacy in the new market situation are correlated with an unusual freedom of movement. A woman may leave her husband if she feels that she is being ill treated, or merely because she is no longer comfortable in his compound, and, in such cases, the children accompany her. This holds whether she returns to her father's house or moves in with another man in another village. Indeed, a woman may have several of these "secondary" husbands, in several villages. However, a woman who develops a reputation for moving too capriciously will be held cheaply, and may have difficulty in finding a man to accept her in his household. This, along with other factors to be considered below, leads to a peculiar and growing sequence of polygynous, polyandrous, and minimally extended nuclear family households.

Freedom of Women and Significance of Maternal Line

The free and easy movement of women (with children) may not only be connected with the fact that they are the money makers, but could, conceivably, be reinforced by the possibility that the Anaguta are a society in transition from matrilineal to patrilineal descent.[7] The strong tendency toward Hawaiian usage would be congruent with this possibility, and with the fact that the sacred medicine bundles (*wahbees*), the most potent of protective objects, which every Anaguta inherits at birth and cherishes throughout his life, are passed down through the mother's line. Furthermore, children enjoy special emotional bonds with their maternal relatives, although these are diffused, not institutionalized. The inheritance of most property and prerogatives is formally patrilineal.

The "Patriarchal" Character of Compounds

The male head of the compound is, traditionally, symbolic of extended family unity. He oversees the work in the fields and the distribution and storage of food. He arranges for the marriage of his children and younger siblings, and is consulted in cases of domestic strife within and among compounds. He may pray to his ancestral spirits, on behalf of the compound, and even to God, in times of immediate family crisis. Moreover, he represents the compound on the council of the patriclan. The head of a compound is the only person likely to have two wives, and is always referred to as "Elder" (*Pozo*), in recognition of his importance. However, an increasing number of these "patriarchs" are not technically members of the third age-grade, and this embarrasses fellow clan members; for the compound is the primary social and subsistence unit in a primarily subsistence economy.

Division of Labor

Within the compound, the customary division of labor among the Anaguta is as follows. Women discharge the domestic tasks, do light hoeing in the gardens, weeding in the fields, along with some broadcast sowing, and supplementary gathering of fruits and nuts; they winnow and pound the grain, and cook beer. Men clear and burn over the bush, and do the heavy hoeing, soil preparation, planting, and terracing, along with supplementary hunting and fishing. However, the division in horticultural labor is by no means

[7] Murdock (1959, pp. 90, 96-97) postulates a general matrilineal to patrilineal transition among Plateau Nigerians as symptomatic of the fundamental matrilineality of the Bantu. His argument is plausible, but omits contemporary factors in trying to account for what he terms "utterly unique" marriage customs. These may be alternatively expressed as phenomena of breakdown, although transitional elements could be operative in part. The point is that Murdock speculates only ethnologically in terms of logical-historical sequences, and ignores the immediate influences of the market, etc.

absolute, and either sex may assist the other in conventionally delegated tasks.

The women mold pots, make closely woven reed baskets, and tan skins; formerly, they wove cloth from a native species of wild cotton on a rudimentary loom. Men manufacture a variety of tools and weapons, including bows and arrows, walking sticks, pipes, mats, musical instruments, shields, women's headtrays, and so on; they build individual huts, but the cooperative work groups construct the compounds. Anaguta men report that they once worked and smelted tin, but evidence is lacking. On the other hand, it is clear that iron smelting was formerly a male activity, since chunks of the smelted metal are found in abandoned compounds and even in caves. Today, the blacksmiths purchase iron in the markets or from Hausa traders, melt it down, and hammer hoes, knives, bells, and ornaments. But smithing, which descended in particular families, is not reproducing itself. Remaining smiths are elders, and their wares, including inferior substitutes, are available in the markets of Jos. A decline in material culture and skills is evident, both in the specialized areas of pottery and smithing and in the more generally distributed crafts. At one time Anaguta women were known throughout the High Plateau for their skill as potters; but pots are now small, hastily constructed, crudely fired, and are being replaced by cheap European utensils. A few of the older women use the loom, but the technique is rapidly being forgotten; European-style blankets today replace the native robes and coverings worn during the cold spells of the dry season and, perhaps, in the past, for ceremonial purposes.

Crops and Domestic Animals

The staple crop is *acha* (*Digitaria excillif*), hungry rice, a grass-like, hardy cereal grain, which requires little water and a minimum of soil preparation. It is the first crop to be planted (by broadcast seeding) in March-April, at the beginning of the rainy season, through June; one variety is harvested in September-October, the later types until the end of December, at the inception of the dry season when hunting and bush clearing begin. The cycle of *acha* growth is heavily ritualized, and parts of the plant, presumably having sacred qualities, are used in other ceremonies. The ash, especially prepared, also serves as a kind of salt, and *acha* porridge (*gwate*), laced with greens, is the dominant food. *Tamba* (*Eleusine coracana*), like *acha*, described as being somewhere between a grass and a grain, is grown during the same period, but is neither so widely used, nor ritually valued. Bulrush millet and Guinea corn round out the important grains, and are utilized primarily to make beer. Mound-grown cassava, yams, and coco yams, requiring a good deal of heavy labor, are the major root crops, and supplement the diet. Relatively insignificant gardens of tomatoes, onions, peppers, and European potatoes are market crops, cultivated and tended by the women.

A few chickens and goats are kept, basically for sacrificial purposes at the ancestral shrines; neither eggs nor goat's milk are consumed, although roasted goat flesh is ritually divided, and the tanned skin of the animal is worn by the elders. Anaguta villagers occasionally contribute to the purchase of a Fulani-owned cow, which is then slaughtered and eaten by all the village residents. Watch dogs are kept as pets, and may, on rare occasions, go into the pot.

THE ECONOMIC TRANSFORMATION OF THE COMPOUND

Theoretical Discussion

The shrinkage of available land, along with the imposition of taxes, has seriously disrupted the customary round of labor and labor's primary locus, the compound. A chain of new social usages, that may be termed deteriorative, has developed. It should first be understood that the Anaguta did not have, aboriginally, nor do they now practice, an internal market economy, although they may have been marginally engaged in bartering in the markets of adjacent groups. Correlatively, they lacked money or any other abstract means of internal exchange. This is not only an historical inference, for the older usages are still current. All reciprocal obligations involving material goods, whether for the services of a medicine man or a blacksmith, in traditional compensation for injury, or in simple exchange, are paid in kind, that is, in grain, domestic animals, or labor. Such exchanges are properly viewed as discharging an economic function within a ramifying network of personal relationships; that is, they are never merely economic. There was, however, no elaborate system of barter. Save for iron tools, provided by the blacksmiths, compounds within the patriclans were economically self-sufficient.

It is only relative to the external, contemporary political economy that the Anaguta have come to behave in terms of money and markets. Their taxes, fines, or fees cannot be paid in kind, and market purchases must be made in currency. They handle money ingenuously; for example, they count by the duodecimal system, and thus may reckon 24 rather than 20 shillings to a pound, assimilating their unit of 12 to the Arabic-European 10. This calibration of the decimal to the duodecimal system is conceptually accurate, but expensive.

The Commercialization of Women's Work

As the available land diminishes, the need to supplement diet by purchasing food stuffs increases the pressure toward earning cash. But, from the beginning, as we have seen, the Anaguta male avoided work in the towns, the mines, or other European residences and installations. The job of accumulating money to pay the £1½ male head tax and to make small purchases in the market became women's work. Three sources of income were developed. First, the sale of firewood for cooking and heating purposes to African residents in Jos and the Saban Gari, (nights in the dry season are cold on the High Plateau); second, the cultivation of garden vegetables and their sale, along with a few eggs and chickens; and, third, the preparation and sale of millet beer. In each case, the women, typically, carry these products on their headtrays to Jos or New Town markets. Occasionally, they venture as far as Naraguta town, or even Tilden Fulani in Bauchi Province. But Hausa middlemen make sporadic forays into Anaguta territory in order to purchase European vegetables.

The Shift in the Position of Women

Since the women provide the money with which to pay taxes, they are also more sensitive to events that may increase the burden, and have developed what may be termed a more pragmatic awareness of the tribe's relation to the civil power. Thus, when all woodcutting was prohibited in the forest reserve, the women marched down from the hills and assembled before the courthouse in a silent, formidable, and dense mass, unnerving the chief and council, all of whom made speeches pledging sympathy; and similar demonstrations took place when it was rumored that women were going to be taxed in the Northern Region. This does not mean, however, that the women are more flexible in accommodating themselves to the culture growing up around them. They do not become petty traders; rather, in earning their shillings, they pay the minimal tribute to the civilization being kept at bay.

The way in which women became actively engaged in the earning of money seems to be as follows. The manufacture of millet beer had always been a female task. In the past generation, with the shrinkage of lands and the decline in hunting, fishing, and gathering, the dependence upon *acha* became even stronger than in the past. Periods of near famine before the late fall harvest increased in duration and intensity. Gradually, millet beer, which had been a ceremonial and social drink, became a necessary nutriment, supplying quick energy, along with certain vitamins and minerals. Gunn (1953, p. 80), discussing the Birom, sums this up: ". . . beer has the consistency of porridge and considerable food-value, while the process of fermentation provides a supply of 'protective elements' which would otherwise be lacking in a diet which includes no dairy-products; beer is thus, perhaps, the chief factor in promoting the cultivation of millet, as it is a better grain than *acha* for brewing."

But one should not underrate the fact that the Pagans drank because they enjoyed getting drunk, particularly in the face of a disintegrating tradition. Millet beer, then, served to dull hunger, made people gay, and could be conveniently transported and sold. It was natural enough for the women to become the marketers. Women also organize millet beer parties in compounds that are short of cash, contributing their labor to the needy family in preparing great quantities of the beverage, which is then sold in penny portions. This is a highly specialized type of transaction, held only in emergency, and cannot be considered in a commercial context. Millet beer parties are simply a transformation of cooperative usage; they serve as occasions for helping one compound after another to meet its fiscal obligations, and no profit is involved.

With reference to firewood, the women had, customarily, collected twigs and branches for their own domestic use, and helped clear the land of small brush after the men had done the heavy work. Furthermore, the carrying of head loads, except in rare cases, was considered to be women's work; and a woman may walk as far as twelve miles, with a 30-pound load of firewood on her head, that may sell for half a dozen shillings in Jos. The collection and sale of firewood, then, was an extension of several converging feminine activities.

The care of small garden plots is a similar situation. These plots can be cultivated with a light-weight woman's hoe, are close to the compound, and vegetables are of no importance in subsistence. Therefore, the sale of vegetables also became a female vocation; and the pattern of each of these cash crops, which in their totality represent only an insignificant fraction of Anaguta produce, was mutually reinforcing.

There are two other elements in the marginal "commercialization" of female activity worth considering. Men would have found the work involved in each case beneath their dignity, since it was composed of traditionally feminine roles and, furthermore, they had no intention of being drawn away from their native haunts into foreign markets. More generally, it is well known that in periods of intense cultural disorganization or readjustment, when the worldly status of males declines, women—the psychobiological vehicles of survival—frequently become the economic and social pivots of the group under stress, that is, families become mother-centered.[8] To a certain extent, this has occurred among the Anaguta. Women, by supplying cash, even in minute quantities, shield their husbands and are thereby valued in a new way. This factor, in combination with the relative scarcity of women, has generated a shift in the relations between the sexes. In the compounds that still function traditionally, psychological equality prevails. The division of labor is not regarded as invidious. Wives and husbands speak freely in each other's company; daily decisions are jointly discussed. The contrast in atmosphere between a conventional Hausa and a well-functioning Pagan household is striking, precisely because of the difference in the behavior of the women, and the intrafamilial relations that flow from that social fact. But, in the more typical Anaguta compound today, although equality among peers of the same sex prevails, women tend toward psychological domination, which has nothing whatever to do with a presumed phase of matrilineal descent. Their apparent scarcity and unquestionable unreliability as sexual partners, the general decline in population (which puts a premium on childbirth), and their involvement with the commercial market are the obvious reasons. The last point deserves emphasis, because women are not the major breadwinners. The men remain basically responsible for the growing of *acha* and millet. It is, then, the marginal association of women with the money economy and concomitant shifts in Anaguta culture which contribute to female "license."

The Instability of the Compound

The circulation of women, for reasons already discussed, along with the ecological drive toward migration into the valley and lowlands, are converting the extended family compound into a grotesquely unstable social organism. Conventionally designed for polygyny, it may, during any given period, be polyandrous, and today tends steadily toward the minimal extension of a single nuclear family.

[8] As, in varying degrees, among New York Jews, Boston Irish, Harlem Negroes, California and Iroquois Indians, etc.

Fig. 83. This view of Manza Valley shows several compounds and farm plots, some enclosed by euphorbia hedges.

Fig. 84. Cassava, or manioc, a root crop of New World origin, is cultivated by the Anaguta. The plants are grown in high ridges to conserve moisture around the tubers.

Fig. 85. Little food is grown beyond subsistence requirements. Guinea corn or sorghum may be cultivated up to the very doors of the houses.

Fig. 86. This domestic scene shows no European influence. The thatched hut, pots, baskets, wooden mortars, and woman attired only in a G-string are all aboriginal.

Fig. 87. This Anaguta boy proudly holds his native-type hoe which has an iron blade and wooden handle.

Fig. 88. The Uja, the tribal Anaguta Priest Chief. Uninfluenced by Islam or Christianity, traditional religious functionaries have considerable power.

Fig. 89. The Anaguta are less factionalized between "conservative" elders and "progressive" youths than many primitive peoples. This young man wears a headdress of leather strips, buttons, twine, and small feathers.

Fig. 90. The *Dodo* wears costume made from husks of Guinea corn after the harvest.

Fig. 91. Potential access to the products of the industrial world has not eliminated the bow and arrow carried by the man in the foreground.

Fig. 92. Aboriginal basketry containers and winnowing trays as well as pots continue in use. Occasionally articles of European manufacture, such as the metal drum in the background, make an incongruous picture.

Fig. 93. Guinea corn is pounded in a wooden mortar by women who chant rhythmically while they work.

Fig. 94. Scarified Anaguta elder wearing traditional skin toga smokes his pipe.

Fig. 95. Anaguta dancers at festive celebration. The leg ornaments consist of palm nuts containing seeds which rattle.

NUCLEAR FAMILIES

Traditional Basis of the Compound

Within the compound, the nuclear family is the immediate affiliative unit. Under ordinary social conditions, the compound was, for all practical purposes, indivisible. The nuclear families, of which it is composed, never lost their identity. Although each nuclear family cultivates specific fields or plots, labor among them is interchangeable, and the identification is irrelevant to distribution, since the compound, as a whole, traditionally holds all land, subject to the approval of the clan. Each family was conceived as a primarily nurturant, maternal grouping, consisting of the mother, children, and father. But where the father's role, in the compounds at large, had symbolic primacy, his role in his conjugal family was more idiosyncratic and less culturally significant. His children, as noted, were members of his clan, but had close emotional ties with their maternal relatives, and each child's protective charms, or medicine bundles, were inherited through the mother. Moreover, the nuclear family was a generically named unit; Anaguta themselves stress the significance of the immediate family, and in delineating it within the compounds, emphasize its feminine character and maternal function. However, these variations in descent and allegiance were, within the traditional compound, complementary. It is only under newly developing conditions that they become disruptive.

Ecological Background of Disaffiliation

The schismatic potential is realized within an increasing number of compounds because of the following factors. To begin with, in the valleys and lowlands, and even on steeply terraced plots, the annual burning of the bush is obviated by the use of manure, received from the Fulani in exchange for (tsetse fly–free) pasturage.[9] The use of fertilizer, along with the scarcity of land available for expansion, leads to the continuous occupation of certain compounds in circumscribed areas of cultivation. Since the heavy labor in burning over the bush is no longer necessary, a small labor force, composed of both sexes, becomes viable. If planting or harvesting has to be done very rapidly, or if the members of a compound are ill or otherwise incapable of meeting work demands, the village work group may still be called upon, usually as a last resort. This transformation to a type of sedentary horticulture is, of course, furthered by crop rota-

[9] It is not unusual to see Fulani cattle grazing almost vertically on the steep slopes of hills when lowland grass has been burnt out during the dry season, or in dry spells during the summer.

tion and the system of fallowing. Technically speaking, then, a compound consisting of a husband, wife, children, and one other male, perhaps a younger brother, would be sufficient to handle horticultural tasks in the valley and lowlands; and, as a matter of fact, such nuclear families, extended minimally, either collaterally or lineally, have become common. The act of migration itself, from the hillsides to the lowlands and valley, speeds the process. For the downmigrants usually split off from larger existent compounds, leaving a less viable group behind, whereas in former times they might descend to work the bottom lands and return to their compounds in the evening. Thus, the personnel setting up the new compound is limited, and the original compound has also been diminished.

Character of New Relations

Of the 350-odd Anaguta compounds, about 225 occupy the downlands, averaging about 6.6 persons per unit; the remaining 125 hill compounds average just over seven residents, and were, obviously, once larger, while the newer groups seem to be stabilized at their present size.

In almost every case, it is the younger people, perhaps a younger brother or son, their wives and children, who migrate, and the parents and older siblings who choose to remain behind. The migration of compounds, reduction in their size, and fixed residence also weaken primogeniture. The mature males of the extended families in the valley and lowlands are now in a position to begin to regard their fields as "private" property. Further, recourse to the patriclan to get new lands becomes less significant, because of the relative permanency of the new nucleated settlements. The strain on primogeniture frays the integrity of the compound, the patrilineal functioning of the clans, and the patrilocality of residence. Eventually, it could lead to severe land hunger, tenancy, other forms of agricultural wage labor, and a sort of micro-class system. But it is unlikely that the society of the valley will persist long enough for these changes to occur.

The people in the hills feel the pinch of hunger more sharply than those of the downlands because of the lower crop yield, intensified by the greater age and diminished size of their labor force, but they manage to survive by cooperating, when necessary, on a broader scale than had been the case before. Thus, one nuclear development compounds another. But, with this essential difference: in the hills, cooperative traits persist in the face of privation; in the downlands, they wither because, in a certain sense, they have ceased to be necessary.

CULTURAL EFFECTS OF THE SHIFT IN THE SOCIAL ECONOMY

Theoretical Discussion

The shift in the social economy is related to an apparent change in ideology, more precisely, an adaptation of ideology to a new socio-economic condition. Under traditional circumstances, the cooperative Anaguta economy functioned on the principle of "to the laborer goes the fruit," a principle emerging out of the socio-economic-technical matrix. Every man had the right, obligation, and training to work; cooperative work resulted in a general equality of distribution. Even when an individual, because of illness or, very rarely, delinquency, failed to contribute, the communalistic, non-acquisitive compound, clan, village, and tribal system continued to function and supported the non-participant until it became unbearable. However, when the cooperative system begins to break down, and the labor necessary for subsistence can be drawn from smaller groups, "privatization" sets in, not because of the sudden growth of an acquisitive sense, but, on the contrary, *because it is assumed that each man deserves the fruits of his labor.* If it is no longer necessary for the previous system to function in order to achieve this end, or if it cannot so function, and if large-scale cooperative labor has become irrelevant, then the specific demands of the previous society will soon cease to be recognized. But, it is important to emphasize that this results from application of an aboriginal principle to a novel condition, and not because of the sudden growth of an acquisitive or "capitalistic" consciousness. Objectively, that is, from the outside, it may appear otherwise, but the Anaguta and, presumably, primitive peoples elsewhere sense no discontinuity in principle; and it is this which blinds them to the pitfalls of the new economy into which they are entering. It is only in more developed situations, where, for example, cash crops, a cash economy, and/or radically new instruments or conditions of labor have completely changed the character of the society, and if some success in accumulation has taken place, that the private entrepreneurial psychology, as we know it in Western culture, may be said to exist. But this, with a solitary exception, has not yet happened among the Anaguta.

A Family Case in Point

THE SOCIOECONOMIC TRAP

The point seems important enough to elaborate by a specific, personal example. The family of one of my interpreters, Audu, was the only "upwardly mobile" family among the Anaguta. Audu was hell-bent on improving his worldly status, which meant becoming a nominal Nigerian, a consumer of European goods, and an employee of the Zaria Tobacco Company. But he believed in nothing except appearances, and he was unskilled at them, for he was an absolutely new bourgeois. Yet, he was a sad and poignant figure, groping his way into the outer world, away from a people that scorned it, condemned by their indifference to be a weak, unhonored pioneer. Both parents were long deceased; the older brother, Sako, who was middle-aged, had assumed the father's place and it was he who was responsible for the family's upward and outward thrust.

Atypically Anaguta, Sako had, from childhood, been awed by and drawn to the white man's technology. Many years before, out of curiosity he had walked 20 miles to a mining station, and there had heard a radio, but he was ridiculed as a spinner of tales when he tried to describe it at home. When the Europeans began to come in greater numbers, and Jos took shape as a city, he realized that the Anaguta would have to adapt themselves to the new ways if they were to survive. Despite his dissenting view of their situation, he never lost caste among his own people, probably because they sensed that his interest was not self-serving. Indeed, he was highly respected by his tribesmen and was said to have the capacity, a warrior's supreme gift, to become invisible in moments of crisis. When he was still a young man, they had seen him pull a leopard off a child; as he grabbed its tail, he vanished and the animal fled. And how ironic it was that Sako, one of the few possessors of the gift, which could have rendered him invulnerable in the struggle against the enemies of the Anaguta, should have been aware of the need to come to terms with the superior power that was encircling his people. Yet, they had clubbed him severely and left him for dead when he enrolled Audu as the first and, for years, the only Anaguta student at the Gwong Primary School, but he neither struck back nor changed his course.

There were other incidents over the years, but Sako survived them with self-respect. After he had become a regular visitor to our compound, he had been charged by a younger man of his lineage with betraying tribal secrets and had been publicly slapped. It was said —and with truth, for I had explained my mission to all who would listen—that I was being given rituals, part of the living body of the people. But the man who slapped Sako—and there was no greater insult from a junior to a senior man—was considered a malcontent, jealous of his position, and secretly interested in getting closer to the Europeans. So Sako was praised for ignoring the insult. On another occasion, Sako had invited me to a most solemn ritual—the symbolic re-enactment of the Anaguta's victory over the Fulani, which helped keep the Islamic horsemen off the Plateau. We had both been under attack that afternoon; he, verbally, by members of the family that had accused him of disloyalty, and I, by a warrior who had made several passes at my head with a tomahawk. The majority of people present stood by observing but not looking directly at us. When we stood our ground, the tension broke, and we were never to be troubled again. Still Sako, the conciliator, continued to be considered the honorable enemy of his people's intentions. He was quite conservative, even exemplary, as a husband, a father, a worker, and a believer. Thus, his unique desire to accommodate the Anaguta to the outer society was conceived as particularly threatening.

However, Sako was not successful. His efforts had been narrowed to the scope of his own family. Audu might escape his Anaguta identity, but he was not influencing his tribesmen, and Umaru, the middle brother, who came to live with us, was also preparing to abandon his people as they were bent on abandoning the world. Both Umaru and Audu were in a tragic or, rather, pitiful situation, since they, in their own way, lacked awareness. They had learned the need for change as the only salvation from a strong brother. But they had no support from their own people and were faced with indifference on the outside. Inevitably, with little moral or material capital, finding themselves and their people inadequate, ignorant of the shape of the society into which they were emerging, lacking modern, specialized skills, and with little chance of developing any, and ashamed of themselves, they could only hope to survive by bluff, self-deception, and other modes of cheating. Audu had not worked on the land for years; as he had been his brother's pioneer in elementary school, he was the only Anaguta to have attended secondary school. With luck, this deracinated, yet uncultivated man might become a clerk or a minor civil servant in a country full of peasants.

What happened to Umaru I, an unwitting agent of change, saw with my own eyes. Umaru had learned a distaste for manual labor from Audu, who had, in turn, absorbed it from the colonial environment in which he moved. A nominal Christian like Audu, by the time he joined our compound he already considered himself superior to his tribe. He was bursting with abstract piety and eager to get ahead, but he spent every last penny on European clothing, utterly ignoring his wife, who roamed our backyard naked and finally left him to return to her brother's compound with their two small sons, which threatened to break up the uniquely settled marriage of Umaru's sister, and caused a good deal of social indignation. This disturbed him, but not too much, because he was at that time engaged in wooing a young Anaguta woman who had married a Birom, had lived briefly in Kaduna, and had returned home in disillusionment. She had a sophisticated Hausa air, wore pretty robes, and was, by general consensus, empty-headed. Finally Umaru's behavior, which had been satisfactory as an informant, became impossible as an Anaguta. His money wages had enabled him to neglect his land; he was unable to hire outsiders to work the land, as no Anaguta sold his agricultural labor. Nor, to my surprise, would his relatives or friends maintain his compound in his willful absence. If he had been ill they would have been glad to help, or if he had needed extra hands they would have organized a work group, but this was sheer neglect, and even if he intended to return one day, they felt no obligation to encourage that degree of delinquency. And one day the breach was made formal when Sako, on a routine visit to our compound, brought Umaru's hoe with him and handed it over without a word. Social relations remained friendly enough between Umaru and his kinsmen, but he was now on his own.

On the other hand, Umaru never shared a shilling with his friends or relatives. At first, this struck me as pure greed. But I came to realize that the logic was as impeccably traditional as that of his kinsmen when they returned the hoe. Umaru was now a wage worker; he was earning his keep by his own efforts, he was not living on traditional land. No fellow tribesman was contributing in any way toward Umaru's livelihood; thus they had no right to share in his wages. The above-mentioned unspoken principle of Anaguta economics—to the laborer shall go the fruit—was now being applied in a quite different context. Umaru accepted this, but he did so naïvely. For he was no longer functioning in a cooperative society; he had no guarantee of productive work, and he had no sense of the intricacy of the new system which would not reward him in direct proportion to his efforts. That is to say, Umaru had no conception of a market economy, the capitalist order, or of his absolutely insignificant bargaining power. As we have seen, the Anaguta had never developed internal markets, had no system of currency, and were almost exclusively subsistence cultivators. Umaru had not even the chance to acquire the elementary shrewdness of the peasant in selling to the city. Nor was he capable of a depersonalized business exchange; that was not the way goods and services were circulated among his people. Even though he gloried in being a paid employee, he, and Audu also, regarded me as a protector, a father, a brother, a kinsman. Objectively, Umaru had exchanged a little compound for a big one which required less work, afforded more prestige, and had many more amenities. He had moved from one world to another; my compound was the flimsiest of shelters, and my heart sank for him and the innumerable others like him whose grand and simple expectations had been, and would be, shattered as they climbed out of what was left of aboriginal society into the modern world. I could not explain all this to Umaru. He was right in believing that he had no place to which to return, he could not go backwards, and who was I to tell him that he had little chance of going forward in the way he had anticipated. So I watched him as he luxuriated in his new European vest and trousers, or in his Hausa cap and gown, jaunty, confident, feeling free, but really rootless—neither Anaguta, nor Nigerian, nor Pagan, nor Christian, a man losing his identity in the pursuit of an illusion.

SYSTEMIC MARITAL DISCORD

Umaru's family is also useful in further illustrating the marital complexities that are rampant among the Anaguta, and which symbolize the very heart of their dilemma. Before Umaru had come to work with me, his compound in the valley consisted of his nuclear family—self, wife and two small sons. The older brother's compound, also in the valley, was composed of Sako, his two wives, three children, and his younger brother. If, when Umaru's wife had left him, she had formed a liaison with a secondary husband in another village, and Umaru had, in turn, taken a secondary wife, the compounds involved would not have changed in size, but the composition would have been altered in a way which has become routine among the Anaguta. The compound which the wife had joined would now be polygynous, while Umaru's household would have been reduced to himself and a more or less transient visiting wife. However, if Umaru's sister had returned to his compound, on the reciprocal break-up of her marriage, then Umaru would have been host to two women, plus his sister's children and, almost certainly, within a short time, his sister's lover.

There is still another possibility which is, in fact, realized among several Anaguta compounds: had Umaru permanently abandoned his compound, and had his sister stayed on, it is probable that she would eventually have been joined by one or more bachelor lovers, who would then be recognized as her "husbands," and the compound would have become polyandrous. A polyandrous compound also develops when a woman, on the death of her husband, returns to her older brother's or father's compound, with successive events paralleling those mentioned. This would not, however, affect the affiliation of her children by her first "exchange" husband; they would remain members of their father's clan and village, now physically attenuated (because of migration), and would participate in the ceremonial and marital procedures involved. But any children issuing from her later liaisons in her brother's compound would probably become members of her patriclan, since polyandrous unions within the compound are just as unstable as the secondary husband affairs. Summing up, the only consistently applied marital and descent rule is that pursued along the path of an exchange marriage. And even here, exceptions occur in awkward cases, so that very young children of a ruptured exchange may be incorporated into the mother's patriclan. In secondary marriages, the only convention seems to be one of mutual convenience and agreement.

For a complex of ecological, economic, and social reasons, then, it is apparent that the average Anaguta compound in the valley and lowlands is diminishing in size and is constantly shifting its composition; and, reactively, the compounds in the hills are also being reduced in size and changed in nature. Neither process is understood by the Anaguta; both develop anarchically. The valley and the lowlands are communities in suspension, formally criss-crossed by diffused relationships with their old villages; and no recognized connection among Manza or Aholl compounds of different villages has yet developed. Also, a few detached Birom and Jarawa families have moved into Manza, further diluting Anaguta associations.

Moreover, the dependence upon manure, and thus upon the Cattle Fulani, a totally new factor in Anaguta culture generally, and specifically an ironic shift in the relations between Anaguta and Fulani, has begun to give the lowlands a common character, while fixing the people more firmly in the new environment. This dependence splits the compounds from each other, as indicated, and even introduces a basic competitive element, since each family must make arrangements with the Fulani for fertilizing its particular fields, including its ancillary commercial gardens. That is to say, the Anaguta as a group no longer command the exploitation of their central valley and adjacent lowlands; the cooperative habits and structures of two-thirds of their population have been directly or indirectly attenuated, and no systematic forms, promising Anaguta continuity, are taking their place.

Part IV. General Conclusion

We have made an effort to describe the way in which Anaguta identity has collapsed on each level of behavior, from the tribe to the nuclear family, reduced to its raw maternal material. The unstable mother-centered family is the precipitate of the interactive changes occurring throughout the whole society, the latter surviving as a hollow shell on a shifting maternal base. In such a situation, if new, internally integrative structures are not formed, the people will cease to exist as an entity, as an ethnic group. Individuals may survive physically, in greater or lesser number, but in a short time, even the memory of the past will have disappeared. Thus, compounded by the probability of drastic physical reduction, Anaguta culture is becoming extinct.

The mature Anaguta whom I knew were aware of this and had chosen not to collaborate with the civilizing process. When they are compelled by law or other social imperatives, they respond minimally. The choice of extinction is the result of a series of tactical decisions in what they conceive as a battle to provide themselves with a little cultural space. But we must always remember that to the Anaguta birth and death, man and nature, the present, the past, and the future, the thing and the person are related in ritual cycles which remold the finality of any experience with which they are objectively faced. Thus, they are able to confront situations which would panic a Western group, made brittle by the certainty of its secular commitments. This is the point that the Senegalese novelist C. H. Kane makes in *L'Aventure Ambiguë* (1962), in a dialogue between a traditional and a Europeanized African:

"His world [our poorest peasant] does not admit of accident. It is more reassuring than yours, despite appearances."

"Maybe. Unhappily for us, it is my universe which is the true one. The earth is not flat. Its banks do not overlook the abyss. The sun is not a lamp hung in a bowl of blue porcelain. The universe which science has revealed to the West is less immediately human than ours, but admit that it's more solid. . . ."

"Your science has revealed a world round and perfect, of infinite movement. It has reconquered that world from chaos. But I think it has also left you open to despair."

"Not at all. It has freed us from fears . . . puerile and absurd."

"Absurd? The absurd is your world. . . ."

Our dilemma, revealed in a stroke by the novelist, is to reconcile the world, the *traditional* world which we perceive with all our senses and describe in metaphors, with the conceptions of modern science, of contemporary industrial society. Conceptions have a social history; perceptions are in the nature of the species (Diamond, 1960, p. 37). The sun *is* a lamp hung in a bowl of blue porcelain, it is also an explosive thermonuclear field wherein hydrogen continuously transforms into helium. Both realities are human realities; we learn from examining the Anaguta and ourselves that to deny either is self-defeating.

EPILOGUE: TWO CONTRASTING MODES OF ACCULTURATION

The Afusare of Jarawan-Jos (Reflexive)

The dynamics of Anaguta adaptation are not duplicated among neighboring peoples, such as the Jarawa and the Nyango-Irigwe. The more intricate analysis of the situation of each of these groups would require intensive study in the field, but there are certain gross distinctions that can be made now.

Among the Hill Jarawa (Afusare) of the village of Jarawan-Jos in the Gwong Village Area, the response to civilization has been, from a Western point of view, far more flexible than that of the Anaguta. We may call it *adaptive-individualistic-reflexive.* Jarawa in the village of Jarawan-Jos, which is the largest of the villages in the Gwong area, are faced with an ecological situation roughly similar to that of their neighbors; that is, extensive, shifting horticulture has been severely curtailed. However, the problems of forest reserves and down-migration are not involved, since the people of Jarawan-Jos occupy an undulating downland. It is possible that the micro-environmental structure of Anaguta territory, an interior valley watered by a stream and surrounded on three sides by hills, affording good pasturage and protection to Fulani cattle, may be a factor in the gross differences in the reactions of the respective tribes. The Anaguta had, so to speak, an interior retreat. But, be that as it may, intensive cultivation, through the use of fertilizer, has become the Jarawa rule, as among the Anaguta.

The Jarawa have responded to both Hausa and European influences on a massive scale. Jarawa men find it prestigious to wear Hausa robes, and frequently protest Islam, while the younger adults look down on the elders, and show little regard for their religious beliefs or ritual usages; Christianity is also spreading.

The residents of Jarawan-Jos are becoming peasants, and a few, at very high cultural speed, have already developed further into individualized, cash-dependent farmers. Vegetables and root crops are grown extensively for the European and African markets. In a few cases, subsistence cropping has diminished to a dangerous point; a householder is likely to put all his efforts into market produce, converting the latter into cash—which is not difficult in the Jos area—and then impoverish himself by spending heavily on consumer items other than food. With the breakdown of the cooperative, socio-economic matrix, he is, even if cautious in his spending, always in danger of becoming money-poor.

Cash is usually converted quickly into consumer goods—clothing, bicycles, bedsteads, door locks, and so on—and these are conspicuously displayed. Compounds in Jarawan-Jos are often white-washed, a glass pane may be inserted into a square hole in a mud wall, pictures from ancient English Sunday supplements may be hung in the interior; on one occasion I found a map of Manhattan from an old telephone book pinned to a wall. Padlocked doors of corrugated metal are sometimes placed across the entrance of private dwellings and storage huts, not only as a protection against burglary, but as a sign of the new acquisitive mentality.

Whereas the position of women has become "dominant" among the Anaguta, for reasons outlined, Jarawa women, in the more modern households, have become subordinate. Since cash cropping among the Jarawa has become the major prestige and breadwinning activity, while field-subsistence cropping has declined, the men have taken over the commercial sphere without much apparent soul-searching. That, together with the greater influence of Mohammedanism, has led to a reinforcement of paternal authority; and the number of wives, and the favors afforded them, have become signs of affluence and distinction. Conversely, a number of unmarried Jarawa women and widows have become prostitutes, selling their charms in the Saban Gari, or in Jos itself, for a few shillings with which they purchase millet beer or food and pay room rent. This is in striking contrast to the Anaguta women, who, despite their traditional "promiscuity," become neither prostitutes nor specialized petty traders, as the unattached Jarawa women are likely to do in the town markets.

The increase of paternal authority and the mushrooming of the money economy have, then, tended to convert women into property, either prized, as in the compound, or degraded, as among the "surplus" women who can no longer find a place in the society.

Correlated to this growing commercial-consumer orientation is the desire to rise in the social scale. Education is seen as a means of upward mobility, and Jarawa children are heavily represented in all neighboring schools.

Individual Jarawa have begun to hire labor to cultivate their gardens, and at the same time they purchase the land of fellow tribesmen, although the latter practice is not yet widespread. The increasing individualization and commercialization of holdings and the greater adaptability that the Jarawa have shown to the market and the city have resulted in a significant migration of Jarawa to the Saban Gari and to Jos. This migration usually involves nuclear families, and the most menial jobs are undertaken in order to earn a livelihood. And this, in turn, accelerates the process in the village by which subsistence cultivators are rapidly becoming peasants and farmers. In contrast with the case of the Anaguta, the evolving acculturation patterns of the Jarawa of Jos are clear—they are eagerly becoming truck farmers in the suburbs, manual laborers in the city, prostitutes and drifters in the New Town.

No matter what specific conditioning factors are shared by Anaguta and Afusare or are unique to either people, at the root of the general difference in acculturation is the Jos Jarawa decision to adapt to the new civilization, along lines of least resistance, that is, in a highly individualized and reflexive way. This "passive" response reflects the values, without challenge, of the dominant marketing economy.

The Nyango-Irigwe (Self-Directing)

The people of the Nyango Village Area of the Irigwe tribe, previously members, like the Anaguta and Jarawa, of the Birom Federation, have made a remarkable effort to accommodate themselves, as a group, to the contemporary commercial-industrial culture emanating from Jos. Their mode, in contrast to that of the Jarawa, may be characterized as *adaptive-cooperative-reflective*; it is against the grain of the marketplace, and required a good deal of foresight and planning. The Nyango-Irigwe occupy a series of villages about 20 miles southwest of Jos, on the edge of the Zaria escarpment. A mission station and a primary school are located in their major village, and the majority of the children attend. Both institutions are singularly respectful of Nyango traditions, encouraging Irigwe children to acknowledge their holidays, and to participate in the celebrations, at least as a token. The mission tends to act as a bridge between cultures, as a midwife of change. While it did not establish the policy, the mission recognized and helped elaborate attitudes that had previously begun to develop among the Nyango-Irigwe.

It is noteworthy that the ritual and subsistence rounds are not yet jeopardized by ecological factors in the native villages. Yet, some years ago, a group of younger men, married and unmarried, migrated to Jos, under the leadership of a "chief," and set up a Nyango quarter in a suburb west of the town. The chief, who was simply the oldest and one of the most vigorous of the young men, was literate in Hausa and English, and had, through mission contacts, been trained as a sanitary inspector. For a short while, he remained the major breadwinner of the migrant group. But the younger men were not without resources; they, along with their village peers, constituted a dance troupe which rented itself out for performances at various civic functions in the town and, also, held recitals for which an admission fee was charged. This traditional expression, then, was converted into a socioeconomic asset in the new environment. Today, Nyango dancers are known throughout the Northern Region for their disciplined exuberance and the artistry of their movements, and the shows they put on, under private auspices and on public occasions, are eagerly attended. The dances have not been watered down; native dress and ornamentation are worn, and the traditional context is taught to new members of the troupe and explained to the audience. The dance serves as a continuously renewed link between the native villages and the new suburb, helps maintain solidarity among the Nyango of the town, and is, of course, a source of income.

The sanitary inspector (the chief) was able to recommend fellow Nyango for related municipal posts, and their combined influence enabled tribesmen to find still other employment; a few were apprenticed to artisans. As the Nyango quarter became viable, it developed an internal structure. A council hall was built, where the chief and other senior men deliberated the problems of the community, and in which meetings attended by the whole neighborhood took place. Moreover, other Nyango migrated with the good wishes of, and in most cases after having received some instruction from, the mission. But the Jos Nyango did not sever their physical ties with the native villages. They return on weekends to their native compounds, the dance troupe frequently performs back home, and they are present at all major festivals.

During their stay in town, Jos Nyango (or Miango, as they are known in the area) wear European clothing and do their best to find semi-skilled and skilled labor, although they will not work in the minefields. Of course, this situation has its limitations. As the movement to town accelerates and the Nyango quarter grows, the number of able-bodied men and women in the villages is bound to decline, and the population of the compounds will increase in age and diminish in number. Already, there are signs of disapproval on the part of the older resident Nyango toward the younger migrants, but it is of a tolerant kind, composed more of pride and sorrow than of anger for the untraditional success of the younger generation. Yet, there is a Nyango consensus on the need for what is happening. The Jos Nyango are, on their part, impeccably respectful of their own background and, in the urban environment, maintain their pride in their ethnic identity.

The Nyango, then, have not permitted themselves to become disorganized by acculturation; they maintain cooperative forms in the town—dance earnings, for example, are parceled out equally, with the surplus going to the "tribal union." A community hall has been built from collective funds, the authority of the chief and maturer men is recognized on important matters, and Nyango recommend employment to and assist each other in times of need. Most dwellings accommodate more than a single nuclear family; relatives from the country and unemployed friends and relatives in town are taken in. Gifts of food and consumer goods flow between village and town. Furthermore, other Pagans, including Jarawa and Birom, who have drifted anarchically to Jos, are drawn into the Nyango-Irigwe orbit, which contributes a bit toward Pagan solidarity.

It is, of course, difficult to predict the degree to which the cohesiveness and respect for tradition which mark Nyango change in Jos can be maintained. A great deal depends upon the nature of the political economy that develops in Plateau Province and the North at large. If a tendency toward cooperative forms develops, the Nyango situation could be stabilized indefinitely. Should more private and anarchic commercial forms prevail, centralized state control be established, or the present neo-feudal structure of the Northern Region persist, then the type of effort being made by the Nyango will probably be short-lived. But Nyango-Irigwe themselves understand this, and seem determined to maintain their evolving pattern. They are politically active in opposition to the Northern Peoples' Congress, the conservative instrument of the Fulani-Hausa upper crust, the most powerful political party in Nigeria, and the senior partner in the national coalition government. They are united in their desire for an independent Middle Belt state and have allied themselves to the more progressive, cooperative-oriented, southern-derived parties. Moreover, they have denied Birom primacy, and have tried to array themselves, under the nominal leadership of the Anaguta in Gwong, in order to achieve greater self-determination in local politics. The Nyango-Irigwe have even been able to produce a representative in the Northern Assembly without any particular official encouragement.

The Anaguta Decision

In contrast to the two modes of adaptive acculturation pursued by the Jarawa and the Nyango, each being antithetical, the present process among the Anaguta may be described as *maladaptive-cooperative-evasive*. The objective situation faced by the Anaguta did not differ in its generality from that confronting the Jos Jarawa or the Nyango-Irigwe. Like the Nyango, the Anaguta had resources which they could conceivably have utilized—the local school, an unusual emphasis on competitive dancing, proximity to Jos, yet sufficient distance to maintain a relatively traditional base, and there were missions available, along with British contacts, if they had desired to pursue them. Thus, the case of the Anaguta, in conjunction with adjacent peoples, helps reveal the literally decisive, or voluntaristic, component in human history.

Sources Cited

Ames, C. G.
1934 *Gazeteer of Plateau Province*, Jos.

Bello, Sir Ahmadu (Sardauna of Sokoto)
1962 *My Life*, Cambridge.

Blankenheimer, B., *et al.*
1957 *Investment in Nigeria*, U.S. Dept. of Commerce, Washington, D.C.

Boelaert, E.
1947 *La Situation Démographique des Nkundo-Mungo*, Centre d'Etudes des Problèmes Sociaux-Indigènes, Elisabethville.

Buchanan, K. M., and J. C. Pugh
1955 *Land and People in Nigeria: The Human Geography of Nigeria and Its Environmental Background*, London.

Burger, Samuel
1963 "Kwashiorkor," *The Sciences*, Vol. III, pp. 4-7.

Burns, Sir Alan
1955 *History of Nigeria*, London.

Census of Nigeria
1931 Vol. II, London, 1932-33.

Commission of Inquiry
1952 *Report of the Native Courts (Northern Provinces)*, Lagos.

Cook, A. N.
1943 *British Enterprise in Nigeria*, Philadelphia.

Crocquevielle, J.
1953 "Etude Démographique de Quelques Villages Likouala," *Population*, No. 3, pp. 491-510.

Cronje, Suzanne
1963 "Nigerian Cattle and Northern Wealth," *West Africa*, No. 2430, p. 1469.

Culwick, A. T., and G. M. Culwick
1938–39 "A Study of Population in Ulanga, Tanganyika Territory,"

Sociological Review, Vol. XXX, pp. 365-79 (1938); Vol. XXXI, pp. 329-43 (1939).

Davies, J. G.
1944 *The Birom Tribe* (unpublished MS).

Diamond, Stanley
1951 *Dahomey: A Proto-State in West Africa*, Ph.D. thesis, Columbia University. (In press.)
1960 "Anaguta Cosmography, the Linguistics and Behavioral Implications," *Anthropological Linguistics*, Vol. II, pp. 31-38.
1962a "Consideraciones Sobre la Herencia del Colonialismo: Ghana y la Nigeria Septentrional," *Revista de Ciencias Sociales*, Vol. VI, pp. 393-429.
1962b "Northern Nigeria: Still a Key but Not a Showpiece," *Africa Today*, Vol. IX, pp. 7-9.
1962c "Collapse in the West, Nigeria II," *Africa Today*, Vol. IX, pp. 6-8.
1962d "The Conflict with Ghana, Nigeria III," *Africa Today*, Vol. IX, pp. 10-15.
1963a "The Weight of the North, Nigeria IV," *Africa Today*, Vol. X, pp. 4-5, 15.
1963b "His Life, Thus Far: The Sardauna of Sokoto, Nigeria V," *Africa Today*, Vol. X, pp. 12-14.
1963c "The Trial of Awowolo," *Africa Today*, Vol. X, pp. 22-28.
1963d "Modern Africa: The Pains of Birth," *Dissent*, Vol. X, pp. 169-76.
1963e "The Search for the Primitive," *Man's Image in Medicine and Anthropology* (ed. Iago Galdston), pp. 62-115, New York.

Dorjahn, Vernon R.
1959 "The Factor of Polygyny in African Demography," *Continuity and Change in African Cultures* (eds. W. R. Bascomb and M. J. Herskovits), pp. 87-112, Chicago.

Eliade, Mircea
1961 *The Sacred and the Profane*, New York.

Fage, J. D.
1956 *An Introduction to the History of West Africa*, Cambridge.

Flint, J. E.
1960 *Sir George Goldie and the Making of Nigeria*, London.

Frankel, S. Herbert
1938 *Capital Investment in Africa*, London.

Greenberg, Joseph H.
1955 *Studies in African Linguistic Classification*, New Haven.
1959 "Africa as a Linguistic Area," *Continuity and Change in African Cultures* (eds. W. R. Bascomb and M. J. Herskovits), pp. 15-27, Chicago.

Gunn, Harold D.
1953 *Peoples of the Plateau Area of Northern Nigeria*, International African Institute, London.

Hailey, (Lord)
1950–53 *Native Administration in the British African Territories*, 5 vols., London.
Hawkins, E. K.
1958 *Road Transport in Nigeria*, London.
Hodgkin, Thomas
1960 *Nigerian Perspectives, an Historical Anthology*, London.
Kane, Cheikh Hamidon
1962 *L'Aventure Ambiguë*, Paris.
Lugard, Lady Flora Shaw
1905 *A Tropical Dependency*, London.
Lugard, Lord F. J. D.
1918 *Political Memoranda*, London, 1919.
1919 *Report on the Amalgamation of Northern and Southern Nigeria and Administration, 1912-1919*, London, 1920.
1922 *The Dual Mandate in British Tropical Africa*, Edinburgh and London.
Meek, C. K.
1925 *The Northern Tribes of Nigeria*, Vol. II, London.
Middleton, Dorothy
1964 *Victorian Lady Travelers*, London.
Mission Socio-Economique Centre-Oubangui
1960 "Enquête Démographique Centre-Oubangui 1959," *Méthodologie-Résultats Provisoires*, Paris.
Murdock, G. P.
1959 *Africa: Its People and Their Cultural History*, London, New York, Toronto.
Myrdal, Gunnar
1957 *Economic Theory and Underdeveloped Regions*, London.
Niven, C. R.
1958 *A Short History of the Yoruba Peoples*, London, New York, Toronto.
Oosterwal, G.
1961 *People of the Tor: A Cultural-Anthropological Study on the Tribes of the Tor Territory (Northern Netherlands New Guinea)*, Assen, The Netherlands.
Post, K. W. J.
1963 *The Nigerian Federal Election of 1959*, Nigerian Institute of Social and Economic Research, London.
Romaniuk, A.
1961 "L'Aspect Démographique de la Sterilité des Femmes Congolaises," *Studia Universitatis Lovanium*, Leopoldville.
Stapleton, G. Brian
1958 *The Wealth of Nigeria*, London.
Temple, O. and C. (eds.)
1919 *Notes on the Tribes, etc., of the Northern Provinces of Nigeria: Anaguta*, Capetown.
United Africa Company, Ltd.
1950 *Statistical and Economic Review*, No. 5.

ADDITIONAL BIBLIOGRAPHY

Austin, Dennis
1957 *West Africa and the Commonwealth*, London.
Awowolo, Obafemi
1947 *Path to Nigerian Freedom*, London.
Bauer, P. T.
1954 *West African Trade*, Cambridge.
1957 *Economic Analysis and Policy in Underdeveloped Countries*, Durham, N.C.
Bovill, E. W.
1933 *Caravans of the Old Sahara*, London.
1958 *The Golden Trade of the Moors*, London.
Cairncross, Alexander
1953 *Home and Foreign Investment 1870-1913*, Cambridge.
Coleman, James
1958 *Nigeria, Background to Nationalism*, Berkeley.
Cowan, L. Gray
1958 *Local Government in West Africa*, New York.
Davidson, Basil
1953 *The New West Africa*, London.
Deane, Phyllis
1953 *Colonial Social Accounting*, Cambridge.
Department of Mines
1957 *Annual Report of the Mines Department* (for the year ending March 31, 1956), Lagos.
1957 *Mining and Mineral Resources in Nigeria*, Lagos.
1967 "Africa in the Perspective of Political Anthropology," *The Transformation of East Africa* (eds. Stanley Diamond and Fred Burke), New York.
Dike, K. O.
1956 *Trade and Politics in the Niger Delta 1830-1885*, London.
Greenidge, C. W. W.
1958 *Slavery*, New York.
Hogben, S. J.
1930 *The Muhammadan Emirates of Nigeria*, London.
Hunton, William A.
1957 *Decision in Africa*, New York.
International Bank for Reconstruction and Development
1955 *Economic Development of Nigeria.*
Mair, Lucy
1936 *Native Policies in Africa*, London.
Nurkse, Ragnar
1957 *Problem of Capital Formation in Underdeveloped Countries.*
Pedler, F. J.
1951 *West Africa*, London.
1955 *Economic Geography of West Africa*, London, New York, Toronto.

Perham, Margery
1937 *Native Administration in Nigeria*, London.
1948 *Mining, Commerce and Finance in Nigeria*, London.
n.d. *The Native Economies of Nigeria*, Vol. I, London.
Smith, M. G.
1955 *The Economy of Hausa Communities of Zaria*, London.
1959 "The Hausa System of Social Status," *Africa*, Vol. XXIX, pp. 239-52.
Strachey, John
1959 *The End of Empire*, London.
United Africa Company, Ltd.
1949–58 *Statistical and Economic Review*, Nos. 4, 6, 11, 12, 13, 14, 15, 17, 19, 20, 21.
United Nations
1951 *Measures for the Economic Development of Underdeveloped Countries.*
United Nations Department of Economic and Social Affairs
1954–60 *Economic Developments in Africa* (annual reports).
Wheare, Joan
n.d. *The Nigerian Legislative Council*, London.
Wieschhoff, H. A.
1944 *Colonial Policies in Africa*, Philadelphia.
Yeld, E. R.
1960 "Islam and Social Stratification in Northern Nigeria," *British Journal of Sociology*, Vol. XI, pp. 112-27.

Index